Principles of Auditing

Principles of Auditing

Fourth Canadian Edition

O. Ray Whittington
San Diego State University

Kurt Pany
School of Accountancy
Arizona State University

Walter B. Meigs
University of Southern California

Robert F. Meigs
School of Accountancy
San Diego State University

Wai P. Lam
Faculty of Business Administration
University of Windsor

IRWIN
Homewood, IL 60430
Boston, MA 02116

This symbol indicates that the paper in this book is made from recycled paper. Its fiber content exceeds the recommended minimum of 50% waste paper fibers as specified by the EPA.

Sponsoring editor: Roderick T. Banister
Project editor: Paula M. Buschman
Production manager: Irene H. Sotiroff
Cover designer: Trish Lawrence
Art manager: Kim Meriwether
Compositor: Bi-Comp, Inc.
Typeface: 10/12 Times Roman
Printer: R. R. Donnelley & Sons Company

ISBN 0-256-09964-2
Library of Congress Catalog Number: 91–77507

Printed in the United States of America
1 2 3 4 5 6 7 8 9 DOC 9 8 7 6 5 4 3 2

Preface

The fourth Canadian edition of *Principles of Auditing* has been substantially revised to reflect the rapidly changing audit environment. The revisions are not only directed toward audits of financial statements but also include increased coverage of internal, compliance, and operational auditing. The breadth of coverage in this edition makes the introductory auditing course both broader and more interesting. Our goal is to provide a textbook well suited for the introductory one-semester auditing course.

The first 10 chapters emphasize the philosophy and environment of the auditing profession. Attention is given to the nature and purpose of auditing, auditing standards, professional conduct, auditors' legal responsibility and liability, and the approach followed in performing audits of financial statements. These initial chapters devote special attention to auditors' decision processes in internal control, audit sampling, and accumulating audit evidence. Chapters 11 through 17 deal with internal control cycles and obtaining evidence about the various financial statement accounts; they emphasize a risk-based approach to selecting appropriate auditing techniques. In Chapters 18 and 19, we present the auditors' reporting responsibilities and special auditing and accounting services, such as reviews and compilations of financial statements and reporting on future-oriented financial statements. Chapter 20, new to this edition, presents expanded coverage of internal, compliance, and operational auditing.

FEATURES OF THIS EDITION

This edition of *Principles of Auditing* includes a variety of learning and instructional aids. Among the major features of this edition are:

Study Objectives for each chapter, which provide a concise summary of the most important concepts to master.

Analytical and Discussion Cases, which provide intriguing case-study situations often based on actual auditing dilemmas. These cases acquaint students with the process of analyzing realistic auditing problems and illustrate the need for exercising professional judgment in the many gray areas characteristic of the auditing practice. These cases, labeled "Group IV" problem material, are provided in 11 chapters of the textbook.

We have increased the number of **illustrations, tables,** and **flowcharts** in this edition. These displays visually summarize key points. The number of **Illustrative Cases,** which use actual business examples to illustrate key concepts, also has been increased.

Our discussion in the first chapter of the role of the auditor in our economy covers the broad concept of the attest function and focuses on how audits of financial statements relate to that function. The chapter also discusses various types of audits and auditors, as well as the public accounting profession.

The second and third chapters cover professional and ethical standards. The second chapter is new but it covers some of the materials, such as the auditors' report and generally accepted auditing standards, that were in Chapter 1 in the previous editions. Our discussion of ethical standards emphasizes emerging issues illustrating the need for judgment in evaluating situations that might impair the auditor's independence.

Attention has been given in this edition to **international auditing standards.** These standards are becoming much more important as countries attempt to create international markets for securities.

In this edition, the discussion of audit evidence has been brought to the front of the textbook. This allows the students to get an understanding of the relationships between financial statement assertions, evidence about control risk, and evidence to restrict detection risk. These relationships are emphasized throughout the remainder of the textbook.

The chapter on internal control has been completely rewritten to reflect the CICA pronouncement in this area. Similarly, the chapter on auditors' reports has been revised to reflect the changes in the standard audit report.

The chapter on the audit of electronic data processing systems includes internal control and audit considerations for systems varying in complexity from microcomputer systems to sophisticated advanced computer systems.

Our easy-to-understand chapter on audit sampling emphasizes basic concepts of importance to every auditor. The chapter presents both statistical and nonstatistical approaches to sampling. For those more interested in statistical techniques, two detailed appendixes present the computational aspects of the audit risk model and probability-proportional-to-size sampling.

Our new Chapter 20—on internal, operational, and compliance auditing—discusses the professional standards established by the Institute of

Internal Auditors, the scope of internal auditors' work, and the nature of their reports. The chapter also describes the purpose and nature of operational audits, and its final section includes the compliance audit engagements performed by auditors.

Both text discussion and problem material have been updated to reflect the most recent legal and professional requirements that affect independent auditors, including provisions of the Canada Business Corporations Act and pronouncements of the Auditing Standards Board of the Canadian Institute of Chartered Accountants. In addition, developments in the United States that are relevant to the Canadian auditing environment are presented.

END-OF-CHAPTER PROBLEM MATERIAL

The questions, problems, and case materials at the end of each chapter are divided as follows: Group I—Review Questions; Group II—Questions Requiring Analysis; Group III—Problems; and Group IV—Analytical and Discussion Cases.

The *Review Questions* are closely related to the material in the chapter and provide a convenient means of determining whether students have grasped the major concepts and details contained in that chapter.

The *Questions Requiring Analysis* call for thoughtful consideration of realistic auditing situations and the application of generally accepted auditing standards. A number of these Group II questions are taken from CA, CPA, and other professional examinations, and others describe actual audit situations. These questions, generally shorter than those in Group III, tend to stress value judgments and conflicting opinions.

Many of the Group III *Problems* have been drawn from CA, CPA, and CIA examinations. In selecting these problems, consideration was given to ones appearing in recent professional exams. Many of the problems are new, but some problems from previous editions were retained (often with modification) if they were superior to others available. Problems requiring extensive working papers and quantitative applications have been minimized, and short case-type questions have been emphasized.

ANALYTICAL AND DISCUSSION CASES

These cases involve controversial situations that do not lend themselves to clear-cut answers. Students are required to analyze the case and then logically formulate and justify their personal positions on the issues involved. The cases acquaint students with the professional literature, develop analytical and communications skills, and demonstrate that several diverse, yet defensible, positions may be argued persuasively in a given situation. *Analytical and Discussion Cases* appear as Group IV problem material at the end of Chapters 1, 2, 5, 6, 7, 9, 10, 11, 13, 15, and 19.

REFERENCES TO AUTHORITATIVE SOURCES

Numerous references are made to the pronouncements and other published materials of the Canadian Institute of Chartered Accountants, the Institute of Chartered Accountants of Ontario, the American Institute of Certified Public Accountants, the Institute of Internal Auditors, the Financial Accounting Standards Board, and the U.S. Securities and Exchange Commission. The cooperation of the Canadian Institute of Chartered Accountants, the Institute of Chartered Accountants of Ontario, the Institute of Internal Auditors, and the American Institute of Certified Public Accountants in permitting the use of their published materials and of the questions from the CICA Uniform Final Examinations, the Uniform CPA Examinations, and the CIA examinations brings to this text an element of authority not otherwise available.

CONTRIBUTIONS BY OTHERS

I would like to express my sincere thanks to the many users of the preceding editions who have offered helpful suggestions for this edition. Especially helpful were the advice and suggestions of the following reviewers:

Catherine Koch—Northern Alberta Institute of Technology

David Richards—*Saskatchewan Institute of Arts, Sciences and Technology*

Philip Paradis—*Northern Alberta Institute of Technology*

Bruce Densmore—*Mount Saint Vincent University*

John Edds—*Brock University*

I would also like to acknowledge the advice and suggestions of Ross Johnston and Trim Shastri, my colleagues at the University of Windsor.

Wai P. Lam

Contents

CHAPTER 2
Professional Standards   38

CHAPTER 3
Professional Ethics   68

CHAPTER 4
Auditors' Legal Responsibility and Liability   **136**

CHAPTER 5
Planning the Audit and Designing Audit Programs   **187**

CHAPTER 6
Evidence: What Kind and How Much?   231

CHAPTER 7
Internal Control   268

CHAPTER 9

354

CHAPTER 10
Audit Working Papers: Examination of the General Records **411**

CHAPTER 13
Inventories and Cost of Goods Sold   549

CHAPTER 14
Property, Plant, and Equipment: Depreciation and Depletion   595

CHAPTER 15
Accounts Payable and Other Liabilities   627

CHAPTER 17
Further Verification of Revenue and Expenses: Completing the Audit   *705*

Chapter 1

The Role of the Auditor in Our Economy

After studying this chapter, you should be able to:

- Describe the nature of the attest function.
- Describe the nature of financial statement audits.
- Explain why audits are demanded by society.
- Describe the various types of audits and types of auditors.
- Describe the public accounting profession and how public accounting firms are typically organized and the responsibilities of auditors at the various levels in the organization.
- Describe the major organizations that have an effect on the public accounting profession.

Dependable financial information is essential to the very existence of our society. The investor making a decision to buy or sell securities, the banker deciding whether to approve a loan, the government obtaining revenue based on income tax returns, all are relying upon information provided by others. In many of these situations, the goals of the providers of information run directly counter to those of the users of the information. Implicit in this line of reasoning is recognition of the social need for independent auditors—individuals of professional competence and integrity who can tell us whether the information on which we rely constitutes a fair picture of what is really going on.

1

One of our purposes in this chapter is to make clear the nature of independent (external) audits and the auditing profession. We begin with a discussion of the broader concept of the *attest* engagement, of which audits are an important type. We will explore types of audits other than the examination of financial statements and note the impact of the Institute of Internal Auditors (IIA) and the Office of the Auditor General of Canada. Also we will examine other types of professional services, and the nature and organization of public accounting firms. Finally, we will highlight the influence exerted on the public accounting profession by the Canadian Institute of Chartered Accountants (CICA) and by other organizations.

What Is the Attest Function?

To *attest* to information means to provide assurance of its fairness and reliability.[1] More formally, the American Institute of Certified Public Accountants (AICPA) in the United States has defined an attest engagement as one in which

> a practitioner is engaged to issue or does issue a written communication that expresses a conclusion about the reliability of a written assertion that is the responsibility of another party.

A financial statement audit is, by far, the most common type of attest engagement. However, public accountants attest to a wide range of other types of information, including the reasonableness of financial forecasts, the adequacy of internal control, and compliance with laws and regulations.

Illustrative Case

Public accountants have attested to the assertion that a supermarket chain has the lowest overall prices in that city. The public accountants selected a sample of approximately 1,000 items and compared the prices to those of the various other major supermarkets. Representatives of the supermarket chain stated that the credibility added by the public accountants has helped to convince consumers that the chain's prices are indeed the lowest.

---

[1] The CICA is currently working on the "attest" project.

FIGURE 1–1   The Attest Function

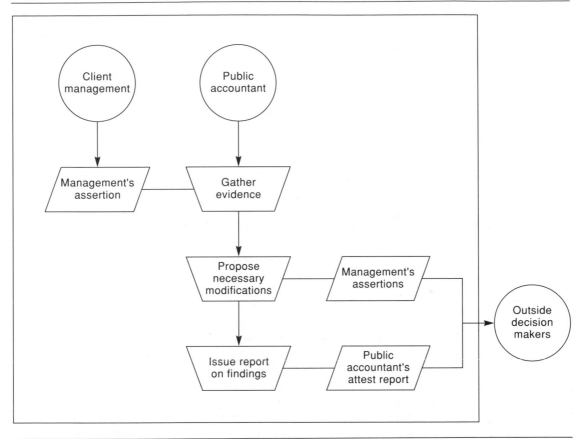

The nature of the attest function is essentially the same, regardless of the information being examined. Figure 1–1 describes the attest function, which always begins with an assertion by management; for example, management may assert that the company's financial statements follow generally accepted accounting principles. The public accountants gather evidence that enables them to provide assurance on the fairness and dependability of management's assertion. Then they issue a report summarizing their findings.

The amount of evidence obtained by the public accountants and the content of the attest report depend on the nature of the engagement. The standards of the CICA recognize three forms of attestation engagements—examinations, reviews, and the performance of specific agreed-upon auditing procedures. An *examination,* referred to as an audit when it involves financial statements, financial information, or compliance with agreements and regulations, results in the highest form of assurance that a public accountant can provide about management's assertion. In an examination, the public accountants select from all evidence a combination that limits to a low level the risk that they will not find a *material misstatement* of an assertion. A *review* is substantially less in scope of procedures than an examination, and is designed to lend only a limited, or moderate, amount of assurance about the assertion. If an examination or review does not meet the client's needs, the public accountants and a specified user of the information may mutually decide on specific *agreed-upon auditing procedures* that the public accountants will perform.

Throughout this chapter, we will focus on the attest function as it relates to an audit of financial statements. Other types of attest services are discussed in Chapters 19 and 20.

What Is a Financial Statement Audit?

In a financial statement audit, the public accountants undertake to gather evidence and provide the highest level of assurance for management's assertion that the financial statements follow generally accepted accounting principles, or some other appropriate basis of accounting. An audit involves searching and verifying the accounting records and examining other evidence supporting those financial statements. By obtaining an understanding of the company's internal control and by inspecting documents, observing assets, making enquires within and outside the company, and performing other audit procedures, the auditors will gather the evidence necessary to issue an audit report. That audit report states that it is the public accountants' opinion that the financial statements are fairly presented, in all material respects, in accordance with generally accepted accounting principles. The flowchart in Figure 1–2 illustrates an audit of financial statements.

The evidence gathered by the auditors focuses on whether the financial statements are fairly presented in accordance with generally accepted accounting principles. More specifically, an audit will address the assertions that the assets listed in the balance sheet really exist, that the company has title to these assets, and that the valuations assigned to these assets have been established in conformity with generally accepted accounting principles. Evidence will be gathered to show that the balance sheet contains *all the liabilities* of the company; otherwise, the balance sheet might be grossly misleading because certain important liabilities had been accidentally or deliberately omitted. Similarly, the auditors will gather evidence about the income statement. They will demand evidence that the reported sales really occurred, that the goods were actually shipped to customers, and that the recorded costs and expenses are appli-

FIGURE 1–2 Audit of Financial Statements

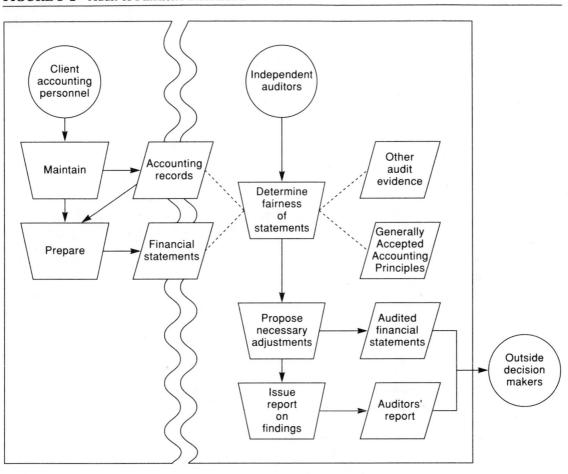

cable to the current period and that all expenses have been recognized. Only if sufficient evidence exists in support of all of these significant assertions are found to be fairly stated can the auditors conclude that the financial statements are presented in accordance with generally accepted accounting principles.

The audit procedures comprising an examination will vary considerably from one engagement to the next. Many of the procedures appropriate to the audit of a small retail store would not be appropriate for the audit of a giant corporation such as Canadian Pacific. Auditors perform audits of all types of business enterprise, and of nonprofit organizations as well. Banks and breweries, factories and stores, colleges and churches, airlines and labour unions—all of these are regularly visited by auditors. The selection of the procedures best suited to each audit requires the exercise of professional skill and judgment.

Economic Decision Making Requires Dependable Information

A decision by a bank to make a loan to a business is usually based on careful study of the company's financial statements along with other information. The bank's purpose in making the loan is to earn interest and to collect the principal of the loan at maturity. But what if the financial statements submitted by the company along with its loan application are not dependable? Assume, for example, that the financial statements overstate current assets and annual earnings, and omit major liabilities. Assume also that the bank, acting on the basis of such misleading information, makes the loan. The end result is likely to be that the bank does not receive the expected interest income and may have to write the loan off as a loss.

A major portion of our economy today is characterized by large corporate organizations that have gathered capital from millions of investors and that control economic resources spread throughout the country or even throughout the world. Top management in the corporate headquarters is remote from the operations of company plants and branches and must rely on financial statements and other reports to control the company's resources. In brief, the decision makers in a large organization cannot get much information on a firsthand basis. They must rely on information provided by others, and this fact increases the risk of receiving undependable information.

The millions of individuals who have entrusted their savings to corporations by investing in securities rely upon annual and quarterly financial statements for assurance that their invested funds are being used honestly and efficiently. Even greater numbers of people entrust their savings to banks, insurance companies, and pension funds, which in turn invest the money in corporate securities. Thus, directly or indirectly, almost everyone has a financial stake in corporate enterprise, and the public interest demands prompt, ***dependable*** financial reporting on the operations and the financial health of publicly owned corporations.

The revenue of the federal government is derived in large part from income taxes based on the reported incomes of individuals and corporations. The information on tax returns is provided by taxpayers and may be biased because of the self-interest of the providers. The government attempts to compensate for this inherent weakness through verification by audits carried out by Revenue Canada, Taxation.

Good accounting and financial reporting aid society in allocating its resources in the most efficient manner. The goal is to allocate our limited capital resources to the production of those goods and services for which demand is greatest. Economic resources tend to be attracted to the industries, the areas, and the organizational entities that are shown by accounting measurements to be capable of using more resources to the best advantage. Inadequate accounting and inaccurate reporting, on the other hand, conceal waste and inefficiency and thereby prevent our economic resources from being allocated in a rational manner.

Credibility—The Contribution of the Independent Auditor to Financial Reporting

The contribution of the independent auditor is to give credibility to financial statements. *Credibility,* in this usage, means that the financial statements can be *believed;* that is, they can be relied upon by outsiders, such as shareholders, creditors, government, and other interested third parties.

Audited financial statements are now the accepted means by which business corporations report their operating results and financial position. The word *audited* when applied to financial statements means that the balance sheet, statements of income and retained earnings, and statement of changes in financial position are accompanied by an audit report prepared by independent public accountants, expressing their professional opinion as to the fairness of the company's financial statements.

Financial statements prepared by management and transmitted to outsiders without first being audited by independent accountants leave a credibility gap. In reporting on its own administration of the business, management can hardly be expected to be entirely impartial and unbiased, any more than a football coach could be expected to serve as both coach and official referee in the same game.

Unaudited financial statements may have been honestly but carelessly prepared. Liabilities may have been overlooked and omitted from the balance sheet. Assets may have been overstated as a result of arithmetical errors or through violation of generally accepted accounting principles. Net income may have been exaggerated because revenue expenditures were capitalized or because sales transactions were recorded in advance of delivery dates.

Finally, there is the possibility that unaudited financial statements have been deliberately falsified in order to conceal theft and fraud or as a means of inducing the reader to invest in the business or to extend credit. Although deliberate falsification in financial statements is not common, it does occur and can cause disastrous losses to persons who rely upon such misleading statements.

For all these reasons (accidental errors, deviation from accounting principles, unintentional bias, and deliberate falsification), unaudited annual financial statements are much less reliable than statements which have been examined by independent auditors.

Major Auditing Developments of the 20th Century

Although the objectives and concepts that guide present-day audits were almost unknown in the early years of the 20th century, audits of one type or another have been made throughout the recorded history of commerce and of government finance. The original meaning of the word *auditor* was "one who hears" and was appropriate to the era during which governmental accounting records were approved only after a public reading in which the accounts were read aloud. From medieval times on through the Industrial Revolution, audits were made to determine whether persons in positions of fiscal responsibility in government and commerce were acting and reporting in an honest manner.

During the Industrial Revolution, as manufacturing concerns grew in size, their owners began to use the services of hired managers. With this separation of the ownership and management groups, the absentee owners turned increasingly to auditors to protect themselves against the danger of unintentional errors, as well as fraud committed by managers and employees. Bankers were the primary outside users of financial reports (usually only balance sheets), and they were also concerned with whether reports were distorted by errors or fraud. Before 1900, consistent with this primary objective to detect errors and fraud, audits often included a study of all, or almost all, recorded transactions.

In the first half of the 20th century, the direction of audit work tended to move away from fraud detection toward a new goal of determining whether financial statements gave a full and fair picture of financial position, operating results, and changes in financial position. This shift in emphasis was a response to the increasing number of shareholders and the corresponding increased size of corporate entities. In addition to the new shareholders, the auditor became more responsible to governmental agencies, stock exchanges representing these new investors, and other parties who might rely upon the financial information. No longer were bankers the only important outside users of audited financial data. The fairness of reported earnings began to assume primary importance.

As large-scale corporate entities developed rapidly in Canada, Great Britain, and the United States, auditors began to sample selected transactions, rather than study all transactions. Auditors and business managers gradually came to accept the proposition that careful examination of relatively few transactions selected at random would give a cost-effective, reliable indication of the accuracy of other, similar transactions.

In addition to sampling, auditors became aware of the importance of effective internal control. A company's internal control consists of the policies and procedures established to provide reasonable assurance that the objectives of the company will be achieved, including the objective of preparing reliable financial statements. Auditors found that by studying the client's internal control, they could identify areas of strength as well as areas of weakness. *The stronger the internal control, the less testing of financial statement account balances was required by the auditors.* For any accounts or any phase of financial operations in which controls were weak, the auditors learned that they must expand the nature and extent of their tests of the account balance.

With the increased reliance upon sampling and internal control, professional standards began to emphasize limitations on auditors' ability to detect fraud. The profession recognized that audits designed to discover fraud would be too costly. Good internal control and surety bonds were recognized as better fraud protection techniques than audits.

Beginning in the 1960s, the detection of large-scale fraud assumed a larger role in the audit process. Professional standards began to use the term *irregularities* to describe fraudulent financial reporting (also called *management fraud*) and misappropriation of assets (also called *defalcations*). This shift in emphasis to taking a greater responsibility for the detection of irregularities resulted from (1) a dramatic increase in governmental pressure to assume more responsibility for large-scale frauds, (2) a number of successful lawsuits claiming that management fraud had improperly gone undetected by the independent auditors, and (3) a belief by public accountants that audits should be expected to detect material fraud.

The increasing use of computers since the 1960s has not altered the auditor's responsibility for detecting errors and fraud. The nature of audit procedures has been affected, however, as auditors have been required to develop new approaches to considering internal control and testing account balances.

Many of the ideas mentioned in this brief historical sketch of the development of auditing will be analyzed in detail in later sections of this book. Our purpose at this point is merely to orient ourselves with a quick, overall look at some of the major auditing developments of the 20th century:

1. A shift in emphasis to the determination of fairness in financial statements.
2. Increased responsibility of the auditor to third parties, such as governmental agencies, stock exchanges, and an investing public numbered in the millions.

3. A change in auditing method from detailed examination of individual transactions to use of sampling techniques, including statistical sampling.
4. Recognition of the need to consider the effectiveness of internal control as a guide to the direction and amount of testing and sampling to be performed.
5. Development of new auditing procedures applicable to electronic data processing systems, and use of the computer as an auditing tool.

Types of Audits

Audits are often viewed as falling into four major types: (1) audits of financial statements, (2) compliance audits, (3) operational audits, and (4) comprehensive audits.

Audits of Financial Statements.   The audit of financial statements (which is our primary concern) ordinarily covers the balance sheet and the related statements of income, retained earnings, and changes in financial position. The goal is to determine whether these statements have been prepared in conformity with generally accepted accounting principles. Financial statement audits are normally performed by firms of public accountants; the user groups include management, investors, bankers, creditors, financial analysts, and government agencies.

Compliance Audits.   The performance of a compliance audit is dependent upon the existence of verifiable data and of recognized criteria or standards established by an authoritative body. A familiar example is the audit of an income tax return by an auditor of Revenue Canada. Such audits seek to determine whether a tax return is in compliance with tax laws and regulations. The findings of the auditors are transmitted to the taxpayer by means of assessment notices.

Operational Audits.   An operational audit is a study of some specific unit of an organization for the purpose of measuring its performance. The operations of the receiving department of a manufacturing company, for example, may be evaluated in terms of its *effectiveness,* that is, its success in meeting its stated goals and responsibilities. Performance is also judged in terms of *efficiency,* that is, success in using to best advantage the resources available to the department. Because the criteria for effectiveness and efficiency are not as clearly established as are generally accepted accounting principles or tax regulations, an operational audit tends to require more subjective judgment than do audits of financial statements or compliance audits. Operational auditing is discussed in detail in Chapter 20.

Comprehensive Audits.   A comprehensive audit encompasses the determination of (1) the fair presentation of financial statements, (2) compliance with legislative and related authorities, and (3) due regard for the economy and efficiency in the administration of resources and the effectiveness of programs (commonly known as *value-for-money*). Since the audit for the fair presentation of financial statements has been discussed earlier, we shall focus our attention on the value-for-money aspect of the comprehensive audit. The objective of a value-for-money audit is to assess management's accountability for the **economy** and **efficiency** of the entrusted resources and the achievement of objectives (**effectiveness**). Economy measures the relationship between resources acquired and their costs. Thus, economy is achieved when the appropriate resources are acquired at the lowest possible cost. Efficiency reflects the relationship between inputs and outputs. It is considered efficient when a maximum amount of output is produced from a given input or a minimum amount of input yields a maximum amount of output. Effectiveness refers to the accomplishment of a set goal or objective. Therefore, the degree of effectiveness is judged by the extent to which the goal is achieved.

Comprehensive auditing owes its origin to the Office of the Auditor General of Canada. It was designed primarily for organizations in the public sector such as government agencies and departments and Crown corporations. However, comprehensive auditing also can be applied to organizations in the private sector, especially not-for-profit organizations.

Types of Auditors

Although our interest is primarily in the audit of financial statements by public accountants, other professional accountants carry on large-scale auditing programs. Among these other well-known types of auditors are internal auditors, auditors of the offices of the Canadian or provincial auditor general and the auditors of Revenue Canada.

Internal Auditors.   Nearly every large corporation maintains an internal auditing staff. A principal goal of the internal auditors is to investigate and evaluate the effectiveness with which the various organizational units of the company are carrying out their assigned functions. Much attention is given by internal auditors to the study and appraisal of internal control.

The internal auditing staff often reports to an audit committee of the board of directors, and also to the president or another high executive. This strategic placement high in the corporate structure helps assure that the internal auditors will have ready access to all units of the business, and that their recommendations will be given prompt attention by department heads. It is imperative that the internal auditors be independent of the department heads and other line executives whose work they review.

Thus, it would be less desirable for the internal auditing staff to be under the authority of the chief accountant or controller. Regardless of their reporting level, however, internal auditors are not independent in the same sense as external (independent) auditors. The internal auditors are employees of the company in which they work, subject to the restraints inherent in the employer-employee relationship.

A large part of the work of the internal auditors consists of operational audits; in addition, however, they may conduct numerous compliance audits. The number and kind of investigative projects varies from year to year. Unlike the external auditors, who are committed to verify each significant item in the annual financial statements, the internal auditors are not obligated to repeat their audits on an annual basis.

The Institute of Internal Auditors (IIA) is the international organization of internal auditors. It has developed various standards relating to internal auditing and it administers the certified internal auditor (CIA) examination. Chapter 20 provides more discussion of internal auditing and the CIA examinations.

Auditors of the Auditor General's Office.   The House of Commons has long had its own auditing staff—the Office of the Auditor General, established in 1878 and headed by the auditor general. The auditor general, as an officer of Parliament, is the auditor of the accounts of Canada. One of the auditor general's major responsibilities is to report to the House of Commons annually on the fairness of the financial statements of Canada. The work of the auditor general encompasses not only expressing opinions on financial statements but also examining and reporting on compliance with legislative and other authorities and conducting value-for-money audits. These three components are currently referred to as *comprehensive audits*. Accordingly, the auditor general's staff audits government departments and agencies as well as Crown corporations, such as Canadian Broadcasting Corporation and Atomic Energy of Canada Limited.

Each provincial government also has its own auditing staff headed by an auditor general whose duties and responsibilities to a large extent parallel those of the auditor general of Canada. In recent years, a number of municipalities (e.g., Edmonton and Montreal) have created the position of auditor general and have assigned them broad audit mandates.

The work and experience of the audit staff employed by these legislative auditors at the federal and provincial levels are accepted as adequate and sufficient practical training requirements by such accounting organizations as the Institute of Chartered Accountants, the Associations of Certified General Accountants, and the Societies of Certified Management Accountants. Consequently, many CA, CGA, and CMA students are currently employed by these offices.

Auditors of Revenue Canada.   Revenue Canada, Taxation, is responsible for enforcement of the federal tax laws. Its auditors conduct compliance audits of the income tax returns of individuals and corporations to determine that income has been computed and taxes paid as required by federal income tax laws. Although these audits include some simple individual tax returns that can be completed in a short time, they also include audits of very large corporations involving highly complex tax issues. The experience of these audits *may* be recognized as acceptable practical training requirements by such accounting organizations as the Associations of Certified General Accountants and the Societies of Certified Management Accountants.

The Accounting Profession

A number of professional accounting organizations in Canada provide education and training leading to a certificate in accountancy. Notably, these are the provincial Institutes of Chartered Accountants,[2] Societies of Management Accountants (formerly the Societies of Industrial Accountants), and Certified General Accountants' Associations. The national organizations of these three accounting bodies are the Canadian Institute of Chartered Accountants, the Society of Management Accountants of Canada, and the Certified General Accountants' Association of Canada. Members of these organizations receive their respective professional designations as chartered accountants (CAs), certified management accountants (CMAs), and certified general accountants (CGAs). The education, training, and examination requirements vary considerably among the three professional organizations. Also, the Institutes of Chartered Accountants place more emphasis on public accounting, the Societies of Management Accountants are primarily interested in management accounting, and the Certified General Accountants' Associations are interested in management accounting as well as public accounting.

Professional Accountants and Top Corporate Executives

While most professional accountants devote their careers to public, private, and government accounting, many have become top corporate executives. The chairpersons, presidents, and directors of many large and well-known corporations in Canada have a professional accounting designation. These top executives run the leading corporations in almost all

---

[2] The provincial organization of chartered accountants in Quebec is called Order of Chartered Accountants of Quebec. For the sake of simplicity, the term *institute* is used to include the Quebec organization. Also, the term *provincial institutes* is used to include the Bermuda Institute, the Yukon Territory Institute, and the Northwest Territories Institute.

industries—banking, commerce, manufacturing, airline, insurance, publication, brewery, mining, and real estate. Thus, a background in accounting can be a stepping stone to top management.

Illustrative Case

Among the well-known top corporate executives with a professional accounting background are Laurant Beaudoin, FCA,* chairman and CEO (chief executive officer) of Bombardier; James Black, FCA, chairman of Molson; William Bradford, FCGA, president and CEO of North American Life Assurance; Donald G. Campbell, FCA, chairman of McLean Hunter; John Cleghorn, FCA, president of Royal Bank of Canada; Norman T. Currie, FCA, president and CEO of Maple Leaf Mills; Rhys T. Eyton, FCA, chairman and CEO of Canadian Airlines International; John Goudie, CMA, FSMAC, chairman of Alberta and Southern Gas; Gordan Gray, FCA, chairman of Royal LePage; Melvin Hawkrigg, FCA, chairman of Trilon Financial; Paul Ivanier, Ph.D., CA, president and CEO of Ivaco; Lucille Johnstone, CGA, president and COO (chief operating officer) of Rivtow Straits; Frank Knowles, CA, president and COO of Power Corp.; Wayne McLeod, FCA, vice-chairman and president, CCL Industries; Claude Taylor, FCMA, Chairman of Air Canada; Adam Zimmerman, FCA, vice-chairman of Noranda.

In addition, a number of individuals hold multiple directorships of large, well-known corporations. Some examples (since listing all the corporations would be lengthy, only three directorships are mentioned for each individual): John W. Adams, FCA, LL.D. (C.T. Financial Services, Canada Trust, F. W. Woolworth-U.S.); Marcel Belanger, FCA (BCE Inc., Hudson's Bay, John Labatt); Warren Chippindale, FCA (Alcan Aluminum, BCE Inc., Molson); Robert Despres, FCGA, FSMAC (Domtar, Norcen Energy, Provigo); Geno Francolini, FCA, LL.D. (Bell Canada, Laidlaw Transportation, Schneider Corp.); and Richard Haskayna, FCA (Manufacturers Life, Royal LePage, Canadian Imperial Bank of Commerce).

---

* Note: The *F* preceding the professional designation CA, CGA, or CMA means *Fellow*, which is awarded to the members for their outstanding service and the distinction they have brought to the profession.

THE PUBLIC ACCOUNTING PROFESSION

The public accounting profession encompasses all of the persons who are licensed or entitled to be licensed to practise public accounting. The licensing requirements for the practice of public accounting vary among the provinces. In some provinces, only chartered accountants are effectively allowed to practise public accounting. In other provinces, either the practice is open to both chartered accountants and members of other accounting organizations such as the Certified General Accountants' Association or there are no qualifications required at all to practise. However, most of those in the practice of public accounting are chartered accountants.

In granting a license to practise public accounting, the government assumes that the public interest will be protected by an official identification of competent professional accountants who offer their services to the public. The opinion of an independent public accountant concerning the fairness of a set of financial statements is the factor that causes these statements to be generally accepted by bankers, investors, and government agencies. To sustain such confidence, the independent public accountant must be a professional person of the highest integrity and competence.

Since most public accountants are chartered accountants, the chartered accountancy profession is used to demonstrate the public accounting profession and the public accounting firm.

The Chartered Accountant—Professional Requirements and Career Opportunities

Specific requirements as to education and public accounting experience differ somewhat among the provinces. Generally, a university degree, a minimum of one to two years' practical training in public accounting, and certain additional education and examination requirements at the provincial level are required before a student is eligible to write the national uniform final examination. A candidate for a CA certificate usually must have a minimum of two years of public accounting experience and pass the national uniform final examination. This latter consists of four papers, each about four hours in duration. The examination is given once a year and covers a wide range of topics in the areas of accounting, finance, taxation, and auditing, with a significant emphasis on the current literature in all these areas.

Although a majority of students-in-accounts hold business degrees, usually with a major in accounting, a significant number of students hold degrees in other disciplines, such as the arts, science, mathematics, and engineering. At present, more than 12,000 students in Canada are pursuing their certification as chartered accountants.

Once a student is admitted to the membership of a provincial institute, and thus the CICA, a variety of rewarding opportunities are available. He or she may choose a career in public accounting, industry, management consulting, government, or teaching. Of course, a CA in public accounting is not limited to the performance of audits; he or she may also provide professional services in fields such as taxation and management consulting, as discussed in more detail later in this chapter.

Organization of Public Accounting Practices

Most public accounting practices are organized as partnerships, although a CA may also practise as a sole practitioner or, if allowed by law as in the provinces of Alberta and British Columbia, as a member of a professional corporation. In comparison with a sole proprietorship, the partnership form of organization offers several advantages. When two or more CAs join forces, the opportunity for specialization is increased and the scope of services offered to clients may be expanded to include such areas as tax planning and management-advisory services. Also, qualified members of the audit staff may be rewarded by admission to the partnership. Providing an opportunity to become a part owner of the practice is an important factor in CA firms' ability to attract and retain competent personnel. A partnership also provides opportunities for professional growth through the exchange of ideas and frequent discussions among partners concerning audit problems and the issues confronting the profession.

In past decades, provincial laws generally prohibited professionals from organizing their practices as corporations. This prohibition was founded on the premise that professionals should not be able to "hide behind the corporate veil" and avoid taking personal responsibility for their professional acts. However, the opposition to incorporation of public accountants' practices has changed in recent years. The provinces of Alberta and British Columbia as well as the Yukon Territory now permit chartered accountants to organize their public practices as corporations. The Alberta legislation requires that shareholders and directors of a *professional corporation* must be members of the profession who are licensed to practise and that shareholders have no limited liability. The officers of a professional corporation, however, do not have to be members of the profession. In British Columbia, these corporations are incorporated under the province's Companies Act and therefore are allowed to have *limited* liability. Since the Institute of Chartered Accountants of British Columbia is unable to have the limited liability provision waived, it requires these corporations to have *mandatory* liability insurance, currently at a minimum of $500,000. Because of these developments and the fact that certain other provinces are contemplating similar action, the *Rules of Professional Conduct* of the provincial institutes have been changed to permit their members to associate with professional corporations. While a professional corporation may provide certain benefits for public accountants, the main benefit appears to be the minimization of income taxes.

In the United States, most states recognize the professional corporation as a permissible form of organization for a public accounting firm.

It should be emphasized that a *professional corporation* differs from a *traditional corporation* in a number of respects. For example, all shareholders and directors of a professional corporation must be licensed practitioners of the profession. In addition, the professional corporation must carry adequate liability insurance to cover damages caused by negligent actions.

While the professional corporation concept is gaining acceptance in both Canada and the United States, it is still more common for public accounting firms to remain sole proprietorships or partnerships.

CA Firms: Size and Services

CA firms organized as partnerships vary in size from local offices with as few as two partners to international organizations with thousands of partners. Only a very large international public accounting firm can perform an audit of a large business with subsidiaries, plants, and branches in many different countries. Most large corporations are audited by these large firms. Until 1989, there were eight of these international firms. However, mergers have reduced them to the "Big Six." Although these firms offer a wide range of services, auditing represents a large, if not the largest, share of their work. Annual revenue of one of these international firms is in the billions of dollars. In alphabetical order, the six firms are Arthur Andersen & Co., Coopers & Lybrand, Deloitte & Touche, Ernst & Young, KPMG Peat Marwick, and Price Waterhouse. In addition to the Big Six, there are other international firms and many national, regional, and local public accounting firms that offer a wide variety of auditing, tax planning, and management advisory services. In terms of size, CA firms are often grouped in the following categories.

Local Firms.   Local firms typically have one or two offices, include only one or a few CAs as partners, and serve clients in a single city or area. Such firms emphasize income tax, management advisory services, and accounting services. Auditing is usually only a small part of the practice and tends to involve small business concerns that need audited financial statements to support applications for bank loans.

Regional Firms.   Many local firms have become regional firms by opening additional offices in neighbouring cities or provinces and increasing the number of professional staff. Merger with other local firms is often a route to regional status. This growth is often accompanied by an increase in the amount of auditing as compared to other services.

National Firms.   CA firms with offices in most major cities in Canada are called *national firms*. Generally, these firms operate in more than five provinces.

Large CA Firms.   The large CA firms usually have offices in major cities and in more than one province, and most of them, through their international affiliations, also have offices in major cities throughout the world. Since only a large firm has sufficient staff and resources to audit a large corporation, the largest CA firms audit nearly all of the largest corporations in Canada. Although these firms offer a wide range of services, auditing represents more than a substantial share of their work. The annual revenue of a large firm runs into hundreds of millions of dollars. The 10 largest CA firms, based on a recent report in *The Financial Post 500,* are

Peat Marwick Thorne, Deloitte & Touche, Ernst & Young, Price Water-house, Coopers & Lybrand, Doane Raymond Pannell Associates, BDO Ward Mallette, Arthur Andersen & Co., Dunwoody & Co., and Fuller Jenks Landau/MacKay.[3]

Other Types of Professional Services.   In addition to auditing, CA firms offer other types of services to their clients, including tax services, management advisory services, accounting and review services, and personal financial planning. CA firms tend to specialize in particular types of services depending on their size and the expertise of their personnel.

Tax Services.   Tax services that are performed by CA firms fall into two broad categories: compliance work and tax planning. Compliance work involves preparing the federal and provincial tax returns of corporations, partnerships, individuals, and estates and trusts. Tax planning, on the other hand, involves consulting with clients on how to structure their business affairs to legally minimize the amount and postpone the payment of their taxes.

Management Advisory Services.   CA firms offer a variety of services that are designed to improve the effectiveness and efficiency of their clients' operations. Initially, these services developed as a natural extension of the audit, and primarily involved consulting on accounting and internal control systems. In recent years, CA firms have expanded by offering a host of services that tend to be more operational. Examples are developing strategic planning models and management information systems and performing executive search services.

Accounting and Review Services.   Audits are expensive. For a small business, the cost of an audit will run into the thousands of dollars; for large corporations, the cost may exceed a million dollars. The most common reason for a small business to incur the cost of an audit is the influence exerted by a bank that insists upon audited financial statements as a condition for granting a bank loan. If a small business is not in need of a significant amount of bank credit, it may see little need for an independent audit.

An alternative is to retain a CA firm to perform other services, such as the compilation or review of financial statements. To compile financial statements means to prepare them; this service is often rendered when the client does not have accounting personnel capable of preparing statements. The CA firm issues a "notice to reader" on the financial

---

[3] "Top Accounting Firms," *The Financial Post 500,* Summer 1991; p. 162. The ranking can change somewhat in a short time due to a change in a firm's revenue, which was used as the basis for ranking. For example, the recent merger of Doane Raymond and Pannell Kerr MacGillivary has propelled the merged firm to the number 5 position (the two firms were number 6 and 11 before the merger), with revenue in excess of $200 million. Also, BDO Ward Mallette and Dunwoody & Co. will be merged in early 1992 to form BDO Dunwoody Ward Mallette.

statements that provides *no assurance* that the statements are presented fairly in accordance with generally accepted accounting principles.

A review of financial statements by a CA firm is substantially smaller in scope than an audit and is designed to provide *limited assurance* on the credibility of the statements. It stresses enquiries by the CA, discussion with client personnel, and applying analytical procedures on financial and nonfinancial data. These types of procedures are useful in bringing to light any unreasonable relationships among financial statement amounts. Compilations and reviews are discussed in Chapter 19.

Personal Financial Planning.　CA firms also may advise individuals on their personal financial affairs. For example, a CA firm may review a client's investment portfolio and evaluate whether the nature of the investments meets the client's financial objectives. The CA firm might also advise the client on the nature and amount of insurance coverage that is appropriate.

Responsibilities of the Professional Staff

Human resources—the competence, judgment, and integrity of personnel—represent the greatest asset of any public accounting firm. The professional staff of a typical public accounting firm includes partners, managers, senior accountants, and staff assistants.

Partners.　The principal responsibility of the partner is to maintain contacts with clients. These contacts include discussing with clients the objectives and scope of the audit work, resolving controversies that may arise as to how items are to be presented in the financial statements, and attending the client's shareholders' meetings to answer any questions regarding the financial statements or the auditors' report. Other responsibilities of the partner include recruiting new staff members, general supervision of the professional staff, reviewing audit working papers, and signing the audit reports.

Specialization by each partner in a different area of the firm's practice is often advantageous. One partner, for example, may become expert in tax matters and head the firm's tax department; another may concentrate in bankruptcy; and a third may devote full time to design and installation of data processing systems.

The partnership level in a public accounting firm is comparable to that of top management in an industrial organization. Executives at this level are concerned with the long-run well-being of the organization and of the community it serves. They should and do contribute important amounts of time to civic, professional, and educational activities in the community. Participation in the provincial institute of chartered accountants and in the CICA is, of course, a requisite if the partners are to do their share in building the profession. Contribution of their specialized skills and professional judgment to leadership of civic organizations is equally necessary in developing the economic and social environment in which business and professional accomplishment is possible.

An important aspect of partners' active participation in various business and civic organizations is the prestige and recognition that such participation may bring to their firms. Many clients select a particular public accounting firm because they have come to know and respect one of the firm's partners. Thus, partners who are widely known and highly regarded within the community may be a significant factor in attracting business to the firm.

Managers.   In large public accounting firms, managers or supervisors perform many of the duties that would be discharged by partners in smaller firms. A manager may be responsible for supervising two or more concurrent audit engagements. This supervisory work includes reviewing the audit working papers and discussing with the audit staff and with the client any accounting and auditing problems that may arise during the engagement. The manager is responsible for determining the audit procedures applicable to specific audits and for maintaining uniform standards of work. Often, managers have the administrative duties of compiling and collecting the firm's billings to clients.

Familiarity with tax laws and corporate and securities legislation, as well as a broad and current knowledge of accounting theory and practice, are essential qualifications for a successful manager. Like the partner, the audit manager may concentrate in specific industries or other areas of the firm's practice.

Senior Auditors.   The senior, or "in charge," auditor is an individual qualified to assume responsibility for the planning and conducting of an audit and the writing of the audit report, subject to review and approval by the manager and partner. In conducting the audit, the senior will delegate most audit tasks to assistants based on an appraisal of each assistant's ability to perform particular phases of the work. A well-qualified university graduate with a formal education in accounting may progress from staff assistant to senior auditor in two or three years, or even less.

One of the major responsibilities of the senior is on-the-job staff training. When assigning work to staff assistants, the senior should make clear the end objectives of the particular audit operation. By assigning assistants a wide variety of audit tasks and by providing constructive criticism of the assistants' work, the senior should try to make each audit a significant learning experience for the staff assistants.

The review of working papers as rapidly as they are completed is another duty of the senior in charge of an audit. This enables the senior to control the progress of the work and to ascertain that each phase of the engagement is adequately covered. At the conclusion of the examination, the senior will make a final review, tracing all items from individual working papers to the financial statements.

The senior will also maintain a continuous record of the hours devoted by all members of the staff to the various phases of the examination. In addition to maintaining uniform professional standards of work, the senior is responsible for preventing the accumulation of excessive staff-hours on inconsequential matters and for completing the entire engagement within budgeted time, if possible.

Staff Assistants.   The first position of a university graduate entering the public accounting profession is that of a staff assistant. Staff assistants usually encounter a variety of assignments that fully utilize their capacity for analysis and growth. Of course, some routine work must be done in every audit engagement, but graduates with thorough training in accounting need have no fear of being assigned for long to extensive routine procedures when they enter the field of public accounting. Most firms are anxious to assign more and more responsibility to younger staff members as rapidly as they are able to assume it.

The audit staff members of all public accounting firms attend high-quality training programs that are either developed ''in house'' or sponsored by professional organizations. One of the most attractive features of the public accounting profession is the richness and variety of experience acquired even by the beginning staff member. Because of the quality of experience gained by chartered accountants as they move from one audit engagement to another, many business concerns select individuals from the public accounting field to fill such executive positions as controller treasurer, or vice-president-finance.

Professional Development for CA Firm Personnel

A major problem in public accounting is keeping abreast of current developments within the profession. New business practices, new pronouncements by the Auditing Standards Board and the Accounting Standards Board, and changes in the tax laws are only a few of the factors that require members of the profession continually to update their technical knowledge.

A CA firm must make certain that the professional staff remains continuously up to date on technical issues. To assist in this updating process, most large public accounting firms maintain a separate professional development section.

Professional development sections offer a wide range of seminars and educational programs to personnel of the firm. The curriculum of each program is especially designed to suit the needs and responsibilities of participants. Partners may attend programs focusing on the firm's policies on audit quality control or means of minimizing exposure to lawsuits; on the other hand, programs designed for staff assistants may cover audit procedures or use of the firm's microcomputers. In addition to offering educational programs, the professional development section usually publishes a newsletter or journal for distribution to personnel of the CA firm and other interested persons.

In the United States, many public accounting firms that are too small to maintain their own professional development departments have banded together into associations of CPA firms. These associations organize education programs, distribute information on technical issues, and engage in other professional activities that are designed to meet the needs of their members. Since the costs of the association's professional activities are shared by all members, the firms are provided with many of the benefits of having their own professional development department at a fraction of the cost.

Continuing Education—The CA's Response to Change

The need for CAs to expand their knowledge and improve their skills continues throughout their professional careers. In recognition of this need, all provincial institutes encourage their members to take appropriate professional development courses. Professional development sections of CA firms, the CICA, various provincial institutes of chartered accountants, and many universities provide numerous programs which meet the continuing education needs. Home study materials providing continuing education needs are also available through the CICA.

Seasonal Fluctuations in Public Accounting Work

One of the traditional disadvantages of the public accounting profession has been the concentration of work during the "busy season" from December through April, followed by a period of slack demand during the summer months. This seasonal trend is caused by the fact that many companies keep their records on a calendar-year basis and desire auditing services immediately after the December 31 closing of the accounts. Another important factor is the spring deadline for filing of income tax returns.

Auditors often work a considerable number of hours of overtime during the busy season. Some public accounting firms pay their staff a premium for overtime hours. Other firms allow their staff to accumulate the overtime in an "overtime bank" and to "withdraw" these hours in the form of additional vacation time during the less busy times of the year.

Relationships with Clients

The wide-ranging scope of public accountants' activities today demands that CAs be interested and well informed on economic trends, political developments, sports events, and many other topics that play a significant part in business and social contact. Although an in-depth knowledge of accounting is a most important qualification of the CA, an abiliy to meet people easily and to gain their confidence and goodwill may be no less important in achieving success in the profession of public accounting. The ability to work effectively with clients will be enhanced by a sincere interest in their problems and by a relaxed and cordial manner.

The question of the auditors' independence inevitably arises in considering the advisability of social activities with clients. The partner in today's public accounting firm may play golf or tennis with the executives of client companies and other business associates. These relationships may make it easier to resolve differences of opinions that arise during the audit, if the cient has learned to know and respect the CA partner. This mutual understanding need not prevent the CA from standing firm on matters of accounting principle. This is perhaps the "moment of truth" for the practitioners of a profession.

However, the CA must always remember that the concept of independence embodies an *appearance* of independence. This appearance of independence may be impaired if an auditor becomes excessively involved in social activities with clients. For example, if a CA frequently attends lavish parties held by a client or dates an officer or employee of a client corporation, the question might be raised as to whether the CA will appear independent to outsiders. This dilemma is but one illustration of the continual need for judgment and perspective on the part of an auditor.

The Canadian Institute of Chartered Accountants and Provincial Institutes of Chartered Accountants

The history of the accounting profession in Canada stems from Scottish and English practices. In the early 1880s, two accounting organizations were formally established—the Association of Accountants in Montreal in 1880 and the Institute of Chartered Accountants of Ontario in 1883. As other provincial accounting organizations were formed, there was a need to coordinate activities, strengthen relationships, and promote common standards of education, training, and admission qualifications. Consequently, a national organization, the Dominion Association of Chartered Accountants, was formed in 1902; and in 1949 its name was changed to the Canadian Institute of Chartered Accountants (CICA).

The CICA is governed by a 29-member board of governors, and its affairs are administered by the executive officers elected by the board. Its organization reflects the federalism of Canada. Thus, members of the various provincial institutes automatically become members of the national institute. While its primary objective is to promote and maintain high professional standards, the CICA not only serves the accounting profession at the national and international level but also provides significant input to the public and private sectors throughout Canada regarding business practices, government legislation, and significant national policies and issues on which the public can expect leadership from the profession.

Through its *Handbook,* research studies, and various publications and its concern and involvement with national standards of education and business practices, the CICA performs a wide range of activities and carries out a variety of functions. All of these are designed to assist its members to better serve their clients or employers and to secure and enhance a uniform high level of competence throughout the profession.

The provincial institutes are responsible for the educational, training, and examination requirements for their students as well as the maintenance of high standards of performance for members as set forth in their *Codes of Ethics* or *Rules of Professional Conduct*. The affairs of each provincial institute are managed and conducted by a council, whose members are elected annually by the members of the provincial institute.

Although the profession of public accounting is a century old in Canada, it is one of the fastest growing. Membership in the CICA has more than doubled in the past decade and is now in excess of 50,000. Despite this tremendous growth, the demand for the services of CAs appears to be growing.

The *CICA Handbook*

Since its inception, the CICA has been concerned with the development of accounting and auditing practices for the enhancement of reliable and informative financial reporting. At present, three groups, the Accounting Standards Board, the Auditing Standards Board, and the Public Sector Accounting and Auditing Committee, are authorized by the institute's Board of Governors to issue recommendations in the *Handbook*. The Accounting Standards Board is responsible for the development and promulgation of accounting principles, and its recommendations are contained in the "Accounting Recommendations" section of the *Handbook*. The Auditing Standards Board is responsible for topics in the auditing areas, and its recommendations appear in the "Auditing Recommendations" section. Since the Accounting and Auditing Standards boards focus primarily on issues relating to the private sector, the Public Sector Committee is responsible for recommendations on those accounting and auditing issues related to governmental and other entities in the public sector. These recommendations are considered as generally accepted accounting principles and auditing standards of the profession. A departure from these recommendations by any member must be justified on valid grounds, and the responsibility for justification rests with the individual member. The

Handbook states that "where the accounting treatment or statement presentation does not follow the recommendations in this *Handbook,* the practice used should be explained in notes to the financial statements with an indication of reasons why the recommendation concerned was not followed."[4]

The issuance of a recommendation by a board is generally preceded by thorough research on its conceptual validity and practicality. An exposure draft on the recommendation is then published to solicit comments and suggestions from institute members and other interested parties. All comments and suggestions are then given serious consideration. Only after due deliberation and with the approval of at least two thirds of the board members will a recommendation be incorporated into the *Handbook*.

The Accounting Standards Board normally comprises 13 members, with terms of office ranging from one to three years. The board members include a cross section of individuals with various backgrounds and occupations: eight members are appointed by the CICA, and one member is appointed by each of these organizations; the Society of Management Accountants of Canada, Certified General Accountants' Association of Canada, Financial Executives Institute Canada, Canadian Academic Accounting Association, and Canadian Council of Financial Analysts.[5] The Auditing Standards Board is smaller, normally having only 11 members, at least eight of whom will be in public practice, with the rest from industry, government, and academe, with terms of office ranging from one to three years. The Public Sector Accounting and Auditing Committee comprises 19 members where terms also range from one to three years. Also, at least 10 of the members must be from government; the balance of its membership may include legislators, economists, financial analysts and academics. The terms of office also range from one to three years. Since the subject matter of the three committees is interrelated to a large extent, their activities are coordinated by the Joint Steering Committees.

Provincial Securities Acts and Securities Commissions

Although the securities acts vary somewhat from province to province, their primary objective is to ensure proper protection of the investing public and adequate financial statement disclosure. A provincial securities commission generally is charged with administering and enforcing the requirements and regulations set forth in the province's act, including audits, investigations and appeals, registration procedures, trading in securities, takeover bids, and insider trading. The various securities acts and commissions appear to depend largely on the accounting profession for

---

[4] The Canadian Institute of Chartered Accountants, *CICA Handbook* (Tornoto), p. 202.

[5] The Certified General Accountants' Association of Canada has declined to appoint its representative to serve on the Board.

the development of sound financial reporting. While national policy statements representing the views of the administrators of provincial securities commissions are issued from time to time, those related to financial reporting and accounting principles are primarily based on the *CICA Handbook* recommendations. For example, *National Policy Statement No. 27,* issued in December 1972, states:

> Where the term "generally accepted accounting principles" is used, either in Securities Legislation, Regulations, and Companies Legislation and Regulations, the Securities Administrators will regard pronouncements by the Accounting and Auditing Research Committee [subsequently changed to the Accounting Standards Board and the Auditing Standards Board] of the Canadian Institute of Chartered Accountants to the extent set out in the research recommendations in the "CICA Handbook" as "generally accepted accounting principles."

Public Accounting and the Certified Public Accountant in the United States

In recognition of the public trust imposed on independent public accountants, each state in the United States recognizes public accountancy as a profession and issues the certificate of Certified Public Accountant (CPA). The CPA certificate is a symbol of technical competence. This official recognition by the state is comparable to that accorded to the legal, medical, and other professions. A CPA certificate is issued by state and territorial governments to those individuals who have demonstrated, through written examinations and the satisfaction of educational and experience requirements, their qualifications for entry into the public accounting profession.

In addition to passing an examination and meeting certain educational requirements, the candidate for a CPA certificate in many states must also complete from one to five years of public accounting experience. The requirements as to amount of education and public accounting experience differ considerably among the various states.

American Institute of Certified Public Accountants

The AICPA is the national organization of certified public accountants engaged in research and in promoting high professional standards of practice in the United States. Throughout its existence, the AICPA has contributed enormously to the evolution of generally accepted accounting principles as well as to the development of auditing standards. The many technical divisions and committees of the institute (such as the Auditing Standards Board—ASB) provide a means of focusing the collective experience and ability of the profession on current problems. Such governmental agencies as the Securities and Exchange Commission (SEC) and the Internal Revenue Service continually seek the advice and cooperation of the institute in improving laws and regulations relating to accounting and auditing matters.

Division for CPA Firms. The AICPA has a division in which the members are CPA firms, rather than individual CPAs. The Division for Firms was created for the purpose of improving the quality of practice in CPA firms of all sizes. The Division for Firms has two sections: the Private Companies Practice Section and the SEC Practice Session. Membership is voluntary; a CPA firm may join either section or both. Each section has its own membership requirements, which include mandatory peer review. The formation of two sections for CPA firms reflects the belief that audits for large corporations subject to SEC regulations involve problems that are significantly different from those that arise in audits for small private companies. The SEC Practice Section has more rigorous membership requirements than does the Private Companies Practice Section. This new division of the AICPA represents a significant step in the American accounting profession's efforts at self-regulation.

Research and Publications of the AICPA—Auditing Literature. Among the most important AICPA publications bearing directly on the work of the CPA are the *Statements on Auditing Standards*. These authoritative pronouncements on auditing matters are issued by the Auditing Standards Board (ASB) and are referred to as SAS. The ASB also issues *Statements on Standards for Attestation Engagements* (*SSAE*). These statements provide CPAs with guidance for attesting to information other than financial statements, such as financial forecasts. Another important set of pronouncements serving as guides to the independent auditor are the *Statements on Standards for Accounting and Review Services* (*SSARS*). These pronouncements deal with the responsibility of CPAs when they are associated with unaudited financial statements.

Peer Review. A peer review occurs when one CPA firm arranges for a critical review of its practices by another CPA firm. Such an external review clearly offers a more objective evaluation of the quality of performance than could be made by self-review. The purpose of this concept is to encourage rigorous adherence to the best professional standards. It signifies the interest of the profession in effective self-regulation. It is required for CPA firms belonging to the SEC Practice Section of the AICPA.

Financial Accounting Standards Board. Auditors must determine whether financial statements are prepared in compliance with generally accepted accounting principles. The AICPA has designated the Financial Accounting Standards Board as the body with power to set forth these principles. Thus *FASB Statements,* exposure drafts, public hearings, and research projects are all of major concern to the public accounting profession.

U.S. Securities and Exchange Commission

The SEC is an agency of the U.S. government. It administers the Securities Act of 1933, the Securities Exchange Act of 1934, and other legislation concerning securities and financial matters. The first objective of the SEC is to protect investors and the public by requiring full disclosure of financial information by companies offering securities for sale to the public. A second objective is to prevent misrepresentation, deceit, or other fraud in the sale of securities.

The term *registration statement* is an important one in any discussion of the impact of the SEC on accounting practice. To *register* securities means to qualify them for sale to the public by filing with the SEC financial statements and other data in a form acceptable to the Commission. A registration statement contains *audited financial statements,* including a balance sheet for a two-year period and income statements for a three-year period. To aid the commission in discharging this responsibility, the securities acts provided for an examination and report by an *independent* public accountant. Thus, from its beginning the Securities and Exchange Commission has been a major user of audited financial statements and has exercised great influence on the development of accounting principles, on the strengthening of auditing standards, and especially on the concept of independence. If the SEC believes that a given registration statement does not meet its standards of disclosure, it may require amendment of the statement or it may issue a stop order preventing sale of the securities.

To improve the quality of the financial statements filed with it and the professional standards of the independent accountants who report on these statements, the SEC has adopted a basic accounting regulation known as *Regulations S-X* and entitled *Form and Content of Financial Statements*.

Since many large Canadian companies have their securities traded in the U.S. stock exchanges and are governed by the requirements of the SEC, it is important that there be a sound understanding of these requirements.

KEY TERMS

Accounting Standards Board (ASB)   The unit authorized by the CICA to issue recommendations with respect to matters of accounting practices. The board's recommendations are recognized as an authoritative source of generally accepted accounting principles.

agreed-upon procedures engagement　An attest engagement in which the public accountants agree to perform restricted procedures for a specified party.

American Institute of Certified Public Accountants (AICPA)　The national professional organization of CPAs engaged in promoting high professional standards and improving the quality of financial reporting in the United States.

assertion　A representation or declaration, typically made by the management of an entity.

attest engagement　An engagement in which a practitioner is engaged to express a conclusion about the reliability of an assertion that is the responsibility of another party.

audit of financial statements　An examination designed to provide the highest level of assurance that the financial statements follow generally accepted accounting principles, or another acceptable basis of accounting.

Auditing Standards Board (AuSB)　The unit authorized by the CICA to issue recommendations with respect to matters of auditing practices. The board's recommendations constitute a body of generally accepted auditing standards and practices.

Canadian Institute of Chartered Accountants (CICA)　The national organization of chartered accountants engaged in promoting and maintaining high professional standards of practice and providing significant input to the public and private sectors regarding business practices, government legislation, and other significant national policies and issues.

certified general accountant (CGA)　A member of the Certified General Accountants' Association.

Certified General Accountants' Association of Canada　A national organization of certified general accountants whose interests include both management and public accounting.

certified public accountant (CPA)　A person licensed by the state in the United States to practise public accounting as a profession, based on having passed the Uniform CPA Examination and having met certain education and experience requirements.

chartered accountant (CA)　A member of a provincial Institute/Order of Chartered Accountants and the CICA.

CICA Handbook　A publication of the Canadian Institute of Chartered Accountants. It contains the recommendations of the Accounting Standards Board, the Auditing Standards Board, and the Public Sector Accounting and Auditing Committee, as well as accounting/auditing guidelines.

compilation of financial statements Presenting in the form of financial statements information that is the representation of management without undertaking to express any assurance on the statements.

compliance audit An audit to determine whether financial statements, income tax returns, or other financial reports are in compliance with established criteria.

comprehensive auditing A new concept encompassing both compliance and operational auditing and having the objectives of determining the fairness of financial statements and the economy, effectiveness, and efficiency of operations.

examination An attest engagement designed to provide the highest level of assurance on an assertion. An examination of financial statements is referred to as an *audit*.

fraud Misrepresentation by a person of a material fact, known by that person to be untrue or made with reckless indifference as to whether it is true, with intent to deceive and with the result that another party is injured.

generally accepted accounting principles (GAAP) Concepts, practices, or standards established primarily by the CICA and accepted by the accounting profession as essential to proper financial reporting.

independence A most important factor in auditing standards, which prohibits public accountants from expressing an opinion on financial statements of an enterprise unless they are independent with respect to such enterprise; independence in appearance is impaired by a material financial interest, service as an officer or trustee, loans to or from the enterprise, and various other relationships suggesting a conflict of interest.

operational audit A review of a department or other unit of a business or governmental organization to measure the efficiency of operations.

Provincial Certified General Accountants' Association A provincial organization of CGAs (in Quebec, the Professional Corporation of Certified General Accountants) incorporated under provincial legislation.

Provincial Institute of Chartered Accountants A provincial organization of CAs (in Quebec, the Order of Chartered Accountants) incorporated under a provincial act and empowered to confer the CA designation on its members.

Provincial Securities Commission A provincial government unit whose primary objective is to ensure proper protection of the investing public and adequate financial statement disclosure.

public accountant A person who is licensed or otherwise permitted by provincial laws to engage in the practice of public accounting, the primary function of which is to attest to the fairness of financial statements.

Public Sector Accounting and Auditing Committee The unit authorized by the CICA to issue recommendations on the accounting and auditing matters related to governmental and other entities in the public sector. The committee's recommendations constitute a body of generally accepted standards.

review An engagement designed to lend only a limited degree of assurance relating to an assertion. As discussed in further detail in Chapter 19, the procedures performed are generally limited to discussions, enquiries, and analytical procedures.

Securities and Exchange Commission (SEC) A government agency in the United States authorized to review financial statements of companies seeking approval to issue securities for sale to the public.

Statements on Auditing Standards (SAS) A series of statements issued by the Auditing Standards Board of the AICPA. These statements are considered to be interpretations of generally accepted auditing standards in the United States.

GROUP I: REVIEW QUESTIONS

1-1. What is the principal use and significance of an audit report to a large corporation with securities listed on a stock exchange? To a small family-owned enterprise?

1-2. Is an *independent status* possible for internal auditors as compared with the independence of a public accounting firm? Explain.

1-3. The attest function is said to be the principal reason for the existence of a public accounting profession. What is meant by attesting to a client's financial statements?

1-4. What is the most common type of attest engagement? What is most frequently being "asserted" by management on this type of engagement?

1-5. What does an operational audit try to measure? Does an operational audit involve more or fewer subjective judgments than a compliance audit or an audit of financial statements? Explain. To whom is the report usually directed after completion of an operational audit?

1-6. Distinguish between a compliance audit and an operational audit.

1-7. What is a comprehensive audit?

1-8. Explain the terms *economy, efficiency,* and *effectiveness* for a value-for-money audit.

1-9. CA firms are sometimes grouped into categories of local firms, regional firms, and national firms. Explain briefly the characteristics of each. Include in your answer the types of services stressed in each group.

1–10. Contrast the objectives of auditing at the beginning of this century with the objectives of auditing today.

1–11. Describe briefly the responsibilities of the Auditor General Office of Canada.

1–12. Why should the province license public accountants?

1–13. List the three major accounting professions in Canada and their respective interests.

1–14. Apart from auditing, what other professional services are offered by public accounting firms?

1–15. What are the advantages of organizing a public accounting firm as a partnership rather than a sole proprietorship?

1–16. How does a professional corporation differ from the traditional corporation?

1–17. Describe the various levels or grades of accounting personnel in a large public accounting firm.

1–18. Distinguish between the responsibilities of a senior auditor and a staff assistant.

1–19. List three of the more important responsibilities of a partner in a public accounting firm.

1–20. What were some of the factors that caused auditors to adopt a sampling technique rather than make a complete review of all transactions?

1–21. Describe several business situations that would create a need for a report by an independent public accountant concerning the fairness of a company's financial statements.

1–22. Spacecraft Inc., a large corporation, is audited regularly by a CA firm and also maintains an internal auditing staff. Explain briefly how the relationship of the CA firm to Spacecraft differs from the relationship of the internal auditing staff to Spacecraft.

1–23. Briefly explain the role of the Canadian Institute of Chartered Accountants?

GROUP II: QUESTIONS REQUIRING ANALYSIS

1–24. The self-interest of the provider of financial information (whether an individual or a business entity) often runs directly counter to the interests of the user of the information.

   a. Give an example of such opposing interests.

   b. What may be done to compensate for the possible bias existing because of the self-interest of the individual or business entity providing the financial information?

1–25. Evaluate the following quotation: "Every business, large or small, should have an annual audit by a public accounting firm. To forgo an audit because of its cost is false economy."

1–26. The role of the auditor in our economy has changed over the years in response to changes in our economic and political institutions. Consequently, an audit today is quite different from an audit performed in the year 1900. Classify the following phrases into two groups: (1) phrases more applicable to an audit performed in 1900 and (2) phrases more applicable to an audit performed today.

   a. Complete review of all transactions.

   b. Assessment of internal control.

   c. Auditors' attention concentrated on balance sheet.

   d. Emphasis upon use of sampling techniques.

   e. Determination of fairness of financial statements.

   f. Audit procedures to prevent or detect fraud on the part of all employees and managers.

   g. Influence of stock exchanges and the investing public upon use of independent auditors.

   h. Generally accepted auditing standards.

   i. Bankers and short-term creditors as principal users of audit reports.

   j. Pressure for more disclosure.

1–27. Select the best answer for each of the following items and give reasons for your choice.

   a. Which of the following has primary responsibility for the fairness of the representations made in financial statements?

   (1) Client's management.

   (2) Independent auditor.

   (3) Audit committee.

   (4) CICA.

   b. What is the most important benefit of having an annual audit by a CA firm?

   (1) Provides assurance to investors and other outsiders that the financial statements are dependable.

   (2) Enables officers and directors to avoid personal responsibility for any misstatements in the financial statements.

   (3) Meets the requirements of government agencies.

   (4) Provides assurance that illegal acts, if any exist, will be brought to light.

   c. Governmental auditing, in addition to including audits of financial statements, often includes audits of efficiency, effectiveness, and:

   (1) Adequacy.

   (2) Evaluation.

   (3) Accuracy.

   (4) Economy.

    d. In general, internal auditors' independence will be greatest when they report directly to the:
    (1) Financial vice-president.
    (2) Corporate controller.
    (3) Audit committee of the board of directors.
    (4) Corporate shareholders.

    e. Operational audits often have an objective of determining whether an entity's:
    (1) Internal control structure is adequately operating as designed.
    (2) Operational information is in accordance with generally accepted governmental auditing standards.
    (3) Financial statements present fairly the results of operations.
    (4) Specific operating units are functioning efficiently and effectively.

(AICPA, adapted)

GROUP III: PROBLEMS

1–28.   For the purposes of this problem, you are to assume the existence of four types of auditors: external auditor, auditor general, Revenue Canada auditor, and internal auditor. Also assume that the work of these various auditors can be grouped into five classifications: audits of financial statements, compliance audits, operational audits, value-for-money audit, and management advisory services.

    For each of the following topics, you are to state the type of auditor most probably involved. Also identify the topic with one of the above classes of work.

    You should organize your answer in a three-column format as follows: Column 1, list the number of the topic; Column 2, list the type of auditor involved; and Column 3, list the class of work.

    1. Financial statements of a small business to be submitted to a bank in support of a loan application.

    2. Financial statements of a large bank listed on the Toronto Stock Exchange to be distributed to shareholders.

    3. Review of the management directive stating the goals and responsibilities of a corporation's mail-handling department.

    4. Review of costs and accomplishments of a military research program carried on within the Air Force to determine whether the program was effective, efficient, and economical.

5. Analysis of the accounting system of a small business with the objective of making recommendations concerning installation of a computer-based system.

6. Determination of fairness of financial statements for public distribution by a corporation that has a professional-level internal auditing staff.

7. Review of the activities of the receiving department of a large manufacturing company, with special attention to efficiency of materials inspection and promptness of reports issued.

8. Review of tax return of corporate president to determine whether charitable contributions are adequately substantiated.

9. Examination of the financial statements of Canada.

1–29. Each auditing term (or organizational name) in Column One below bears a close relationship to a term in Column Two.

Column One	**Column Two**
1. Operational audit.	*a.* Compliance audit.
2. Internal control.	*b.* Attest function.
3. Office of the Auditor General of Canada.	*c.* Material information.
	d. Credibility.
4. Disclosure.	*e.* Accounting service.
5. Major reason for existence of public accounting profession.	*f.* Measurement of effectiveness and efficiency of a unit of an organization.
6. Revenue Canada.	*g.* Basis for sampling and testing.
7. Audited financial statements.	*h.* Auditing staff reporting to the House of Commons.
8. Compilation of financial statements.	

Required:

You are to identify the most closely related terms in Columns One and Two. Organize your answer in a two-column format by copying the numbers and terms in Column One as given. Then, rearrange the sequence of terms in Column Two so that each line of your schedule will contain two closely related terms.

1–30. Feller, the sole owner of a small hardware business, has been told that the business should have financial statements audited by an independent CA. Feller, having some bookkeeping experience, has personally prepared the company's financial statements and does not understand why such statements should be audited by a CA. Feller discussed the matter with Farber, a CA, and asked Farber to explain why an audit is considered important.

Required:

a. Describe the objectives of an independent audit.

b. Identify five ways in which an independent audit may be beneficial to Feller.

(AICPA, adapted)

1–31. Will Williams, a college senior, has begun the interviewing process. He has discovered a great variety of organizations in search of "accounting majors." He finds that various CA firms, corporations, Office of the Auditor General of Canada, and Revenue Canada are all interviewing candidates at his school.

He has come to you and asked for your advice. He has suggested that although he has had only one class session of auditing, he already realizes that it is going to be a great course. But, he also especially enjoyed his tax and accounting systems courses.

Required:

Compare and contrast his possibilities with CA firms, corporations, the Office of the Auditor General of Canada, and Revenue Canada if he wishes to emphasize the following areas of expertise:

a. Taxation.

b. Auditing.

c. Systems design.

For example, first compare and contrast his likely responsibilities with each of the above organizations if he chooses to emphasize taxation.

1–32. In a discussion between Peters and Ferrel, two auditing students, Peters made the following statement:

"A CA is a professional person who provides an independent expert opinion on the fairness of financial statements. To maintain an attitude of mental independence and objectivity in all phases of audit work, it is advisable that the CA not fraternize with client personnel. The CA should be courteous but reserved and dignified at all times. Indulging in social contacts with clients outside of business hours will make it more difficult to be firm and objective if the CA finds evidence of fraud or of unsound accounting practices."

Ferrel replied as follows:

"You are 50 years behind the times, Peters. An auditor and a client are both human beings. The auditor needs the cooperation of the client to do a good job; you're much more likely to get cooperation if you're relaxed and friendly rather than being cold and impersonal. Having a few beers or going to a football game or other similar social activities with a client won't keep the CA from being independent. It will make the working relationship a lot more comfortable, and will probably cause the client to recommend the CA to other business people who need auditing services. In other words, the approach you're recommending should be called 'How to Avoid Friends and Alienate Clients.' ''

Evaluate the opposing views expressed by Peters and Ferrel.

Chapter 2

Professional Standards

Chapter Objectives

After studying this chapter, you should be able to:
- Describe the generally accepted auditing standards.
- Explain the key elements contained in the generally accepted auditing standards.
- Discuss the auditors' responsibility for detection of errors, fraud and illegal acts.
- Explain the key elements of the auditors' standard report.
- Discuss the other types of reports that are issued by auditors.
- Describe the quality control standards and their purposes.
- Discuss the status of international auditing standards.

Standards are rules approved and adopted by various individuals and organizations. Standards relating to the accounting profession concern themselves both with the public accountants' professional qualities and with the judgment exercised by public accountants in the performance of their professional engagements.

Our purpose in this chapter is to make clear the nature of generally accepted auditing standards and quality control standards. In our discussion of the generally accepted auditing standards, we consider in detail the nature of the independent auditors' report—that brief but important document that emerges as the end product of an audit engagement. The auditors' report is what gives credibility to a set of financial statements and makes them acceptable to investors, bankers, government, and other users.

GENERALLY ACCEPTED AUDITING STANDARDS (GAAS)

Standards are authoritative rules for measuring the *quality* of performance. The existence of generally accepted auditing standards is evidence that auditors are very concerned with the maintenance of a uniformly high quality of audit work by all independent public accountants. If every public accountant has adequate technical training and performs audits with skill, care, and professional judgment, the prestige of the profession will rise, and the public will attribute more and more significance to the auditors' opinion attached to financial statements.

What are the standards developed by the public accounting profession? The CICA has set forth the basic framework in the following eight *generally accepted auditing standards:*

General standard:

> The examination should be performed and the report prepared by a person or persons having adequate technical training and proficiency in auditing, with due care and with an objective state of mind.

Examination standards:

(i) The work should be adequately planned and properly executed. If assistants are employed, they should be properly supervised.

(ii) A sufficient understanding of internal control should be obtained to plan the audit. When control risk is assessed below maximum, sufficient appropriate audit evidence should be obtained through tests of controls to support the assessment.

(iii) Sufficient appropriate audit evidence should be obtained, by such means as inspection, observation, enquiry, confirmation, computation, and analysis, to afford a reasonable basis to support the content of the report.

Reporting standards:

(i) The report should identify the financial statements and distinguish between the responsibilities of management and the responsibilities of the auditor.

(ii) The report should describe the scope of the auditor's examination.

(iii) The report should contain either an expression of opinion on the financial statements or an assertion that an opinion cannot be expressed. In the latter case, the reasons therefor should be stated.

(iv) Where an opinion is expressed, it should indicate whether the financial statements present fairly, in all material respects, the financial position, results of operations, and changes in financial position in accordance with an appropriate disclosed basis of accounting, which except in special circumstances should be generally accepted accounting principles. The report should provide adequate explanation with respect to any reservation contained in such opinion.

Application of Auditing Standards

In addition to setting forth the generally accepted auditing standards, the CICA Auditing Standards Board provides explanations of the applicability of the standards and the term *disclosed basis of accounting*.

Applicability of the Standards

The auditing standards . . . apply to engagements in which the objective is the expression of an audit opinion on financial statements. The general and examination standards are also applicable to other types of audit engagements.

The general standard . . . is intended to express the spirit of the related rule(s) of professional conduct of each provincial Institute or Order, to which rule(s) the auditor is referred.

Disclosed Basis of Accounting

Reporting standard (*iv*) . . . contains a reference to "an appropriate disclosed basis of accounting, which except in special circumstances should be generally accepted accounting principles." [There are] circumstances where the auditor should express his opinion as to the conformity of the financial statements with generally accepted accounting principles. There are [also] special circumstances where a different basis of accounting may be appropriate, for example in financial statements:

(*a*) prepared in accordance with regulatory legislation; and
(*b*) prepared in accordance with contractual requirements such as may be set out in trust indentures or buy/sell agreements.

In special circumstances where a basis of accounting other than generally accepted accounting principles is appropriate, the auditor would express his opinion as to the conformity of the financial statements with such appropriate disclosed basis of accounting. The auditor would express a reservation of opinion on financial statements which did not disclose information appropriate and adequate in the circumstances.

The eight standards set forth by the Auditing Standards Board also include such intangible and subjective terms of measurement as "*adequate* planning," "*sufficient* understanding of internal control," "*sufficient appropriate* audit evidence," and "*adequate* explanation." To decide under the circumstances of each audit engagement what is adequate, sufficient, and appropriate requires the exercise of professional judgment. Auditing cannot be reduced to rote; the exercise of judgment by the auditor is vital at numerous points in every examination.

However, the formulation and publication of carefully worded auditing standards are an immense aid in raising the quality of audit work, even though these standards require professional judgment in their application.

Training and Proficiency

How does the independent auditor achieve the "adequate technical training and proficiency in auditing" required by the general standard? This requirement is usually interpreted to mean university education in accounting and auditing, substantial public accounting experience, ability to use procedures suitable for computer-based systems, and participation in continuing education programs. A technical knowledge of the industry in which the client operates is also part of the personal qualifications of the auditor. It follows that a CA firm must not accept an audit engagement without first determining that members of its staff have the technical training and proficiency needed to function effectively in the particular industry.

An Objective State of Mind, or Independence

An opinion by an independent public accountant as to the fairness of a company's financial statements is of no value unless the accountant is truly objective or independent. Consequently, the general standard states that "the examination should be performed and the report prepared . . . with an objective state of mind." This requirement is perhaps the most essential factor in the existence of a public accounting profession.

An "objective state of mind," or "independence," comprises two distinct considerations: *in fact* and *in appearance.* Independence in fact refers to the ability of public accountants to maintain an unbiased and impartial mental attitude in all aspects of their work, whether or not existing circumstances might have an apparent effect on their objectivity. Independence in appearance relates to the public accountants' freedom from conflict of interest which a third party may infer from circumstantial evidence. Independence in appearance is considered to be lacking; for example, if auditors owned shares of stock in a company which they audited, or if their fees are contingent on the results of the audit, or if they served as members of the board of directors, or if one client represents a major portion of the auditors' income. Auditors should therefore avoid any relationship with a client that would cause an outsider who had knowledge of all the facts to doubt their independence. Thus, it is not enough that the auditors be independent in fact. They must also be independent in appearance; that is, they must conduct themselves in such a manner that informed members of the public will have no reason to doubt their independence.

Due Care

The general standard also requires due care in the conduct of the audit and in the preparation of the audit report. It requires the auditors to carry out every step of the audit engagement in an alert and diligent manner. Full compliance with this requirement would rule out any negligent acts or material omissions by the auditors. Of course, auditors, as well as members of other professions, inevitably make occasional errors in judgment, but this human element does not justify indifference or inattention to professional responsibilities.

Examination Standards—Accumulating Evidence

The three examination standards relate to accumulating and evaluating evidence sufficient for the auditors to express an opinion on the financial statements. One major type of evidence is the client's internal control. By obtaining an understanding and testing of internal control, the auditors can judge whether the internal control offers assurance that the financial statements will be free from material errors and fraud. A second major type of evidence consists of information that substantiates the amounts on the financial statements being audited. Examples of such evidence include written confirmations from outsiders and firsthand observation of assets by the auditors. The gathering and evaluating of evidence lies at the very heart of the audit process and is a continuing theme throughout this textbook.

Adequate Planning and Supervision

Adequate planning is essential to a satisfactory audit. Some portions of the examination can be performed prior to the end of the year under audit; some information may be compiled by the client's staff and made available for the auditors' review. The appropriate number of audit staff of various levels of skill and the time required of each need to be determined in advance of the examination. These are but a few of the elements of planning the audit.

Most of the work of an audit is carried out by staff members with limited experience. The key to successful use of relatively new staff members is close supervision at every level. This concept extends from providing specific written instructions to staff members all the way to an overall review by the partner in charge of the engagement.

Sufficient Understanding of Internal Control

Excellent internal control provides strong assurance that the client's records are dependable and that its assets are protected. When the auditors find this type of strong internal control, the quantity of other evidence required is much less than if controls were weak. Thus, the auditor's understanding of internal control has great impact on the planning of the audit and on the nature, extent, and timing of the auditing procedures.

Sufficient Appropriate Audit Evidence

The third examination standard requires that the auditors gather sufficient appropriate audit evidence to have a basis for expressing an opinion on the financial statements. The term *appropriate* refers to the quality of the evidence; some forms of evidence are stronger and more convincing than others. In Chapter 6, we shall explore at length the meaning of this standard.

The Reporting Standards

The four reporting standards establish some specific directives for preparation of the auditors' report. The report must specifically identify the financial statements, distinguish the responsibilities between management and the auditor, state the scope of the examination and state whether the financial statements are in conformity with generally accepted accounting principles. The report must contain an opinion on the financial statements as a whole, or must contain a denial of an opinion. Adequate informative disclosure in the financial statements is to be assumed unless the audit report states otherwise. These basic reporting standards are considered more fully in Chapter 18.

Summary of the Eight Generally Accepted Auditing Standards

The basic concepts embodied in generally accepted auditing standards are summarized in Figure 2–1. Keep in mind, however, that these standards represent the *minimum* requirements for all audit engagements.

FIGURE 2–1   Summary of Eight Generally Accepted Auditing Standards

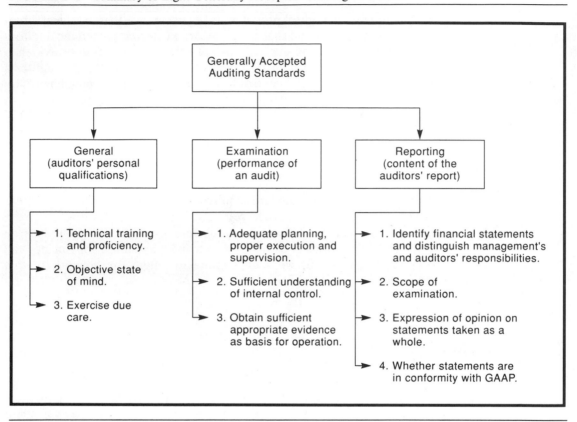

THE AUDITORS' RESPONSIBILITY FOR DETECTING MISSTATEMENTS

For financial statements to be in accordance with generally accepted accounting principles, they must be free from material misstatements. Therefore, the auditors have a responsibility to detect various types of misstatements, including errors, fraud, and those caused by certain illegal acts. Section 5135 of the *CICA Handbook* delineates the auditors' responsibility to detect and communicate misstatements in financial statements, as a result of errors and fraud.

Errors and Fraud.   Section 5135 of the *CICA Handbook* defines the term *error* as an unintentional misstatement in financial statements such as a mistake in the application of accounting principles. *Fraud,* on the other hand, is defined as an intentional misstatement in financial statements by omission of disclosure or theft of assets through such means as the use of deception to manipulate, falsify, or alter accounting records or documents.

Section 5135 further states that generally accepted auditing standards require the auditors to design their audit procedures to reduce the risk of not detecting a material misstatement resulting from error or fraud to an appropriately low level. Accordingly, the auditors must exercise due care in planning, performing, and evaluating the results of audit procedures. They also must exercise the proper degree of professional skepticism by not assuming unquestioned honesty and good faith on the part of management.

The auditors should inform the appropriate level of management about any material misstatements. For example, if fraud is detected, the level of management to inform is usually at least one level above those suspected to be involved in the fraud. Also, the audit committee of the client's board of directors should be informed of any significant misstatements.

An audit must provide reasonable assurance, not absolute assurance, of detecting a material misstatement of the financial statements. The auditors are in no way an insurer and their audit reports do not constitute a guarantee. Audits providing absolute assurance would be too costly.

Illegal Acts by Clients.   Laws and regulations vary in their relation to the client's financial statement. Certain laws have a direct effect on the financial statements and are considered on every audit. An example is the income tax law, which affects the amount of income tax expense in the financial statements of most clients. The auditors' responsibility for detecting violations of these laws is greater than their responsibility to detect illegal acts arising from laws that only indirectly affect the client's financial statements, such as violations of the Combines legislation. An illegal act may need to be reflected in the client's financial statements, and may even affect the future viability of the client's business.

It has been suggested that the CICA should provide guidance on the auditors' responsibility for client's illegal acts.[1] The AICPA in the United States, however, has stated in *SAS 54* that an audit carried out in accordance with generally accepted auditing standards should be designed to provide reasonable assurance of detecting illegal acts having a material *direct* effect on the determination of financial statement amounts—this is the same responsibility the auditors have for material errors and fraud. An audit does not generally provide a basis for detecting violations of laws or regulations which have an ***indirect*** effect on the financial statement amounts. Unfortunately, the media and the public sometimes tend to blame auditors because illegal acts by a client company are not brought to light during an audit. Only those persons who understand the scope and limitations of an audit realize that audits by their very nature cannot be

---

[1] CICA, *Report of the Commission to Study the Public's Expectations of Audits* (Toronto, 1988), pp. 99–102.

relied on to detect all types of illegel acts by the client. Of course, audit procedures such as reading minutes of the board of directors and enquiring of management and the client's legal counsel sometimes will result in the discovery of certain illegal acts. Also, the auditors are alert throughout their audit for information that raises a question regarding the possibility of illegal acts, such as transactions that are unauthorized or improperly recorded, investigations of governmental agencies, and excessive or unusual payments.

Under no circumstances should the auditors condone or ignore actions they know to be dishonest or illegal. This does not mean that the auditors should report such acts to governmental authorities; it does mean that they should not permit their firm's name to be associated with financial statements that are misleading or that conceal legally indefensible actions by a client.

If the auditors have knowledge of dishonest or clearly illegal actions by a client, they should attempt to assess the impact of the actions on the financial statements. This usually requires consulting legal counsel or other specialists. The auditors should also discuss the situation with top management and notify the audit committee of the board of directors so that proper action can be taken, including making any necessary disclosures or adjustments to the financial statements. If the client fails to take appropriate corrective action, the auditors should withdraw from the engagement. This action on the part of the auditors makes clear that they will not be associated in any way with dishonourable or illegal activities.

THE AUDITORS' REPORT

The end product of an audit of a business entity is a report expressing the auditors' opinion on the client's financial statements. In 1990 the Auditing Standards Board made a number of changes in the profession's reporting standards. The auditors' **standard report** (also called a *standard unqualified report*) that resulted from these changes consists of three paragraphs. The first paragraph identifies the financial statements and clarifies the responsibilities of management and the auditors and is referred to as the **introductory paragraph.** The second paragraph, which describes the nature of the audit, is called the **scope paragraph;** the final paragraph, the **opinion paragraph,** is a concise statement of the auditor's opinion based on the audit.

The auditors' report is addressed to the person or persons who retained the auditors; in the case of corporations, the appointment of an auditing firm is usually made by the shareholders.

Auditors' Report

To the Shareholders of XYZ Limited:

We have audited the balance sheet of XYZ Limited as at December 31, 19––, and the statements of income, retained earnings, and changes in financial position for the year then ended. These financial statements are the responsibility of the company's management. Our responsibility is to express an opinion on these financial statements based on our audit.

We conducted our audit in accordance with generally accepted auditing standards. Those standards require that we plan and perform an audit to obtain reasonable assurance whether the financial statements are free of material misstatement. An audit includes examining, on a test basis, evidence supporting the amounts and disclosures in the financial statements. An audit also includes assessing the accounting principles used and significant estimates made by management, as well as evaluating the overall financial statement presentation.

In our opinion, these financial statements present fairly, in all material respects, the financial position of the Company as at December 31, 19––, and the results of its operations and the changes in its financial position for the year then ended in accordance with generally accepted accounting principles.

Windsor, Ontario
February 26, 19––

Blue, Gray + Company
Chartered Accountants

The Introductory Paragraph of the Auditors' Report

To gain a full understanding of the introductory paragraph of the auditors' report we need to emphasize the following two points:

1. The client company is primarily responsible for the financial statements.

The management of a company has the responsibility of maintaining adequate accounting records and of preparing proper financial statements for the use of shareholders and creditors. Even though the financial statements are sometimes constructed and typed in the auditors' office, primary responsibility for the statements remains with management.

The auditors' product is their report. It is a separate document from the client's financial statements, although the two are closely related and transmitted together to shareholders and to creditors.

Once we recognize that the financial statements are the statements of the company and not of the auditors, we realize that the auditors have no right to make changes in the financial statements. What action, then, should the auditors take if they do not agree with the presentation of a material item in the balance sheet or income statement? Assume, for example, that the allowance for doubtful accounts is not sufficient (in the auditors' opinion) to cover the probable collection losses in the accounts receivable.

The auditors will first discuss the problem with management and point out why they believe the valuation allowance is inadequate. If management agrees to increase the allowance for doubtful accounts, an adjusting entry is made for that purpose, and the problem is solved. If management is not convinced by the auditors' arguments and declines to increase the doubtful accounts allowance, the auditors will probably *qualify* their opinion by stating in the report that the financial statements reflect fairly the company's financial position and operating results, *except for the effects of not providing an adequate provision for doubtful account losses.* Usually such issues are satisfactorily disposed of in discussions between the auditors and the client, and a qualification of the auditors' opinion is avoided. A full consideration of the use of qualifications in the auditors' report is presented in Chapter 18.

2. The auditors render a report on the financial statements, not on the accounting records.

The primary purpose of an audit is to provide assurance to the users of the financial statements that these statements are reliable. Auditors do not express an opinion on the client's accounting records. The auditors' investigation of financial statement items includes reference to the client's accounting records, but is not limited to these records. The auditors' examination includes observation of tangible assets, inspection of such documents as purchase orders and contracts, and the gathering of evidence from outsiders (such as banks, customers, and suppliers), as well as analysis of the client's accounting records.

It is true that a principal means of establishing the validity of a balance sheet and income statement is to trace the statement figures to the accounting records and back through the records to the original evidence of transactions. However, the auditors' use of the accounting records is only a means to an end—and merely a part of the audit. It is, therefore, appropriate for the auditors to state in their report that they have made an audit of the *financial statements* rather than to say that they have made an audit of the accounting records.

The Scope Paragraph of the Auditors' Report

The scope paragraph describes the nature of the audit. It states that the audit was conducted in accordance with generally accepted auditing standards and points out that while an audit is meant to provide *reasonable assurance* that the financial statements are free of material misstatement, the procedures are applied on a test basis. Thus, an audit cannot provide *absolute assurance* that the financial statements are free from material misstatement.

The Opinion Paragraph of the Auditors' Report

The opinion paragraph consists of only one sentence, which is restated here with certain significant phrases shown in boldface italics:

> *In our opinion,* these financial statements *present fairly, in all material respects,* the financial position of the company as at December 31, 19––, and the results of its operations and the changes in its financial position for the year ended in accordance with *generally accepted accounting principles.*

Each of the emphasized phrases has a special significance. The first phrase, "in our opinion," makes clear that the auditors are expressing nothing more than an informed opinion; they are not guaranteeing or certifying that the statements are accurate, correct, or true. In an earlier period of public accounting, the wording of the audit report contained the phrase "We certify that . . . ," but this expression was discontinued on the grounds that it was misleading. To "certify" implies a positive assurance of accuracy, which an audit simply does not provide.

The auditors cannot guarantee the correctness of the financial statements because the statements themselves are largely matters of opinion rather than of absolute fact. Furthermore, the auditors do not make a complete and detailed examination of all transactions. Their examination is limited to a program of tests that leaves the possibility of some errors going undetected. Because of limitations inherent in the accounting process and because of practical limitations of time and cost in performing an audit, the auditors' work culminates in the expression of an opinion and not in the issuance of a guarantee of accuracy. The growth of public accounting and the increased confidence placed in audited statements by all sectors of the economy indicate that the auditors' opinion is usually sufficient assurance that the statements may be relied upon.

The Financial Statements "Present Fairly, in All Material Respects . . ."

Since many of the items in financial statements cannot be measured exactly, the auditors cannot say that the statements present exactly or correctly the financial position or operating results. The meaning of "present fairly" as used in the context of the auditors' report has been much discussed in court cases and in auditing literature. Some accountants believed that financial statements were fair if they conformed to GAAP; others insisted that fairness was a distinct concept, broader than mere compliance with GAAP. This discussion led to an earlier CICA recommendation of a "two-part" opinion; that is, "present fairly" and "in accordance with GAAP" were to be judged separately. However, the CICA subsequently changed its recommendation and now takes the position that the judgment on "present fairly" can be applied only within the framework of generally accepted accounting principles.[2] In the opinion of the authors, the essence of the CICA position is to equate the quality of *presenting fairly* with that of *not being misleading* or *not being materially misstated.* Financial statements must not be so presented as to lead users to forecasts or conclusions that a company and its independent auditors know are unsound or unlikely.

What Is "Material"?   Auditors cannot issue an unqualified opinion on financial statements that contain *material* deficiencies. The term *material* may be defined as "sufficiently important to influence decisions made by reasonable users of financial statements." In the audit of a small client—such as a condominium property owners' association—$1,000 might be considered material. On the other hand, in the audit of an IBM or a General Motors an amount of $1 million might be considered to be immaterial.

In practice, one of the most significant elements of professional judgment is the ability to draw the line between material and immaterial departures from good accounting practices. The auditor who raises objections over immaterial items will soon lose the respect of both clients and associates. On the other hand, the auditor who fails to identify and disclose material deficiencies in financial statements may be liable for the losses of those who rely upon the audited statements. In short, applying the concept of materiality is one of the most complex problems faced by auditors.

Materiality depends upon both the *dollar amount* and the *nature of the item.* For example, a $500,000 error in the balance of the Cash account is far more important than a $500,000 error in the balance of Accumulated Depreciation. If a corporation sells assets to a member of top management and then buys the assets back at a higher price, this *related party trans-*

---

[2] CICA, *CICA Handbook,* sec. 5400.16.

action warrants disclosure even though the dollar amounts are not large in relation to the financial statements as a whole. The reason for requiring disclosure of such a transaction—that is, the risk of management impropriety—is based more on the nature of the transaction than upon the dollar amount.

Adequate Informative Disclosure. If financial statements are to present fairly, in all material respects, the financial position and operating results of a company, there must be adequate disclosure of all essential information. A financial statement may be misleading if it does not give a complete picture. For example, if an extraordinary item arising from the expropriation of land and buildings were combined with operating income and not clearly identified, the reader might be misled as to the earning power of the company.

Generally Accepted Accounting Principles

In our study of the main ideas contained in the auditors' report, the next key phrase to be considered is "generally accepted accounting principles." The wording of the audit report implies that generally accepted accounting principles represent a concept well known to auditors and sophisticated users of financial statements. Examples of such principles have long been agreed upon; the cost principle, the realization principle, the matching concept, the going-concern assumption, and other principles are familiar to every accounting student. However, no official list of accounting principles exists, and a satisfactory concise definition is yet to be developed.[3]

At present, the recommendations of the CICA Accounting Standards Board constitute a major authoritative source. These *CICA Handbook* recommendations are recognized as generally accepted accounting principles by the Canada Business Corporations Act and the provincial securities commissions.

When an accounting principle is not covered by the recommendations in the *CICA Handbook,* the auditors may refer to a variety of sources:

1. Accounting practices that are in widespread use.
2. Broad theoretical concepts that underlie most accounting practices.
3. Standards published by the International Accounting Standards Committee.

---

[3] The definition of generally accepted accounting principles in the *CICA Handbook* is far too broad as it "encompasses not only specific rules, practices, and procedures relating to particular circumstances but also broad principles and conventions of general application" (sec. 1000.60).

4. Standards published by authorized bodies in other jurisdictions, for example, *Statements of Financial Accounting Standards* issued by the Financial Accounting Standards Board in the United States.
5. Research studies published by recognized accounting bodies.
6. Accounting literature—textbooks and journals.

Other Types of Auditors' Reports

The form of auditors' report discussed in this chapter is called a *standard report.* Such a report contains an unqualified opinion issued by the auditors. An unqualified opinion denotes that the examination was adequate in scope and that the financial statements present fairly the financial position and results of operations in conformity with generally accepted accounting principles. Under these circumstances, the auditors are taking *no exceptions* and inserting *no qualifications* in the report.

An unqualified opinion is the type of report the client wants and also the type auditors prefer to issue. In some audits, however, the circumstances do not permit the auditors to give their unqualified opinion on the financial statements. As alternatives to an unqualified opinion, auditors may issue a *qualified opinion,* an *adverse opinion,* or a *denial of opinion.*

The auditors issue a *qualified opinion* on financial statements when there is some limitation on their examination, or when one or more items in the financial statements are not presented in accordance with generally accepted accounting principles. The limitation or exception must be significant but not so material as to overshadow an overall opinion on the financial statements.

An *adverse opinion* states that the financial statements are not fairly presented. In practice an adverse opinion is rare, because it would be of little use to the client. If the financial statements contain such material departures from generally accepted accounting principles, as to warrant an adverse opinion, this situation will be discussed between the auditors and the client's management. The management probably will agree to make the changes necessary to avoid an adverse opinion or will decide to terminate the audit engagement and thus avoid paying additional audit fees.

The auditors will issue a *denial of opinion* if they are unable to determine the overall fairness of the financial statements. This type of report results from very significant limitations in the scope of the auditors' examination or limitations that are imposed by the client.

QUALITY CONTROL FOR ACCOUNTING FIRMS IN CANADA AND THE UNITED STATES

In its desire to maintain high professional standards and to signify the profession's interest in effective self-regulation, the accounting profession in both Canada and the United States has taken steps to enhance the quality of its members' performance. Also, accounting firms in both countries have strengthened their internal review programs to ensure high standards of quality control over their auditing and other engagements. These review programs generally involve an appraisal by the firm's own review team of the work of its members or offices. Constructive criticisms and suggestions are given to those whose work has been reviewed so that their performance can be improved.

Quality Control in Canada

To ensure that high standards of performance are not only being maintained but also are seen to be so, the chartered accountancy profession has established a program of quality control called ***practice inspection*** (also called *practice review*). Practice inspection means that the work of a CA firm on auditing and accounting engagements is reviewed in a careful and constructive manner by an independent external party. This practice inspection program is administered by each provincial institute through its practice inspection (or similar) committee. It is mandatory on all the practising members of the provincial institute. Thus, all CA firms in each province are subject to practice inspection.[4]

While there are slight differences among the practice inspection programs of the various provincial institutes, the programs generally cover an inspection of the auditing and accounting engagements. A practice inspection generally involves a review of the engagement files and other relevant documents relating to the auditing and accounting services rendered by CA practitioners. The provincial institute is responsible for assigning independent CAs to carry out such an inspection. The results of the inspection are discussed and reported to the practitioners inspected as well as to the provincial institute's practice inspection (or similar) committee. The reports may include recommendations to assist the practitioners to improve their performance. In those cases where the inspection reveals serious failure to maintain professional standards, the institute's professional conduct committee is advised.

The amount of work required in an inspection depends on whether the CA firm has documented its quality control policies and procedures. The areas that should be documented include the following:

1. File and statement preparation, including appropriate forms, documentation, and second-person review.
2. Objectivity.
3. Maintenance of professional skills and standards through professional development, review of periodicals, self-study, and other aids.

---

[4] All provincial institutes have a practice inspection or practice review requirement.

4. Staff recruiting, advancement, and supervision, including the planning and budgeting of time, the assignment of personnel, on-the-job training, and staff progress reviews.
5. Outside consultation as necessary, such as consultation with practice advisers, other practitioners, and non-CA specialists.
6. Office administration as it relates to the supervision of internal quality control, liability insurance, file retention, professional conduct, and the acceptance and continuation of engagements.

For firms or offices with proper documentation, the inspectors will review the adequacy of the quality control policies and procedures and will perform compliance tests on a sample of working paper files and other related areas to ensure adherence to the established policies and procedures. On the other hand, where firms and offices lack proper documentation, the inspectors will perform more extensive review and testing.

Quality Control in the United States

To ensure that a CPA firm's quality control policies and procedures are adequate to provide reasonable assurance of the firm's conformity with generally accepted auditing standards, the AICPA has issued *Statement on Quality Control Standards 1,* identifying nine elements or areas of quality control: independence, assigning personnel to engagements, consultation, supervision, hiring, professional development, advancement, acceptance and continuation of clients, and inspection.[5] The AICPA did not require specific quality control procedures. In fact, it stated that the specific procedures should depend upon the size of the firm, the number of offices, and the nature of the firm's practice. Thus, the quality control procedures employed by a 200-office international firm will differ considerably from those employed by a single-office firm that only audits small businesses. Technically, the AICPA's quality control *Statement* applies only to auditing and accounting services for which professional standards have been established by the AICPA. As a practical matter, however, every CPA firm should have quality control procedures applicable to *every aspect of its practice.* In the broad sense, the concept of "quality control" means that CPA firms should establish controls to provide assurance that they meet their responsibilities to their clients and to the public.

---

[5] AICPA, *Statement on Auditing Standards 25,* "The Relationship of Generally Accepted Auditing Standards to Quality Control Standards" (New York, 1979), AU 161; and AICPA, *Statement on Quality Control Standards 1,* "System of Quality Control for a CPA Firm" (New York, 1979), Professional Standards QC 10.

Division for CPA Firms.   Another major step taken by the AICPA toward establishing quality control standards within the profession was the formation of the AICPA Division for CPA Firms. Previously, CPAs joined the AICPA only as individuals; no mechanism existed for enforcing professional standards for CPA firms. In the Division for CPA Firms, membership is granted to CPA firms, not to individual CPAs.

The Division for CPA Firms actually includes two separate sections, the *SEC Practice Section* and the *Private Companies Practice Section.* CPA firms voluntarily join either, or both, sections based on the type of clients that they serve. Both sections require member firms to establish and maintain an adequate system of quality control and adhere to certain membership requirements. For example, the SEC Practice Section requires audit partners on SEC audit clients to be rotated at least every seven years. Audit engagements for such clients must be subjected to review by a second partner. Members of the SEC Practice Section are also prohibited from performing certain management advisory services for SEC audit clients, including executive recruiting activities. Regular *peer reviews* and mandatory continuing education for firm personnel are part of the membership requirements of both firm sections.

The executive committees of the two sections have the power to sanction member firms for substandard performance. These sanctions may include additional personnel education requirements, fines, and expulsion from the division.

The Public Oversight Board.   A vital part of the SEC Practice Section is the Public Oversight Board, which is made up of prominent individuals who are not members of the accounting profession. The board oversees the activities of the SEC Practice Section and can intervene when the members of the board think that the public's interest is not being served. Periodic reports inform the SEC and Congress about the activities of the Public Oversight Board.

Peer Reviews.   An important feature of the AICPA Division for Firms is the mandatory peer reviews that are required periodically of members of both sections. Member firms must subject their practice to an intensive review of their quality control policies and procedures by another CPA firm, or a review team authorized or appointed by one of the peer review committees of the two sections.

A peer review involves a study of the adequacy of the firm's established quality control policies and tests to determine the extent of the firm's compliance with these policies. In large part, these tests consist of a review of working paper files and audit reports for selected engagements. These engagements are evaluated for compliance with established quality control policies and generally accepted auditing standards.

The reviewers also examine many internal records of the CPA firm. They are especially interested in records concerning the promotion of employees, continuing education of firm personnel, staffing of audit engagements, client acceptance, and the employment of professional personnel. Based on the reviewers' study and tests of the quality controls, they issue a report that includes an opinion as to the adequacy of the reviewed firm's quality control system. Suggestions for improvement to the system are outlined in a letter issued by the reviewers to the reviewed firm.

INTERNATIONAL STANDARDS SETTING

Auditing standards are currently determined on a country-by-country basis. However, as securities markets around the world are becoming more multinational, a need has developed for common auditing standards. The International Federation of Accountants (IFAC) is a worldwide organization of national accounting bodies (e.g., the CICA) from approximately 80 countries, established to help foster a coordinated worldwide accounting profession with harmonized standards. One of its committees, the International Auditing Practices Committee (IAPC) issues pronouncements that provide procedural and reporting guidance to auditors.

The pronouncements of the IAPC do not override the national auditing standards of its members. Rather they are meant to foster the development of consistent worldwide auditing standards. Members from countries that do not have such standards are encouraged to adopt IAPC standards; members from countries that already have such standards are encouraged to compare them to IAPC standards and to seek to eliminate any material inconsistencies.

The international auditing standards setting process is at an early stage of development. Yet, one might expect rapid progress as multinational securities offerings and stock markets develop. Ultimately, we may find an audit in conformity with IAPC standards to be acceptable for multinational securities offerings in all of the participating nations.

The International Audit Report. The reporting guidance of the IAPC is similar to that included in Canadian standards. However, the report itself is somewhat different, as illustrated on the next page.

In addition to its format of only two paragraphs, the international report includes several other differences when compared to a Canadian report. First, it may be signed using the personal name of the auditor, the firm, or both—as is done in the above illustration. Second, note the lack of certain disclosures in the audit report (e.g., the responsibilities of management and of the auditors).

> **Auditors' Report to the Shareholders of ABC Corporation**
>
> We have audited the accompanying balance sheet of ABC Corporation as of December 31, 19--, and the related statements of income, retained earnings, and cash flows for the year then ended in accordance with International Auditing Guidelines.
>
> In our opinion, the financial statements present fairly the financial position of ABC Corporation as of December 31, 19--, and the results of its operations and its cash flows for the year then ended in accordance with International Accounting Standards.
>
> February 17, 19--
> Toronto, Ontario, Canada
>
> *Robert Rotter*
> Blue, Gray & Company

KEY TERMS

adverse opinion An opinion issued by the auditors that the financial statements they have examined *do not present fairly* the financial position, results of operation, or changes in financial position in accordance with generally accepted accounting principles.

auditors' standard report A very precise document designed to communicate exactly the character and limitations of the responsibility being assumed by the auditors; in standard form, the report consists of an introductory paragraph, a scope paragraph, and an opinion paragraph, which cover the basic financial statements.

denial of opinion A form of report in which the auditors state that they do not express an opinion on the financial statements; it should include a separate paragraph stating the auditors' reasons for denying an opinion and disclosing any reservations they may have concerning the financial statements.

disclosure Making public all material information about financial affairs.

Division for CPA Firms A division of the AICPA providing a mechanism to regulate CPA firms. Firms may voluntarily join either or both sections; the SEC Practice Section and the Private Companies Practice Section.

error An unintentional misstatement in financial statements.

fraud An intentional misstatement in the financial statements.

generally accepted auditing standards (GAAS) A set of eight standards adopted by the CICA and binding on its members—designed to ensure the quality of the auditors' work.

illegal acts Violations of laws or governmental regulations.

independence A most important auditing standard, which prohibits CAs from expressing an opinion on financial statements of an enterprise unless they are independent with respect to such enterprise; independence is impaired by a material financial interest, service as an officer or trustee, loans to or from the enterprise, and various other relationships.

internal control A company's control environment, accounting system, and control policies and procedures that are established to provide reasonable assurance that the company's objectives will be achieved.

International Auditing Practices Committee (IAPC) A committee of the International Federation of Accountants, established to issue guidance on auditing and reporting practices that is intended to improve the degree of uniformity of auditing practices and related services throughout the world.

International Federation of Accountants A worldwide organization of national accounting bodies established to help foster a coordinated worldwide accounting profession with harmonized standards. Currently the organization consists of representatives from approximately 80 countries.

peer review The study and evaluation of a CPA firm's quality control policies and procedures by another CPA firm or a team of qualified CPAs.

practice inspection Review by independent CA inspectors of the CA practitioners' work on auditing and accounting engagements. Its objective is to encourage rigorous adherence to the high standards of the profession and to signify the interest of the profession in effective self-regulation.

Public Oversight Board An independent group of prominent nonaccountants who monitor the activities of the SEC Practice Section to provide assurance that the section is serving the public's interest.

qualified opinion The appropriate form of audit report when there is a limitation in the scope of the audit or the financial statements depart from GAAP significantly enough to require mention in the auditors' report, but not so materially as to necessitate the expression of an adverse opinion or the denial of an opinion.

quality control standards Standards for establishing quality control policies and procedures that provide reasonable assurance that all of the accounting firm's audits are conducted in accordance with generally accepted auditing standards.

unqualified opinion   The form of audit report issued when the examination was adequate in scope and the auditors believe that the financial statements present fairly the financial position, operating results, and changes in financial position in conformity with generally accepted accounting principles.

GROUP I: REVIEW QUESTIONS

2–1.   When a public accounting firm completes an audit of a business and issues a report, does it express an opinion on the client's accounting records, financial statements, or both? Give reasons.

2–2.   What is the difference between generally accepted accounting principles (GAAP) and generally accepted auditing standards (GAAS)? Give an example of a generally accepted accounting principle and an example of a generally accepted auditing standard falling under the subheading of *examination standards.*

2–3.   The generally accepted auditing standards established by the CICA list first the requirement that "the examination should be performed and the report prepared by a person or persons having adequate technical training and proficiency in auditing." What would be the usual avenues for an individual to meet these personal qualifications?

2–4.   You are to evaluate the following quotation:
"If a CA firm completes an examination of Adam Company's financial statements following generally accepted auditing standards and is satisfied with the results of the audit, an *unqualified* audit report may be issued. On the other hand, if no audit is performed of the current year's financial statements, but the CA firm has performed satisfactory audits in prior years, has confidence in the management of the company, and makes a quick review of the current year's financial statements, a qualified report may be issued."
Do you agree? Give reasons to support your answer.

2–5.   Pike Limited has had an annual audit performed by the same firm of public accountants for many years. The financial statements and copies of the audit report are distributed to shareholders each year shortly after completion of the audit. Who is primarily responsible for the fairness of these financial statements? Explain.

2–6.   Draft the standard form of audit report commonly issued after a satisfactory examination of a client's financial statements.

2–7.   Davis & Co., Chartered Accountants, after completing an audit of Samson Corporation decided that it would be unable to issue an unqualified opinion. What circumstances might explain this decision?

2–8.   State the principal assertions made by the auditors in the opinion paragraph of the auditors' standard report.

2–9.   Alan Weston, CA, completed an examination of Kirsten Manufacturing Limited and issued an unqualified audit report. What does this tell us about the extent of the auditing procedures included in the examination?

2–10. A CA firm does not guarantee the financial soundness of a client when it renders an opinion on financial statements, nor does the CA firm guarantee the absolute accuracy of the statements. Yet the CA firm's opinion is respected and accepted. What is expected of the CA firm in order to merit such confidence?

(AICPA, adapted)

2–11. If a CA firm has made a thorough professional examination of a client's financial statements, should it not be able to issue a report dealing with facts rather than the mere expression of an opinion? Explain.

2–12. Explain briefly the auditors' responsibility for detecting error and fraud committed by clients.

2–13. What is the International Auditing Practices Committee? What is purpose of its pronouncements? Do these pronouncements establish standards which override a member nation's auditing standards?

2–14. Briefly describe two differences between an international audit report and one based on Canadian reporting standards.

2–15. What action has the CA profession taken to ensure quality control by CA firms and why? Explain fully.

2–16. What is meant by the term *practice inspection?*

2–17. What areas of the quality control policies and procedures should be documented?

GROUP II: QUESTIONS REQUIRING ANALYSIS

2–18. An objective state of mind or independence is a most essential element of an audit by a firm of chartered accountants. Describe several situations in which the CA firm might find it somewhat difficult to maintain this independent point of view.

2–19. Jane Lee, a director of a large corporation with large numbers of shareholders and lines of credit with several banks, suggested that the corporation appoint as controller John Madison, a chartered accountant on the staff of the auditing firm that had made annual audits of the corporation for many years. Lee expressed the opinion that this move would effect a considerable saving in professional fees because annual audits would no longer be needed. She proposed to give the controller, if appointed, an internal auditing staff to carry on such continuing investigations of accounting data as appeared necessary. Evaluate this proposal.

2–20. Select the best answer for each of the following items and give reasons for your choice.

    a. The three generally accepted auditing standards classified as examination standards may be summarized as:

        (1) The need to maintain an independence in mental attitude throughout the audit.

        (2) The criteria for audit planning and evidence gathering.

        (3) The criteria for the content of the auditors' report on financial statements.

        (4) The competence, independence, and professional care to be exerted while performing the audit.

    b. Which of the following most directly determines the specific audit procedures that a CA will perform to obtain the reasonable assurance necessary to express an opinion?

        (1) The audit program.

        (2) The CA's judgment.

        (3) Generally accepted auditing standards.

        (4) The CA's working papers.

    c. Which of the following is **not** explicitly included in an unqualified standard audit report?

        (1) The CA's opinion that the financial statements comply with generally accepted accounting principles.

        (2) That generally accepted auditing standards were followed during the audit.

        (3) That the internal control of the client was satisfactory.

        (4) The subjects of the audit.

    d. The general standard of the generally accepted auditing standards requires that:

        (1) The auditors maintain an objective state of mind.

        (2) The audit be conducted in conformity with generally accepted accounting principles.

        (3) Assistants, if any, be properly supervised.

        (4) The auditor obtain an understanding of the internal control.

                           (AICPA, adapted)

2–21. Reed, CA, accepted an engagement to audit the financial statements of Smith Limited. Reed's discussions with Smith's new management and the predecessor auditor indicated the possibility that Smith's financial statements may be misstated due to the possible occurrence of errors, fraud, and illegal acts.

Required:

a. Identify and describe Reed's responsibilities to detect Smith's errors and fraud. Do *not* identify specific audit procedures.

b. Identify and describe Reed's responsibilities to report Smith's errors and fraud.

c. Describe Reed's responsibilities to detect Smith's material illegal acts. Do *not* identify specific audit procedures.

(AICPA, adapted)

GROUP III: PROBLEMS

2–22. Joe Rezzo, a college student majoring in accounting, helped finance his education with a part-time job maintaining all accounting records for a small business, White Company, located near the campus. Upon graduation, Rezzo joined the audit staff of a national CA firm. However, he continued to perform all accounting work for White Company (with the CA firm's permission) during his leisure time. Two years later, Rezzo passed his CA examination, received his CA certificate, and decided to give up his part-time work with White Company. He notified White that he would no longer be available after preparing the year-end financial statements.

On January 7, Rezzo delivered the annual financial statements as his final act for White Company. The owner then made the following request: "Joe, I am applying for a substantial bank loan, and the bank loan officer insists upon getting audited financial statements to support my loan application. You are now a CA, and you know everything that's happened in this company and everything that's included in these financial statements, and you know they give a fair picture. I would appreciate it if you would write out and sign the standard audit report and attach it to the financial statements. Then I'll be able to get some fast action on my loan application."

Required:

a. Would Rezzo be justified in complying with White's request for an auditor's opinion? Explain.

b. If you think Rezzo should issue the audit report, do you think he should first perform an audit of the company despite his detailed knowledge of the company's affairs? Explain.

c. If White had requested an audit by the national CA firm for which Rezzo worked, would it have been reasonable for that firm to accept and to assign Rezzo to perform the audit? Explain.

2–23.   The following audit report is deficient in several respects.

To Whom It May Concern:

We have examined the accounting records of Garland Corporation for the year ended June 30, 19––. We counted the cash and marketable securities, studied the accounting methods in use (which were consistently followed throughout the year), and made tests of the ledger accounts for assets and liabilities. The internal control contained no weaknesses.

In our opinion the balance sheet and income statement present correctly the financial condition of the Corporation at June 30, 19––.

The accounting records of Garland Corporation are maintained in accordance with accounting principles generally observed throughout the industry. Our examination was made in accordance with generally accepted auditing standards, and we certify the records and financial statements without qualification.

Required:

You are to criticize the report systematically from beginning to end, considering each sentence in turn. Use a separate paragraph with identifying heading for each point, for example, Paragraph 1, Sentence 1. You may also wish to make comments on the overall contents of each paragraph and upon any omissions. Give reasons to support your views. After completing this critical review of the report, draft a revised report, on the assumption that your examination was adequate in all respects and disclosed no significant deficiencies.

2–24.   Bart James, a partner in the CA firm of James and Day, received the following memorandum (shown on the next page) from John Gray, president of Gray Manufacturing Corporation, an audit client of many years.

Required:

Put yourself in Bart James's position and write a reply to this client's request. Indicate clearly whether you are willing to accept the engagement and explain your attitude toward this proposed extension of the auditor's attest function. (In drafting your letter, keep in mind that Gray is a valued audit client whose goodwill you want to maintain.)

Dear Bart:

I have a new type of engagement for you. You are familiar with how much time and money we have been spending in installing equipment to eliminate the air and water pollution caused by our manufacturing plant. We have changed our production process to reduce discharge of gases, we have changed to more expensive fuel sources with less pollution potential, and we have discontinued some products because we couldn't produce them without causing considerable pollution.

I don't think the shareholders and the public are aware of the efforts we have made, and I want to inform them of our accomplishments in avoiding danger to the environment. We will devote a major part of our annual report to this topic, stressing that our company is the leader of the entire industry in combating pollution. To make this publicity more convincing, I would like to retain your firm to study what we have done and to attest as independent accountants that our operations are the best in the industry as far as preventing pollution is concerned.

To justify your statement, you are welcome to investigate every aspect of our operations as fully as you wish. We will pay for your services at your regular audit rates and will publish your "pollution opinion" in our annual report to shareholders immediately following some pictures and discussion of our special equipment and processes for preventing industrial pollution. We may put this section of the annual report in a separate cover and distribute it free to the public. Please let me know at once if this engagement is acceptable to you.

2–25. John Clinton, owner of Clinton Company, applied for a bank loan and was informed by the banker that audited financial statements of the business must be submitted before the bank could consider the loan application. Clinton then retained Arthur Jones, CA, to perform an audit. Clinton informed Jones that audited financial statements were required by the bank and that the audit must be completed within three weeks. Clinton also promised to pay Jones a fixed fee plus a bonus if the bank approved the loan. Jones agreed and accepted the engagement.

The first step taken by Jones was to hire two accounting students to conduct the audit. He spent several hours telling them exactly what to do. Jones told the students not to spend time reviewing internal controls but instead to concentrate on proving the mathematical accuracy of the ledger accounts and summarizing the data in the accounting records that support Clinton Company's financial statements. The students followed Jones's instructions and after two weeks gave Jones the financial statements that did not include any footnotes. Jones reviewed the statements and prepared an unqualified audit report. The report, however, did not refer to generally accepted accounting principles.

Required:
List on the left side of the sheet of paper the generally accepted auditing standards that were violated by Jones, and indicate how the actions of Jones resulted in a failure to comply with each standard. Organize your answer as follows:

Generally accepted auditing standards	*Actions by Jones resulting in failure to comply with generally accepted auditing standards*
(1) The examination should be performed and the report prepared by a person or persons having adequate technical training and proficiency in auditing, with due care, and with an objective state of mind.	(1)
	(AICPA, adapted)

2–26. The business activities of Casa Royale Inc. consist of the administration and maintenance of approximately 400 condominiums and common property owned by individuals in a suburban residential development. Revenue consists of monthly fees collected from each condominium owner, plus some miscellaneous revenue. The principal expenses are property taxes and maintenance of all the buildings, shrubbery, swimming pools, lakes, parking lots, and other facilities. The furniture, fixtures, and equipment owned by the corporation and used to perform its maintenance functions represent about 25 percent of its total assets of $400,000.

The corporation retained Howard Smith, CA, to perform an audit of its financial statements for the current year and received from him the audit report as shown on the next page.

The note to the financial statements referred to in the audit report read as follows: "The plant assets (equipment, furniture, and fixtures) necessary for administration and maintenance were acquired in various years going back as far as the origin of the company 10 years ago. Therefore, the records do not lend themselves readily to application of standard auditing procedures and are not included in our engagement of independent auditors. These

---

Auditors' Report

To the Shareholders of Casa Royale Inc.:

I have audited the balance sheet of Casa Royale Inc. as at December 31, 19––, and the statements of income, retained earnings, and changes in financial position for the year then ended. These financial statements are the responsibility of the company's management. My responsibility is to express an opinion on these financial statements based on my audit.

I conducted my audit in accordance with generally accepted auditing standards. Those standards require that I plan and perform an audit to obtain reasonable assurance whether the financial statements are free of material misstatement. An audit includes examining, on a test basis, evidence supporting the amounts and disclosures in the financial statements. An audit also includes assessing the accounting principles used and significant estimates made by management, as well as evaluating the overall financial statement presentation.

As further amplified in Note 3 to the financial statements, my engagement did not include an examination of records relating to furniture, fixtures, equipment, or other assets indicated on the balance sheet.

In my opinion, except for the effects of such adjustments, if any, as might have been determined to be necessary had I been able to examine evidence regarding plant assets, these financial statements present fairly, in all material respects, the financial position of Casa Royale Inc. as at December 31, 19––, and the results of its operations and the changes in its financial position for the year then ended in accordance with generally accepted accounting principles.

Howard Smith, CA

Howard Smith, CA

---

assets are being depreciated using the straight-line method over various estimated useful lives.''

Required:

a. What type of audit report did the CA issue? Was this the appropriate type of report under the circumstances? Explain.

b. What contradiction, if any, exists between the scope paragraph of the audit report and the note to the financial statements? Do you consider the note to be a reasonable statement? Why or why not?

c. Did the omission of the examination of plant assets from the audit engagement have any bearing on the evidence needed by the auditor in order to express an opinion on the income statement? Explain fully.

GROUP IV: ANALYTICAL AND DISCUSSION CASE

2–27.   Enormo Corporation is a large multinational audit client of your CA firm. One of Enormo's subsidiaries, Ultro Ltd., is a successful electronics assembly company that operates in a small Caribbean country. The country in which Ultro operates has very strict laws governing the transfer of funds to other countries. Violations of these laws may result in fines or the expropriation of the assets of the company.

During the current year, you discover that $50,000 worth of foreign currency was smuggled out of the Caribbean country by one of Ultro's employees and deposited in one of Enormo's bank accounts. Ultro's management generated the funds by selling company automobiles, which were fully depreciated on Ultro's books, to company employees.

You are concerned about this illegal act by Ultro's management and decide to discuss the matter with Enormo's management and the company's legal counsel. Enormo's management and board of directors seemed to be unconcerned with the matter and expressed the opinion that you were making far too much of a situation involving an immaterial dollar amount. They also believe that it is unnecessary to take any steps to prevent Ultro's management from engaging in illegal activities in the future. Enormo's legal counsel indicated that the probability was remote that such illegal acts would ever be discovered, and that if discovery occurred, it would probably result in a fine that would not be material to the client's consolidated financial statements.

Your CA firm is ready to issue its opinion on Enormo's consolidated financial statements for the current year, and you are trying to decide on the appropriate course of action regarding the illegal act.

Required:
a. Discuss the implication of these illegal acts by Ultro's management.
b. Describe the courses of action that are available to your CA firm regarding this matter.
c. State your opinion as to the course of action that is appropriate. Explain.

Chapter 3

Professional Ethics

Chapter Objectives

After studying this chapter, you should be able to:

- Describe the reasons that professions establish professional ethics.
- Describe the criteria by which accountants merit recognition as a profession.
- Identify the fundamental principles underlying the *Rules of Professional Conduct*.
- Describe each of the rules in the *Rules of Professional Conduct*.
- Explain the concepts and rationale underlying the major rules of the *Rules of Professional Conduct*.

The Need for Professional Ethics

All recognized professions have developed codes of professional ethics. The fundamental purpose of such codes is to provide members with guidelines for maintaining a professional attitude and conducting themselves in a manner that will enhance the professional stature of their discipline.

To understand the importance of a code of ethics to public accountants and other professionals, one must understand the nature of a profession as opposed to other vocations. Unfortunately, there is no universally accepted definition of what constitutes a profession; yet, for generations, certain types of activities have been recognized as professions, while others have not. Medicine, law, engineering, architecture, and theology are examples of disciplines long accorded professional status. Public accounting is a relative newcomer to the ranks of the professions, but it has achieved widespread recognition in recent decades.

All of the recognized professions have several common characteristics, and to a great extent it is these characteristics which distinguish the professions from other disciplines. The following characteristics, contained in the "Foreword" of the various provincial institutes' *Rules of Professional Conduct,* constitute the criteria by which chartered accountancy merits recognition as a profession.[1]

1. There is mastery by the practitioners of a particular intellectual skill, acquired by lengthy training and education.
2. The foundation of the calling rests in public practice—the application of the acquired skills to the affairs of others for a fee.
3. The calling centres on the provision of personal services rather than entrepreneurial dealing in goods.
4. There is an outlook, in the practice of the calling, which is essentially objective.
5. There is acceptance by the practitioners of a responsibility to subordinate personal interests to those of the public good.
6. There exists a developed and independent society or institute, comprising the members of the calling, which sets and maintains standards of qualification, attests to the competence of the individual practitioner, and safeguards and develops the skills and standards of the calling.
7. There is a specialized code of ethical conduct, laid down and enforced by that society or institute, designed principally for the protection of the public.
8. There is a belief, on the part of those engaged in the calling, in the virtue of interchange of views, and in a duty to contribute to the development of their calling, adding to its knowledge and sharing advances in knowledge and technique with their fellow members.

The most important of these characteristics may be summarized as *(a)* a responsibility to serve the public, *(b)* a complex body of knowledge, *(c)* standards of admission to the profession, and *(d)* a need for public confidence. Let us briefly discuss each.

Responsibility to Serve the Public.   The public accountant is the representative of the public—creditors, shareholders, consumers, employees, and others—in the financial reporting process. The role of the independent auditor is to assure that financial statements are *fair to all parties* and not biased to benefit one group at the expense of another. This responsibility to serve the public interest must be a basic motivation for the professional. If a public accountant's primary concern were to maximize income, he or she

---

[1] As mentioned in Chapter 1, since most public accountants are chartered accountants, the chartered accountancy profession is used to illustrate the public accounting profession.

would presumably work for the benefit of creditors, investors, management, or whichever group offered the highest fee.

There is a saying in public accounting that "the public is our only client." This expression is an oversimplification, since the entity being audited pays the auditor's fee and is, in fact, the client. Yet the saying conveys an ideal which is essential to the long-run professional status of public accounting. Public accountants must maintain a high degree of objectivity (independence) from their client (the company) if they are to be of service to the larger community. Objectivity is perhaps the most important concept embodied in public accounting's code of professional ethics.

Complex Body of Knowledge.   Any practitioner or student of accounting has only to look at the abundance of authoritative pronouncements governing financial reports to realize that accounting is a complex body of knowledge. One reason why such pronouncements continue to proliferate is that accounting must reflect what is taking place in an increasingly complex environment. As the environment changes—such as the trend toward business combinations in the 1960s and the increase in litigation and governmental regulation in more recent years—accounting principles and auditing practices must adapt. The continued growth in the "common body of knowledge" for practicing accountants has led to the need for continuing education requirements for public accountants. The need for technical competence and familiarity with current standards of practice is embodied in the code of professional ethics.

Standards of Admission to the Profession.   Attaining a license to practise as a public accountant requires an individual to meet minimum standards for education and experience. The individual must also pass a set of professional examinations showing mastery of the body of knowledge described above. Once licensed, public accountants must adhere to the ethics of the profession or risk disciplinary action.

Need for Public Confidence.   A physician, lawyer, public accountant, and all other professionals must have the confidence of the public to be successful. To the public accountant, however, public confidence is of special significance. The public accountant's product is *credibility;* without public confidence in the attestor, the attest function serves no useful purpose.

Illustrative Case

A national survey of a large number of business people on the ethical conducts of sixteen professional and business groups ranks accountants first, followed by dentists and doctors. The others include corporate officers, lawyers, realtors, union leaders, newspaper reporters, and politicians.

Professional ethics in public accounting, as in other professions, has developed gradually and is still in a process of change as the practice of accounting itself changes. Often new concepts are added as a result of unfortunate incidents which reflect unfavourably upon the profession, although not specifically in violation of existing standards.

Professional Ethics in Public Accounting

A principal factor in maintaining high professional standards of practice has been the development of rules of professional conduct by the provincial institutes. Careless work or lack of integrity on the part of any CA is a reflection upon the entire profession. Consequently, members of the profession have acted in unison through their provincial organizations to devise rules of professional conduct. These rules provide practical guidance to the individual member in maintaining a professional attitude. In addition, they give assurance to clients and to the public that the profession intends to maintain high standards and to enforce compliance by individual members.

Evidence that public accounting has achieved the status of a profession is found in the willingness of its members to accept voluntarily standards of conduct more rigorous than those imposed by law. These standards cover the relationships of the CA with clients, with fellow practitioners, and with the public. To be effective, a body of professional ethics must be comprehensive, attainable, and enforceable; it must consist not merely of abstract ideals but of attainable goals and practical working rules which can be enforced.

In the short run the restraints imposed on the individual CA by a body of professional ethics may sometimes appear to constitute a hardship. From a long-run point of view, however, it is clear that the individual practitioner, the profession as a whole, and the public all benefit from the existence of a well-defined body of professional ethics.

The *Rules of Professional Conduct*

The *Rules of Professional Conduct* of the various provincial institutes essentially consist of three parts. The first part, "Foreword," discusses the distinguishing characteristics of the chartered accountancy profession and the fundamental principles underlying the rules, and provides brief clarifications on definitions, application of rules, and the importance of the interpretations of the rules. The second part, "Rules of Professional Conduct," is a group of enforceable ethical standards. The third part, "Interpretations," represents the interpretations of the rules issued by the provincial institute council for the guidance of its members and students.

The *Rules of Professional Conduct,* by their very nature, set forth a **minimum** level of acceptable conduct. Consequently, CAs should strive for conduct beyond that indicated merely by prohibitions. The conduct toward which CAs should strive is embodied in the following fundamental principles underlying the rules:

1. A member or student shall conduct himself or herself at all times in a manner which will maintain the good reputation of the profession and its ability to serve the public interest.
2. A member or student shall perform his or her professional services with integrity and care and accept an obligation to sustain his or her professional competence by keeping himself or herself informed of, and complying with, developments in professional standards.
3. A member who is engaged in an attest function such as an audit or review of financial statements shall hold himself or herself free of any influence, interest, or relationship, in respect of his or her client's affairs, which impairs his or her professional judgment or objectivity or which, in the view of a reasonable observer, would impair the member's professional judgment or objectivity.
4. A member or student has a duty of confidence in respect of the affairs of any client and shall not disclose, without proper cause, any information obtained in the course of his or her duties, nor shall he or she in any way exploit such information to his or her advantage.
5. The development of a member's practice shall be founded upon a reputation for professional excellence, and the use of methods of advertising which do not uphold professional good taste, which could be characterized as self-promotion, and which solicit, rather than inform, is not in keeping with this principle.
6. A member shall act in relation to any other member with the courtesy and consideration due between professional colleagues and which, in turn, he or she would wish to be accorded by the other member.

These principles may be summarized as *(a)* responsibilities to the public and the profession; *(b)* integrity, due care, and competence; *(c)* objectivity; and *(d)* responsibilities to clients and colleagues.

RULES OF CONDUCT

Applicability and Enforcement of Rules

While most of the *Rules of Professional Conduct* are applicable to those members practising public accounting, many are also applicable to all members and students. The applicability of the rules is stated in the Foreword of the provincial institute's *Rules of Professional Conduct.*

A member not engaged in the practice of public accounting must observe these rules except where the wording of any rule makes it clear that it relates specifically to the practice of public accounting or there is a specific exception made in a particular rule.

Where the term "professional services" is used it means, in its application to a member not engaged in the practice of public accounting, those of his or her activities where the public or his or her associates are entitled to rely on his or her membership in the Institute as giving him or her particular competence.

A member is responsible to the Institute for compliance with these rules by others associated with him or her in the public practice of the functions covered by the rules who are either under his or her supervision or share with him or her proprietary interest in the practice, and must not permit others to carry out on his or her behalf acts which, if he or she carried them out himself or herself, would place him or her in violation of the rules.

A member who is resident outside Canada is expected to abide by the rules of the organized accounting profession in the jurisdiction in which he or she resides and to ensure that his or her actions do not bring disrepute upon the Institute.

Each provincial institute is empowered by its bylaws to enforce compliance with the *Rules of Professional Conduct* by its members. The institute's professional conduct, discipline, and appeal committees are charged with the responsibility of the administration, enforcement, and disciplinary processes. A member or student who is found guilty of violating any provisions of the rules will be admonished, reprimanded, suspended, or expelled. A member who is expelled from the institute will lose his or her CA certificate. Obviously, neither the institute nor its members should take such penalty lightly, for the damage to the individual's professional reputation can be very serious.

Interpretations of *Rules of Professional Conduct*

In order to ensure that the *Rules of Professional Conduct* are properly and clearly understood, interpretations of the rules are issued by the council of the provincial institute. These interpretations provide further information and guidance for members and students and constitute an integral part of the rules. Each member and student should be extremely familiar with such interpretations. Since the interpretations are generally lengthy, they will not be discussed here but are included as an Appendix to this chapter.[2]

---

[2] Since the interpretations are uniform for most provincial institutes, and since the provincial institutes are responsible for the enforcement of the rules, the interpretations of the Ontario Institute have been arbitrarily selected for purposes of illustration. Members and students should, of course, refer to their respective institutes' interpretations for guidance.

Specific Rules

The following *Rules of Professional Conduct* are classified into four categories: *(a)* general, *(b)* standards of conduct affecting the public interest, *(c)* relations with fellow members and with nonmembers engaged in public accounting, and *(d)* organization and conduct of a professional practice.[3]

General

101 Members and students and, where applicable, professional corporations shall comply with the bylaws, regulations and rules of professional conduct of the Institute as they may be from time to time and with any order or resolution of the Council or officers of the Institute under the bylaws.

102(1) A member or student who has been:

(*a*) convicted of an offence of fraud, theft, forgery, or income tax evasion; or

(*b*) found guilty of violating the provisions of any securities legislation; or

(*c*) convicted of any criminal or similar offence for conduct in or relating to their professional capacity, or for conduct in circumstances where there was reliance on their membership in or association with the Institute; or

(*d*) discharged absolutely or upon condition after pleading guilty to or being found guilty of an offence described in (*a*), (*b*), or (*c*) above

shall promptly inform the Institute of the fact of the conviction, finding of guilt or discharge, as the case may be, when the right of appeal has been exhausted or expired.

(2) This rule of professional conduct applies in respect of an event which occurs after the 10th day of June, 1991.

103 A member or student or any person who applies to become a member or student shall not sign or associate himself or herself with any letter, report, statement or representation relating to his or her application for admission or re-admission to membership, or relating to his or her application for registration or re-registration as a student, which he or she knew, or should have known, was false or misleading.

104 A member or student shall promptly reply in writing to any letter from the Institute in which a written reply is specifically requested.

(Continued)

---

[3] For the same reasons as stated in footnote 2, the *Rules of Professional Conduct* of the Ontario Institute are used as illustration. Members and students should, of course, refer to their respective institutes' *Rule of Professional Conduct* for guidance. Also, both the rules and interpretations are subject to change from time to time.

Standards of Conduct Affecting the Public Interest

201.1 A member or student shall conduct himself or herself at all times in a manner which will maintain the good reputation of the profession and its ability to serve the public interest.

.2 Notwithstanding any other provisions of the bylaws or these rules of professional conduct, in the event a member or student is charged under Rule 201.1 on account of an offence referred to in Rule 102, when a certificate of conviction or certified copy of the original information or indictment as provided for in Bylaw 87(2)(*af*) with respect to the offence set out in Rule 102 is filed with the discipline or appeal committee, there is a rebuttable presumption the member or student charged failed to maintain the good reputation of the profession and its ability to serve the public interest.

.3 No person registered as a student shall be engaged on his or her own or in association with others in the practice of public accounting provided that this rule shall not prohibit a student from engaging in the practice of public accounting as an employee in a designated office of a practising member qualified to employ students.

202 A member or student shall perform his or her professional services with integrity and due care.

203.1 A member shall sustain his or her professional competence by keeping informed of, and complying with, developments in professional standards in all functions in which the member practises or is relied upon because of his or her calling.

.2 A member or student shall co-operate with officers, servants, or agents of the Institute who have been appointed to arrange or conduct:

(*a*) a practice inspection; or

(*b*) an investigation on behalf of the professional conduct committee.

204.1 A member engaged as an auditor to express an opinion on financial statements or on financial or other information shall hold himself or herself free of any influence, interest, or relationship which, in respect of the engagement, impairs the member's professional judgment or objectivity or which, in the view of a reasonable observer, would impair the member's professional judgment or objectivity.[4]

.2 A member engaged to conduct a review of financial statements or financial or other information and to issue a review engagement report shall hold himself or herself free of any influence, interest, or relation-

---

[4] It should be noted that the specific interpretations of objectivity or independence, as used in federal and some provincial business corporations acts, may differ somewhat. Some acts are more restrictive than the council's interpretations. A member should be familiar with the specific act under which his or her client company is incorporated. To the extent that the act is more restrictive, the auditor should comply with such statutory requirement.

(Continued)

ship which, in respect of the engagement, impairs the member's professional judgment or objectivity or which, in the view of a reasonable observer, would impair the member's professional judgment or objectivity.

.3 A member engaged in the public practice of acting as a trustee in bankruptcy, a liquidator, a receiver, a receiver-manager, or any other aspect of insolvency practice, shall hold himself or herself free of any influence, interest, or relationship which, in respect of the engagement, impairs the member's professional judgment or objectivity or which, in the view of a reasonable observer, would impair the member's professional judgment or objectivity.

.4 A member engaged in the practice of public accounting or any related function, in providing professional services other than those specifically provided for in Rules 204.1 or 204.2 or 204.3, shall disclose any influence, interest, or relationship which, in respect of the engagement, would be seen by a reasonable observer to impair the member's professional judgment or objectivity and such disclosure shall be made in the member's written report or other written communication accompanying financial statements or financial or other information and the disclosure shall indicate the nature of the influence or relationship and the nature and extent of the interest.

205 A member or student shall not

(*a*) sign or associate himself or herself with any letter, report, statement, representation, or financial statement which he or she knows, or should know, is false or misleading, whether or not the signing or association is subject to a disclaimer of responsibility, nor

(*b*) make or associate himself or herself with any oral report, statement, or representation which he or she knows, or should know, is false or misleading.

206 A member engaged in the practice of public accounting shall perform his or her professional services in accordance with generally accepted standards of practice of the profession, including the Recommendations set out in the *CICA Handbook*.

207 A member engaged in the practice of public accounting or the public practice of a function not inconsistent with public accounting shall inform his or her clients or associates in such practice of any business connections, any affiliations, and any interests of which they might reasonably expect to be informed but this does not necessarily include disclosure of professional services the member may be rendering or proposing to render to other clients.

208 A member or student shall not, in connection with any transaction involving a client or an employer, hold, receive, bargain for, become entitled to, or acquire any fee, remuneration, or benefit without the client's or employer's knowledge and consent.

(Continued)

209 A member or student shall not take any action, such as acquiring any interest, property, or benefit, in connection with which he or she makes improper use of confidential knowledge of a client's affairs obtained in the course of his or her duties.

210.1 A member or student shall not disclose or use any confidential information concerning the affairs of any client, former client, employer, or former employer except:

(*a*) when properly acting in the course of his or her duties;

(*b*) when such information should properly be disclosed for purposes of Rule 211;

(*c*) when such information is required to be disclosed by order of lawful authority or, in the proper exercise of their duties, by the Council, the professional conduct committee, or any subcommittee thereof, the discipline committee, the appeal committee, or the practice inspection committee; or

(*d*) when justified in order to defend himself or herself or his or her associates or employees, as the case may be, against any lawsuit or other legal proceeding or against alleged professional misconduct or in any legal proceeding for recovery of unpaid professional fees and disbursements, but only to the extent necessary for such purpose.

.2 A member engaged to perform a particular service may contract for the services of a person not employed by the member to assist in the performance of that service, provided the member first obtains the written agreement of that person to carefully and faithfully preserve the confidentiality of any information acquired for the purposes of the engagement and not to make use of such information other than as shall be required in the performance of such services.

211 A member shall bring to the attention of the professional conduct committee any apparent breach of these rules of professional conduct or any instances involving doubt as to the competence, reputation or integrity of a member, student or applicant, provided that this rule shall not apply to

(*a*) a trivial matter, or

(*b*) a member exempted from this rule for the purpose and to the extent specified by Council, or

(*c*) a member who is under a specific legal requirement imposed by or pursuant to statutory authority which would preclude the disclosure of confidential information.

212.1 A member or student who receives, handles, or holds money or other property as a trustee, receiver, or receiver/manager, guardian, administrator/manager, or liquidator shall do so in accordance with the terms of the engagement, including the terms of any applicable trust, and the law relating thereto and shall maintain such records as are necessary to account properly for the money or other property; unless

(Continued)

otherwise provided for by the terms of the trust, money held in trust shall be kept in a separate trust bank account or accounts.

.2 A member or student in the course of providing professional services shall handle with due care any property entrusted to him or her.

213 A member or student shall not knowingly lend himself or herself or his or her name or services to any unlawful activity.

214 A member shall not quote a fee for any professional services unless requested to do so by a client or a prospective client, and no quote shall be made until adequate information has been obtained about the assignment.

215 A member engaged in the practice of public accounting shall not offer or agree to render any professional service for a fee contingent on the results of such service, nor shall the member represent that he or she does any professional service without fee except services of charitable, benevolent, or similar nature.

216 Other than in relation to the sale and purchase by a member of an accounting practice, a member engaged in the practice of public accounting or a student while employed by a member engaged in the practice of public accounting shall not directly or indirectly pay to any person who is not an employee of the member or who is not a public accountant a commission or other compensation to obtain a client, nor shall the member or student accept directly or indirectly from any person who is not a public accountant a commission or other compensation for a referral to a client of products or services of others.

217.1 A member may advertise, but shall not do so, directly or indirectly, in any manner

(*a*) which the member knows, or should know, is false or misleading, or

(*b*) which contravenes professional good taste or fails to uphold normal professional courtesy, or

(*c*) which makes unfavorable reflections on the competence or integrity of the profession or any member thereof, or

(*d*) which includes a statement the contents of which the member cannot substantiate.

.2 A member engaged in the practice of public accounting shall not

(*a*) endorse, other than in expressing a considered professional opinion in the course of an engagement, or

(*b*) consent to or allow the use of the member's name, or the name of the firm or organization with which the member is associated, in the public promotion of

any commercial product or service of others.

218 A member shall retain for a reasonable period of time such working papers, records, or other documentation which reasonably evidence the nature and extent of the work done in respect of any professional engagement.

(Continued)

**Relations with Fellow Members and with Non-members Engaged
in Public Accounting**

301.1 A member engaged in the practice of public accounting shall not adopt any method of obtaining or attracting clients which tends to bring disrepute on the profession.

    .2 A member shall not directly or indirectly or through a party acting on behalf of and with the knowledge of the member solicit any professional engagement which has been entrusted to another member engaged in the practice of public accounting or who carries on a business or practice which constitutes a related function.

302.1 A member shall not accept an engagement with respect to the practice of public accounting or the public practice of a function not inconsistent with public accounting, where the member is replacing another member or public accountant, without first communicating with such person and enquiring whether there are any circumstances the member should take into account which might influence the member's decision whether or not to accept the engagement.

    .2 The incumbent member shall respond promptly to the communication referred to in Rule 302.1.

303.1 A member shall upon written request of the client supply on a timely basis reasonable information to the member's successor about the work done or being assumed.

    .2 A member who is a predecessor on an engagement shall cooperate with the successor, recognizing the client's interests are paramount, and shall transfer promptly to the client or, on the client's instructions, to the successor, all books, documents, and other property belonging to the client which are in the member's possession.

304 A member who accepts any engagement jointly with another member shall accept joint and several responsibility for any portion of the work to be performed by either; no member shall proceed in any matter within the terms of such joint engagement without due notice to the other member.

305 A member engaged in the practice of public accounting shall, before commencing any engagement for a client of another member who is the duly appointed auditor or accountant, first notify such auditor or accountant of the engagement, unless the client makes an unsolicited request that such notification not be given. In the event such request is made, written evidence thereof shall be obtained by the member before commencing the engagement.

306.1 A member who accepts an engagement, whether by referral or otherwise, from a client of a member who has a continuing relationship with that client shall not take any action which would tend to impair the position of the other member in the ongoing work with the client.

    .2 A member who receives an engagement for services by referral from another member shall not provide or offer to provide any additional

(Continued)

services to the referring member's client without the consent of the referring member; the interest of the client being of overriding concern, the referring member shall not unreasonably withhold such consent.

Organization and Conduct of a Professional Practice

401   A member, or, where permitted, a professional corporation, shall not engage in the practice of public accounting, or in the public practice of any function not inconsistent therewith, under a name or style which is misleading as to the nature of the organization (proprietorship, partnership, or, where permitted, corporation) or the nature of the functions performed.

402   A member engaged in the practice of public accounting as a sole proprietor, or, where permitted, a professional corporation, shall practise under the member's own name and, where permitted in special circumstances by the Council, may, with the predecessor's written authorization, practise under the name of a predecessor sole proprietor or, on a temporary basis, some other predecessor firm name as well as under the member's own name.

403.1   Subject to the provisions of Rule 403(2), any firm name shall be limited to:
(*a*) the names of professional colleagues who are or were previously partners of the firm or any predecessor firm, provided that the number of names used does not exceed the number of partners currently active with the firm,
(*b*) the names of persons who have practised as public accountants in Canada or any other country, provided each person named practised with the firm or any predecessor firm and the person or his or her legal representative has authorized the use of the name,
(*c*) part or all of the name, including a non-personal name, of the international partnership of which the firm is a partner or affiliate, provided that the name has been approved by the Council
and the term "& Co." or appropriate similar wording may be used where the number of partners currently active with the firm exceeds the number of names used in the firm name.

403.2   Notwithstanding the provisions of Rule 403(1), a firm may use an additional name, including a non-personal name, to meet the international needs of clients, if the additional name is
(*a*) part or all of the name of the international partnership of which the firm is a partner, or affiliate, or
(*b*) part or all of the name of a foreign-based partner or affiliate name
provided the registered name of the firm in Ontario is clearly and prominently associated with the additional name in the signature of any report or any other communication and the Council has given its approval to the use of such additional name.

(Continued)

404.1 The practice of public accounting shall be carried on under the descriptive style of either "chartered accountant(s)" or "public accountant(s)"; regardless of the functions actually performed, the use of either descriptive style, in offering services to the public, shall be regarded as carrying on the practice of public accounting for the purposes of these rules of professional conduct.

.2(*a*) Each office in Ontario of any member or firm[5] of members engaged in the practice of public accounting shall be under the personal charge and management of a member who is a public accountant and who shall normally be in attendance in such office during such times as the office is open to the public.

(*b*) A member shall not operate a part-time office except in accordance with such terms and conditions established by Council.

.3 Each office in Ontario of any firm engaged in the practice of public accounting and composed of one or more members sharing proprietary interest with other public accountants who are not members shall practise under the style of "public accountants" and shall be under the personal charge and management of a member or other public accountant who shall normally be in attendance in such office during such times as the office is open to the public.

405 A member shall not associate in any way with any firm practising as chartered accountants in Ontario unless:

(*a*) all partners resident in Ontario are members,

(*b*) at least one partner is a member, and

(*c*) all the partners are professional colleagues[6] or professional corporations provided each such corporation is recognized and approved for the practice of public accounting by the provincial institute in the province concerned.

406 A member engaged in the practice of public accounting or a related function who is associated with non-members in such practice shall be responsible to the Institute for any failure of such non-members, in respect of such practice, to abide by the rules of professional conduct of the Institute.

407 A member shall not hold out or imply that the member has an office in any place where the member is in fact only represented by another public accountant or a firm of public accountants and, conversely, a member who only represents a public accountant or a firm of public accountants, shall not hold out or imply that the member maintains an office for such public accountant or such firm.

408 A member shall not be associated in any way with any corporation engaged in Canada in the practice of public accounting, except to the

[5] Members are referred to the bylaws definition of "firm" as meaning a partnership.

[6] Members are referred to the bylaws definition of "professional colleague" as a member or a member of a provincial institute.

(Continued)

extent permitted in Rule 420 and in clauses (1), (2), and (3) of this rule:

(1) A member or the member's firm

    (*a*) may be the auditor(s) of the corporation,

    (*b*) may be the appointed accountant(s) to prepare the financial statements of the corporation,

    (*c*) may give tax advice to the corporation with respect to the financial affairs of the corporation.

(2) A member, other than a practising member, may be associated with a corporation which provides taxation services involving advice and counselling in an expert capacity provided such services are only a small part of the corporation's activities.

(3) A member may be associated with a professional corporation engaged in the practice of public accounting in a province other than Ontario if the corporation is recognized and approved for such practice by the provincial institute in the province concerned and the corporation does not engage in the practice of public accounting in Ontario.

Without limiting the generality of the foregoing, a member shall be deemed to be associated with a corporation engaged in Canada in the practice of public accounting even though the corporation provides a public accounting service only to another member or to a public accountant.

409–419 Reserved for future use.

420.1 A member engaged in the practice of a related function shall adhere to the rules of professional conduct, and the rules of professional conduct shall apply to such member as if the related function were the practice of public accounting.

420.2 For the purpose of the rules of professional conduct, a related function shall be any member's business or practice that is cross-referenced to

    (*a*) the member's public accounting practice, or

    (*b*) another business or practice that is cross-referenced to the member's public accounting practice,

whether carried on through an organization separate from the member's public accounting practice or as a separate department or division of such practice.

420.3 In respect of clause (2), "cross-referenced" means

    (*a*) any reference in the advertising or promotional or other material of the member's public accounting practice that is made to any other business or practice of the member; or

    (*b*) any reference in the advertising or promotional or other material of any other business or practice of the member that is made to

        (i) the member's public accounting practice; or

        (ii) any business or practice of the member that is referenced in any advertising or promotional or other material of the member's public accounting practice; or

(Continued)

> (c) any use of a name or logo or any possession of features or characteristics by any business or practice of a member which, in the view of a reasonable observer, would imply that an association or relationship exists between such business or practice and
>
> >   (i) the member's public accounting practice; or
> > (ii) any other business or practice of the member to which there is any reference made in the advertising or promotional or other material of the member's public accounting practice.
>
> 420.4 A member may associate with a related function as a proprietor, as a partner, or as a director, officer, or shareholder of a corporation and may associate with a non-member for this purpose.
>
> 420.5 A related function shall not be designated "chartered accountant(s)" or "public accountant(s)".
>
> 420.6 A related function designated as "management consultant(s)" or "trustee(s) in bankruptcy" shall be carried on under a personal name or names or under a corporate derivative of any such personal name or names.
>
> 421 Any member engaged in the practice of public accounting who is associated as a proprietor or partner of a related function business, or as a director, officer, or shareholder of a corporation carrying on a related function, shall be responsible to the Institute for any failure of the related function business or corporation or any non-member associated with either of them, to abide by the rules of professional conduct as if such related function business, corporation or nonmember were a member engaged in the practice of public accounting.

ANALYSIS OF *RULES OF PROFESSIONAL CONDUCT*

Some of the rules stated in the *Rules of Professional Conduct* are self-explanatory, but discussion and illustration may be necessary to a full understanding of several others.

Objectivity

Rule 204 is concerned with the problem of objectivity, which has two distinct aspects.[7] First, public accountants must *in fact* be objective toward any enterprise they audit or review. Second, the relationships of

---

[7] The term *objectivity* is sometimes referred to as *independence*. The Canada Business Corporations Act and some provincial business corporations acts use the term *independence*. Thus, the terms *objectivity* and *independence* are used interchangeably in this chapter and the rest of the textbook.

public accountants with audit or review clients must be such that they will *appear* objective to third parties.

Objectivity in fact refers to the public accountant's ability to maintain an unbiased and impartial mental attitude or state of mind in all aspects of work, whether or not existing circumstances might have an apparent effect on his or her objectivity. As such, objectivity in fact is not subject to objective measurement and therefore can be judged only by the public accountant.

Objectivity in appearance refers to the public accountant's freedom from conflict of interest which third parties may infer from circumstantial evidence. It is a third party's perception of the public accountant's objectivity based on the facts of a given situation. For example, if a public accountant owns shares in the corporation being audited, he or she is most likely to be perceived by third parties as lacking objectivity. Whether the public accountant can maintain an objective state of mind is beside the question; he or she *does not appear* to be objective because of his or her conflict of interest, being a shareholder and the auditor of the same corporation. Since objectivity in fact is subjective and difficult to prove, objectivity in appearance has become more important in judging the public accountant's objectivity. A public accountant who is lacking objectivity in appearance is not qualified to serve as an auditor under the Canada Business Corporations Act.[8] An investor or banker using audited financial statements would prefer that the audit be performed by a public accountant who had no financial or management interest in the company and therefore had no conflict of interest. Moreover, this may also be beneficial to the public accountant. For example, if a public accountant failed to discover a material misstatement in the financial statements, the reaction of creditors, investors, and the public would be far more critical if it were discovered that the public accountant was also part owner of the company, even if that ownership interest were small. Under these circumstances the publicity which always stems from such a case would surely lessen public confidence in the public accounting profession.

The following paragraphs illustrate some of the more common situations where the conflict of interest is considered to be significant enough to impair the auditor's objectivity. Although these situations parallel the situations contained in the Council Interpretations of the Ontario Institute, students may find it useful to refer to the interpretations in the Appendix to this chapter.

---

[8] *Canada Business Corporations Act and Regulations,* sec. 155. This legal requirement only prohibits the auditor from having material interest in the securities of the client corporation. For a comparison with the *Rules of Professional Conduct,* see the section on the independence of the auditor in the Canada Business Corporation Act in this chapter.

Investment Interest in Audit Clients.   An auditor's investment in shares, bonds, mortgages, and notes of an audit client or its associates, either direct or indirect, creates a conflict of interest. In this situation, an auditor may be in a position to issue an opinion or to influence the client's financial statements for personal financial gain at the expense of his or her capacity as auditor. Thus, a reasonable third-party observer will question the auditor's ability to maintain an impartial attitude in his or her work. Such an investment is not limited to the auditor but also applies to his or her immediate family and to partners and their immediate families. The term *immediate family* means the spouse, son, daughter, and other relatives living in the same home as the auditor or his or her partners.

Nonaudit Functions and Services.   Certain functions and services are incompatible with the auditing function. These include functioning as a director, officer, or employee of an audit client; serving as a trustee of a profit-sharing or pension plan of an audit client; or serving as an executor or trustee of an estate or trust which holds a material interest in an audit client. The auditor's involvement in these functions and services creates a conflict of interest situation. For example, being both an auditor and a director of the same corporation means that the auditor has to evaluate the work of management of which he or she is a part. This raises the question of the auditor's ability to remain impartial in fulfilling the auditing function. Such a conflict of interest would also exist if members of the immediate families of the auditor or his or her partners functioned as directors or officers of an audit client; however, members of these immediate families may work as employees of an audit client without creating a conflict of interest.

Business Transactions and Relationships.   It would be unreasonable to expect the auditor to refrain from carrying out any business transaction or relationship with an audit client under terms and conditions that are normal for the business. However, the auditor should avoid conflict of interest situations such as these: situations where the auditor is involved in business transactions under *special* terms and conditions that are not available to others or in substantial amounts that do not bear a reasonable relationship to his or her income and financial position and situations where the auditor accepts a commission or other remuneration from third parties for arranging the sale of securities or insurance to an audit client. In such situations, the auditor's impartiality is in question because the auditor may stand to gain by placing his or her personal interest ahead of the interests of the client and other parties. Of course, the auditor's immediate family and partners and their immediate families should also avoid such situations.

Other Conflict of Interest Situations.   It is impossible to describe all the situations that impair the appearance of objectivity. However, three special situations deserve some attention: activities of retired partners, client gifts, and litigation.

The activities of retired partners may affect the objectivity of the CA firm. These partners usually receive retirement benefits from the CA firm and may continue to function as part of its management. Such retirement benefits would not affect the firm's objectivity if the retired partners held a direct or indirect financial interest in or a position with an audit client, provided that the benefit payments were determined at the date of the partners' retirement in accordance with the terms of the partnership agreement and were not affected by subsequent events. However, a conflict of interest would arise if the retired partners held a direct or indirect financial interest in or a position with an audit client and continued to maintain an association with their CA firm, for example, by being part of the firm's management, by using the office space in the firm's offices, or by otherwise remaining actively involved in the firm's operational activities.

A third party may question the objectivity of a CA firm in situations in which a partner or his or her professional staff accepts an expensive gift from an audit client. It would appear that special considerations might be tied to the acceptance of such gifts, and the auditor might not act with impartiality. To avoid this implication of lack of objectivity, auditors should decline all but token gifts from audit clients.

Litigation involving the client and the auditors may also affect the objectivity of auditors. The relationship between the auditors and client management must be characterized by complete candor and full disclosure. A relationship with these characteristics may not exist when litigation places the auditors and client management in an adversary position. Auditors in litigation with a client must evaluate the situation to determine whether the significance of the litigation affects the client's confidence in the auditors or the auditors' objectivity.

Does Rendering of Management Advisory Services Threaten the Auditors' Independence?   A problem to be considered in rendering management advisory services is the possible threat to the auditors' independence when both auditing and a variety of consulting services are performed for the same client. Can a public accounting firm that renders extensive management advisory services for a client still maintain the objective status so essential in an audit and in the expression of an opinion on the client's financial statements?

A CA who serves as a part-time controller for a client and assumes a *decision-making* role in the client's affairs is not in a position to make an independent audit of the financial statements. On the other hand, public accounting firms have long been rendering certain purely *advisory* services to management while continuing to perform audits in an objective manner that serves the public interest. Advisory services can generally be distinguished from management proper; the work of the consultant or adviser consists of such functions as conducting special studies and investigations, making suggestions to management, pointing out the existence of weaknesses, outlining various alternative corrective measures, and making recommendations. Such advisory services should not affect the objectivity of the public accounting firm. However, if an auditor becomes deeply and continuously involved in rendering a great many management advisory services for a given client, the relationship could conceivably become so significant that third parties may doubt his objectivity in his work as an auditor.

Objectivity—A Matter of Degree.   The concept of objectivity is not absolute; no auditors could claim complete objectivity toward a client. Rather, objectivity is relative—a matter of degree. As long as the auditors work closely with client management and are paid fees by their clients, complete objectivity can be considered merely an ideal. Auditors must strive for the greatest degree of objectivity consistent with their environment.

Recent developments have served to increase the auditor's objectivity in dealings with management. One of these developments is the widespread adoption of audit committees by corporations. In fact, many corporations are required by federal and a number of provincial corporations acts to have audit committees, as discussed in Chapter 4. Members of these audit committees are selected from the company's board of directors. Ideally, audit committee members are outside directors; that is, board members who are not also officers of the company. The functions of the audit committee include nominating the independent auditors, reviewing the scope of the auditors' services, reviewing audit findings, and resolving conflicts between the auditors and management.

A second development that has strengthened the auditor's objectivity is the provision in the federal and some provincial business corporations acts regarding the rights of the auditor when he or she resigns or is dismissed. The auditor is entitled under these acts to inform the shareholders of the reasons for the resignation or dismissal. This is similar to the SEC requirement in the United States that public companies must file an informative disclosure (Form 8-K) describing the reason for a change in auditors. The discharged auditors may also respond if they disagree with management's analysis.

The legislative provisions regarding audit committees and the auditor's right to representation on his or her resignation or dismissal probably discourage corporations from willful dismissal of auditors. For example, a corporation may dismiss an auditor because the corporation is *shopping for accounting principles.* Shopping for accounting principles occurs when a company changes from one accounting firm to another that is more likely to sanction a disputed accounting principle. A company's management might search for auditors, for example, who would accept a questionable inventory valuation method as being in accordance with generally accepted accounting principles. Consequently, auditors who are consulted on a question of accounting or auditing by a company other than a client should be sure they are aware of all the facts and circumstances before responding. This would include obtaining permission from the company's management to make enquiries of the current auditors. Although cases in which management has actually shopped for accounting principles may not be common, it is clear that if management can change auditors casually and without explanation, undue pressure is placed on auditors' objectivity.

Advertising and Tendering

At present, all provincial institutes allow advertising by their members. A few years ago, advertising in any form was considered unprofessional. However, the change in public attitude and in legislation has created an environment where certain forms of advertising by professionals are in the best interest of the public, the clients, and the professions. Accordingly, members of these provincial institutes may now advertise their services as long as the advertising is informative, factual, and dignified. More specifically, Rule 217 stipulates that the advertising should not be "false or misleading," should not contravene "professional good taste," should not make "unfavourable reflections on the competence or integrity of the profession," and should not "involve a statement the contents of which" cannot be substantiated.

Since acceptable advertising must be informative, factual, and dignified, CAs should review their advertising very carefully to ensure that they have complied with the professional ethical standards. Acceptable advertising includes indications of the types of services offered, certificates and degrees of members of the firm, and fees for services. Such advertising provides useful information to potential clients in their preliminary assessment of the firms with which they may wish to deal.

Unethical advertising is advertising which is false or misleading, is not in professional good taste, reflects negatively on the profession, or contains a statement that cannot be substantiated. Among the characteristics of unethical advertising are the use of inaccurate or outdated information, flamboyancy, and extravagant and self-laudatory claims of superiority or uniqueness.

The change in attitude and legislation that has affected the advertising of professional services has also led to the removal of the rule prohibiting bidding or tenders for professional services. All provincial institutes now allow bidding or tendering as long as it is done in a professional manner.

In the United States, the AICPA also permits its members to advertise their services as long as the advertising is not false, misleading, or deceptive. Until 1978, advertising by CPAs was strictly forbidden by the *Rules of Professional Ethics*. However, this prohibition was dropped because it was deemed a possible violation of the U.S. federal antitrust laws. These laws also led to the repeal of the rule restricting competitive bidding.

Practice Inspection

Rule 203 of the provincial institutes requires that members maintain their professional competence. To ensure that this is not only being done but is also seen to be done, a new concept called *practice inspection* (also called *practice review*) has been implemented. Practice inspection means that the work of a CA firm on auditing and accounting engagements is reviewed in a careful and constructive manner by an independent external party. The objective of such inspection is to encourage rigorous adherence to the high professional standards and to signify the interest of the profession in effective self-regulation. Practice inspection is now required for CA firms in all provinces.

Each provincial institute administers its own practice inspection requirement. A practice inspection generally involves a review of the engagement files and other relevant documents relating to the auditing and accounting services rendered by CA practitioners. The review is carried out by inspectors who are independent CAs, and the reports are submitted to the practitioners inspected and to the practice inspection (or similar) committee of the provincial institute. These reports may include suggestions and recommendations to assist the practitioners in improving their performance. In cases where the inspection reveals *serious failure* to maintain professional standards by the practitioners, the institute's professional conduct committee is advised.

The amount of work required in an inspection depends on whether the CA firm has documented its quality control policies and procedures. The areas that should be documented include the following:

1. File and statement preparation, including appropriate forms, documentation, and second-person review.
2. Objectivity.
3. Maintenance of professional skills and standards through professional development, review of periodicals, self-study, and other aids.
4. Staff recruiting, advancement, and supervision, including the planning and budgeting of time, the assignment of personnel, on-the-job training, and staff progress reviews.
5. Outside consultation as necessary, such as consultation with practice advisers, other practitioners, and non-CA specialists.
6. Office administration as it relates to the supervision of internal quality control, liability insurance, file retention, professional conduct, and the acceptance and continuation of engagements.

For firms or offices with proper documentation, the inspectors will review the adequacy of the quality control policies and procedures and will perform compliance tests on a sample of working paper files and other related areas to ensure adherence to the established policies and procedures. On the other hand, where firms and offices lack proper documentation, the inspectors will perform more extensive review and testing.

Responsibilities to the Public and to Clients

Auditing Standards and Accounting Principles.   Rule 206 obligates a CA performing an audit to comply with the CICA Auditing Standards Board's eight generally accepted auditing standards, discussed in Chapter 1. It also requires the CA to recognize the recommendations of the CICA Accounting Standards Board as generally accepted accounting principles.

The consequences of this rule are a strengthening of the authority of the CICA and its Accounting Standards Board and Auditing Standards Board and a lessening of the opportunity for wide variations in the quality of auditing services or the options available for accounting principles.

Contingent Fees.   Rule 215 prohibits a CA from rendering any professional service on a contingent fee basis. For example, a company in need of an auditor's report to support its application for a bank loan might offer to make the auditor's fee contingent upon approval of the loan by the bank. Such an arrangement would affect the auditor's objectivity, both in fact and in appearance. There would be the potential temptation for the auditor to abandon an objective viewpoint and lend support to the statements prepared by management, and the conflict of interest would probably cause informed third parties to doubt the auditor's objectivity.

Confidential Client Information.   Rule 210 stresses the confidential nature of information obtained by CAs from their clients. The nature of public accountants' work makes it necessary for them to have access to their clients' most confidential financial affairs. However, this right of access carries with it the necessity for confidentiality; otherwise, clients will not allow public accountants to have access to such information. Public accountants may gain knowledge of impending business combinations, proposed financing, prospective stock splits or dividend changes, contracts being negotiated, and other confidential information which, if disclosed or otherwise improperly used, could bring the accountants quick monetary profits. Of course, the clients would be financially injured, as well as embarrassed, if the CAs were to leak such information. Accountants must not only keep quiet as to their clients' business plans, but they rarely even mention in public the names of their clients. Any loose talk by public accountants concerning the affairs of their clients would immediately brand them as lacking in professional ethics. On the other hand, the confidential relationship between the CA and the client is *never* a justification for the CA to cooperate in any deceitful act. The personal integrity of the CA is essential to the performance of the attest function.

The communications between CAs and their clients are confidential, but they are not *privileged* under common law, as are communications with lawyers, clergymen, or physicians. The difference is that disclosure of legally privileged communications cannot be required by a subpoena or court order. Thus, auditors may be compelled to disclose their communications with clients in court proceedings.

Illegal Acts by Clients.   Rule 213 requires that a CA "shall not knowingly lend himself or herself or his or her name or services to any unlawful activity." We must also emphasize that unswerving commitment to honourable behavior is the essence of ethical conduct. If CAs permit doubts to arise about their personal integrity, they have destroyed their usefulness as independent auditors. This concept should govern the CAs' reaction when they encounter illegal or possibly illegal acts by a client. Under no circumstances should the CAs condone or ignore actions they *know* to be illegal. This does not necessarily mean that the CAs should report such acts to governmental authorities; it does mean that they should not permit their firm's name to be associated with financial statements that conceal illegal actions by a client.

If the CAs have knowledge of clearly illegal actions by a client, they should discuss the situation with the client so that action can be taken to remedy the situation and they should make disclosures or adjustments to the financial statements. In most cases this may mean discussing the situation with the audit committee of the board of directors. If the client fails to take corrective action, the CAs should withdraw from the engagement. This action on the part of the CAs makes clear that they will not be associated in any way with illegal activities.

Responsibilities to Colleagues

Society's impression of a profession is affected by the way its members conduct their professional affairs. Cutthroat competition, solicitation, or general lack of cooperation among its members casts a poor image on any profession. Currently, a number of rules govern responsibilities to colleagues to ensure goodwill and mutual cooperation among members of the profession.

Rules 301 to 306 ban solicitation and encroachment by one public accountant on the practice of another. The need for such a prohibition is apparent; without it, distrust and hostility would pervade relationships among public accountants. It would be considered a form of solicitation, for example, if a firm of public accountants circulated its technical publications to parties other than its clients and close associates without a direct request from those parties.

When there is a change of appointment, there should be complete cooperation between the incumbent and the successor accountants. Before accepting an appointment, the successor should enquire of the incumbent whether there are any circumstances that might influence the decision to accept the appointment. An awareness that enquiries with a company's incumbent accountant must precede acceptance of a new client will perhaps serve as a deterrent to encroachment by one public accountant upon the practice of another.

These rules should discourage overly aggressive, unprofessional actions by public accountants in seeking to attract new clients currently served by others. Also, they should safeguard against the undesirable practice known as "shopping for accounting principles."

Independence of the Auditor in the Canada Business Corporations Act

The Canada Business Corporations Act uses the term *independence* rather than *objectivity* to describe the auditor's lack of conflict of interest. Section 155 of the act stipulates that a person must be independent to be qualified as an auditor of a corporation, unless a court exempts such a requirement. Independence is considered "a question of fact," and the following facts constitute nonindependence:

> a person is deemed not to be independent if he or his business partner
>
> (i) is a business partner, a director, an officer or an employee of the corporation, or any of its affiliates, or a business partner of any director, officer or employee of any such corporation or any of its affiliates,
> (ii) beneficially owns or controls, directly or indirectly, a material interest in the securities of the corporation or any of its affiliates, or
> (iii) has been a receiver, receiver-manager, liquidator or trustee in bankruptcy of the corporation or any of its affiliates within two years of his proposed appointment as auditor of the corporation.

The concept of independence (objectivity) required by the act differs from that set forth in the *Rules of Professional Conduct* in three aspects. First, the act defines independence in terms of independence in appearance, while the rules encompass both independence in appearance and independence in fact. Second, the act allows the auditor to have **immaterial** interest in the client's securities, while the rules do not allow **any** interest in the client's securities. Third, the act disqualifies from serving as auditor a person who has been a receiver, receiver-manager, liquidator, or trustee in bankruptcy of the corporation or any of its affiliates within the past two years.[9] The interpretations of the *Rules of Professional Conduct,* however, state that a CA *may not* act as trustee in bankruptcy of a company if he or she has been the auditor within the past two years. Also, the rules do not preclude a CA who is or has acted as auditor for a client from accepting an appointment as receiver, receiver-manager, or liquidator of that client. If an auditor accepts an appointment as receiver, receiver-manager, or liquidator, he would resign his audit position, as otherwise he would be expressing an opinion on operating results for which he was responsible. Obviously, the auditor must follow a statutory prohibition in cases where it applies.

The CA as Tax Adviser—Ethical Problems

Since the *Rules of Professional Conduct* contain no specific provisions for tax practices, what are the responsibilities of the CA in serving as tax adviser? The CA has a primary responsibility to the client, namely, to see that the client pays the proper amount of tax and no more. The CA may properly resolve questionable issues in favour of the client as long as the solution is within the reasonable interpretation of the tax laws and regulations and the client is appropriately advised of the implications involved; the CA is not obliged to maintain the posture of independence required in audit work. When CAs express an opinion on financial statements, they must be unbiased; however, freedom from bias is not required in serving as a tax adviser. On the other hand, CAs must adhere to the same standards of truth and personal integrity in tax work as in all other professional activities. Any departure from these standards on a tax engagement would surely destroy the reputation of CAs, especially in performing their work as independent auditors.

A second responsibility of CAs on a tax engagement is to ensure that the information contained in the tax returns is not false or misleading, whether or not the returns are signed by CAs. This is required by Rule 205, which states that "a member or student shall not sign or associate himself or herself with the letter, report, statement, representation or financial statement which he or she knows, or should know, is false or misleading, whether or not the signing or association is subject to a disclaimer of responsibility."

---

[9] Certain provincial corporations acts contain the same or similar requirements. For example, see the Ontario Business Corporations Act.

To comply with this responsibility, what steps must the CAs take? The CAs are not required to perform an audit; knowledge of the tax return may be limited to information supplied to them by the taxpayer. However, if this information appears unreasonable or contradictory, the CAs are obligated to make sufficient investigation to resolve these issues. Information which appears plausible to a layperson might appear unreasonable to CAs, who are experts in evaluating financial data. CAs are not obligated to investigate any and all information provided by the taxpayer, but they cannot ignore clues which cast doubt on the accuracy of these data.

Unless CAs approach tax engagements with full recognition of the responsibilities imposed on them by the profession, they may quickly destroy public confidence in the profession. The interests of the taxpayer and the interests of the government are directly opposed, and this conflict of interest requires a most careful delineation of the responsibility of CAs. Because of public confidence in the high professional standards of CAs and the reputation of the profession for integrity, any financial data to which CAs lend their names gains a measure of credibility even though no examination is made and no opinion is expressed. Such public confidence is an invaluable asset of the profession, and it deserves to be guarded with the greatest care.

KEY TERMS

appeal committee A committee of the provincial institute that is responsible for confirming, rejecting, or changing the findings and any orders of the discipline committee.

audit committee A committee of a corporation's board of directors that nominates independent auditors, reviews audit findings, monitors activities of the internal auditing staff, and intervenes in any disputes between management and the independent auditors. Generally, the majority of audit committee members are outside directors, that is, directors who do not also serve as corporate officers. In Canada, many corporations are required by federal and provincial corporations acts to have audit committees.

council An elected governing body of the provincial institute whose function is to carry out the objectives of the institute.

council interpretations (of the *Rules of Professional Conduct*) Specific guidelines issued by the council of the provincial institute regarding the scope and applications of the *Rules of Professional Conduct*.

discipline committee A committee of the provincial institute that is responsible for administering and enforcing the *Rules of Professional Conduct*.

in dependence: See **objectivity.**

practice inspection   Review of the CA practitioners' work on auditing and accounting engagements by independent CA inspectors. Its objective is to encourage rigorous adherence to the high standards of the profession and to signify the interest of the profession in effective self-regulation.

profession   An activity which involves a responsibility to serve the public, which has a complex body of knowledge, which sets standards of admission to the profession, and which has a need for public confidence.

professional conduct committee   A committee of the provincial institute that is responsible for initiating disciplinary work on ethical matters and referring them to the discipline committee for appropriate action.

objectivity   This rule, one of the most important in the *Rules of Professional Conduct,* prohibits CAs from expressing an opinion on the financial statements of an enterprise unless they are objective with respect to that enterprise. Objectivity has two aspects—objectivity in fact and objectivity in appearance. A biased state of mind impairs objectivity in fact, and a conflict of interest impairs objectivity in appearance.

Rules of Professional Conduct   A group of enforceable ethical standards developed for members by the provincial institutes of the chartered accountancy profession to enable them to maintain a professional attitude and to conduct themselves in a manner which will enhance the professional stature of their discipline.

shopping for principles   Undesirable conduct in which some enterprises discharge one independent auditing firm after seeking out another firm that will sanction a disputed financial statement presentation or disclosure.

GROUP 1: REVIEW QUESTIONS

3–1.   What is the basic purpose of a code of ethics for a profession?

3–2.   Briefly describe the key elements in each of the six fundamental principles underlying the *Rules of Professional Conduct.*

3–3.   In Chapter 2 the eight generally accepted auditing standards were discussed. How do *Rules of Professional Conduct* relate, if at all, to these eight generally accepted auditing standards?

3–4.   Sara Kole, CA, has been requested by the president of Noyes Limited, a closely held corporation and audit client, to cosign Noyes's cheques with the Noyes treasurer when the president is away on business trips. Would Kole violate the *Rules of Professional Conduct* if she accepted this request? Explain.

3–5.   Is it ethical for a CA firm to determine its fee for audit services in connection with a bond issuance as a percentage of the proceeds of the bond issue? Explain.

3–6.   Laura Clark, wife of Jon Clark, CA, is a life insurance agent. May Jon Clark refer audit clients needing officer life insurance to Laura Clark or to another life insurance agent who will share a commission with Laura Clark? Explain.

3–7.   Generally, what kind of advertising is allowed by the accounting profession? Explain.

3–8.   Briefly explain the meaning and objective of practice inspection.

3–9.   Cary Beal, a CA in public practice, has proposed to enter into an arrangement with Susan Dunlap, a management specialist. Dunlap would seek engagements to study companies' operations and suggest where improvements might be made. If the study indicates deficiencies in the accounting system, Dunlap would recommend Beal to perform the proposed services. Beal would pay Dunlap compensation for the referral. Would such an arrangement violate the *Rules of Professional Conduct?* Explain.   (AICPA, adapted)

3–10.   Briefly describe the two legislative developments that strengthen the auditor's objectivity (independence).

3–11.   Describe the differences in defining the concept of independence by the Canada Business Corporations Act and the *Rules of Professional Conduct*.

3–12.   Must a CA maintain an objective and impartial mental attitude when preparing a client's income tax return? Explain.

3–13.   The preparation of a fraudulent income tax return by a CA would specifically violate four of the *Rules of Professional Conduct*. Which rules?

3–14.   In preparing a client's income tax return, a CA feels that certain expenses are unreasonably high and probably are overstated. Explain the CA's responsibilities in this situation.

GROUP II: QUESTIONS REQUIRING ANALYSIS

3–15.   Sally Adams, CA, is an auditor with a large CA firm. Her husband, Steve Adams, plans to accept a position as controller of Coast Corporation, an audit client of Sally's firm. Comment upon whether the CA firm's independence will be impaired assuming that Sally Adams is:

a. A partner in the CA firm.

b. An audit manager of the CA firm.

c. A staff auditor without managerial responsibilities.

3–16. Tracy Smith, CA, is in charge of the audit of Olympic Fashions, Inc. Seven young members of the CA firm's professional staff are working with Smith on this engagement, and several of the young auditors are avid skiers. Olympic Fashions owns two condominiums in Quebec City, which it uses primarily to entertain clients. The controller of Olympic Fashions has told Smith that she and any of her audit staff are welcome to use the condominiums at no charge any time that they are not already in use. How should Smith respond to this offer? Explain.

3–17. Harvey Jackson publishes a well-known book entitled *The Best of Everything*. In his book, Jackson lists retailers of products and services who have demonstrated excellence in service to their customers. Carl Swift, a CA in public practice, has been nominated for listing in Jackson's book. Should Swift allow his name to be associated with such a publication? Explain.

3–18. Harris Fell, CA, was engaged to audit the financial statements of Wilson Corporation. Fell had half-completed the audit when he had a dispute with the management of Wilson Corporation and was discharged. Hal Compton, CA, was promptly engaged to replace Fell. Wilson Corporation did not compensate Fell for his work to date; therefore, Fell refused to allow Wilson Corporation's management to examine his working papers. Certain of the working papers consisted of adjusting journal entries and supporting analysis. Wilson Corporation's management had no other source of this information. Did Fell or Compton act properly? Explain fully.

3–19. Since the accounting profession is one of the learned professions, its members are regarded as highly competent, disciplined, and responsible professionals. If this is so, why is it still necessary for the profession to establish and enforce the *Rules of Professional Conduct?* Explain fully.

3–20. Rule 204 of the *Rules of Professional Conduct* of the institute states that a member who is engaged to express an opinion on financial statements shall hold himself or herself free of any influence, interest or relationship, in respect of the client's affairs, which impairs his or her professional judgment or objectivity or which, in the view of a reasonable observer, has that effect. What is the rationale for this rule, and how is this rule related to the two important aspects of the auditor's objectivity? Explain briefly.

3–21. Ward Nolan retired from the large CA firm of Oates, Pyle & Co. after an association of 20 years. Nolan then accepted directorships in several corporate clients of Oates, Pyle & Co. Nolan has requested permission from the managing partners of Oates, Pyle & Co. to maintain a small office in the firm's suite, to receive mail and telephone calls through the firm, and to perform occasional consulting services for the firm on a fee basis. May the managing partner of Oates, Pyle & Co. ethically grant Nolan's request? Explain.

3–22. Mark Riley, CA, of Riley & Co., was requested by John Gray, president of Gray Industries Ltd., to call at his office to discuss the possibility of having Riley's CA firm perform an annual audit of Gray Industries. During the discussion, Riley made the following statement:

"We will need to contact your former auditors, Green and Handler, regarding our appointment as your auditors; we will be able to get a lot of helpful background information from them. Also, by referring to their working papers, we can save a great deal of time in establishing the beginning balances of accounts this year, and consequently our audit fee will be much less than it would be if we had to develop such information from the accounting records."

Gray replied as follows: "No, I prefer that you start from scratch and develop on your own all the information you need. I realize this will require more audit time, but we are willing to pay for it. Frankly, I don't feel our former auditors were too competent; that's why we are inviting you to take over our audit work. I prefer that you do not contact the Green and Handler CA firm at all. Just do whatever is necessary to develop your own working papers from our records."

How should Mark Riley, CA, respond to John Gray's statements? Explain fully.

3–23. Select the best answer for each of the following. Explain the reasons for your selection.

a. In which of the following situations would a CA firm be in violation of the *Rules of Professional Conduct* in determining its fee?

(1) A fee based on whether or not the CAs' report leads to the approval of the client's application for a bank loan.

(2) A fee to be established at a later date by the court due to the bankruptcy of the client.

(3) A fee based upon the nature of the engagement rather than upon the actual time spent on the engagement.

(4) A fee based on the fee charged by the client's former auditors.

b. Who makes the ultimate decision as to whether or not CAs maintain an appearance of independence from their audit clients?

(1) Auditors.

(2) Client.

(3) Audit committee.

(4) Public.

c. Which of the following best describes why publicly traded corporations follow the practice of having the outside auditor nominated by the audit committee of the board of directors?

(1) To comply with the recommendations of the CICA.

(2) To emphasize auditor independence from the management of the corporation.

(3) To encourage a policy of rotation of the independent auditors.

(4) To provide the corporate owners with an opportunity to voice their opinion concerning the quality of the auditing firm selected by the directors.

d. Glen Page, CA, accepted the audit engagement of Todd Corporation. During the audit, Page became aware of his lack of competence required for the engagement. What should Page do?

(1) Deny an opinion.

(2) Issue an adverse opinion.

(3) Suggest that Todd Corporation engage another CA to perform the audit.

(4) Rely on the competence of client personnel.

(AICPA, adapted)

GROUP III: PROBLEMS

3–24. CA is a member of a committee responsible for reviewing situations which may require disciplinary action against other chartered accountants. The following unrelated situations have come to the committee's attention:

a. A chartered accountant placed an advertisement in a professional magazine. The advertisement carried the slogan "Better audit service."

b. During the annual meeting of a public company, a chartered accountant, who had just been appointed auditor of the company, commented that his predecessor, another chartered accountant, had been an "incompetent auditor."

c. During the trial of a businessman charged with income tax evasion, the businessman testified that his income tax affairs had been arranged entirely according to the advice of his tax adviser, a chartered accountant.

Required:

State the factors that you believe should govern CA's reaction to each of the above situations. (CICA, adapted)

3–25.   Donald Westerman is president of Westerman Corporation, a manufacturer of kitchen cabinets. He has been approached by Darlene Zabish, a partner with Zabish and Co., CAs, who suggests that her firm can design a payroll system for Westerman which will either save his corporation money or be free. More specifically, Ms. Zabish proposes to design a payroll system for Westerman on a contingent fee basis. She suggests that her firm's fee will be 25 percent of the savings in the cost of the payroll system for each of the next four years. After four years Westerman will be able to keep all future savings. Westerman Corporation's payroll system costs currently are approximately $200,000 annually and the corporation has not previously been a client of Zabish.

   Westerman discussed this offer with his current CA, Bill Zabrinski, whose firm annually audits Westerman Corporation's financial statements. Zabrinski states that this is a relatively simple task, and that he would be willing to provide the service for $30,000.

   Required:
   a.   Would either Zabish or Zabrinski violate the *Rules of Professional Conduct* by offering to provide these services? Explain.
   b.   Now assume that Westerman has indicated to Zabrinski that he was leaning toward accepting Zabish's offer. Zabrinski then offered to provide the service for 15% of Westerman's savings for the next three years. Would performing the engagement in accordance with the terms of this offer violate the *Rules of Professional Conduct?* Explain.

3–26.   James Daleiden, CA, is interested in expanding his practice through acquisition of new clients. For each of the following independent cases, indicate whether Daleiden would violate the *Rules of Professional Conduct* by engaging in the suggested practice and explain why. If more information is needed to arrive at a final determination, indicate the nature of such information.
   a.   Daleiden wishes to form a professional corporation and use the name AAAAAAAA the CAs, so as to obtain the first ad in the yellow pages of the telephone book.
   b.   Daleiden wishes to prepare a one page flyer which he will have his son stuff on the windshields of each car at the Pleasant Valley shopping mall. The flyer will outline the services provided by Daleiden's firm and will include a $50 off coupon for services provided on the first visit.
   c.   Daleiden has a thorough knowledge of the tax law. He has a number of acquaintances that prepare their own tax returns. He proposes to offer to review these returns before they are

filed with Revenue Canada. For this review, he will charge no fee unless he is able to identify legal tax savings opportunities. He proposes to charge each individual 1/3 of the tax savings he is able to identify.

d. Daleiden and his associates audit a number of municipalities. He proposes to contact other CAs and inform them of his interest in obtaining more audits of this type. He offers a $500 "finders fee" to CAs who forward business to him.

3-27. Roland Company, a retail store, has utilized your services as independent auditor for several years. During the current year, the company opened a new store; in the course of your annual audit, you verify the cost of the fixtures installed in the new store by examining purchase orders, invoices, and other documents. This review brings to light an understated invoice nearly a year old in which a clerical error by the supplier, Western Showcase, Inc., caused the total of the invoice to read $28,893.62 when it should have read $82,893.62. The invoice was paid immediately upon receipt without any notice of the error, and subsequent statements and correspondence from Western Showcase, Inc., showed that the account with Roland Company had been paid in full. Assume that the amount in question is material in relation to the financial position of both companies.

Required:
a. What action should you take in this situation?
b. If the client should decline to take any action in the matter, would you insist that the unpaid amount of $54,000 be included in the liabilities shown on the balance sheet as a condition necessary to your issuance of an unqualified audit report?
c. Assuming that you were later retained to make an audit of Western Showcase, Inc., would you utilize the information gained in your examination of Roland Company to initiate a reopening of the account with that company?

3-28. Auditors must not only appear to be independent; they must also be independent in fact.

Required:
a. Explain the concept of an "auditor's independence" as it applies to third-party reliance upon financial statements.
b. (1) What determines whether or not an auditor is independent in fact?
    (2) What determines whether or not an auditor appears to be independent?

   c. Explain how an auditor may be independent in fact but not appear to be independent.

   d. Would Joe Marks, a CA, be considered independent for an examination of the financial statements of a:

     (1) Church for which he is serving as treasurer without compensation? Explain.

     (2) Women's club for which his wife is serving as treasurer-accountant if he is not to receive a fee for the examination? Explain   (AICPA, adapted)

3–29. An audit client, March Corporation, requests that John Day, CA, conduct a feasibility study to advise management of the best way the corporation can use electronic data processing equipment and which computer, if any, best meets the corporation's requirements. Day is technically competent in this area and accepts the engagement. Upon completion of Day's study, the corporation accepts his suggestions and installs the computer and related equipment that he recommended.

Required:

   a. Discuss the effect that acceptance of this management advisory services engagement would have upon John Day's independence in expressing an opinion on the financial statements of March Corporation.

   b. A local company printing data processing forms customarily offers a commission for recommending it as supplier. The client is aware of the commission offer and suggests that Day accept it. Would it be proper for Day to accept the commission with the client's approval? Discuss.   (AICPA, adapted)

3–30. Lauren Brown, CA, has been requested by the management of Walker Corporation, an audit client, to perform a nonrecurring engagement involving the implementation of an information and control system. Walker's management requests that, in setting up the new system and during the period before conversion to the new system, Brown:

(1) Counsel on potential expansion of business activity plans.

(2) Search for and interview new personnel.

(3) Hire new personnel.

(4) Train personnel.

In addition, Walker's management requests that, during the three months subsequent to the conversion, Brown:

(5) Supervise the operation of the new system.

(6) Monitor client-prepared source documents and make changes in basic data generated by the system as Brown may deem necessary without concurrence of the client.

Required:

a. If Brown completes the engagement for implementation of the system, as outlined, before she begins the audit of Walker Corporation, is her independence impaired? Explain.

b. Which of the services may Brown perform and remain independent with respect to Walker Corporation?

c. If Walker Corporation was Brown's tax client and not her audit client, could Brown implement the system as outlined and continue to perform tax services for the client? Discuss.

(AICPA, adapted)

3–31. In each of the following four *unrelated* circumstances, explain what course of action a CA should follow in order to discharge his or her professional and ethical responsibilities.

a. CA is employed by a firm of chartered accountants practising in a small town. Early in 1992, he reviews with the principal shareholder the draft audited 1991 financial statements of G Ltd., a building contractor. CA notes that the company's deteriorating cash position is so serious that he believes that the company is facing bankruptcy.

CA subsequently reviews the draft audited 1991 financial statements of K Ltd., also a client, and notes that the company has a large overdue account receivable from G Ltd., against which no allowance for doubtful accounts has been provided. When CA questions the owner of K Ltd. on the collectibility of the account, CA is convinced that the owner is not aware of the actual financial condition of G Ltd.

b. CA is approached by J, an insurance agent, with the following proposal. When counselling his clients on the purchase of keyman life insurance, CA will refer his clients to J. In return, J will pay CA 10 percent of his commission on all policies sold through such referrals. In addition, J will undertake to refer to CA certain of his clients who require estate planning services. J points out that he has a similar arrangement with X, another chartered accountant, and that, in fairness to all concerned, he will refer to CA only those clients for which CA offers a lower fee than that offered by X.

c. CA is in charge of the audit of P Ltd., a public company. An economist who is doing research for a thesis on the financial operations of firms in the same industry as P Ltd. asks CA whether he would contribute any information or views on the financial operations of P Ltd. The economist promises to keep confidential any information received from CA.

d. R Ltd. is a small mining company whose principal shareholders are actively promoting the company's shares. CA, the auditor of the company for several years, is in the company's offices conducting his test of control before the year-end when he discovers a copy of a set of interim financial statements recently prepared and apparently sent to the company's bank. These were prepared by the company's accounting staff without CA's knowledge. They are clearly marked "unaudited," and CA's name does not appear on them. A quick scrutiny reveals that the statements appear to overstate net income by a material amount. (CICA, adapted)

3–32. "Professional status as a chartered accountant in Canada carries with it an obligation to maintain a position of independence (objectivity)."

Required:

Outline the rules and guidelines pertaining to the professional standards of independence that apply to the chartered accountant as an auditor. What other services can a chartered accountant provide to a client, and what are their implications with respect to his or her independence as an auditor? (CICA, adapted)

APPENDIX

THE INSTITUTE OF CHARTERED ACCOUNTANTS OF ONTARIO Council Interpretations*
(under powers contained in Bylaw 3)

INTRODUCTION

Administration of the rules of professional conduct, and their enforcement, is the responsibility of the professional conduct committee. It is one of the prime functions of such a committee to give guidance to individual members and students on questions of ethics. When in doubt, therefore, members and students should not hesitate to seek advice from the committee concerning any problem of an ethical nature or concerning the ethical propriety of a proposed course of action in connection with their professional work. Arising from the committee's experience with ethical problems, the council publishes, from time to time, council interpretations (CIs) on professional conduct matters. These interpretations are made by resolution under the authority of Bylaw 3 and are issued for the information and guidance of members and students. They should be read in conjunction with the rules of professional conduct, including the Foreword and the Application section. The council has not published interpretations on all of the rules of professional conduct.

---

* Adopted by the council June 11, 1973, and revised from time to time.

CI 101—COMPLIANCE WITH BYLAWS*

Employing Students

1 Bylaw 97 provides that the office of a practising member must be approved for the instruction of students before any offer of employment is made to a student. A breach of this bylaw is a breach of Rule 101 and, as such, exposes a member to disciplinary action.

2** An administrative procedure has been established whereby cases are not considered to be a contravention of Bylaw 97 when the member and person acknowledge, in writing, prior to the contract of employment that:
   • the member's office is not designated to train students;
   • the person cannot be registered as an Institute student until the firm receives approval, and the person will not receive credit for practical experience until that time.

3† Two or more offices of the same firm may be designated as a single unit for the purpose of obtaining approval for the training of students provided that the following criteria are met prior to granting such designation:
   • a consistency of both policies and procedures followed in each office of the unit must be documented;
   • the firm must designate a central reporting office for personnel functions and designate a member who is responsible for all personnel matters and functions for the unit.
   • a sufficiency of chargeable hours and a diversity of clientele must be available within the unit to support the training of students in accordance with the standards and requirements otherwise established pursuant to the bylaws.

CI 102—CRIMINAL OR SIMILAR OFFENCES

Incorporating Companies

1 The act of preparing and filing documents of incorporation for Ontario companies by persons other than lawyers has been held to be contrary to the Solicitors Act, in that it is part of the practice of law. A member of the Institute was tried and found guilty under Part XVI of the Criminal Code on a charge that he practised as a solicitor or, for gain or

---

* CI 101, pars. 2 and 3, deleted October 1977.

** CI 101(2) added March 18, 1981.

† CI 101(3) added September 6, 1983.

reward, acted as a solicitor, contrary to the Solicitors Act, since he had incorporated a number of companies.

2 Quite apart from the legal position, the relationship existing in this province between the members of the legal profession and members of the Institute is a favourable one, built on the basis of mutual respect for and understanding of each other's fields of endeavour. Members of the Institute should avoid any action which might be interpreted as contrary to the Solicitors Act.

3* The law has developed over the years whereby a Court dealing with a person who pleads guilty to or is found guilty of a criminal offence (other than an offence for which the minimum punishment is prescribed by law or which is punishable by imprisonment for fourteen years or for life), may, if it finds it to be in the best interest of the accused and not contrary to the public interest, instead of convicting the person, discharge him absolutely or upon conditions prescribed in a probation order. By including a reference to such discharges in the rules of professional conduct, the Institute is able to take disciplinary action if it deems it to be appropriate in those cases where a discharge has been granted for an offence which affects, or is perceived to affect, the professional conduct of the member or student involved.

CI 201—GENERAL STANDARDS OF CONDUCT

Public Accountancy Act

1 All members who offer public accounting services in Ontario, whether full or part-time, should be familiar with the provisions of the Public Accountancy Act and must ensure that they obtain a licence to practise before offering services to the public; the licence must be kept up to date during the time that such services are offered.

Law Society Reports

2 Members who are asked to report to the Law Society of Upper Canada concerning lawyer's trust accounts should note that these reports can be signed only by a licensed public accountant.

3 The Law Society report requires the public accountant to certify certain specific items set out in the form of report; a member requiring clarification or guidance concerning these requirements should contact the Law Society.

---

* CI 102(3) added June 14, 1982.

Employment Agencies Act

4 The Employment Agencies Act, and regulations thereto, requires that those who, for a fee, procure persons for employment or employment for persons must obtain a licence under the legislation to perform the service. A licence is required for each office in Ontario undertaking such assignments.

Criticism of a Professional Colleague or Other Public Accountant

5 During the course of his professional work, a member may on occasion find that he has a responsibility to criticize a professional colleague or other public accountant; such criticism may be direct, or may be implied by material adjustments to a client's accounts considered necessary to correct work performed by the professional colleague or other public accountant. It may be, however, that there are facts or explanations known to the professional colleague or other public accountant concerned which would have a bearing on the matter.

6 A member, unless limited or restricted in writing in special circumstances by the terms of his engagement, shall first submit any proposed criticism to the professional colleague or other public accountant involved so that any eventual criticism takes into account all the available information. This is a step dictated by considerations both of professional courtesy and of simple prudence.

7 When a member does criticize a professional colleague or other public accountant, and due to limitations or restrictions in writing by the terms of his engagement he has not been permitted to submit his criticism to his professional colleague or other public accountant, the member should be on record with the person placing the restriction that such consultation has not taken place.

Refer also to Rule 306.

Selection of Professional Advisers

8* When a client decides, for any reason, to change from one practitioner to another, the change should be facilitated on the basis of the following fundamental assumptions:
  • the client's interests should be placed ahead of the personal interest of the member;

* As amended June 11, 1979.

- the client is free to have his work performed by the practitioner of his choice;
- the fee for professional services cannot be estimated until adequate information is available about the assignment;
- professional courtesy and co-operation should be maintained between members in complying with the client's wishes.

Responding to Requests by Prospective Clients

9* When approached by a prospective client, a member may meet with him to discuss the proposed engagement and, subject to paragraphs 10 to 12 below, to evaluate the work required to carry out the assignment. The member approached should satisfy himself by suitable enquiry that he is aware of the position of any incumbent, and whether or not a decision to terminate an existing engagement has been made.

10* As the prospective client will wish to discuss with the member the services that may be needed or available, the member approached may provide the prospective client with information which will help him in making his selection. There is no objection to the member supplying such information and giving factual information as to his organization, the skills available therein and his per diem rates based on his standard rates for all clients. However, a member must not indicate or imply that he has exclusive knowledge or ability when in fact such knowledge or ability may be available from other practitioners.

11* The prospective client will also wish to obtain some indication of the cost of the services. Normally, professional fees are based on the time required to perform the services undertaken and a member discussing a possible assignment is rarely in a position to quote a fee or fee range until he has become more familiar with the requirements of the client, e.g., in an audit assignment he would need to familiarize himself with the prospective client's accounting policies and procedures and internal control, while in an accounting assignment he would be required to make an assessment of the prospective client's books and records and the application of his policies. Unless the member has so familiarized himself or made such an assessment, he cannot estimate the time required to carry out the professional responsibilities imposed by any statute or by the standards required by the profession, or by both.

12* Members are reminded that in accepting assignments from new clients they must comply with the requirements of Rules of Professional Conduct 302 and 304, where applicable.

---

* As amended June 11, 1979.

Resignation of Auditors

13** On occasion, the question arises of the duty of a chartered accountant appointed to act as an auditor of a corporation, who is asked by the directors to resign before reporting.

14** In Company, Corporation and Business Corporation Acts the statutory provisions with regard to auditors form a very important part of the legislation. The whole background of corporation legislation makes it clear that the auditor fulfills an essential statutory and independent function and assumes statutory duties when he accepts his appointment. It is the council's view that, as a general rule, the proper course for an appointed auditor to follow is the completion of his statutory duties: having been appointed by the shareholders, he should report, as required in the legislation. He should lay down his duties only when a successor has been properly appointed, after he has been relieved or disqualified.

15** This being the proper course, the question remains whether there are exceptions when a duly authorized auditor may resign at the request of a board of directors without fulfilling his statutory duties. The answer depends on the circumstances. Certainly, the auditor of a company should not lightly resign under such circumstances, and should not resign at all, before reporting to the shareholders, if he has any reason to believe that his resignation is required by reason of any sharp practice, impropriety or concealment which it is his duty to report upon.

16** However, exceptional circumstances may exist in a particular case which would justify an auditor in acceding to a request for his resignation; one example would be where he has reason to believe that if a special meeting of the shareholders was called to relieve him of his appointment the necessary percentage of shareholders specified in the governing statute would require his resignation—in such a case it may not be necessary for the auditor to insist on a special meeting being called.

17** In summary, the auditor of a company is appointed to represent the shareholders and has a duty to them, he should never lightly resign his appointment before reporting and should not resign at all before reporting if he has reason to suspect that his resignation is required by reason of any sharp practice, impropriety or concealment, which it is his duty to report upon. Subject to that general statement, however, there may be exceptional circumstances in a particular case which would justify his resignation and this will be a matter of individual judgment in each case.

** Amended June 11, 1979, and transferred from CI 301.

Non-member Public Accountants

18*   It is emphasized that the approaches outlined in this Interpretation are to be followed, where applicable, not only in dealing with fellow members and professional colleagues but in dealing with licensed public accountants generally.

Refer also to Rule 302.

CI 202—INTEGRITY AND DUE CARE**

CI 203—PROFESSIONAL COMPETENCE

Refer to Rule 206 and CI 206, *Professional Standards*.

ADDENDUM TO COUNCIL INTERPRETATION 204†

This addendum sets out amendments to Council Interpretation 204 which have been adopted by the Council. An updated Council Interpretation 204 will be published following completion of certain reviews requested by the Council:

- In respect of Council interpretations dealing with objectivity, contingency fees, commissions and finder's fees.
- To update and standardize the wording of the interpretations, including those noted immediately above.

Until the updated Council Interpretation 204 is issued, this addendum forms an integral part of the *ICAO Member's Handbook*.

COUNCIL INTERPRETATION 204

An introductory note has been added to the interpretation, as follows:

Members are advised that as a result of the amendment of Rule of Professional Conduct 204 at the Annual General Meeting in June 1988 the objectivity requirements now apply to members engaged to issue a review engagement report. While the term ''express an opinion'' is used in this interpretation, members should note that the interpretation also applies and provides guidance to members engaged to issue a review engagement report.

---

* Amended June 11, 1979, and transferred from CI 301.

** CI 202 deleted March 18, 1981, included in *Rules of Professional Conduct* as Rule 218.

† July 1989.

A special committee has been established to review objectivity. Accordingly, Council Interpretation 204 will not be amended until the Council has acted upon the special committee's report.

Former paragraph 13 has been deleted and a new paragraph 13 has been added, as follows:

A member is not permitted to establish or use a trust as a means to hold investments he otherwise would be prohibited from holding due to client relationships. This includes such trusts or family trusts established by the member or on his behalf which hold investments the member or his immediate family would be prohibited from holding due to client relationships.

The Council considers, however, that a member would not be in breach of Rule 204 if a trust, an estate, a custodianship or a guardianship, in which he, or any of his partners, or his or their immediate families, has a beneficial interest, held, in market or board lots, investments similar to those listed in paragraph 4(*a*) hereof in an audit client or any associate thereof, provided that the member or his partners or his or their immediate families did not have direct or indirect control over the investment policies of the trust, estate, custodianship or guardianship.

The Council also considers that a member would not be in breach of Rule 204 only by reason of the fact that he or any of his partners, or his or their immediate families, serves on the governing body of an organization which may hold an interest in an audit client or in any associate of an audit client of the member or his firm, provided that

(*i*) the holding of such interest does not make the organization an "insider" of the audit client or any associate thereof within the terms of the *Business Corporations Act of Ontario,* 1982; and

(*ii*) the member serving on the governing body refrains from participating in discussions and decisions relating to investments in the audit client or any associate thereof.

Any member who serves in any such position, where the organization concerned holds a material interest in an audit client or any associate thereof, should consider his position carefully; if the circumstances are such that his appearance of objectivity is impaired then the member, or his firm, would be expected to resign the position of auditor if the conflict could not otherwise be resolved.

CI 204—OBJECTIVITY

1   Rule 204 requires that a member engaged to express an opinion on financial statements hold himself free of any influence, interest or relationship, in respect of his client's affairs, which impairs his pro-

fessional judgment or objectivity or which, in the view of a reasonable observer, has that effect.

2   This is one of the principles expressed in the foreword to the rules and the foreword includes some exposition of the reasoning underlying the principle and thus underlying the rule. The "reasonable observer" does not, of course, exist as an individual. The term simply expresses the standard by which impairment, or the possibility of impairment, can be judged. The standard is that of a reasonable man having knowledge of all the facts involved and applying judgment objectively—that is, as an impartial observer.

3   To provide guidance for members, the council issues this Interpretation to set out how, in its opinion, a reasonable observer might be expected to view certain situations.

4*   The council believes that a member would not be complying with Rule 204 if he or his partners in a public accounting practice were engaged to express an opinion on financial statements of a client, and any of the following circumstances were present:

(a) In the case of a corporate client, he or any of his partners or his or their immediate families, directly or indirectly, had any investment in:
   • shares of the corporation or any associate thereof,
   • bonds or debentures of the corporation or any associate thereof (but not such other evidence of indebtedness as annuity contracts, insurance policies or guaranteed investment receipts),
   • mortgages of the corporation or any associate thereof, or
   • notes or other advances to the corporation or any associate thereof.

(b) Where the client is any other type of organization, he or any of his partners or his or their immediate families, directly or indirectly, had any investment in the organization, or any affiliate thereof, similar to those listed in (a) above.

(c) He or any of his partners was a director, officer, or employee of the client organization or of any associate thereof, or a member of his or their immediate families was a director or officer of the client organization or of any associate thereof.

   For purposes of this Interpretation:
   (i) The term "immediate family" when used to indicate a relationship with any person means:
      • any spouse, son or daughter of that person who has the same home as that person; or
      • any other relative of that person or of his spouse who has the same home as that person.

---

* Amended October 26, 1973.

(ii) the term "associate" means in relation to a corporate client:
- any affiliate thereof,
- any "investor" (whether or not it is an affiliate), as that term is defined in subparagraph (*b*) of paragraph 3050.03 of the Recommendations contained in the *CICA Handbook,* where the investor uses the equity method on the bases recommended in Section 3050 thereof to account for its investment in the corporate client and where the amounts relating to the corporate client reflected in the annual financial statements of the investor constitute more than 5% of total assets or gross revenues of the investor, or
- any "investee" as that term is defined in subparagraph (*c*) of paragraph 3050.03 and where the corporate client is an investor and uses the equity method in the same circumstances as described in the case of the "investor" referred to above.

(iii) The term "affiliate" has the same meaning as is given to the term "affiliated body corporate" in The Business Corporations Act (RSO 1970 c. 53), except that the meaning is extended to include any unincorporated body.

5   Where one or more close relatives of a member, even if not having the same home as the member, hold a material interest in any organization, the member, and his firm, is unlikely to have the appearance of objectivity. The facts in each case determine whether or not there appears to be an acceptable degree of objectivity; the professional conduct committee is willing to give rulings in individual cases.

6*   A member would not be complying with Rule 204 if he or his partners in a public accounting firm were members of a private mutual fund or an investment club which held any investments, set out in 4(*a*) above, of a client of the member or any of his partners. A member would not be in violation of Rule 204, however, if he or his partners invest in a public mutual fund not audited by the member or his partners, which held investments of a client of the member or his partners, nor would a member be in violation if he held qualifying shares in a social club such as a golf or curling club where the shareholding is a prerequisite of membership.

7   *Borrowings*—a member would not be considered to violate Rule 204 if he was engaged to report on financial statements of an institution (such as a chartered bank, trust company, finance or acceptance company) from which he or any of his partners, or his or their immediate families, had borrowed funds in the normal course of business, by way of a loan or mortgage, provided that the amount

---

* CI 204(6) as amended June 9, 1975.

borrowed bears a reasonable relationship to the borrower's income and his net worth and that the loan is of the sort that would be granted to other customers of the institution in the normal course of events. This assumes, of course, the absence of any specific statutory prohibition on such borrowing by the auditor of the institution, his partners or his or their immediate families.

8   *Commercial transactions*—similarly, a member would not be considered in breach of Rule 204 if he was engaged to report on the financial statements of a client with whom he or any of his partners, or his or their immediate families, carried out a commercial transaction, provided that the transaction was on the same terms and conditions as are normally allowed to other customers—this would include receiving the client's normal terms for payment of accounts. The member or any of his partners, or his or their immediate families, should not receive any special treatment or preference over and above that granted to other customers.

9* *Deposits and shareholdings in savings and loan institutions, cooperatives, caisses populaires and credit unions*—a member would not be considered to be in violation of Rule 204 if he was engaged to report on financial statements of a savings and loan institution, co-operative, caisses populaires, a credit union or similar institution in which he or any of his partners, or his or their immediate families, had deposited funds in the normal course of business, provided that the amount deposited bears a reasonable relationship both to the borrower's income and net worth and to the total assets of the institution. This assumes, of course, the absence of any specific statutory prohibitions on such deposits by the auditor of the institution, his partners or his or their immediate families. If such deposits entitle the depositor to vote at the annual or special meetings of the institution, this right to vote should not be exercised. In some cases, it may be necessary for the depositor in such institutions to hold a share in the institution. The holding of such a qualifying share by a member, or any of his partners, or his or their immediate families would not disqualify the member from reporting on financial statements of such institutions, provided that the vote attaching to that share is not exercised at annual or special meetings of the institution.

10 *Non-profit-seeking organizations*—any non-profit-seeking organization which is incorporated under the provisions of Part III of The Ontario Corporations Act (RSO 1970, Ch. 89 as amended) or within Part II of the Canada Corporations Act (RSC 1970 c. C-32) is subject to statutory provisions which preclude a member or his firm serving

---

* CI 204(9) added June 9, 1975, subsequent paragraphs renumbered.

as auditor if the member or any of his partners is an officer or director of the organization.

11*

12** *Executor/trustee/trusts*—occasions may arise where the acceptance by a member or any of his partners, or his or their immediate families, of a position as executor or trustee, might create a conflict with Rule 204. For example, a member would face a conflict of interest if he or any of his partners or a member of his or their immediate families was:

(*a*) the auditor of the related trust or estate; or

(*b*) an executor or trustee of an estate or trust which held a material interest in an organization or in an associate of an organization of which the member or his firm was the auditor; or

(*c*) a trustee of a profit sharing plan of an audit client or of any associate thereof; or

(*d*) a trustee of a pension plan of an audit client or of any associate thereof; or

(*e*) a trustee of a private charitable foundation which held a material interest in an organization or in an associate of an organization of which the member or his firm was the auditor.

In circumstances of this nature, the member, or his firm, would be expected to resign the position of auditor, if the conflict with the position of executor or trustee could not otherwise be resolved.

13† The council considers, however, that a member would not be in breach of Rule 204 if a trust, an estate, a custodianship or a guardianship, in which he, or any of his partners, or his or their immediate families, has a beneficial interest, held, in market lots, investments similar to those listed in paragraph 4(*a*) hereof in an audit client or any associate thereof, provided that the member or his partners or his or their immediate families did not have direct or indirect control over the investment policies of the trust, estate, custodianship or guardianship.

The council also considers that a member would not be in breach of Rule 204 only by reason of the fact that he or any of his partners, or his or their immediate families, serves on the governing body of an organization which may hold an interest in an audit client or in any associate of an audit client of the member or his firm, provided that (i) the holding of such interest does not make the organization an "insider" of the audit client or any associate thereof within the terms

---

* CI204(11) deleted March 18, 1981.

** CI 204(12) amended May 16, 1974.

† CI 204(13) amended May 16, 1974.

of the Business Corporations Act of Ontario and (ii) the member serving on the governing body refrains from participating in discussions and decisions relating to investments in the audit client or any associate thereof. Any member who serves in any such position, where the organization concerned holds a material interest in an audit client or any associate thereof, should consider his position carefully; if the circumstances are such that his appearance of objectivity is impaired, then the member, or his firm, would be expected to resign the position of auditor if the conflict could not otherwise be resolved.

14   ***Retired partners***—a member or his partners would not be considered to violate Rule 204 if they were making payments to a retired partner who holds a direct or indirect financial interest in, or a position or an appointment with, client provided such payments to the retired partner were determined as of the date of retirement in accordance with the terms of the partnership agreement and are not affected by subsequent events.

15   ***Application of Ontario Business Corporations Act***—members are cautioned that the provisions of The Business Corporations Act (Ontario)(Section 170) impose somewhat more restrictive requirements (in respect of audit appointments to corporations covered by the Act) than those set out in this Interpretation. The council has made known to the provincial government its view that the Act requires amendment in this respect, since it is the council's feeling that the section imposes unrealistic and impractical restrictions. The relevant provisions are:

Section 170*

(1) No person shall be appointed or act as auditor of a corporation who is a director, officer or employee of the corporation or of an affiliate of the corporation or who is a partner, employer or employee of any such director, officer or employee or who is a related person to any director or officer of the corporation or of an affiliate of the corporation. R.S.O. 1960, c.71, s.81(1), amended.

(2) No person shall be appointed or act as auditor of a corporation if he or any partner or employer of or related person to him beneficially owns, directly or indirectly, any securities of the corporation or of a subsidiary thereof or, if the corporation is a subsidiary, any securities of its holding corporation.

(3) Subsection 2 does not apply to a person, partner, employer or related person, as the case may be, if the person, partner, employer or related

(Continued)

person is not empowered to decide whether securities of the corporation or its holding corporation, as the case may be, are to be beneficially owned, directly or indirectly, by him, or if he is not entitled to vote in respect thereof.

(4) Where, on the date this section comes into force, an auditor or his partner, employer or related person owns securities as set out in Subsection 2, notwithstanding Subsection 2, he may for a period of two years from the date this section comes into force continue to act as auditor if he discloses in the report required under Subsection 2 of Section 171 that he or his partner, employer or related person so owns such securities but, at the expiration or such period, he shall cease to act as auditor unless he or his partner, employer or related person, as the case may be, has disposed of such securities.

(5) No person shall be appointed a receiver or a receiver and manager or liquidator of any corporation of which he or any partner or employer of or a related person to him is the auditor or has been auditor within the two years preceding his appointment as receiver or receiver and manager or liquidator.

(6) No person who is appointed a trustee of the estate of corporation under the Bankruptcy Act (Canada) or any partner or employer of or a related person to him shall be appointed or act as auditor of the corporation.

---

* This section is replaced by Section 151 of the *Business Corporations Act* of Ontario. The relevant provisions of Section 151 are as follows:

151.—(1) Subject to Subsection 5, a person is disqualified from being an auditor of a corporation if he is not independent of the corporation, all of its affiliates, or of the directors or officers of the corporation and its affiliates.

(2) For the purposes of this section,
   (a) independence is a question of fact; and
   (b) a person is deemed not to be independent if he or his business partner,
      (i) is a business partner, director, officer or employee of the corporation or any of its affiliates, or a business partner of any director, officer or employee of the corporation or any of its affiliates,
      (ii) beneficially owns directly or indirectly or exercises control or direction over a material interest in the securities of the corporation or any of its affiliates, or
      (iii) has been a receiver, receiver and manager, liquidator or trustee in bankruptcy of the corporation or any of its affiliates within two years of his proposed appointment as auditor of the corporation.

(3) An auditor who becomes disqualified under this section shall, subject to Subsection 5, resign forthwith upon becoming aware of his disqualification.

(4) An interested person may apply to the court for an order declaring an auditor to be disqualified under this section and the office of auditor to be vacant.

(5) An interested person may apply to the court for an order exempting an auditor from disqualification under this section and the court may, if it is satisfied that an exemption would not unfairly prejudice the shareholders, make an exemption order on such terms as it thinks fit, which order may have retrospective effect.

16   ***Commissions and finder's fees***—from time to time members may be asked by investment dealers, and possibly by insurance brokers, to act as agents or sub-agents for the sale of securities or the placement of insurance. A member in public practice receives fees from his clients for his services which, in some cases, will include advice on the utilization of surplus funds and, often, counselling on insurance coverages. There is bound to be a conflict of interest between this position and that of acting as an agent or sub-agent for the sale of securities or the placement of insurance.* In the opinion of the council, acceptance by a practising member of a commission or other remuneration from third parties for such agency services, would be incompatible with the principle of objectivity which is fundamental to our profession.

17   Instances have also occurred where third parties have offered to pay finder's fees to practising members in connection with arranging a client's mortgage or other financing or in connection with the purchase or sale of a business by a client. A practising member should not accept such a fee without his client's knowledge and consent.

18   In the rare instances where a practising member is able to render independent advice to two or more clients who are parties to the same transaction, the member must inform each of his clients that his services have been retained by other parties to the transaction and that he will derive fees from such parties.

Member Acting as Trustee under the Bankruptcy Act or as Liquidator, Receiver, or Receiver/Manager

19   ***Trustee under the Bankruptcy Act***—members who hold, or have held, an appointment as auditor, accountant or business adviser may be asked to act as trustee in the bankruptcy of the client or as trustee under a proposal to be made by the client to creditors under the Bankruptcy Act. A potential conflict of interest may exist in such circumstances because the member, in carrying out his duties, may have acquired confidential information concerning his client's affairs which he would be duty-bound to pass on to the creditors.

20   Notwithstanding that there will likely in fact be no conflict of interest existing in such appointments, council is aware that many creditors facing losses tend to be highly critical of all persons who were in any

---

* Note: The Insurance Act prohibits the payment of compensation by an insurer, agent or broker to anyone not licensed as an agent for placing or negotiating insurance. The acceptance of fees or other compensation by a person not licensed under this act is an offence under the act, which renders such a person subject to a penalty.

way connected with the insolvent debtor, including those who have had knowledge of his financial affairs. Where a member acts as trustee under the Bankruptcy Act and he has previously acted for the client in another capacity, doubt may be raised in the business community concerning a "possible conflict of interest," even though the doubt may not be justified by the facts.

21   Council considers that, as a profession, we should avoid not only possible conflicts of interest, but also any position which to a reasonable observer would have the appearance of a conflict of interest. Accordingly, a member or his associate may not be a trustee in bankruptcy, or in a proposal, for a client while holding, or within two years of having held, the position of auditor of that client. Furthermore, when a member or his associate has acted for a client in any capacity other than as auditor, he should accept an appointment as trustee only when he can act with objectivity. As a guide, and without attempting to cover all circumstances, it probably would be inadvisable for a member acting as an accountant (say, preparation of unaudited financial statements) or business adviser (say, advice on taxation and other financial matters) to be appointed a trustee under the Bankruptcy Act if he had been advising such client within the preceding two-year period; on the other hand, a member acting as a business adviser (say, consideration of financial reorganization which involved a proposal to creditors under the Bankruptcy Act) may readily be able to act with objectivity as a trustee under a proposal that was related to the reorganization. Before accepting an assignment under the Bankruptcy Act, a member should also be satisfied that his or his associates' relationship with any other clients having an interest in the bankrupt estate is not such as to impair his objectivity.

22   The attention of members is drawn to Section 170(6) of the *Business Corporations Act,* 1970 (Ontario) which precludes a trustee of the estate of a bankrupt corporation from being auditor of that corporation.

23   *Liquidator*—the council believes that there is no inherent conflict of interest between the positions of auditor, accountant or business adviser, and that of liquidator. A liquidator is appointed to act on behalf of the shareholders or owners in realizing the value of the assets of the company, meeting its debts and distributing any balance to the shareholders. The dictates of normal commercial ethics and law apply and, within these bounds, it is the duty of the liquidator to act in the interest of the shareholders or owners, while seeing that all legal liabilities are settled. A member may, therefore, *in the absence of a statutory prohibition* (see Section 170[5] of the Business Corporations Act, 1970 [Ontario]) act as liquidator for a company of which he or an associate holds or has held the position of auditor, accountant or business adviser, provided that he can act with objectivity.

24   An auditor who accepts an appointment as liquidator would, of course, resign his audit position as otherwise he would be expressing an opinion on the results of the business which he was responsible for liquidating.

25   ***Receiver, receiver/manager***—the council believes that there is not normally a conflict of interest which would preclude a member or his associate, who is acting or who has acted as auditor, accountant or business adviser for a client, from accepting an appointment as receiver or receiver/manager of such client in the absence of a statutory prohibition (see Section 170[5] of the Business Corporations Act, 1970 [Ontario]), provided that he can act with objectivity. In fact, the member's specialized knowledge of the client's affairs may well make him the logical appointee.

26* If a member is asked to act as a receiver or receiver/manager by the shareholders or owners and he is not prevented by statute, or by some other conficting circumstances, he may accept the appointment. A member who proposes to accept such an appointment where it is being made by parties other than the shareholders or owners of the client, or former client, must observe the following requirements:

(*a*) The offer of appointment must not be accepted without first having secured the consent of the client or former client. Where a corporation is involved, if it is impracticable to seek the consent of the shareholders, the consent of a responsible officer of the corporation must first be secured. It must be made clear, in seeking such consent, that the terms of the appointment may require the member to place his responsibility to the shareholders and/or management second to those attached to the new appointment, and that he may have to disclose information which he may have obtained as auditor, accountant or business adviser and which may conceivably affect the position of the shareholders and/or management.

(*b*) The discussion should be followed up immediately by a letter to the client or former client reiterating the member's position.

(*c*) The member must make it known to those who are appointing him that he has complied with the above requirements, so that his position is clear to all concerned. A copy of the letter to the client or former client, in which the member's position is set out, should be filed with those persons who are making the appointment.

27   An auditor who accepts an appointment as receiver or receiver/ manager would, of course, resign his audit position as otherwise he would be expressing an opinion on the results of the business which he was responsible for operating. In any event, a member shall not accept any appointment unless he can act with objectivity.

---

* CI 204(26) amended June 9, 1975.

General

28   Frequently, secured creditors require assistance in disposing of assets which have been seized as security for a debt owing. A member should be guided by the foregoing provisions of this Interpretation before accepting an appointment to act as agent for a secured creditor in administering or disposing of such assets.

29   References to "members" in this Interpretation are to be read as applying equally to firms and as applying also as between partners in the same or associated firms. Reference to trustee in bankruptcy, liquidator, receiver or receiver/manager would apply equally to companies incorporated to perform these functions.

CI 204a—AUDIT APPOINTMENTS UNDER THE ONTARIO ELECTION FINANCES REFORM ACT[1]

CI 204B—AUDIT APPOINTMENTS UNDER THE CANADA ELECTIONS ACT[1]

CI 205—FALSE OR MISLEADING STATEMENTS

A member who is employed other than in public practice is subject to Rule 205 just as is the member in public practice. It is recognized that under exceptional circumstances, this may place such a member in a difficult position *vis-à-vis* the organization with which he is employed; however, a member fails in his professional duty if he allows himself to be associated with financial statements or other documents which he knows, or should know, are false or misleading.

CI 206—GENERALLY ACCEPTED STANDARDS OF PRACTICE*

1   The phrase "generally accepted standards of practice of the profession" as used in Rule 206 means the standards, principles and practices accepted by the profession generally which apply to accounting, financial reporting, auditing, review and compilation engagements. The *CICA Handbook* sets out authoritative Recommendations which cover many, but not all, of these standards, principles and practices.

2   A member must exercise professional judgment to determine whether or not the Recommendations of the *CICA Handbook* apply to a particular matter. This would include taking into account any guidance and other relevant information that may be obtained by considering the sources listed in paragraph 4 of this interpretation.

---

[1] Since these Interpretations deal with the auditor's independence in two special settings and follow the same reasoning as that followed in CI 204, they have been omitted from this Appendix.

* Former CI 206 deleted and replaced with current CI 206 June 12, 1989.

3 When the Recommendations of the *CICA Handbook* apply to a particular matter, a member must exercise professional judgment in determining whether, in rare and unusual circumstances, the literal application of the Recommendations to the particular matter might result in misleading financial information.

4 When the Recommendations in the *CICA Handbook* do not apply to a particular matter, a member should take into account:
- background material and suggestions as to other practices which the *CICA Handbook* describes as desirable;
- accounting guidelines published by the CICA Accounting Standards Steering Committee;
- auditing and related service guidelines published by the CICA Auditing Standards Steering Committee;
- auditing and accounting guidelines published by the Institute of Chartered Accountants of Ontario;
- auditing, accounting and reporting requirements of any governing statute or regulation;
- practice in analogous situations;
- standards published by bodies authorized to establish financial accounting or auditing standards in other jurisdictions or internationally;
- CICA research and technique studies; and
- other sources of accounting literature such as text books and journals.

The relative importance of these various sources is a matter of professional judgment in the circumstances.

5 A member performing professional services in the context of a public sector entity should take into account the Recommendations issued by the CICA Public Sector Accounting and Auditing Committee. The Recommendations in auditing issued by the CICA Public Sector Accounting and Auditing Committee supplement the Recommendations of the *CICA Handbook*.

6 A member reporting on financial information of any enterprise required to file such information with a regulatory authority should comply with any specific audit or accounting requirements or regulation prescribed by such authority. In the exceptional circumstance where it is not possible or reasonable to comply with any specific audit or accounting requirements or regulation, a member should communicate the problem to the client; and, if requested to do so by the client and where appropriate, should communicate the problem to the regulatory authority. Further, the member should consider the impact and consequences of the problem in preparing the report.

CI 207—INFORMING CLIENT OF BUSINESS CONNECTIONS

Refer to Rule 204 and CI 204, paragraphs 16 to 18, *Commissions and Finder's Fees*.

CI 208—FEE FOR TRANSACTION INVOLVING CLIENT

Refer to Rule 204 and CI 204, paragraphs 16 to 18, *Commissions and Finder's Fees*.

CI 209—IMPROPER USE OF CONFIDENTIAL KNOWLEDGE OF CLIENTS' AFFAIRS

Refer to Rule 204 and CI 204, paragraphs 16 to 18, *Commissions and Finder's Fees*.

CI 210—CONFIDENTIALITY

Legal Privilege

1 Members and students should be aware of a judgment of the Supreme Court of Ontario (*Cronkwright* v. *Cronkwright* [1970] # O.R. 784). Mr. Justice Wright, in the course of the action, recognized a duty on professional persons or other persons in a position of confidence and testifying at a trial to ask the court for a ruling before divulging information obtained by them in their confidential capacity.

2 While His Lordship qualified his comments as being "my personal opinion" and while that opinion was not essential to his decision on the point in issue and is therefore not binding on other courts, a member or student testifying at a trial could quite properly point to this opinion in requesting a ruling of this kind. Indeed, as His Lordship stated, he has "a duty" to do so.

Information about Client's Affairs

3 Members and students who may be asked by a banker, or other third party, to pass on information concerning a client's affairs should clearly understand that the information requested must not be divulged without the client's consent. The third party's request for information, or for authority to make such an approach direct, should be made to the client.

CI 214—TENDERS FOR PROFESSIONAL APPOINTMENTS

Refer to Rule 301 and CI 301, *Professional Appointments*.

CI 217—ADVERTISING AND COMMUNICATIONS*

General Policy

1 Council is of the opinion that it is in the public interest and in the interest of all members of the Institute that members and firms be allowed to advertise specific services available and the fees charged. Members should be able to receive publicity, identifying them as members of the Institute, in areas which reflect their competence and knowledge, in matters which are within the scope of activities of members of the Institute, and in matters of civic or public interest. The Council wishes to ensure that advertising and publicity will contribute to public respect for the profession and thus to the professional standing of all members. It is the responsibility of the member to ensure that any material published is factual, and that any commentary is not misleading.

2 As guidance to members engaged in the practice of public accounting, Council sets out below its interpretation of what is acceptable conduct in a number of areas. Unless specifically noted, this interpretation applies to members otherwise engaged or employed, and to firms or corporations engaged in the practice of functions related to public accounting ("related function" organizations) if they are associated with members or firms engaged in the practice of public accounting. The interpretation seeks to ensure that advertising is accurate and factual, and that it is to inform rather than to solicit.

3 Members, firms and "related function" organizations that engage public relations, recruiting or other agents are responsible for ensuring that no activity for which the agent is engaged contravenes the rules of professional conduct and related interpretations. While there are matters in which the use of skilled assistance can be advantageous, members should recognize that there is an inherent danger of contravention of the rules and interpretations and that close control must be exercised by members to avoid breaches. Public relations, recruitment and advertising copy should be closely scrutinized by members engaging the services of consultants or other agents to ensure that it contains nothing objectionable.

4 The generality of the word "advertise" in Rule 217 is not intended to prohibit any member, firm or "related function" organization from being the subject of or being referred to in any *bona fide* news story (including interviews and commentaries) or to prohibit the publishing by any member, firm or related function organization of any work (including any professional paper, report, article, etc.) related to his services, as a chartered accountant or the practice of public accounting or in his

---

* As amended June 11, 1979.

business or practice of any related functions (as referred to in Rules 408 and 409.1 of the Rules of Professional Conduct), provided that none of the contents of such news story or work violates the requirements of Rule 301.

False or Misleading Advertising

5* Members, firms, and "related function" organizations must ensure, at all times, that any public reference (in advertising, stationery, reports, etc.) to themselves, their firms, or their services is accurate. Without restricting the generality of the foregoing, the following examples are given of situations which will be regarded as false or misleading advertising:

- any reference which implies that the practising unit is larger than it is, by use of plural descriptions or other misleading use of words;
- any implication that a member is a partner of a firm, when he is not, by the inclusion of his name in public announcements without a clear designation that he is not a partner;
- any implication that a member is entitled to practise as a public accountant, by including his name in public announcements of a practising firm if he is not licensed as a public accountant;
- any reference to representation or association which is not in conformity with the facts;
- the use of obsolete or out of date information;
- any reference to particular services of any member, firm, or "related function" organization where the member, firm, or corporation is not currently able to provide those services;
- any statement by a member or firm that his practice is restricted to one or more functions, if he accepts one or more assignments in practice functions outside those to which the statement indicated his practice is restricted.

6 Any listing of, or reference to, fees which is intended for the information of the public (including prospective clients) must not be misleading. Without restricting the generality of the foregoing, the following examples are given of situations which will be regarded as false or misleading advertising:

- any advertisement of fee information if service at the fee(s) specified will not be available on an ongoing basis for a reasonable length of time after such advertisement appears;
- the quotation of specific fee information if service at the fee(s) specified is conditional upon the acceptance by the client of other services, if such condition is not disclosed;

---

* CI 217(5) amended June 9, 1986.

- any advertisement of a "rate per hour" or fee or fee range for specified services, which does not give a reasonable description of the services included;
- any advertisement of fee information which quotes an unqualified "average rate," fee or fee range for services when a particular assignment might likely be billed at an amount significantly higher than the advertisement suggests;
- any advertisement of fee information, using terms such as "from $X" where the fees, rates or ranges actually charged for services performed bear little or no relation to those advertised.

7 Members, firms, and "related function" organizations must ensure that any public reference to themselves, their services or accomplishments, whether written or oral, are clear and completely factual, and contain no innuendo, implication, or assertion that is likely to be misunderstood, or to mislead a reasonable observer.

Professional Good Taste

8* Members, firms, and "related function" organizations should ensure that any advertising takes into account the following considerations:
- advertising should not be flamboyant;
- name plates, announcements, and professional cards should be of a reasonable size, appropriate to their purpose;
- advertisements for staff, or any other purpose, should not be extravagant or self-laudatory;
- advertising should not appear in media which might tend to lower public respect for the profession.

Unfavourable Reflections

9 Since any member, firm, or "related function" organization may be able to offer services similar to those offered by others, it is not appropriate for any member, firm, or "related function" organization to claim superiority or uniqueness with respect to any other member, firm, or "related function" organization. Members should not seek to differentiate their practices by self-laudatory puffery.

10**

11**

---

* CI 217(8) amended December 10, 1981, and April 15, 1983.

** CI 217(10) and 217(11) deleted June 10, 1985.

Endorsements

12* The word "endorse" in Rule of Professional Conduct 217.2 is to have its ordinary dictionary meaning, but is not intended to include a considered professional opinion given in the normal course of an engagement such as:
- may be incorporated in a prospectus or annual report; or
- the recommendation to a client with respect to a specific brand of product or the normal use of a particular product by a firm; or
- the sale by a firm of computer hardware or software developed by others.

In respect of involvement with products such as computer hardware and software, a member must not consent to or allow his name or the name of his public accounting firm or "related function" to be used in the advertising of others to assist them in the marketing of their products. However, the normal use of a particular product by a firm, or the sale by a firm of computer hardware or software developed by others, is not an endorsement of the product. Members are cautioned that "consent to or allow" the use of a name may be considered to be given in a variety of ways including by acquiescence. Rule of Professional Conduct 217.2 applies to endorsements such as those made to the general public.

The word "others" in this rule includes clients and non-clients alike; however, the word does not include a separate organization carrying on business as a related function as referred to in Rule of Professional Conduct 408.1.

Clients and Close Associates

13** Rule of Professional Conduct 217.3 permits members to mail, deliver or otherwise send promotional or other informational material, including letters, brochures, or technical or other publications to people with whom they have real and substantial business or personal relationships.

The rule is designed to allow the public to be served and to promote professional relationships between members, consistent with the Institutes long-standing prohibition against solicitation.

In that rule of professional conduct, the word "client" means a person or other legal entity such as a corporation, association, trust,

---

* CI 217(12) added February 25, 1983, and amended June 13, 1988.
** CI 217(13) added February 24, 1984, and amended June 15, 1987, and June 12, 1989.

or partnership, which or who retains or engages the member to provide professional services. The relationship ends when the engagement is complete or when some other apparent break in the relationship occurs. In the case of an audit, or other engagement wherein services are provided on a regular periodic basis, the client relationship continues until the member has become aware that the engagement has been terminated.

The word "close" means proximate in time and purpose. The word "associate" includes a colleague or one who is united with or identified with a member by a community of interest in a particular way.

By illustration, the following would be "close associates":
- the member's bankers, lawyers, insurance agents, or other people with whom the member or his firm has an active business relationship;
- a client's lawyers, bankers, financial advisers, and, in the case of a corporation, its senior management, with whom a member has a professional relationship arising from the engagement;
- alumni of member's firm;
- people with whom the member has developed a close personal relationship as a result of the member's social or community activities, such as fellow volunteer board members of a charitable or community organization.

Seminar Sponsorship

14* Members and firms engaged in the practice of public accounting may serve the interests of the public and members of the Institute by presenting educational and informational seminars on subjects within their particular expertise. Members and firms, therefore, may arrange, promote, present, or otherwise be responsible for such seminars, with or without a fee, subject to the rules of professional conduct.

Members and firms should recognize that seminars must not be utilized to directly or indirectly solicit any professional engagement which has been entrusted to another public accountant or a member who carries on a related function business or practice.

Seminars may be advertised in compliance with Rule of Professional Conduct 217. Such advertising may invite members of the public to request brochures, letters or other descriptive, promotional or infor-

---

* CI 217(14) formerly 217 (13), added June 13, 1983, renumbered February 4, 1984, and amended June 15, 1987, and June 12, 1989.

mational material from the member or firm responsible for the seminar. Responding to an advertisement for or attending a seminar does not, by itself, make the respondent or attendee a client or close associate of the member or firm responsible for the seminar.

Existing clients or close associates of the member or firm and persons who have made an express request may be provided with seminar brochures, letters, or other descriptive, promotional, or informational material of the member or firm.

Providing seminar brochures, letters, or other descriptive, promotional, or informational material, by or on behalf of a member or firm responsible for a seminar, to those who are not existing clients or close associates and have not requested such material will be considered indirect solicitation and contrary to Rules of Professional Conduct 217.3 and 301.

A member who participates in a seminar arranged for or promoted by a non-member shall ensure that any reference to him or to his firm at the seminar and in its promotion complies with the rules of professional conduct.

CI 301—PROFESSIONAL APPOINTMENTS*

Entrusted Engagements

1   Members are not permitted to solicit a professional engagement which has been entrusted to another public accountant because to permit such solicitation in the practice of public accounting could result in an impairment of the standard of integrity reasonably necessary for the protection of the public.
2   Rules of Professional Conduct 408.2 and 408.3 require members engaged in a related function to adhere to the rules of professional conduct and to ensure that any firm, corporation, or non-member associated with the member in the related function adheres to the rules of professional conduct.
3   The prohibition of soliciting applies to any professional engagement which has been entrusted to another public accountant or member who carries on a business or practice which constitutes a related function.
4   A professional engagement ends when the services which have been undertaken are completed or when some other apparent break in the relationship occurs. In the case of engagements wherein services are provided on a regular periodic basis such as but not limited to audits,

---

* CI 301 amended June 11, 1979, June 15, 1987, and June 13, 1988.

non-audit reviews, and annual tax compliance, the relationship continues until the member or the person so engaged has become aware that the engagement has been terminated.

Non-entrusted Engagements

5 The solicitation of a prospective professional engagement which has not yet been entrusted to a public accountant or to a person engaged in a related function must not offend those rules of professional conduct which require integrity, prohibit conflicts of interest, govern advertising, or otherwise regulate the members.

6 It is the responsibility of a member engaged in the practice of public accounting or a related function to determine, in a manner consistent with the rules of professional conduct, whether an engagement has been entrusted to another public accountant or a person engaged in a related function.

Tendering

7 A member responding to an invitation to tender is not in breach of Rule of Professional Conduct 301 solely by reason of such response.

8 A member approached by a prospective client is not in breach of Rule of Professional Conduct 301 solely because he discusses a possible professional engagement with, or responds to a request for information from, such prospective client.

Computer Hardware and Software

9 Members in public practice may be involved with computer hardware and software, not only in consulting and sales but also in installations of systems. It is acceptable for members in public practice to make arrangements with manufacturers or dealers to install or consult on behalf of such manufacturers or dealers. It would be contrary to Rule of Professional Conduct 301 for a member to enter into an agreement with a manufacturer or other third party where the manufacturer or third party solicits, on behalf of the member, any professional engagement which has been entrusted to another public accountant.

10 A member's engagement by a manufacturer or dealer as a part of the consulting process before a sale is not considered solicitation since the member is essentially part of the sales team of the manufacturer or dealer. It is not necessary that the member contact the incumbent auditor or accountant pursuant to Rule 305. Billings should be for-

warded to the manufacturer or dealer, rather than the purchaser. It is not appropriate for the member to provide the manufacturer or dealer with the firm's or member's promotional material for distribution to third parties.

11 Where dealers sell products at a fixed price, either for a set number of hours or to complete the installation and implementation, the relationship is acceptable provided the member's fees are charged to the dealer. It is not necessary that the member contact the incumbent auditor or accountant pursuant to Rule 305. If the customer is to be charged by the member, then it is necessary to contact the incumbent auditor or accountant.

12 It is not considered to be solicitation if a member is engaged by the customer after the sale to perform consulting or installation services. It is necessary that the member contact the incumbent auditor or accountant pursuant to Rule 305, however.

CI 302—COMMUNICATION WITH INCUMBENT PUBLIC ACCOUNTANT

Changes in Professional Appointments

1* Many members in the practice of public accounting are unclear on the purpose of Rule 302 which relates to changes in professional appointments, their impression being that on receipt of a communication from a proposed successor they may object to him assuming the appointment and thus prevent the change. There is no such intention; the purpose of the rule is as follows:

(*a*) It protects a potential successor from accepting an appointment before he has knowledge of the circumstances under which the previous accountant's services were discontinued. Knowledge of these circumstances might well influence him against accepting the engagement which is offered.

(*b*) If two separate practitioners are dealing with the same client, one as incumbent and one as successor, they should only do so in complete cooperation. There should be no period when each one believes he is the incumbent. They must both be aware of the proposed change before the successor accountant accepts the appointment. In all circumstances relating to changes in professional appointments the recommended procedure outlined in paragraph 2—below—should be followed.

2** When a member has been asked by a prospective client to accept a professional appointment it is recommended that he advise the client

---

* CI 302.1 formerly 301.9, amended October 26, 1973, renumbered June 11, 1979.

** CI 302.2 amended October 26, 1973, further amended June 9, 1975, and June 11, 1979.

that the incumbent should be notified of the proposed change by the client. The member should then enquire of the incumbent whether there are any circumstances he should take into account which might influence his decision whether or not to accept the appointment. The member should not take up any work on the account until he has communicated with the incumbent, except that in the client's interest, acceptance of the offered appointment should not be unduly delayed through the failure of the incumbent to reply, if every reasonable effort has been made to communicate with him. As a matter of professional courtesy the incumbent should respond promptly to a communication of this nature. If there are no circumstances that the member should be made aware of, a simple response to this effect is all that is necessary. If, on the other hand, the incumbent is aware of circumstances that the member should take into account which might influence his decision whether or not to accept the appointment, he will need to consider first the question of confidentiality. If it appears that the circumstances cannot be disclosed because of confidentiality, the response to the member should state that there are, in the opinion of the incumbent, circumstances which should be taken into account, but that they cannot be disclosed without the consent of the client.[2] Although the circumstances which the incumbent has in mind may be matters of public record, the incumbent must still consider whether confidentiality precludes him from disclosing the exact circumstances to his successor. Where confidentiality is in doubt, legal advice should be sought.

3*

4*

5† The attention of members is drawn to the provisions of Section 166 of the Canada Business Corporations Act:

> 166. Any oral or written statement or report made under this Act by the auditor or former auditor of a corporation has qualified privilege.

The apparent purpose of this provision is to provide the auditor or former auditor with legal protection against liability which might otherwise flow from a statement or report made by him pursuant to the

---

[2] Section 162(7) of the Canada Business Corporations Act requires the successor auditor to obtain a written statement of the circumstances and the reasons why, in the predecessor auditor's opinion, he is to be replaced. For a more detailed discussion, see Chapter 4.

* CI 302(3) and (4) deleted March 18, 1981.

† Added June 11, 1979.

provisions of the Act. A member wishing to rely on this provision should first ascertain that the corporation of which he is the auditor or former auditor was incorporated or continued under the above statute during the period he was an auditor. Further, members should note that the question whether the auditor or former auditor is entitled to the protection afforded by the provision can be answered only in particular cases. Accordingly, it is recommended that a member wishing to place reliance on S 166 should, for his own protection, take legal advice as to whether the report or statement he wishes or may be called upon to make is of the kind that is referred to in the statute.

CI 305—ASSIGNMENTS FOR CLIENTS OF ANOTHER PUBLIC ACCOUNTANT

Refer also to Rule 201 and CI 201, paragraphs 5 to 7, *Criticism of a Professional Colleague or other Public Accountant.*

CI 401—INTERNATIONAL ARRANGEMENTS*

1   The nature of public practice and the requirements of international commerce have led to the situation where many members of firms have representation or other arrangements with a person or organizations in other countries, and public references to such relationships appear on member's or firm's professional stationery and in their name plates, directory listings, announcements, and brochures. This interpretation sets out guidance for the use of such references.

International Firms

2   Where a member or firm participates in an organization which is practising public accounting internationally with professional engagements accepted and reports or opinions being issued in the international name, then it is appropriate for the member or firm to refer to such international name, if desired, on professional stationery and in name plates, directory listings, announcements, and brochures by using the term "Internationally," or "International firm." General references to "offices throughout the world" or "offices in principal cities throughout the world" imply broad coverage and should be used only where the international organization is practising public accounting in many countries.

---

* CI 401 added June 11, 1979, and amended June 9, 1986.

International Representation Arrangements

3* A member or firm may have an arrangement with another person or organization whereby one acts for the other in a particular location, and the assignment, by agreement, may be in the name of one of them. In such circumstances it is appropriate, if desired, for the member or firm to refer to the fact of such representation on professional stationery and elsewhere by a suitable reference to the location and the name and/or address and professional designation of the representative, with a description of the relationship as being "Represented by." General references such as "represented throughout the world," which may not be factual and may be misleading, should be avoided. In any public reference to representation, the representative must be a person or organization practising public accounting.

International Associations

4* Members and firms may associate themselves with international organizations which do not practice public accounting as such but which consist of members who are practising public accounting and which exist primarily to provide their members with access to international public accounting services. In these cases it is appropriate to make public reference on professional stationery and elsewhere to membership in a bonafide international organization by using a term such as "a member of (name), and international association of accounting firms". Terms such as "internationally" or "international firm" should not be used. General references such as "members throughout the world" should be used only where there are in fact members of the organization in many countries. References such as "represented throughout the world" should be avoided unless they are factual and not misleading.

Name Approval

5* While approval of representation arrangements and participation in international organizations is not required, it should be noted that approval of international names (CI 401[2]) may be necessary under the provisions of Rule of Professional Conduct 406(4)(*b*).

---

* CI 401(3), (4), and (5) added June 11, 1979, and amended June 9, 1986.

CI 403—PART-TIME AND "CONVENIENCE" OFFICES*

CI 405—OBTAINING OR ATTRACTING CLIENTS

Organizations Offering Tax Services

> 1 Any arrangement made by practising members with an organization offering tax services to the public, which results in a franchise or referral scheme whereby that organization benefits from supplying clients to a practitioner, would be objectionable as a form of indirect solicitation.

> Refer also to Rule 217 and C1 217, *Publicity and Advertising,* and Rule 301.

CI 406—PARTNERSHIPS

> Refer to Rule 401 and C1 401, *Misleading Names.*

CI 407—ASSOCIATION WITH A CORPORATION ENGAGED IN THE PRACTICE OF PUBLIC ACCOUNTING**

> In Rule 407, the term "corporation engaged in Canada in the practice of public accounting" does not include a corporation primarily engaged in the publishing business which publishes information on the subject of auditing, accounting or taxation.

---

* CI 403 amended October 1977 and deleted March 19, 1981.

** CI 407—new October 1977.

Chapter 4

Auditors' Legal Responsibility and Liability

Chapter Objectives

After studying this chapter, you should be able to:

- Describe the audit requirement mandated by the Canada Business Corporations Act and its underlying rationale.
- Explain the auditors' statutory rights and responsibilities and rationale therefor.
- Identify the responsibilities of directors and auditors regarding subsequent discovery of errors in financial statements.
- Describe the nature, purposes, and functions of the audit committee.
- Define the major legal concepts that relate to auditors' liability.
- Describe the criteria under which the auditor is liable to clients and third parties under common law.
- Describe the auditor's responsibility for the detection of fraud and error.
- Describe the accountant's legal liability for accounting and review services, and business advisory services.
- Explain the auditor's liability under the securities acts of the United States.

Legal Responsibility and Liability

Public accountants must comply with certain statutory and contractual requirements in their professional engagements. These requirements delineate their legal responsibility. Of course, they should also observe the rules of professional conduct and generally accepted auditing standards discussed in the previous chapters. Those who fail to fulfill their professional and legal responsibility satisfactorily may be faced with legal action. Thus, public accountants must be keenly aware of their legal responsibility and liability.

LEGAL RESPONSIBILITY

The auditors' legal responsibility can be statutory, contractual, or both. Statutory responsibility is based on the mandatory audit requirement in the federal or provincial business corporations act. Contractual responsibility derives from an agreement mutually decided upon by the auditor and the client. Both may also agree to certain functions in addition to the statutory requirements; in such a case, the auditor will be responsible to the client for both the statutory and the additional contractual requirements.

A business corporation may be incorporated under the federal or a provincial business corporations act. Certain types of corporations such as banking, insurance, and trust are incorporated under special acts. The auditors must be familiar with the specific act applicable to each of their clients. The discussion of the auditors' responsibility in the following sections of this chapter is related to the Canada Business Corporations Act because it governs some of the largest corporations and is one of the most recently revised corporation acts in Canada. It is also similar to some provincial acts, such as the Ontario Business Corporations Act.

Mandatory Audit Requirement

Sections 160 and 162 of the Canada Business Corporations Act require a corporation that is offering or has offered its securities to the public, or with gross revenues exceeding $10 million, or with assets exceeding $5 million, to appoint an auditor by an ordinary resolution of its shareholders at the first and all succeeding annual shareholders' meetings. Section 163 specifies that under certain circumstances the shareholders of a corporation not governed by Section 160 and by unanimous consent may choose not to appoint an auditor. The auditor's qualifications are stipulated in Section 161, which was briefly discussed in Chapter 3.

The details of these four sections are on the next two pages.

The main reason underlying these sections of the Canada Business Corporations Act regarding an independent audit on the annual financial statements of publicly held corporations is to ensure the reliability and credibility of these statements so that the interests of the shareholders and other investors are adequately safeguarded. It should be noted that the act

160. (1) Copies to Director—A corporation
   (*a*) any of the securities of which are or were a part of a distribution to the public, remain outstanding and are held by more than one person, or
   (*b*) the gross revenues of which, as shown in the most recent financial statements referred to in Section 155, [see pages 150–51], exceed ten million dollars or the assets of which as shown in those financial statements exceed five million dollars,
   shall, not less than twenty-one days before each annual meeting of shareholders or forthwith after the signing of a resolution under paragraph 142(1)(*b*) in lieu of the annual meeting, and in any event not later than fifteen months after the last date when the last preceding annual meeting should have been held or a resolution in lieu of the meeting should have been signed, send a copy of the documents referred to in Section 155 to the Director.
   (2) Affiliates.—For the purposes of paragraph (1)(*b*), the gross revenues and assets of the corporation include the gross revenues and assets of its affiliates.
   (3) Exemption.—A corporation may apply to the Director for an order exempting the corporation from the application of subsection (2) in such circumstances as may be prescribed.
   (4) Further disclosure.—If a corporation referred to in subsection (1)
   (*a*) sends to its shareholders, or
   (*b*) is required to file with or send to a public authority or a stock exchange
   interim financial statements or related documents, the corporation shall forthwith send copies thereof to the Director.
   (5) Subsidiary corporation exemption.—A subsidiary corporation is not required to comply with this section if
   (*a*) the financial statements of its holding corporation are in consolidated or combined form and include the accounts of the subsidiary; and
   (*b*) the consolidated or combined financial statements of the holding corporation are included in the documents sent to the Director by the holding corporation in compliance with this section.
   (6) Offence.—A corporation that fails to comply with this section is guilty of an offence and liable on summary conviction to a fine not exceeding five thousand dollars.
161. (1) Qualification of auditor.—Subject to Subsection (5), a person is disqualified from being an auditor of a corporation if he is not independent of the corporation, any of its affiliates, or the directors or officers of any such corporation or its affiliates.
   (2) Independence.—For the purpose of this section,
   (*a*) independence is a question of fact; and

(*Continued*)

   (*b*) a person is deemed not to be independent if he or his business partner

    (i) is a business partner, a director, an officer or an employee of the corporation or any of its affiliates, or a business partner of any director, officer or employee of any such corporation or any of its affiliates,

    (ii) beneficially owns or controls, directly or indirectly, a material interest in the securities of the corporation or any of its affiliates, or

    (iii) has been a receiver, receiver-manager, liquidator or trustee in a bankruptcy of the corporation or any of its affiliates within two years of his proposed appointment as auditor of the corporation.

 (3) Duty to resign.—An auditor who become disqualified under this section shall, subject to Subsection (5), resign forthwith after becoming aware of his disqualification.

 (4) Disqualification order.—An interested person may apply to a court for an order declaring an auditor to be disqualified under this section and the office of auditor to be vacant.

 (5) Exemption order.—An interested person may apply to a court for an order exempting an auditor from disqualification under this section and the court may, if it is satisfied that an exemption would not unfairly prejudice the shareholders, make an exemption order on such terms as it thinks fit, which order may have retrospective effect.

162. (1) Appointment of auditor.—Subject to section 163, shareholders of a corporation shall, by ordinary resolution, at the first annual meeting of shareholders and at each succeeding annual meeting, appoint an auditor to hold office until the close of the next annual meeting.

 (2) Eligibility.—An auditor appointed under Section 104 [auditor appointed by directors to hold office until the first annual meeting of shareholders] is eligible for appointment under Subsection (1).

 (3) Incumbent auditor.—Notwithstanding Subsection (1), if an auditor is not appointed at a meeting of shareholders, the incumbent auditor continues in office until his successor is appointed.

 (4) Remuneration.—The remuneration of an auditor may be fixed by ordinary resolution of the shareholders or, if not so fixed, may be fixed by the directors.

163. (1) Dispensing with auditor.—The shareholders of a corporation that is not required to comply with section 160 may resolve not to appoint an auditor.

 (2) Limitation.—A resolution under Subsection (1) is valid only until the next succeeding annual meeting of shareholders.

 (3) Unanimous consent.—A resolution under Subsection (1) is not valid unless it is consented to by all the shareholders, including shareholders not otherwise entitled to vote.

 (4) Exemption from appointing auditor.—A corporation that is a wholly-owned subsidiary of a holding body corporate may apply to the Director for an order exempting the corporation from appointing an auditor in such circumstances as may be prescribed.

focuses the auditor's qualification in terms of independence in appearance only while the general standard of the generally accepted auditing standards requires the auditor to be independent both in fact and in appearance, to be competent in auditing, and to exercise due care.

Auditors' Statutory Rights and Responsibilities

Sections 168, 169, 170, and 172 of the federal business corporations act delineate the auditors' rights and responsibilities. The specifics of these sections are:

168. (1) Right to attend meeting.—The auditor of a corporation is entitled to receive notice of every meeting of shareholders and, at the expense of the corporation, to attend and be heard thereat on matters relating to his duties as auditor.

(2) Duty to attend.—If a director or shareholder of a corporation, whether or not the shareholder is entitled to vote at the meeting, gives written notice, not less than ten days before a meeting of shareholders, to the auditor or a former auditor of the corporation, the auditor or former auditor shall attend the meeting at the expense of the corporation and answer questions relating to his duties as auditor.

(3) Notice to corporation.—A director or shareholder who sends a notice referred to in Subsection (2) shall send concurrently a copy of the notice to the corporation.

(4) Offence.—An auditor or former auditor of a corporation who fails without reasonable cause to comply with Subsection (2) is guilty of an offence and liable on summary conviction to a fine not exceeding five thousand dollars or to imprisonment for a term not exceeding six months or to both.

(5) Statement of auditor.—An auditor who
   (a) resigns,
   (b) receives a notice or otherwise learns of a meeting of shareholders called for the purpose of removing him from office,
   (c) receives a notice or otherwise learns of a meeting of directors or shareholders at which another person is to be appointed to fill the office of auditor, whether because of the resignation or removal of the incumbent auditor or because his term of office has expired or is about to expire, or
   (d) receives a notice or otherwise learns of a meeting of shareholders at which a resolution referred to in section 163 is to be proposed.
   is entitled to submit to the corporation a written statement giving

(Continued)

the reasons for his resignation or the reason why he opposes any proposed action or resolution.

(6) Circulating statement.—The corporation shall forthwith send a copy of the statement referred to in Subsection (5) to every shareholder entitled to receive notice of any meeting referred to in Subsection (1) and to the Director unless the statement is included in or attached to a management proxy circular required by Section 150.

(7) Replacing auditor.—No person shall accept appointment or consent to be appointed auditor of a corporation if he is replacing an auditor who has resigned, been removed or whose term of office has expired or is about to expire until he has requested and received from that auditor a written statement of the circumstances and the reasons why, in that auditor's opinion, he is to be replaced.

(8) Exception.—Notwithstanding Subsection (7), a person otherwise qualified may accept appointment or consent to be appointed as auditor of a corporation if, within fifteen days after making the request referred to in that subsection, he does not receive a reply.

(9) Effect of non-compliance.—Unless Subsection (8) applies, an appointment as auditor of a corporation of a person who has not complied with Subsection (7) is void.

169. (1) Examination.—An auditor of a corporation shall make the examination that is in his opinion necessary to enable him to report in the prescribed manner on the financial statements required by this Act to be placed before the shareholders, except such financial statements or part thereof that relate to the period referred to in subparagraph 155(1)(*a*)(*ii*).

(2) Reliance on other auditor.—Notwithstanding section 170, an auditor of a corporation may reasonably rely on the report of an auditor of a body corporate or an unincorporated business the accounts of which are included in whole or in part in the financial statements of the corporation.

(3) Reasonableness.—For the purpose of subsection (2), reasonableness is a question of fact.

(4) Application.—Subsection (2) applies whether or not the financial statements of the holding corporation reported on by the auditor are in consolidated form.

170. (1) Right to information.—On the demand of an auditor of a corporation, the present or former directors, officers, employees, or agents of the corporation shall furnish such

(*a*) information and explanations, and

(*b*) access to records, documents, books, accounts, and vouchers of the corporation or any of its subsidiaries as are, in the opinion of the auditor, necessary to enable him to make the examination and reports required under Section 169 and that the directors, officers, employees or agents are reasonably able to furnish.

(*Continued*)

> (2) Idem.—On the demand of the auditor of a corporation, the directors of the corporation shall
>
> (*a*) obtain from the present or former directors, officers, employees and agents of any subsidiary of the corporation the information and explanations that the present or former directors, officers, employees and agents are reasonably able to furnish and that are, in the opinion of the auditor, necessary to enable him to make the examination and report required under Section 169; and
>
> (*b*) furnish the auditor with the information and explanations so obtained.
>
> 172. Qualified privilege (defamation).—Any oral or written statement or report made under this Act by the auditor or former auditor of a corporation has qualified privilege.

The main thrust of these sections is to strengthen the auditor's position, which in turn would enhance the reliability and credibility of audited financial statements, for the protection of shareholders and other investors.

Two items in Section 168 deserve special attention: first, the auditor's right and duty to attend the shareholders' meetings; and second, the right and duty of the predecessor and successor auditors in the change of appointment. The first item is significant because it provides a formal and direct channel of communication between the auditor and shareholders whereby the auditor has the opportunity to explain and respond to matters concerning his or her duties. This would contribute to the effective and efficient functioning of the auditor. The second item is significant because it provides the auditor who resigns or is being asked to resign with the opportunity to explain his or her position. Also, the successor auditor is required to request and to receive a written statement from the predecessor auditor concerning the circumstances and reasons for his or her resignation or removal. This would probably serve as a deterrent to unreasonable dismissal of the auditor. The auditor's position would be further strengthened if the Canada Business Corporations Act had compelled the predecessor auditor to respond to the successor auditor's request. The act permits the auditor to accept the appointment if he or she does not receive a response from the predecessor auditor within 15 days after making such a request. The act, however, goes beyond the rules of professional conduct by requiring the auditor to disclose the ***circumstances and reasons*** for the replacement rather than to state whether there are circumstances for the successor auditor to consider before accepting the engagement. To the extent that this legal requirement overrides the auditor's right to maintain professional confidentiality, he or she may decline to respond. However, if the predecessor auditor does respond, the successor auditor should seek legal advice on the matter.

The provisions in Section 169 concerning the auditor's examination and right to rely on other auditors warrant further elaboration. First, the auditor is responsible for an examination of the client's financial statement. In addition, the auditor is also responsible for the opinion on such statements based on his or her examination. The reporting standards and contents of these financial statements are governed by the following regulations of the Canada Business Corporations Act.

General

44. The financial statements referred to in paragraph 155(1)(*a*) of the Act shall, except as otherwise provided by this Part, be prepared in accordance with the standards, as they exist from time to time, of the Canadian Institute of Chartered Accountants set out in the *C.I.C.A. Handbook*.

45. The auditor's report referred to in Section 169 of the Act shall, except as otherwise provided by this Part, be prepared in accordance with the standards of the Canadian Institute of Chartered Accountants set out in the *C.I.C.A. Handbook*.

Contents of Financial Statements

46. (1) The financial statements referred to in section 155 of the Act shall include at least
     (*a*) a balance sheet;
     (*b*) a statement of retained earnings;
     (*c*) an income statement; and
     (*d*) a statement of changes in financial position.
   (2) Financial statements need not be designated by the names set out in paragraphs (1)(*a*) to (*d*).

Reporting Classes of Business

47. (1) In this section, "corporation" means a corporation that carries on a diversified as distinct from an integrated business and that sends its financial statements to the Director pursuant to subsection 160(1) of the Act.
   (2) The financial statements of a corporation shall disclose separately or in a schedule thereto a summary of financial information for each class of business the revenue from which is 10 percent or more of the corporation's total revenues for the period.
   (3) The financial statements or schedule referred to in Subsection (2) shall contain a note stating that the directors of the corporation have determined its classes of business at a meeting of directors and have recorded them in the minutes of the meeting.

(Continued)

> (4) Subject to Subsection (5), the classes of business referred to in Subsection (2) shall be designated in accordance with the Statistics Canada Standard Industrial Classification Code.
>
> (5) Where the directors of the corporation do not adopt the Statistics Canada Standard Industrial Classification Code to identify the corporation's classes of business, the financial statements or a note thereto shall contain a description of the basis used to determine the corporation's classes of business.
>
> (6) Subsections (1) to (5) do not apply to any corporation that discloses segmented information in accordance with the standards as they exist from time to time of the Canadian Institute of Chartered Accountants set out in the *C.I.C.A. Handbook.*

Regulations 48, 49, and 50 prescribe certain circumstances under which a corporation may be exempted from public disclosure of its financial statements.

It is important to stress that the Canada Business Corporations Act requires financial statements to be prepared in accordance with the standards set out in the *CICA Handbook*. This statutory sanction of the standards of the accounting profession strengthens the authority of the CICA and its Accounting Standards Board and Auditing Standards Board, and, at the same time, it places an added heavy responsibility on the accounting profession to provide sound accounting and reporting standards.

Second, the auditor of a parent or holding corporation may ***reasonably*** rely on the auditor's report of a subsidiary or an affiliate. *Reasonableness* is defined by the Canada Business Corporations Act as "a question of fact." To establish such reasonableness, the auditor of the parent or holding corporation should make "a professional judgment as to the competence of his professional colleague, and it is for him to decide how he will satisfy himself on the matter."[1] But how does the auditor decide on the matter? Section 6930 of the *CICA Handbook* provides certain guidelines for the primary auditor (the auditor of the parent or holding corporation) in the reliance on the secondary auditor (the subsidiary or affiliate auditor). These guidelines require the primary auditor:

1. To consider the professional qualifications, competence, and integrity of the secondary auditor.
2. To communicate with the secondary auditor regarding such matters as the requirements of the primary auditor and any significant audit problems encountered by the secondary auditor.

---

[1] Robert W. V. Dickerson et al., *Proposals for a New Business Corporations Law for Canada* (Ottawa: Queen's Printer, 1971), I, p. 111.

3. To read the report of the secondary auditor and the related financial statements.
4. To obtain a written communication from the secondary auditor acknowledging the primary auditor's intention to rely on the secondary auditor's report and setting out the representations required by the primary auditor.
5. To review the work of the secondary auditor.

The materiality of the subsidiary or affiliate, as well as the existence of agency relationships between the primary and secondary auditors, will govern the extent to which the primary auditor applies the guidelines identified above. A discussion of reliance on other auditors is presented in Chapter 18.

Section 170 of the Canada Business Corporations Act grants the auditor the right to demand the information needed to perform his or her duties. The auditor is allowed to have access to records, documents, books, accounts, and vouchers of the corporation or any of its subsidiaries, and to obtain information and explanations from the *present* or *former* directors, officers, employees, or agents of the corporation. The necessity of this right is obvious, for without it the scope of the audit may be limited or restricted by the corporation.

Section 172 gives the auditor a "qualified privilege" for any oral or written statement or report made under the Canada Business Corporations Act. This protects the auditor from legal action for slander or libel, provided that the auditor's statement or report is made in good faith and without malice. Thus, it encourages the auditor to make full and frank statements on matters related to the examination and his or her opinion on the financial statements. Since the auditor is probably entitled to such a "qualified privilege" under common law, this provision is to ensure that he or she is aware of the common-law position.[2]

Subsequent Discovery of Errors in Financial Statements

Section 171 contains two important provisions: first, the rights and responsibilities of the auditor and directors of a corporation with regard to subsequent discovery of errors in published financial statements; and, second, the audit committee. The first item is discussed below, and the second in the next section.

The details of the first provision are on page 146. This provision imposes on the auditor, director, and officer of a corporation a duty to take necessary action to inform the shareholders and probably other users of the errors they discover in published financial statements of the corpora-

---

[2] Ibid., p. 112.

171. (6) Notice of errors.—A director or an officer of a corporation shall forthwith notify the audit committee and the auditor of any error or mis-statement of which he becomes aware in a financial statement that the auditor or a former auditor has reported on.

(7) Error in financial statements.—If the auditor or former auditor of a corporation is notified or becomes aware of an error or mis-statement in a financial statement on which he has reported, and if in his opinion the error or mis-statement is material, he shall inform each director accordingly.

(8) Duty of directors.—When upon Subsection (7) the auditor or former auditor informs the directors of an error or mis-statement in a financial statement, the director shall
   (a) prepare and issue revised financial statements; or
   (b) otherwise inform the shareholders and, if the corporation is one that is required to comply with Section 160, it shall inform the Director of the error of mis-statement in the same manner as it informs the shareholders.

(9) Offence.—Every director or officer of a corporation who knowingly fails to comply with Subsection (6) or (8) is guilty of an offence and liable on summary conviction to a fine not exceeding five thousand dollars or to imprisonment for a term not exceeding six months or to both.

tion. This is essential to ensure the continuing reliability and credibility of financial statements. A further discussion on the subsequent discovery of errors in financial statements is presented in Chapter 6.

Audit Committee

Section 171 requires a corporation that is offering or has offered its securities to the public to have an audit committee. The specific provisions are:

171. (1) Audit committee.—Subject to Subsection (2), a corporation described in Subsection 102(2) [requiring a corporation offering its securities to the public to have no fewer than three directors] shall, and any other corporation may, have an audit committee composed of not less than three directors of the corporation, a majority of whom are not officers or employees of the corporation or any of its affiliates.

(2) Exemption.—A corporation may apply to the Director for an order authorizing the corporation to dispense with an audit committee,

(Continued)

> and the Director may, if he is satisfied that the shareholders will not be prejudiced by such an order, permit the corporation to dispense with an audit committee on such reasonable conditions as he thinks fit.
>
> (3) Duty of committee.—An audit committee shall review the financial statements of the corporation before such financial statements are approved under Section 158 [approval by one or more directors].
>
> (4) Auditor's attendance.—The auditor of a corporation is entitled to receive notice of every meeting of the audit committee and, at the expense of the corporation, to attend and be heard thereat; and, if so requested by a member of the audit committee, shall attend every meeting of the committee held during the term of office of the auditor.
>
> (5) Calling meeting.—The auditor of a corporation or a member of the audit committee may call a meeting of the committee.

The most salient rationale for establishing an audit committee is the need to assure the independence or objectivity of the external auditor. This need arises because the close relationship between the auditor and management frequently poses a threat to the auditor's independence. The audit committee, composed chiefly or entirely of nonofficer directors, provides a degree of objectivity and a direct channel of communication between the auditor and directors, and thus will help to minimize or avert this threat to the auditor's independence.[3]

In practice, the objectives and functions of an audit committee usually are broader than those set forth or implied in the statutory requirements. The most important objectives are:

1. To assist the board of directors regarding the review of the results of the external audit.
2. To perform as an independent review function of the corporation's operations and its annual financial statements before their submission to the board of directors for approval.
3. To assist the board of directors regarding the review of the annual financial statements.
4. To give attention to the internal control functions of the corporation.
5. To enhance the external auditors' independence by giving additional attention to their audit function.

---

[3] Ontario, Legislative Assembly, *1967 Interim Report of the Select Committee on Company Law* (Toronto, 1967), pp. 91–92. Also see Ontario, *Report of the Royal Commission— Atlantic Acceptance Corporation Limited* (Toronto, 1967), IV, p. 1512, which noted that with an audit committee the auditor would have been more independent of management and "it was probable that the story of Atlantic Acceptance would have been different."

6. To provide outside directors with direct and regular contact with the external auditors.

Although the functions of an audit committee may vary from corporation to corporation, the most important functions should include:

1. Discuss with the external auditors, before the audit, its scope, purpose, and the procedures to be included.
2. Review with the external auditors their evaluation of the corporation's internal control systems.
3. Review with the external auditors regarding the problems they encountered, any restrictions on their work, cooperation received, their findings, and their recommendations.
4. Review the corporate annual financial statements before their submission to the board of directors for approval.
5. Review the scope of internal audit procedures with the chief internal auditor.
6. Review interim financial reports to shareholders before these reports are approved by the board of directors.

Since the creation of an audit committee introduces a new organizational unit within the corporate structure, it gives rise to a new set of relationships among the auditor, directors, and management. An audit committee, in performing a variety of its functions, should take extreme care not to encroach upon management's operating duties. Any unnecessary and unwarranted encroachment would eventually undermine the effective functioning of the committee.

Audit committees usually are small, three members being most common. This perhaps reflects the thinking that a small committee would make in-depth discussions on important matters more effective and efficient. The committee generally meets at least once or twice a year, usually with the auditor in attendance. These meetings are devoted to the discussion of the functions cited earier.

In general, audit committees are considered useful for most corporations, including not-for-profit organizations, and are effective in fulfilling their objectives and functions. They represent a positive force in assuring the auditor's independence from management and enhance the reliability and credibility of corporate financial statements. They can also contribute other benefits, such as resolving major disagreements between auditors and management and providing added protection for the directors of the corporation, especially for outside (nonofficer) directors, in discharging their responsibilities.

In addition to the federal business corporations act, other provincial acts such as the Ontario, Manitoba, Saskatchewan, and British Columbia acts also contain an audit committee provision. It appears that the audit committee is now well established in Canada.[4]

Other Statutory Requirements Relevant to the Auditor

The following sections of the Canada Business Corporations Act are related to such matters as the preparation, maintenance, and form of corporate records, the duty of care of corporate directors and officers, annual financial statements and their approval, removal of the auditor, and the court-appointed auditor. Some of these sections, such as Sections 155 and 158, have been referred to earlier. Auditors should be quite familiar with these sections.

---

20. (1) Corporate records.—A corporation shall prepare and mantain, at its registered office or at any other place in Canada designated by the directors, records containing
    (*a*) the articles and the by-laws, and all amendments thereto, and a copy of any unanimous shareholder agreement;
    (*b*) minutes of meetings and resolutions of shareholders;
    (*c*) copies of all notices required by Section 106 or 113; and
    (*d*) a securities register complying with section 50.
    (2) Directors' records.—In addition to the records described in Subsection (1), a corporation shall prepare and maintain adequate accounting records and records containing minutes of meetings and resolutions of the directors and any committee thereof.
    (3) Records of continued corporations.—For the purposes of paragraph (1)(*b*) and Subsection (2), where a body corporate is continued under this Act, "records" includes similar records required by law to be maintained by the body corporate before it was so continued.
    (4) Place of directors' records.—The records described in subsection (2) shall be kept at the registered office of the corporation or at such other place as the directors think fit and shall at all reasonable times be open to inspection by the directors.
    (5) Records in Canada.—Where accounting records of a corporation are kept at a place outside Canada, there shall be kept at the registered office or other office in Canada accounting records adequate to enable the directors to ascertain the financial position of the corporation with reasonable accuracy on a quarterly basis.

(*Continued*)

---

[4] In the United States, the New York Stock Exchange requires its listed companies to have an audit committee composed exclusively of outside directors.

(6) Offence.—A corporation that, without reasonable cause, fails to comply with this section is guilty of an offence and liable on summary conviction to a fine not exceeding five thousand dollars.

22. (1) Form of records.—All registers and other records required by this Act to be prepared and maintained may be in a bound or loose-leaf form or in a photographic film form, or may be entered or recorded by any system of mechanical or electronic data processing or any other information storage device that is capable of reproducing any required information in intelligible written form within a reasonable time.

(2) Precautions.—A corporation and its agents shall take reasonable precautions to

(*a*) prevent loss or destruction of,

(*b*) prevent falsification of entries in, and

(*c*) facilitate detection and correction of inaccuracies in the registers and other records required by this Act to be prepared and maintained.

(3) Offence.—A person who, without reasonable cause, contravenes this section is guilty of an offence and liable on summary conviction to a fine not exceeding five thousand dollars or to imprisonment for a term not exceeding six months or to both.

23. Corporate Seal.—An instrument or agreement executed on behalf of a corporation by a director, an officer or an agent of the corporation is not invalid merely because a corporate seal is not affixed thereto.

122. (1) Duty of care of directors and officers.—Every director and officer of a corporation in exercising his powers and discharging his duties shall

(*a*) act honestly and in good faith with a view to the best interests of the corporation; and

(*b*) exercise the care, diligence and skill that a reasonably prudent person should exercise in comparable circumstances.

(2) Duty to comply.—Every director and officer of a corporation shall comply with this Act, the regulations, articles, by-laws and any unanimous shareholder agreement.

(3) No exculpation.—Subject to Subsection 146(4), no provision in a contract, the articles, the by-laws or a resolution relieves a director or officer from the duty to act in accordance with this Act or the regulations or relieves him from liability for a breach thereof.

155. (1) Annual financial statements.—Subject to Section 156, the directors of a corporation shall place before the shareholders at every annual meeting

(*a*) comparative financial statements as prescribed relating separately to

(i) the period that began on the date the corporation came into existence and ended not more than six months before the annual meeting or, if the corporation has completed a fi-

(Continued)

nancial year, the period that began immediately after the end of the last completed financial year and ended not more than six months before the annual meeting, and

(ii) the immediately preceding financial year;

(*b*) the report of the auditor, if any; and

(*c*) any further information respecting the financial position of the corporation and the results of its operations required by the articles, the by-laws or any unanimous shareholder agreement.

(2) Exception.—Notwithstanding paragraph (1)(*a*), the financial statements referred to in subparagraph (1)(*a*)(ii) may be omitted if the reason for the omission is set out in the financial statements, or in a note thereto, to be placed before the shareholders at an annual meeting.

156. Exemption.—A corporation may apply to the Director for an order authorizing the corporation to omit from its financial statements any item presecribed, or to dispense with the publication of any particular financial statement prescribed, and the Director may if he reasonably believes that disclosure of the information therein contained would be detrimental to the corporation, permit such omission on such reasonable conditions as he thinks fit.

157. (1) Consolidated statements.—A corporation shall keep at its registered office a copy of the financial statements of each of its subsidiary bodies corporate and of each body corporate the accounts of which are consolidated in the financial statements of the corporation.

(2) Examination.—Shareholders of a corporation and their agents and legal representatives may on request therefor examine the statements referred to in Subsection (1) during the usual business hours of the corporation, and may make extracts therefrom, free of charge.

(3) Barring examination.—A corporation may, within fifteen days of a request to examine under Subsection (2), apply to a court for an order barring the right of any person to so examine, and the court may, if it is satisfied that such examination would be detrimental to the corporation or a subsidiary body corporate, bar such right and make any further order it thinks fit.

(4) Notice to Director.—A corporation shall give the Director and the person asking to examine under Subsection (2) notice of an application under Subsection (3), and the Director and such person may appear and be heard in person or by counsel.

158. (1) Approval of financial statements.—The directors of a corporation shall approve the financial statements referred to in section 155 and the approval shall be evidenced by the signature of one or more directors.

(2) Condition precedent.—A corporation shall not issue, publish or

(Continued)

circulate copies of the financial statements referred to in section 155 unless the financial statements are

(a) approved and signed in accordance with Subsection (1); and

(b) accompanied by the report of the auditor of the corporation, if any.

164. (1) Ceasing to hold office.—An auditor of a corporation ceases to hold office when

(a) he dies or resigns; or

(b) he is removed pursuant to Section 165.

(2) Effective date of resignation.—A resignation of an auditor becomes effective at the time a written resignation is sent to the corporation, or at the time specified in the resignation, whichever is later.

165. (1) Removal of auditor.—The shareholders of a corporation may by ordinary resolution at a special meeting remove from office the auditor other than an auditor appointed by a court under Section 167.

(2) Vacancy.—A vacancy created by the removal of an auditor may be filled at the meeting at which the auditor is removed or, if not so filled, may be filled under Section 166.

166. (1) Filling vacancy.—Subject to Subsection (3), the directors shall forthwith fill a vacancy in the office of auditor.

(2) Calling meeting.—If there is not a quorum of directors, the directors then in office shall, within twenty-one days after a vacancy in the office of auditor occurs, call a special meeting of shareholders to fill the vacancy and, if they fail to call a meeting or if there are no directors, the meeting may be called by any shareholder.

(3) Shareholders filling vacancy.—The articles of a corporation may provide that a vacancy in the office of auditor shall only be filled by vote of the shareholders.

(4) Unexpired term.—An auditor appointed to fill a vacancy holds office for the unexpired term of his predecessor.

167. (1) Court appointed auditor.—If a corporation does not have an auditor, the court may, on the application of a shareholder or the Director, appoint and fix the remuneration of an auditor who holds office until an auditor is appointed by the shareholders.

(2) Exception.—Subsection (1) does not apply if the shareholders have resolved under Section 163 not to appoint an auditor.

Auditors' Contractual Responsibilites

Auditors' contractual responsibilities stem from three different types of engagements—statutory, statutory with additional agreements, and non-statutory. For the first type, the statutory responsibilities are the auditors' contractual responsibilities. The second type of engagement requires the auditors to be responsible for both the statutory requirements and other additional functions agreed upon by the auditors and their clients. The terms of the third engagement depend completely on the auditors and their clients. The terms of the contract, once agreed upon by auditors and clients, are binding on both parties. In all engagements, the auditors should make certain that the parties to the contract understand clearly and precisely what the terms are. To avoid misunderstanding, the contract, usually in the form of an engagement letter, should be in writing and should be confirmed by the client. In the case of repeat engagements, the auditors should confirm in writing the terms of the contract with their clients every year to ensure that any changes in the contract are not overlooked.

LEGAL LIABILITY

We live in an era of litigation, in which persons with real or fancied grievances are likely to take their grievances to court. In this environment, investors and creditors who suffer financial reversals find auditors, as well as lawyers and corporate directors, tempting targets for lawsuits alleging professional malpractice. Auditors must approach every engagement with the prospect that they may be required to defend their work in court. Even if the court finds in favour of the auditors, the costs of defending a legal action can be very substantial. As a result, the cost of professional liability insurance has escalated greatly.

Costs are not the only concern in this area; lawsuits can be extremely damaging to a professional's reputation. In extreme cases, the auditors may even be tried criminally for malpractice. Every man and woman considering a career in public accounting should be aware of the legal liability inherent in the practice of this profession.

In the following sections, we discuss some of the most important concepts and considerations in determining CAs' legal liability to their clients and to the third parties who rely upon audited financial statements. However, a comprehensive study of auditors' liability is far beyond the scope of a single chapter in an auditing textbook. Rather, it is a topic that CAs continue to study throughout their professional careers.

Vulnerability of Accountants to Lawsuits

The potential liability of public accountants to persons who might be injured as a result of professional malpractice (negligence) may greatly exceed that of physicians or other professional groups. One reason for this is the potentially large number of injured parties. If a physician or lawyer is negligent, the injured party usually is only the professional's patient or client. If a public accountant is negligent in expressing an opinion on financial statements, literally hundreds or thousands of investors may sustain losses.

Litigation against public accountants is a global phenomenon and judgments of millions of dollars against them can well exceed their professional liability insurance. Consequently, public accountants are having difficulty in obtaining the desired insurance coverage, even at very high premiums, and may find themselves personally liable for any judgment in excess of their insurance. The following excerpts from an editorial aptly illustrate this situation:

The *Cambridge Credit* case in Australia concluded with the appeal judge's observation that the massive award ($145 million Australian) against [the accounting firm . . . would make all its partners] vulnerable to the devastating bankruptcy proceedings that might cause their assets, including their homes, to be seized and sold. . . . The partners of Alexander Grant, the tenth largest U.S. firm, are currently facing . . . a $300 million (U.S.) lawsuit. . . . [The amounts of the U.S. "Big Six" firms'] litigation and out-of-court settlements over the last five years . . . range from $1.5 million for Arthur Young [now, Ernst & Young] . . . to $137 million for Arthur Anderson.

Some large accounting firms in Canada and the United States have reported premium increases of as much as 125% over last year, with their coverage being reduced by up to 30%. And, beyond certain limits, coverage simply isn't available at any price.[5]

---

[5] Editorial, "Risky Business," *CA Magazine*, February 1986, p. 3.

In fact, the burden of litigation may lead to the downfall of an accounting firm. As well, the partners of the firm may be liable for their share of the firm's debts.

Illustrative Case

Laventhol and Horwath, the seventh-ranked public accounting firm in the United States, filed for protection from creditors under the U.S. Federal Bankruptcy Act in 1991. This was unprecedented in the history of public accounting. One of the contributing factors to Laventhol's predicament seemed to be the consequence of lawsuits against it. It was reported that over the past few years, the firm paid more than $50 million in litigation settlements. At the time of filing for protection under the bankruptcy act, there were 100 litigation claims against Laventhol, including the multi-million-dollar lawsuit over its audit on Jim and Tammy Bakker's PTL ministry.

In Canada, the amount of pending lawsuits against public accountants can run into millions of dollars. Some of the largest firms of chartered accountants have paid multi-million-dollar out of court settlements or are currently facing multi-million-dollar lawsuits.

Definition of Terms

Discussion of auditors' liability is best prefaced by a definition of some of the common terms of business law. Among these are the following:

Negligence is violation of legal duty to exercise a degree of care that an ordinarily prudent person would exercise under similar circumstances with resultant damages to another party. For the CA, negligence is failure to perform a duty in accordance with applicable professional standards. For practical purposes, negligence may be viewed as "failure to exercise due professional care."

Gross negligence[6] is the lack of even slight care, indicative of a *reckless disregard* for one's professional responsibilities. Substantial failures on the part of an auditor to comply with generally accepted auditing standards might be interpreted as gross negligence. Many jurisdictions in the United States consider gross negligence equivalent to *constructive fraud*.

Fraud is defined as misrepresentation by a person of a material fact, known by that person to be untrue or made with reckless indifference as to whether the fact is true, with the intention of deceiving the other party and with the result that the other party is injured. Rule 205 of *Rules of Professional Conduct* (discussed in Chapter 3) states that a CA shall not knowingly misrepresent facts. A CA found to have violated this provision might be sued for fraud by the client or another injured party. Charges of fraud might also be made against a CA who violates Rule 206.

Constructive fraud differs from fraud as defined above in that constructive fraud does not involve a misrepresentation with intent to deceive. Gross negligence on the part of an auditor may be interpreted by the courts as constructive fraud.

Privity is the relationship between parties to a contract. A CA firm is in privity with the client it is serving.

Engagement letter is the written contract summarizing the contractual relationships between auditor and client. The engagement letter typically specifies the scope of the professional services to be rendered, expected completion dates, and the basis for determination of the CA's fee. Engagement letters will be discussed more fully in Chapter 5.

---

[6] *Gross negligence* is a term more relevant in the United States, where it may be used as grounds for an action against an accountant by a person other than the client. It is important to be familiar with this term because it is used in the U.S. cases discussed in this chapter.

Breach of contract is failure of one or both parties to a contract to perform in accordance with the contract's provisions. A CA firm might be sued for breach of contract, for example, if the firm failed to deliver its audit report to the client by the date specified in the engagement letter. Negligence on the part of the CAs also constitutes breach of contract.

A *third-party beneficiary* is a person—not the promisor or promisee—who is named in a contract or intended by the contracting parties to have definite rights and benefits under the contract in the United States. For example, if Warren & Co., CPAs, is engaged to examine the financial statements of Arthur Company and to send a copy of its audit report to Third National Bank, the bank is a third-party beneficiary under the contract between Warren & Co. and Arthur Company in the United States.

Proximate cause exists when damage to another is directly attributable to a wrongdoer's act. The issue of proximate cause may be raised as a defense in litigation. Even though a CA firm might have been negligent in rendering services, it will not be liable for the plaintiff's loss if its negligence was not the proximate cause of the *plaintiff's* loss.

Plaintiff is the party claiming damages and bringing suit against the defendant.

Contributory negligence is negligence on the part of the plaintiff that has contributed to his or her having incurred a loss. Contributory negligence may be used as a defense, because the court may limit or bar recovery by a plaintiff whose own negligence contributed to the loss.

Common law is unwritten law that has developed through court decisions; it represents judicial interpretation of a society's concept of fairness. For example, the right to sue a person for fraud is a common law right.

Litigation Placed in Perspective

As we discuss auditors' liability for negligence, gross negligence, and fraud, there may be a tendency to conclude that CAs are often careless in rendering professional services. This is simply not the case. The overwhelming majority of engagements are completed successfully by CAs without any allegations of improper conduct. However, in any endeavor as complex as auditing, it is inevitable that some mistakes will be made. Any large CA firm that performs thousands of audits will, at one time or another, find that it has issued an unqualified auditor's report on financial statements that were, in some respect, misleading. Also, investors who have sustained large losses become desperate to recover their losses by any means possible. Thus, if bringing suit against a company's CAs offers even a remote chance of recovery, the injured parties are likely to initiate legal action.

CAs must recognize occasional allegations of misconduct as a fact of life. Some of the lawsuits brought against CAs will be frivolous—desperate attempts by plaintiffs to recover their losses. Others will have some basis in fact—judgmental errors made by the CAs during the engagement. No matter how careful CAs are, every large CA firm will occasionally find itself as a defendant in litigation.

Notice in our definitions of terms that *negligence, gross negligence,* and *fraud* each represent different *degrees of improper performance* by the CA. The extent to which the CAs' services are found to be improper is one of the factors that determines the parties to whom the CAs are liable for losses proximately caused by their improper actions. Liability may arise from improper performance on any type of engagement—an audit, tax services, accounting services, or management advisory services. However, CAs are *never liable to any party* if they perform their services with *due professional care.* Having exercised due professional care (sometimes called *due diligence*) is a *complete defense* against any charge of improper conduct.

Auditors' Liability to Their Clients

When CAs take on any type of engagement, they are obliged to render due professional care. This obligation exists whether or not it is specifically set forth in the written contract with the client. Thus, CAs are liable to their clients under common law for any losses proximately caused by the CAs' *failure to exercise due professional care.* That is, to recover its losses, an injured client need only prove that the auditors were guilty of *negligence* and that the auditors' negligence was the proximate cause of the client's losses.

A Canadian case, *Toromont Industrial Holding, Ltd.,* involved the liability of the auditors to a client because of negligence. The parties were a CA firm and its client, Cimco Ltd., which was controlled by Toromont. The action against the CA firm for negligence was brought by Toromont on behalf of Cimco. The High Court of Justice of Ontario ruled in June 1975 that the CA firm was negligent and was in breach of its duty to its client, with a resulting damage of $7,967. The counter-claim by the CA firm for audit fees of $4,750 was disallowed in view of the admitted negligence of the defendant.

A similar case in the United States is the *Westec* case. Westec Corporation was a rapidly growing, diversified company, and the market price of its stock increased from $2 per share to more than $67 per share over a two-year span. The stock's market price thereafter began to decline. Westec Corporation subsequently entered into corporate reorganization under Chapter 10 of the Bankruptcy Act. On behalf of Westec and its shareholders, the bankruptcy trustee sued the CPA firm. The trustee charged the CPA firm with negligence in conducting the audits and with consequently failing to discover significant related-party transactions, fictitious sales of assets, and improper application of the pooling-of-interests accounting method for business combinations completed by Westec. The CPA firm subsequently settled the trustee's suit by a payment of $1,875,000 to compensate for damages to Westec and its shareholders and by withdrawing a claim for fees and interest totaling approximately $133,000.

Not all damages paid by public accounting firms for negligence to their clients result from lawsuits. Litigation is extremely costly in demands upon the time of public accountants involved as well as expenditures for legal fees. Therefore, some public accounting firms have made payments to aggrieved clients voluntarily, before the clients initiated a suit.

Auditors' Liability to Third Parties

The liability of public accounting firms to third parties not in privity has developed under the common law. The responsibility of auditors to third parties who may rely on the audit report has evolved through several significant court cases. These cases involve the auditors' liability to third parties for negligence, gross negligence, and fraud. Since court decisions in the United Kingdom and the United States are cited in Canadian court decisions (for example, the decision of the Supreme Court of Canada in *Haig* v. *Bamford et al.* in 1976), it is important to discuss cases in those two countries as well as Canada. The principal aspects of the following cases, arranged in chronological order, are discussed.

In *Ultramares* v. *Touche & Co.,* 255 N. Y. 170 [1931], in the United States, the defendant CPAs issued an unqualified opinion on the balance sheet of a company engaged in the importation and sale of rubber. On the basis of the CPAs' opinion, Ultramares, a factor, made a number of loans to the company. Shortly thereafter, the company was declared bankrupt, and Ultramares sued the CPAs for negligence. Even though the case was ultimately settled out of court, Justice Cardozo established the principle that auditors could be held liable to any third party for *gross negligence* (constructive fraud) or fraud.

However, Justice Cardozo also held that the auditors could not be liable for negligence to the plaintiff, a third party identifiable only in a general way.

If liability for negligence exists, a thoughtless slip or blunder, the failure to detect a theft or forgery beneath the cover of deceptive entries, may expose accountants to a liability in an indeterminate amount for an indeterminate time to an indeterminate class.

In *Hedley Byrne & Co. Ltd*. v. *Heller & Partners Ltd*. [1963] 2 all ER 575, in the United Kingdom, Hedley Byrne & Co. Ltd., a third-party advertising agency, sued Heller & Partners Ltd., a banking company, for negligence. The plaintiff suffered a loss resulting from relying on the defendant's favourable references on a client company which subsequently went into liquidation. The plaintiff's action failed because the defendant had expressly disclaimed any responsibility for his references. The observations of the court on the broader issue of negligence to third parties are especially significant to auditors. The court stated that anyone making negligent statements in a business or professional capacity would be liable to third parties that were known or should have been known to him.

> [I]f in a sphere in which a person is so placed that others could reasonably rely upon his judgment or his skill or upon his ability to make careful enquiry, a person takes it upon himself to give information or advice to, or allows his information or advice to be passed on to, another person, who, as he knows or should know, will place reliance upon it, then a duty of care shall arise.

Hence, the defence of privity of contract may be invalid if the auditors know or should know that certain third parties will be relying on their report. To prove whether the auditors know or should know the third parties, a principle called the ***Hedley Byrne*** principle of foreseeability or special relationship is used. Its influence on Canadian court decisions is evident in two cases discussed later.

In another case in the United States, *Rusch Factors, Inc*. v. *Levin*, 284 F. Supp. 85 [1968], the court extended these rights to any limited class of persons who could be foreseen to rely on the auditors' report, despite the auditors' lack of knowledge of the specific third parties. This principle of auditor liability for ordinary negligence to a limited class of foreseen third parties was also supported by the American Law Institute's *Second Restatement of the Law of Torts,* which guides many courts in common-law rulings.

In *Haig* v. *Bamford et al*. [1972] 6 W.W.R. 557 in Canada, the Saskatchewan court found the accountants liable to a third party for negligence. The third party, Haig, relied on the accountants' audit report and invested $20,075 in an apparently profitable company which in fact was losing money. The profit figure was distorted by an erroneous treatment of a customer's advances as sales. The accountants submitted the auditors' report on the financial statements without performing an audit, the performance of which would have discovered the error. After the error was revealed and when the company was in financial trouble, Haig invested another $2,500 in an attempt to save the company. The attempt proved futile, and the company ceased operation shortly thereafter.

The court found the accountants negligent and, in applying the *Hedley Byrne* principle of foreseeability, held the accountants liable to Haig, for both the original investment ($20,075) and the additional investment ($2,500), because they knew or ought to have known that a third party would be relying on the financial statements.

> On the facts I hold that the defendants knew or ought to have known that [the auditors' report] would be used by a potential investor. Although Haig was not in the picture when the defendants were preparing [the report], he must be included in the category of persons who could be foreseen by the defendants as relying on [the report] in a matter affecting their economic interests. The defendants therefore had a duty to Haig. The negligence which I have found was a breach of that duty, and it follows therefore that the defendants are liable.

The successful appeal of the accountants in the Saskatchewan Court of Appeal was reversed by the Supreme Court of Canada in 1976 (*Haig* v. *Bamford et al.* [1977] 1 SCR 466). In reinstating the trial judge's decision that the defendants were negligent and therefore liable, the Supreme Court stated:

> The outcome of this appeal rests, it would seem, on whether, to create a duty of care, it is sufficient that the accountants knew that the information was intended to be disseminated among a specific group or class, . . . or whether the accountants also needed to be apprised of the plaintiff's identity.
>
> The increasing growth and changing role of corporations in modern society has been attended by a new perception of the social role of the profession of accounting. . . . The complexities of modern industry combined with . . . the separation of ownership from management . . . have led to marked changes in the role and responsibilities of the accountant, and in the reliance which the public must place upon his work. The financial statements of the corporations upon which he reports can affect the economic interests of the general public as well as of shareholders and potential shareholders.
>
> With the added prestige and value of his services has come, as the leaders of the profession have recognized, a concomitant and commensurately increased responsibility to the public. It seems unrealistic to be oblivious to these developments. It does not necessarily follow that the doors must be thrown open and recovery permitted whenever someone's economic interest suffers as the result of a negligent act on the part of an accountant. . . . [I]t appears that several possible tests could be applied to involve a duty of care
>
> *(Continued)*

on the part of accountants vis-à-vis third parties; (i) foreseeability of the use of the financial statements and the auditor's report thereon by the plaintiff and reliance thereon; (ii) actual knowledge of the limited class that will use and rely on the statement; (iii) actual knowledge of the specific plaintiff who will use and rely on the statement.

The choice in the present case, it seems to me, is between test (ii) and test (iii), actual knowledge of the limited class or actual knowledge of the specific plaintiff. I have concluded on the authorities that test (iii) is too narrow and that test (ii), actual knowledge of the limited class, is the proper test to apply in this case.

In the present case the accountants knew that the financial statements were being prepared for the very purpose of influencing . . . a limited number of potential investors. The names of the potential investors were not material to the accountants. What was important was the nature of the transaction or transactions for which the statements were intended, for that is what delineated the limits of potential liability.

The court then allowed Haig to recover the $20,075 but not the additional investment of $2,500 because he was then fully aware of the true state of affairs of the company. Thus, a duty of care arises when the auditor has actual knowledge of the limited class of third parties.

In another Canadian case, *Toromont Industrial Holdings Ltd. et al.* v. *Thorne, Gunn, Helliwell & Christenson* [1975] 3–10 OR, the plaintiff, a third party, sued the auditors for about $1.6 million in damages for the auditors' negligence. The High Court of Justice of Ontario held that the auditors were not liable for the damages, but this was only because the plaintiff failed to prove any loss flowing from the auditors' negligence.

In order for there to be liability for negligent misrepresentation, there must be first a duty of care; second, a negligent misrepresentation; third, reliance on the misrepresentation by the plaintiff; and fourth, loss resulting from that reliance. Since *Hedley Byrne & Co. Ltd.* v. *Heller & Partners Ltd.* . . . , liability for negligent misrepresentation can arise whenever there is *a special relationship* existing between the parties which casts a duty on the one making the statement to exercise reasonable care. The *defendant through one of its partners was aware that the plaintiff was relying on the financial statements* in connection with the purchase of the shares, and *this knowledge was enough to create a special relationship imposing a duty of care on the defendant*. (Emphasis added.)

The court also found that the audited financial statements did reflect the true financial position of the company at the time, but the auditors' report was false because ''no adequate audit had in fact been completed for the year in question'' and ''the defendant [had been] too prone to accept the advice of the management of [the company] in conducting their audit.''

The plaintiff appealed the decision, but the Ontario Court of Appeal upheld the ruling of the High Court of Justice. Thus, a duty of care arises when there is a special relationship between the auditor and the third parties.

In a recent Canadian case, *Albert Dupuis* v. *Pan American Mines Ltd. et al.* [1979] C.S. 421 à 440, the Superior Court of the Province of Quebec held that the auditors who expressed an opinion on the consolidated balance sheet and the pro forma consolidated balance sheet included in a prospectus owed a duty of care to a purchaser of shares, a third party, for negligence. Although the plaintiff, Albert Dupuis, sued a number of parties involved in the prospectus, including Pan American Mines Ltd. (Pan Am), its eight directors, and its wholly owned U.S. subsidiary Central Mining Corporation, he finally brought action against only the auditors and the lawyers. The negligence charge was based on the failure of Central Mining's auditors to obtain sufficient information in checking the titles of certain mining claims; to confirm with Pyramid Planners Assurance Company, a prospective lender, a commitment to lend Central Mining $1 million; and to secure information about Pyramid's ability to fulfill this commitment. Since both the parent auditors, a Canadian CA firm, and the subsidiary auditors, a CPA firm in the United States, were members of an international group of accounting firms, the court held that the former was responsible for the latter's negligence and was liable to the plaintiff, a third party.

In rendering his decision, the judge stated:

> It has been suggested to the Court that the standard of care applicable to the conduct of auditors requires reasonable care and competence; and that they are liable in damage to their clients if the performance of their work indicates lack of reasonable care but to third parties, they are liable only for fraud.
>
> When an auditor prepares a Balance Sheet which he knows is going to be inserted in a company Prospectus offering stock for sale, *I believe he has a duty to make sure that the contents of that Balance Sheet are accurate so that prospective investors will not be led into error by it.* (Emphasis added.)

Thus, the judge awarded the plaintiff the sum of $89,266.91 for the loss on his purchases of the Pan Am shares, together with interest and costs.

Some of the observations made by a lawyer writing up this case are worthy of note.

> The judgment clearly holds that a purchaser of shares, who suffers economic loss as a result of negligent misrepresentations in financial statements pre-

pared for the prospectus by an auditor who failed to exercise the required standard of due skill and care, may recover the loss from the auditor.

This appears to go beyond the point decided by the Supreme Court of Canada in *Haig* v. *Bamford.* . . . But *Haig* v. *Bamford* was not a prospectus case.

It is curious that a decision of such importance does not refer to *Haig* v. *Bamford,* or indeed to any other legal precedent.[7]

---

[7] Hugh Rowan, Q.C., "Third Party Liability Extended?" *CA Magazine,* August 1979, pp. 78–82.

From the analysis of the above cases it appears that, under common law, bankers and other creditors or investors who utilize financial statements covered by an audit report can recover damages from the auditors if it can be shown that the auditors were guilty of *fraud* or ***gross negligence*** in the performance of their professional duties. Fraud is obviously present if the auditors surrender their objectivity and cooperate with the client to give outsiders a false impression of the financial position or operating results of the business. In the United States, gross negligence exists if the auditors have not conducted an examination of any real substance and consequently have no real basis for an opinion. To express an opinion in their role of independent experts when in fact they have no basis for an opinion is considered gross negligence and provides a basis for legal action by the injured third parties.

Moreover, the auditors can be held liable for negligence to a limited class of third parties if the auditors have actual knowledge of such third parties or if there exists a special relationship between the auditors and the third parties. Thus, either of these two criteria determines whether the auditors owe a duty of care to third parties. In addition, the auditors may be held liable for negligence to a third-party investor in a prospectus issue.

The Burden of Proof. Legal actions under common law require the plaintiffs to bear most of the burden of affirmative proof. Thus, the plaintiffs must prove that they sustained losses, that they relied on audited financial statements which were misleading, that this reliance was the proximate cause of their losses, and that the auditors were negligent. The auditors named as defendants in a common-law action are in the position of having to refute the charges brought by the plaintiffs.

In the United States, certain third parties have the same rights as a client in litigation against the auditors. A third-party beneficiary is in privity with the CPA firm and with the client being audited, and therefore has the same rights as the client under common law. Thus, an aggrieved third-party beneficiary need prove only that (1) the auditors were guilty of ordinary negligence and (2) losses were sustained as a result of reliance on the auditors' opinion. In Canada, however, the only persons who are in privity with the CA firm and thus are entitled to sue on a contract are the actual parties to the contract, except in special situations where one of the parties to the contract acts as an agent or trustee for the third party. A third-party beneficiary is therefore *not* in privity with the CA firm. Thus, the third-party beneficiary position in the United States is quite different from that in Canada.

Auditors' Responsibility for the Detection of Fraud and Error

Auditors' liability to clients most often arises from their failure to uncover an embezzlement or fraud being perpetrated against the client by client employees. A client who has sustained such losses may allege that the auditors were negligent in not uncovering the scheme and sue the auditors for the amount of the loss. The key factor in determining whether the auditors are liable is *not* just whether the auditors failed to uncover the fraud. Rather, the issue is whether this failure *stems from the auditors' negligence.*

Section 5135 of the *CICA Handbook* delineates the auditors' responsibility to detect and communicate misstatements in financial statements such as error or fraud. It defines the term *error* as an unintentional misstatement in financial statements such as a mistake in the application of accounting principles. *Fraud*, on the other hand, is defined as an intentional misstatement in financial statements by omission of disclosure or theft of assets through such means as the use of deception to manipulate, falsify, or alter accounting records or documents.

Section 5135 further states that generally accepted auditing standards require the auditors to design their audit procedures to reduce the risk of not detecting a material misstatement such as error or fraud to an appropriately low level. Accordingly, the auditors must exercise due care in planning, performing, and evaluating the results of audit procedures. They also must exercise the proper degree of professional skepticism by not assuming unquestioned honesty and good faith on the part of management.

If the auditors suspect that error and fraud exist, they should obtain sufficient evidence to either confirm or dispel their suspicion. They should also assess the effect that the error or fraud may have on the financial statements and on their opinion. Of course, the auditors should inform management in writing of their findings on a timely basis. When the auditors encounter or suspect fraud involving the client's management, they should report their findings to one level above those involved and to the board of directors or its audit committee. Since any fraud involving management, especially at a high level, reflects negatively on management's integrity and good faith, the auditors must consider whether it is possible or practical to complete their examination. They should also consider seeking legal advice as to their responsibilities and their appropriate course of action.

There are certain circumstances that may suggest the possibility of error and fraud. Section 5135 provides the following examples:

---

1. Unrealistic time deadlines for audit completion imposed by management.
2. Reluctance by management to engage in frank communication with appropriate third parties, such as regulators and bankers.
3. Limitation in audit scope imposed by management.
4. Identification of important matters not previously disclosed by management.
5. Conflicting or unsatisfactory evidence provided by management or employees.
6. Unusual documentary evidence such as handwritten alterations to documentation or handwritten documentation which would usually be electronically printed.
7. Information provided unwillingly or after unreasonable delay.
8. Seriously incomplete or inadequate accounting records.
9. Unsupported transactions.
10. Unusual transactions, by virtue of their nature, volume or complexity; particularly, if they occurred close to the year-end.
11. Significant unreconciled differences between control accounts and subsidiary records or between physical count and the related account balance which were not appropriately investigated and corrected on a timely basis.
12. Inadequate control over computer processing. For instance, too many processing errors or delays in processing results and reports.
13. Significant differences from expectations disclosed by analyical procedures.
14. Fewer confirmation responses than expected or significant differences revealed by confirmation responses.

If the auditors encounter one or more of the above circumstances in an audit, they should seek reasonable assurance that material error or fraud does not in fact exist.

Of course, it should *not imply* that auditors were negligent whenever errors or fraud are later found to exist in audited financial statements. Auditors do not guarantee the accuracy of financial statements; they merely express an opinion as to the fairness of the statements. Furthermore, auditors do not make a complete and detailed examination of all records and all transactions. To do so would entail an almost prohibitive cost, which would certainly not be warranted under ordinary business conditions.

The nature and extent of the auditors' examination are determined by the auditors' judgment after obtaining an understanding and testing of the client's internal control. There can never be absolute assurance that errors or fraud did not exist among the transactions not included in the auditors' tests. Also, the possibility exists that documents have been so skillfully forged or fraud so expertly concealed that the application of normal auditing techniques would not reveal such incidents. When the auditors have made their examination in accordance with generally accepted auditing standards, they have fulfilled their professional responsibility and consequently should not be liable for failure to detect the existence of fraud or error.

In the United States, the AICPA's *SAS 53* (AU 316) requires that auditors (1) design their examination to *search* for errors and irregularities that would have a *material effect* on the financial statements and (2) exercise due professional care in the planning and conducting of their examination. If the auditors' tests indicate that material errors and irregularities may exist, they should discuss the matter with appropriate levels of the client's management. In addition, the auditors should extend their audit procedures to determine whether such material errors or irregularities do exist and, if so, their effects upon the financial statements.

Accountants' Liability for Accounting and Review Services

To this point we have discussed the liability of public accounting firms that serve their clients as independent auditors. Public accounting firms are also associated with unaudited financial statements. For example, public accountants may be engaged to prepare or review the financial statements of nonpublic companies. When a public accounting firm is engaged, as accountants, to perform financial statement services, there is always a danger that the client or third parties will misunderstand the extent of the public accountants' involvement with the financial statements. Thus, it is essential for the public accounting firms and their clients to have a clear understanding as to the nature, extent, and limitation of the engagement. The terms mutually agreed upon by the two parties should be in writing to avoid future misunderstanding. The risks for an accounting engagement was brought into sharp focus by the *1136 Tenants' Corporation* v. *Rothenberg* case in the United States. In this common-law case, an incorporated apartment cooperative, which was owned by its shareholder-tenants and managed by a separate realty agent, orally retained a CPA firm for a period of 17 months to perform services leading to the preparation of financial statements for the cooperative, also including letters containing tax information to the shareholders. The CPA firm's fee was to be only $600 per year.

The CPA firm submitted financial statements of the corporation for one full year and the first six months of the following year. The financial statements bore the notation "subject to comments in letter of transmittal." The referenced letter of transmittal read in part:

> Pursuant to our engagement, we have reviewed and summarized the statements of your managing agent and other data submitted to us by . . . [the agent], pertaining to 1136 Tenants' Corporation. . . .
>
> The following statements were prepared from the books and records of the Corporation. No independent verifications were undertaken thereon.

The client corporation later sued the CPA firm for damages totaling $174,000 for the firm's alleged failure to discover defalcations of the corporation's funds committed by the managing agent. The client contended that the CPAs had been retained to render all necessary accounting **and auditing** services for it. The CPAs maintained that they had been engaged to do write-up work only, although a working paper they had prepared supporting accrued expenses payable in the balance sheet included an entry for "audit expense."

The New York state trial court ruled in favour of the plaintiff client, as did the Appellate Court of New York. The latter found that the CPA's working papers indicated that the CPAs had examined the client's bank statements, invoices, and bills and had made notations concerning "missing invoices." The New York Court of Appeals affirmed the decision.

In summary, the court held the CPAs liable because it found that they had led their client to believe that they were performing an audit. Consequently, the courts held the CPAs responsible for performing their work in accordance with generally accepted auditing standards, which they clearly had not done. More importantly, however, the court also concluded that the CPAs had a duty to follow up on significant problems (the missing invoices) uncovered during their engagement. Thus, it is probable that the CPA firm would have been held liable to its client *even if the court had recognized that the firm was not performing an audit.* Whenever CPAs encounter evidence that their client may be sustaining a loss through embezzlement or other irregularities, they should warn the client immediately.

There are many lessons for public accounting firms in the *1136 Tenants' Corporation* case.

1. Public accountants who prepare unaudited financial statements should adhere closely to the Rules of Professional Conduct. Rule 205 states that CAs shall not sign or associate themselves with financial statements which they know, or should know, are false or misleading.

2. Engagement letters are as essential for accounting services as they are for independent audits. Oral arrangements for accounting services are of scant assistance when there is a dispute as to the nature of the services to be rendered by the public accounting firm to the client.

3. A public accountant engaged to perform *accounting* services that include unaudited financial statements should be alert for, and follow up on, such unusual items as missing invoices. As professional persons, public accountants are bound to exercise due professional care, even though their engagements do not encompass independent audits of the client's financial statements.

4. Public accountants should *clearly* and *concisely* communicate their conclusions on unaudited financial statements, using whenever possible standardized language set forth in the *CICA Handbook,* Section 8100. In addition, each page of the financial statements and footnotes should be marked "unaudited."

Accountants' Liability for Business Advisory Services

It now appears that public accountants are incurring a risk for liability to their clients not only for auditing and accounting and review services but also for business advisory services. A recent decision by the Supreme Court of Ontario held an accountant and his firm liable to the client for negligence for his advice on an investment.[8]

In this case, a newly established restaurant was losing money since its inception and needed an infusion of capital from potential investors. Certain financial data about the restaurant were given to the investors' accountant to determine the advisability of making the investment. These data included (1) unaudited financial statements for the period March 29 (the date of incorporation) to September 30, 1978; (2) a projected statement of earnings and surplus for October 1, 1978 to September 30, 1979; (3) a projected cash flow statement for October 23, 1978 to September 30, 1979; and (4) a list of accounts payable. Based on these data, the two investors invested $35,000 in the restaurant. Despite this infusion of capital and a bank loan of $15,000, the restaurant continued to lose money and, after a fire in December 1979, ceased operation.

The critical issue in this case was whether the accountant should have noticed and questioned a $9,000 decrease in accounts payable between the *September 30, 1978,* unaudited balance sheet and the *October 23, 1978* to September 30, 1979, projected cash flow statement. It was suggested that the substantial decrease in accounts payable in a span of less than a month should have alerted the accountant that something was amiss and that further information should have been obtained to explain such a decrease.

---

[8] Hugh Rowan, Q.C., "Caught in the Ever-Widening Net of Liability," *CA Magazine,* February 1986, pp. 64–68.

Had this been done, he would have discovered that the amount of accounts payable had increased in October 1978, by about $17,000, and that the restaurant was losing about $24,000 in October 1978. If such information were obtained, the investors would not have made the investment. Accordingly, the judge concluded that

[the accountant] and [his firm] Clarkson, Gordon & Co. were liable to [the two investors for the loss of] $47,000 . . . plus interest and costs.[9]

---

[9] Ibid., p. 68.

In support of his conclusion, the judge stated:

I cannot avoid the conclusion that [the accountant's] performance . . . fell short of that which was required of a reasonably competent chartered accountant in the circumstances, with the result that the advice he gave was incomplete and therefore unsound: the financial position of the [restaurant] was materially worse than he realized.[10]

---

[10] Ibid.

The accountant and his firm appealed the decision but it was settled before it reached the Ontario Court of Appeal.[11] Consequently, whether a higher court would affirm or reverse this decision remains an unanswered question.

Auditors' Liability under the Securities Acts of the United States

Legal actions against auditors which are brought under the U.S. securities acts tend to shift much of the burden of proof to the auditors. The plaintiffs must prove only that they sustained losses and that the financial statements were misleading. The auditors must then bear the burden of proof to show that they were not negligent or that the misleading financial statements were not the proximate cause of the plaintiffs' losses. For these and other reasons, in considering specific cases involving auditors' liability to third parties in the United States, it is important to determine whether the legal action is being brought under the statutes administered by the Securities and Exchange Commission (SEC).

---

[11] Ibid.

Auditors' Liability under the U.S. Securities Acts.   The Securities Act of 1933 and the Securities Exchange Act of 1934 place heavy responsibility on independent public accountants who prepare or examine any part of a registration statement or periodic report required under the acts. The inclusion of an untrue statement of material fact, or failure to state a material fact when such omission makes the statement misleading, opens the door to legal action against the public accountants by any person acquiring the security.

The 1933 Act requires a company intending to offer its securities for sale to the public to first file a *registration statement* with the Securities and Exchange Commission (SEC).[12] The 1933 Act states that both the company filing the registration statement and its auditors may be held liable to the initial purchasers of the securities in the event that the registration statement is found to contain material misstatements or omissions.[13] The wording of section 11(*a*) of the act on this point is as follows:

> In case any part of the registration statement, when such part became effective, contained an untrue statement of a material fact or omitted to state a material fact required to be stated therein or necessary to make the statements therein not misleading, any person acquiring such security (unless it is proved that at the time of such acquisition he knew of such untruth or omission) may . . . sue.

The 1933 Act offers protection only to a limited group of investors—those who initially purchase a security (stock or bond) offered for sale to the public. However, the act gives these initial investors the right to recover losses caused by the auditors' *ordinary negligence* as well as gross negligence or fraud and shifts much of the burden of proof from the plaintiff to the defendant. The plaintiffs (security purchasers) need only prove that (1) they sustained a loss and (2) the registration statement was misleading. They *need not* prove that they relied upon the registration statement or that the auditors were negligent. If auditors are to avoid liability for the plaintiffs' losses, they must affirmatively prove that either (1) they were not negligent (the "due negligence" defense), (2) their negligence was not the proximate cause of the plaintiff's losses, or (3) the plaintiff knew of the financial statement misstatement when the securities were purchased. Thus, the 1933 Act establishes the highest level of auditor liability. Not only are the auditors liable for losses caused by acts of

---

[12] The 1933 Act requires registration statements to be filed by any company that will offer securities for sale to the public through the mails or interstate commerce. There are certain exceptions, however, for charitable institutions, and other not-for-profit organizations.

[13] The auditors are liable for misstatements or omissions in only those portions of the registration covered by their examination and report.

ordinary negligence, but they must ***prove their innocence,*** rather than merely refuting the accusations of the plaintiffs.

The 1934 Act requires all companies under SEC jurisdiction to file audited annual financial statements with the SEC.[14] The act also creates potential liability for the filing company and its auditors to anyone who buys or sells the company's securities in the event that these annual statements are found to be misleading. Thus, the 1934 Act offers recourse against the auditors to a far greater number of investors than does the 1933 Act.

Section 18(*a*) of the 1934 Act provides the following liability for misleading statements:

> Any person who shall make or cause to be made any statement in any application, report, or document filed pursuant to this . . . (Act) or any rule or regulation thereunder . . . , which statement was at the time and in the light of the circumstances under which it was made false or misleading with respect to any material fact, shall be liable to any person (not knowing that such statement was false or misleading) who, in reliance upon such statement, shall have purchased or sold a security at a price which was affected by such a statement, for damages caused by such reliance, ***unless the person sued shall prove that he acted in good faith*** and had no knowledge that such statement was false or misleading. [Emphasis added.]

In addition, Rule 10*b*–5 promulgated by the SEC under Section 10(*b*) of the act reads as follows:

> It shall be unlawful for any person, directly or indirectly, . . .
> (1) to employ any device, scheme, or artifice to defraud,
> (2) to make any untrue statement of a material fact or to omit to state a material fact necessary in order to make the statements made . . . not misleading, or
> (3) to engage in any act, practice, or course of business which operates or would operate as a fraud or deceit upon any person, in connection with the purchase or sale of any security.

Most lawsuits against certified public accountants have been filed under Section 18(*a*) and Rule 10*b*–5. Section 18(*a*) states that defendants may be liable unless they prove that they "acted in good faith," which means that they were not ***grossly*** negligent. Thus, Section 18(*a*) establishes liability for gross negligence or fraud, but ***not for ordinary negligence.*** The wording of

---

[14] Companies with total assets exceeding $3 million and 500 or more shareholders are under SEC jurisdiction. Almost all publicly owned corporations fall into this category.

Rule 10*b*–5 appears to create liability only for fraudulent misrepresentations. In some court decisions, however, the rule was interpreted more broadly and auditors have been held liable for losses caused by ordinary negligence even when fraudulent intent was not established. In 1976, however, the U.S. Supreme Court clarified auditors' liability under Rule 10*b*–5 in the *Hochfelder* v. *Ernst* case.

Hochfelder v. *Ernst.*

This landmark case is one of the few court decisions that has served to reduce, rather than expand, auditors' liability to third parties. The suit was brought by a group of investors against the CPA firm that for 21 years had audited the financial statements of First Securities Company of Chicago, a small brokerage firm. The president of First Securities, who was also its majority shareholder, committed suicide, leaving a note stating that the firm was insolvent and disclosing a fraud that he had perpetrated upon several investors. The president had persuaded the investors to mail him their personal cheques, the funds from which he was to invest in escrow accounts yielding high returns to the investors. There were no such escrow accounts in the accounting records of First Securities Company; instead, the president converted the investors' cheques to his own use immediately upon receipt.

The investors filed suit under SEC Rule 10*b*–5 (and the related Securities Exchange Act of 1934 Section 10[*b*]) against the CPA firm, charging it with ***ordinary negligence,*** and thus with responsibility for the investors' losses in the fraud. The plaintiffs did ***not accuse the CPA firm of fraud or intentional misconduct.***

The basis for the plaintiffs' charge of negligence was that the CPA firm failed to discover a weakness in First Securities Company's internal control that enabled the company's president to carry on the fraud. The control weakness, called the "mail rule," was the president's policy that ***only he*** could open mail addressed to him at First Securities, or addressed to First Securities to his attention. (It is common practice at financial institutions for ***all*** incoming mail to be opened in the mailroom, in part to avoid the possibility of employees' perpetrating some type of fraud.)

The U.S. district court which heard the case dismissed it, holding that there was no issue of material fact as to whether the CPA firm had conducted its audits of First Securities in accordance with generally accepted auditing standards. The U.S. Court of Appeals reversed the district court and ruled that the CPA firm was liable for damages for aiding and abetting the First Securities president's fraud because the CPA firm had breached its duty of enquiry and disclosure regarding the First Securities internal control weakness.

The U.S. Supreme Court reversed the court of appeals, deciding that an action for damages under Section 10(*b*) of the 1934 Act and the related SEC Rule 10*b*–5 was not warranted in the absence of ***intent to deceive, manipulate, or defraud*** on the CPA firm's part. In the Court's opinion, Mr. Justice Powell wrote:

> The words "manipulative or deceptive" used in conjunction with "device or contrivance" strongly suggest that (Section) 10(*b*) was intended to proscribe knowing or intentional misconduct.
>
> * * * * *
>
> When a statute speaks so specifically in terms of manipulation and deception, and of implementing devices and contrivances—the commonly understood terminology of intentional wrongdoing—and when its history reflects no more expansive intent, we are quite unwilling to extend the scope of the statute to negligent conduct.

Based upon this ruling, auditors can no longer be held liable for ordinary negligence under Section 10(*b*) and Rule 10*b*–5 of the 1934 Act. On the surface, the decision seems to imply that Rule 10*b*–5 creates liability only for acts of fraud. However, several lower federal courts subsequently have held auditors liable for *gross negligence,* on the premise that gross negligence constitutes intent to deceive.

Auditors' Criminal Liability under the U.S. Securities Acts.   Both the Securities Act of 1933 and the Securities Exchange Act of 1934 include provisions for *criminal charges* against persons violating provisions of the act. These provisions are found in Section 17(*a*) of the Securities Act of 1933 and Section 32(*a*) of the Securities Exchange Act of 1934.

The *Continental Vending Machine Corporation* civil case was accompanied by a celebrated criminal case involving three members of the CPA firm that audited Continental's financial statements. The criminal charges rocked the profession because there was no intent to defraud on the part of the CPAs; they were convicted of criminal fraud on the basis of gross negligence. The verdict of guilty was affirmed by a U.S. court of appeals, and the U.S. Supreme Court refused to review the case. The three CPAs were later pardoned by the president of the United States.

The principal facts of the *Continental Vending* case (*United States* v. *Simon,* 425 F.2d 796 [1969]) are as follows. The U.S. government's case of fraud against the three CPAs hinged upon a footnote to Continental's audited financial statements which read:

> The amount receivable from Valley Commercial Corp. (an affiliated company of which . . . [Continental's president] is an officer, director, and stockholder) bears interest at 12 percent a year. Such amount, less the balance of the notes payable to that company, is secured by the assignment to the Company of Valley's equity in certain marketable securities. As of . . . [the date of the auditors' report] . . . the amount of such equity at current market quotations exceeded the net amount receivable.

The U.S. government charged that the CPAs should have insisted that the note be worded as follows:

> The amount receivable from Valley Commercial Corp. (an affiliated company of which . . . [Continental's president] is an officer, director, and stockholder), which bears interest at 12 percent a year, was uncollectible at . . . [the balance sheet date], since Valley had loaned approximately the same amount to . . . [Continental's president] who was unable to pay. Since that date . . . [Continental's president] and others have pledged as security for the repayment of his obligation to Valley and its obligation to Continental (now $3,900,000, against which Continental's liability to Valley cannot be offset) securities which, as of . . . [the date of the auditors' report] . . . , had a market value of $2,978,000. Approximately 80 percent of such securities are stock and convertible debentures of the Company.

The receivable from Valley amounted to $3.5 million, of which more than $2.1 million was included in current assets (totaling $20.1 million), with the $1.4 million balance in other assets. The amount payable to Valley was slightly more than $1 million, of which about one half was included in total current liabilities of $19 million and the remainder in long-term debt.

The CPA firm had been auditors for Continental for several years. The court found that the CPAs had been concerned with the amounts receivable from and payable to Valley for at least five years, especially as they involved loans to Continental's president; yet the CPAs had continued to issue opinions on Continental's financial statements despite the continued growth of the receivable from Valley. The court also found that the CPAs were not furnished audited financial statements for Valley, in spite of their repeated requests, and that the CPAs had never themselves been auditors for Valley. In response to the defendant CPAs' claims that they had no motive for the alleged fraud, the U.S. government demonstrated to the appellate court's satisfaction that the CPAs were motivated to preserve their firm's reputation and to conceal the alleged derelictions of their predecessors and themselves in preceding years.

The *Continental Vending* case has significant implications for the public accounting profession. Not only is civil liability an ever-present hazard for public accountants, but criminal charges may also be involved.

The SEC's Regulation of Accountants.   The SEC has issued rules for the appearance and practice of CPAs, lawyers, and others before the commission under the statutes it administers. Rule of Practice 2(*e*), giving the SEC the power of suspension and disbarment, has the following wording:

> The Commission may deny, temporarily or permanently, the privilege of appearing or practicing before it in any way to any person who is found by the Commission . . . (1) not to possess the requisite qualifications to represent others, or (2) to be lacking in character or integrity or to have engaged in unethical or improper professional conduct.

On several occasions, the commission has taken punitive action against public accounting firms when it has found the audit work deficient with regard to financial statements filed with the commission. These actions against public accounting firms usually arise when a listed corporation encounters financial difficulties and it later appears that misleading financial statements had served to conceal for a time the losses being incurred by the company. In recent years the SEC has taken action against CPA firms by use of the consent decrees in which the CPAs have agreed to certain penalties or restrictions. For example, a CPA firm may agree under pressure from the SEC not to accept new clients during a specified period and permit a review of its practice.

The Public Accountants' Posture in an Era of Litigation

It is apparent that lawsuits will continue to plague the public accounting profession, as they have the legal and medical professions. The question thus is, What should be the public accountants' reaction to this era of litigation?

In the opinion of the authors, positive actions helpful to public accountants in withstanding threats of possible lawsuits include the following:

1. Greater emphasis upon compliance with the public accounting profession's generally accepted auditing standards and *Rules of Professional Conduct*. Close analysis of the court cases and other actions described in this chapter discloses numerous instances in which the auditors appear not to have complied fully with one or more auditing standards and *Rules of Professional Conduct*.
2. Retain legal counsel that is familiar with public accountants' legal liability. They should thoroughly discuss all potentially dangerous situations with their legal counsel and should carefully consider their counsel's advice.
3. Maintenance of adequate liability insurance coverage. Although liability insurance coverage should not be considered a substitute for the public accountants' compliance with the preceding recommendations, public accountants must protect themselves against possible financial losses from lawsuits. Adequate liability insurance is essential.

4. Thorough investigation of prospective clients. As indicated in preceding sections of this chapter, many court cases involving public accountants have been accompanied by criminal charges against top management of their clients. Public accountants should use great care in screening prospective clients to avoid the risks involved in professional relationships with the criminally inclined.

5. Obtain a thorough knowledge of the client's business. One of the major causes of audit failures has been a lack of understanding by auditors of the client's business and of industry practices.

6. Use of engagement letters for all professional services. Controversies over what services are to be rendered by a public accountant can be minimized by a clearly written contract describing the agreed-upon services. Engagement letters are discussed in Chapter 5.

7. Exercise extreme care in audits of clients in financial difficulties. Creditors and shareholders of companies that are insolvent or in bankruptcy are likely to seek scapegoats to blame for their losses. As the court cases described in this chapter demonstrate, litigation involving public accountants tends to centre around auditing of clients who later become bankrupt.

KEY TERMS

audit committee   A committee of a corporation's board of directors that nominates independent auditors, reviews audit findings, monitors activities of the internal auditing staff, and intervenes in any disputes between management and the independent auditors. Generally, the majority of audit committee members are outside directors, that is, directors who do not serve as corporate officers. In Canada, many corporations are required by federal and provincial corporations acts to have audit committees.

common law   Unwritten legal principles developed through court decisions.

constructive fraud   Performing duties requiring due care with such recklessness that persons believing the duties to have been completed carefully are being misled. Differs from fraud in that constructive fraud does not involve knowledge of misrepresentations within the financial statements.

due diligence   A public accounting firm's contention that its audit work was adequate to support its opinion on financial statements included in a registration statement filed with the SEC under the Securities Act of 1933.

errors   An unintentional misstatement in the financial statements.

fraud An intentional misstatement in the financial statement. Legally, the term *fraud* is defined as misrepresentation by a person of a material fact, known by that person to be untrue or made with reckless indifference as to whether the fact is true, with intent to deceive and with the result that another party is injured.

gross negligence Lack of even slight care or reckless disregard for responsibilities.

negligence Violation of a legal duty to exercise a degree of care that an ordinarily prudent person would exercise under similar circumstances, with resultant damages to another party.

GROUP I: REVIEW QUESTIONS

4–1. Why does the Canada Business Corporations Act provide an audit requirement for corporations offering securities to the public?

4–2. Contrast the auditor's qualification required by the Canada Business Corporations Act and the generally accepted auditing standards established by the Canadian Institute of Chartered Accountants.

4–3. Describe fully the auditor's statutory rights and responsibilities.

4–4. Briefly describe the statutory rights and duties of the predecessor and successor auditors in the change of appointment. Are they the same as those set forth in the Interpretations of the *Rules of Professional Conduct?*

4–5. Briefly describe the reasons for each of the following provisions in the Canada Business Corporations Act:

(*a*) The auditor's right and duty to attend the shareholders' meetings.

(*b*) The right and duty of the predecessor and successor auditors in the change of an audit appointment.

(*c*) The auditor's right to have access to records and documents and to obtain information from directors, officers, and employees of the corporation.

(*d*) The auditor's "qualified privilege" for any oral or written statement or report.

4–6. What are the statutory rights and responsibilities of the auditor, director, or officer of a corporation regarding subsequent discovery of errors in the published financial statements?

4–7. What is the significance of the statutory sanction of the *CICA Handbook* recommendations?

4–8.   With respect to the audit committee, discuss:

(*a*) Its composition.

(*b*) The rationale for its establishment.

(*c*) Its purposes and functions.

(*d*) The rights and duties of the auditor.

4–9.   Assume that a large public accounting firm exercises due professional care on every engagement. Can the firm reasonably expect that it will never face a lawsuit accusing the firm of professional misconduct? Explain.

4–10.   What is meant by the term *privity?* How does privity affect the auditor's liability under common law?

4–11.   Describe the criteria for determining the auditors' liability to clients under common law.

4–12.   Describe the criteria for determining the auditors' liability to third parties for negligence under common law.

4–13.   Describe how the courts determine that the auditors owe a duty of care to third parties in each of the following cases:

(*a*) *Haig* v. *Bamford et al.*

(*b*) *Toromont Industrial Holdings Ltd. et al.* v. *Thorne, Gunn, Helliwell & Christenson.*

4–14.   Compare the auditors' common-law liability to clients with their common-law liability to third parties.

4–15.   Briefly explain whether the decision in the *Pan American Mines Ltd.* case expands the scope of the auditors' liability to third parties for negligence.

4–16.   Should auditors who are engaged in the examination of the client's financial statements thoroughly investigate suspected material fraud? Explain.

4–17.   Is privity a valid defence regarding third-party charges of negligence against an auditor? Explain.

4–18.   In the *1136 Tenants* case, what was the essential difference in the way the client and the public accountant viewed the work to be done in the engagement?

4–19.   How was the *Continental Vending* case unusual with respect to penalties levied against auditors?

4–20.   Are engagement letters needed both for audits and for accounting and review services performed by public accountants? Explain.

GROUP II: QUESTIONS REQUIRING ANALYSIS

4–21.   In connection with current problems relating to external accounting statements, it has been stated that "the bulk of the problems can be traced to a single crucial flaw in the basic structure [of the financial disclosure process]: despite the fact that external accounting statements are meant to report on managerial operation of owner resources, it is management that controls the content of these reports.

"The obvious question is: What about the shareholders' auditor in this situation? My hypothesis is that the auditor is just not sufficiently independent to overcome the power position of management."

Required:
Analyze and comment on the relative positions of, and the causes of the potential conflict between, management and the shareholders' auditor.

(CICA, adapted)

4–22. It is now doubtful that an auditor can defend a challenge to his opinion simply by having adhered to generally accepted auditing standards and by stating that the financial statements have been presented fairly in accordance with generally accepted accounting principles.

Required:
Discuss the above statement, and indicate its implications for the auditing profession.

(CICA, adapted)

4–23. Rogers and Green, CAs, admit they failed substantially to follow generally accepted auditing standards in their audit of Martin Corporation. "We were overworked and understaffed and never should have accepted the engagement," said Rogers. Does this situation constitute fraud on the part of the CA firm? Explain.

4–24. The partnership of Porter, Potts & Farr, CAs, was engaged by Revolutionary Products, Inc., a closely held corporation, to perform an audit of the company's financial statements. The engagement letter said nothing about the CA firm's responsibility for fraud detection. Porter, Potts & Farr performed its examination in a careful and competent manner, following generally accepted auditing standards and using appropriate auditing procedures and tests under the circumstances.

Subsequently, it was discovered that the client's chief accountant was engaged in major fraudulent activities. However, only an investigation specifically designed to discover possible fraud would have revealed these activities. Revolutionary Products asserts that Porter, Potts & Farr is liable for the fraud.

Required:
Is Porter, Potts & Farr liable? Explain.

(AICPA, adapted)

4–25. Jensen, Inc., filed suit against a CA firm, alleging that the auditors' negligence was responsible for failure to disclose a large fraud that had been in process for several years. The CA firm responded that it may have been negligent, but that Jensen, Inc., was really to blame because it had completely ignored the CA firm's repeated recommendations for improvements in Jensen's internal control.

    If the CA firm was negligent, is it responsible for the loss sustained by the client? Does the failure by Jensen, Inc., to follow the CA's recommendations for better internal controls have any bearing on the question of liability? Explain.

4–26. Susan Harris is a new assistant auditor with the CA firm of Sparks, Watts, and Wilcox. On her third audit assignment, Harris examined the documentation underlying 60 disbursements as a test of control over purchasing, receiving, vouchers payable, and cash disbursement procedures. In the process, she found five disbursements for the purchase of materials with no receiving reports in the documentation. She noted the exceptions in her working papers and called them to the attention of the senior auditor. Relying on prior experience with the client, the senior auditor disregarded Harris's comments, and nothing further was done about the exceptions.

    Subsequently, it was learned that one of the client's purchasing agents and a member of its accounting department were engaged in a fraudulent scheme whereby they diverted the receipt of materials to a public warehouse while sending the invoices to the client. When the client discovered the fraud, the conspirators had obtained approximately $700,000, of which $500,000 was after the completion of the audit.

Required:
Discuss the legal implications and liabilities to Spark, Watts, and Wilcox as a result of the above facts.

                                      (AICPA, adapted)

4–27. The CA firm of Hanson and Brown was expanding very rapidly. Consequently, it hired several staff assistants, including James Small. Subsequently, the partners of the firm became dissatisfied with Small's production and warned him that they would be forced to discharge him unless his output increased significantly.

    At that time Small was engaged in audits of several clients. He decided that to avoid being fired, he would reduce or omit entirely some of the required auditing procedures listed in audit programs prepared by the partners. One of the CA firm's clients, Newell Corporation, was in serious financial difficulty and had adjusted several of its accounts being examined by Small to appear financially sound. Small prepared fictitious working papers in his home at night to support purported completion of auditing procedures assigned to him, although he in fact did not examine the Newell adjusting entries. The CA firm rendered an unqualified opinion on Newell's financial statements, which were grossly misstated. Several creditors, relying upon the audited financial statements, subsequently extended large sums of money to Newell Corporation.

Required:
Would the CA firm be liable to the creditors who extended the money in reliance on the erroneous financial statements if Newell Corporation should fail to pay the creditors? Explain.

(AICPA, adapted)

4–28.   In conducting the examination of the financial statements of Farber Corporation, Anne Harper, CA, discovered that George Nance, the president who was also one of the principal shareholders, had borrowed substantial amounts of money from the corporation. Nance indicated that he owned 51 percent of the corporation, that the money would be promptly repaid, and that the financial statements were being prepared for internal use only and would not be distributed to the other six shareholders. He requested that these loans not be accounted for separately in the financial statements but be included in the other current accounts receivable. Harper acquiesced in this request. Nance was correct as to his shares ownership and the fact that the financial statements were for internal use only. However, he subsequently became insolvent and was unable to repay the loans.

Required:
What was Harper's liability? Explain.

(AICPA, adapted)

4–29.   Wanda Young, doing business as Wanda Young Fashions, engaged the CA partnership of Scott & Green to examine her financial statements. During the examination, Scott & Green discovered certain irregularities that would have indicated to a reasonably prudent auditor that James Smith, the chief accountant, might be engaged in a fraud. However, Scott & Green, not having been engaged to discover fraud, submitted an unqualified opinion in its report and did not mention the potential fraud problem.

Required:
What are the legal implications of the above facts as they relate to the relationship between Scott & Green and Wanda Young? Explain.

(AICPA, adapted)

4–30.   "As increasing numbers of lawsuits against auditors are demonstrating, the public accountant incurs very real risks as auditor of a corporation. In his own interest, he should be more aware of the factors that must be considered in any attempt to measure the risk of an audit engagement."

Required:
What factors affect the risk of a specific audit engagement? Explain each briefly.

(CICA, adapted)

GROUP III: PROBLEMS

4–31.   Donald & Co. (DC) is the auditor of Change Limited, a widely held public company incorporated under the Canada Business Corporations Act. DC feels that it must qualify the 1992 financial statements because of auditing scope limitations. When the directors of Change Limited become aware of the situation, they immediately ask DC to resign before reporting and ask Gibson & Co. (GC) to accept the appointment as auditor of Change Limited for the 1992 fiscal year.

Required:
Discuss the professional and legal duties and responsibilities of Donald & Co. and Gibson & Co.

(CICA, adapted)

4–32.   Austin & Co. is the auditor of Silex Products. During the past three audits, Austin & Co. has repeatedly warned Silex's top management of serious weaknesses in the company's internal control over cash disbursements. Management has not, however, taken any corrective action.

During the current year's audit, the CAs were negligent in failing to test inventory for obsolescence. Certain items were in fact obsolete, and as a result, inventory was overstated by a material amount in the company's audited financial statements for the year.

Shortly after the audit, Silex learned that two employees in its accounting department had been embezzling money for the last two years. The scheme involved authorizing cash disbursements to fictitious people, recording these disbursements in various expense accounts, and then arranging to have the cheques cashed. Each of the improper disbursements was for a relatively small amount, but the cumulative effects of the fraud was material in each of the last two years. Silex has brought suit against Austin & Co. for the amount of its losses in this cash fraud.

Required:

(a) Without regard to the above case, briefly describe the auditors' responsibility for the detection of fraud and errors within the accounting records and financial statements of a client.

(b) Suggest two arguments that the auditors might make in court that might lessen or eliminate their liability for the client's losses in the embezzlement scheme.

(c) What argument might Silex advance to indicate that the auditors were negligent in failing to discover the embezzlement scheme?

4–33. Risk Capital Limited, a publicly held corporation, was considering the purchase of a substantial amount of treasury stock held by Sunshine Corporation, a closely held corporation. Initial discussions with the Sunshine Corporation began late in 199X.

Wilson and Wyatt, CAs, Sunshine's public accountants, regularly prepared quarterly and annual unaudited financial statements. The most recently prepared unaudited financial statements were for the fiscal year ended September 30, 199X.

On November 15, 199X, after protracted negotiations, Risk Capital agreed to purchase 100,000 shares of no-par, Class A treasury stock of Sunshine at $12.50 per share. However, Risk Capital insisted upon audited statements for the calendar year 199X. The contract specifically provided: "Risk Capital shall have the right to rescind the purchase of said stock if the audited financial statements of Sunshine for calendar year 199X show a material adverse change in the financial position of the Corporation."

At the request of Sunshine, Wilson and Wyatt audited the company's financial statements for the year ended December 31, 199X. The December 31, 199X, audited financial statements furnished to Sunshine by Wilson and Wyatt showed no material adverse change from the September 30, 199X, unaudited statements. Risk Capital relied upon the audited statements and purchased the treasury stock of Sunshine. It was subsequently discovered that as of the balance sheet date, the audited statements contained several misstatements and that in fact there had been a material adverse change in the financial position of the corporation. Sunshine has become insolvent, and Risk Capital will lose virtually its entire investment.

Risk Capital seeks recovery against Wilson and Wyatt.

Required:

(a) Discuss each of the theories of liability that Risk Capital will probably assert as its basis for recovery.

(b) Assuming that only negligence by Wilson and Wyatt is proven, will Risk Capital prevail? State yes or no and explain.

(AICPA, adapted)

4–34. Meglow Corporation, a closely held manufacturer of dresses and blouses, sought a loan from Busch Factors. Busch had previously extended $50,000 credit to Meglow but refused to lend any additional money without obtaining copies of Meglow's audited financial statements.

Meglow contacted the CA firm of Seavers & Dean to perform the audit. In arranging for the examination, Meglow clearly indicated that its purpose was to satisfy Busch Factors as to the corporation's sound financial condition and to obtain an additional loan of $100,000. Seavers & Dean accepted the engagement, performed the examination in a negligent manner, and rendered an unqualified opinion. If an adequate examination had been performed, the financial statements would have been found to be misleading.

Meglow submitted the audited financial statements to Busch Factors and obtained an additional loan of $70,000. Busch refused to lend more than that amount. After several other factors also refused, Meglow finally was able to persuade Maxwell Department Stores, one of its customers, to lend the additional $30,000. Maxwell relied upon the financial statements examined by Seavers & Dean.

Meglow is now in bankruptcy, and Busch seeks to collect from Seavers & Dean the $120,000 it loaned Meglow. Maxwell seeks to recover from Seavers & Dean the $30,000 it loaned Meglow.

Required:
(a) Will Busch recover? Explain.
(b) Will Maxwell recover? Explain.

(AICPA, adapted)

4–35. Mark Williams, CA, was engaged by Jackson Financial Development Corporation to audit the financial statements of Apex Construction Limited, a small, closely held corporation. Williams was told when he was engaged that Jackson Financial needed reliable financial statements that would be used to determine whether or not to purchase a substantial amount of Apex Construction's convertible debentures at the price asked by the estate of one of Apex's former directors.

Williams performed his examination in a negligent manner. As a result of his negligence, he failed to discover a substantial fraud by Carl Brown, the Apex controller. Jackson Financial purchased the debentures, but would not have if the fraud had been discovered. After discovery of the fraud, Jackson Financial promptly sold them for the highest price offered in the market at a $70,000 loss.

Required:
(a) What liability does Williams have to Jackson Financial? Explain.
(b) If Apex Construction also sues Williams for negligence, what are the probable legal defences Williams' lawyer would raise? Explain.
(c) Will the negligence of Mark Williams, CA, as described above, prevent him from recovering on a liability insurance policy covering the practice of his profession? Explain.

(AICPA, adapted)

4–36. Cragsmore & Company, a medium-sized partnership of CAs, was engaged by Marlowe Manufacturing, Inc., to examine its financial statements for the year ended December 31, 199X.

Before preparing the audit report William Cragsmore, a partner, and Joan Willmore, a staff senior, reviewed the disclosures necessary in the notes to the financial statements. One note involved the terms, costs, and obligations of a lease between Marlowe and Acme Leasing Corporation.

Willmore suggested that the note disclose the following: "The Acme Leasing Corporation is owned by persons who have a 35 percent interest in the capital stock and who are officers of Marlowe Manufacturing, Inc."

On Cragsmore's recommendation, this was revised by substituting "minority shareholders" for "persons who have a 35 percent interest in the capital stock and who are officers."

The audit report and financial statements were forwarded to Marlowe Manufacturing for review. The officer-shareholders of Marlowe who also owned Acme Leasing objected to the revised wording and insisted that the note be changed to describe the relationship between Acme and Marlowe as merely one of affiliation. Cragsmore acceded to this request.

The audit report was issued on this basis with an unqualified opinion. But the working papers included the drafts that showed the changes in the wording of the note.

Subsequent to delivery of the audit report, Marlowe suffered a substantial uninsured fire loss and was forced into bankruptcy. The failure of Marlowe to carry any fire insurance coverage was not noted in the financial statements.

Required:
What legal problems for Cragsmore & Company are suggested by these facts? Discuss.

(AICPA, adapted)

4–37. Charles Worthington, the founding and senior partner of a successful and respected CA firm, was a highly competent practitioner who always emphasized high professional standards. One of the policies of the firm was that all reports by members or staff be submitted to Worthington for review.

Recently, Arthur Craft, a junior partner in the firm, received a phone call from Herbert Flack, a close personal friend. Flack informed Craft that he, his family, and some friends were planning to create a corporation to engage in various land development ventures; that various members of the family are presently in a partnership (Flack Ventures), which holds some land and other assets; and that the partnership would contribute all of its assets to the new corporation and the corporation would assume the liabilities of the partnership.

Flack asked Craft to prepare a balance sheet of the partnership that he could show to members of his family, who were in the partnership, and to friends, to determine whether they might have an interest in joining in the formation and financing of the new corporation. Flack said he had the partnership general ledger in front of him and proceeded to read to Craft the names of the accounts and their balances at the end of the latest month. Craft took the notes he made during the telephone conversation with Flack, classified and organized the data into a conventional balance sheet, and had his secretary type the balance sheet and an accompanying letter on firm stationery. He did not consult Worthington on this matter or submit his work to him for review.

The transmittal letter stated: "We have reviewed the books and records of Flack Ventures, a partnership, and have prepared the attached balance sheet at March 31, 199X. We did not perform an examination in conformity with generally accepted auditing standards, and therefore do not express an opinion on the accompanying balance sheet." The balance sheet was prominently marked "unaudited." Craft signed the letter and instructed his secretary to send it to Flack.

Required:

What legal problems are suggested by these facts? Explain.

(AICPA, adapted)

Chapter 5

Planning the Audit and Designing Audit Programs

After studying this chapter, you should be able to:

- Explain an auditor's responsibilities when planning an audit.
- Describe the manner in which an audit is affected by the auditors' assessment of audit risk and materiality.
- Identify and explain the components of audit risk.
- Distinguish between the systems portion of the audit program and the substantive test part.
- Describe the general objectives of audit programs for financial statement accounts.
- Explain the way in which the general objectives of audit programs are used to develop the specific objectives that are then used to determine the audit procedures to be applied to an account.
- Describe the major steps in the audit process.

How do auditors determine whether a prospective client is reputable? After accepting an audit client, how do auditors go about planning the engagement and preparing the initial audit program? When one considers the professional responsibility and potential legal liability involved, it becomes obvious that auditors do not merely accept a new audit client and then arrive at the client's premises to "start auditing." The first examination standard states:

> The work should be *adequately planned* and *properly executed*. If assistants are employed, they should be *properly supervised*. [Emphasis added.]

The concept of adequate planning includes investigating a prospective client before deciding whether to accept the engagement, obtaining an understanding of the client's business operations, and developing an overall strategy to organize, coordinate, and schedule the activities of the audit staff. Although much planning is done before beginning the actual audit work, the planning process continues throughout the engagement. Whenever a problem is encountered during the audit, the auditors must plan their response to the situation.

Section 5150 of the *CICA Handbook* on "Planning and Supervision" suggests that the auditor, in planning the audit, needs to consider the following:

1. The terms of the engagement and the expected date of the report.
2. The nature of the client's business, including applicable statutory and contractual requirements.
3. The experience gained during previous audit engagements.
4. The accounting policies and degree of complexity of the accounting system.
5. Materiality and the components of audit risk.
6. Any involvement of other auditors.
7. Any involvement of internal auditors and persons having special expertise.
8. The intended reliance on internal control.
9. The level of experience and the number of audit staff for the engagement.
10. The timing and effectiveness of performing the audit procedures.

This chapter describes the dynamic process of planning the audit, beginning with the acceptance of a client and proceeding through the design of the audit program. It also provides an overview of the entire audit.

CLIENT ACCEPTANCE

Public accounting is a competitive profession, and most public accounting firms are anxious to obtain new clients. However, a public accounting firm's principal product is its reputation for credibility. No auditor can afford to be associated with clients who are engaging in management fraud or other misleading practices.

The continuing wave of litigation involving auditors underscores the need for public accounting firms to develop policies for investigating prospective clients *before accepting an engagement.* The auditors should investigate the history of the prospective client, including such matters as the identities and reputations of the directors, officers, and major shareholders, its financial statements and audit reports.

Auditors should also consider the financial strength and credit rating of a prospective client in order to help assess the overall risk of association with that business entity. This overall risk is often referred to as *business risk.* The incentive for management to overstate operating results is increased when the client company is in a weak financial position or is greatly in need for additional capital. When an audit client goes bankrupt, the auditors often are named as defendants in lengthy and costly lawsuits. For that reason, many auditors choose to avoid engagements entailing a relatively high risk of overstated operating results or of subsequent litigation; others may accept such engagements, recognizing the need to expand audit procedures to compensate for the unusual levels of risk.

Communication with Predecessor Auditors

The predecessor auditors are an excellent source of information about a prospective client. Both the *Rules of Professional Conduct* and business corporations legislation require the successor auditors to make certain enquiries of the predecessor auditors before accepting the engagement. As mentioned in Chapter 3, the *Rules of Professional Conduct* require that the successor auditors enquire of the incumbent auditors whether there are any circumstances that might influence the decision to accept the engagement. Also, the Canada Business Corporations Act, as pointed out in Chapter 4, requires that the successor auditors request a written statement from the predecessor auditors concerning the circumstances and reasons for the predecessors' resignation or removal. To ensure that the predecessor auditors are not in violation of confidentiality by providing the relevant information, the successor auditors should ask the prospective client to authorize the predecessor to respond frankly and fully of the enquiries made by the successor auditor. If a prospective client is reluctant to authorize such communications with the predecessor auditors, the successor auditors should seriously consider the implications in deciding whether or not to accept the engagement.

When permission has been granted, the successor auditors' enquiries will include questions about disagreements with management over accounting principles, the predecessors' understanding of the reasons for the change in auditors, and other matters that will assist the successor auditors in deciding whether to accept the engagement. This communication is extremely important as it aids the successor auditors in evaluating the integrity of management.

Other Communications

The auditors may also make enquiries of other third parties in obtaining background information about a prospective audit client. For example, the client's banker can provide information regarding the client's financial history and credit rating. The client's legal counsel can provide information about the client's legal environment, including such matters as pending litigation and regulatory requirements.

Obtaining the Engagement

After the auditors have collected the necessary information on the potential client, they will be in a position to assess the various risks involved with the audit and determine whether to attempt to obtain the engagement. Often, they will be asked to submit a proposal which will include information on the nature of services that the public accounting firm will offer, the qualifications of the firm's personnel, and other information to convince the prospective client to select the firm. The firm may even be asked to make an oral presentation to the prospective client's management to provide a basis for the selection.

Fee Arrangements.   When the business engages the services of independent public accountants, it will usually ask for an estimate of the cost of the audit. In supplying this estimate, the public accountants will give first consideration to the time probably required for the audit. Staff time is the basic unit of measurement of audit fees. Each public accounting firm develops a per hour or per diem fee schedule for each category of audit staff, based on direct salaries and such related costs as payroll taxes and insurance. The direct rate is then increased for allocated overhead costs and a profit element.

In addition to basic per diem or per hour fees, clients are charged for direct costs incurred by the public accounting firm for staff travel, report processing, and other out-of-pocket expenditures.

Estimating a fee for an audit thus usually involves the application of the firm's daily or hourly rates to the estimated time required. Since the exact number of days cannot be determined in advance, the auditors may merely give a rough estimate of the fee. Or they may multiply the rates by the estimated time, add an amount for unforeseen problems, and quote a range or bracket of amounts within which the total fee will fall. Once the auditors have given an estimate of the fee to a client, they naturally feel some compulsion to keep the charges within this limit.

Per diem rates for audit work vary considerably in different sections of the country, and even within a given community, in accordance with the reputation and experience of the accounting firm. Of course, the salaries paid to audit staff members are much less than the rates at which audit time is billed to clients. In many firms, salaries represent about 40 percent of billing rates; the remainder is required to cover the cost of nonbillable time when auditors are not assigned, overhead expenses of the office, and a profit to the partners.

Engagement Letters.   The preliminary understandings with the client should be summarized by the auditors in an *engagement letter,* making clear the nature of the engagement, any limitations on the scope of the audit, work to be performed by the client's staff, scheduled dates for performance and completion of the examination, and the basis for computing the auditors' fee. When the engagement letter is accepted by the authorized client official, it represents an *executory contract* between the auditor and the client. Engagement letters do not follow any standard form; an example of such a letter is presented in Figure 5–1.

The use of engagement letters is not limited to audit engagements. Professional standards for accounting and review services also require that the accountant have an understanding with the client as to the nature of the services to be performed. *This understanding preferably should be in writing and signed by the client and the public accountant.*

Illustrative Case

In the *1136 Tenants' Corporation* v. *Rothenberg* case in the United States, an incorporated apartment cooperative sued its CPAs for failing to detect embezzlement losses caused by a managing agent. The CPAs maintained they had been engaged only to do write-up work and not to perform any audit procedures. The court found that the CPAs had not made it sufficiently clear to the client that the engagement did not include audit procedures and held the CPAs liable for damages totaling $174,000. (The CPAs' fee for the engagement had been only $600.) Had the CPAs clearly set forth the scope of the engagement in an engagement letter, the case might never have been brought to court.

AUDIT PLANNING

Once the client has been obtained, the planning process intensifies as the auditors concentrate their efforts on obtaining a detailed understanding of the client's business and developing an overall audit strategy.

FIGURE 5–1 Engagement Letter

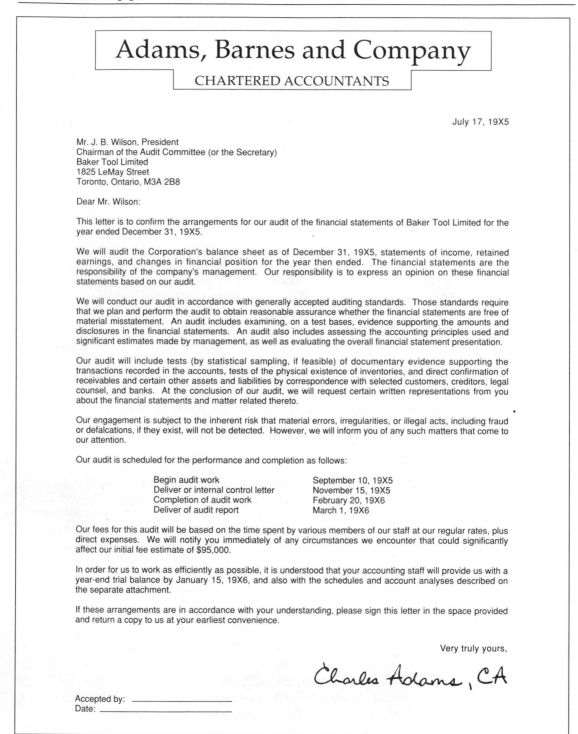

Adams, Barnes and Company
CHARTERED ACCOUNTANTS

July 17, 19X5

Mr. J. B. Wilson, President
Chairman of the Audit Committee (or the Secretary)
Baker Tool Limited
1825 LeMay Street
Toronto, Ontario, M3A 2B8

Dear Mr. Wilson:

This letter is to confirm the arrangements for our audit of the financial statements of Baker Tool Limited for the year ended December 31, 19X5.

We will audit the Corporation's balance sheet as of December 31, 19X5, statements of income, retained earnings, and changes in financial position for the year then ended. The financial statements are the responsibility of the company's management. Our responsibility is to express an opinion on these financial statements based on our audit.

We will conduct our audit in accordance with generally accepted auditing standards. Those standards require that we plan and perform the audit to obtain reasonable assurance whether the financial statements are free of material misstatement. An audit includes examining, on a test bases, evidence supporting the amounts and disclosures in the financial statements. An audit also includes assessing the accounting principles used and significant estimates made by management, as well as evaluating the overall financial statement presentation.

Our audit will include tests (by statistical sampling, if feasible) of documentary evidence supporting the transactions recorded in the accounts, tests of the physical existence of inventories, and direct confirmation of receivables and certain other assets and liabilities by correspondence with selected customers, creditors, legal counsel, and banks. At the conclusion of our audit, we will request certain written representations from you about the financial statements and matter related thereto.

Our engagement is subject to the inherent risk that material errors, irregularities, or illegal acts, including fraud or defalcations, if they exist, will not be detected. However, we will inform you of any such matters that come to our attention.

Our audit is scheduled for the performance and completion as follows:

Begin audit work	September 10, 19X5
Deliver or internal control letter	November 15, 19X5
Completion of audit work	February 20, 19X6
Deliver of audit report	March 1, 19X6

Our fees for this audit will be based on the time spent by various members of our staff at our regular rates, plus direct expenses. We will notify you immediately of any circumstances we encounter that could significantly affect our initial fee estimate of $95,000.

In order for us to work as efficiently as possible, it is understood that your accounting staff will provide us with a year-end trial balance by January 15, 19X6, and also with the schedules and account analyses described on the separate attachment.

If these arrangements are in accordance with your understanding, please sign this letter in the space provided and return a copy to us at your earliest convenience.

Very truly yours,

Charles Adams, CA

Accepted by: _____
Date: _____

Obtaining an Understanding of the Client's Business

When should a health club recognize its revenue from the sale of lifetime memberships? Is a company organized to produce a motion picture a going concern? Is it appropriate for a real estate developer to use the percentage-of-completion method of revenue recognition? What is a reasonable life for today's most advanced computer system? We will not attempt to answer these questions in this textbook; we raise them simply to demonstrate that the auditors must obtain a good working knowledge of an audit client's business and its industry if they are to design an effective strategy to allow them to issue an opinion on the fairness of its financial statements.

After the engagement is accepted, the auditors must obtain a detailed understanding of such factors as the client's financial position and operating results, organizational structure, accounting policies and procedures, financial policies and capital structure, product lines, and methods of production and distribution. In addition, the auditors should be familiar with matters affecting the industry within the client operates, including economic conditions and financial trends, inherent types of risk, governmental regulations, changes in technology, and widely used accounting methods. Without such a knowledge of the client's business environment, the auditor would not be in a position to evaluate the appropriateness of the accounting principles in use or the reasonableness of the many estimates and assumptions embodied in the client's financial statements.[1]

Numerous sources of information on prospective clients are available to the auditors. CICA audit and accounting publications, trade publications, and governmental agency publications are useful in obtaining an orientation in the client's industry. Previous audit reports, annual reports to shareholders, securities commission filings, and prior years' tax returns are excellent sources of financial background information. Informal discussions between the auditor-in-charge and key officers of the prospective client can provide information about the history, size, operations, accounting records, and internal controls of the enterprise.

Tour of Plant and Offices.   Another useful preliminary step for the auditors is to arrange an inspection tour of the plant and offices of a prospective client. This tour will give the auditors some understanding of the plant layout, manufacturing processes, principal products, and physical safeguards surrounding inventories. During the tour, the auditors should be alert for signs of potential problems. Rust on equipment may indicate that plant assets have been idle; excessive dust on raw materials or finished goods may indicate a problem of obsolescence. A knowledge of the physical facilities will assist the auditors in planning how many audit staff members will be needed to participate in observing the physical inventory.

---

[1] CICA, *CICA Handbook* (Toronto), Section 5140, "Knowledge of the Client's Business."

The tour affords the auditors an opportunity to observe firsthand what types of internal documentation are used to record such activity as receiving raw materials, transferring materials into production, and shipping finished goods to customers. This documentation is essential to the auditors' consideration of internal control.

In going through the offices, the auditors will learn the location of various accounting records. The auditors can ascertain how much subdivision of duties is practical within the client organization by observing the number of office employees. In addition, the tour will afford an opportunity to meet the key personnel whose names appear on the organization chart. The auditors will record the background information about the client in a *permanent file* available for reference in future engagements.

Illustrative Case

Volkswagen AG reported that "criminal manipulation" of its foreign-exchange positions has cost the firm as much as $259 million. The fraud prompted the resignation of the company's chief financial officer and the firing of its foreign-exchange manager. The auditors did not detect the irregularities until fraudulent contracts came due and were rejected by banks. An insider suggested that auditors often don't know enough about complicated currency instruments to detect such problems.

Developing an Overall Audit Strategy

After obtaining a knowledge of the client's business, the auditor-in-charge should formulate an overall audit strategy for the upcoming engagement. The best audit strategy is the approach that results in the most *efficient* audit—that is, an effective audit performed at the least possible cost to the client. Section 5130 of the *CICA Handbook*, "Materiality and Audit Risk," states that in planning an audit, the auditors must consider carefully the appropriate levels of *materiality* and *audit risk*.

Materiality.   Materiality, for planning purposes, is the auditor's preliminary estimate of the smallest amount of misstatement that would probably influence the judgment of a reasonable person relying upon the financial statements. Auditors must modify their opinion whenever there are *material* deficiencies in the client's financial statements. However, they may issue an unqualified report if the deficiencies are *immaterial*.

In planning the audit, auditors should design their audit procedures to avoid wasting time searching for immaterial misstatements that cannot affect their report. For example, some auditors do not investigate the amount of prepaid expenses on the premise that *any* error in this account *cannot be material* in relation to the financial statements.

While planning the audit, the auditors may also become aware of a number of accounting expediencies followed by the client which may result in immaterial misstatements. The concept of materiality often allows auditors to pass over such conceptual accounting errors as:

1. Charging all purchases of office supplies directly to expense accounts and making no effort to record as an asset the small quantities of office supplies remaining on hand at year-end.
2. Charging low-cost items such as small tools or desk-top calculators directly to expense accounts.
3. Not accruing liabilities for payroll taxes when the period ends between payroll dates. Many companies follow this policy in order to keep their accounting records consistent with the deductibility of payroll taxes for income tax purposes.

The auditors need to carefully consider the likelihood that the effects of these accounting expediencies may differ materially from results obtained following generally accepted accounting principles. Accounting expediencies are not acceptable simply because the client's management says the amounts involved are immaterial or because the amounts involved were considered immaterial in the past.

Illustrative Case

For many years a company had maintained its small tools as a set amount in a "tools inventory" asset account. Tools were expensed as purchased based on the assumption that annual purchase approximated annual "depreciation." Consistent with this, no inventory of tools was taken annually.

The auditors had agreed with the above accounting approach for several years. However, when the company began to grow, the client agreed with the auditors' request for a year-end count of the inventory of tools on hand. The asset account was subsequently written up approximately 80 percent based on the count.

Auditors use various approaches in determining a materiality measure for planning purposes. Some auditors rely upon judgment to estimate the amount that would materially distort the individual financial statements. The auditors may, for example, estimate that a $100,000 misstatement of the income statement is material, while a $200,000 misstatement of the balance sheet is material. Since most misstatements affect equally the balance sheet and the income statement, the auditors would then design their audit to detect the smallest misstatement that would be material to any one of the financial statements, in this case $100,000. Auditors may also use *rules of thumb* related to a financial statement base, such as net income or total sales, to develop these estimates of materiality.

Illustrative Case

Based on the research publications of the accounting professions in both Canada and the United States, it is suggested that a common rule of thumb for planning materiality is 5 to 10 percent of pretax income. Other rules of thumb are .5 to 1.5 percent of a larger of total assets or total revenues.

Some auditors use a sliding scale based on total assets or total revenues in which the percentage decreases with the size of the company. Thus, for example, as the size of a client doubles, materiality increases, but it does not double in amount.

The materiality estimates we have discussed to this point are those used to *plan the audit.* Because it is difficult to anticipate the nature of misstatements that the auditors might find, many auditors use quantitative measures such as those described. When subsequently *evaluating the results of audit procedures,* however, auditors must consider both quantitative and qualitative aspects of detected misstatements. For example, an illegal payment of an otherwise immaterial amount might be material if it might result in a material fine to the company.

Audit Risk. The term *audit risk* refers to the possibility that the auditors may unknowingly fail to appropriately modify their opinion on financial statements that are materially misstated. At the overall financial statement level, audit risk is the chance that a material misstatement exists in the financial statements, and the auditors do not detect the misstatement with their audit procedures.

In developing an audit plan, the auditors must consider factors that affect audit risk. An essential concept here is that the risk of misstated statements is higher for some audits than for others. Auditors are aware that very few audits involve material misstatements of financial statements, but when such misstatements do exist, they can result in millions of dollars of potential liability to the auditors. Experience has shown that many undetected misstatements of financial statements are intentional irregularities, rather than unintentional errors.

Illustrative Case

An analysis of 456 court cases filed against CPAs in the United States indicates that management fraud was present approximately 44 percent of the time. Other employee defalcations were believed to be present 2 percent of the time. An assortment of accounting and auditing errors was alleged in the remaining cases.

Figure 5–2 presents a list of risk factors, or "red flags," which may indicate a higher-than-normal risk of misstated financial statements. While none of these risk factors in and of itself would normally indicate the existence of a misstatement with certainty, each one should be considered by the auditors in planning the audit.

FIGURE 5–2 Financial Statement Audit Risk Factors

Management Characteristics

—Management operating and financing decisions are dominated by a single person.
—Management attitude toward financial reporting is unduly aggressive.
—Management turnover (particularly senior accounting personnel) is high.
—Management places undue emphasis on meeting earnings projections.
—Management's reputation in the business community is poor.

Operating Characteristics

—Profitability of entity relative to its industry is inadequate or inconsistent.
—Sensitivity of operating results to economic factors (inflation, interest rates, unemployment, etc.) is high.
—Rate of change in entity's industry is rapid.
—Direction of change in entity's industry is declining with many business failures.
—Organization is decentralized without adequate monitoring.
—Internal or external matters that bring into question the entity's ability to continue in existence are present.

Engagement Characteristics

—Many contentious or difficult accounting issues are present.
—Significant difficult-to-audit transactions or balances.
—Significant and unusual related party transactions not in the ordinary course of business.
—Nature, cause (if known), or the amount of known and likely misstatements detected in the audit of prior period's financial statements is significant.
—New client with no prior audit history or sufficient information is not available from the predecessor auditor.

Source: AICPA, *Statement on Auditing Standards 53*, "The Auditor's Responsibility to Detect and Report Errors and Irregularities" (New York, 1988), AU 316.

In addition, Section 5135.09 of the *CICA Handbook* suggests the following risk factors for misstatements:

1. Unrealistic time deadlines for audit completion imposed by management.
2. Reluctance by management to engage in frank communication with appropriate third parties, such as regulators and bankers.
3. Limitation in audit scope imposed by management.
4. Identification of important matters not previously disclosed by management.
5. Conflicting or unsatisfactory evidence provided by management or employees.

6. Unusual documentary evidence such as handwritten alterations to documentation or handwritten documentation which would usually be electronically printed.
7. Information provided unwillingly or after unreasonable delay.
8. Seriously incomplete or inadequate accounting records.
9. Unsupported transactions.
10. Unusual transactions, by virtue of their nature, volume or complexity; particularly, if they occurred close to the year-end.
11. Significant unreconciled differences between control accounts and subsidiary records or between physical count and the related account balance which were not appropriately investigated and corrected on a timely basis.
12. Inadequate control over computer processing. For instance, too many processing errors or delays in processing results and reports.
13. Significant differences from expectations disclosed by analytical procedures.
14. Fewer confirmation responses than expected or significant differences revealed by confirmation responses.

Considering the Risk of Misstatement of Account Balances

Various types of misstatements may occur in individual accounts. Section 5300.17 of the *CICA Handbook* suggests that financial statement items embody the following assertions by management:

Existence—that an asset or a liability of the company exists at a given date.

Occurrence—that a transaction took place which pertains to the company.

Completeness—that there are no unrecorded assets, liabilities, or transactions.

Ownership—that an asset is owned by the company at a given date.

Valuation—that an asset or liability is recorded at an appropriate carrying value.

Measurement—that a revenue or expense transaction is recorded in the proper amount and allocated to the proper period.

Statement presentation—that an item is disclosed in accordance with generally accepted accounting principles (or, where applicable, with another appropriate basis of accounting).

Thus, for any particular item or account, if all of these assertions are accurate, the overall assertion that the account is presented in conformity with generally accepted accounting principles is achieved. Misstatements may occur, however, relating to any one or more of the individual assertions.

At the individual account balance level, *audit risk* is the chance that (1) a material misstatement in an assertion has occurred and (2) that the auditors do not detect the misstatement. The risk of the occurrence of a material misstatement may be separated into two components—inherent risk and control risk. *Inherent risk* refers to the possibility of a material misstatement occurring in an assertion assuming no related internal controls. *Control risk* is the risk that a material misstatement in an assertion will not be prevented or detected on a timely basis by the company's internal control. The risk that the auditors will not detect the misstatement with their audit procedures is referred to as *detection risk.* That is, detection risk is the risk that the auditors' procedures will lead them to conclude that a material misstatement does *not* exist in an assertion when in fact such misstatement does exist.

Note that while detection risk relates directly to the effectiveness of the auditors' procedures, inherent and control risk are functions of the client and its environment. In planning the audit, the auditors must assess the extent of inherent and control risks, and then plan sufficient audit procedures to reduce detection risk to the appropriate level. In this way, the overall audit risk will be sufficiently low to justify the auditors' opinion that the financial statements are not materially misstated. For example, if the auditors believe that the client's internal controls over the existence assertion for accounts receivable are poor, resulting in a high level of control risk relating to that assertion, the auditors may compensate by increasing the substantive procedures for receivables and, thereby, reducing detection risk.

Analytical Procedures. Analytical procedures involve comparisons of financial statement balances and ratios for the year with auditor expectations developed from sources such as the client's prior years' financial statements, published industry statistics, and budgets. When used for planning purposes, analytical procedures assist the auditors in planning the nature, timing, and extent of audit procedures that will be used for the specific accounts. The approach used is one of obtaining an understanding of the client's business and transactions, and identifying areas that may represent risks relevant to the audit. The auditors will then plan a more thorough investigation of these potential problem areas, and perform a more effective audit. Section 5300.31 of the *CICA Handbook* suggests that the auditors perform analytical procedures as a part of the planning process for an audit.

An example of the use of an analytical procedure for planning purposes is the comparison of the client's inventory turnover for the current year with comparable statistics from prior years. A significant decrease in inventory turnover might lead the auditors to consider the possibility that the client has excessive amounts of inventory. As a result, the auditors would plan a more extensive search for inventory items that may be obsolete. Analytical procedures are discussed in detail in Chapter 6.

First-Year Procedures.   A new client should be informed as to the extent of investigation of the beginning balances of such accounts as plant and equipment and inventories. To determine the propriety of depreciation expense for the current year and the proper balances in plant and equipment accounts at the balance sheet date, the auditors must investigate the validity of the property accounts at the beginning of the current period. Similarly, if the auditors are unable to obtain satisfactory evidence for the balance of *beginning inventory,* it may be necessary to qualify or deny an opinion on the income statement in the first audit of a new client.

When satisfactory preceding-year audits of the business have been performed by reputable predecessor auditors, the auditors may be able to accept the opening balances of the current year with a minimum of verification work. In other cases, in which no satisfactory recent audit has been made, an extensive analysis of transactions of prior years will be necessary to establish account balances as of the beginning of the current year. In these later situations, where appropriate, the client should be made to understand that the scope and cost of the initial audit may exceed that of repeat engagements, which will not require analysis of past years' transactions. Communication with the predecessor can also provide the successor auditors with background information about the client and details about the client's internal control.

Use of the Client's Staff.   The auditors should obtain an understanding with the client as to the extent to which the client's staff, including the internal auditors, can help prepare for the audit. The client's staff should have the accounting records up to date when the auditors arrive. In addition, many audit working papers can be prepared for the auditors by the client's staff, thus reducing the cost of the audit and freeing the auditors from routine work. The auditors may set up the columnar headings for such working papers and give instructions to the client's staff as to the information to be gathered. These working papers should bear the label *Prepared by Client,* or *PBC,* as well as the initials of the auditor who verifies the work performed by the client's staff. Working papers prepared by the client should never be accepted at face value; such papers must be reviewed and tested by the auditors so that they maintain their independent status.

Among the tasks that may be assigned to the client's employees are the preparation of a trial balance of the general ledger, preparation of an aged trial balance of accounts receivable, analyses of accounts receivable written off, lists of property additions and retirements during the year, and analyses of various revenue and expense accounts. Many of these working papers may be in the form of computer spreadsheets and other computerized data files.

Other Auditors.   When a portion of the client is audited by another public accounting firm (e.g., a subsidiary in a distant city) efforts must be coordinated. For example, if the accounts of the subsidiary are to be consolidated with the overall enterprise, and if that subsidiary is audited by another accounting firm, the auditors must coordinate timing of necessary reports and procedures to be performed. Chapter 4 briefly discusses using the work of other auditors, and Chapter 18 addresses this topic in further detail.

Arranging Specialists. Public accountants may lack the qualifications necessary to perform certain technical tasks relating to the audit. For example, judging the valuation of a diamond inventory may require employing a specialist in gem appraisal. Effective planning involves arranging for the appropriate use of specialists both inside and outside of the client organization. Using the work of specialists will be discussed in detail in Chapter 6.

Audit Plans

The planning process is documented in the audit working papers through the preparation of *audit plans, audit programs,* and *time budgets.* These "planning, execution, and supervision" working papers serve a dual purpose. First, they provide documentary evidence of the accounting firm's compliance with the "adequate planning" requirement of the first examination standard. Second, these working papers provide the auditor-in-charge with a means of coordinating, scheduling, executing, and supervising the activities of the audit staff members involved in the engagement.

An audit plan is an overview of the engagement, outlining the nature and characteristics of the client's business operations and the overall audit strategy. Although audit plans differ in form and content among accounting firms, a typical plan includes details on the following:

1. Description of the client company—its structure, nature of business, and organization.
2. Objectives of the audit (e.g., statutory audit, special-purpose audit).
3. Nature and extent of other services, such as preparation of tax returns, to be performed for the client.
4. Timing and scheduling of the audit work, including determining which procedures may be performed before the balance sheet date, what must be done on or after the balance sheet date, and setting dates for such critical procedures as cash counts, accounts receivable confirmations, and inventory observation.
5. Work to be done by the client's staff.
6. Staffing requirements during the engagement.
7. Target dates for completing major segments of the engagement, such as the consideration of internal control, tax returns, the audit report, and filings with government authorities.
8. Any special problems to be resolved in the course of the engagement, such as those revealed by analytical procedures.

9. Preliminary judgments about materiality and risk levels for the engagement.

The audit plan is normally drafted before starting work at the client's offices. However, the plan may be modified throughout the engagement as special problems are encountered and as the auditors' consideration of internal control lead to identification of areas requiring more or less audit work.

Time Budgets for Audit Engagements

Public accounting firms usually charge clients on a time basis, and detailed time records must therefore be maintained on every audit engagement. A time budget for an audit is constructed by estimating the time required for each step in the audit program for each of the various grades of auditors and totaling these estimated amounts. Time budgets serve other functions in addition to providing a basis for estimating fees. The time budget communicates to the audit staff those areas the manager or partner feel are critical and require more time. It also is an important tool of the audit senior—it is used to measure the efficiency of staff assistants and to determine at each stage of the engagement whether the work is progressing at a satisfactory rate.

There is always pressure to complete an audit within the estimated time. The staff assistant who takes more than the normal time for a task is not likely to be popular with supervisors or to win rapid advancement. Ability to do satisfactory work when given abundant time is not a sufficient qualification, *for time is never abundant in public accounting.*

The development of time budgets is facilitated in repeat engagements by reference to the preceding year's detailed time records. Sometimes time budgets prove quite unattainable because the client's records are not in satisfactory condition, or because of other special circumstances that arise. Even when time estimates are exceeded, there can be no com-

---

Illustrative Case

A problem for some public accounting firms is staff members' understating the hours they have actually worked—a practice informally called *eating time*. One study revealed that over 50 percent of respondents in the profession complete work on their own time without reporting the chargeable hours. This is generally accomplished by arriving early, staying late, or working through lunch or on weekends without recording the extra hours on the time sheet. Such a practice results in several problems for the firm, including underbilling of clients, unrealistic future time budgets, and lower staff morale. This is a particularly difficult problem to eliminate since the in-charge auditors tend to benefit from the practice, because the audit engagement is completed in less time than was budgeted.

promise with qualitative standards in the performance of the audit work. The accounting firm's professional reputation and its legal liability to clients and third parties do not permit any shortcutting or omission of audit procedures to meet a predetermined time estimate.

Planning a Recurring Engagement

Planning a repeat engagement is far easier than planning for a first audit of a new client. The auditor-in-charge of a repeat engagement usually was involved in the previous year's audit and has a good working knowledge of the client's business. Also, the previous year's audit working papers contain a wealth of information useful in planning the recurring engagement. For example, the audit plan provides background information about the client and explains the overall strategy employed in the last audit. The prior year's audit program shows in detail the procedures performed and the length of time required to perform them. In addition, last year's working papers substantiate the beginning balances for the current year's audit.

While the prior year's working papers are extremely useful in planning the new engagement, the auditor-in-charge should not merely duplicate last year's audit program. Each audit should be a learning experience for the auditors, enabling them to design a more efficient audit in the following year. Also, the auditors may need to modify their approach to the audit for any changes in the client's operations or business environment.

DESIGNING AUDIT PROGRAMS

An audit program is a detailed list of the audit procedures to be performed in the course of the examination. A tentative audit program is developed as part of the advance planning of an audit. This tentative program, however, requires frequent modification as the audit progresses. For example, the nature, extent, and timing of test procedures are influenced by the auditor's assessment of control risk. Thus, not until the consideration of internal control has been completed can a final version of the audit program be drafted. Even this final version may require modification if the auditors revise their preliminary estimates of materiality or risk for the engagement, or if the substantive tests disclose unexpected problems.

The Audit Trail

In developing audit procedures, the auditors are assisted by the organized manner in which accounting systems record, classify, and summarize data. The flow of accounting data begins with the recording of thousands of individual transactions on such documents as invoices and cheques. The information recorded on these original documents is summarized in journals, and at the end of each month, the amounts in the journals are posted to ledger accounts. At the end of the year, the balances in the ledger accounts are arranged in the form of financial statements.

In thinking of the accounting records as a whole, we may say that a continuous trail of evidence exists—a trail of evidence that links the thousands of individual transactions comprising a year's business activity with the summary figures in the financial statements. In a manual accounting system, this *audit trail* consists of source documents, journal entries, and ledger entries. An audit trail also exists within a computer-based accounting system, although it may have a substantially different form; this will be discussed in Chapter 8.

Just as hikers may walk in either direction along a mountain path, auditors may follow the audit trail in either of two directions. For example, the auditors may follow specific transactions from their origin forward to their inclusion in the financial statement summary figures. This approach provides the auditors with assurance that all transactions have been properly interpreted and processed.

On the other hand, the auditors may follow the stream of evidence back to its sources. This type of verification consists of tracing the various items in the statements (such as cash, receivables, sales, and expenses) back to the ledger accounts, and from the ledgers on back through the journals to original documents, evidencing transactions. This process of working backward from the financial statement figures to be detailed evidence of individual transactions provides assurance that financial statement figures are based upon valid transactions.

Although the technique of working along the audit trail is a useful one, bear in mind that the auditors must acquire other types of evidence obtained from sources other than the client's accounting records.

Organization of the Audit Program

The audit program usually is divided into two major sections. The first section deals with the procedures to assess the effectiveness of the client's internal control (the systems portion), and the second section deals with the substantiation of specific financial statement amounts, as well as the adequacy of financial statement disclosures.

The Systems Portion of the Program. The systems portion of the audit program is generally organized around the major *transaction cycles* of the client's internal control. For example, the systems portion of the audit program for a manufacturing company might be subdivided into separate programs for such areas as (1) sales and collections cycle, (2) purchases and disbursements cycle, (3) production cycle, (4) payroll cycle, and (5) financing cycle.

To illustrate one of these transaction cycles, let us consider sales and collections. The procedures used in processing sales transactions might include receipt of a customer's purchase order, preparation of the sales order, credit approval, shipment of merchandise, preparation of sales invoices, recording the sale, recording the account receivable, billing, and handling and recording the cash received from the customer.

Audit procedures in the systems portion of the program typically include preparation of flowcharts for each transaction cycle, tests of the significant internal controls, identification of strengths and weaknesses, and the assessment of control risk for the various financial statement assertions.

In conjunction with their consideration of internal control, the auditors will make appropriate modification in the substantive test portion of the audit program. For example, as a result of weaknesses in internal control over the proper recording of sales, the auditors may assess control risk for assertion of existence of accounts receivable to be high, and decide to send additional accounts receivable confirmations.

The Substantive Test Portion of the Program.   The portion of the audit program aimed at substantiating financial statement amounts usually is organized in terms of major balance sheet topics, such as cash, accounts receivable, inventories, and plant and equipment. Considering the importance of the income statement, why do audit programs emphasize the substantiation of balance sheet items? In part, this method of organizing the work may be a carryover from the days when the auditors' objective was verification of the balance sheet alone. Even though present-day auditors are very much concerned with the reliability of the income statement, they still find the balance sheet approach to be an effective method of organizing their substantive audit procedures.

One advantage of the balance sheet approach is that highly appropriate evidence generally is available to substantiate assets and liabilities. Assets usually are subject to direct verification by such procedures as physical observation, inspection of externally created documentary evidence, and confirmation by outside parties. Liabilities usually can be verified by externally created documents, confirmation, and inspecting paid cheques after the liabilities have been paid.

In contrast, consider the nature of revenues and expenses in double-entry accounting. The entry to record revenues or expenses has two parts: first, the recognition of the revenue or expense; and second, the corresponding change in an asset or liability account. Revenues and expenses have no tangible form; they exist only as entries in the client's accounting records, representing changes in owners' equity. Consequently, the best evidence supporting the existence of revenues or expenses usually is the verifiable change in the related asset or liability account.

Indirect Verification of Income Statement Accounts.   Figure 5–3 shows the relationship between income statement accounts and the related

FIGURE 5–3

Income Statement Items		Cash Transactions		Balance Sheet Items		
Revenue	=	Cash receipts from customers	−	Beginning balance of Accounts Receivable	+	Ending balance of Accounts Receivable
Cost of goods sold	=	Cash payments for merchandise	−	Beginning balance of Accounts Payable	+	Ending balance of Accounts Payable
			+	Beginning balance of Inventory	−	Ending balance of Inventory
Expenses	=	Cash payments for expenses	−	Beginning balances of Accrued Expenses	+	Ending balances of Accrued Expenses
			+	Beginning balances of Prepaid Expenses	−	Ending balances of Prepaid Expenses

Financial statement relationships

Auditors' approach to substantiation

- Verify indirectly by substantiating right-hand side of equation; also by analytical procedures and (if possible) direct computations. *(Income Statement Items)*
- Substantiate by testing transactions; also by reconciliations of cash accounts. *(Cash Transactions)*
- Substantiate by reference to last year's audit working papers. *(Beginning balances — Balance Sheet Items)*
- Substantiate by substantive tests in current year. *(Ending balances — Balance Sheet Items)*

changes in cash or other balance sheet items. By substantiating the changes in the asset and liability accounts, the auditors indirectly verify revenue, cost of goods sold, and expenses. For example, most revenue transactions involve a debit to either Cash or Accounts Receivable. If the auditors are able to satisfy themselves that all cash receipts and all changes in accounts receivable during the year have been properly recorded, they have indirect evidence that revenue transactions have been accounted for properly.

Direct Verification of Income Statement Accounts. Not all of the audit evidence pertaining to income statement accounts is indirect. The verification of a major balance sheet item often involves several closely related income statement accounts that can be verified through computation or other direct evidence. For example, in substantiating the marketable securities owned by the client, it is a simple matter to compute the related interest revenue, dividends revenue, and gains or losses on sales of securities. In substantiating the balance sheet items of plant assets and accumulated depreciation, the auditors make computations that also substantiate depreciation expense. Uncollectible accounts expense is substantiated in conjunction with the balance sheet item Allowance for Doubtful Accounts. In addition to these computations, the auditors' *analytical procedures* provide direct evidence as to the reasonableness of various revenues and expenses.

Comparison of the Systems Approach and the Substantive Approach. Auditing literature frequently refers to a public accounting firm's following a systems approach or a substantive approach to an audit. The *systems approach* involves extensive testing of the design and operating effectiveness of internal controls to justify low-control risk assessments; the substantive approach relies more heavily upon substantive testing to restrict detection risk as the basis for the auditors' opinion. Actually, almost all audits involve a blend of procedures aimed at testing the effectiveness of internal controls and substantive testing. Thus, *systems approach* and *substantive approach* are relative terms, indicating the emphasis that a particular accounting firm places in the systems and substantive portions of its audit program on a given engagement. Some firms may lean toward one approach or the other as a matter of firm policy. However, in the audit of a client with weak internal control, the resulting high level of control risk allows the auditors no choice but to emphasize the substantive approach.

Objectives of Audit Programs

An audit program is designed to accomplish certain objectives with respect to each major account in the financial statements. These objectives follow directly from the assertions that are contained in the clients financial statements. Recall that those assertions are:

1. *Existence.*
2. *Occurrence.*
3. *Completeness.*
4. *Ownership.*
5. *Valuation.*
6. *Measurement.*
7. *Statement presentation.*

From these assertions, general objectives may be developed for each major type of balance sheet account, including assets, liabilities, and owners' equity.

General Objectives of Audit Programs for Asset Accounts

The audit program for each financial statement account must be tailored to accomplish the specific audit objectives for that account. The specific objectives for auditing cash are not identical to the specific objectives for auditing inventory. Although the specific audit objectives and, therefore, the audit procedures differ for each account, it is useful to realize that each audit program follows basically the same approach to verifying the balance sheet items and related income statement amounts. The audit program for every asset category includes procedures designed to accomplish the following *general objectives:*

Audit Program for Asset Accounts Stated in Terms of General Objectives

I. Consideration of internal control.
II. Substantiate account balances (substantive tests).
   A. Establish the *existence* of assets.
   B. Establish that the company has *ownership* of the assets.
   C. Establish *completeness* of recorded assets.
   D. Determine the appropriate *valuation* of the assets.
   E. Establish the *clerical accuracy* of the underlying records.
   F. Determine the appropriate financial *statement presentation* of the assets.

These general objectives are *common to all audit programs for asset accounts.* Changes in these audit objectives, with respect to audit programs for liability and owners' equity accounts, will be discussed in later chapters.

Substantiation of Account Balances

The central purpose of the auditors' consideration of internal control is to assess control risk for each major *assertion* concerning a financial statement account to determine the nature, extent, and timing of the audit work necessary to substantiate the account balance. In subsequent chapters, considerable attention will be given to the consideration of internal control; let us now discuss the objectives of the auditors' substantiation procedures.

Existence of Assets

The first step in substantiating the balance of an asset account is to verify the existence of the asset. For assets such as cash on hand, marketable securities, and inventories, existence of the asset usually may be verified by physical inspection, and by tracing backwards from the recorded entry to the documents created when the assets were acquired, referred to as *vouching*.

When assets are in the custody of others, such as cash in banks and inventory on consignment, the appropriate audit procedure may be direct confirmation with the outside party. The existence of accounts receivable normally is verified by confirming with customers the amounts receivable. Verifying the existence of intangibles is more difficult; the auditors must gather evidence that costs have been incurred and that these costs represent probable future economic benefits.

Ownership of the Assets

Usually, the same procedures that verify existence also establish the company's ownership of the asset. For example, confirming cash balances in bank accounts establishes existence of the cash and the company's ownership rights to that cash. Similarly, inspecting marketable securities verifies both existence and ownership because the registered owner's name usually appears on the face of the security certificate.

With other assets, such as plant and equipment, physical inspection establishes existence *but not ownership.* Plant and equipment may be rented or leased rather than owned. To verify the client's ownership of plant assets, the auditors must inspect documentary evidence such as property tax bills, purchase documents, and deeds.

The client may not hold legal title to all assets that are appropriately included in the financial statements. Instead, the client may own *rights* to use the assets, conveyed by contracts such as leases. The ownership of these rights may be established by reviewing the underlying contracts.

Establishing Completeness

Designing substantive tests that are effective at detecting assets that are not recorded in the client's accounting records is difficult. Thus, the auditors often find it preferable to rely heavily on tests of the client's internal controls to establish the completeness of recorded assets.

Many tests for unrecorded assets involve *tracing* from the source documents created when the assets were acquired to entries recording the assets in the accounting records. To test for unrecorded accounts receivable, for example, the auditors may select a sample of shipping documents issued during the year and trace the details to recorded sales transactions. Observation is important to testing the completeness of recorded physical assets. During their observation of the client's physical inventory, the auditors are alert for inventory items that are not counted and included in the inventory summary.

Analytical procedures also may be used to bring conditions to light that indicate that all assets may not be recorded. For example, a low gross profit percentage for the current year in comparison to prior years may indicate that the client has a substantial amount of unrecorded inventory.

Verifying the Cutoff of Transactions.   As a part of the auditors' procedures for establishing completeness as well as existence of recorded assets, the auditors will verify the client's cutoff of transactions included in the period. The financial statements should reflect all transactions occurring through the end of the period and none that occur subsequently. The term *cutoff* refers to the process of determining that transactions occurring near the balance sheet date are assigned to the proper accounting period.

The impact of cutoff errors upon the financial statements varies with the nature of the error. For example, a cutoff error in recording acquisitions of plant assets affects the balance sheet, but probably does not affect the income statement since depreciation usually is not recorded on assets acquired within a few days of year-end. On the other hand, a cutoff error in recording shipments of merchandise to customers affects both inventory and the cost of sales. In order to improve their financial picture, some clients may "hold their records open" to include in the current year cash receipts and revenue from the first part of the next period.

To verify the client's cutoff of transactions, the auditors should review transactions recorded shortly before and after the balance sheet date to ascertain that these transactions are assigned to the proper period. When such documents as cheques, receiving reports, and shipping documents are serially numbered, noting the last serial number issued during the period will assist the auditors in determining that a proper cutoff has been made in recording transactions.

Direction of Testing.   In the above discussion of the existence and completeness assertions, two similar tests are described. In one test, *existence*

FIGURE 5–4   Direction of Tests

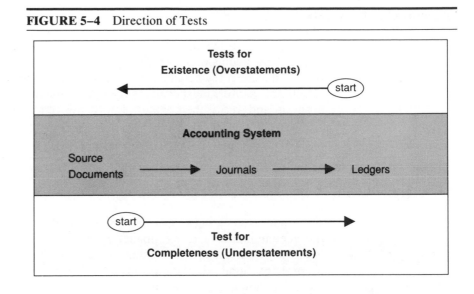

of assets was verified by *vouching* from the recorded entry to the source documents. In the second test, the *completeness* of recording of assets was verified by *tracing* from the source documents to the recorded entry. Figure 5–4 illustrates these concepts.

In the first test, the auditors are looking for unsupported entries in the journals (or ledgers). Vouching from right to left on Figure 5–4 one might identify journal entries that are not supported and, possibly, are not valid. Note that transactions that are not supported *can never* be found by tracing forward from source documents to the journal entries (left to right).

In the second test, the auditors are determining the *completeness* of posted transactions. If a transaction was never recorded, the omission can be detected only by tracing in the direction from the source documents to the journals and ledgers. Transactions improperly omitted from ledger accounts cannot be brought to light by tracing existing ledger entries back to their source. Of course, some errors, such as transposition errors in entering transactions and postings to the wrong account, may be discovered by tracing or vouching.

Valuation of Assets

Determining the proper valuation of assets requires a thorough knowledge of generally accepted accounting principles. The auditors must not only establish that the accounting method used to value a particular asset is generally accepted but also determine that the method of valuation is appropriate in the circumstances. Once the auditors are satisfied as to the appropriateness of the method, the auditors will perform procedures to test the accuracy of the client's application of the method of valuation to the asset.

Most assets are valued at cost. Therefore, a common audit procedure is to vouch the acquisition cost of assets to paid cheques and other documentary evidence. If the acquisition cost is subject to depreciation or amortization, the auditors must evaluate the reasonableness of the cost allocation program and verify the computation of the remaining unallocated cost. Assets valued at lower of cost and market necessitate an investigation of current market prices as well as acquisition costs.

Clerical Accuracy of Records

The amount appearing as an asset on a financial statement is almost always the accumulation of many smaller items. For example, the amount of inventory on a financial statement might consist of the cost of thousands or, perhaps, hundreds of thousands of individual products. Before auditing these individual items, the auditors must test the clerical accuracy of the underlying records to determine that they accumulate to the total appearing in the general ledger and, therefore, the amount in the financial statements. The auditors often use their generalized audit software (computer) programs to perform these tests of clerical accuracy of the records.

Statement Presentation

Even after all dollar amounts have been substantiated, the auditors must perform procedures to assure that the financial statement presentation conforms to the requirements of authoritative accounting pronouncements and the general principle of adequate disclosure. Procedures falling into this category include the review of subsequent events; search for related party transactions; investigation of contingencies; review of disclosure of such items as accounting policies, leases, and pledged assets; and review of the categories and descriptions used on all of the financial statements.

An Illustration of Program Design

The above general objectives apply to all types of assets. Audit procedures for a particular asset account must be designed to accomplish the *specific audit objectives* regarding that asset. These specific objectives vary with the nature of the asset and the generally accepted accounting principles that govern its valuation and presentation.

In designing an audit program for a specific account, the auditors start by developing general objectives from the financial statement assertions. Then, specific objectives are developed for the account under audit and,

FIGURE 5–5 Relationship of Assertions, Objectives, and Procedures

Management Assertions	General Audit Objectives for Assets	Specific Audit Objectives for Accounts Receivable	Example Audit Procedures
Existence and occurrence	Existence of assets	All receivables exist	Confirm a sample of accounts receivables by direct communication with debtors
Ownership	Ownership of assets	The client has rights to the receivables	
Completeness	Completeness	All receivables are recorded	Compare a sample of shipping documents to related sales invoices
Valuation	Valuation of assests	Receivables are presented at net realizable value	Investigate the credit ratings for delinquent and large receivables accounts
Measurement	Proper cutoff	Sales and receivables recorded in the proper period	Test the sales transactions shortly before and after the year end date
	Clerical accuracy of records	Receivables records are accurate and agree with general ledger	Obtain an aged trial balance of receivables, test its clerical accuracy, and reconcile to the ledgers
Statement presentation	Financial statement presentation	Receivables are properly presented in the balance sheet, including the appropriate disclosures	Review standard bank confirmations for indications of receivables pledged for loans

finally, audit procedures are designed to accomplish each specific audit objective. Figure 5–5 provides a description of this process for accounts receivables and illustrates the relationship between management assertions, audit objectives, and audit procedures.

Figure 5–5 includes only one example of audit procedure for each specific objective. Usually, additional procedures must be performed to accomplish the audit objectives. For example, the audit objective of determining that receivables are properly presented in the balance sheet is not achieved solely by a procedure focusing on the disclosure of pledged accounts. The audit program must include procedures that focus on other aspects of presentation and disclosure, such as procedures designed to identify receivables from related parties.

The audit objectives relating to the auditors' consideration of internal control are not included in Figure 5–5. The auditors' consideration of internal control can provide evidence regarding any of the assertions for an account. Any evidence provided by internal control regarding an assertion results in a reduction in the extent of the substantive tests required to accomplish the related objective.

In Chapters 11 through 14, we will consider the audit work to be done on the major asset categories, beginning with cash and concluding with plant assets and intangible assets. Specific audit objectives and a sample audit program will be presented for each asset caetgory to provide a framework for our discussion. It is important to remember that the audit programs presented in the textbook are merely illustrations of *typical* audit procedures. In actual practice, audit programs must be tailored to each client's business environment and internal control. The audit procedures comprising audit programs may vary substantially from one engagement to the next.

Verification of Related Income Statement Accounts

Income statement amounts often can be verified conveniently in conjunction with the substantiation of the related asset account. For example, after notes receivable have been verified, the related interest revenue can be substantiated by mathematically computing the interest applicable to the notes. In other cases, income statement amounts are determined by the same audit procedures used in determining the valuation of the related asset. Determining the undepreciated cost of plant assets, for example, necessitates computing (or testing) the depreciation expense for the period. Similarly, determining the net valuation of accounts receivable involves estimating the amount of the uncollectible accounts expense.

Some income statement items, such as sales revenue, do not lend themselves to verification of such direct audit procedures. However, when the auditors establish that accounts receivable are legitimate assets and have been properly recorded, they have substantial *indirect* evidence that sale transactions also have been properly measured.

THE AUDIT PROCESS

Although specific audit procedures vary from one engagement to the next, the fundamental steps underlying the audit process are essentially the same in almost every engagement:

1. Obtain an understanding of internal control sufficient to plan the audit.
2. Assess control risk and design additional tests of controls.
3. Perform additional tests of controls.
4. Reassess control risk and design substantive tests.
5. Perform substantive tests and complete the audit.
6. Form an opinion and issue the audit report.

1. Obtain an understanding of internal control sufficient to plan the audit. The second examination standard states:

> A sufficient understanding of internal control should be obtained to plan the audit. When control risk is assessed below maximum, sufficient appropriate audit evidence should be obtained through tests of controls to support the assessment.

The nature and extent of the audit work to be performed on a particular engagement depends largely upon the effectiveness of the client's internal control in preventing material misstatements in the financial statements. Before auditors can evaluate the effectiveness of the internal control, they need a knowledge and understanding of how it works: what procedures are performed and who performs them, what controls are in effect, how various types of transactions are processed and recorded, and what accounting records and supporting documentation exist. Thus, an assessment of the client's internal control system or structure is a logical first step in every audit engagement.

Sources of information about the client's internal control include interviews with client personnel, audit working papers from prior years' engagements, plant tours, and the client's manuals. In gathering information about the internal control, it is often useful to study the sequence of procedures used in processing major categories of transaction cycles.

A working knowledge of the client's internal control is needed throughout the audit; consequently, the auditors usually prepare working papers fully describing their understanding of the system. Frequent reference to these working papers will be made to aid in designing audit procedures, ascertaining where documents are filed, familiarizing new audit staff with the system, and as a refresher in beginning next year's engagement.

The description of internal control is usually prepared in the form of systems flowcharts. As an alternative to flowcharts, parts of the system may be described by written narratives or by the completion of specially designed questionnaires. All of these working papers are illustrated and discussed in Chapter 7.

2. Assess control risk and design additional tests of controls. After analyzing the design of the internal control, the auditors must decide whether it seems strong enough as designed, to prevent or to detect and correct material misstatements. In terms of the audit risk model, the auditors make an assessment of control risk for each significant assertion. If they assess internal control to be weak (control risk is high), they will rely primarily on substantive tests to reduce audit risk for the assertion to an acceptable level. On the other hand, if the internal control seems capable of preventing or detecting and correcting material misstatements, the auditor must decide which additional controls, if any, can efficiently be tested.

3. Perform additional tests of controls. Audit tests may be performed to determine whether key internal control procedures have been *properly designed and are operating effectively.* To illustrate a *test of a control,* consider the control procedure in which the accounting department accounts for the serial sequence of all shipping documents before preparing the related journal entries. The purpose of this control is to provide assurance that each shipment of merchandise is recorded in the accounting records (i.e., to assure the completeness of recorded sales and accounts receivable). As a test of the control procedure, the auditors account for the serial sequence of shipping documents on a test basis and select a sample of shipping documents prepared at various times throughout the year and inspect the related sales invoices and journal entries.

Notice that a test of an internal control measures the effectiveness of a particular *control procedure;* it *does not* substantiate the dollar amount of an account balance. Actually, a particular control procedure may affect several financial statement amounts. If, for example, the test described above indicates that the accounting department does not effectively account for the serial sequence of shipping documents, the auditors should be alert to the possibility of material misstatements in sales revenue, accounts receivable, cost of goods sold, and inventories.

4. Reassess control risk and design substantive tests. After completing their tests of controls, the auditors are in a position to reassess control risk based on the results of the tests, and determine the *nature, extent,* and *timing* of the substantive tests necessary to complete the audit. *Substantive tests* are procedures designed to substantiate the fairness of specific financial statement assertions. Examples of substantive tests include confirmation of accounts receivable and observation of how the client takes physical inventory. A major objective of internal control is to produce accurate and reliable accounting data. Thus, auditors should make an intensive investigation of account balances in areas for which internal control is weak; however, they are justified in performing less extensive testing of financial statement assertions for which they have determined that controls are operating effectively. This process of deciding upon the matters to be emphasized during the audit, based upon the assessment of internal control, means that the auditors will modify their audit program by expanding substantive tests in some areas and by reducing them in others.

Not all weaknesses in internal control require action by the auditors. For example, poor internal control over a small petty cash fund is not likely to have a material impact upon the fairness of the financial statements. On the other hand, if one employee is responsible for initiating cash disbursements and also for signing cheques, this combination of duties might result in material error in the financial statements and substantial fraud. In each instance, the auditors must exercise professional judgment in determining whether to modify the nature, extent, and timing of their audit procedures and whether to make recommendations to the client for improving internal control.

When significant deficiencies in internal control are discovered, the auditors should communicate the details to the client. In general, significant weaknesses should be communicated to top management and to the audit committee of the board of directors. In addition, an *internal control letter* is often issued in which the auditors discuss the deficiencies in greater detail and provide management with workable suggestions for improvements in the system. If the assessment of internal control is completed before the balance sheet date, the auditors' recommendations may be implemented quickly enough to contribute to the reliability of the financial statements for the year under audit.

5. Perform substantive tests and complete the audit. Some procedures for verifying account balances may be performed early in the audit. However, only after having completed the assessment of internal control are the auditors in a position to complete the procedures necessary to substantiate account balances.

6. Form an opinion and issue the audit report. Although the audit report is dated as of the date of substantial completion of the examination, it is not actually issued on that date.[2] Since the audit report represents an acceptance of considerable responsibility by the public accounting firm, a partner must first review the working papers from the engagement to ascertain that a thorough examination has been completed, and decide the type of report that is appropriate. If the auditors are to issue anything other than an unqualified opinion of standard form, considerable care must go into the precise wording of the audit report. Consequently, the audit report is usually issued a week or more after the date of the report.

Relationship between Tests of Controls and Substantive Tests

Tests of controls provide auditors with evidence as to whether prescribed internal control procedures are in use and operating effectively. The results of these tests assist the auditors in evaluating the *likelihood* of material misstatements having occurred. Substantive tests, on the other hand, are designed to *detect* material errors if they exist in the financial statements. The amount of substantive testing done by the auditors is greatly influenced by their assessment of the likelihood that material errors exist.

---

[2] CICA, *CICA Handbook* (Toronto), section 5405.03.

To illustrate, assume that a client's procedures manual indicates that the finished goods warehouse is to be locked at all times and accessible only to authorized personnel. Through tests of controls consisting of enquiry and observation, the auditors learn that the warehouse often is unlocked and that several employees who are not authorized to be in the warehouse regularly eat lunch there. As the client's internal control procedure is not operating properly, the auditors should recognize that the *risk* of inventory shortages is increased. However, the tests of controls have *not* determined that an inventory shortage does, in fact, exist.

The principal substantive test to detect shortages of inventories is the auditors' observation of a physical inventory taken by the client. As part of this observation, the auditors make test counts of various items. In our case of the unlocked warehouse, the auditors' test has shown that internal control cannot be relied upon to prevent shortages. Therefore, the auditors should increase the number of test counts in an effort to verify the existence of inventory.

Timing of Audit Work

The value of audited financial statements is enhanced if the statements are available on a timely basis after the year-end. To facilitate an early release of the audit report, auditors normally begin the audit well before the balance sheet date. The period before the balance sheet date is termed the *interim period.* Audit work that can always be performed during the interim period includes the consideration of internal control, issuance of the *internal control* letter, and substantive tests of transactions that have occurred to the interim date.

Interim tests of certain financial statement balances, such as accounts receivable, may also be performed, but this results in additional risk that must be controlled by the auditors. Significant errors or fraud could arise in these accounts during the *remaining period* between the time that the interim test was performed and the balance sheet date. Thus, to rely on the interim test of a significant account balance, the auditors must be confident regarding the effectiveness of the client's internal controls over that account, or perform additional tests of the account during the remaining period.

Performing audit work during the interim period has numerous advantages in addition to facilitating the timely release of the audited financial statements. The independent auditors may be able to assess internal control more effectively by observing and testing controls at various times throughout the year. Also, they can give early consideration to accounting problems. Another advantage is that interim auditing creates a more uniform workload for public accounting firms. With a large client, the auditors may have office space within the client's buildings and carry on auditing procedures throughout the entire year.

KEY TERMS

analytical procedures   Substantive tests that involve comparisons of financial data for the current year to that of prior years, budgets, nonfinancial data, or industry averages. From a planning standpoint, analytical procedures help the auditors obtain an understanding of the client's business, and identify financial statement amounts that appear to be affected by errors or irregularities, or other potential problems.

audit plan   A broad overview of an audit engagement prepared in the planning stages of the engagement. Audit plans usually include such matters as the objectives of the engagement, nature of the work to be done, a time schedule for major audit work and completion of the engagement, and staffing requirements.

audit program   A detailed list of the audit procedures to be performed in the course of an audit engagement. Audit programs provide a basis for assigning and scheduling audit work and for determining what work remains to be done.

audit risk   The risk that the auditors may unknowingly fail to appropriately modify their opinion on financial statements that are materially misstated.

business risk   The overall risk to the public accounting firm of association with a particular audit client. The primary elements involved are the risk of loss of reputation and litigation if the client has financial difficulties.

control risk   The risk of a material misstatement occurring in an account and not being prevented or detected on a timely basis by internal control.

detection risk   The risk that the auditors' procedures will lead them to conclude that a financial statement assertion is not materially misstated, when in fact such misstatement does exist.

engagement letter   A formal letter sent by the auditors to the client at the beginning of an engagement summarizing the nature of the engagement and the scope of audit. It may also include such items as work to be done by the client's staff and the basis for the audit fee. The purpose of engagement letters is to avoid misunderstandings, and they are essential on nonaudit engagements as well as audits.

inherent risk   The risk of material misstatement of a financial statement assertion, assuming there were no related internal controls.

interim period   The time interval from the beginning of audit work to the balance sheet date. Many audit procedures can be performed during the interim period to facilitate early issuance of the audit report.

management assertions   Representations of management that are communicated, explicitly or implicitly, by the financial statements.

predecessor auditor   The public accounting firm that formerly served as auditor but has resigned from the engagement or has been notified that its services have been terminated.

substantive approach (to an audit)   An approach to auditing in which the auditors' opinion is based primarily upon the evidence obtained by substantiating the individual financial statement assertions. This approach places less emphasis upon the consideration of internal control than does the systems approach and is particularly appropriate when internal control is weak.

substantive tests   Tests of account balances and transactions designed to detect any material errors in the financial statements. The nature, timing, and extent of substantive testing is determined by the auditors' consideration of the client's internal control.

successor auditor   An auditor who has accepted an engagement or who has been invited to make a proposal for an engagement to replace the public accounting firm that formerly served as auditors.

systems approach (to an audit)   An approach to auditing in which the auditors place a relatively high degree of reliance upon their consideration of the client's internal control and, therefore, perform a minimum of substantive testing. Whether an auditor follows a systems approach or a substantive approach is merely a matter of degree; every engagement involves both an assessment of control risk and substantive testing.

tests of control   Audit procedures designed to determine whether a particular policy or procedure operates in a manner that would prevent or detect material misstatements.

time budget   An estimate of the time required to perform each step in the audit program.

transaction cycle   The sequence of procedures applied by the client in processing a particular type of recurring transaction. The term *cycle* reflects the idea that the same sequence of procedures is applied to each similar transaction. The auditors' consideration of internal control often is organized around the client's major transactions cycles.

GROUP I: REVIEW QUESTIONS

5–1.   What information should a public accounting firm seek in its investigation of a prospective client?

5–2.   What topics should be discussed in a preliminary meeting with a prospective audit client?

5–3.   Are auditors justified in relying upon the accuracy of working papers prepared for them by employees of the client?

5–4. In planning an audit the auditors must consider those factors that affect the risk of the particular engagement. List three risk factors relating to each of the following: management characteristics, operating characteristics, engagement characteristics.

5–5. State the purpose and nature of an engagement letter.

5–6. Criticize the following statement: "Throughout this audit, for all purposes, we will define a 'material amount' as $500,000."

5–7. Define and differentiate between an **audit plan** and an **audit program.**

5–8. Should a separate audit program be prepared for each audit engagement, or can a standard program be used for most engagements?

5–9. "An audit program is desirable when new staff members are assigned to an engagement, but an experienced auditor should be able to conduct an examination without reference to an audit program." Do you agree? Discuss.

5–10. Suggest some factors that might cause an audit engagement to exceed the original time estimate. Would the extra time be charged to the client?

5–11. What problems are created for a public accounting firm when audit staff members underreport the amount of time spent in performing specific auditing procedures?

5–12. What is a management assertion? List the assertions embodied in the financial statements.

5–13. Why is audit work usually organized around balance sheet accounts rather than income statement items?

5–14. Identify the general objectives of the auditors' substantiation procedures with respect to any major asset category.

5–15. What is meant by making a proper year-end **cutoff?** Explain the effects of errors in the cutoff of sales transactions in both the income statement and the balance sheet.

5–16. What are the purposes of the audit procedures of (*a*) tracing a sample of journal entries forward into the ledgers and (*b*) vouching a sample of ledger entries back into the journals?

5–17. Charles Halstead, CA, has a number of clients who desire audits at the end of the calendar year. In an effort to spread his work load more uniformly throughout the year, he is preparing a list of audit procedures that could be performed satisfactorily before the year-end balance sheet date. What audit work, if any, might be done in advance of the balance sheet date?

5–18. What are analytical procedures? How are such procedures useful to auditors in planning an audit?

5–19. Define and differentiate between a test of a control and a substantive test.

GROUP II: QUESTIONS REQUIRING ANALYSIS

5–20.   When planning an audit, the auditors must assess the levels of risk and materiality for the engagement. Explain how the auditors' judgments about these two factors affect the auditors' planned audit procedures.

5–21.   Morgan, CA, is approached by a prospective audit client who wants to engage Morgan to perform an audit for the current year. In prior years, this prospective client was audited by another CA. Identify the specific procedures that Morgan should follow in deciding whether or not to accept this client.

(AICPA, adapted)

5–22.   How does a knowledge of the client's business help the auditors in planning and performing an examination in accordance with generally accepted auditing standards?

5–23.   Arthur Samuels, CA, agreed to perform an audit of a new client engaged in the manufacture of power tools. After some preliminary discussion of the purposes of the audit and the basis for determination of the audit fee, Samuels asked to be taken on a comprehensive guided tour of the client's plant facilities. Explain specific ways that the knowledge gained by Samuels during the plant tour may help in planning and conducting the audit.

5–24.   A CA has been asked to audit the financial statements of a company for the first time. All preliminary discussions have been completed between the CA, the company, the predecessor auditor, and all other necessary parties. The CA is now preparing an engagement letter. List the items that should be included in the engagement letter.

(AICPA, adapted)

5–25.   The audit plan, the audit program, and the time budget are three important working papers prepared early in an audit. What functions do these working papers serve in the auditor's compliance with generally accepted auditing standards? Discuss.

5–26.   The first examination standard requires, in part, that "the work should be adequately planned." An effective tool that aids the auditor in adequately planning the work is an audit program. What is an audit program and what purposes does it serve?

(AICPA, adapted)

5–27.   How can a CA make use of the preceding year's audit working papers in a recurring examination?

5–28.   Ann Knox, president of Knox Corporation, is a close friend of a client of yours. In response to a strong recommendation of your audit work by her friend, Ann Knox has retained you to make an audit of Knox Corporation's financial statements. Although you have had extensive auditing experience, you have not previously audited a company in the same line of business as Knox Corporation.

Ann Knox informs you that she would like to have an estimate of the cost of the audit. List all the steps you would take in order to have an adequate basis for providing an estimate of the audit fee for the Knox Corporation engagement.

(AICPA, adapted)

5–29. Select the best answer for each of the following. Explain the reasons for your selection.

a. When a CA is approached to perform an audit for the first time, the CA should make inquiries of the predecessor auditor. This procedure is necessary because the predecessor auditor may be able to provide information that will assist the successor auditor in determining whether:

(1) The predecessor's work should be utilized.

(2) The company follows a policy of rotating its auditors.

(3) The predecessor is aware of any weaknesses in internal control.

(4) The engagement should be accepted.

b. Appointing the independent auditors early will enable:

(1) A more thorough examination to be performed.

(2) A sufficient understanding of internal control to be obtained.

(3) Sufficient appropriate audit evidence to be obtained.

(4) A more efficient examination to be planned.

c. Which portion of an audit may **not** be completed before the balance sheet date?

(1) Tests of controls.

(2) Issuance of an internal control letter.

(3) Substantive testing.

(4) Assessment of control risk.

d. Which of the following should the auditors obtain from the predecessor auditor before accepting an audit engagement?

(1) Analysis of balance sheet accounts.

(2) Analysis of income statement accounts.

(3) All matters of continuing accounting significance.

(4) Facts that might bear on the integrity of management.

e. As one step in testing sales transactions, an auditor traces a random sample of sales journal entries to debits in the accounts receivable subsidiary ledger. This test provides evidence as to whether:

(1) Each recorded sale represents a bona fide transaction.

(2) All sales have been recorded in the sales journal.

(3) All debit entries in the accounts receivable subsidiary ledger are properly supported by sales journal entries.

(4) Recorded sales have been properly posted to customer accounts.

(AICPA, adapted)

5–30. Financial statements contain certain broad assertions regarding the accounts and classes of transactions included in the statements.

Required:

a. Who makes the assertions?

b. List and describe each of the assertions.

5–31. Auditing literature frequently makes reference to the substantive approach and the systems approach to auditing.

a. Distinguish between the substantive approach and the systems approach to an audit.

b. Explain the circumstances under which each approach would be most appropriate.

5–32. Listed below are several of the auditors' general objectives in performing substantive tests of an asset account:

Establish the existence of assets.

Establish that the company has ownership of the assets.

Establish the completeness of recorded assets.

Determine the appropriate valuation of the assets.

Establish the clerical accuracy of the underlying records.

Determine the appropriate financial statement presentation of the assets.

Required:

Indicate the general objective (or objectives) of each of the following audit procedures:

a. Count cash on hand.

b. Locate on the client's premises a sample of the equipment items listed in the subsidiary plant and equipment ledger.

c. Obtain a listing of shipping documents to recorded sales transactions.

d. Trace a sample of shipping documents to recorded sales transactions.

e. Obtain a letter of representations from management stating that no inventory or accounts receivable have been pledged to secure specific liabilities.

f. Vouch selected purchases of securities to brokers' advices.

5–33. Richard Foster, an assistant auditor, was assigned to the year-end audit work of Sipher Corporation. Sipher is a small manufacturer of language translation equipment. As his first assignment, Foster was instructed to test the cutoff of year-end sales transactions. Since Sipher uses a calendar year-end for its financial statements, Foster began by obtaining the computer-generated sales ledgers and journals for December and January. He then traced ledger postings for a few days before and after December 31 to the sales journals, noting the dates of the journal entries. Foster noted no journal entries that were posted to the ledger in the wrong accounting period. Thus, he concluded that the client's cutoff of sales transactions was effective.

Required:
Comment on the validity of Foster's conclusion. Explain fully.

GROUP III: PROBLEMS

5–34. The president of R Ltd. has just telephoned CA to ask if CA would "do an audit of the company." The president explained that R Ltd. had applied for a substantial bank loan and had been informed that the bank would require audited financial statements of the company. CA's name had been selected by the president from a list of local CA firms supplied by the bank.

The president indicated that the company had never had an audit and that he was not sure what the audit would involve and what benefits would result from it. He asked CA to come to the company's offices to discuss the terms and arrangements for the engagement with him and other officers of the company.

Required:
a. CA intends to explain carefully to the officers of R Ltd. the extent and limits of the responsibilities he would assume if he accepted the audit engagement. What points would he make?
b. What other matters would CA want to discuss at the meeting?
(CICA)

5–35. CA was recently appointed auditor of W Ltd., a public company. He had been approached by the audit committee of the board of directors and had communicated with the company's previous auditor before indicating that he would be prepared to accept the appointment. He attended the shareholders' meeting at which he was appointed but has not yet visited the company's offices.

Required:
List the matters that CA should attend to between the time of his

appointment and the commencement of his detailed audit work in order to plan an effective audit of W Ltd.

(CICA)

5–36.   Valley Finance Company opened four personal loan offices in neighbouring cities on January 2. Small cash loans are made to borrowers who repay the principal with interest in monthly instalments over a period not exceeding two years. Ralph Norris, president of the company, uses one of the offices as a central office and visits the other offices periodically for supervision and internal auditing purposes.

Required:
Assume that you agreed to examine Valley Finance Company's financial statements for the year ended December 31. No scope limitations were imposed.
a. How would you determine the scope necessary to complete your examination satisfactorily? Discuss.
b. Would you be responsible for the discovery of fraud in this examination? Discuss.

(AICPA, adapted)

5–37.   You are invited by John Bray, the president of Cheviot Corporation, to discuss with him the possibility of your conducting an audit of the company. The corporation is a small, closely held manufacturing organization that appears to be expanding. No previous audit has been made by independent public accountants. Your discussions with Bray include a review of the recent monthly financial statements, inspection of the accounting records, and review of policies with the chief accountant. You also are taken on a guided tour of the plant by the president. He then makes the following statement:

"Before making definite arrangements for an audit, I would like to know about how long it will take and about how much it will cost. I want quality work and expect to pay a fair price, but since this is our first experience with independent auditors, I would like a full explanation as to how the cost of the audit is determined. Will you please send me a memorandum covering these points?"

Write the memorandum requested by John Bray.

5–38.   Precision Industries Inc. is a manufacturer of electronic components. When a purchase order is received from a customer, a salesclerk prepares a serially numbered sales order and sends copies to the shipping and accounting departments. When the merchandise is shipped to the customer, the shipping department prepares a serially numbered shipping advice and sends a copy to the accounting department. Upon receipt of the appropriate documents, the accounting department records the sale in the accounting records. All shipments are ***FOB shipping point.***

Required:

a. How can the auditors determine whether Precision Industries Inc. has made a proper year-end cutoff of sales transactions?

b. Assume all shipments for the first five days of the following year were recorded as occurring in the current year. If not corrected, what effect will this cutoff error have upon the financial statements for the current year?

5–39. You are a new staff assistant with the London office of a national public accounting firm. Yesterday you read an article in *The Bay Street Journal* in which the managing partner of your firm's Toronto office discussed the problems caused for the public accounting profession by auditors underreporting the number of hours worked on audits.

You found this article interesting because of the experience you are having on the audit of Regal Industries, one of your office's largest clients. The audit work at Regal is being run by Mark Thomas, a very hard-working senior who is highly regarded within your office. Thomas made senior in record time and has established a reputation for bringing in jobs on schedule. Four staff assistants, including yourself, are working under Thomas. At the end of the engagement, Thomas will write a performance report on each assistant, which will be placed in the assistant's personnel file. The manager on the engagement also writes a performance evaluation of each assistant and on Thomas. You have heard, however, that managers usually agree with whatever the senior has said about an assistant's performance.

The budgeted time estimates for almost every audit procedure being performed at Regal seem too short. No one is able to finish anything on schedule. Last week, Thomas approached all the staff assistants about working Saturday to "catch up." He said that he was going to work a short day on Saturday and would not report the hours on his time sheet. He said that if you would do the same, he would buy lunch after you finished up on Saturday. You and two other assistants agreed. The fourth assistant, Dave Scott, declined, saying that he was going to a baseball game on Saturday.

The work on Saturday ran smoothly, and it was nice to wear jeans instead of dress clothes. You did quit a little early, although it was about 3:30, not noon. Afterwards, Thomas bought everyone lunch at a popular restaurant.

During the following workweek, you noticed that Thomas seemed quite friendly toward you and the other two assistants who had worked on Saturday. He was also complimentary of your work. He was not complimentary of Scott's work; in fact, you heard him comment to the engagement manager that he thought Scott would be a "short-timer," a phrase used to describe staff assistants who do not last long in public accounting. You were not too sympathetic to Scott's plight, however, as you and the other staff assistants also feel that Scott's work on the engagement has been substandard.

It is now Thursday afternoon, and Thomas has just asked the three of you who worked last Saturday if you will do the same thing again this week. He did not ask Scott. Again, Thomas offered to buy lunch if you would leave the hours off your time sheets. You suspect that Thomas has read the article in *The Bay Street Journal,* because he seemed a little defensive about asking you to underreport your time. He pointed out that you are not paid by the hour anyway, so leaving the extra hours off of your time sheet "doesn't really cost you anything."

Required:
a. Briefly explain why the managing partner of an office would probably oppose the practice of underreporting hours worked by the audit staff.

b. Briefly explain why a senior might *not* oppose the practice.

c. Explain how you think the other two staff assistants asked to work again on Saturday will probably respond. If you would respond differently, explain.

d. Suggest quality control procedures that you think could be implemented by a CA firm to discourage the underreporting of time by audit staff members.

5–40. McKay Company found its sales rising rapidly after the opening of a large manufacturing operation in its territory. To finance the increase in accounts receivable and the larger inventory required by the increased volume of sales, the company decided for the first time in its history to seek a bank loan. The manager of the local bank informed McKay Company that an audit by a CA would be a necessary prerequisite to approval of the loan application. Jill McKay, sole proprietor of the business, engaged the newly formed CA firm of Marshall and Wills to conduct the audit and provide the report requested by the bank. McKay Company had not previously been audited.

From the beginning of the audit engagement, nothing seemed to go well. Robert Corning, the staff accountant sent out by Marshall and Wills to begin the work, found that the accounting records were not up to date or in balance. He worked for a week assisting the McKay Company accountant to get the accounting records in shape. The problem was not reported to the partners until the following week because Marshall was out of town and Wills was suddenly taken ill. In the meantime, the McKay accountant complained to Jill McKay that the auditor was impeding his work.

After the audit work was well under way during the second week, McKay refused to permit the auditor to confirm accounts receivable, which were the largest current asset. He also stated that the pressure of current business prevented interrupting operations for the taking of a physical inventory. Corning protested that confirmation of accounts receivable and observations of a physical inventory were mandatory auditing procedures, but Jill McKay rejected this protest.

Upon his return to town Marshall was informed of the difficulties and went immediately to McKay's office. He explained to McKay that the ommission of work on receivables and inventories would force the auditors to deny an opinion on the financial statements. McKay became quite angry; she asserted that she could borrow the money she needed from her mother-in-law and thereby eliminate the need for any bankers or auditors in her business. McKay ordered Marshall and Corning off the premises and asserted that she would pay them nothing. Marshall replied that he had the McKay Company general ledger and other accounting records in his own office and that he would not return them until he received payment in full for all time expended, at the firm's regular per diem rates for Corning plus a charge for his own time.

Evaluate the actions taken by Marshall and Wills in this case, and advise Marshall on the action to be taken at this point.

GROUP IV: ANALYTICAL AND DISCUSSION CASE

5–41. Tammy Potter, a new partner with the regional CA firm of Tower & Tower, was recently appointed to the board of directors of a local civic organization. The chairman of the board of the civic organization is Lewis Edmond, who is also the owner of a real estate development firm, Tierra Corporation.

Potter was quite excited when Edmond indicated that his corporation needed an audit, and he wished to discuss the matter with her. During the discussion, Potter was told that Tierra Corporation needed the audit to obtain a substantial amount of additional financing to acquire another company. Presently, Tierra Corporation is successful, profitable, and committed to growth. The audit fee for the engagement should be substantial.

Since Tierra Corporation appeared to be a good client prospect, Potter tentatively indicated that Tower & Tower wanted to do the work. Potter then mentioned that Tower & Tower's policies require an investigation of new clients and approval by the managing partner, Lee Tower.

Potter obtained the authorizations of Edmond to make the necessary enquiries for the new client investigation. Edmond was found to be a highly respected member of the community. Also, Tierra corporation was highly regarded by its banker and its lawyer, and the Dun & Bradstreet report on the corporation reflected nothing negative.

As a final part of the investigation process, Potter contacted Edmond's former tax accountant, Bill Turner. Potter was surprised to discover that Turner did not share the others' high opinion of Edmond. Turner related that on an income tax audit 10 years ago, Edmond was questioned about the details of a large capital loss reported on the sale of a tract of land to a trust. Edmond told Revenue Canada that he had lost all of the supporting documentation for the transaction, and that he had no way of finding out the names of the principals of the trust. A search by an auditor of Revenue Canada revealed that the land was recorded in the name of Edmond's married daughter and that Edmond himself was listed as the trustee. Revenue Canada disallowed the loss and Edmond was assessed a civil fraud penalty. Potter was concerned about these findings, but eventually concluded that Edmond had probably matured to a point where he would not engage in such activities.

Required:

a. Present arguments supporting a decision to accept Tierra Corporation as an audit client.

b. Present arguments supporting a decision *not* to accept Tierra Corporation as an audit client.

c. Assuming that you are Lee Tower, set forth your decision regarding acceptance of the client, identifying those arguments from (*a*) or (*b*) that you found most persuasive.

Chapter 6

Evidence: What Kind and How Much?

After studying this chapter, you should be able to:

- Explain the concepts of appropriateness and sufficiency as they apply to audit evidence.
- Describe the types of procedures used to obtain audit evidence.
- Describe the characteristics of accounts with high inherent risk.
- List and describe the types of evidence used to restrict detection risk.
- Describe the auditors' approach to auditing accounting estimates.
- Describe the appropriate auditing procedures for subsequent events.
- Describe the auditors' responsibilities for subsequent discovery of errors in financial statements and for related party transactions.

During financial statement audits, the auditors gather and evaluate evidence to form an opinion on whether financial statements follow the appropriate criteria, usually generally accepted accounting princples. To express their opinion, enough evidence must be gathered to adequately restrict audit risk and provide an adequate basis for an opinion on the financial statements. In short, gathering sufficient appropriate audit evidence is the very essence of auditing.

SUFFICIENT APPROPRIATE AUDIT EVIDENCE

The third examination standard states:

> *Sufficient appropriate audit evidence* should be obtained by such means as inspection, observation, enquiry, confirmation, computation and analysis, to afford a reasonable basis to support the content of the report. (Emphasis added.)

What constitutes "sufficient appropriate audit experience"? This question arises repeatedly during the planning and performance of every audit. When an auditor is accused of negligence in the performance of an audit, the answer to this question will often determine the auditor's innocence or guilt. To provide auditors with guidelines for answering this question, the CICA's Auditing Standards Board has issued a section on "Audit Evidence" in the *Handbook* specifically addressing the nature, appropriateness, and sufficiency of audit evidence. For example, Section 5300.10 of the *CICA Handbook* on *"Audit Evidence"* states that the auditor's judgment as to what is sufficient appropriate audit evidence, particularly with respect to substantive testing, is influenced by the following factors:

1. Materiality.
2. Inherent risk and control risk considerations.
3. The experience gained during previous audit examinations as to the reliability of the client's records and representations.
4. The persuasiveness of the evidence.
5. Fraud or error found while performing his auditing procedures.

Procedures to Obtain Audit Evidence

Audit evidence is *any information that corroborates or refutes* an assertion. The audit evidence supporting the assertions in a company's financial statements consists of the underlying accounting data and all corroborating information available to the auditors. Auditors use a variety of audit procedures to obtain corroborating information. In Chapters 11 through 17, these procedures will be discussed in detail as they apply to specific accounts. Here we will briefly recap a number of audit procedures.

Physical examination means to view physical evidence of an asset. For example, the auditors might physically examine plant equipment or inventory items to obtain evidence as to their existence or condition.

Confirmation is the process of obtaining evidence by written, direct communication with the debtor, creditor, or other party to the transaction.

Tracing is the process of establishing the completeness of transaction processing by following a transaction forward through the accounting records. For example, the auditors may trace from a source document to the subsequent recorded transaction.

Vouching is the process of establishing the accuracy of recorded transactions by following a transaction back to supporting documents from a prior processing step. For example, the auditors may select recorded purchase transactions in the purchases journal and vouch them to supporting evidence such as invoices, paid cheques, and receiving reports. The direction of testing for vouching is the reverse of that used for tracing. Vouching is also referred to as *tracing back*.

Reperformance is the process of repeating a client activity. For example, the auditors may recalculate depreciation, or reperform a bank account reconciliation. Other examples of reperformance include footing, cross-footing, and extending. *Footing* is the process of proving the totals of a vertical column of figures, such as the total of daily sales for the month from the sales journal. *Cross-footing,* on the other hand, is the process of proving the total of a horizontal row. An example of cross-footing is determining that withholdings plus net pay is equal to gross pay for an employee in the payroll journal. *Extending* is the process of recomputing by multiplication. To extend the client's inventory listing is to multiply the quantities in units by the cost per unit. The resultant product is the extension.

Observation is the process of viewing a client activity. For example, the auditors may observe the application of internal control procedures such as the client's inventory-taking procedures. The distinction between physical examination and observation is that for observation to be performed, an activity must be involved. Thus, while physical examination and observation both may involve inventory, observation would require a client activity (e.g., counting) to be occurring. In practice, the term *observation* is sometimes used to refer to both types of procedures.

Inspection involves a reading or point-by-point review of a document or record. For example, the auditors may inspect a loan agreement. The terms *examine, read,* and *scan* are often used to describe applications of the inspection technique.

Reconciliations are used to establish agreement between two sets of independently maintained but related records. Thus, the ledger account for Cash in Bank is reconciled with the bank statement, and the home office record of shipments to a branch office is reconciled with the record of receipts maintained by the branch.

Enquiries are questions directed toward appropriate client personnel. The responses to the questions may be oral or in writing. An example of the enquiry technique is the auditors' questioning of the client's controller about the segregation of duties for cash receipts. The term *enquiry* is also sometimes used to refer to the technique of questioning parties outside the organization. For example, a letter of audit enquiry may be sent to the client's lawyer.

Analytical procedures are evaluations of financial information made by a study of expected relationships among financial and nonfinancial data.

Sufficiency—A Matter of Judgment

The term *sufficient* relates to the *quantity* of evidence the auditors should obtain. The amount of evidence that is considered sufficient to support the auditors' opinion is a matter of professional judgment. However, the following considerations may be useful in evaluating the sufficiency of audit evidence:

1. The amount of evidence that is sufficient in a specific situation varies inversely with the appropriateness of the evidence available. Thus, the more appropriate the evidence, the less the amount of evidence that is needed to support the auditors' opinion.
2. The need for audit evidence is closely related to the concept of materiality. The more material a financial statement amount, the greater the need for evidence as to its validity. Conversely, little or no evidence is needed to support items that are not material.
3. In every audit engagement, there is an element of risk that the auditors may overlook material error and issue an unqualified report when one is not warranted. This risk varies from one engagement to the next, depending upon such factors as the client's financial condition, internal control, the line of business, and the integrity of management. As the *relative risk* associated with a particular engagement increases, the auditors should require more evidence to support their opinion. In some special audit engagements, the auditors are aware in advance that fraud is suspected and that the accounting records may include fictitious or altered entries. Perhaps the auditors have been engaged because of a dispute between partners or because of dissatisfaction on the part of shareholders with the existing management. The risk involved in such engagements will cause the auditors to assign different weight to various types of evidence than they otherwise would. Chapter 5 presented the factors that indicate a high overall risk of errors and fraud in financial statements.

Appropriateness—A Relative Term

The appropriateness of audit evidence refers to its *quality* or *reliability*. To be appropriate, evidence must be both *valid* and *relevant*. The relative appropriateness of different types of evidence may vary greatly. Several factors contribute to the quality of evidence, including the following:

1. When auditors obtain evidence from independent sources *outside of the client company,* the reliability of the evidence is increased.
2. *Strong internal control* contributes substantially to the quality of accounting records and other evidence created within the client organization.
3. The quality of evidence is enhanced when the auditors obtain the information *directly*—that is, by firsthand observation, correspondence, or computation, rather than by obtaining the information secondhand.

In addition, the appropriateness of audit evidence is increased when the auditors are able to obtain additional information to support the original evidence. Thus, several pieces of related evidence may form a package of evidence that has greater appropriateness than do any of the pieces viewed individually.

TYPES OF AUDIT EVIDENCE

When conducting audits, the auditors gather a combination of many types of evidence to adequately restrict audit risk. As described in Chapter 5, audit risk at the account balance level has three components—inherent risk, control risk, and detection risk. The evidence that the auditors gather pertaining to each of these risks differs. As a starting point, it is helpful to recognize that while the auditors gather evidence to assess inherent and control risk, they gather evidence to restrict detection risk to the appropriate level. Therefore, detection risk is the only risk that is completely a function of the effectiveness of the evidence gathered through the auditors' procedures.

Evidence about Inherent Risk

Just as risk differs for various audits, it also differs for various accounts within a given audit. *Inherent risk,* the risk of material error before considering internal control, is one source of this difference.

The very nature of some accounts makes the inherent risk of misstatement of those accounts greater than for others. Assume that in a given business the balance of the Cash account amounts to only one tenth that of the Buildings account. Does this relationship indicate that the auditors should spend only one tenth as much time in the verification of cash as in the verification of the buildings? Cash is much more susceptible to error or theft than are buildings, and the great number of cash transactions affords an opportunity for errors to be well hidden. The amount of time devoted to the verification of cash balances and of cash transactions during the year will generally be much greater in proportion to the dollar amounts involved than will be necessary for assets such as buildings.

Illustrative Case

Bruce Henry, a resident of Windsor, owned a 90 percent stock interest in a Halifax automobile agency. The other 10 percent of the stock was owned by James Barr, who also had a contract to act as general manager of the business. As compensation for his managerial services, Barr received a percentage of net income rather than a fixed salary. The reported net income in recent years had been large and increasing each year, with correspondingly larger payments to Barr as manager. However, during this period of reported rising income, the cash position of the business as shown by the balance sheet had been deteriorating rapidly. Working capital had been adequate when Barr took over as manager, but was now critically low.

Henry, the majority shareholder in Windsor, was quite concerned over these trends. He was further disturbed by reports that Barr was spending a great deal of time in Las Vegas and that he had placed several relatives on the payroll of the automobile agency. Henry decided to engage a CA firm to audit the business. He explained fully to the CAs his doubts as to the fairness of the reported net income and his misgivings as to Barr's personal integrity. Henry added that he wished to buy Barr's shareholdings, but first needed some basis for valuing the stock.

An audit initiated under these circumstances obviously called for a greater amount of evidence and a greater degree of caution by the auditors than would normally be required. Oral evidence from Barr could not be given much weight. Documents created within the business might very possibly have been falsified. In brief, the degree of inherent risk was great, and the auditors' approach was modified to fit the circumstances. More evidence and more conclusive evidence was called for than in a more routine audit of an automobile agency.

The outcome of the audit in question was a disclosure of a gross overstatement of inventories and the reporting of numerous fictitious sales. Commission payments were also found to have been made to persons not participating in the business.

Evidence about Control Risk

It is not practical for the auditors to examine every invoice, cheque, or other piece of documentary evidence. To do so would make an audit far too expensive. The solution lies in a study of the methods and procedures by which the company controls its accounting processes. If these procedures are well designed and consistently followed, the financial statements will be accurate and complete. An adequate internal control promotes accuracy and reliability in the accounting data. Errors are quickly and automatically brought to light by the built-in proofs and cross-checks that are inherent in the system.

To obtain an understanding of the client's internal controls and to determine whether these procedures are designed and operating effectively, the auditors use a combination of knowledge obtained from previous audits, and enquiry, inspection, observation, and reperformance procedures performed during the current year.

If the auditors find that the client company has designed effective internal control for a particular account and that the prescribed practices are being consistently followed in day-to-day operations, they will assess control risk for the related assertions to be low, and thereby accept a higher level of detection risk. Thus, the adequacy of the client's internal control is a major factor in determining how much evidence the auditors will gather to restrict detection risk.

Evidence That Restricts Detection Risk

On all audits, a primary portion of the time is devoted to performing procedures that restrict detection risk—the risk that the auditors' procedures will fail to detect a material misstatement of the financial statements. The *major* types of evidence that are gathered to restrict detection risk may be summarized as follows:

1. Physical evidence.
2. Documentary evidence.
   a. Documentary evidence created outside the client organization and transmitted directly to the auditors.
   b. Documentary evidence created outside the client organization and held by the client.
   c. Documentary evidence created and held within the client organization.
3. Accounting records.
4. Analytical procedures.
5. Computations.
6. Evidence provided by specialists.
7. Oral evidence.
8. Client letters of representations.

1. Physical evidence

Actual examination provides the best evidence of physical existence of certain assets. The amount of cash on hand is verified by counting; inventories are also observed and counted. The existence of property and equipment, such as automobiles, buildings, office equipment, and factory machinery, may also be established by physical examination.

At first thought, it might seem that physical examination of an asset would be conclusive verification, but this is often not true. For example, if the cash on hand to be counted by the auditors includes cheques received from customers, counting provides no assurance that all of the cheques will prove to be collectible when deposited. There is also the possibility that one or more worthless cheques may have been created deliberately by a dishonest employee as a means of concealing from the auditors the existence of a cash shortage.

The observation of the client's count of inventory may also leave some important questions unanswered. The quality and condition of merchandise or of goods in process are vital in determining salability. If the goods counted by the auditors contain hidden defects or are obsolete, a mere counting of units does not substantiate the dollar value shown on the balance sheet. Since auditors examine such widely differing businesses as breweries, mines, and jewelry stores, it is not possible for them to become expert in appraising the products of all their clients. However, they should be alert to any clues that raise a doubt as to the quality or condition of inventories. Auditors sometimes request clients to hire independent specialists to provide the auditors with information on quality or condition of inventories.

Illustrative Case

During the observation of the physical inventory of a company manufacturing semiconductors— small chips of photographically etched silicon that channel electricity along microscopic pathways—one of the auditors counted semiconductors purportedly worth several hundred thousand dollars. He then asked why apparently identical appearing semiconductors on another wall were not being counted. The client informed him that these semiconductors were defective and could not be sold. To the auditor, the defective semiconductors were identical in appearance with those included in the count. Shortly thereafter the auditor entered academics.

In the case of plant and equipment, the auditors' physical examination verifies the existence of the asset, but gives no proof of ownership. A fleet of automobiles used by salespeople and company executives, for example, might be leased rather than owned. Also, physical examination does not substantiate the cost of the plant assets.

In summary, physical examination provides evidence as to the *existence* of certain assets, but generally needs to be supplemented by other types of evidence to determine the ownership, proper valuation, and condition of these assets. For some types of assets, such as accounts receivable or intangible assets, even the existence of the asset cannot be verified through physical evidence.

2. Documentary evidence

The most important type of evidence relied upon by auditors consists of documents. The worth of a document as evidence depends in part upon whether it was created within the company (e.g., a sales invoice) or came from outside the company (as in the case of a vendor's invoice). Some documents created within the company (e.g., cheques) are sent outside the organization for endorsement and processing; because of this critical review by outsiders, these documents are regarded as very reliable evidence.

In appraising the reliability of documentary evidence, the auditors should consider whether the document is of a type that could easily be forged or created in its entirety by a dishonest employee. A share certificate evidencing an investment in marketable securities is usually elaborately engraved and would be more difficult to falsify. On the other hand, a note receivable may be created by anyone in a moment merely by filling in the blank spaces in one of the standard note forms available at any bank.

Documentary Evidence Created Outside the Client Organization and Transmitted Directly to the Auditors.   The best quality of documentary evidence consists of documents created by independent parties outside the client's organization and transmitted directly to the auditors without passing through the client's hands. For example, in the verification of accounts receivable, the customer is requested by the client to write directly to the auditors to confirm the amount owed to the auditors' client.

Confirmations of third parties can address any of the assertions about a particular financial statement amount. However, they do not address all assertions equally well. For example, confirmations are generally effective at addressing the assertion of existence of the amounts, but not effective at addressing the appropriate valuation of the amounts. To improve the reliability of confirmations, the auditors should carefully design the confirmation forms to request the appropriate information and make it easy for the recipient to respond. Also, the confirmation should be specifically addressed to an individual in the outside organization that has access to the information being confirmed. To assure that the customer's reply comes directly to the auditors and not to the client, the auditors will enclose with the confirmation request a return envelope addressed to the auditors' office. If the replies were addressed to the auditors at the client's place of business, an opportunity would exist for someone in the client's organization to misplace the customer's letter, to intercept the customer's letter and alter the amount of indebtedness reported, or even destroy the letter.

Another type of document created outside the client's organization and transmitted directly to the auditors is a letter from the client's lawyers describing any pending litigation. Again, the client requests the outsider to furnish the information directly to the auditors in an envelope addressed to the auditors' office, and the auditors mail the request.

Documentary Evidence Created Outside the Client Organization and Held by the Client.   Many of the externally created documents referred to by the auditors will be in the client's possession. Examples include bank statements, vendors' invoices and statements, property tax bills, notes receivable, contracts, customers' purchase orders, and share and bond certificates. In deciding how much reliance to place upon this type of evidence, the auditors should consider whether the document is of a type that could be easily created or altered by someone in the client's employ.

The auditors should be particularly cautious in accepting as evidence any documents that have been altered in any way. Of course, an alteration may have been made by the company originating the document to correct an accidental error. In general, however, business concerns do not send out documents marred by errors and corrections. The auditors cannot afford to overlook the possibility that an alteration on a document may have been made deliberately to misstate the facts and to mislead auditors or others who relied upon the document.

In pointing out the possibility that externally created documents in the client's possession *might* have been forged or altered, it is not intended to discredit this type of evidence. Externally created documents in the possession of the client are used extensively by auditors and are considered, in general, as a stronger type of evidence than documents created by the client.

Documentary Evidence Created and Held within the Client Organization. No doubt the most dependable single piece of documentary evidence created within the client's organization is a paid cheque. The cheque bears the endorsement of the payee and a perforation or stamp indicating payment by the bank. Because of this review and processing of a cheque by outsiders, the auditors will usually look upon a paid cheque as a strong type of evidence. The paid cheque may be viewed as evidence that an asset was acquired at a given cost, or as a proof that a liability was paid or an expense incurred.

Most companies place great emphasis on proper internal control of cash disbursements by such devices as the use of serial numbers on cheques, signature (or two signatures) by responsible officials, and separation of the cheque-signing function from the accounting function. This emphasis on internal control over cash payments lends additional assurance that a paid cheque is a valid document.

Most documents created within the client organization represent a lower quality of evidence than a paid cheque because they circulate only within the company and do not receive critical review by an outsider. Examples of internally created documents that do not leave the client's possession are sales invoices, shipping notices, purchase orders, receiving reports, and credit memoranda. Of course, the original copy of a sales invoice or purchase order is sent to the customer or supplier, but the carbon copy available for the auditors' inspection has not left the client's possession.

The degree of reliance to be placed on documents created and used only within the organization depends on the adequacy of the internal control. If the accounting procedures are so designed that a document prepared by one person must be critically reviewed by another, and if all documents are serially numbered and all numbers in the series accounted for, these documents may represent reasonably good evidence. Adequate internal control will also provide for extensive subdivision of duties so that no employee handles a transaction from beginning to end. An employee who maintains records or creates documents, such as credit memoranda, should not have access to cash. Under these conditions there is no incentive for an employee to falsify a document, since the employee creating documents does not have custody of assets.

On the other hand, if internal control is weak, the auditors cannot place as much reliance on documentary evidence created within the organization and not reviewed by outsiders. If an employee is authorized to create documents such as sales invoices and credit memoranda and also has access to cash, an incentive exists to falsify documents to conceal a theft. If documents are not controlled by serial numbers, the possibility arises that the auditors are not being given access to all documents or that duplicates are being used to support fictitious transactions. There is the danger not only of fictitious documents created to cover theft or error by an employee but also the possibility, however remote, that management is purposely presenting misleading financial statements and has prepared false supporting documents for the purpose of deceiving the auditors.

3. Accounting records as evidence.

When auditors attempt to verify an amount in the financial statements by tracing it back through the accounting records, they will ordinarily carry this process through the ledgers to the journals and vouch the items to such basic documentary evidence as a paid cheque, invoice, or other original papers. To some extent, however, the ledger accounts and the journals constitute worthwhile evidence in themselves.

The dependability of ledgers and journals as evidence is indicated by the extent of internal control covering their preparation. Whenever possible, subsidiary ledgers for receivables, payables, and plant equipment should be maintained by persons not responsible for the general ledger. All general journal entries should be approved in writing by the controller or other official. If ledgers and journals are produced by an electronic data processing system, the safeguards described in Chapter 8 should be in effect. When controls of this type exist and the records appear to be well maintained, the auditors may regard the ledgers and journals as affording some support for the financial statements.

As a specific example, assume that the auditors wish to determine that the sale of certain old factory machinery during the year under audit was properly recorded. By reference to the subsidiary ledger for plant and equipment, they might ascertain that the depreciation accumulated during the years the machine was owned agreed with the amount cleared out of the Accumulated Depreciation account at the time of sale. They might also note that the original cost of the machine as shown in the plant ledger agreed with the credit to the Plant and Equipment control account when the machine was sold, and that the proceeds from sale were entered in the cash receipts journal. Assuming that the plant ledger, general ledger, and the cash receipts journal are independently maintained by three different employees, or are produced by an electronic data processing department with effective internal control, the agreement of these records offers considerable evidence that the sale of the machine was a legitimate transaction and properly recorded. Whether the auditors should go beyond this evidence and examine original documents, such as the bill of sale or a work order authorizing the sale, would depend upon the relative importance of the amount involved and upon other circumstances of the audit.

In addition to journals and ledgers, other accounting records providing evidence for external auditors include sales summaries, trial balances, interim financial statements, and operating and financial reports prepared for management.

4. Analytical procedures.

Analytical procedures involve evaluations of financial statement information by a study of relationships among financial and nonfinancial data. Essentially, the process of performing analytical procedures consists of four steps:

1. Develop an expectation of an account balance.
2. Determine the amount of difference from the expectation that can be accepted without investigation.
3. Compare the company's account balance with the expected account balance.
4. Investigate significant deviations from the expected account balance.

Techniques used in performing analytical procedures range in sophistication from straightforward comparisons and ratios to complex models involving many relationships and data from many previous years. Examples of analytical procedures include comparisons of revenue and expense amounts for the current year to those of prior periods, to industry averages, to budgeted levels, and to relevant nonfinancial data, such as units produced or hours of direct labour. A more sophisticated analytical procedure might involve the development of a multiple regression model to estimate the amount of sales for the year using economic and industry data. In addition, analytical procedures may involve computations of percentage relationships of various items in the financial statements, such

---

Illustrative Case

In performing analytical procedures for a marine supply store, the auditors noticed that uncollectible accounts expense, which normally had been running about 1 percent of net sales for several years, had increased in the current year to 4 percent of net sales. This significant variation caused the auditors to make a careful investigation of all accounts written off during the year and those presently past due. Most of the uncollectible accounts examined were found to be fictitious, and the cashier-bookkeeper then admitted that he had created those accounts to cover up his abstraction of cash receipts.

as gross profit percentages. When the relationships turn out as expected, auditors are provided with evidence that the data being reviewed are free from material error. On the other hand, unusual fluctuations in these relationships may indicate serious problems in the financial statements and should be investigated fully by the auditors. Thus, Section 5300.31 of the *CICA Handbook* suggests that analytical procedures "can be effective in identifying possible financial statement misstatements" in the planning, executing, and evaluating phrases of the audit.

Comparisons with Industry Averages.   Average statistics for various industries are available through such reporting services as Dun & Bradstreet's *Key Business Ratios*. Such averages provide a potentially rich source of information for analytical procedures. Comparisons with industry statistics may alert auditors to classification errors, improper applications of accounting principles, or other misstatements in specific items in the client's financial statements. In addition, these comparisons may highlight the client's strengths and weaknesses relative to similar companies, thus providing the auditors with a basis for making constructive recommendations to the client.

One problem with the use of industry averages for analytical procedures is the degree of comparability. Other companies in the same industry may be larger or smaller, engage in other lines of business that affect their financial ratios, or use different accounting methods than does the auditors' client. Thus, auditors should carefully consider the extent of comparability before drawing conclusions based upon comparisons with industry averages.

Comparisons with Internal Client Data.   Every audit client generates internal information that may be used in performing analytical procedures. Forecasts, production reports, and monthly performance reports are but a few data sources that may be expected to bear predictable relationships to financial statement amounts. In establishing these relationships, auditors may use dollar amounts, physical quantities, ratios, or percentages. Separate relationships may be computed for each division or product line.

Trend analysis is a technique for identifying consistent patterns in the relationships of data from successive time periods. For example, a review of the client's sales for the past three years might reveal a consistent growth rate of about 7 percent. This information would assist the auditors in evaluating the reasonableness of the sales reported in the client's income statement for the current year.

Timing of Analytical Procedures.   Analytical procedures are used at various times throughout the audit. They are useful in the early *planning* phase for assisting in planning the nature, timing, and extent of other audit procedures and directing the auditors' attention to areas requiring special investigation. Some of the problems that may be brought to light by the application of specific analytical procedures are illustrated in Figure 6–1. Analytical procedures also may be applied during the audit as *substantive tests* to provide evidence as to the reasonableness of specific account balances. Finally, analytical procedures are performed at the end of the engagement as a final overall review to evaluate the reasonableness of the audited figures. This last application provides assurance that the auditors have not "failed to see the forest because of the trees."

The quality or appropriateness of evidence obtained from analytical procedures depends upon the strength of the relationships among the data being compared. However, analytical procedures usually are highly efficient in that they may be performed quickly and inexpensively (often on a microcomputer using audit software) in relation to the value of the evidence obtained.

FIGURE 6–1   Potential Problems Disclosed by Analytical Procedures

Analytical Procedure	*Potential Problems*
1. Comparison of inventory levels for the current year to that of prior years.	Misstatement of inventory; inventory obsolescence problem.
2. Comparison of research and development expense to the budgeted amount.	Misclassification of research and development expenses.
3. Comparison of accounts receivable turnover for the current year to that of prior years.	Misstatement of sales or accounts receivable.
4. Comparison of the client's gross profit percentage to published industry averages.	Misstatement of sales and accounts receivable; misstatement of cost of goods sold and inventory.
5. Comparison of production records in units to sales.	Misstatement of sales; misstatement of inventory.
6. Comparison of interest expense to the average outstanding balance of interest bearing debt.	Understatement of liabilities; misstatement of interest expense.

5. Computations.

Another form of audit evidence consists of computations made independently by the auditors to prove the arithmetical accuracy of the client's records. Computations differ from analytical procedures. Analytical procedures involve the analysis of relationships among financial data, whereas computations simply verify mathematical processes. In its simplest form, an auditor's computation might consist of footing a column of figures in a sales journal or in a ledger account to prove the column total.

Independent computations may be used to prove the accuracy of such client calculations as earnings per share, depreciation expense, allowance for uncollectible accounts, revenue recognized on a percentage-of-completion basis, and provisions for income taxes. The computation of a client's pension liability normally involves actuarial assumptions and computations beyond an auditor's area of expertise. Therefore, auditors usually enlist the services of an actuary to verify this liability.

6. Evidence provided by specialists.

We have pointed out that auditors may not be experts in such technical tasks as judging the quality of a client's inventory or making the actuarial computations to verify pension liabilities. Other phases of an audit in which auditors lack the special qualifications necessary to determine the fairness of the client's representations include assessing the probable outcome of pending litigation and estimating the number of barrels of oil in an underground oil field.

In Section 5360 of the *CICA Handbook*, "Using the Work of a Specialist," the CICA recognized the necessity for auditors to consult with experts, when appropriate, as a means of gathering appropriate audit evidence. A *specialist* may be defined as a person or firm possessing special skill or knowledge in a field other than accounting or auditing, giving as examples actuaries, appraisers, lawyers, engineers, and geologists. It is desirable that the specialist consulted by the auditors be unrelated to the client; however, in some instances it is acceptable for the specialist to have an existing relationship with the client. For example, the most logical specialist to consult regarding pending litigation would be the client's legal counsel. In any event, the auditors are responsible for ascertaining the professional qualifications and reputation of the specialist consulted.

Auditors cannot accept a specialist's findings blindly; they must obtain an understanding of the methods or assumptions used by the specialist and test accounting data furnished to the specialist by the client. The auditors may accept the specialist's findings as competent audit evidence unless their tests cause them to believe the findings are unreasonable. However, the auditors should not refer to the specialist in their audit report unless the specialist's findings affect the type of audit report being issued.

7. Oral evidence.

Throughout their examination the auditors will ask a great many questions of the officers and employees of the client's organization. Novice auditors are sometimes afraid to ask questions for fear of seeming to be uninformed and inexperienced. Such an attitude is quite illogical; even the most experienced and competent auditors will ask a great many questions. These questions cover an endless range of topics—the location of records and documents, the reasons underlying an unusual accounting procedure, the probabilities of collecting a long past-due account receivable.

The answers auditors receive to these questions constitute another type of evidence. Generally, oral evidence is not sufficient in itself, but it may be useful in disclosing situations that require investigation or in corroborating other forms of evidence. For example, after making a careful analysis of all past-due accounts receivable, an auditor will normally sit down with the credit manager and get that official's views on the prospects for collection of accounts considered doubtful. If the opinions of the credit manager are in accordance with the estimates of uncollectible accounts losses that have been made independently by the auditor, this oral evidence will constitute significant support of the conclusions reached. In repeat examinations of a business, the auditor will be in a better position to evaluate the opinions of the credit manager based on how well the manager's estimates in prior years have worked out.

8. Clients letters of representations.

At the conclusion of the examination, auditors obtain from the client a written letter of representations summarizing the most important oral representations made during the engagement. Many specific items are included in this representations letter. For example, management usually represents that all liabilities known to exist are reflected in the financial statements. Most of the representations fall into the following broad categories:

1. All accounting records, financial data, and minutes of directors' meetings have been made available to the auditors.
2. The financial statements are complete and prepared in conformity with generally accepted accounting principles.
3. All items requiring disclosure (such as contingencies and related party transactions) have been properly disclosed.

While the *CICA Handbook* is silent on this matter, *SAS 19* (AU 333) of the AICPA, ''Client Representations,'' requires auditors to obtain a representations letter on every engagement and provides suggestions as to its form and content. These letters are dated as of the date of the audit report and usually are signed by both the client's chief executive officer and chief financial officer.

A client representations letter is a low grade of audit evidence and *should never be used as a substitute for performing other audit procedures.* The financial statements already constitute written representations by the client; hence, a representations letter does little more than assert that the original representations were correct.

Although representations letters are not a substitute for other necessary auditing procedures, they do serve several important audit purposes. One purpose is to *remind the client officers of their primary and personal responsibility for the financial statements.* Another purpose is to document in the audit working papers the client's responses to many questions asked by the auditors during the engagement. Also, a representation by management may be the only evidence available with respect to management's

---

Illustrative Case

The income statement of National Student Marketing Corporation (NSMC) in the United States included total gains of $370,000 from the sale of two subsidiary companies to employees of the subsidiaries. Consideration for the sales was notes receivable collateralized by 7,700 shares of NSMC stock. Because both subsidiaries had been operating at substantial losses, NSMC's external auditors obtained written representations from three officers of NSMC that there were no indemnification or repurchase commitments given to the purchasers.

   The SEC of the United States criticized the auditors for too great reliance on management representations regarding the sales. The SEC considered the sales to be sham transactions that would have been brought to light had the auditors sufficiently extended their auditing procedures. NSMC had executed various side agreements to assume all risks of ownership after the "sale" of one subsidiary, and had agreed to make cash contributions and guarantee a bank line of credit after the "sale" of the other subsidiary. Further, the NSMC stock collateralizing the notes receivable had been given to the subsidiaries' "purchasers" by officers of NSMC.

---

future intentions. For example, whether maturing debt is classified as a current or a long-term liability may depend upon whether management has both the ability and the *intention* to refinance the debt.

Evidence about Accounting Estimates

The auditors must be especially careful in considering financial statement accounts that are affected by estimates made by management (often referred to as *accounting estimates*), particularly those in which a wide range of accounting methods are considered acceptable. Examples of accounting estimates include allowances for loan losses and obsolete inventory, and estimates of warranty liabilities. Making accounting estimates is management's responsibility, and such estimates are generally more susceptible to material misstatement than financial statement amounts which are more certain in amount. While the *CICA Handbook* is silent on this matter, the AICPA's *SAS 57* (AU 342), "Auditing Accounting Estimates," requires the auditors to determine that (*a*) all necessary estimates have been developed, (*b*) the accounting estimates are reasonable, and (*c*) the accounting estimates are properly accounted for and disclosed.

   Determining whether all necessary estimates have been developed and accounted for properly (Steps *a* and *c*) requires a knowledge of the client's business and the applicable generally accepted accounting principles. When evaluating the reasonableness of accounting estimates (Step *b*), one or a combination of the following three basic approaches may be taken:

1. Reviewing and testing management's process of developing the estimates—this will often involve reviewing the steps performed by management and considering their reasonableness.

2. Independently developing an estimate of the amount to compare to management's estimate.
3. Reviewing subsequent events or transactions bearing on the estimate, such as examining actual payments made subsequent to year-end.

The wide range of potential accounting methods complicates transactions involving accounting estimates. Pensions, leases, and long-term construction contracts are just a few examples of transactions with complex accounting methods that vary depending on the nature of the agreements and the specific circumstances. It is the auditors' responsibility to evaluate whether the accounting rules followed are appropriate in the circumstances. While it sounds so basic as to almost be trivial, it is essential that the auditors understand the transactions in which their clients are involved. In practice, this requirement is onerous since the auditors may be involved in a variety of audits, requiring knowledge of a host of different accounting methods and estimates.

Illustrative Case

The financial difficulties of the financial institution industry during the late 1980s and early 1990s present a good example of the potential risk to auditors presented by accounting estimates. A number of bank and trust companies (savings and loan organizations in the United States) ran into financial difficulties due in large part to making loans which subsequently proved to be uncollectible.

Two banks went bankrupt and their auditors were sued for the alleged misleading financial statements resulting from inadequate provision for loan losses. These lawsuits were later settled, out of court, for millions of dollars.

The Cost of Obtaining Evidence

Auditors should consider the cost of alternative auditing procedures in determining an efficient and economic audit for the benefit of the client. Cost is not the primary factor influencing the auditors in deciding what evidence should be obtained, but cost is always an important consideration.

The cost factor may preclude gathering the ideal form of evidence and necessitate the substitution of other forms of evidence that are of lesser quality, yet still satisfactory. For example, assume that the auditors find that the client has a large note receivable from a customer. What evidence should the auditors obtain to be satisfied that the note is authentic and will be paid at maturity? One alternative is for the auditors to correspond directly with the customer and obtain written confirmation of the amount, maturity date, and other terms of the note. This confirmation is evidence that the customer issued the note and regards it as a valid obligation. Second, the auditors might test the collectibility of the note by obtaining a credit report on the customer from Dun & Bradstreet or from a local credit association. They might also obtain copies of the customer's most recent financial statements accompanied, if possible, by the opinion of an external auditor. To carry our illustration to an extreme, the auditors might obtain permission to make an audit of the financial statements of the customer. The cost of conducting this separate audit could amount to more than the note receivable the auditors wished to verify.

The point of this illustration is that auditors ***do not*** always insist upon obtaining the strongest possible evidence. They do insist upon obtaining evidence that is adequate under the circumstances. The more material the item to be verified or more risk is involved, the stronger the evidence required by the auditors, and the greater the cost they may be willing to incur in obtaining it.

EVIDENCE PROVIDED BY SUBSEQUENT EVENTS

Evidence not available at the close of the period under audit often becomes available before the date of the audit report (the date of substantial completion of the examination). The auditors' opinion on the fairness of the financial statements may be changed considerably by the ***subsequent events***. The term ***subsequent event*** refers to an event or transaction that occurs between the date of the balance sheet and the date of the audit report. Subsequent events may be classified into two broad categories: (1) those providing additional evidence as to facts existing on or before the balance sheet date and (2) those involving facts coming into existence after the balance sheet date.[1]

Type 1 Subsequent Events. The first type of subsequent event provides additional evidence as to ***conditions that existed at the balance sheet date*** and affects the estimates inherent in the process of preparing financial statements. This type of subsequent event requires that the financial statement amounts be ***adjusted*** to reflect the changes in estimates resulting from the additional evidence.

As an example, let us assume that a client's accounts receivable at December 31 included one large account and numerous small ones. The large amount due from the major customer was regarded as good and collectible at the year-end, but during the course of the audit engagement the customer entered bankruptcy. As a result of this information, the auditors might have found it necessary to insist on an increase in the

---

[1] CICA, *CICA Handbook* (Toronto), Section 3820.

December 31 allowance for uncollectible accounts. The bankruptcy of the customer shortly after the balance sheet date indicates that the financial strength of the customer had probably deteriorated before December 31, and the client was simply in error in believing the receivable to be good and collectible at that date. Evidence becoming available after the balance sheet date should be used in making judgments about the valuation of receivables on the balance sheet date.

Other examples of this first type of subsequent event include the following:

1. Customers' cheques included in the cash receipts of the last day of the year prove to be uncollectible and are charged back to the client's account by the bank. If the cheques were material in amount, an adjustment of the December 31 cash balance may be necessary to exclude the cheques now known to be uncollectible.
2. A new three-year union contract signed two weeks after the balance sheet date provides evidence that the client has materially underestimated the total cost to complete a long-term construction project on which revenue is recognized by the percentage-of-completion method. The amount of income (or loss) to be recognized on the project in the current year should be recomputed using revised cost estimates.
3. Litigation pending against the client is settled shortly after the balance sheet date, and the amount owed by the client is material. This litigation was to be disclosed in notes to the financial statements, but no liability had been accrued because at year-end no reasonable estimate could be made of the amount of the client's loss. Now that appropriate evidence exists as to the dollar amount of the loss, this contingent loss meets the criteria for accrual in the financial statements, rather than mere footnote disclosure.[2]

Type 2 Subsequent Events. The second type of subsequent event involves conditions *coming into existence after the balance sheet date.* These events do not require adjustment to the dollar amounts shown in the financial statements, *but they should be disclosed if the financial statements otherwise would be misleading.* To illustrate, assume that shortly after the balance sheet date a client sustains an uninsured fire loss destroying most of its plant assets. The carrying value of plant assets should not be reduced in the balance sheet because these assets were intact at year-end. However, those analyzing the financial statements would be misled if they were not advised that most of the plant assets are no longer in a usable condition.

---

[2] Section 3290 of the *CICA Handbook* requires accrual of contingent losses in the accounting records when both of the following criteria are met: (1) It is likely that a future event will confirm that an asset has been impaired or a liability incurred at the date of the financial statements, and (2) the amount of losses can be reasonably estimated.

Not all events occurring after the balance sheet date warrant adjustment to or disclosure in the financial statements. For example, assume that the following events occurred between the balance sheet date and the date of the audit report:

1. Business combination with a competing company.
2. Early retirement of bonds payable.
3. Adoption of a new pension plan requiring large, near-term cash outlays.
4. Death of the company treasurer in an airplane crash.
5. Introduction of a new line of products.
6. Plant closed by a labour strike.

Although these events may be significant in the future operations of the company and of interest to many who read the audited financial statements, none of these occurrences has any bearing on the results of the year under audit, and their bearing on future results is not easily determinable. The question facing the external auditors is: Which, if any, of these events should be reflected in footnotes to the financial statements in order to achieve adequate informative disclosure?

It is generally agreed that subsequent events involving business combinations, substantial casualty losses, and other significant changes in a company's financial position or financial structure should be disclosed in footnotes. Otherwise the financial statements might be misleading rather than informative. Consequently, the first three of the preceding examples (combination with a competing company, early retirement of bonds payable, and adoption of a new pension plan) should be disclosed in notes to the financial statements. The last three subsequent events (personnel changes, product line changes, and strikes) are *not disclosed in footnotes* unless particular circumstances make such information essential to the proper interpretation of the financial statements.

Pro Forma Statements as a Means of Disclosure. Occasionally subsequent events may be so material that supplementary *pro forma financial statements* should be prepared giving effect to the events as if they had occurred as of the balance sheet date. The pro forma statements (usually a balance sheet only) may be presented in columnar form next to the audited financial statements. This form of disclosure is used only when the subsequent event has a pervasive effect upon the asset structure, the capital structure, or the future activities of the business. An example would be a business combination or a sale of a significant segment of the business.

Distinguishing between the Two Types of Subsequent Events. In deciding whether a particular subsequent event should result in adjustment to the financial statements or footnote disclosure, the auditor should carefully consider *when the underlying conditions came into existence.* For example, assume that shortly after the balance sheet date, a major customer of the audit client declares bankruptcy, with the result that a large receivable previously considered fully collectible now appears to be uncollectible. If the customer's bankruptcy resulted from a steady deterioration in financial position, the subsequent event provides evidence that the receivable actually was uncollectible at year-end, and the allowance for doubtful accounts should be increased. On the other hand, if the customer's bankruptcy stemmed from a casualty (such as a fire) occurring after year-end, the conditions making the receivable uncollectible came into existence after the balance sheet date. In this case, the subsequent event should be disclosed in a note to the financial statements.

Auditors' Responsibility for Subsequent Events

The external auditors are responsible to ensure that those subsequent events (the events occurred between the balance sheet date and the audit report date) that require adjustment to or disclosure in the financial statements have been identified and appropriately presented in the financial statements. During the period between the balance sheet date and the audit report date (the subsequent period), the auditors should determine that proper cutoffs of cash receipts and disbursements and sales and purchases have been made, and should examine supporting evidence to aid in the evaluation of assets and liabilities as of the balance sheet date. In addition, they should perform the following review, enquiry, and related procedures regarding subsequent events:

1. Reviewing and scanning records of transactions and events to the extent necessary.
2. Reading the latest available interim financial statements, comparing them with the financial statements being reported upon, and making any other comparisons appropriate in the circumstances.
3. Reading the minutes of meetings of shareholders, the board of directors, and appropriate committees, and enquiring of officials about matters dealt with at those meetings for which minutes are not yet available.
4. Enquiring of management as to:
   a. Whether there are any significant changes in commitments or contingencies (including contingent gains and losses).
   b. Whether there has been any significant change or proposed change in the assets, share capital, long-term debt, or working capital.
   c. Whether any unusual accounting adjustments have been made in the subsequent period.
   d. The current status of items in the financial statements that were accounted for on the basis of tentative, preliminary, or inconclusive data.

5. Considering the necessity of any further communication with legal counsel and, if applicable, secondary auditors.
6. Enquiring of appropriate officials, generally the chief executive officer and the chief financial officer, as to whether any subsequent events have occurred that in their opinion would require adjustment to or disclosure in the financial statements, and obtaining written confirmation (dated on or after the auditor's report date) of their representations.[3]

The auditors, in determining the extent of the above procedures, should take the following factors into consideration:

1. The nature of the business of the client and the matters likely to affect it.
2. Audit findings to date.
3. The quality of the records and controls.
4. The length of the subsequent period.
5. Their assessment of the likelihood that management may have failed to identify subsequent events that require adjustment to or disclosure in the financial statements.[4]

Moreover, the auditors are responsible to evaluate facts or events after the date of their audit report that came to their attention before the release of their report.[5] Suppose, for example, that the auditors' report for a December 31 audit is dated February 3. On February 12, before their report is released, the auditors were informed by the client that a lawsuit, which had been footnoted as a contingent loss in the December 31 financial statements, had been settled on February 11 by a substantial payment by the client. The auditors would have to insist that the contingent loss be changed to a real liability in the December 31 balance sheet and that the footnote be revised to show the settlement of the lawsuit subsequent to the balance sheet date. If the client agreed, the auditors would ***double-date*** their report "February 3, except for Note _____, as to which date is February 11." Alternatively, the auditors might decide to return to the client's facilities for further review of subsequent events through February 11; in this case, the audit report would bear that date only. However, if the item affected by a subsequent event is adjusted in the financial statements and a footnote is not required, the auditors can use the original date for their report, which is February 3.

Double-dating extends the auditors' responsibility for disclosure through the later date ***only with respect to the specified item.*** Using the later

---

[3] CICA, *CICA Handbook* (Toronto), Section 6550.04.

[4] Ibid., Section 6550.03.

[5] Ibid., Section 5405.02.

FIGURE 6–2   Subsequent Events

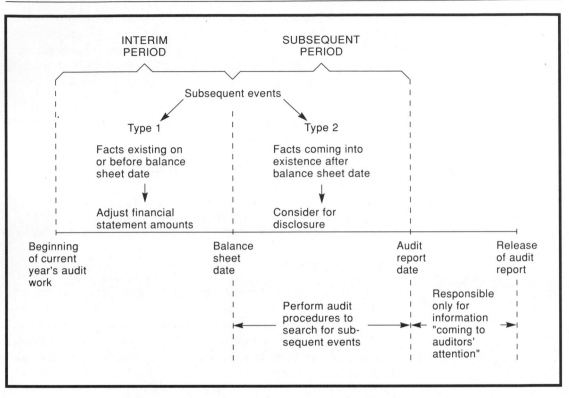

date for the date of the report will extend the auditors' responsibility with respect to all areas of the financial statements.

Figure 6–2 summarizes the auditors' responsibilities for subsequent events among the relevant dates: the balance sheet date, the date of the audit report, and the date upon which the audit report is actually released.

The Auditors' Subsequent Discovery of Errors Existing at the Date of Their Report

After the release of their report, if the auditors learn that the audited financial statements contained a material error or misstatement, they should notify their client. For example, Section 171 of the Canada Business Corporations Act requires a director or an officer of a company who is aware of any error or misstatement in the financial statements to inform the auditors accordingly. When the auditors are notified or otherwise become aware of the material error or misstatement, they are responsible for ensuring that each director of the company is likewise informed. The directors are then responsible for either issuing revised financial statements or informing the shareholders by other appropriate means.

When the financial statements are revised, the auditors' responsibility regarding the evidence to be examined and the dating and content of the audit report depends on the error or misstatement. If the error was an isolated one, the auditors should examine the evidence related to the error and double-date their report.[6] On the other hand, if the error was so pervasive as to undermine the auditors' reliance on the audit evidence supporting the original financial statements, they should reevaluate the previous evidence and update their work, and issue a new report with a new date.[7] This new report should indicate that the previous report has been withdrawn and that the financial statements have been revised.[8] In addition, an explanation of the revision should be made either in the audit report or in a footnote to the financial statements; in the latter case, the audit report should refer to such a footnote.[9]

Subsequent Discovery of Omitted Audit Procedures

What actions should the auditors take if after issuing an audit report they find that they have failed to perform certain significant audit procedures? The omission of appropriate audit procedures in a particular engagement might be discovered during a practice inspection review or other subsequent review of the auditors' working papers. Unlike the situation described in the previous section, the auditors do not have information indicating that the financial statements are in error. Instead, the subsequent review has revealed that they may have issued their audit report without having gathered sufficient and appropriate audit evidence. While the CICA is silent on the issue, the AICPA in the United States addresses this sensitive problem by stating that if the auditors believe their report is still being relied upon by third parties, they should attempt to perform the omitted procedures.[10] Because of the legal implications of these situations, the auditors should consider consulting their legal counsel.

Evidence for Related Party Transactions

How should auditors react if a corporation buys a parcel of real estate from one of its executive officers at an obviously excessive price? This situation illustrates the problems that may arise for auditors when the client com-

---

[6] Ibid., Section 5405.17.

[7] Ibid.

[8] Ibid.

[9] Ibid.

[10] AICPA, *Statement on Auditing Standards 46*, "Consideration of Omitted Procedures after the Report Date" (New York, 1983), AU 390.

pany enters into *related party transactions*. The term *related party* refers to the client entity and any other party with which the client may deal where one party has the ability to influence the other to an extent that may prevent one party to the transaction from pursuing its own separate interests fully.[11] Related parties include officers, directors, principal owners, and members of their immediate families; and affiliated companies, such as subsidiaries. A related party transaction is any transaction between related parties (except for normal compensation arrangements, expense allowances, and similar transactions arising in the ordinary course of business).

The primary concern of the auditors is that material related party transactions be *adequately disclosed* in the client's financial statements or footnotes. Disclosure of related party transactions should include the nature of the relationship; a description of the nature and extent of the transactions, including dollar amounts; and amounts due to and from related parties, together with terms and manner of settlement.

Since transactions with related parties are not conducted at arm's length, the auditors should be aware that the *economic substance* of these transactions may differ from their form. For example, a long-term, interest-free loan to an officer includes in substance an element of executive compensation equal to a realistic interest charge. If the auditors believe that related party transactions were executed at unrealistic prices or terms, and the dollar amounts are material, they must insist upon adequate disclosure in the financial statements to properly describe the substance of the transactions.

While there is no auditing pronouncement in Canada, AICPA in the United States suggests guidelines for identifying related parties and related party transactions.[12] Common methods of identifying related parties include making enquiries of management and reviewing securities commission filings, shareholders' listings, and conflict-of-interest statements obtained by the client from its executives. A list of all known related parties should be prepared at the beginning of the audit so that the audit staff may be alert for related party transactions throughout the engagement. This list is retained in the auditors' permanent file for reference and updating in successive engagements.

KEY TERMS

(Note: The first portion of this chapter defines a number of audit procedures. Those terms are not repeated in this glossary.)

---

[11] Ibid., Section 3840.

[12] AICPA, *Statement on Auditing Standards 45*, "Omnibus Statement on Auditing Standards—1983" (New York, 1983), AU 334.

analytical procedures Evaluations of financial information made by a study of plausible relationships among both financial and nonfinancial data. Typical analytical procedures involve comparisons of current financial data to that of prior periods, to industry averages, to budgeted performance, and to nonfinancial data.

appropriateness The appropriateness of audit evidence relates to its quality. To be appropriate, evidence must be both valid and relevant.

audit evidence Any information that corroborates or refutes an assertion in financial statements.

letter of representations A single letter or separate letters prepared by officers of the client company at the auditors' request setting forth certain representations about the company's financial position or operations.

material Of substantial importance. Significant enough to affect evaluations or decisions by users of financial statements. Information that should be disclosed in order that financial statements constitute a fair presentation. Involves both qualitative and quantitative considerations.

pro forma financial statements Financial statements that give effect to subsequent events as though they had occurred as of the balance sheet date.

related party transaction A transaction in which one party has the ability to influence significantly the management or operating policies of the other party, to the extent that one of the transacting parties might be prevented from pursuing fully its own separate interests.

relative risk The danger in a specific audit engagement of substantial error and misstatement in the accounts and the financial statements.

specialist A person or firm possessing special skill or knowledge in a field other than accounting or auditing, such as an actuary.

subsequent event An event occurring between the date of the balance sheet and the date of the audit report.

sufficient Sufficient audit evidence is a measure of the quantity of the evidence.

GROUP I: REVIEW QUESTIONS

6–1. In a conversation with you, Mark Rogers, CA, claims that both the *sufficiency* and the *appropriateness* of audit evidence are a matter of judgment in every audit. Do you agree? Explain.

6–2. "The gathering of evidence by auditors is guided by the generally accepted auditing standards. To comply with these standards, the auditors must obtain the strongest possible evidence for each item in the financial statements, regardless of the cost or difficulties that may be encountered.''

Do you agree with the two sentences quoted above? Explain.

6–3. What are the factors that may influence the auditors' judgment on the sufficiency and appropriateness of audit evidence, particularly with respect to substantive testing?

6–4. Distinguish between the components of audit risk that the auditors gather evidence to assess versus the component of audit risk that they collect evidence to restrict.

6–5. Identify and explain the considerations that guide the auditors in deciding how much evidence they must examine as a basis for expressing an opinion on a client's financial statements.

6–6. ''The best means of verification of cash, inventory, office equipment, and nearly all other assets is a physical count of the units; only a physical count gives the auditors complete assurance as to the accuracy of the amounts listed on the balance sheet.'' Evaluate this statement.

6–7. As part of the verification of accounts receivable as of the balance sheet date, the auditors might inspect copies of sales invoices. Similarly, as part of the verification of accounts payable, the auditors might inspect purchase invoices. Which of these two types of invoices do you think represents the stronger type of evidence? Why?

6–8. In verifying the asset accounts Notes Receivable and Marketable Securities, the auditors examined all notes receivable and all share certificates. Which of these documents represents the stronger type of evidence? Why?

6–9. When in the course of an audit may the auditor find it useful to apply analytical procedures?

6–10. List and briefly describe three approaches to auditing accounting estimates that are included in the financial statements.

6–11. Give at least four examples of *specialists* whose findings might provide appropriate evidence for the external auditors.

6–12. What are the major purposes of obtaining letters of representations from audit clients?

6–13. ''In deciding upon the type of evidence to be gathered in support of a given item on the financial statements, the auditors should not be influenced by the differences in cost of obtaining alternative forms of evidence.'' Do you agree? Explain.

6–14. The cost of an audit might be significantly reduced if the auditors relied upon a representations letter from the client instead of observing the physical counting of inventory. Would this use of a representations letter be an acceptable means of reducing the cost of an audit?

6–15. What are subsequent events?

6–16. List three procedures that the auditors should perform to determine subsequent events.

6–17. List the five factors that the auditors should consider in determining the extent of the audit procedures for subsequent events.

6–18. What are *related party transactions?*

6–19. What disclosures should be made in the financial statements regarding material related party transactions?

6–20. Evaluate the following statement: ''Identifying related parties and obtaining a client letter of representations are two required audit procedures normally performed on or closest to the date of the audit report.''

GROUP II: QUESTIONS REQUIRING ANALYSIS

6–21. When gathering audit evidence, auditors use various types of audit procedures. List 8 of these procedures and provide an example of each.

6–22. Analytical procedures are extremely useful in the initial audit planning stage:

Required:

a. Explain why analytical procedures are considered substantive tests.

b. Explain how analytical procedures are useful in the initial audit planning stage.

c. Should analytical procedures be applied at any other stages of the audit process? Explain.

d. List several types of comparisons an auditor might make in performing analytical procedures.

(AICPA, adapted)

6–23. When analytical procedures disclose unexpected changes in financial relationships relative to prior years, the auditors consider the possible reasons for the changes. Give several possible reasons for the following significant changes in relationships:

a. The rate of inventory turnover (ratio of cost of goods sold to average inventory) has declined from the prior year's rate.

b. The number of days' sales in accounts receivable has increased over the prior year.

(AICPA, adapted)

6–24. Comment on the appropriateness of each of the following examples of audit evidence. Arrange your answer in the form of a separate paragraph for each item. Explain fully the reasoning employed in judging the appropriateness of each item.

     a. Copies of client's sales invoices.

     b. Auditors' independent computation of earnings per share.

     c. Paid cheques returned with a bank statement.

     d. Response from customer of client addressed to auditors' office confirming amount owed to client at balance sheet date.

     e. Letter of representations by the chief financial officer of client company stating that all liabilities of which she has knowledge are reflected in the company's accounts.

6–25. Marshall Land Company owns substantial amounts of farm and timber lands, and consequently property taxes represent one of the more important types of expense. What specific documents or other evidence should the auditors examine in verifying the Property Taxes Expense account?

6–26. One of the assets of Vista Corporation is 6,000 acres of land in a remote area of the Arizona desert. The land is held as a long-term investment and is carried in the accounting records at a cost of $200 per acre. A recent topographical map prepared by the U.S. Soil Conservation Service shows the land to be nearly flat with no standing bodies of water. The land is accessible only by aircraft or four-wheel-drive vehicles. Evaluate the merits of the auditors personally observing this land as a means of obtaining audit evidence.

6–27. Auditors are required on every engagement to obtain a letter of representations from the client.

     Required:

     a. What are the objectives of the client's representations letter?

     b. Who should prepare and sign the client's representations letter?

     c. When should the client's representations letter be obtained?

6–28. What would you accept as satisfactory documentary evidence in support of entries in the following?

     a. Sales journal.

     b. Sales returns register.

     c. Voucher or invoice register.

     d. Payroll register.

     e. Cheque register.

(AICPA, adapted)

6–29. Select the best answer for each of the following questions. Explain the reasons for your selection.

     a. As part of their examination, auditors obtain a letter of representations from their client. Which of the following is *not* a valid purpose of such a letter.

       (1) To increase the efficiency of the audit by eliminating the need for other audit procedures.

     (2) To remind the client's management of its primary responsibility for the financial statements.

     (3) To document in the audit working papers the client's responses to certain verbal inquiries made by the auditors during the engagement.

     (4) To provide evidence in those areas dependent upon management's future intentions.

b. Which of the following statements best describes why auditors investigate related party transactions?

     (1) Related party transactions generally are illegal acts.

     (2) The substance of related party transactions may differ from their form.

     (3) All related party transactions must be eliminated as a step in preparing consolidated financial statements.

     (4) Related party transactions are a form of management fraud.

c. On March 15, the auditor has substantially completed the audit of a client's financial statements for the year ended December 31. On April 1, before the release of the auditor's report, an event occurred that the client and auditor agree should be disclosed in a footnote to the December 31 financial statements. The auditor has not otherwise reviewed events subsequent to the date of the report. The auditor's report should be dated:

     (1) April 1.

     (2) December 31, except for the footnote, which should be dated April 1.

     (3) March 15, except for the footnote, which should be dated April 1.

     (4) March 15.

d. Which event that occurred after the balance sheet date but prior to the release of the auditor's report would not require disclosure in the financial statements?

     (1) Sale of a capital stock issue.

     (2) A significant drop in the quoted market price of the company's capital stock.

     (3) Destruction of a factory as a result of a fire.

     (4) Settlement of litigation when the event giving rise to the claim took place after the balance sheet date.

e. Of the following, which is the *least* persuasive type of audit evidence?

     (1) Confirmations mailed by outsiders to the auditors.

     (2) Correspondence between the auditors and suppliers.

     (3) Copies of sales invoices inspected by the auditors.

     (4) Cancelled cheques returned in the year-end bank statement directly to the client.

f. Analytical procedures are most likely to detect:
   (1) Weaknesses of a material nature in internal control.
   (2) Unusual transactions.
   (3) Noncompliance with prescribed control procedures.
   (4) Improper separation of accounting and other financial duties

(AICPA, adapted)

6–30. John Reed is engaged in the audit of Brooke Corporation. While reviewing the company's notes payable, Reed encounters a three-year, 16 percent note in the amount of $1.5 million payable to Alan Davis, president of Brooke Corporation. The note was issued in conjunction with the purchase of a parcel of commercial real estate from Davis during the current year at a total price of $2.5 million. Discuss the audit significance of these findings and the actions, if any, that Reed should take.

6–31. The auditor's opinion on the fairness of financial statements may be affected by subsequent events.

Required:

a. Define what is commonly referred to in auditing as a subsequent event, and describe the two general types of subsequent events.

b. Identify those auditing procedures that the auditor should apply at or near the date of the audit report to disclose significant subsequent events.

(AICPA, adapted)

6–32. On July 27, 1992, Arthur Ward, CA, issued an unqualified audit report on the financial statements of Dexter Limited for the year ended June 30, 1992. Two weeks later, Dexter mailed annual reports, including the June 30 financial statements and Ward's audit report, to 150 shareholders and to several creditors of Dexter Limited. Dexter Limited's shares are not actively traded on national exchanges or over the counter.

On September 5, the controller of Dexter Limited informed Ward that an account payable for consulting services in the amount of $170,000 had inadvertently been omitted from Dexter's June 30 balance sheet. As a consequence, net income for the year ended June 30 was overstated $90,500, net of applicable income taxes. Both Ward and Dexter's controller agreed that the misstatements were material to Dexter's financial position at June 30, 1992, and operating results for the year then ended.

Required:

What should Arthur Ward's course of action be in this matter? Discuss.

GROUP III: PROBLEMS

6–33. Assume that the auditors find serious weaknesses in the internal control of Oak Canyon, Inc., a producer and distributor of fine wines. Would these internal control weaknesses cause the auditors to rely more or less upon each of the following types of evidence during their audit of Oak Canyon?

   a. Documents created and used only within the organizaton.

   b. Physical evidence.

   c. Evidence provided by specialists.

   d. Analytical procedures.

   e. Accounting records.

   Required:

   For each of the above five items, state your conclusion and explain fully the underlying reasoning.

6–34. The financial statements of Wayne Company indicate that large amounts of notes payable to banks were retired during the period under audit. Evaluate the reliability of each of the following types of evidence supporting these transactions:

   a. Debit entries in the Notes Payable account.

   b. Entries in the cheque register.

   c. Paid cheques.

   d. Notes payable bearing bank perforation stamp PAID and the date of payment.

   e. Statement by client's treasurer that notes had been paid at maturity.

   f. Letter received by auditors directly from bank stating that no indebtedness on part of client existed as of the balance sheet date.

6–35. During your examination of the accounts receivable of Hope Ranch, a new client, you notice that one account is much larger than the rest, and you therefore decide to examine the evidence supporting this customer's account. Comment on the relative reliability and adequacy of the following types of evidence:

   a. Computer printout from accounts receivable subsidiary ledger.

   b. Copies of sales invoices in the amount of the receivable.

   c. Purchase order received from customer.

   d. Shipping document describing the articles sold.

   e. Letter received by client from customer acknowledging the correctness of the receivable in the amount shown on client's accounting records.

   f. Letter received by auditors directly from customer acknowledging the correctness of the amount shown as receivable on client's accounting records.

6–36. Robertson Limited had accounts receivable of $200,000 at December 31, 1991, and had provided an allowance for uncollectible accounts of $6,000. After performing all normal auditing procedures relating to the receivables and to the valuation allowance, the external auditors were satisfied that this asset was fairly stated and that the allowance for uncollectible accounts was adequate. Just before completion of the audit work late in February, however, the auditors learned that the entire plant of Thompson Corporation, a major customer, had been destroyed by a flood early in February and that as a result Thompson Corporation was hopelessly insolvent.

The account receivable from Thompson Corporation in the amount of $44,000 originated on December 28; terms of payment were net 60 days. The receivable had been regarded as entirely collectible at December 31, and the auditors had so considered it in reaching their conclusion as to the adequacy of the allowance for uncollectible accounts. In discussing the news concerning the flood, the controller of Robertson Limited emphasized to the auditors that the probable loss of $44,000 should be regarded as a loss of the following year, 1992 and not of 1991, the year under audit.

What action, if any, should the auditors recommend with respect to the receivable from Thompson Corporation?

6–37. In connection with your examination of the financial statements of Hollis Mfg. Corporation for the year ended December 31, 1993, your review of subsequent events disclosed the following items:

(1) January 7, 1994. The mineral content of a shipment of ore en route to Hollis Mfg. Corporation on December 31, 1993, was determined to be 72 percent. The shipment was recorded at year-end at an estimated content of 50 percent by a debit to Raw Materials Inventory and a credit to accounts payable in the amount of $82,400. The final liability to the vendor is based on the actual mineral content of the shipment.

(2) January 15, 1994: Culminating a series of personal disagreements between Ray Hollis, the president, and his brother-in-law, the treasurer, the latter resigned, effective immediately, under an agreement whereby the corporation would purchase his 10 percent share ownership at book value as of December 31, 1993. Payment is to be made in two equal amounts in cash on April 1 and October 1, 1994. In December, the treasurer had obtained a divorce from his wife, who is Ray Hollis's sister.

(3) January 31, 1994: As a result of reduced sales, production was

curtailed in mid-January and some workers were laid off. On February 5, 1994, all the remaining workers went on strike. To date the strike is unsettled.

Required:
Assume that the above items came to your attention before the date of your audit report on Feburary 15, 1994. For each of the above items, discuss the disclosure that you would recommend for the item, listing all details that you would suggest should be disclosed. Indicate those items or details, if any, that should not be disclosed. Give your reasons for recommending or not recommending disclosure of the items or details.

(AICPA, adapted)

6–38. One of the examination standards requires the auditor to obtain sufficient appropriate audit evidence to afford a reasonable basis to support the content of his or her report.

Required:
a. Identify the general source of audit evidence available to the auditor.
b. Comment on the degree of reliance that the auditor may place on evidence originating from each source.
c. Give an example of the type of evidence that would originate from each source.
   Arrange your answers in the following format:

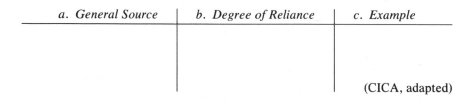

a. General Source	*b. Degree of Reliance*	*c. Example*

(CICA, adapted)

6–39. In the examination of financial statements, auditors must judge the validity of the audit evidence they obtain.

Required:
Assume that the auditors have considered internal control and found it satisfactory.
a. In the course of examination, the auditors ask many questions of client officers and employees.
   (1) Describe the factors that the auditors should consider in evaluating oral evidence provided by client officers and employees.
   (2) Discuss the validity and limitations of oral evidence.

> *b.* Analytical procedures include the computation of various balance sheet and operating ratios for comparison to prior years and industry averages. Discuss the validity and limitations of ratio analysis as evidence.
>
> *c.* In connection with an examination of the financial statements of a manufacturing company, the auditors are observing the physical inventory of finished goods, which consists of expensive, highly complex electronic equipment. Discuss the validity and limitations of the audit evidence provided by this procedure.

(AICPA, adapted)

6–40.   In connection with her examination of the financial statements of Flowmeter Inc. for the year ended December 31, 1993, Joan Hirsch, CA, is aware that certain events and transactions that took place after December 31, 1993, but before she issues her report dated February 28, 1994, may affect the company's financial statements.

The following material events or transactions have come to her attention:

a. On January 3, 1994, Flowmeter Inc. received a shipment of raw materials from the United States. The materials had been ordered in October 1993 and shipped FOB shipping point in November 1993.

b. On January 15, 1994, the company settled and paid a personal injury claim of a former employee as the result of an accident that had occurred in March 1993. The company had not previously recorded a liability for the claim.

c. On January 25, 1994, the company agreed to purchase for cash the outstanding stock of Porter Electrical Co. The business combination is likely to double the sales volume of Flowmeter Inc.

d. On February 1, 1994, a plant owned by Flowmeter Inc. was damaged by a flood, resulting in an uninsured loss of inventory.

e. On February 5, 1994, Flowmeter Inc. issued to an underwriting syndicate $2 million in convertible bonds.

Required:
For each of the above items, indicate how the event or transaction should be reflected in Flowmeter's financial statements and explain the reasons for selecting this method of disclosure.

(AICPA, adapted)

6–41.   CA is the auditor of F. Ltd., which has a December 31 year-end. On February 15, CA is in the process of finalizing his auditor's report dated January 31, 1993, when he becomes aware of a subsequent event which occurred on February 10, 1993, CA's investigation shows that the event did occur and it is material. However, management prefers not to disclose the subsequent event.

Required:
What factors should CA take into account before signing and releasing his report?

(CICA, adapted)

GROUP IV: ANALYTICAL AND DISCUSSION CASE

6–42. The existence of risk is implicit in the phrase "in our opinion" which appears in the auditors' standard report. The auditors accept some risk that the audit opinion rendered may be in error. In planning and executing an audit, the auditors strive to reduce this risk to a level that is acceptable to the client and the public.

The auditors do this by obtaining sufficient appropriate audit evidence as required by generally accepted auditing standards. However, specific guidelines as to what constitutes "sufficient appropriate audit evidence" have not yet been fully developed by the profession.

Required:
a. Identify the key issues raised by listing them in a logical manner.
b. Discuss the judgmental and risk factors and their relationship with what constitutes "sufficient appropriate audit evidence."

(CICA, adapted)

Chapter 7

Internal Control

After studying this chapter, you should be able to:

- Define internal control for a business.
- Describe the major components of a client's internal control: the overall control environment, the control systems consisting of the accounting system and control procedures.
- Explain the characteristics of effective internal control.
- Describe the auditors' consideration of internal control.
- Explain the techniques used by auditors to obtain an understanding of internal control and describe the results in their working papers.
- Explain how the auditors assess control risk and the related audit strategy.
- Describe the auditors' responsibility for communication of internal control weakness to client.

The second examination standard states:

> A sufficient understanding of internal control should be obtained to plan the audit. When control risk is assessed below maximum, sufficient appropriate audit evidence should be obtained through tests of control to support the assessment.

Our consideration of internal control in this chapter has three major objectives: first, to explain the meaning and significance of internal control; second, to discuss the major components of a client's internal control; and third, to show how auditors go about obtaining an understanding of internal control to meet the requirements of the second examination standard. No attempt is made in this chapter to present in detail the internal control procedures applicable to particular kinds of assets or to particular types of transactions, such as purchases or sales. Detailed information along those lines will be found in succeeding chapters as each phase of the audit is presented.

As discussed in Chapter 1, internal control has attained greatest significance in large-scale business organizations. Accordingly, the greater part of the discussion in this chapter is presented in terms of the large corporation. A separate section is presented at the end of the chapter, however, dealing with the problem of achieving internal control in a small business.

The Meaning of Internal Control

Many people interpret the term *internal control* as the measures taken by a business to prevent employee fraud. Actually, such measures are only a part of internal control. In the broadest sense, an organization's internal control (also referred to as *internal control structure* or *system*) consists of the policies and procedures established to provide *reasonable assurance* that the *organization's objectives* will be achieved.[1] The concept of *reasonable assurance* recognizes that no internal control is perfect and that the cost of an entity's internal control should not exceed the benefits expected to be derived. As one might expect, when considering internal control, an *organization's objectives* include safeguarding assets and providing reliable, timely financial information. But internal control extends beyond the accounting and financial functions; its scope is companywide and touches all activities of the organization. It includes the methods by which top management delegates authority and assigns responsibility for such functions as selling, purchasing, accounting, and production. Internal control also includes the program for preparing, verifying, and distributing to various levels of management those current reports and analyses that enable executives to maintain control over the variety of activities and functions that constitute a large corporate enterprise. The use of budgetary techniques, production standards, inspection laboratories, time and motion studies, and employee training programs involves engineers and many others far removed from accounting and financial activities; yet all of these devices are part of the mechanism referred to as internal control.

Business Corporations Legislation and Internal Control

As discussed in Chapter 4, Section 20 of the Canada Business Corporations Act requires corporations to maintain certain corporate records such as bylaws and minutes as well as "adequate accounting records." Section

---

[1] *CICA Handbook* section 5200.03 defines internal control as consisting "of the policies and procedures established and maintained by management to assist in achieving its objective of ensuring, as far as practical, the orderly and efficient conduct of the entity's business."

22(2) of the act further requires corporations to take "reasonable precautions to (*a*) prevent loss or destruction of, (*b*) prevent falsification of entries in, and (*c*) facilitate detection and correction of inaccuracies in . . . other records." Thus, a strong internal control, long considered vital to the operation of a business organization, is recognized by business corporations legislation.

Similarly, federal legislation in the United States requires corporations under its jurisdiction to have a strong internal control, mainly as a result of certain actions taken by corporations which were regarded as either illegal or unethical. In the mid-1970s, a number of American corporations acknowledged having made payments (which could be interpreted as bribes) to officials in foreign countries. In most cases, the payments were legal under the laws of the countries in which they were made, but they were not in accordance with American standards of business ethics. In some instances, these questionable payments were made without the authorization or knowledge of top executives of the corporations involved.

In the Foreign Corrupt Practices Act of 1977, the U.S. Congress ordered an end to this practice. Payments to foreign officials for the purpose of securing business were specifically prohibited. However, the act goes far beyond the issue of illegal payments and requires *every corporation under the jurisdiction of the SEC to maintain a system of internal accounting control that will provide reasonable assurance that transactions are executed only with the knowledge and authorization of management.* In addition, the act requires the system of internal control to limit the use of corporate assets to those purposes approved by management. Finally, the act calls for accounting records to be reconciled at reasonable intervals with assets actually on hand. These requirements are designed to prevent the creation of secret slush funds or other misuses of corporate resources. Violations of the act can result in fines up to $1 million and imprisonment of the responsible individuals. Since Canadian companies listed on the U.S. stock exchanges are subject to the SEC regulations, the Foreign Corrupt Practices Act will affect these Canadian companies as well.

Means of Achieving Internal Control

Internal control structures or systems vary significantly from one organization to the next. The specific control features used depend upon such factors as the size, nature of operations, and objectives of the organization for which the structure or system was designed. Yet certain features are essential to satisfactory internal control in almost any large-scale organization. For purposes of financial statement audits, the relevant features are generally those that pertain to the entity's ability to *collect, record, process,* and *report* financial information or data. These features may be divided into three elements: (1) the *control environment,* (2) the *accounting system,* and (3) *control procedures.*[2]

CONTROL ENVIRONMENT

The control environment is the collective effect of various overall factors that establish, enhance, or reduce the effectiveness of specific control policies and procedures. The control environment reflects the overall attitude, awareness, commitment, and actions of the board of directors, management, owners, and others concerning the importance of control and the way it is used in the entity. Control environment factors include management's philosophy and operating style; function of the board of directors and its committees, particularly the audit committee; the company's organizational structure; systems development methodology; personnel policies and practices; methods of assigning authority and responsibility; management control methods; an internal audit function; and management reaction to external influences.

Management Philosophy and Operating Style

Managements differ in both their philosophies toward financial reporting and their attitudes toward taking business risks. Some managements are extremely aggressive in financial reporting and place great emphasis on meeting or exceeding earnings projections. They may be willing to undertake activities with high risk on the prospects of high returns. Other managements are extremely conservative and risk averse. These differing philosophies and operating styles may have an impact on the overall reliability of the financial statements. Therefore, this factor is important to the auditors' assessment of the entity's control environment.

Function of Board of Directors and Its Committees, Particularly the Audit Committee

The manner in which the board of directors and its audit committee perceive and carry out their respective functions can affect the operating management's attitude and behaviour in many areas, including business activities and financial reporting. Thus, an active board of directors and a strong audit committee can be an important and integral part of the control environment. Not only can the board play its proper role in planning and overseeing business activities and financial reporting; it can also reduce

---

[2] As noted earlier in the chapter, the accounting system and control procedures together are also called the "control systems."

the risk of material misstatement that may be associated with a dominant management.

As discussed in Chapter 4, an audit committee is composed of members of the board of directors, the majority of whom are neither officers nor employees of the client organization. Because of this independence from management, audit committees help maintain a direct line of communication between the board of directors and the entity's external and internal auditors. They also monitor top management of the organization by overseeing the accounting and financial reporting policies and practices, serving as a deterrent to management override of the established internal controls or to the commission of fraud by management.

Organizational Structure

Another control environment factor is the entity's organizational structure. A well-designed organizational structure provides a basis for planning, directing, and controlling operations. It divides authority, responsibilities, and duties among members of an organization by dealing with such issues as centralized versus decentralized decision making and appropriate segregation of duties among the various departments. When management decision making is centralized and dominated by one individual, that individual's moral character is extremely important to the auditors. When a decentralized style is used, procedures to monitor the decision making of the many managers involved become more important.

Illustrative Case

During an examination of Foster Limited, the auditors' study of organizational lines of authority and their use of an internal control questionnaire disclosed that the receiving department personnel were under the direction of the purchasing agent. Accounts payable department employees had also been instructed to accept informal memoranda from the purchasing agent as evidence of receipt of merchandise and propriety of invoices.

Because of this deficiency in internal control, the auditors made a very thorough examination of purchase invoices and came across a number of large December invoices from one supplier bearing this notation: "Subject to adjustment at time of delivery of merchandise." Investigation of these transactions disclosed that the merchandise had not yet been delivered, but the invoices had been paid. The purchasing agent explained that he had requested the advance billing in an effort to reduce taxable income for the year under audit, during which profits had been higher than usual. Further investigation revealed that the purchasing agent held a substantial personal interest in the supplier making the advance billings, and that top management of the client company was not aware of this conflict of interest.

Organizational responsibilities should be segregated so as to separate responsibilities for (1) *authorization* of transactions, (2) *recordkeeping* for transactions, and (3) *custody* of assets. In addition, to the extent possible, *execution* of the *operation* involved should be segregated from these responsibilities. The effectiveness of such structure is usually obtained by having designated department heads who are evaluated on the basis of the performance of their respective departments. The top executives of the major departments should be of equal rank and should report directly to the president or to an executive vice president. The partial organization chart in Figure 7–1 illustrates such an arrangement. If, for example, the controller were a line subordinate to the vice president of production, the organizational independence of the accounting department would be greatly impaired.

Responsibilities of Finance and Accounting Departments. Finance and accounting are the two departments most directly involved in the financial affairs of a business enterprise. The division of responsibilities between these departments illustrates the separation of the accounting function from operations and also from the custody of assets. Under the direction of the *treasurer,* the finance department is responsible for financial operations and custody of liquid assets. Activities of this department include planning future cash requirements, establishing customer credit policies, and arranging to meet the short- and long-term financing needs of the business. In addition, the finance department has custody of bank accounts and other liquid assets, invests idle cash, handles cash receipts, and makes cash disbursements. In short, the finance department *conducts* financial activities.

The accounting department, under the authority of the *controller,* is responsible for all accounting functions and the design and implementation of internal control. With respect to financial activity, the accounting department *records* financial transactions but does not handle financial assets. Accounting records establish *accountability* over assets, as well as provide the information necessary for financial reports, tax returns, and daily operating decisions. With respect to internal control, the accounting department maintains the independent records with which quantities of assets and operating results are compared. Often, this reconciliation function is performed by the *operations control group* or some other subdepartment within accounting.

Many of the subdepartments often found within accounting are illustrated in figure 7–1. It is important for many of these subdepartments to be relatively independent of one another. For example, if the operations control group reconcile assets on hand to the accounting records, it is essential that the operations control personnel not maintain those records.

FIGURE 7–1 Partial Organization Chart

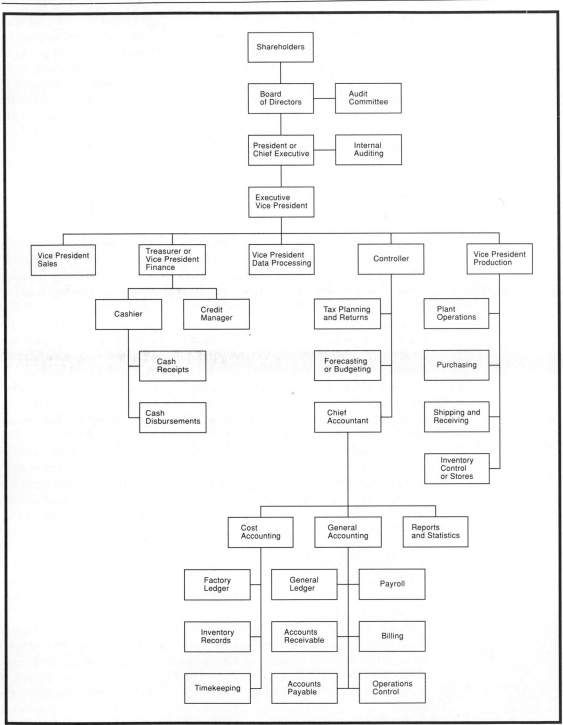

Systems Development Methodology

The methods by which the systems are developed, established, monitored, and modified affect the control environment. When the appropriate methodologies are used to develop, establish, use, and monitor the systems and procedures, the resulting financial information is likely to be more relevant, reliable, and timely. Also, difficulties and problems arising from these systems and procedures can usually be anticipated or at least corrected on a more timely basis.

Personnel Policies and Practices

Ultimately, the effectiveness of an internal control environment is affected by the characteristics of its personnel. Thus, personnel management policies and practices for hiring, training, evaluating, promoting, and compensating employees have a significant effect on the effectiveness of the control environment. Effective personnel policies and practices often can enhance the effectiveness of specific policies and procedures or mitigate other weaknesses in the control environment.

When employees of the organization have a high degree of integrity and competence and a good knowledge of the established policies and procedures, they will perform their duties with care and understanding. The personnel policies and practices should ensure that only individuals with competence and integrity are hired and that they are assigned responsibilities commensurate with their qualifications. Also, they should be given the resources necessary to carry out their assigned responsibilities. For example, they should be given an opportunity to secure an understanding of the policies and procedures relating to their positions so that errors and misunderstandings can be minimized.

Fidelity Bonds. Effective personnel management is not a guarantee against losses from dishonest employees. It is often the most trusted employees who engineer large embezzlements. The fact that they are so highly trusted explains why they have access to cash, securities, and company records and are in a position that makes embezzlement possible.

Fidelity bonds are a form of insurance in which a bonding company agrees to reimburse an employer, within limits, for losses attributable to theft or embezzlement by bonded employees. Most employers require employees handling cash or other negotiable assets to be bonded. Individual fidelity bonds may be obtained by concerns with only a few employees; larger concerns may prefer to obtain a blanket fidelity bond covering many employees. Before issuing fidelity bonds, underwriters investigate thoroughly the past records of the employees to be bonded. This service offers added protection by preventing the employment of persons with dubious records in positions of trust. Bonding companies are much more likely to prosecute fraud cases vigorously than are employers; general awareness of this fact is another deterrent against dishonesty on the part of bonded employees.

Methods of Assigning Authority and Responsibility

Personnel within an organization need to have a clear understanding of their responsibilities and the rules and regulations that govern their actions. Therefore, to enhance the control environment, management develops employee job descriptions, computer systems documentation, and clearly defines authority and responsibility within the enterprise. Policies also may be established regarding such matters as acceptable business practices, conflicts of interest, and codes of conduct.

Management Control Methods

Management control methods are used to exercise control over the authority delegated to others. Such methods involve developing plans and monitoring the progress towards accomplishment of those plans. A financial forecast and budgeting system is a prime example of a management control method. A financial forecast for an enterprise is an estimate of the expected financial position, results of operations, and cash flows for one or more future periods. It establishes definite goals, providing management with a yardstick for evaluating and controlling actual performance. During the year, monthly reports may be prepared comparing actual operating results with forecast figures. These reports should be accompanied by explanations of all significant variations between forecast and actual results, with a definite fixing of responsibility for such variances.

Internal Audit

Another basic component of the control environment is an internal auditing staff. Internal auditors investigate and appraise the internal control and the efficiency with which the various units of the business are performing their assigned functions, and they report their findings and recommendations to top management. As representatives of top management, the internal auditors are interested in determining whether each branch or department has a clear understanding of its assignment, is adequately staffed, maintains good records, protects cash and inventories and other assets properly, cooperates harmoniously with other departments, and in general carries out effectively its designated function. The manner in which the external auditors use the work of internal auditors is discussed later in this chapter; the internal auditing profession is discussed in Chapter 20.

Management Reaction to External Influences

As mentioned earlier in this chapter, the Canadian Business Corporations Act requires corporations to establish and maintain internal control over their accounting records. Also, other legislative and regulatory bodies impose compliance and monitoring requirements on corporations; for example, bank regulatory agency examinations are imposed on banks. These external influences may have a positive impact on management's consciousness and attitude in conducting and reporting the corporation's operations. Moreover, these influences may encourage management to establish certain policies and procedures to improve the control environment.

THE ACCOUNTING SYSTEM

The accounting system consists of the methods and records established to identify, assemble, analyze, classify, record, and report an entity's transactions and to maintain accountability for the related assets and liabilities. An accounting system should include methods and records to accomplish the following objectives:

1. Identify and record all valid transactions.
2. Describe on a timely basis the transactions in sufficient detail to permit proper classification of transactions for financial reporting.
3. Measure the value of transactions in a manner that permits recording their proper monetary value in the financial statements.
4. Determine the time period in which transactions occurred to permit recording of transactions in the proper accounting period.
5. Present properly the transactions and related disclosures in the financial statements.

In addition to the typical system of journals, ledgers, and other recordkeeping devices, an accounting system should include a chart of accounts and a manual of accounting policies and procedures. A *chart of accounts* is a classified listing of all accounts in use, accompanied by a detailed description of the purpose and content of each. A *manual of accounting policies and procedures* states clearly in writing the methods of initiating, authorizing, recording, and summarizing transactions. In combination, the chart of accounts and manual of accounting policies and procedures should allow proper and uniform handling of transactions.

CONTROL PROCEDURES

In addition to the control environment and the accounting system, management establishes other controls over particular types of transactions and assets. While there are many specific control procedures that may be implemented by a company, they may be categorized as procedures for (1) proper authorization of transactions and activities, (2) appropriate segregation of duties, (3) adequate documentation and recording of transactions and events, (4) effective safeguards over access to and use of *assets* and *records,* and (5) independent checks on performance and proper valuation of recorded amounts.

Authorization of Transactions

Authorization of transactions may be either general or specific. *General authorization* occurs when management establishes criteria for acceptance of a certain type of transaction. For example, top management may establish general price lists and credit policies for new customers. Transactions with customers that meet these criteria may be *approved* by the credit department. *Specific authorization* occurs when transactions are authorized on an individual basis. For example, top management may consider individually and specifically authorize any sales transaction in excess of a specified amount, say $100,000.

Segregation of Duties

A fundamental concept of internal control is that *no one department or person* should handle all aspects of a transaction from beginning to end. We have already discussed the segregation of responsibilities among departments. In a similar manner, no individual should perform more than one of the functions of *authorizing* transactions, *recording* transactions, and maintaining *custody* over assets. Also, to the extent possible, individuals performing the specific *operation* should be segregated from these functions. The goal is to reduce the opportunities to allow any person to be in a position to both perpetrate and conceal errors or fraud in the normal course of his or her duties.

A credit sales transaction may be used to illustrate appropriate authorization and segregation procedures. Top management may have generally authorized the sale of merchandise at specified credit terms to customers who meet certain requirements. The credit department may approve the sales transactions after ascertaining that the extension of credit and terms of sale are in compliance with company policies. Once the sale is approved, the shipping department performs the operation by obtaining custody of the merchandise from the inventory stores department and shipping it to the customer. The accounting department uses copies of the documentation created by the sales, credit, and shipping departments as a basis for recording the transaction and billing the customer. With this segregation of duties, no one department or individual can initiate and execute an unauthorized transaction.

Adequate Documentation

A system of well-designed forms and documents is necessary to create a record of the activities of all departments. In the case of a credit sales transaction, the accounting department receives copies of internal documents prepared by the sales, credit, and shipping departments to properly record the transaction.

An internal control device of wide applicability is the use of serial numbers on documents. Serial numbers provide control over the number of documents issued. Cheques, tickets, sales invoices, purchase orders, shipping reports, stock certificates, and many other business papers can be controlled in this manner. For some documents, such as cheques, it may be desirable to account for the sequence used, by a monthly or weekly inspection of the documents issued. For other documents, as in the case of serially numbered admission tickets, control may be achieved by noting the last serial number issued each day, and thereby computing the total value of tickets issued during the day. Adequate safeguarding and numerical control should be maintained at all times for unissued prenumbered documents.

Safeguards over Assets and Records

Only properly authorized individuals should be allowed access to the company's assets. Direct physical access to assets may be controlled through the use of safes, locks, fences, and guards. Improper indirect access to assets, generally accomplished by falsifying financial records, must also be controlled. This may be accomplished by securing documents, accounting records, and computer data files and monitoring their use.

Illustrative Case

A manufacturer of golf clubs operated a large storeroom containing thousands of sets of golf clubs ready for shipment. Detailed perpetual inventory records were maintained by the employee in charge of the storeroom. A shortage of several sets of clubs developed as a result of theft by another employee who had acquired an unauthorized key to the storeroom. The employee responsible for the storeroom discovered the discrepancy between the clubs in stock and the quantities of clubs as shown by the records. Fearing criticism of his record-keeping, he changed the inventory records to agree with the quantities on hand. The thefts continued, and large losses were sustained before the shortages were discovered. If the inventory records had been maintained by someone not responsible for physical custody of the merchandise, there would have been no incentive or opportunity to conceal a shortage by falsifying the records.

Independent Checks on Performance and Proper Valuation

The accuracy of the work of various individuals in a company may be verified by independent checks on performance and valuation such as clerical checks, computer program controls, independent review reports, and reconciliations. When the accounting and custodial departments are relatively independent, the work of each department serves to verify the accuracy of the work of the other. Periodic comparisons should be made of accounting records and the physical assets on hand. Investigation as to the cause of any discrepancies will uncover weakness either in procedures for safeguarding assets or in maintaining the related accounting records. If the accounting records were not independent of the custodial department, the records could be manipulated to conceal waste, loss, or theft of the related assets.

Figure 7–2 illustrates the use of an independently maintained record to establish accountability for assets. It is not essential that *all three* parties in the diagram (A, B, and C) be employees of the company; one or more may be an outside party or a mechanical device. For example, if A is a bank with custody of cash on deposit, B would be the company employees maintaining records of cash receipts and disbursements, and C might be a computer program that performs periodic bank reconciliations. Or, if A is a salesclerk with custody of cash receipts from sales, B could be a cash

FIGURE 7–2   Establishing Accountability for Assets

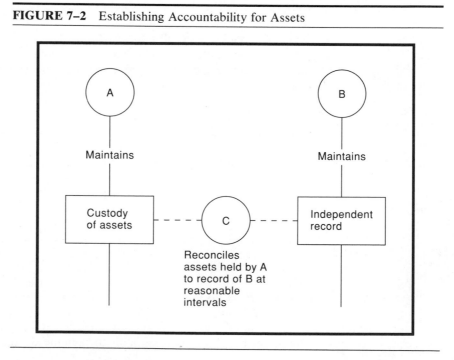

register with a locked-in tape, and C could be the departmental supervisor. Regardless of the nature of the parties involved, the principle remains the same: accounting records should be maintained independently of custody of the related assets and should be compared at reasonable intervals to asset quantities on hand.

Limitations of Internal Control

Internal control can do much to protect against both error and fraud and assure the reliability of financial data. Still, it is important to recognize the existence of inherent limitations in any internal control. Errors may be made in the performance of control procedures as a result of carelessness, misunderstanding of instructions, or other human factors. Without active participation in management by the board of directors and an effective internal audit department, top management can easily override internal control. Also, those control procedures dependent upon separation of duties may be circumvented by collusion among employees. Moreover, most controls tend to be directed at regularly recurring types of transactions, and the efficiency of controls may vary with volume of transactions or changes of staff. Finally, the extent of the internal controls adopted by a business is limited by cost considerations. It is not feasible from a cost standpoint to establish a control system that provides absolute protection from fraud, errors, and waste; *reasonable assurance* in this regard is the best that generally can be achieved.

THE AUDITORS' CONSIDERATION OF INTERNAL CONTROL

The second examination standard requires the auditors to obtain a sufficient understanding of internal control to plan the audit, to assess control risks, and to determine the nature, timing and extent of substantive procedures or tests to be performed. Thus, the auditors' understanding of their clients' internal control provides a basis both (1) to *plan* the audit and (2) to *assess control risk*. However, the auditors consideration of internal control is very complex. Figure 7–3 is a flowchart that highlights the major steps in the auditors' consideration of internal control, including the planning and assessing processes.

In planning an audit, it is essential that the auditors have a sufficient understanding of the client's control environment, accounting system, and control procedures. This understanding encompasses both the *design* of policies, procedures, and records, and a knowledge of whether they have been *placed in operation* by the client. With this knowledge the auditors are able to (1) identify the types of potential misstatements of the financial statements, (2) consider factors that affect the risk of material misstatements, and (3) design effective substantive tests of the financial statement balances. It is difficult to imagine designing tests of financial

FIGURE 7–3 The Auditors' Consideration of Internal Control

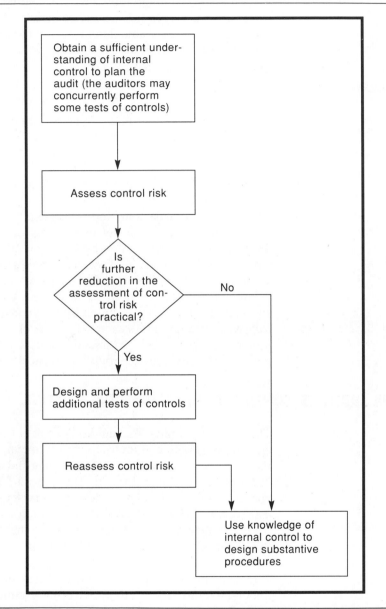

statement balances without an understanding of internal control. For example, auditors who do not understand the client's policies and procedures for executing and recording credit sales would have a difficult time substantiating the balances of accounts receivable and sales.

The auditors' understanding of internal control also provides a basis for their assessment of control risk—the risk that material misstatements will not be prevented or detected by the client's internal control. If the auditors determine that the client's internal control is effective, they will assess control risk to be low. The auditors can then accept a higher level of detection risk, and substantive testing can be decreased. Conversely, if internal controls are weak, control risk is high and the auditors must increase the extent of their substantive tests to limit the level of detection risk. Therefore, the auditors' understanding of internal control is a major factor in determining the nature, extent, and timing of substantive procedures necessary to verify the financial statement assertions.

Since adequate internal control is a major factor in an audit, the question arises as to what action the auditors should take when internal control is found to be seriously deficient. Can the auditors complete a satisfactory audit and properly express an opinion on the fairness of financial statements of a company in which control risk is considered to be extremely high? The answer to this question depends on whether the auditors believe that inherent risk is at a satisfactory level so that substantive procedures can be designed that will reduce audit risk to an acceptable level. For example, the auditors of a small business with a limited segregation of duties often rely largely upon an approach of restricting detection risk through substantive tests of financial statement assertions, rather than relying on tests of internal control.

Obtain an Understanding of Internal Control

In every audit, the auditors must obtain an understanding of internal control sufficient to plan the audit—this includes an understanding of the control environment, the accounting system, and control procedures.

Control Environment.   The auditors must obtain sufficient knowledge to understand management's and the board of directors' attitudes, awareness, commitment, and actions concerning the control environment. It is important that the auditors concentrate on the substance of controls, rather than their form. For example, a budgetary reporting system may provide reports, but the reports may not be analyzed and acted upon by management.

Accounting System.   To understand the accounting system the auditors must first understand the major types of transactions engaged in by the entity. Next, the auditors must become familiar with the treatment of those transactions, including how they are initiated, the related accounting records, and the manner of processing the transactions. Finally, the auditors must understand the financial reporting process used to prepare the financial statements, including the approaches used to make accounting estimates and disclosure.

Control Procedures. While obtaining an understanding of the control environment and the accounting system, the auditors will generally obtain some information about the client's control procedures. For example, while obtaining an understanding of documents relating to cash transactions, it is likely that the auditors will discover whether the bank accounts are reconciled. Auditors must use their judgment as to whether it is necessary to devote additional attention to obtaining an understanding of other control procedures.

The auditors may need to understand and test specific control procedures to audit certain assertions. For example, when auditing a charitable organization that receives significant cash donations, the auditors may be unable to effectively plan the audit for the completeness assertion for cash contributions without understanding and testing control procedures related to cash receipts. For other assertions, the auditors may conclude that it would be too costly to audit the assertions and thus may use only substantive procedures.

Transaction Cycles. In obtaining an understanding of the client's accounting system and the related control procedures, auditors generally find it useful to subdivide the overall system into its major transaction cycles. The term *transaction cycle* refers to the policies and the sequence of procedures for processing a particular type of transaction. For example, the accounting system in a manufacturing business might be subdivided into the following major transaction cycles:

1. *Sales and collection cycle*—including procedures and policies for obtaining orders from customers, approving credit, shipping merchandise, preparing sales invoices, recording revenue and accounts receivable, billing, and handling and recording cash receipts.
2. *Purchase or acquisition cycle*—including procedures for initiating purchases of inventory, other assets, or services; placing purchase orders; inspecting goods upon receipt and preparing receiving reports; recording liabilities to vendors; authorizing payment; and making and recording cash disbursements.
3. *Production cycle*—including procedures for storing materials, placing materials into production, assigning production costs to inventories, and accounting for the cost of goods sold.
4. *Payroll cycle*—including procedures for hiring, firing, and determining pay rates; timekeeping; computing gross payroll, payroll taxes, and amounts withheld from gross pay; maintaining payroll records and preparing and distributing paycheques.
5. *Financing cycle*—including procedures for authorizing, executing, and recording transactions involving bank loans, leases, bonds payable, and capital stock.

The transaction cycles within a particular company depend upon the nature of the company's business activities. A bank, for example, has no production cycle, but has both a lending cycle and a demand deposits cycle. Also, different auditors may elect to define a given company's transaction cycles in different ways. For example, the sales and collection cycle may alternatively be defined as two separate transaction cycles for (1) the processing and recording of credit sales and (2) the handling and recording of cash receipts. The important point to recognize is that subdividing internal control into transaction cycles enables the auditor to focus upon the internal control procedures that affect the reliability of specific assertions in the financial statements.

Sources of Information about Internal Control.   How do auditors gain an understanding of the client's internal control? Auditors obtain information about internal control by *enquiry* of appropriate client personnel, *inspecting* various entity documents and records, and *observing* control activities and operations as they are performed. In repeat engagements, their investigation for the current year will stress areas shown as having questionable controls in prior years. It is imperative, however, that auditors recognize that the pattern of operations in an ever-changing one—internal controls that were adequate last year may now be obsolete.

Auditors may ascertain the duties and responsibilities of client personnel by inspecting organization charts and job descriptions, and interviewing client personnel. Many clients have procedures manuals and flowcharts describing the approved practices to be followed in all phases of operations. Another excellent source of information is in the reports, working papers, and audit programs of the client's internal auditing staff.

The auditors' understanding of internal control encompasses not only the design of the policies and procedures, but also whether they have been placed in operation. The term *placed in operation* means that the policy or procedure actually exists and is in use; that is, it does not just exist in theory or on paper.

While obtaining an understanding of internal control, the auditors may also obtain information on the operating effectiveness of various controls. *Operating effectiveness* deals with (1) how a control is applied, (2) the consistency with which it is applied; and (3) by whom. The distinction between knowing that a control has been *placed in operation* and obtaining evidence on its *operating effectiveness* is important. To properly plan the audit, auditors *are* required to determine that the major controls have been placed in operation; they *are not* required to evaluate their operating effectiveness. However, if the auditors wish to assess control risk at a level lower than the maximum, they must have evidence of the operating effectiveness of the controls. This evidence is obtained by performing *tests of controls,* which are discussed later in this chapter.

As the external auditors obtain a working knowledge of internal control to plan the audit, they must document the information in their working papers. The form and extent of this documentation is affected by the size and complexity of the client, as well as the nature of the client's internal control. The documentation usually takes the form of internal control questionnaires, written narratives, or flowcharts.

Internal Control Questionnaire. The traditional method of describing internal control is to fill in a standardized internal control questionnaire. Many public accounting firms have developed their own questionnaires for this purpose. The questionnaire usually contains a separate section for each major transaction cycle, enabling the work of completing the questionnaire to be divided conveniently among several audit staff members.

Most internal control questionnaires are designed so that a "no" answer to a question indicates a weakness in internal control. In addition, questionnaires may provide for a distinction between major and minor control weaknesses, indication of the sources of information used in answering questions, and explanatory comments regarding control deficiencies. Thus, these questionnaires have the advantage of highlighting the weaknesses. Other advantages are that they are comprehensive and easy to complete. A disadvantage of standardized internal control questionnaires is their lack of flexibility. They often contain many questions that are "not applicable" to specific systems, particularly systems for small companies. To compensate for this, many accounting firms have a separate internal control questionnaire for small companies. Also, the situation in which an internal control strength compensates for a weakness in the system is not obvious from examining a completed questionnaire. An internal control questionnaire relating to cash receipts is illustrated in Figure 7–4.

Written Narrative of Internal Control. An internal control questionnaire is intended as a means for the auditors to document their understanding of internal control. If completion of the questionnaire is regarded as an end in itself, there may be a tendency for the auditors to fill in the "yes" and "no" answers in a mechanical manner, without any real understanding or study of the problem. For this reason, some public accounting firms prefer to use written narratives or flowcharts in lieu of, or in conjunction with, questionnaires. Also, written narratives are tailor-made for the client's system and require a penetrating analysis of the system. Written narratives usually follow the flow of each major transaction cycle, identifying the employees performing various tasks, documents prepared, records maintained, and the division of duties. Figure 7–5 is a written narrative, describing internal control over cash receipts.

Flowcharts of Internal Control. Many public accounting firms now consider *systems flowcharts* to be more effective than questionnaires or narrative descriptions in developing an understanding of a client's data process-

FIGURE 7–4

INTERNAL CONTROL QUESTIONNAIRE
CASH RECEIPTS - SALES CYCLE

Client *Bennington Co., Inc.*   Audit Date *December 31, 199X*

Names and Positions of Client Personnel Interviewed:
Lorraine Martin - Cashier; Helen Ellis - head bookkeeper; Wm. Dale - Manager

QUESTION	NOT APPL.	YES	NO	MAJOR	MINOR	REMARKS
1. Are all persons receiving or disbursing cash bonded?		✓				*H. Ellis is head bookkeeper*
2. Is all incoming mail opened by a responsible employee who does not have access to accounting records?			✓	✓		*See mitigating control in #13*
3. Does the employee assigned to opening of incoming mail prepare a list of all cheques and money received?			✓		✓	
4. a) Is a copy of the listing of mail receipts forwarded to the accounts receivable department for comparison with the credits to customers' accounts?	✓					
b) Is a copy of this list turned over to an employee other than the cashier for comparison with the cash receipts records?	✓					
5. Are receipts from cash sales and other over-the-counter collections recorded by sales registers, point-of-sale terminals, and serially numbered receipts?	✓					
6. Are the daily totals of cash registers or other mechanical devices verified by an employee not having access to cash?	✓					
7. Are physical facilities and mechanical equipment for receiving and recording cash adequate and conducive to good control?		✓				
8. Is revenue from investments, rent, concessions, and similar sources scheduled in advance so that nonreceipt on due date would be promptly investigated?	✓					
9. Do procedures for sale of scrap materials provide for direct reporting to accounting department concurrently with transfer of receipts to cashier?	✓					
10. Are securities and other negotiable assets in the custody of someone other than the cashier?	✓					
11. Are collections by branch offices deposited daily in a bank account subject to withdrawal only by home office executives?	✓					
12. Are each day's receipts deposited intact and without delay by an employee other than the accounts receivable bookkeeper?		✓				
13. Are the duplicate deposit slips or tickets returned by the bank and compared with the cash receipts record and mailroom list of receipts by an employee other than the cashier or accounts receivable bookkeeper?		✓				*W. Dale Manager*
14. Are the duplicate deposit slips or tickets properly filed and available for inspection by auditors?		✓				*Chronological sequence*
15. Are NSF cheques or other items returned by the bank delivered directly to an employee other than the cashier and promptly investigated?		✓				*W. Dale Manager*
16. Is the physical arrangement of offices and accounting records designed to prevent employees who handle cash from having access to accounting records?			✓			*Small Company doesn't permit this*

Prepared by *V. M. Harris*   Date *Sept 6, 9X*   Manager Review _____   Date _____

Senior Review _____   Date _____   Partner Review _____   Date _____

FIGURE 7–5

Bennington Co., Inc.
Cash Receipts Procedures
December 31, 199X

All cash receipts are received by mail in the form of cheques. Lorraine Martin, cashier, picks up the mail every morning at the post office and delivers it unopened to Helen Ellis, the head bookkeeper.

Ellis opens and distributes the mail. Customers' cheques are given to Martin, who records the remittances in the cash receipts journal, prepares duplicate deposit slips, and mails the day's receipts intact to First National Bank. The bank returns the validated duplicate deposit slips by mail, and Ellis files them in chronological order. Ellis posts the accounts receivable subsidiary ledger from the cash receipts journal on a daily basis.

Any customers' cheques charged back by the bank are given by Ellis to the manager, William Dale, who follows up and redeposits the cheques. Ellis also forwards monthly bank statements unopened to Dale. Dale reconciles the monthly bank statement, compares the dates and amounts of deposits with the entries in the cash receipts journal, and reviews the propriety of sales discounts recorded in the cash receipts journal.

Martin, Ellis, and Dale are all bonded.

2 M.H.
September 6, 9X

FIGURE 7–6 Widely Used Flowcharting Symbols

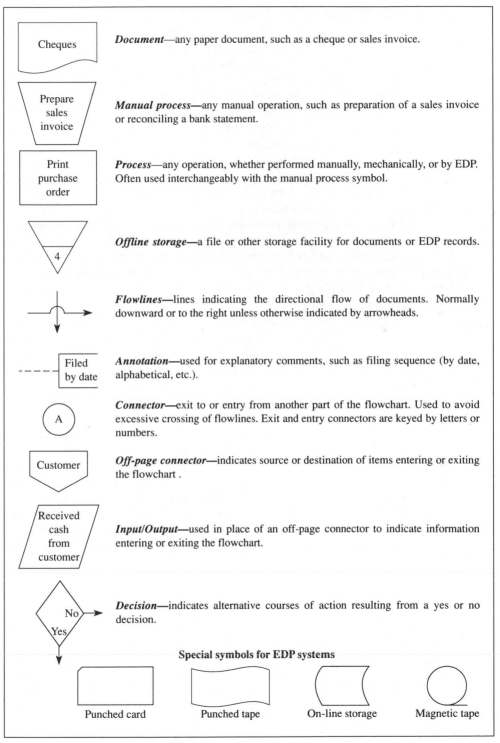

Document—any paper document, such as a cheque or sales invoice.

Manual process—any manual operation, such as preparation of a sales invoice or reconciling a bank statement.

Process—any operation, whether performed manually, mechanically, or by EDP. Often used interchangeably with the manual process symbol.

Offline storage—a file or other storage facility for documents or EDP records.

Flowlines—lines indicating the directional flow of documents. Normally downward or to the right unless otherwise indicated by arrowheads.

Annotation—used for explanatory comments, such as filing sequence (by date, alphabetical, etc.).

Connector—exit to or entry from another part of the flowchart. Used to avoid excessive crossing of flowlines. Exit and entry connectors are keyed by letters or numbers.

Off-page connector—indicates source or destination of items entering or exiting the flowchart .

Input/Output—used in place of an off-page connector to indicate information entering or exiting the flowchart.

Decision—indicates alternative courses of action resulting from a yes or no decision.

Special symbols for EDP systems

Punched card   Punched tape   On-line storage   Magnetic tape

ing system and the related internal controls. A systems flowchart is a diagram—a symbolic representation of a system or a series of procedures with each procedure shown in sequence. To the experienced reader, a flowchart conveys a clear image of the system, showing the nature and sequence of procedures, division of responsibilities, sources and distribution of documents, and types and location of accounting records and files. The standard symbols used in systems flowcharting are illustrated in Figure 7–6; however, the symbols used and flowcharting technique vary somewhat among different public accounting firms.

Separate systems flowcharts are prepared for each major transaction cycle. In addition, each flowchart is subdivided into vertical columns representing the various departments (or employees) involved in processing the transactions. Departmental responsibility for procedures, documents, and records is shown by reviewing the related flowcharting symbol beneath the appropriate departmental heading. Flowcharts usually begin in the upper-left-hand corner; directional flowlines then indicate the sequence of activity. The normal flow of activity is from top to bottom and from left to right. These basic concepts of systems flowcharting are illustrated in Figure 7–7.

The special advantage of a flowchart over a questionnaire or a narrative is that a flowchart provides a clearer, more specific portrayal of the client's system. There is less opportunity for misunderstanding, blank spots, or ambiguous statements when one uses lines and symbols rather than words to describe internal control. Furthermore, in each successive annual audit, updating a flowchart is a simple process requiring only that the auditor add or change a few lines and symbols.

A possible disadvantage of flowcharts is that internal control weaknesses are not identified as prominently as in questionnaires. A "no" answer in an internal control questionnaire is a conspicuous red flag calling attention to a dangerous situation. A flowchart may not provide so clear a signal that a particular internal control is absent or is not being properly enforced. For that reason, some accounting firms use both flowcharts and questionnaires to describe internal control. The flowchart clearly depicts the system, while the questionnaire serves to remind the auditors of controls that should be present in the system.

Walk-Through Test. After describing internal control in their working papers, the auditors will generally verify that the system has been placed in operation by performing a walk-through of each transaction cycle. The term *walk-through* refers to tracing several transactions (perhaps only one or two) through each step in the cycle. To perform a walk-through of the sales and collection cycle, for example, the auditors might begin by selecting several sales orders and following the related transactions through the client's sequence of procedures. The auditors would determine whether such procedures as credit approval, shipment of merchandise, preparation of sales invoices, recording of the accounts receivable, and

FIGURE 7–7

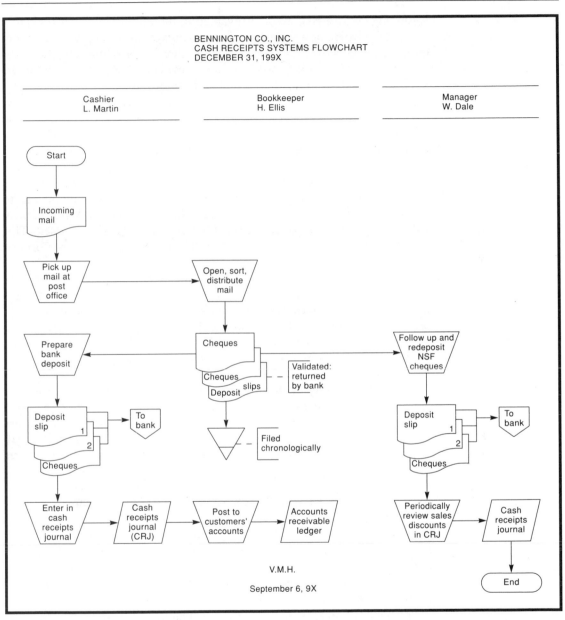

BENNINGTON CO., INC.
CASH RECEIPTS SYSTEMS FLOWCHART
DECEMBER 31, 199X

Cashier L. Martin	Bookkeeper H. Ellis	Manager W. Dale

Start

Incoming mail

Pick up mail at post office

Open, sort, distribute mail

Prepare bank deposit

Cheques

Cheques

Deposit slips

Validated: returned by bank

Follow up and redeposit NSF cheques

Deposit slip 1 2

Cheques

To bank

Filed chronologically

Deposit slip 1 2

Cheques

To bank

Enter in cash receipts journal

Cash receipts journal (CRJ)

Post to customers' accounts

Accounts receivable ledger

Periodically review sales discounts in CRJ

Cash receipts journal

End

V.M.H.

September 6, 9X

processing of the customers' remittances were performed by appropriate client personnel and in the sequence indicated in the audit working papers. If the auditors find that the system functions differently from the working paper description, they will amend the working papers to describe the actual system.

Assessing Control Risk

Assessing control risk involves evaluating the effectiveness of a client's internal control policies and procedures in preventing or detecting material misstatements in the financial statements. Recall from Chapter 6 that most of the external auditors' work involves evaluating evidence about the various financial statement assertions. Therefore, the auditors assess control risk in terms of the seven financial statement assertions—existence, occurrence, completeness, ownership, valuation, measurement, and statement presentation.

The auditors may assess control risk at maximum or below maximum. Control risk is assessed at maximum for a particular financial statement assertion when the internal control policies and procedures do not address the assertion or are unlikely to be effective or when it is inefficient to evaluate the effectiveness of these policies and procedures. When control risk is assessed at maximum, a *substantive audit approach* is used. This approach involves an audit strategy of obtaining evidence by performing substantive procedures only.

On the other hand, control risk is assessed at below the maximum for a particular financial statement assertion when the auditors (1) have identified the relevant internal control policies and procedures that are likely to prevent or detect material misstatements in that assertion and (2) plan to perform tests of controls to evaluate the operational effectiveness of such policies and procedures. When control risk is assessed at below the maximum, a *combined audit approach* is used. This approach involves an audit strategy of obtaining evidence by performing both tests of controls and substantive procedures.

The process of considering control risk may be viewed as (*a*) assess control risk and design additional tests of controls, (*b*) perform tests of controls, and (*c*) reassess control risk and design substantive procedures or tests.

Assess Control Risk and Design Additional Tests of Controls.   After documenting their understanding of internal control for purposes of planning the audit, the auditors arrive at a *planned assessed level of control risk* for the various financial statement assertions. For assertions for which control risk appears high, the auditors may simply plan to assess control risk at the maximum level; no tests of controls but substantive procedures need to be performed.

For financial statement assertions for which control risk appears to be lower, the auditors may plan to assess control risk at less than the maximum. To assess control risk at less than the maximum for a particular assertion, the auditors must have evidence of the operating effectiveness of the controls; they must test the controls. In determining the planned assessed level of control risk, the auditors must consider whether it is efficient to perform these tests necessary to support the lower *assessed level of control risk.* The auditors compare the estimated cost of performing the necessary tests of controls with the expected resulting benefit in the form of decreased substantive testing. Accordingly, substantive procedures are also performed.

While performing procedures to obtain an understanding of the design of internal controls, the auditors may already have gained some evidence of the operating effectiveness of various controls. If so, such procedures serve as tests of controls and may justify an *assessed level of control risk* at less than the maximum for certain assertions. Often, however, additional tests of controls will be necessary to justify an assessment of control risk at the planned level.

Perform Additional Tests of Controls.   Tests of controls are used by the auditors to obtain evidence about whether a particular policy or procedure operates in a manner that would prevent or detect material misstatements. Therefore, tests of controls are used to evaluate both the *design effectiveness* and *operating effectiveness* of controls.

The audit procedures used to test the effectiveness of internal control policies and procedures include (1) *enquiries* of appropriate client personnel, (2) *inspection* of documents and reports, (3) *observation* of the application of accounting policies or procedures, and (4) *reperformance* of the policy or procedure. It should be remembered that tests of controls focus on the performance of policies and procedures rather than upon financial statement amounts of completed transactions. For example, assume that the client has implemented the control procedure of requiring a second person to review the quantities, prices, extensions, and footing of each sales invoice. The purpose of this control procedure is to prevent material errors in the billing of customers and the recording of sales transactions. To test the effectiveness of this control procedure the auditors may make enquiries, inspect related documents, and observe application of the procedure. They might also select a sample of, say 30 sales invoices prepared throughout the year. They would compare the quantities shown on each invoice to the quantities listed on the related shipping documents, compare unit prices to the client's price lists, and verify the extensions and footings. The results of this test provide the auditors with evidence as to the existence and valuation of the recorded sales and accounts receivable. If numerous errors are found in the invoices, the auditors will expand their substantive procedures with respect to existence and valuation of accounts receivable and sales transactions.

The control procedure described above leaves documentary evidence of performance, allowing it to be tested by sampling. Other internal control procedures must be tested entirely through observation by the auditors and enquiry of client personnel. Segregation of duties, for example, is tested by observing the client's employees as they perform their duties and by enquiring who performed those duties throughout the period under audit. The auditors also should determine whether employees performed incompatible functions when other employees were absent from work on sick leave or vacation.

Reassess Control Risk and Design Substantive Tests.   After the auditors have carried out their tests of controls, they are in a position to perform a reassessment of control risk. Based on this reassessment, the auditors will determine an *assessed level of control risk* for the various assertions. If this differs from the *planned assessed level of control risk* for any assertions, modifications will then be made to the nature, timing, and extent of the substantive tests in the audit program. For example, for areas in which control risk is assessed at a higher level than planned, the auditors may decide to use tests involving evidence from parties outside, rather than inside, the company being audited. Also, year-end rather than interim period tests may be relied on, and the extent of procedures may be increased.

The auditors' assessment of control risk will have identified those assertions with maximum control risk and those assertions for which control risk is considered to be less than the maximum. The auditors will document these conclusions, as well as the basis for those assessments of control risk that are less than the maximum. These results are often summarized on a working paper that provides space for the auditors' assessment of control risk and references to the modifications in substantive procedures. A working paper used to summarize the auditors' assessment of control risk is illustrated in Figure 7-8. Notice that the extensions and limitations of audit procedures are described in detail to facilitate drafting a final version of the audit program.

Decision Aids for Audit Program Modification

Modifying audit programs for strengths and weaknesses in internal control, while considering other factors such as levels of materiality and risk, involves complex judgments. How many additional items should the auditors sample to compensate for high control risk? Is control risk for a particular account low enough to make it feasible to test the account at an interim date rather than at year-end? Without guidance from the accounting firm, different auditors within that firm might arrive at different answers to these questions. In fact, research on these types of audit judgments has revealed just that; there is a good deal of variance in auditors' program decisions.

Public accounting firms initially reacted to this problem by developing firm policies that put limits on individual auditor's decisions. The establishment of minimum audit sample sizes for particular types of tests is an example of such a policy. More recently, accounting firms have attempted to add even more structure to auditors' program decisions through the use

FIGURE 7–8   Understanding Internal Control, Control Risk Assessment, and Impact on Substantive Tests

WP Index _CR-1_

Understanding Internal Control, Control Risk Assessment, and Impact on Substantive Procedures

Client   _Arntco, Inc._   Balance Sheet Date   _Dec. 31, 1992_

Completed by: _R.W._   Date: _Sept. 15, 1992_   Reviewed by: _K.J._   Date: _Oct. 28, 1992_

We obtained sufficient knowledge of the design of the control environment, the accounting system, and control procedures to plan the audit, and determined that the policies and procedures have been placed in operation.

Workpapers related to our understanding of internal control are included at _Perm. Files ICS-1_ through _ICS-7_. Except as noted below, and on the reference workpapers, we have assessed control risk to be at the maximum and have designed our substantive audit procedures accordingly.

For those significant assertions related to the account balances indicated below, we have assessed control risk at less than the maximum, and the effects of such assessment have been reflected in our audit program. For assertions for each account balance or class of transactions where control risk has been assessed at less than the maximum, tests of controls have been performed to provide audit evidence sufficient to evaluate the effectiveness of the policies and procedures relevant to the various assertions.

CASH   **WORKPAPER REF __**

ACCOUNTS RECEIVABLE   **WORKPAPER REF _C-2_**

Control risk is assessed as slightly below the maximum for the following assertions: existence and valuation (other than for net realizable value which risk is assessed at the maximum). Control risk for completeness is assessed as moderate. Accordingly, primary audit evidence for existence, ownership and valuation (other than net realizable value) will be obtained by year-end confirmation of all key items (over $3,500), a nonstatistical representative sample of the remaining population (see workpaper C-5) and cutoff tests at year-end. Evidence about the net realizable value objective will be obtained by procedures set forth in the audit program, which consider subsequent cash collections, the aged trial balance, analytical procedures, and review of specific accounts with the owner-manager. Audit evidence for completeness will be obtained by application of (1) year-end cutoff tests and (2) analytical procedures applied to sales (see workpaper C-6).

INVENTORY   **WORKPAPER REF _D-5_**

Prior experience and tests of controls indicate good controls over physical counts and pricing of material items in inventory. These tests of controls provide sufficient evidence to support a low control risk assessment for the existence and valuation assertions.

:
:
:

EXPENSE ACCOUNTS   **WORKPAPER REF __**

Adapted from _AICPA Audit Guide: Consideration of the Internal Control Structure in a Financial Statement Audit_ (New York, 1990).

of decision aids or guides. A *decision aid* is a checklist or standard form that helps the auditors make a particular decision by ensuring that they consider all relevant information or assisting them in combining the information to make the decision. By reducing the variance in auditors' program judgments, decision aids promote the performance of audits that meet firm and professional requirements.

Consideration of the Work of Internal Auditors

Many of the audit procedures performed by internal auditors are similar in nature to those employed by external auditors. This raises the question of how the work of the internal auditors affects the external auditors' work.

The internal audit function is an important aspect of the client's control environment. Therefore, the external auditors consider the existence and quality of an internal audit function in their assessment of the client's internal control. Through its contribution to internal control, the work of the internal auditors may reduce the amount of audit testing performed by the external auditors.

The external auditors first obtain an understanding of the work of the internal auditors to determine its relevance to the audit. They make enquiries about such matters as the internal auditors' activities and audit plans. If the external auditors conclude that the internal auditors' work is relevant and it would be efficient to consider it, they assess the *competence* and *objectivity* of the internal audit staff, and *evaluate the quality of their work*.

In evaluating the competence of the internal auditors, the external auditors consider the educational level and professional experience of the internal audit staff. They also appraise the internal auditors' policies, programs, and checklists, and the extent to which their activities are supervised and reviewed. Objectivity is evaluated by considering the organizational status of the director of internal audit, including whether the director reports to an officer of sufficient status to ensure broad audit coverage and has direct access to the audit committee of the board of directors. The internal auditors' policies for assigning staff to audit areas are also reviewed.

After evaluating the competence and objectivity of the internal auditors, the external auditors evaluate and test their work. This investigation and evaluation provides the external auditors with a sound basis for determining the extent to which they may limit their audit procedures.

In addition to reducing the extent of the external auditors' substantive procedures, the internal auditors' work may affect the external auditors' procedures when obtaining an understanding of the client's internal control and assessing control risk. However, the external auditors should perform sufficient procedures to support their opinion on the financial statements. Regardless of the extent of the internal auditors' work, the external auditors must perform direct testing of those financial statement assertions with a high risk of material misstatement. Judgments about assessments of inherent and control risks, the materiality of misstatements, the sufficiency of tests performed, and other matters affecting the opinion must be those of the external auditors. Also, they should be directly involved in evaluating audit evidence that requires significant subjective judgment.

To reduce the time and cost of an audit, the internal auditors may provide direct assistance to the external auditors in preparing working papers and performing certain audit procedures. The external auditors, however, should supervise and evaluate any audit work done for them by the internal auditors.

Preparation of an Internal Control Letter

Deficiencies in internal control brought to light by the auditors' consideration of internal control should be communicated to the client along with the auditors' recommendations for corrective action. Discussions with management are the most effective way for auditors to communicate their findings to the client and explore possible courses of action. The content of these discussions is formally summarized and conveyed in writing to the client in a report called an *internal control (management) letter.* This report is a valuable reference document for management and may also serve to minimize the auditors' legal liability in the event that a major fraud or other loss results from a weakness in internal control. For these reasons, it is important that the *appropriate representative of the client be made aware of significant weaknesses* discovered in the audit. In the United States, the AICPA's *SAS 60* (AU325) *requires* auditors to advise the client's audit committee of the board of directors of *material weaknesses* in internal control.

Many public accounting firms place great emphasis on providing clients with a thorough and well-planned internal control letter. These firms recognize that such a report can be a valuable and constructive contribution to the efficiency of the client's operations. The quality of the auditors' recommendations reflects their professional expertise and creative ability and the thoroughness of their investigation. No specific format exists for the preparation of internal control letters.

Internal Control in the Small Company

The preceding discussion of internal control and its assessment by the external auditors has been presented in terms of large corporations. In the large concern, excellent internal control may be achieved by extensive subdivision of duties, so that no one person handles a transaction completely from beginning to end. In the very small concern, however, with only one or two office employees, there is little or no opportunity for division of duties and responsibilities. Consequently, internal control tends to be weak, if not completely absent, unless the owner/manager recognizes the importance of internal control and participates in key activities.

Because of the absence of adequate internal control in small concerns, the external auditors must make a much more detailed examination of accounts, journal entries, and supporting documents than is required in larger organizations. Although it is well to recognize that internal control can never be adequate in a small business, this limitation is no justification for ignoring available forms of control. Auditors can make a valuable contribution to small client companies by encouraging the installation of such control procedures as are practicable in the circumstances. The following specific practices are almost always capable of use in even the smallest businesses:

1. Record all cash receipts immediately.
   a. For over-the-counter collections, use cash registers easily visible to customers. Record register readings daily.
   b. Prepare a list of all mail remittances immediately upon opening of the mail and retain this list for subsequent comparison with bank deposit slips or tickets and entries in the cash receipts journal.
2. Deposit all cash receipts intact daily.
3. Make all payments by serially numbered cheques, with the exception of small disbursements from petty cash.
4. Reconcile bank accounts monthly and retain copies of the reconciliations in the files.
5. Use serially numbered documents such as sales invoices, purchase orders, shipping reports, and receiving reports.
6. Issue cheques to vendors only in payment of approved invoices that have been matched with purchase orders and receiving reports.
7. Balance subsidiary ledgers with control accounts at regular intervals; prepare and mail customers' statements monthly.
8. Prepare comparative financial statements monthly in sufficient detail to disclose significant variations in any category of revenue or expense.
9. Account for the numerical sequence of all prenumbered documents such as purchase orders, shipping reports, receiving reports, sales invoices, and cheques.

Adherence to these basic control practices significantly reduces the risk of material errors or major fraud going undetected. If the size of the business permits a segregation of the duties of cash handling and record-keeping, a fair degree of control can be achieved. If it is necessary that one employee serve as both accounting clerk and cashier, then active participation by the owner in certain key functions is necessary to guard against the concealment of fraud or errors. In a few minutes each day, the owner, even though not trained in accounting, can create a significant amount of internal control by personally (1) reading daily cash register totals, (2) reconciling the bank account monthly, (3) signing all cheques and canceling the supporting documents, (4) approving all general journal entries, and (5) critically reviewing comparative monthly statements of revenue and expense.

KEY TERMS

assessed level of control risk The level of control risk used by the auditors in determining the acceptable detection risk for a financial statement assertion and, accordingly, in deciding on the nature, timing, and extent of substantive procedures.

audit decision aids Standard checklists or forms that assist auditors in making audit decisions by ensuring that they consider all relevant information, or aiding them in weighting and combining the information to make a decision.

combined audit approach An audit strategy of assessing control risk below maximum in which audit evidence is obtained through the performance of both tests of controls and substantive procedures.

control risk The possibility that a material misstatement (error or fraud) will occur in a financial statement assertion and not be prevented or detected by the client's internal control.

fidelity bonds A form of insurance in which a bonding company agrees to reimburse an employer for losses attributable to theft or embezzlement by bonded employees.

Foreign Corrupt Practices Act The U.S. federal legislation prohibiting payments to foreign officials for the purpose of securing business. The act also requires all companies under SEC jurisdiction to maintain a system of internal accounting control providing reasonable assurance that transactions are executed only with the knowledge and authorization of management.

incompatible duties Assigned duties that put an individual in a position to both perpetrate and conceal errors or fraud in the normal course of job performance.

internal auditors Corporation employees who design and execute audit programs to test the efficiency of all aspects of internal control. The primary objective of internal auditors is to evaluate and improve the efficiency of the various operating units of an organization rather than to express an opinion as to the fairness of financial statements.

internal control (management) letter A report to management containing the auditors' recommendations for correcting any deficiencies disclosed by the auditors' consideration of internal control. In addition to providing management with useful information, this letter may also help limit the auditors' liability in the event a control weakness subsequently results in a loss by the client.

internal control questionnaire   One of several alternative methods of describing internal control in audit working papers. Questionnaires are usually designed so that "no" answers prominently identify weaknesses in internal control.

internal control (structure or system)   An organization's policies and procedures that have been established to provide reasonable assurance that its related objectives will be achieved. Internal control is composed of the overall control environment, the accounting system, and control procedures.

planned assessed level of control risk   The level of control risk the auditor uses in developing a preliminary audit strategy which includes an appropriate combination of tests of controls and substantive tests.

substantive audit approach   An audit strategy of assessing control risk at maximum in which audit evidence is obtained through the performance of substantive procedures only.

systems flowcharts   A symbolic representation of a system or series of procedures with each procedure shown in sequence. Systems flowcharts are a widely used method of describing internal control.

tests of controls   Tests directed toward the design or operation of an internal control policy or procedure to assess its effectiveness in preventing or detecting material misstatements in the financial statements.

transaction cycle   The sequence of procedures applied by the client in processing a particular type of recurring transaction. The auditors' working paper description of internal control is organized around the client's major transaction cycles.

walk-through of the system   A test of the accuracy and completeness of the auditors' working paper description of internal control. A walk-through is performed by tracing several transactions through each step of the related transaction cycle, noting whether the sequence of procedures actually performed corresponds to that described in the audit working papers.

written narrative of internal control   A written summary of internal control for inclusion in audit working papers. Written narratives are more flexible than questionnaires, but are practical only for describing relatively small, simple systems.

GROUP I: REVIEW QUESTIONS

7–1.   What is the basic purpose of internal control? What measures comprise internal control?

7–2. Identify the three elements of an organization's internal control.

7–3. List the factors that make up an organization's control environment.

7–4. How does separation of the record-keeping function from custody of assets contribute to internal control?

7–5. Name three factors you consider of greatest importance in protecting a business against losses through embezzlement.

7–6. The owner of a medium-sized corporation asks you to state two or three principles to be followed in dividing responsibilities among employees in a manner that will produce strong internal control.

7–7. One basic concept of internal control is that no one employee should handle all aspects of a transaction. Assuming that a general category of transactions has been authorized by top management, how many employees (or departments) should participate in each transaction, as a minimum, to achieve strong internal control? Explain in general terms the function of each of these employees.

7–8. Compare the objectives of the internal auditor with those of the external auditor.

7–9. What reliance, if any, may external auditors place upon the work of a client's internal audit staff?

7–10. What are the purposes of the consideration of internal control required by generally accepted auditing standards?

7–11. A prospective client informs you that all officers and employees of the company are bonded, and he requests that under these circumstances you forgo an assessment of internal control in order to reduce the cost of an audit. Construct a logical reply to this request.

7–12. Suggest a number of sources from which you might obtain the information needed to prepare a description of internal control in the audit working papers.

7–13. Under what circumstances are test of controls *efficient* audit procedures?

7–14. "All experienced auditors would design exactly the same audit program for a particular audit engagement." Do you agree? Explain.

7–15. What is an internal control letter? What is the letter's significance?

7–16. In view of the reliance the auditor places upon internal control, how do you account for the fact that the auditors' standard report makes no reference to internal control in describing the scope of the examination?

7–17. You have discussed with the president of Vista Corporation several material weaknesses in internal control that have come to your attention during your audit. At the conclusion of this discussion, the president states that he will personally take steps to remedy these problems and that there is no reason for you to bring these matters to the attention of the board of directors. He explains that he believes the board should deal with major policy decisions and not be burdened with day-to-day management problems. How would you respond to this suggestion? Explain fully.

GROUP II: QUESTIONS REQUIRING ANALYSIS

7–18.   The consideration of internal control is integral to financial statement audits.

Required:
   a. For what two primary reasons do auditors consider internal control?
   b. How is the auditors' understanding of the client's internal control documented in the audit working papers?
   c. In what circumstances do auditors perform tests of control procedures?

7–19.   Auditors may restrict substantive procedures or tests based on their assessment of control risk.

Required:
   a. Discuss and contrast the concepts of (1) the planned assessed level of control risk, (2) the assessed level of control risk and (3) control risk.
   b. Using internal control for the existence assertion for accounts receivable, provide an example which distinguishes among the three concepts discussed in part a above.

7–20.   The auditors' consideration of internal control begins with obtaining an understanding of the internal control.
   a. Describe the remaining stages of the auditors' consideration.
   b. Provide examples of audit procedures that are performed at each stage (including the stage of obtaining an understanding).

7–21.   Henry Bailey, CA, is planning the audit of The Neighbourhood Store, a local grocery cooperative. Because The Neighbourhood Store is a small business operated entirely by part-time volunteer personnel, internal controls are weak. Bailey has decided that he will not be able to rely on internal control to reduce substantive audit procedures in any area. Under these circumstances, may Bailey omit the consideration of internal control in this engagement?

7–22.   Adherence to generally accepted auditing standards requires, among other things, a proper understanding of the existing internal control. The most common approaches to documenting the understanding of internal control include the use of a questionnaire, preparation of a written narrative, preparation of a flowchart, and combinations of these methods.

Required:

a. Discuss the advantages to the external auditors of documenting internal control by using:

   (1) An internal control questionnaire.

   (2) A written narrative.

   (3) A flowchart.

b. If the external auditors are satisfied after completing their description of internal control that no material weaknesses exist in the system, is it necessary for them to conduct tests of controls? Explain.

(AICPA, adapted)

7–23. The process of gathering audit evidence to support an opinion on a client's financial statements involves several types of testing procedures. In the course of the examination, auditors perform tests of samples of transactions from large-volume populations. Auditors may also audit various types of transactions by tracing a few transactions of each type through all stages of the accounting system.

Required:

What are the audit objectives associated with:

a. A sample of transactions from a large-volume population?

b. Tracing a few examples of each type through all stages of the accounting system?

(AICPA, adapted)

7–24. During your first examination of a medium-sized manufacturing company, the owner, John Bell, explains that in order to establish clear-cut lines of responsibility for various aspects of the business, he has made one employee responsible for the purchasing, receiving, and storing of merchandise. A second employee has full responsibility for maintenance of accounts receivable records and collections from customers. A third employee is responsible for personnel records, timekeeping, preparation of payrolls, and distribution of payroll cheques. Bell asks your opinion concerning this plan of organization. Explain fully the reasons supporting your opinion.

7–25. Internal auditing is a staff function found in virtually every large corporation. The internal audit function is also performed in many smaller companies as a part-time activity of individuals who may or may not be called internal auditors. The differences between the audits by external auditors and the work of internal auditors are more basic than is generally recognized.

Required:

a. Briefly discuss the auditing work performed by the external auditor and the internal auditor with regard to:

(1) Auditing objectives.

(2) General nature of auditing work.

b. In conducting their audit, the external auditors must evaluate the work of the internal auditors. Discuss briefly the reason for this evaluation.

7–26. Select the best answer for each of the following questions. Explain the reason for your selection.

a. Which of the following would be least likely to be considered an objective of internal control?

(1) Checking the accuracy and reliability of accounting data.

(2) Detecting management fraud.

(3) Encouraging adherence to managerial policies.

(4) Safeguarding assets.

b. Which of the following symbols indicate that a file has been consulted?

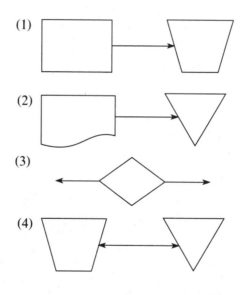

(1)

(2)

(3)

(4)

c. When an external auditor decides that the work performed by internal auditors may have a bearing on the nature, timing, and extent of the external auditor's procedures, the external auditor should evaluate the competence and objectivity of the internal auditors. Relative to objectivity, the external auditor should:

(1) Consider the organizational level to which the internal auditors report the results of their work.

(2) Review the internal auditors' work.

(3) Consider the qualifications of the internal audit staff.

(4) Review the training program in effect for the internal audit staff.

d. Effective internal control in a small company that has an insuf-

ficient number of employees to permit proper subdivision of responsibilities can be improved by:
   (1) Employment of temporary personnel to aid in the separation of duties.
   (2) Direct participation by the owner in key record-keeping and control activities of the business.
   (3) Engaging a public accountant to perform monthly write-up work.
   (4) Delegation to each employee of full, clear-cut responsibility for a separate major transaction cycle.

e. Of the following statements about internal control, which one is *not* valid?
   (1) No one person should be responsible for the custody and the recording of an asset.
   (2) Transactions must be properly authorized before such transactions are processed.
   (3) Because of the cost/benefit relationship, a client may apply control procedures on a test basis.
   (4) Control procedures reasonably ensure that collusion among employees *cannot* occur.

f. Proper segregation of functional responsibilities calls for separation of the
   (1) Authorization, recording, and custodial functions.
   (2) Authorization, execution, and payment functions.
   (3) Receiving, shipping, and custodial functions.
   (4) Authorization, approval, and execution functions.

7–27. During your first examination of a manufacturing company with approximately 100 production employees, you find that all aspects of factory payroll are handled by one employee and that none of the usual internal controls over payroll is observed. What action will you take?

7–28. a. A newspaper article about embezzlement contained this comment, "Both the management of a company and the external auditor have certain responsibilities with respect to the prevention of fraud by employees."

   What is the extent of the responsibilities of each?

   b. What general measures should be taken by management in attempting to prevent fraud by employees?

(CICA, adapted)

GROUP III: PROBLEMS

7–29. At the Main Street Theatre the cashier, located in a box office at the entrance, receives cash from customers and operates a machine that ejects serially numbered tickets. To gain admission to the theatre a customer hands the ticket to a door attendant stationed some 50 feet from the box office at the entrance to the theatre lobby. The attendant tears the ticket in half, opens the door for the customer, and returns the stub to the customer. The other half of the ticket is dropped by the door attendant into a locked box.

Required:
a. What internal controls are present in this phase of handling cash receipts?
b. What steps should be taken regularly by the manager or other supervisor to give maximum effectiveness to these controls?
c. Assume that the cashier and the door attendant decided to collaborate in an effort to abstract cash receipts. What action might they take?
d. Continuing the assumption made in (c) of collusion between the cashier and the door attendant, what features of the control procedures would be likely to disclose the embezzlement?

7–30. Orange Corp., a high technology company, utilizes the following procedures for recording raw materials and transferring them to work in process.
a. Upon receipt of raw materials by stores, the storeskeeper prepares a stock-in report with part number and quantities, files the original by date, and sends a copy to accounting.
b. The inventory accounting clerk uses the stock-in report to post the perpetual inventory records using standard costs, and files the stock-in report by date.
c. Raw materials requisitions, which show part number and quantity, are prepared by the manufacturing clerk and approved by the supervisor of manufacturing. A copy of the requisition is sent to accounting, and the original is filed by job order.
d. The inventory accounting clerk reviews the requisitions for completeness, transfers the cost from raw materials to work in process, and files the requisitions by date.

Required:
Prepare a flowchart which describes the client's system of recording raw materials and transferring them to work in process.

(CIA, adapted)

7–31. Island Trading Co., a client of your accounting firm, has requested your advice on the following problem. It has three clerical employees who must perform the following functions:
(1) Maintain general ledger.
(2) Maintain accounts payable ledger.
(3) Maintain accounts receivable ledger.

(4) Maintain cash disbursements journal and prepare cheques for signature.

(5) Issue credit memos on sales returns and allowances.

(6) Reconcile the bank account.

(7) Handle and deposit cash receipts.

Required:

Assuming that there is no problem as to the ability of any of the employees, the company requests your advice on assigning the above functions to the three employees in such a manner as to achieve the highest degree of internal control. It may be assumed that these employees will perform no other accounting functions than the ones listed and that any accounting functions not listed will be performed by persons other than these three employees.

a. List four possible unsatisfactory combinations of the above-listed functions.

b. State how you would recommend distributing the above functions among three employees. Assume that, with the exception of the nominal jobs of the bank reconciliation and the issuance of credits on returns and allowances, all functions require an equal amount of time.

(AICPA, adapted)

7–32. Prospect Corporation, your new audit client, processes its sales and cash receipts in the following manner:

1. Sales. Salesclerks prepare sales invoices in triplicate. The original and second copy are presented to the cashier, and the third copy is retained by the salesclerk in the sales book. When the sale is for cash, the customer pays the salesclerk, who presents the money to the cashier with the invoice copies.

A credit sale is approved by the cashier from an approved credit list. After receiving the cash or approving the invoice, the cashier validates the original copy of the sales invoice and gives it to the customer. At the end of each day the cashier recaps the sales and cash received, files the recap by date, and forwards the cash and the second copy of all sales invoices to the accounts receivable clerk.

The accounts receivable clerk balances the cash received with cash sales invoices and prepares a daily sales summary. Cash sales are recorded by the accounts receivable clerk in the cash receipts journal, and the daily sales summary is filed by date. Cash from cash sales is included in the daily bank deposit (preparation of the bank deposit is described with cash receipts in the following section). The accounts receivable clerk posts credit sales invoices to the accounts receivable ledger and then sends all invoices to the inventory control clerk in the sales department.

The inventory clerk posts to the inventory control cards and files the sales invoices numerically.

2. Cash receipts. The mail is opened each morning by a mail clerk in the sales department. The mail clerk prepares a remittance advice (showing customer and amount paid) for each cheque and forwards the cheques and remittance advices to the sales department supervisor. The supervisor reviews the remittance advices and forwards the cheques and advices to the accounting department supervisor.

The accounting department supervisor, who also functions as credit manager in approving new credit and all credit limits, reviews all cheques for payments on past-due accounts and then gives the cheques and remittance advices to the accounts receivable clerk, who arranges the advices in alphabetical order. The remittance advices are posted directly to the accounts receivable ledger cards. The cheques are endorsed by stamp and totaled. The total is recorded in the cash receipts journal. The remittance advices are filed chronologically.

After receiving the cash from the previous day's cash sales from the cashier, the accounts receivable clerk prepares the daily deposit slip in triplicate. The original and second copy of the deposit slip accompany the bank deposit, and the third copy is filed by date. The bank deposit is sent directly to National Bank.

Required:

a. Prepare a systems flowchart of internal control over sales transactions as described in part 1 above.

b. Prepare a systems flowchart of internal control over cash receipts as described in part 2 above.

7–33. You have been asked by the board of trustees of a local church to review its accounting procedures. As part of this review you have prepared the following comments relating to the collections made at weekly services and recordkeeping for members' pledges and contributions:

(1) The church's board of trustees has delegated responsibility for financial management and internal audit of the financial records to the finance committee. This group prepares the annual forecast and approves major disbursements, but is not involved in collections or recordkeeping. No internal or independent audit has been considered necessary in recent years because the same trusted employee has kept church records and served as financial secretary for 15 years.

(2) The offering at the weekly service is taken by a team of ushers. The head usher counts the offering in the church office following each service. He then places the offering and a notation of

the amount counted in the church safe. The next morning the financial secretary opens the safe and recounts the offering. He withholds about $100 to meet cash expenditures during the coming week and deposits the remainder of the offering intact. In order to facilitate the deposit, members who contribute by cheque are asked to draw their cheques to cash.

(3) At their request a few members are furnished prenumbered, predated envelopes in which to insert their weekly contributions. The head usher removes the cash from the envelopes to be counted with the loose cash included in the offering and discards the envelopes. No record is maintained of issuance or return of the envelopes, and the envelope system is not encouraged.

(4) Each member is asked to prepare a contribution pledge card annually. The pledge is regarded as a moral commitment by the member to contribute a stated weekly amount. Based upon the amounts shown on the pledge cards, the financial secretary furnishes a receipt to requesting members to support the tax deductibility of their contributions.

Required:

Describe the weaknesses and recommend improvements in procedures for:

a. Offerings given at weekly services.

b. Record-keeping for members' pledges and contributions.

Organize your answer sheets as follows:

Weakness	Recommended Improvement

(AICPA, adapted)

GROUP IV: ANALYTICAL AND DISCUSSION CASE

7–34. You are performing your first audit of Merit Drug Supply Company, a small company that is owned and managed by William Hicks. Merit employs only two other office workers, Tom Howe, the bookkeeper, and Glenda Monroe, the receptionist-secretary.

In your review of internal control over cash receipts, you ascertain that all cash receipts are received and deposited by Hicks. He prepares a list of the details of the receipts that is used by Howe to post the accounts receivable records. Neither Hicks nor Howe have any other incompatible duties in processing cash. You feel that this separation of responsibilities of custody of cash from record-keeping is good, but you are uneasy about relying on controls applied by an owner/manager.

Required:
a. Present arguments for relying on the owner/manager control.
b. Present arguments against relying on the owner/manager control.
c. Express your own opinion, referring back to points from (*a*) or (*b*) that support your opinion.

Chapter 8

Internal Control over EDP Activities

After studying this chapter, you should be able to:

- Identify the characteristics of an EDP system that differ from a manual system.
- Describe the characteristics of various types of computer systems.
- Distinguish between general controls and application controls in an EDP system.
- Discuss the nature of the controls over microcomputers.
- Explain the manner in which the auditors obtain an understanding of internal control in an EDP environment.
- Discuss the ways in which the auditors may test internal controls in an EDP environment.
- Describe the nature of generalized audit software programs and the ways they are used by the auditors.

The rapid growth of electronic data processing (EDP) for business use is having a greater impact on public accounting than perhaps any other event in the history of the profession. No longer is the challenge of auditing EDP activities limited to a few large clients. With the advent of inexpensive microcomputer systems, even the smallest audit clients are likely to use a computer for many accounting functions. Thus, auditors must be prepared to work in an ever-changing environment in which the client's accounting records are maintained on anything from a personal computer to a multi-million-dollar mainframe system.

Although the computer has created some challenging problems for professional accountants, it has also broadened their horizons and expanded the range and value of the services they offer. The computer is more than a tool for performing routine accounting tasks with unprecedented speed and accuracy. It makes possible the development of information that could not have been gathered in the past because of time and cost limitations. When a client maintains accounting records with a complex and sophisticated EDP system, auditors often find it helpful, and even necessary, to utilize the computer in performing many auditing procedures.

This chapter will consider some of the most significant ways in which auditing work is being affected by EDP, but it cannot impart extensive knowledge of technical computer skills. External auditors will find additional familiarity with the computer, including technical skills such as programming, to be of ever-increasing value in the accounting profession.

Nature of an Electronic Data Processing System

Before considering the impact of electronic data processing systems on the work of the independent public accountant, some understanding of the nature of a computer and its capabilities is needed. A business EDP system usually consists of a digital computer and peripheral equipment known as *hardware* and equally essential *software,* consisting of various programs and routines for operating a computer.

Hardware.   The principal hardware component of a digital computer is the *central processing unit* (CPU). The CPU consists of a *control unit,* which processes a program of instructions for manipulating data; a *storage unit* for storing the program of instructions and the data to be manipulated; and an *arithmetic unit* capable of addition, subtraction, multiplication, division, and comparison of data at speeds measured in *microseconds, nanoseconds,* or even *picoseconds.*

Peripheral to the central processing unit are devices for recording input and devices for auxiliary storage, output, and communications. Peripheral devices in direct communication with the CPU are said to be *on-line,* in contrast to *off-line* equipment not in direct communication with the CPU.

A first step in electronic data processing is to convert the data to machine-sensible form. This is the role of recording and input devices, such as card readers, optical scanners, electronic cash registers, and intelligent terminals. Each of these devices either records data in some medium for later reading into the storage unit or communicates data direct to the CPU.

Secondary storage devices are utilized to augment the capacity of the storage unit of the CPU. Examples of secondary storage devices are magnetic tapes and magnetic disk packs. Magnetic disk packs have the advantage of *direct access,* which allows for faster location and retrieval of data. Data on magnetic tapes must be stored sequentially and is retrieved by a systematic search.

Digital computer circuitry has two states in that any given circuit may be "on" or "off." By using an internal code, or machine language, capable of representing with two symbols any kind of data, all data may be expressed internally by the computer by a combination of on and off circuits. An example of a machine language is the *binary* number system.

Machines must also be used to translate the output of the computer back into a recognizable code or language. Output equipment includes printers and display terminals.

Software.   Computer systems use two major types of software: *system software* and *application software.* System software consists of programs that control and coordinate hardware components and provide other support to application software. Important components of system software are utility programs for recurring tasks of data processing, such as sorting, sequencing, and merging of data. The system software known as the *operating system* is important to the control of computer operations because it may be programmed to control access to programs and stored data and to maintain a log of all system activities.

Programs designed to perform a specific data processing task, such as payroll processing, are known as application software. Early application programs are laboriously written in machine language, but today, programming languages such as COBOL (common business-oriented language) are much like English. Programming in COBOL and other *source languages* is made possible by another element of software, the *compiler,* which is a computer program utilized in translating a *source-language program* into machine language. The machine-language version of a program is called an *object program.*

In some ways, computer systems enhance the reliability of financial information. Computers process transactions uniformly and eliminate the human errors that may occur in a manual system. On the other hand, defects in hardware or programs can result in a computer processing all transactions incorrectly. Also, errors or fraud that do occur in computer processing may not be detected by the client's personnel because few people are involved with data processing. Thus, computer hardware precision does not assure that computer output will be reliable. Auditors have the same responsibility in an EDP system as in a manual system, which is to satisfy themselves that the financial statements produced are in conformity with generally accepted accounting principles.

Characteristics of Various Types of EDP Systems

EDP systems differ as to their characteristics. A computer system, regardless of its size, may possess one or more of the following elements:

1. Batch processing.
2. On-line systems.
3. Data base systems.
4. Distributive data processing.

Batch Processing.   When batch processing is used, input data is gathered and processed periodically in discrete groups. An example of batch processing is accumulating all of a day's sales transactions, and processing them as a "batch" at the end of that day. While batch processing systems do not provide up-to-the-minute information, they are often more efficient than other types of systems.

On-line Systems.   On-line systems allow users to have direct (on-line) access to the data stored in the system. When an on-line system is in use, input need not be entered into the computer in batches. Individual transactions may be entered directly from the originators at remote locations. In on-line, real-time (OLRT) systems, transactions are processed immediately and all accounting records are updated instantaneously. These systems are frequently encountered in banks and other financial institutions. On-line, real-time systems allow a teller at any branch to update a customer's account immediately by recording deposits or withdrawals on a computer terminal. At most financial institutions, customers are able to transact business directly with the computer by inserting an identification card in an automatic teller terminal.

The use of an on-line, real-time system results in significant changes in internal control. Original source documents may not be available to support input into the computer, and the overall amount of the hard copy (printed) audit trail may be substantially reduced. Essential controls must be *programmed* into the computer. For example, the validity of data must be checked by the computer as it is entered into the system.

Data Base Systems.   In a traditional computer system, files are maintained for each application. An example of an application file is the master file of accounts receivable, which contains customer account activity for a period of time and information about each customer. Much of the information on this file would also be included on customer files maintained by the sales department. This *data redundancy* is expensive in terms of computer storage cost. Also, data inconsistencies may arise because the information may not be up-to-date on all files.

In *data management systems,* separate files for each computer application are not necessary. Instead, all data are stored in a common data base with each information element being stored only once. This system of data integration eliminates data redundancy, and since the data base is normally stored on a direct access device, the system responds quickly to users' requests for information.

From a control standpoint, it is essential that the data base be secured against improper access to the data. Organizations that use data base systems often create a data base administrator function, with responsibility for administering the data base and controlling access to the data.

Distributive Data Processing (End User Computing).

In *distributive data processing systems,* smaller computers are located throughout the organization to allow users to perform certain information processing in their own departments. The smaller computers are linked to a main computer that allows information and programs to be shared by all the users. A distributive data processing system provides company executives with on-line access to the vast amount of data stored in the company's main computer. They may selectively retrieve data and process it to their personal specifications with microcomputers located in their departments.

In a computer system that has distributive data processing capabilities, data may be altered at any location that can access the system. Weak internal controls at a single location can jeopardize the reliability of the entire system. Accordingly, security should be provided at each location to assure that transactions are initiated and data is accessed only by authorized personnel.

INTERNAL CONTROL IN THE ELECTRONIC DATA PROCESSING SYSTEM

The discussion of internal control in Chapter 7 stressed the need for a proper division of duties among employees operating a manual accounting system. In such a system, no one employee has complete responsibility for a transaction, and the work of one person is verified by the work of another handling other aspects of the same transaction. The division of duties gives assurance of accuracy in records and reports and protects the company against loss from fraud or carelessness.

When a company converts to an EDP system, however, the work formerly divided among many people is performed by the computer. Consolidation of activities and integration of functions are to be expected, since the computer can conveniently handle many related aspects of a transaction. For example, when payroll is handled by a computer, it is possible to carry out a variety of related tasks with only a single use of the master records. These tasks could include the maintenance of personnel files with information on seniority, rate of pay, insurance, and the like; a portion of the timekeeping function; distribution of labour costs; and preparation of payroll cheques and payroll records.

Despite the integration of several functions in an EDP system, the importance of internal control is not in the least diminished. The essential factors described in Chapter 7 for satisfactory internal control in a large-scale organization are still relevant. Separation of duties and clearly defined responsibilities continue to be key ingredients despite the change in organization of activities. These traditional control concepts are augmented, however, by controls written into the computer programs and controls built into the computer hardware.

In auditing literature, internal controls over EDP activities often are classified as either *general controls* or *application controls.* General controls relate to all EDP applications and include such considerations as (*a*) the organization of the EDP department; (*b*) procedures for documenting, testing, and approving the original system and any subsequent changes; (*c*) controls built into the hardware (equipment controls); and (*d*) security for files and equipment. Application controls, on the other hand, relate to specific accounting tasks performed by EDP, such as the preparation of payrolls. Controls of this nature include such measures as controls over input, controls over processing, and controls over output to assure the reliability of the data.

Organizational Controls in an Electronic Data Processing System

Because of the ability of the computer to process data efficiently, there is a tendency to combine many data processing functions in an EDP department. In a manual or mechanical system, these combinations of functions may be considered incompatible from a standpoint of achieving strong internal control. For example, the function of recording cash disbursements is incompatible with the responsibility for reconciling bank statements. Since one of these procedures serves as a check upon the other, assigning both functions to one employee would enable the employee to conceal his or her own errors. A properly programmed computer, however, has no tendency or motivation to conceal its errors. Therefore, what appears to be an incompatible combination of functions may be combined in an EDP department without weakening internal control.

When apparently incompatible functions are combined in the EDP department, compensating controls are necessary to prevent improper human intervention with computer processing. A person with the opportunity to make unauthorized changes in computer programs or data files is in a position to exploit the concentration of data processing functions in the EDP department. For example, a computer program used to process accounts payable may be designed to approve a vendor's invoice for payment only when that invoice is supported by a purchase order and receiving report. An employee able to make unauthorized changes in that program could cause unsubstantiated payments to be made to specific vendors.

EDP programs and data files cannot be changed without the use of EDP equipment. With EDP equipment, however, they can be changed without leaving any visible evidence of the alteration. Thus, the organization plan of an EDP department should prevent EDP personnel from having unauthorized access to EDP equipment, programs, or data files. This is accomplished by providing definite lines of authority and responsibility, segregation of functions, and clear definition of duties for each employee in the department. The organizational structure of a well-staffed EDP department, as illustrated in Figure 8–1, should include the following separation of responsibilities.

Data Processing Management.   A manager should be appointed to supervise the operation of the data processing department. The data processing manager should report to an officer who does authorize transactions for computer processing, perhaps to a vice president of data processing. When EDP is a section within the accounting department, the controller should not have direct contact with computer operations.

Systems Analysis.   Systems analysts are responsible for designing the EDP system. After considering the objectives of the business and the data processing needs of the various departments using the computer output (***user groups***), they determine the goals of the system and the means of achieving these goals. Utilizing system flowcharts and detailed instructions, they outline the data processing system.

FIGURE 8–1   Organization of EDP Department

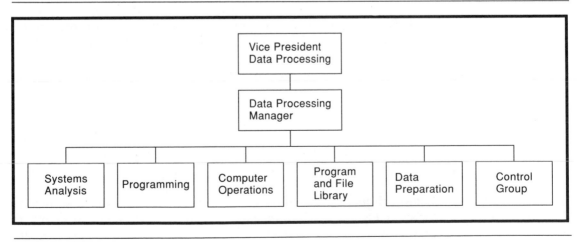

Programming.   Guided by the specifications provided by the systems analysts, the programmers design program flowcharts for computer programs required by the system. They then code the required programs in computer language, generally making use of specialized programming languages, such as COBOL, and software elements, such as assemblers, compilers, and utility programs. They test the programs with *test data* composed of genuine or dummy records and transactions and perform the necessary debugging. Finally, the programmers prepare necessary documentation, such as the computer operator instructions.

Computer Operations.   The computer operators use the computer in accordance with the instructions developed by the programmers. On occasion, the computer operators may have to intervene through the computer console during a run in order to correct an indicated error. The computer's operating system should be programmed to maintain a detailed log of all operator intervention. The separation of computer operations from programming is an important one from the standpoint of achieving internal control. An employee performing both functions would have an opportunity to make unauthorized changes in computer programs.

Program and File Library.   The purpose of the file library is to protect computer programs, master files, transaction (detail) files, and other records from loss, damage, and unauthorized use or alteration. To assure adequate control, the librarian maintains a formal checkout system for making records available to authorized users.

In many systems, the library function is performed by the computer. The computer operators use special code numbers or passwords to gain access to programs and files stored within the system. The computer automatically maintains a log showing when these programs and files are used.

Data Preparation.   Personnel involved with this function prepare and verify input data for processing. A keypunch operation is a traditional example of a data preparation department. Keypunching is primarily associated with *batch processing* systems, in which a group (batch) of transactions is processed at one time. In an *on-line, real-time system,* data may be entered directly into the computer by user groups through remote *terminals* and computer files are immediately updated to reflect the new data. Even in the most sophisticated systems, however, some applications may still be handled by batch processing of transactions entered directly by the user groups.

Control Group.   The control group of a data processing department reviews and tests all input procedures, monitors computer processing, reviews exception reports, handles the reprocessing of exceptions detected by the computer, and reviews and distributes all computer output. This group also reviews the computer log of operator interventions and the library log of program usage. In smaller organizations, control group functions may be performed by the user groups.

Besides segregation of functions, the data processing organization plan should provide for rotation of programmer assignments, rotation of operator assignments, mandatory vacations, and adequate fidelity bonds for EDP employees. At least two of the qualified data processing personnel should be present whenever the computer facility is in use. Careful screening procedures in the hiring of EDP personnel are also important in achieving strong internal control.

Organizational Controls and Computer-Centred Fraud.   The history of computer-centred fraud shows that the persons responsible for frauds in many situations set up the system and control its use as programmer and operator.

Illustrative Case

A programmer for a large bank wrote a program for identifying and listing all overdrawn accounts. Later, as operator of the bank's computer, he was able to insert a "patch" in the program to cause the computer to ignore overdrafts in his own account. The programmer-operator was then able to overdraw his bank account at will, without the overdraft coming to management's attention. The fraud was not discovered until the computer broke down and the listing of overdrawn accounts had to be prepared manually.

The number of personnel and the organizational structure will of course determine the extent to which segregation of duties is possible. As a minimum, the function of programming should be separated from the function of controlling input to the computer programs, and the function of the computer operator should be segregated from functions requiring detailed knowledge or custody of the computer programs. If one person is permitted to perform duties in several of these functions, internal control is weakened, and the opportunity exists for fraudulent data to be inserted in the system.

Access to Assets by EDP Personnel.   Whenever the responsibilities for record-keeping and custody of the related assets are combined, the opportunities for an employee to conceal the abstraction of assets are increased. Since EDP is basically a record-keeping function, it is highly desirable to limit the access of EDP personnel to company assets. However, EDP personnel have direct access to cash if EDP activity includes the preparation of signed cheques. EDP personnel may also have indirect access to assets if, for example, EDP is used to generate shipping orders authorizing the release of inventory.

The combination of record-keeping with access to assets seriously weakens internal control unless adequate *compensating controls* are present. One type of compensating control is the use of predetermined *batch totals,* such as document counts and totals of significant data fields, prepared in departments independent of EDP. For example, if EDP performs the function of printing cheques, another department should be responsible for authorizing the preparation of the cheques. The authorizing department should maintain a record of the total number and dollar amount of cheques authorized. These independently prepared batch totals should then be compared with the computer output before the cheques are released.

It is difficult for compensating controls to eliminate entirely the risk that results from EDP personnel having access to company assets. Auditors should therefore realize that the risk of computer-centred fraud is greatest in those areas in which EDP personnel have access to assets.

Management Fraud.   Organizational controls are reasonably effective in preventing an individual employee from perpetrating a fraud, but they do not prevent fraud involving collusion. If key employees or company officers conspire in an effort to commit fraud, internal controls that rely upon separation of duties can be rendered inoperative.

Illustrative Case

Equity Funding Corporation of America, a company in the United States, went into bankruptcy after it was discovered that the company's financial statements had been grossly and fraudulently misleading for a period of years. A subsidiary of the company had been manufacturing bogus insurance policies on fictitious persons and then selling these policies to other insurance companies. When the fraud was discovered, Equity Funding's balance sheet included more than $120 million in fictitious assets, far exceeding the $75 million net income reported over the 13-year life of the company.

Perhaps the most startling revelation of the Equity Funding scandal was that numerous officers and employees of the company had worked together for years to perpetrate and conceal the fraud. The fictious transactions had been carefully integrated into the company's computer-based accounting system. A wide variety of fraudulent supporting documents had been prepared for the sole purpose of deceiving auditors and governmental regulatory agencies. Upon disclosure of the activities, several members of top management were convicted of criminal charges.

The Equity Funding scandal is often described as a computer-based fraud. It was not because of the use of computers, however, that the company was able to deceive auditors and government investigators. Rather, the fraudulent activities were successfully concealed for a number of years because of the unprecedented willingness of a large number of company officers and employees to participate in the scheme. Collusion of the magnitude existing at Equity Funding would render any system of internal control ineffective.

Documentation

Internal control in an EDP department requires not only subdivision of duties but also the maintenance of adequate documentation describing the system and procedures used in all data processing tasks. An effective system of documentation helps achieve control by providing users and operators with current operating instructions. It also aids programmers in revising existing programs.

The purpose of *system documentation* is to provide an overall description of a processing system including system flowcharts and descriptions of the nature of input, operations, and output. It also establishes responsibilities for entering data, performing control tasks, and correcting and reprocessing exceptions detected by the computer. An example of system documentation is a *user's manual* that provides instructions for user tasks, such as preparing data for processing, applying control procedures, and operating computer terminals.

Another important type of documentation is *program documentation,* which contains a complete description of each application program. As a minimum, program documentation should include:

1. A description of the purpose of the program.
2. A list and explanation of processing controls associated with the program.
3. A record of layouts showing the organization of data on magnetic tapes or disks.
4. Examples of computer output, including exception reports.
5. Program flowcharts showing the major steps and logic of the computer program.
6. Program listings in source language.
7. Program approval and change sheets showing proper authorization for all initial programs and subsequent changes.
8. An operations manual, containing instructions for running the program.
9. Test data utilized in testing and debugging the program.

Complete program documentation may be utilized by systems analysts and programmers for making authorized changes in programs. Computer operators, on the other hand, should have access only to the *operations manual* that contains the instructions for processing the programs. If operators have access to detailed information about programs, the opportunities for an operator to change or patch a program are increased.

Documentation is helpful to the auditors in reviewing the controls over program changes, evaluating controls written into programs, and determining the program logic. The auditors must also refer to format and layout information in the documentation in order to prepare test decks or special audit programs for testing the client's processing programs and computerized files.

Hardware Controls

Modern electronic data processing equipment is highly accurate and reliable. Most errors in computer output result from erroneous input or an error in the program. Auditors, however, should be familiar with the hardware controls within a given system in order to appraise the reliability of the hardware. Hardware (equipment) controls are built into the computer by the computer manufacturer. Among the more common hardware or equipment controls are the following:

1. **Echo check.** The purpose of the echo check is to ensure that peripheral equipment, such as a printer, complies with computer instructions. A signal is returned to the computer verifying the transmitted data or acknowledging the performance of an assigned task.
2. **Self-diagnosis.** Many computers are supplied with hardware or software routines that allow the computer to test its own circuitry. Self-diagnosis routines can identify a defective circuit or memory module before the system fails.
3. **Duplicate process check.** A duplicate process check consists of performing an operation twice and comparing the two results. In the duplicate process check known as *read after write,* the computer reads back data after they have been moved in the system and verifies their accuracy.
4. **Parity check.** Data are processed by the computer in arrays of *bits* (binary digits of 1 or 0). In addition to bits necessary to represent the numeric or alphabetic character, a *parity* bit is added when necessary to make the sum of all the 1 bits always odd or even, depending upon the make of the computer. As data are transferred at rapid speeds between computer components, the parity check is applied by the computer to assure that bits are not lost during the transfer process.

A program of preventive maintenance also is essential to assure the proper functioning of computer hardware.

Security for Files and Equipment

Every EDP system should have adequate security controls to safeguard equipment, files, and programs against loss, damage, and access by unauthorized personnel. When programs or files can be accessed from minicomputers or on-line terminals, users should be required to enter a *secret password* in order to gain access to the system. The computer's operating system should be programmed to maintain a log of all terminal usage and should produce a warning if repeated attempts are made to gain access to data by use of incorrect passwords. The importance of these controls has been illustrated by several highly publicized incidents of youthful "hackers" using home computers to gain entry to both military and commercial computer systems.

Another purpose of security controls is to enable a company to reconstruct its computer-based records in the event that files are lost or damaged. Magnetic tapes of disks can be damaged by exposure to magnetic fields or excessive heat. Also, it is possible that a program or a file will accidentally be erased while it is being processed by the computer. As a precaution against such accidents, duplicate copies should be made of all files and programs. These backup copies should be stored at a separate location from the originals. Records that are updated on-line should be transferred to disks or tapes at regular frequent intervals to prevent significant data loss in the event of power failure.

Files that are periodically updated, such as the accounts receivable files, are called master files. Generally, three generations of master files should be retained to enable reproduction of files lost or destroyed. Under this *grandfather-father-son* principle of file retention, the current updated master file is the *son,* the master file utilized in the updating run that produced the son is the *father,* and the previous father is the *grandfather.* Records of transactions for the current period and for the prior period also should be retained to facilitate updating the older master files in the event that the current master file is accidentally destroyed. The three generations should be stored in separate sections of the file library, or in separate locations, to minimize the risk of losing all three generations at once.

Safeguards are also necessary to protect the equipment against sabotage, fire, and water damage. The best way to prevent deliberate damage is to limit access to the facility to authorized personnel. Outsiders should be kept away from the facility, and EDP personnel should be carefully screened before employment. Management should always be alert to the possibility of damage by a disgruntled employee. Frequently, the location of the computer facility is kept relatively secret. The facility should have no windows and few doors; entrances should be controlled by guards or badge-activated locks. In addition, the computer facilities should be fire resistant, air conditioned, and above likely flood levels.

Controls over Input

Input controls, the first type of application controls, are designed to provide assurance that data received for processing represent properly *authorized* transactions and are *accurate* and *complete* when read into the computer. Control over input begins with proper authorization for initiation of the transactions to be processed. EDP is primarily a record-keeping department and therefore should not be authorized to initiate transactions. When transaction data are originally recorded on hard-copy source documents, such as sales orders, authorization may be indicated by the appropriate person initiating the document. In on-line systems, transaction data may be entered directly into the computer from remote terminal devices located in the departments initiating the transactions. In these cases, access to the terminals must be limited to those persons authorized to initiate transactions. This may be accomplished by assigning to authorized terminal users an identification number that must be entered into the terminal before the computer will accept the input data. Also, the operating system should maintain a log of activity at each terminal to be reviewed by the system's control group for evidence of unauthorized use.

Input validation (edit) checks, such as the following should be performed on data as it is entered:

1. *Limit test.* A test of the reasonableness of a field of data, given a predetermined upper and/or lower limit.
2. *Validity test.* A comparison of data (e.g., employee, vendor, and other codes) against a master file for authenticity.
3. *Self-checking number (digit).* A number containing redundant information, such as the sum of the digits in another number, permitting a check for accuracy when the number is input, or after it has been transmitted from one device to another.

Input validation checks increase the accuracy of input data because any data that fail to meet a test requirement are rejected by the system and revised data are requested from the user. The data can also be tested for completeness as it is entered at a terminal.

Input controls are necessary in batch processing systems to determine that no data are lost or added to the batch. The sequence of serial numbers of source documents comprising each batch should be accounted for. In addition, the following controls help assure the accuracy and completeness of batch processing:

1. *Item (or record count).* A count of the number of items or transactions being input in a given batch.
2. *Control total.* The total of one field of information items in a batch. An example would be total sales of a batch of sales orders.
3. *Hash total.* A total of one field of information for all items in a batch, used in the same manner as a control total. The difference between a hash total and a control total is that a hash total has no intrinsic meaning. An example of a hash total would be the sum of the employee social insurance numbers being input for payroll process.

Provision should be made for verifying the accuracy of the conversion of source documents to machine-readable media. For example, keyed information may be entered a second time, independently, for verification of its accuracy.

Control over Processing

Processing controls are designed to assure the reliability and accuracy of data processing. A major method of achieving control over processing is the use of ***program controls,*** which are written into the computer programs. A number of the input controls described above are programmed as processing controls, including limit tests, validity tests, self-checking numbers, items counts, and control and hash totals. In addition, ***file labels*** may be used to ensure that the proper transaction file or master file is being used on a specific run. A ***header label*** is a machine-readable message on a tape or disk file, identifying the file and the date it was created. A ***trailer file*** is the last record in a file and contains such control devices as an item count and/or control totals. These internal labels are used in conjunction with gummed-paper external labels to prevent operators from accidentally processing the wrong file.

In cases of exceptions or errors disclosed by program controls, the computer processing will halt, or the exceptions will be printed out. Exception reports should be transmitted directly to the control group for follow-up. The control group's responsibility includes ascertaining that corrections of exceptions are properly entered and that duplicate corrections are avoided.

The control group also monitors the operator's activities. A log maintained by the operator should be available for review by the control group. The log records the description of each run, the elapsed time for the run, operator console interventions, machine halts, master files utilized, and so on.

Controls over Output

Output controls are designed to assure the reliability of computer output and to determine that output is distributed only to authorized personnel. Reconciliation of control totals generated by the computer to the totals developed at the input phase is an important aspect of output controls. In some EDP systems, user departments appraise the reliability of output from the data processing department by extensive review and testing. For example, sales invoices generated by the computer may be tested for clerical accuracy and pricing by an accounting clerk. Although these *user controls* can be very effective, it is generally more efficient to implement program controls, and have users merely test the overall reasonableness of the output. Another important output control involves assigning the EDP control group the responsibility for distributing the computer output to the appropriate users, and for following up on the exceptions reported.

Control Responsibilities of the Internal Auditors

An internal audit function should exist separate and distinct from the work of the control group in the data processing department. The control group is primarily concerned with day-to-day maintenance of the internal controls for data processing, whereas the internal auditors are interested in evaluating the overall efficiency of data processing operations and the related internal controls.

The internal auditors should participate in the design of the data processing system to ensure that the system provides a proper *audit trail* and includes adequate internal controls. Once the system becomes operative, internal auditors review all aspects of the system on a test basis to determine that prescribed internal controls are operating as planned. Among other things, the internal auditors will test to determine that no changes are made in the system without proper authorization, programming personnel are functionally separate from computer operating personnel, adequate documentation is maintained, input controls are functioning effectively, and the control group is performing its assigned functions.

Integrated Test Facility.   One method used by internal auditors to test and monitor controls in EDP applications is an *integrated test facility*. An integrated test facility is a subsystem of dummy records and files built into the regular data processing system. These dummy files permit test data to be processed simultaneously with regular (live) input without adversely affecting the live data files or output. The test data, which include all conceivable types of transactions and exceptions, affect only the dummy files and dummy output. For this reason, an integrated test facility is often called the "minicompany approach" to testing the system. Integrated test facilities may be used in either on-line, real-time, or batch processing systems.

The internal auditing staff monitors the processing of test data, studying the effects upon the dummy files, exception reports and other output produced, and the follow-up of exceptions by the control group. An integrated test facility for payroll applications, for example, could be set up by including a fictitious department and records for fictitious employees in the payroll master file. Input data for the dummy department would be included with input data from actual departments. Internal auditors would monitor all output relating to the dummy department, including payroll records, exception reports, and payroll cheques. (In this situation, strict control would be necessary to prevent misuse of the dummy payroll cheques.)

A problem with integrated test facilities is the risk that someone may manipulate the real data files by transferring data to or from the dummy files. Controls should exist to prevent unauthorized access to the dummy files, and the internal auditors should monitor all activity in these files.

Also, the test facility must be carefully designed to ensure that real files are not *inadvertently* contaminated with the fictitious test data.

Control in Microcomputer Systems

The term *microcomputer* refers to a variety of small computers including computer workstations, personal computers, and intelligent terminals. Although technology is reducing the extent of the differences between microcomputers and large computers, microcomputers generally are less flexible, smaller in memory capacity, and slower at processing data than large computers. However, microcomputers have the advantage of giving office personnel and salespeople direct access to the computer without the turnaround time associated with a centralized system. For that reason, even audit clients with sophisticated central systems are likely to use microcomputers for a variety of on-site record-keeping functions.

The advent of microcomputers has resulted in a decentralization of data processing activities. In a microcomputer environment, computers are located in user departments and operated by user personnel who have little or no computer training. Processing usually is performed with commercial software packages, thus eliminating the need for the client to employ programmers. For secondary storage when the computer is operating, microcomputers use hard (rigid) disk drives where programs and files are stored. Floppy (flexible) disks or magnetic tapes are used as *backup* for the hard disk.

Internal control over microcomputers is enhanced when data processing procedures are documented and operators are well trained. To assure that the client can reconstruct financial records, duplicate (backup) diskettes or tapes of files should be made frequently, and stored away from the originals in a secure location. Since microcomputers are located in user departments, there is a greater risk of use by unauthorized personnel. Therefore, the microcomputer's operating system should require the operator to enter authorization codes to gain access to menus that control specific programs and files. As a means of detecting improper activities, there should be an independent review of activity logs generated by the microcomputer. In addition, management should consider locking away critical software or installing a locking on/off switch on the microcomputer to prevent unauthorized use of the machine after business hours.

Impact of EDP on the Audit Trail

In a manual or mechanical data processing system, an audit trail (also referred to as a *transaction trail*) of hard-copy documentation links individual transactions with the summary figures in the financial statements.

Computers, on the other hand, are able to create, update, and erase data in computer-based records without any visible evidence of a change being made. During the early development of EDP systems, this capability led to some concern among accountants that electronic data processing would obscure or even eliminate the audit trail. Although it is technologically possible to design an EDP system that would leave no audit trail, such a system would be neither practical nor desirable. Valid business reasons exist for the inclusion of an audit trail in even the most sophisticated EDP systems. An adequate audit trail is necessary to enable management to direct and control the operations of the business, to permit file reconstruction in the event of processing errors or computer failure, and to accommodate the needs of external auditors and governmental agencies.

An audit difficulty with advanced computer systems is that while an audit trail may still exist, it may not be in printed form; it may be generated only in machine-readable form. Shortly after it is generated, the audit trail information may be transferred to a low-cost storage medium, such as microfiche. Some companies use electronic data interchange (EDI) in which the company and its customers or suppliers use communication links to exchange business data electronically. Source documents, such as invoices, purchase orders, cheques, and bills of lading, are replaced with electronic transactions. For example, in an EDI system a purchase transaction may be automatically initiated by the company's computer by sending an electronic message (purchase order) directly to a supplier's computer system. The auditors should consider such data retention and processing policies in planning the nature, extent, and timing of their audit procedures. Emphasis should be placed on coordinating the efforts of external and internal auditors to assure adequate audit coverage.

Fears that EDP would eliminate the audit trail have not materialized. During the design of an EDP system, management will normally consult with both its internal auditors and external auditors to assure that an adequate audit trail is built into the system. In an EDP system, of course, the audit trail may consist of computer printouts and data stored in machine readable form, rather than the more traditional handwritten source documents, journals, and ledgers.

THE AUDITORS' CONSIDERATION OF INTERNAL CONTROL IN AN EDP SYSTEM

Whether financial statements are produced by a manual, mechanical, or electronic data processing system, the auditors must properly consider internal control. Their consideration provides the auditors with a basis for assessing control risk to determine the nature, extent, and timing of work necessary to complete the audit. In addition, it serves as the basis for the auditors' recommendations to the client for improving the internal control.

Regardless of the type of data processing system used by the client, the auditors' consideration of internal control involves four distinct steps. The auditors must (1) obtain an understanding of internal control sufficient to plan the audit, (2) assess control risk and design tests of controls, (3) perform tests of controls, and (4) reassess control risk and design substantive tests or procedures.

Obtain an Understanding of Internal Control Sufficient to Plan the Audit

As discussed in Chapter 7, the auditors must have a sufficient understanding of internal control to plan the audit, regardless of whether the client has a manual or EDP accounting system. This understanding of internal control should include knowledge about the design of relevant policies, procedures, systems, and records, and whether they have been placed in operation by the client.

Specialized skills may be needed to understand internal control or to design effective audit tests for clients with complex EDP systems. For this reason, many public accounting firms have trained *EDP specialists* who act as consultants to the firm's other auditors. Other public accounting firms may even rely on outside consultants to provide assistance on complex engagements. In either case, the auditor in charge of the engagement should have sufficient computer-related knowledge to review the adequacy of the procedures performed by the specialist. The results of the specialist's procedures must be considered when planning the nature, extent, and timing of other audit procedures.

The auditors' documentation of the client's EDP system varies depending on the complexity of the system. For a client with simple internal control, a written narrative might be adequate. However, the auditors generally document their understanding of EDP systems by the use of systems flowcharts or specially designed internal control questionnaires.

Systems Flowcharts.   As explained in Chapter 7, systems flowcharts are a commonly used technique for documenting internal control in audit working papers. An advantage of flowcharting, with respect to EDP systems, is that the EDP department should have systems flowcharts available for all computer applications as part of the standard documentation.

An illustration of a systems flowchart for sales, accounts receivable, and cash receipts appears in Figure 8–2. The following description of the illustrated procedures and processing steps should be helpful in studying the illustrated flowchart.

1. Orders are received from sales representatives, and sales invoices are generated on an intelligent terminal. A magnetic tape of sales transactions is generated by the terminal as a by-product of sales invoice

FIGURE 8–2   System Flowchart

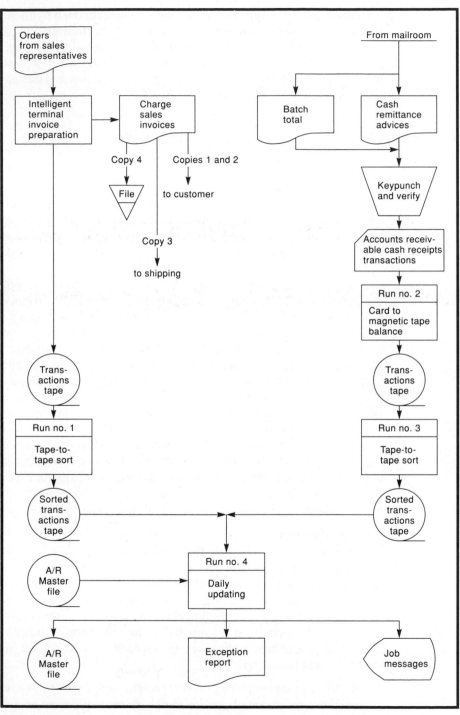

preparation. Two copies of the invoice are mailed to the customer, one copy is sent to the shipping department, and one copy is filed off-line. The items on the magnetic tape are then sorted into the proper sequence on another magnetic tape.

2. Individual cash remittances from customers are received from the mail room and verified to a batch total, which is also received from the mail room. These remittances are keypunched on cards, and the cards are verified. The deck of punched cards is then converted to magnetic tape. The items on the magnetic tape are in turn sorted into proper sequence on another magnetic tape.

3. The accounts receivable master file is updated by processing both the sales transactions tape and the cash receipts transactions tape. A by-product of the updating of the accounts receivable master file is an ***exception report*** for the run and a printout (on an on-line terminal) of any job messages.

The client's documentation of EDP activities usually includes ***program flowcharts*** as well as systems flowcharts. Program flowcharts illustrate the detailed logic of specific computer programs. Auditors capable of interpreting program flowcharts may evaluate the program controls contained in specific computer applications and draw inferences regarding the computer output.

Internal Control Questionnaires for EDP Systems.   The use of internal control questionnaires was discussed in Chapter 7. A specialized EDP internal control questionnaire for the general controls over access to the computer system is illustrated by Figure 8–3.

Auditing around the Computer.   When the client's computer system is relatively simple and produces hard copy documents and records, the auditors may decide that it is efficient to assess control risk at, or near, the maximum and audit around the computer. Using this approach, the auditors will process input data manually on a test basis. The auditors' results are then compared to those obtained by the client's EDP processing, and any discrepancies are investigated. This technique is called ***auditing around the computer*** because the auditors bypass the computer rather than utilizing it in conducting their tests. While auditing around the computer can be an effective approach in certain circumstances, it is unacceptable if the reason for its use is merely the auditors' lack of understanding of the client's computer processing activities.

Assess Control Risk and Design Additional Tests of Controls

After obtaining an understanding of the client's overall control environment, the flow of transactions through the EDP system, and basic control procedures, the auditors are in a position to make a preliminary as-

---

FIGURE 8–3 Control Procedures Questionnaire
General Control Procedures Access to System Resources

	Yes, No, N/A	Comments
1. Does the company have documented policies and procedures for computer security?	_____	_____
2. Are there adequate physical controls to restrict access to the computer room to authorized individuals?	_____	_____
3. Are programmers restricted from access to application programs, job control language, and live data files?	_____	_____
4. Has a test library procedure been established such that programming is not performed using live data files and application programs?	_____	_____
5. Are operators restricted from access to source programs?	_____	_____
6. Are utility programs that can alter data without any audit trail adequately controlled and their use logged for subsequent management reviews?	_____	_____
7. Is there terminal access control software that restricts who can access the system, what programs can be used, and what files the user and/or program can access?	_____	_____
8. Does terminal access control rely on passwords or other identification/ validation processes to control access to the system?	_____	_____
9. Are passwords administered to ensure that they are confidential, unique, and updated to reflect needed changes on a timely basis?	_____	_____
10. Are all significant events (security violations, use of critical software, or system commands, etc.) logged and promptly investigated by appropriate management personnel?	_____	_____

Adapted from AICPA, *Guide for Consideration of the Internal Control Structure in a Financial Statement Audit* (New York, 1990).

sessment of the reliability of the client's internal controls. If it appears that the controls are not adequate to provide a basis for further reductions of control risk, the auditors will omit additional tests of controls. On the other hand, if it appears that the controls will prove sufficiently reliable to justify the audit effort of testing the procedures, the auditors will document those controls before designing and performing the additional tests of controls.

Perform Additional Tests of Controls

The purpose of tests of controls is to provide reasonable assurance that the controls described in the audit working papers are actually operating as planned. Regardless of the nature of the client's data processing system, auditors must conduct tests of those controls they intend to rely on to reduce their assessment of control risk. The nature of the data processing system may, however, affect the specific procedures employed by the auditors in their testing of the controls.

Auditors usually begin their consideration and tests of internal control over EDP systems with the general controls. This is an efficient approach since the effectiveness of specific application controls is often dependent on the existence of effective general controls over all EDP activities. The auditors, for example, would get little audit evidence from testing program controls in an environment where programmers can easily make unauthorized changes in the programs. In the absence of controls over program modification, the auditors have no evidence that the program being tested is identical to the one used to process data during the year. Such weaknesses may limit the auditors' ability to rely on application controls to reduce their assessment of control risk.

Procedures to Test General Controls.   Auditors usually test general controls by observing the performance of duties by client personnel; reviewing authorizations, documentation, and approvals of programs and program changes; inspecting the equipment in use; and observing the security measures in force. The nature of general controls is such that their presence usually must be observed rather than determined by the examination of accounting data.

Procedures to Test Application Controls.   Procedures used to test application controls vary significantly from one system or application to another. In a batch system, for example, input controls may be tested by accounting for the serial sequence of source documents in selected batches, verifying the computation of batch control totals, and comparing control totals to computer output. In an on-line, real-time system, on the other hand, batch data are not available and the auditors must design different tests of controls.

In testing processing controls, the auditors review the procedures performed by the EDP control group and review the working papers of any testing done by the client's internal auditors. To test the effectiveness of significant controls in the computer programs, auditors examine exception reports and activity logs generated by the computer. These documents list the violations of program controls that occurred during computer processing, providing evidence of the application of those controls. The auditors also need to understand and test the manual follow-up procedures used to investigate items listed on the exception reports, because the effectiveness of the program controls depends on effective follow-up on the exceptions. If user controls have been implemented, the auditors also can examine the client's documentation of the procedures to obtain evidence about the effectiveness of program control procedures.

Other techniques for testing program controls involve auditing "through the computer" with the use of *computer-assisted audit techniques*. These techniques include the use of test decks, controlled programs, program analysis, tagging and tracing, and generalized audit software programs. Computer-assisted audit techniques are used by both external and internal auditors.

Test Decks (Data). In the audit of a manual accounting system, the auditors trace sample transactions through the records from their inception to their final disposition. In the audit of an EDP system, a comparable approach is the use of a *test deck*. The test decks developed by the client's programmers may be utilized by the external auditors once they have satisfied themselves by study of flowcharts and printouts that the tests are valid. As an alternative, the auditors may develop their own test decks, but this approach is often too time-consuming to be practicable.

Test decks should include all regular transactions and significant exceptions and errors in a process. Among these exceptions and errors would be missing transactions, erroneous transactions, illogical transactions, out-of-balance batches, and out-of-sequence records. The auditors will carefully appraise the program controls and control group functions with respect to the test deck errors and exceptions. Dummy transactions and records used in test decks can be specially coded, or alternatively, copies of the client's files can be used for testing to avoid contamination of the client's genuine records and files. If the client's computer system includes an integrated test facility, the auditors may use this facility to prevent their test data from contaminating the client's files.

Controlled Programs. As an alternative or supplement to the test-deck approach, the auditors may monitor the processing of current data by using a duplicate program that is held under their control. They then compare their output to that developed by the client's copy of the program. They may also reprocess historical data with their controlled program for comparison with the original output. Reprocessing historical data may alert the auditors to undocumented changes in the client's programs.

Controlled programs are advantageous because the auditor may test the client's program with both genuine (live) and test data. Through controlled programs, auditors may test program controls without risk of contaminating the client's files. Also, the testing may be conducted at an independent computer facility without utilizing the client's computer or data processing personnel.

Program Analysis Techniques.   Many computers will accept programs that can generate computer-made flowcharts of other programs. A trained auditor can examine the flowcharts as a test of the logic of applications programs, and to ensure that the client's program documentation describes the program that is actually being used.

Tagging and Tracing Transactions.   This technique involves "tagging" transactions with an indicator when they are entered into the system. The computer provides the auditors with a printout of the details of the steps in processing tagged transactions. This printout is examined for evidence of unauthorized program steps.

Generalized Audit Software.   Many large public accounting firms have developed *generalized audit software* (computer programs) that may be used to test the reliability of the client's programs as well as to perform many specific auditing functions. This audit software is suited for use on a wide variety of computer systems.

One application of computer audit software is to verify the reliability of the client's programs through a process termed *parallel simulation.* The generalized audit software may be directed to perform processing functions essentially equivalent to those of the client's programs. If the client's program is operating properly, the output of the client's processing of a group of transactions should be equivalent to the output from the generalized audit software package. However, this application is both complex and costly in many cases.

The value of generalized audit software lies in the fact that the auditors are able to conduct independent processing of live data. Often, the verification of the client's output would be too large a task to be undertaken manually, but can be done efficiently through a parallel computer program. Even when manual verification is possible, the use of a parallel program allows the auditors to expand greatly the size of the sample of transactions to be tested. An extensive examination of the client's files may become a feasible and economic undertaking. It is not necessary, however, to duplicate all of the client's data processing. Testing should be performed only to the extent necessary to determine the reliability of the client's financial reporting systems.

Generalized Audit Software and Substantive Testing.   Audit software is available for a wide variety of audit applications. It is most widely used for retrieving data from the client's system for use by the auditors in substantiating account balances. In performing retrieval functions, the audit software *interfaces* with the client's computer files and locates specific data requested by the auditors. The audit software may then be used to rearrange the data in a format more useful to the auditors, compare the data to other files, make computations, and select random samples. Applications of this nature include:

1. Examining the client's records for overall quality, completeness, and valid conditions. In auditing a manual system, the auditors become aware of the general quality, accuracy, and validity of the client's records through visual observation. Since the auditors do not have the same physical contact with computer-based records, the audit software may be used to scan the client's files for various improprieties. For example, the accounts receivable file may be scanned for account balances in excess of credit limits, and the depreciation expense may be recomputed for each item in the plant assets file. The great speed of the computer often makes it possible to perform such calculations for each item in the population, rather than having to rely upon a sample-based test.

2. Rearranging data and performing analyses. The audit software may be used to rearrange the data in the client's files into a format more useful to the auditors. For example, the accounts receivable file may be reorganized into the format of an aged trial balance. Data from the client's files may be printed out in the format of the auditors' working papers. In addition, the audit software can make analytical computations, such as computing turnover ratios to identify slow-moving inventory.

3. Selecting audit samples. Audit samples may be selected from the client's files on a random basis or in accordance with any other criteria specified by the auditors. Examples include selection of the inventory items to be test counted and the accounts receivable to be confirmed. An additional time savings may result if the audit software is used to print out the actual confirmation requests.

4. Comparing data on separate files. When similar data is contained in two or more files, the audit software can compare the files and identify any discrepancies. For example, the changes in accounts receivable over a period of time may be compared to the details of the cash receipts and credit sales transactions files. Also, actual operating results may be compared to forecasts.

5. Comparing the results of audit procedures with the client's records. Data obtained by the auditors may be converted to machine-readable form and compared to the data in computer-based files. For example, the results of the auditors' inventory test counts can be compared to the perpetual inventory file.

Using Audit Software: An Illustration.   To illustrate some of the possible uses of generalized audit software, let us consider a specific example. Assume that an auditor is planning to observe a client's physical count of inventories at a specific date. All inventory is stored either in the client's distribution centre or at a public warehouse. The client maintains computer-based perpetual inventory records, which are updated daily. This inventory file contains the following information:

Part number.	Cost per unit.
Description of item.	Date of last purchase.
Location.	Date of last sale.
Quantity on hand.	Quantity sold during the year.

The client has provided the auditor with a duplicate copy of the inventory file as of the date of the physical count.

The left-hand column in Figure 8–4 indicates typical inventory audit procedures the auditor might perform. The right-hand column indicates how the auditor's generalized audit software might be helpful in the performance of these procedures.

Auditors do not need extensive technical EDP knowledge in order to make use of generalized audit software. They will find it necessary to perform only a modest amount of programming. In fact, many public accounting firms have found that they can train audit staff members to code specification sheets and operate a generalized audit program within a few days. Because of the simplified procedures that have been developed, auditors can, after limited training, program and operate the generalized audit software independently—that is, without assistance from the client's EDP personnel. On occasion, prepackaged software may not be available for a specific audit application. Most large accounting firms, however, have technical support groups that can design software routines to meet the specifications of the audit staff.

As previously mentioned, a number of the larger public accounting firms have developed their own generalized audit software. Similar programs are available to members of the profession from private software companies.

Reassess Control Risk and Design Substantive Tests

Auditors assess internal control to determine the extent to which it may be relied upon to produce reliable accounting data and thereby reduce control risk. This assessment in turn determines the nature, timing, and extent of the substantive testing necessary for the auditors to express an opinion as to the fairness of the financial statements.

FIGURE 8–4   Illustration of the Uses of Generalized Audit Software

Basic Inventory Audit Procedure	*How Generalized Audit Software Might Be Helpful*
1. Observe the physical count, making appropriate test counts.	1. Determine which items are to be test counted by selecting from the inventory file a sample of items that provides the desired dollar coverage.
2. Test the mathematical accuracy of the inventory extensions and footings.	2. For each item in the inventory file, multiply the quantity on hand by the cost per unit and add the extended amounts.
3. Compare the auditors' test counts to the inventory records.	3. Arrange the test counts in a format identical to the inventory file and compare the two files.
4. Compare the client's physical count data to the inventory records.	4. Compare the quantity of each item counted to the quantity on hand in the inventory file.
5. Perform a lower-of-cost-and-market test by comparing a list of current costs per item from vendors to the cost per item in the inventory record.	5. Compare the current costs per unit to the cost per unit in the inventory file; print out the extended value for each item, using the lower of two unit costs, and add extended amounts.
6. Test purchases and sales cutoff.	6. List a sample of items on the inventory file for which the date of last purchase or last sale is on, or immediately before, the date of the physical count.
7. Confirm the existence of items located in public warehouses.	7. List items located in public warehouses.
8. Analyze inventory for evidence of obsolescence or slow-moving items.	8. List items from the inventory file for which the turnover ratio (quantity sold divided by quantity on hand) is low or for which the date of last sale indicates a lack of recent transactions.

Source: AICPA, adapted from Uniform CPA Examination.

Conceptually, considering internal controls over EDP activities is no different from considering other aspects of the system. Substantive testing procedures must be expanded in those areas where internal controls are weak and may be restricted in areas where control is unusually strong. In assessing control over EDP activity, the auditors should consider the controls applied by user departments and internal auditing, as well as controls applied within the EDP department.

Computer Service Centres

Computer service centres (or organizations) provide data processing services to customers who do not do enough data processing to justify having their own computer facilities. Customers usually transmit data in batches to the service centre, and the service centre processes the data and returns the output to the customer.

Some computer centres operate on a time-sharing basis. The subscribers to a commercial time-sharing system can, through their terminals, run programs, store these programs in the computer for subsequent use, use the programs developed by the time-sharing company, and store files of data in the computer for subsequent use. In brief, the user of a time-sharing system has available most of the services that would be available through ownership of a computer.

When a service centre performs data processing for a client, the centre's internal controls interact with the client's control system. Accordingly, the auditors' understanding of the control system must be based, in part, on an understanding of processing activities at the computer service centre. A visit to the centre may be necessary to obtain this understanding. In addition, if the auditors plan to reduce their assessed level of control-risk based on certain controls, they must obtain evidence of their operational effectiveness regardless of whether those controls are applied by the client or by the service centre.

The auditors may find that controls applied by the client are adequate to assure that errors or fraud in transactions are detected. For example, the client's personnel may develop input control totals and compare them to the service centre's output. They may also reperform computer calculations on a test basis. When such controls are adequate, the auditors need test only client controls to reduce their assessment of control risk; there is no need to perform tests of controls at the service centre.

In other situations, the controls performed at the computer service centre are necessary to achieve the client's control objectives. This means that the auditors' assessment of control risk cannot be significantly reduced without evidence that controls at the centre are operating effectively. To obtain this evidence, the auditors may have to perform tests at the service centre.

Reports by Service Auditors. Most service centres perform similar processing services for numerous clients. If the auditors of each client (called *user auditors*) were to visit the service centre for the purpose of examining internal controls, they would ask similar questions and perform similar tests of compliance. It may be advantageous for the service centre to engage its own auditors (called *service auditors*) to examine their system of internal control and issue a report on the centre's system. The user auditors may then elect to rely on this report as an alternative to visiting the service centre themselves.

The *CICA Handbook* Sections 5310 and 5900 on service organizations (service centres) state that service auditors may report on either the design and existence of control procedures or on the design, effective operation, and continuity of control procedure at the service organization. A report on the design and existence of control procedures tells the user auditors whether the control procedures were suitably designed and existed to achieve internal control objectives, but it does not provide a basis for reliance on controls at the service centre. To rely on service centre controls, the user auditors must have evidence that controls *are being effectively applied as prescribed.* This evidence can only be obtained from tests of control effectiveness performed directly by the user auditors, or a report on the results of tests of control effectiveness performed by the service auditors. If the report covers tests of the controls on which the user auditors intend to rely, there usually is no need for the user auditors to perform their own tests at the centre. They may decide to rely solely on the results of the service auditors' tests.

Before relying upon a service auditors' examination, the user auditors should take steps to satisfy themselves as to the professional qualifications, competence, and integrity of the service auditors. In addition, they should enquire of the service centre management and the service auditors as to whether any significant changes have been made in internal control at the service centre subsequent to the service auditors' internal examination.

KEY TERMS

application controls   Internal controls relating to a specific accounting task, such as preparation of a payroll.

batch processing   A system in which like transactions are processed periodically as a group.

control total   A total of one information field for all the records of a batch, such as the total sales dollars for a batch of sales invoices.

data base management system   A system that eliminates data redundancy by storing data for two or more computer applications in an integrated data base.

data communication   In a system with this capability, data may be transmitted between computer devices at different locations.

direct (random) access   A storage technique in which each piece of data is assigned an address and may be retrieved without searching through other stored data. A magnetic disk drive is a direct access device.

distributive data processing (end user computing)   A system that uses data communication to allow users to perform certain data processing activities in their own departments.

electronic data interchange (EDI)   A system in which data is exchanged electronically between the computers of different companies. In an EDI system source documents are replaced with electronic transactions created in a standard format.

file   An organized collection of related records, such as a customer file.

file integrity   The accuracy and reliability of data in a file.

general controls   Internal controls that relate to all EDP applications. The category includes organizational controls, documentation, equipment controls, and security controls.

generalized audit software   A group of computer programs used by auditors to locate and process data contained in a client's EDP-based records. The audit programs perform such functions as rearranging the data in a format more useful to the auditors, comparing records, selecting samples, and making computations. This software is compatible with a wide variety of different computer systems.

hard copy   Computer output in printed form, such as printed listings, reports, and summaries.

hash total   A meaningless control total such as the total of all invoice numbers in a batch of sales invoices, used to determine whether data are lost, added, or processed incorrectly.

header label   A machine-readable record at the beginning of a file that identifies the file.

integrated test facility   A set of dummy records and files included in an EDP system enabling test data to be processed simultaneously with live input.

intelligent terminals   Visual display or keyboard/printer terminals that have a minimum amount of processing capabilities. They are often used to input transactions directly to magnetic tapes or disks for subsequent computer processing.

interface   To run two or more files or programs simultaneously in a manner permitting data to be transferred from one to another.

master file   A file of relatively permanent data or information that is generally updated periodically.

off-line   Pertaining to peripheral devices or equipment not in direct communication with the central processing unit of the computer.

on-line   Pertaining to peripheral devices or equipment in direct communication with the central processing unit of the computer.

on-line system   A system that allows direct access to information on computer files by users of that information.

operating system   Software that coordinates and controls hardware components. Authorization procedures may be programmed into the operating system to restrict access to files and programs to authorized personnel.

patch   A new section of coding added in a rough or expedient way to modify a program.

program analysis techniques   Techniques for testing program controls that involve the examination of computer-generated flowcharts of application programs.

program flowchart   A graphic representation of the major steps and logic of a computer program.

record   A group of related items or fields of data handled as a unit.

record layout   A diagram showing all the fields of data in a record and their arrangement in the record.

self-checking number (digit)   A number that contains a redundant suffixed digit (check digit) permitting the number to be verified for accuracy after it has been transferred from one device or medium to another.

sequential access   A storage technique in which data is read and written in numerical (i.e., account number) sequence. A magnetic tape drive is a sequential storage device.

service auditors' report (of a computer service centre)   A report by an external auditor on the internal controls at a computer service centre. Other auditors make use of this report in assessing the internal control over data processing performed for their clients by the service centre.

tagging and tracing   A technique for testing program controls in which selected transactions are tagged when they are entered for processing. A computer program provides a printout of the steps in processing the tagged transactions that may be reviewed by the auditors.

test deck (data)   A set of dummy records and transactions developed to test the adequacy of a computer program or system.

GROUP I: REVIEW QUESTIONS

8–1.   Describe briefly the internal controls that should be established over the operation of a microcomputer to prevent use by unauthorized personnel.

8–2. EDP systems use two types of software: system software and application software. Explain the difference between these two types of software.

8–3. What are internal and external file labels? Why are they used?

8–4. Describe what is meant by electronic data interchange (EDI). How does EDI affect a company's audit trail?

8–5. Distinguish general controls from application controls and give examples of the types of controls included in each of these broad categories.

8–6. An EDP department usually performs numerous data processing functions that would be separated in a manual system. Does this imply that separation of duties is not a practical means of achieving internal control in a computerized system? Explain.

8–7. Explain briefly "on-line, real-time system."

8–8. Explain briefly the meaning of the term ***documentation*** as used in an EDP department. How might a client's documentation be used by the auditors?

8–9. The number of personnel in an EDP department may limit the extent to which subdivision of duties is feasible. What is the minimum amount of segregation of duties that will permit satisfactory internal control?

8–10. Compare the responsibilities and objectives of the EDP control group to those of the internal auditors with respect to EDP activities.

8–11. Define and give the purpose of each of the following program or equipment controls:

    a. Record counts.

    b. Limit test.

    c. Duplicate processing.

    d. Hash totals.

(AICPA, adapted)

8–12. Distinguish equipment controls from program controls and give examples of each.

8–13. Differentiate between a system flowchart and a program flowchart.

8–14. Auditors should be familiar with the terminology employed in electronic data processing. The following statements contain some of the terminology so employed. Indicate whether each statement is true or false.

    a. A recent improvement in computer hardware is the ability to automatically produce error listings. Previously, this was possible only when provisions for such a report were included in the program.

    b. The control of input and output to and from the EDP department should be performed by an independent control group.

c. An internal-audit computer program that continuously monitors computer processing is a feasible approach improving internal control in OLRT systems.

d. An internal label is one of the controls built into the hardware by the manufacturer of a magnetic tape system.

e. A limit test in a computer program is comparable to a decision that an individual makes in a manual system to judge a transaction's reasonableness.

f. A principal advantage of using magnetic tape files is that data need not be recorded sequentially.

g. A major advantage of disk files is the ability to gain random access to data on the disk.

h. The term ***grandfather-father-son*** refers to a method of computer record security rather than to generations in the evolution of computer hardware.

i. When they are not in use, tapes, disks, and card files should be stored apart from the computer room under the control of a librarian.

8–15. Explain briefly what is meant by a distributive data processing system.

8–16. Is it probable that the use of EDP will eventually eliminate the audit trail, making it impossible to trace individual transactions from their origin to the summary totals in the financial statements? Explain the reasons for your answer.

8–17. Do auditors usually begin their consideration of internal control over EDP activities with a review of general or application controls? Explain.

8–18. Describe the audit technique known as ***tagging*** and ***tracing.*** What is the purpose of the technique?

8–19. What is a service centre? Are the auditors of a client that uses a service centre concerned about the controls applied at the centre? Explain.

GROUP II: QUESTIONS REQUIRING ANALYSIS

8–20. Auditors encounter the use of microcomputers on almost every audit engagement.
  a. How do microcomputers differ from large computers?
  b. When are the auditors concerned with internal control over the use of microcomputers?

8–21. What are the purposes of each of the following categories of application controls?

    a. Input controls.

    b. Processing controls.

    c. Output controls.

(AICPA, adapted)

8–22. One requirement of an effective system of internal control is a satisfactory plan of organization. Explain the characteristics of a satisfactory plan of organization for an EDP department, including the relationship between the department and the rest of the organization.

8–23. Distinguish between batch processing and on-line, real-time (OLRT) processing. In which of these systems is strong internal control over input most easily attained? Explain.

8–24. The use of test decks is one method of performing tests of processing controls in an EDP system. Identify and discuss several other methods by which auditors may test internal processing controls over EDP activity.

8–25. Discuss how generalized audit software can be used to aid the auditor in examining accounts receivable in a fully computerized system.

(AICPA, adapted)

8–26. An integrated test facility (ITF) is a method used by both internal and external auditors for testing EDP system controls. Discuss the advantages and disadvantages of implementing an ITF.

(CICA, adapted)

8–27. Many companies have part or all of their data processing done by computer service centres.

    a. What controls should the company maintain to assure the accuracy of processing done by a service centre?

    b. How do auditors assess internal control over applications processed for an audit client by a service centre?

    c. What is a service auditors' report of a computer service centre?

    d. What two types of reports may be provided by service auditors?

    e. How do user auditors use each type of report?

8–28. Select the best answers for each of the following questions. Explain the reasons for your selection.

    a. When erroneous data are detected by computer program controls, such data may be excluded from processing and printed on an exception report. Which of the following should probably review and follow the exception report?

        (1) EDP control group.

        (2) System analyst.

        (3) Supervisor of computer operations.

        (4) Computer programmer.

b. Which of the following is **not** a characteristic of a batch processed computer system?
  (1) The collection of like transactions that are sorted and processed sequentially against a master file.
  (2) Keypunching of transactions, followed by machine processing.
  (3) The production of numerous printouts.
  (4) The posting of a transaction, as it occurs, to several files, without intermediate printouts.

c. When an on-line, real-time (OLRT) electronic data processing system is in use, internal control can be strengthened by:
  (1) Providing for the separation of duties between keypunching and error listing operations.
  (2) Attaching plastic file protection rings to reels of magnetic tape before new data can be entered on the file.
  (3) Making a validity check of an identification number before a user can obtain access to the computer files.
  (4) Preparing batch totals to provide assurance that file updates are made for the entire input.

d. Which of the following is an advantage of generalized audit software packages?
  (1) They are all written in one identical computer language.
  (2) They can be used for audits of clients that use differing EDP equipment and file formats.
  (3) They have reduced the need for the auditor to study input controls for EDP-related procedures.
  (4) Their use can be substituted for a relatively large part of the required tests of controls.

e. The auditors should be concerned about internal control in a data processing system because:
  (1) The auditors cannot follow the flow of information through the computer.
  (2) Fraud is more common in an EDP system than in a manual system.
  (3) There is usually a high concentration of data processing activity and control by a small number of people in an EDP system.
  (4) Auditors most often "audit around the computer."

f. An auditor will use the EDP test data (test deck) method in order to gain assurances with respect to:
  (1) Input data.
  (2) Machine capacity.
  (3) Procedures contained within the program.
  (4) Degree of keypunching accuracy.

GROUP III: PROBLEMS

8–29.   The Ultimate Life Insurance Company recently established a data base management system. The company is now planning to provide its branch offices with terminals that have on-line access to the central computer facility.

Required:

a. Define a "data base."

b. Give one fundamental advantage of a data base.

c. Describe three security steps to safeguard the data base from improper access through the terminals.

(CICA, adapted)

8–30.   Auditors may audit around or through computers in the examination of the financial statements of clients who utilize computers to process accounting data.

Required:

a. Describe the auditing approach referred to as "auditing around the computer."

b. Under what conditions do auditors decide to audit through the computer instead of around the computer?

c. In auditing through the computer, auditors may use test decks.
   (1) What is a test deck?
   (2) Why do auditors use test decks?

d. How can the auditors be satisfied that the computer programs presented to them for testing are actually those used by the client for processing accounting data?

(AICPA, adapted)

8–31.   Johnson, CA, was engaged to examine the financial statements of Horizon Incorporated, which has its own computer installation. While obtaining an understanding of internal control, Johnson found that Horizon lacked proper segregation of the programming and operating functions. As a result, Johnson intensified the consideration of internal control surrounding the computer and concluded that the existing compensating general controls provided reasonable assurance that the objectives of internal control were being met.

Required:

a. In a properly functioning EDP environment, how is the separation of the programming and operating functions achieved?

b. What are the compensating general controls that Johnson most likely found?

(AICPA, adapted)

8–32. As you are planning the annual audit of Norton Corporation, you are informed that the company has purchased a number of micro-computers for use in various locations. One of the machines has been installed in the stores department, which has the responsibility for disbursing stock items and for maintaining stores records. In your audit, you find that an employee receives the requisitions for stores, disburses the stock, maintains the records, operates the computer, and authorizes adjustments to the total amounts of stock accumulated by the computer.

When you discuss the applicable controls with the department manager, you are told that the microcomputer is assigned exclusively to that department. Therefore, the manager contends that it does not require the same types of controls applicable to large computer systems.

Required:
a. Comment on the manager's contention.
b. Discuss five types of control that would apply to this microcomputer application.

(CICA, adapted)

8–33. A CA's client, The Outsider, Inc., is a medium-sized manufacturer of products for the leisure time activities market (camping equipment, scuba gear, bows and arrows, and so on). During the past year, a computer system was installed, and inventory records of finished goods and parts were converted to computer processing. The inventory master file is maintained on a disk. Each record of the file contains the following information:

Item or part number.

Description.

Size.

Unit of measure code.

Quantity on hand.

Cost per unit.

Total value of inventory on hand at cost.

Date of last sale or usage.

Quantity sold or used this year.

Economic order quantity.

Code number of major vendor.

Code number of secondary vendor.

In preparation for year-end inventory, the client has two identical sets of preprinted inventory count cards. One set is for the client's inventory counts and the other is for the CA's use to make audit test counts. The following information has been keypunched into the cards and interpreted on their face:

Item or part number.

Description.

Size.

Unit of measure code.

In taking the year-end inventory, the client's personnel will write the actual counted quantity on the face of each card. When all counts are complete, the counted quantity will be keypunched into the cards. The cards will be processed against the disk file, and quantity-on-hand figures will be adjusted to reflect the actual count. A computer listing will be prepared to show any missing inventory count cards and all quantity adjustments of more than $100 in value. These items will be investigated by client personnel, and all required adjustments will be made. When adjustments have been completed, the final year-end balances will be computed and posted to the general ledger.

The CA has available generalized audit software that can process both cards and disk files.

Required:

a. In general and without regard to the facts above, discuss the nature of generalized audit software and list the various types of uses of such software.

b. List and describe at least five ways general purpose audit software can be used to assist in the audit of inventory of The Outsider, Inc. (For example, the software can be used to read the disk inventory master file and list items of high unit cost or total value. Such items can be included in the CA's test counts to increase the dollar coverage of the audit verification.)

(AICPA, adapted)

8–34. You will be examining for the first time the financial statements of Central Credit Union for the year ending December 31. The CA firm that examined the credit union financial statements for the prior year issued an unqualified audit report.

At the beginning of the current year, the credit union installed an on-line, real-time computer system. Each teller in the main office and seven branch offices has an on-line, input-output terminal. Customers' mortgage payments and savings account deposits and withdrawals are recorded in the accounts by the computer from data input by the teller at the time of the transaction. The teller keys the proper account by account number and enters the information in the terminal keyboard to record the transaction. The accounting department at the main office has input-output devices. The computer is housed at the main office.

Required:
You would expect the credit union to have certain internal controls in effect because an on-line, real-time computer system is employed. List the internal controls that should be in effect solely because this system is employed, classifying them as:
a. Those controls pertaining to input of information.
b. All other types of computer controls.

(AICPA, adapted)

8–35.   Lee Wong, CA, is examining the financial statements of the Alexandria Corporation, which recently installed an off-line electronic computer. The following comments have been extracted from Wong's notes on computer operations and the processing and control of shipping notices and customer invoices:

To minimize inconvenience Alexandria converted without change its existing data processing system, which utilized tabulating equipment. The computer company supervised the conversion and has provided training to all computer department employees in systems design, operations, and programming.

Each computer run (application) is assigned to a specific employee, who is responsible for making program changes, running the program, and answering questions. This procedure has the advantage of eliminating the need for records of computer operations because each employee is responsible for his or her own computer runs.

At least one computer department employee remains in the computer room during office hours, and only computer department employees have keys to the computer room.

System documentation consists of those materials furnished by the computer company—a set of record formats and program listings. These and the file library are kept in a corner of the computer department.

The corporation considered the desirability of program controls, but decided to retain the manual controls from its existing system.

Company products are shipped directly from public warehouses, which forward shipping notices to general accounting. There a billing clerk enters the price of the item and accounts for the numerical sequence of shipping notices from each warehouse. The billing clerk also prepares daily adding machine tapes (control tapes) of the units shipped and the unit prices.

Shipping notices and control tapes are forwarded to the computer department for keypunching and processing. Extensions are made on the computer. Output consists of invoices (in six copies) and a daily sales register. The daily sales register shows the aggregate totals of units shipped and unit prices, which the computer operator compares to the control tapes.

All copies of the invoice are returned to the billing clerk. The clerk mails three copies to the customer, forwards one copy to the warehouse, maintains one copy in a numerical file, and retains one copy in an open invoice file that serves as a detailed accounts receivable record.

Required:
Describe weaknesses in internal control over information and data flows and the procedures for processing shipping notices and customer invoices, and recommend improvements in these controls and processing procedures. Organize your answer sheets as follows:

Weakness	Recommended Improvement

(AICPA, adapted)

8–36. In a recent survey, executives of companies using computers indicated that they obtained their assurance of the adequacy of internal control over their companies' computer applications primarily by reliance on their external auditors.

Required:
a. What aspects of internal control over these computer applications would not be covered by the normal review of the external auditor?
b. How should management obtain assurance of the adequacy of internal controls over these computer applications without any reliance on the external auditor?

(CICA, adapted)

8–37. M Corporation Ltd. has been following a policy of increasingly computerizing its financial and management information records. Recently, the controller of M Corporation Ltd. approached CA, the company's auditor, with a problem he had encountered that, he felt, jeopardized the success of this policy. He confided to CA that the personnel of the systems and data processing department appeared to view their department as separate from the rest of the company and beyond reproach. He felt that this situation pointed to a need for greater control over compliance with management policy and better safeguards against possible destruction of data as well as an overall review of the computerization policy.

The controller therefore asked CA the following questions:

a. What methods should be used for continuous monitoring of the operations of a systems and data processing department to ensure compliance with management's policies and objectives?

b. What steps could be taken to ensure that only authorized use was made of the computer?

c. What steps could be taken to guard against loss from destruction of computer records by malicious acts?

d. What steps could be taken to ensure the adequacy of security and protection over confidential data, such as executive payrolls and customer lists?

Required:

CA's answers to the controller's five questions.

(CICA, adapted)

8–38. CA is the auditor of GR Ltd., the largest retailer of phonograph records in the city of Q. The company is a wholly owned subsidiary of a nationwide wholesale distributor of records. The ownership of the retail operation enables the parent company's management to keep abreast of changes in consumer buying patterns and tastes, thereby making the distributorship more quickly responsive to changes in demand than would be the case otherwise.

The merchandise inventory of GR Ltd. averages about 140,000 records of 15,000 different titles, 98 percent of which are LPs. The remainder are current 45-rpm singles. In addition, there is a relatively small stock of peripheral items such as record sleeves, cleaners, and catalogues.

In order to provide current information on which LP records are selling, as well as accurate inventory information for stock control, reordering, and financial statement preparation, GR Ltd. recently began using point-of-sale computer terminals operating on-line with the parent company's computer.

All records are identifiable by the manufacturer's alphanumeric code, which identifies the manufacturer as well as the title. For the perpetual inventory system, GR Ltd. converts the alphanumeric code for each LP to a strictly numeric code. This code, which is fixed in length, is printed on labels by the stock clerks and affixed to each record jacket when the record is received and put into stock. Single 45-rpm records and the sundry items are not included in the perpetual inventory system.

When a customer makes a purchase or returns merchandise, the salesclerk keys the following into the terminal:

(1) Four-digit salesclerk identifier code.

(2) ENTER;

(3) One-digit transaction code (sale or return).

(4) Record stock number of a record sold or returned, if an LP; a one-digit code if a 45 single or a sundry item.

(5) ENTER;

(6) Quantity of the specific items being purchased or returned.

(7) × (Multiplication symbol).

(8) Unit price.

(9) ENTER;

(10) Repeats steps (4) through (9) for each item.

(11) TOTAL (terminal displays the merchandise total, adds the automatically computed sales tax, and goods and services tax, and displays the amount due or refundable).

(12) Amount tendered.

(13) ENTER (causing the computer to calculate and display the change due).

(14) OFF.

The transaction is held by the computer without processing until the transaction is terminated by depressing the "off" key. This delay permits the clerk to void the transaction if an error has been made during entry. When the "off" key is depressed, the inventory information (items 3, 4, and 6 above) is used to update the inventory master file, which is on disk. While the transaction is being entered, the terminal prints a sales slip. The sales slip is not released by the terminal until the transaction is completed. Voided sales slips must be approved by the store manager or assistant manager.

As a part of his internal control review, CA has undertaken to assess the controls embodied in GR Ltd.'s inventory system and proposed to use test transactions to determine what controls were operating in the computerized sales entry portion of the system, as described above.

Required:

a. List the controls which should be programmed into the sales entry system described above. List only those programmed controls which relate to the processing of individual sale and return transactions.

b. Describe the transactions which you would include in a test deck (data) in this case, and state which controls each transaction would test.

c. Explain a procedure that CA may follow in conducting the above tests in order to protect the integrity of the GR Ltd. inventory master file.

(CICA, adapted)

Chapter 9

Audit Sampling

After studying this chapter, you should be able to:

- Explain the important similarities and differences between statistical and nonstatistical sampling.
- Describe the basic sampling concepts as applied to audit sampling.
- Explain the effects of changes in various population characteristics and changes in sampling risk on required sample size.
- Plan, perform, and evaluate sampling plans for tests of controls.
- Plan, perform, and evaluate sampling plans for substantive tests.
- Distinguish among attributes, discovery, sequential, variables, and probability-proportional-to-size sampling plans.

In Chapter 6, we discussed the need for sufficient, appropriate audit evidence as the basis for audit reports. As business entities have evolved in size, auditors increasingly have had to rely upon sampling procedures as the only practical means of obtaining this evidence. This reliance upon sampling procedures is one of the basic reasons that audit reports are regarded as expressions of opinion, rather than as absolute certifications of the fairness of financial statements.

Sampling, whether statistical or nonstatistical (judgmental), is the process of selecting a group of items (called the *sample*) from a large group of items (called the *population* or *field*) and using the characteristics of the sample to draw inferences about the characteristics of the entire population of items. The underlying assumption is that the sample is *representative* of the population, meaning that the sample will possess essentially the same characteristics as the population. Basic to audit sampling is ***sampling risk*** —the risk that the auditors' conclusion based on a sample might be different from the conclusion they would reach if they examined every item in the entire population.

Sampling risk is reduced by increasing the size of the sample. In the extreme, when 100 percent of the population is examined, the results obtained are, by definition, perfectly representative, and sampling risk is eliminated entirely. Large samples, however, are costly and time-consuming. A key element in efficient sampling is to balance the sampling risk against the cost of using larger samples.

Auditors may also draw erroneous conclusions because of ***nonsampling errors***—errors due to factors not directly caused by sampling. For example, the auditors may fail to apply appropriate audit procedures, or they may fail to recognize errors in the documents or transactions that are examined. The risk pertaining to nonsampling errors is referred to as ***nonsampling risk***. Nonsampling risk can generally be reduced to low levels through effective planning and supervision of audit engagements and through implementation of appropriately designed quality control procedures within the public accounting firm. The procedures discussed throughout this text help control nonsampling risk. In the remainder of this chapter, we will emphasize sampling risk.

Comparison of Statistical and Nonstatistical Sampling

A sample is said to be nonstatistical (or judgmental) when the auditors estimate sampling risk by using professional judgment rather than by using statistical techniques. This is not to say that nonstatistical samples are haphazard samples. Indeed, both nonstatistical and statistical audit samples should be selected in a way that is expected to result in their being representative of the population. In addition, the misstatements found in either a nonstatistical or a statistical sample should be used to estimate the total amount of misstatement in the population (called the ***projected misstatement***). However, nonstatistical sampling provides no means of ***quantifying*** sampling risk—that is, mathematically measuring the possibility that the actual amount of misstatement in the population is ***significantly greater*** (or ***smaller***) than that indicated by the results of the sample. Thus, the auditors may find themselves taking larger and more costly samples than are necessary, or unknowingly accepting a higher-than-acceptable degree of sampling risk.

The use of statistical sampling does not eliminate professional judgment from the sampling process. In fact, professional judgment is used in the entire statistical sampling process. For example, judgment is used in identifying the controls to be tested, in defining the population to be tested and a "deviation," in determining the maximum tolerable deviation rate, and in evaluating the results. It does, however, allow sampling risk to be measured and controlled. Through statistical sampling techniques, the auditors may specify *in advance* the sampling risk they want in their sample results and may then compute a sample size that controls sampling risk at the desired level. Since statistical sampling techniques are based upon the laws of probability, the auditors are able to control the extent of their risk in relying upon sample results. Thus, statistical sampling may assist auditors in (1) designing efficient samples, (2) measuring the sufficiency of the evidence obtained, and (3) objectively evaluating sample results. However, these advantages are not often obtained without additional costs of training audit staff, designing sampling plans, and selecting items for examination. For these reasons, nonstatistical samples are widely used by auditors, especially for tests of relatively small populations. Both statistical and nonstatistical sampling can help to provide auditors with sufficient appropriate audit evidence.

Random Selection

A common misinterpretation of statistical sampling is to equate this process with random sampling. Random sampling is simply a method of *selecting* items for inclusion in a sample; it can be used in conjunction with either statistical or nonstatistical sampling. To emphasize this distinction, we will use the term *random selection* rather than random "sampling" to refer to the procedure of selecting the items for inclusion in a sample.

The principle involved in unrestricted random selection is that every item in the population has an equal chance of being selected for inclusion in the sample. Although random selection results in an *unbiased sample,* the sample is not necessarily representative. The risk still exists that purely by chance a sample will be selected that does not possess essentially the same characteristics as the population. However, since the risk of a nonrepresentative random sample stems from the laws of probability, this risk may be measured by statistical formulas.

The sample may also not be representative of the actual population because the population being sampled from differs from the correct population. That is, the *physical representation* of the actual population may not be complete. For example, if the auditors are using a computer printout of recorded accounts payable from which to sample, any conclusions based on the sample relate only to the population on that computer printout. The auditors' statistical conclusions do not consider situations such as those in which certain creditors (with balances due) are completely omitted from the printout. It is essential that the auditors consider whether the physical representation includes the entire population.

The concept of a random sample requires that the person selecting the sample will not influence or bias the selection either consciously or unconsciously. Thus, some type of impartial selection process is necessary to obtain a truly random sample. Techniques often used for selecting random samples include *random number tables, random number generators,* and *systematic selection.*

Random Number Tables

Perhaps the easiest method of selecting items at random is the use of a random number table. A portion of a random number table is illustrated in Figure 9–1.

The random numbers appearing in Figure 9–1 are arranged into columns of five digits. Except that the columnar arrangement permits the reader of the table to select numbers easily, the columns are purely arbitrary and otherwise meaningless. Each digit on the table is a random digit; the table does *not* represent a listing of random five-digit numbers. The columnar arrangement is for convenience only.

In using a random number table, the first step is to establish correspondence between the digits in the table and the items in the population. This is most easily done when the items in the population are consecutively numbered. On occasion, however, auditors may find it necessary to renumber the population to obtain correspondence. For example, if transactions are numbered A–001, B–001, and so on, the auditors may assign numbers to replace the alphabetic characters. Next, the auditors must select a starting point and a systematic route to be used in reading the random number table. Any route is permissible, as long as it is followed consistently.

FIGURE 9–1　Table of Random Numbers

Row	*Columns*				
	(1)	*(2)*	*(3)*	*(4)*	*(5)*
1	04734	39426	91035	54839	76873
2	10417	19688	83404	42038	48226
3	07514	48374	35658	38971	53779
4	52305	86925	16223	25946	90222
5	96357	11486	30102	82679	57983
6	92870	05921	65698	27993	86406
7	00500	75924	38803	05386	10072
8	34862	93784	52709	15370	96727
9	25809	21860	36790	76883	20435
10	77487	38419	20631	48694	12638

To illustrate the use of a random number table, assume that a client's accounts receivable are numbered from 0001 to 5,000 and that the auditors want to select a random sample of 200 accounts for confirmation. Using the table in Figure 9–1, the auditors decide the start at the top of Column 2 and to proceed from top to bottom. Reading only the first four digits of the numbers in Column 2, the auditors would select 3942, 1968, and 4837 as three of the account numbers to be included in their sample. The next number, 8692, would be ignored, since there is no account with that number. The next numbers to be included in the sample would be 1148, 592, 2186, and so on.

Duplicate Numbers.   In using a random number table, it is possible that the auditors will draw the same number more than once. If the auditors ignore a number that is drawn a second time and go on to the next number, they are *sampling without replacement.* This term means that an item once selected is not replaced into the population of eligible items, and consequently it cannot be drawn for inclusion in the sample a second time.

The alternative to sampling without replacement is *sampling with replacement.* This method requires that if a particular number is drawn two or more times, the number must be included two or more times in the sample. Sampling with replacement means that once an item has been selected, it is immediately replaced into the population of eligible items and may be selected a second time.

Statistical formulas can be used to compute sample size either with or without replacement. Sampling without replacement is the more efficient technique because it requires slightly smaller sample sizes.

Random Number Generators

Even when items are assigned consecutive numbers, the selection of a large sample from a random number table may be a very time-consuming process. Computer programs called *random number generators* may be used to provide any length list of random numbers applicable to a given population. Random number generators may be programmed to select random numbers with specific characteristics, so that the list of random numbers provided to the auditors includes only numbers present in the population. A random number generator is a standard program in all generalized audit software packages.

Systematic Selection

An approach that is less time-consuming than selecting a random number for each item to be included in the sample is *systematic selection.* This technique involves selecting every *n*th item in the population following one or more *random starting points.*

To illustrate systematic selection, assume that auditors wish to examine 200 paid cheques from a population of 10,000 cheques. If only one random starting point is used, the auditors would select every 50th cheque (10,000 ÷ 200) in the population. As a starting point, the auditors would select at random one of the first 50 cheques. If the random starting point is cheque No. 37, cheque Nos. 37, 87 (37 + 50), and 137 (87 + 50) would be included in the sample, as well as every 50th cheque number after 137. If the auditors had elected to use five random starting points, 40 cheques (200 ÷ 5) would have to be selected from each random start. Thus, the auditors would select every 250th cheque number (10,000 ÷ 40) after each of the five random starting points between one and 250.

Selecting every *n*th item in the population results in a random sample only when positions in the population were assigned in random order. For example, if expensive inventory parts are always assigned an identification number ending in 9, systematic selection could result in a highly biased sample that would include too many expensive items or too many inexpensive items.

To prevent drawing a nonrandom or biased sample when systematic selection is used, the auditors should first determine that the population is arranged in random order. If the population is not in random order, each item to be included in the sample should be selected independently, or the auditors should use several random starting points for their systematic selection process.

The systematic selection technique has the advantage of enabling the auditors to obtain a sample from a population of unnumbered documents or transactions. If the documents to be examined are unnumbered, there is no necessity under this method to number them either physically or mentally, as required under the random number table selection technique. Rather, the auditors merely count off the sampling interval to select the documents or use a ruler to measure the interval. Generalized audit software packages include routines for systematic selection of audit samples from computer-based files.

Stratification

Auditors often *stratify* a population before computing the required sample size and selecting the sample. Stratification is the technique of dividing a population into relatively homogeneous subgroups called *strata*. These strata then may be sampled separately; the sample results may be evaluated separately, or combined, to provide an estimate of the characteristics of the total population. Whenever items of extremely high or low values, or other unusual characteristics, are segregated into separate populations, each population becomes more homogeneous. It is easier to draw a representative sample from a relatively homogeneous population. Thus, it is generally true that a smaller number of items must be examined to evaluate several strata separately than to evaluate the total population.

Besides increasing the efficiency of sampling procedures, stratification enables auditors to relate sample selection to the materiality, turnover, or other characteristics of items and to apply different audit procedures to each stratum. Frequently, auditors examine 100 percent of the stratum containing the most material items.[1] For example, in selecting accounts receivable for confirmation, auditors might stratify and test the population as follows:

Stratum	*Composition of Stratum*	*Method of Selection Used*	*Type of Confirmation Request**
1	All accounts of $10,000 and over	100% confirmation	Positive
2	Wholesale accounts receivable (under $10,000), all numbered with numbers ending in zero.	Random number table selection	Positive
3	All other accounts (under $10,000) in random order	Systematic selection	Negative

* A positive confirmation request asks the respondent to reply, indicating the amount owed; a negative request asks for a response only if the respondent does not agree with the amount indicated on the request. Confirmation of accounts receivable is discussed in more detail in Chapter 12.

Block Samples

A block sample consists of all items in a selected time period, numerical sequence, or alphabetical sequence. For example, in testing internal control over cash disbursements, the auditors might decide to vouch all disbursements made during the months of April and December. In this case, the sampling unit is months rather than individual transactions. Thus, the sample consists of 2 blocks selected from a population of 12. Block sampling cannot be relied upon to produce a representative sample unless a relatively large number of blocks are selected from the population.

---

[1] Any item sufficiently material that it may, by itself, constitute a material misstatement in the balance should be substantiated separately, rather than by reliance upon sample results. Also, some populations (such as minutes of directors meetings) should be examined on a 100 percent basis, rather than on a sampling basis.

Sampling Plans

The statistical sampling procedures used to accomplish specific audit objectives are called *sampling plans*. Sampling plans may be used to estimate many different characteristics of a population, but every estimate is either (1) of an occurrence rate or (2) of a numerical quantity. The sampling terms corresponding to **occurrence rates** and **numerical quantities** are, respectively, **attributes** and **variables.**

Attributes sampling plans are used in testing of internal control procedures. In tests of controls, the auditors are interested in estimating the rate of compliance with (or deviation from) prescribed control procedures. **Variables sampling plans,** on the other hand, are widely used in substantive tests because they provide auditors with an estimate of a numerical quantity, such as an account balance. Sometimes one sampling plan may be used for the **dual purposes** of (1) testing an internal control procedure and (2) substantiating the dollar amount of an account balance. For example, a single sampling plan might be used to evaluate the effectiveness of the client's internal controls over recording the cost of sales and to estimate the total overstatement or understatement of the cost of goods sold account.[2]

In order to understand statistical sampling plans, you must first have a general familiarity with the meanings and interrelationships among certain statistical concepts. One of these concepts, sampling risk, has already been described. Other concepts include **allowance for sampling risk** (or **precision**) and **sample size,** which are presented in the following sections.

Allowance for Sampling Risk (Precision)

Whether the auditors' objective is estimating attributes or variables, the sample results may not be **exactly** representative of the population. Some degree of **sampling error**—the difference between the actual rate or amount in the population and that of the sample—is usually present. In utilizing statistical sampling techniques, auditors are able to measure and control the risk of material sampling error by deciding on the appropriate levels for sampling risk and the allowance for sampling risk.

The allowance for sampling risk is the range, set by + and − limits from the sample results, within which the true value of the population characteristic being measured is likely to lie. For example, assume a sample is taken

---

[2] The size of a sample selected for a dual purpose test should be the larger of the samples that would have been designed for the two separate purposes.

to determine the occurrence rate of a certain type of error in the preparation of invoices. The sample indicates an error rate of 2.1 percent. We have little assurance that the error rate in the population is exactly 2.1 percent, but we know that the sample result probably approximates the population error rate. Therefore, using statistical sampling techniques, we may set an interval around the sample result within which we expect the population error rate to be. An allowance for sampling risk of ±1 percent would indicate that we expect the true population error rate to lie between 1.1 and 3.1 percent.

The wider the interval we allow, the more confident we may be that the true population characteristic is within it. In the preceding example, an allowance for sampling risk ±2 percent would mean that we assume the population error rate to be between .1 percent and 4.1 percent.

The allowance for sampling risk may also be used to construct a dollar value interval. For example, we may attempt to establish the total dollar value of receivables with an interval of ±$10,000. As is discussed later in this chapter, the allowance for sampling risk required by auditors usually is determined in light of the amount of a tolerable misstatement. ***Tolerable misstatement*** is an estimate of the maximum monetary misstatement that may exist in an account that, when combined with the misstatement in other accounts, will not cause the financial statements to be materially misstated.

Sample Size

The size of the sample has a direct effect upon both the allowance for sampling risk and sampling risk. With a very small sample, we cannot have low sampling risk unless we allow a large allowance for sampling risk (precision). On the other hand, a sample of 100 percent of the population allows us no sampling risk with an allowance for sampling risk of zero.

The allowance for sampling risk and sampling risk can be decreased by increasing sample size. In other words, the smaller the allowance for sampling risk or the sampling risk desired by the auditors, the larger the required sample.

Sample size is also affected by certain characteristics of the population being tested. As the population increases in size, the sample size necessary to estimate the population with specified sampling risk and allowance for sampling size will increase, but not in proportion to the increase in population size. In attributes sampling, sample size also increases as the expected population deviation rate increases. Finally, in variables sampling, greater variability among the item values in the population (a larger standard deviation) increases the required sample size. These relationships are summarized in Figure 9–2.

FIGURE 9–2 Factors Affecting Sample Size

Factor	Change in Factor*	Effect upon Required Sample Size
Auditors' requirements:		
Sampling risk	Increase (higher)	Decrease
Allowance for sampling risk	Increase (wider)	Decrease
Population characteristics:		
Size..	Increase	Small increase†
Population deviation rate or Variability of item values	Increase	Increase

* As one factor changes, other factors are assumed to remain constant.
† This assumes sampling without replacement is used. If sampling with replacement is used, the population size has no effect on sample size.

AUDIT SAMPLING FOR TESTS OF CONTROLS

Sampling is used for tests of controls to estimate the frequency of *deviations or exceptions* from a prescribed internal control procedure. As discussed in Chapter 7, sampling cannot be used to test all internal control procedures. In general, sampling can be used only when performance of the internal control procedures leaves *evidence* such as a completed document or the initials of the person performing the procedure. This evidence allows the auditors to determine whether or not the control procedure was applied to each item included in their sample. The deviation rate in the sample can then be used to estimate the deviation rate in the entire population of items processed during the period.

Audit sampling for tests of controls generally involves the following procedures:

1. Determine the objective of the test.
2. Define a deviation.
3. Define the population to be sampled.
4. Determine the method of sample selection.
5. Determine the sample size.
6. Select the sample and examine the sample items.
7. Evaluate the sample results.
8. Document the sampling procedures.

Defining a "Deviation"

When sampling is used for tests of controls, the population usually consists of all transactions subject to a specific control procedure during the period under audit. Deviations are defined as departures from prescribed internal control procedures. The procedures pertinent to auditors are those which affect the likelihood of material misstatement for a financial statement assertion (e.g., the valuation of receivables).

The auditors' interpretation of the estimated deviation rate will depend largely on how they have defined deviations. If deviations are defined to include every departure from prescribed procedures, no matter how trivial, a population could contain a relatively high deviation rate without significantly increasing control risk. On the other hand, if deviations are defined only as fictitious transactions recorded in the accounting records, even a very low occurrence rate has serious implications.

Auditors may combine several types of exceptions in their definition of a deviation. However, it is important that these deviations be of similar audit significance. If both serious and minor types of exceptions are combined in the definition, the significance of the deviation rate to the auditors' assessment of control risk is obscured.

If a document selected for testing cannot be located, the auditors will not in general be able to apply alternative procedures to determine whether the control procedure was applied. Simply selecting another item is ***not*** appropriate. In such circumstances, at a minimum, the misplaced document should be treated as a deviation for evaluation purposes. Also, because the disappearance of documents is consistent with many possible explanations, ranging from unintentional misfiling to material fraud, the auditors must carefully consider the overall implications of the situation.

Sampling Risk for Tests of Controls

In performing tests of control procedures, the auditors are concerned with two aspects of sampling risk:

1. **The risk of assessing control risk too high.** This risk is the possibility that assessed level of control risk based on the sample is greater than the true operating effectiveness of the internal control procedure.
2. **The risk of assessing control risk too low.** This more important risk is the possibility that the assessed level of control risk based on the sample is less than the true operating effectiveness of the internal control procedure.[3]

---

[3] These risks were previously referred to, respectively, in the professional literature as (1) the *risk of underreliance on internal control* and (2) the *risk of overreliance on internal control*.

The risk of assessing control risk too high relates to the ***efficiency*** of the audit process. When the sampling results cause the auditors to assess control risk at a higher level than it actually is, the auditors will perform more substantive testing than is necessary in the circumstance. This unnecessary testing reduces the ***efficiency*** of the audit process, but it does not lessen the ***effectiveness*** of the audit in disclosing material misstatements in the financial statements. The auditors usually do not attempt to directly control the risk of assessing control risk too high.

The risk of ***assessing control risk too low,*** on the other hand, is of utmost concern to the auditors. If the auditors assess control risk to be lower than it actually is, they will inappropriately ***reduce*** the intensity of their substantive tests. An unwarranted reduction in substantive testing lessens the overall ***effectiveness*** of the audit as a means of detecting material misstatements in the client's financial statements. In designing tests of controls, therefore, auditors should ***carefully control the risk of assessing control risk too low.***

The Allowance for Sampling Risk

Tests of controls are designed to provide the auditors with assurance that deviation rates do not exceed acceptable levels. Assume, for example, that the auditors anticipate a deviation rate of 3 percent and stipulate an allowance for sampling risk of ±1 percent. The relevant question is whether the auditors can accept a deviation rate of up to 4 percent, not whether they can accept a deviation rate of less than 2 percent. The lower limit is not pertinent to the objective of the test. For this reason, auditors generally use one-sided tests in attributes sampling; they generally only consider the ***tolerable rate***[4] that will still permit them to assess control risk at the planned level.

Attributes Sampling

Statistical sampling applied to attributes enables auditors to estimate the frequency with which specified characteristics occur within a population. Attributes sampling does not provide dollar information—that is, the sample results do not indicate the dollar amount of the deviations or their effect upon the fairness of the financial statements. For example, the definition of a deviation from a control procedure might include failure to secure management approval for a specific transaction. If an unapproved

---

[4] The term ***tolerable deviation rate*** is used interchangeably with ***tolerable rate*** in the professional standards.

transaction is properly recorded in the accounting records, it is a deviation in internal control but it does not result in a misstatement in the financial statements. The major factors that determine the sample size for an attributes sampling plan include the risk of assessing control risk too low, the tolerable rate, and the expected population deviation rate.

Determining the Risk of Assessing Control Risk Too Low and the Tolerable Deviation Rate.   How do auditors determine the appropriate risk of assessing control risk too low and the tolerable rate for a test of a control? The answer, in short, is ***professional judgment.*** The risk of assessing control risk too low—that is, the risk that the actual deviation rate *exceeds* the tolerable rate—is a critical risk in tests of controls. Since the results of tests of controls play a major role in determining the nature, timing, and extent of other audit procedures, auditors usually specify a low level of risk for these tests. When the degree of assurance desired by the evidence in the sample is high, the auditor should allow for a low level of risk of assessing control risk too low—in practice, often 5 to 10 percent.[5]

Auditors specify the tolerable rate based on (1) the planned assessed level of control risk and (2) the degree of assurance to be obtained by the evidence in the sample. The lower the planned assessed level of control risk (or more assurance to be obtained by the sample), the lower the tolerable deviation rate.

The AICPA's *Audit Sampling Guide* includes the following overlapping ranges to illustrate the relationship between the planned assessed level of control risk and the tolerable rate:

Planned Assessed Level of Control Risk	*Tolerable Rate*
Low	2%–7%
Moderate	6%–12%
Slightly below the maximum	11%–20%
Maximum	omit test

Estimating the Expected Population Deviation Rate.   In addition to the tolerable rate and the risk of assessing control risk too low, the expected population deviation rate affects sample size in attribute sampling. This expected deviation rate is significant because it represents the rate that the auditors expect to discover in their sample from the population.

---

[5] Some sources use the term ***confidence level*** to represent the complement of the risk of assessing control risk too low. Thus, a 95 percent confidence level is identical to a 5 percent risk of assessing control risk too low (100 percent − 5 percent).

In estimating the expected population deviation rate, the auditors often use the sample results from prior years, as documented in their working papers. The auditors may also base the estimate on their experience with similar tests for other clients or on examination of a small pilot sample.

Tables for Use in Attributes Sampling. To enable auditors to use attributes sampling without resorting to complex mathematical formulas, tables such as the ones in Figures 9–3 and 9–4 have been developed. All of the information in these figures is based on a risk of assessing control risk too low of 5 percent. Similar tables are available for other levels of risk, such as 1 percent and 10 percent.

The horizontal axis of Figure 9–3 is the tolerable rate specified by the auditors. The vertical axis is the deviation rate estimated by the auditors to exist within the population. The numbers in the body of the table indicate the *required sample sizes.* The number in parenthesis shown after the required sample size is the allowable number of deviations that may be observed in the sample for the results to support the auditors' planned assessed level of control risk.[6]

To use Figure 9–3, one must stipulate (1) the permissible risk of assessing control risk too low, (2) the expected deviation rate in the population, and (3) the tolerable rate.[7] An appropriate table is selected based on the specified risk of assessing control risk too low. Then, one may read the sample size from the table at the intersection of the stipulated tolerable rate and the expected population deviation rate. For example, assume that the auditors specify a risk of assessing control risk too low of 5 percent, allowing them to use Figure 9–3 to determine sample size. They estimate the deviation rate for the population at 3 percent and specify a 7 percent tolerable rate to justify their planned assessed level of control risk related to this control procedure. Figure 9–3 shows that these specifications indicate a sample size of 129 items, which must contain no more than four control procedure deviations if the auditors' planned control risk assessment is to be justified by the test.

After the sample has been taken, if four or fewer deviations are found in the sample, the results would support the auditors' planned assessed level of control risk. If more than four deviations are found, Figure 9–4 may be used to evaluate the results.

---

[6] Some readers may notice that the number of deviations allowable in a sample sometimes exceeds the estimated deviation rate multiplied by the sample size. This is because the allowable number of deviations is always rounded up to the nearest whole number, as it is not possible to observe a partial deviation in a sample item. The sample sizes have been adjusted to reflect this rounding.

[7] Some tables require the auditors to specify population size. Figures 9–3 and 9–4 assume an infinite population. The effect on sample size when populations are finite but of significant size is not material.

FIGURE 9–3 Statistical Sample Sizes for Tests of Controls 5 Percent Risk of Assessing Control Risk Too Low (with Allowable Number of Deviations in Parentheses)

Expected Population Deviation Rate (in Percentage)	Tolerable Rate										
	2%	3%	4%	5%	6%	7%	8%	9%	10%	15%	20%
0.00%	149(0)	99(0)	74(0)	59(0)	49(0)	42(0)	36(0)	32(0)	29(0)	19(0)	14(0)
0.25	236(1)	157(1)	117(1)	93(1)	78(1)	66(1)	58(1)	51(1)	46(1)	30(1)	22(1)
0.50	*	157(1)	117(1)	93(1)	78(1)	66(1)	58(1)	51(1)	46(1)	30(1)	22(1)
0.75	*	208(2)	117(1)	93(1)	78(1)	66(1)	58(1)	51(1)	46(1)	30(1)	22(1)
1.00	*	*	156(2)	93(1)	78(1)	66(1)	58(1)	51(1)	46(1)	30(1)	22(1)
1.25	*	*	156(2)	124(2)	78(1)	66(1)	58(1)	51(1)	46(1)	30(1)	22(1)
1.50	*	*	192(3)	124(2)	103(2)	66(1)	58(1)	51(1)	46(1)	30(1)	22(1)
1.75	*	*	227(4)	153(3)	103(2)	88(2)	77(2)	51(1)	46(1)	30(1)	22(1)
2.00	*	*	*	181(4)	127(3)	88(2)	77(2)	68(2)	46(1)	30(1)	22(1)
2.25	*	*	*	208(5)	127(3)	88(2)	77(2)	68(2)	61(2)	30(1)	22(1)
2.50	*	*	*	*	150(4)	109(3)	77(2)	68(2)	61(2)	30(1)	22(1)
2.75	*	*	*	*	173(5)	109(3)	95(3)	68(2)	61(2)	30(1)	22(1)
3.00	*	*	*	*	195(6)	129(4)	95(3)	84(3)	61(2)	30(1)	22(1)
3.25	*	*	*	*	*	148(5)	112(4)	84(3)	61(2)	30(1)	22(1)
3.50	*	*	*	*	*	167(6)	112(4)	84(3)	76(3)	40(2)	22(1)
3.75	*	*	*	*	*	185(7)	129(5)	100(4)	76(3)	40(2)	22(1)
4.00	*	*	*	*	*	*	146(6)	100(4)	89(4)	40(2)	22(1)
5.00	*	*	*	*	*	*	*	158(8)	116(6)	40(2)	30(2)
6.00	*	*	*	*	*	*	*	*	179(11)	50(3)	30(2)
7.00	*	*	*	*	*	*	*	*	*	68(5)	37(3)

Note: This table assumes a large population.
* Sample size is too large to be cost-effective for most audit applications. Source: AICPA, "Audit and Accounting Guide," *Audit Sampling* (New York, 1983).

FIGURE 9–4   Statistical Sampling Results Evaluation Table for Tests of Controls: Achieved Upper Deviation Rate at 5 Percent Risk of Assessing Control Risk Too Low

Sample size	Actual Number of Deviations Found										
	0	1	2	3	4	5	6	7	8	9	10
25	11.3	17.6	*	*	*	*	*	*	*	*	*
30	9.5	14.9	19.6	*	*	*	*	*	*	*	*
35	8.3	12.9	17.0	*	*	*	*	*	*	*	*
40	7.3	11.4	15.0	18.3	*	*	*	*	*	*	*
45	6.5	10.2	13.4	16.4	19.2	*	*	*	*	*	*
50	5.9	9.2	12.1	14.8	17.4	19.9	*	*	*	*	*
55	5.4	8.4	11.1	13.5	15.9	18.2	*	*	*	*	*
60	4.9	7.7	10.2	12.5	14.7	16.8	18.8	*	*	*	*
65	4.6	7.1	9.4	11.5	13.6	15.5	17.4	19.3	*	*	*
70	4.2	6.6	8.8	10.8	12.6	14.5	16.3	18.0	19.7	*	*
75	4.0	6.2	8.2	10.1	11.8	13.6	15.2	16.9	18.5	20.0	*
80	3.7	5.8	7.7	9.5	11.1	12.7	14.3	15.9	17.4	18.9	*
90	3.3	5.2	6.9	8.4	9.9	11.4	12.8	14.2	15.5	16.8	18.2
100	3.0	4.7	6.2	7.6	9.0	10.3	11.5	12.8	14.0	15.2	16.4
125	2.4	3.8	5.0	6.1	7.2	8.3	9.3	10.3	11.3	12.3	13.2
150	2.0	3.2	4.2	5.1	6.0	6.9	7.8	8.6	9.5	10.3	11.1
200	1.5	2.4	3.2	3.9	4.6	5.2	5.9	6.5	7.2	7.8	8.4

Note: This table presents upper limits as percentages. This table assumes a large population.
* Over 20 percent.
Source: AICPA, ''Audit and Accounting Guide,'' *Audit Sampling* (New York, 1983).

Figure 9–4 allows auditors to obtain the ***achieved upper deviation rate*** from a sample result. The achieved upper deviation rate is the actual maximum deviation rate which the results obtained in the sample statistically support. When the achieved upper deviation rate is in excess of the tolerable rate, the planned assessed level of control risk relating to the control procedure is not justified. To illustrate evaluation of a sample, assume that 5 deviations are found in the sample of 129. Referring to Figure 9–4, we find that the exact sample size of 129 does not appear. When this happens the auditors may interpolate; use more detailed tables, sometimes generated by generalized audit software; or use the largest sample size listed on the table that does not exceed the sample size actually selected. Using the latter approach, we evaluate the results using a slightly smaller size of 125. Figure 9–4 reveals that when 5 deviations are found for a sample size of 125, the achieved upper deviation rate is 8.3 percent. This tells the auditors that, statistically, there is a 5 percent chance that the actual deviation rate is higher than 8.3 percent. Therefore, there is more than a 5 percent chance that the actual deviation rate exceeds 7 percent, the tolerable rate. The most likely effect on the audit will be an increased assessed level of control risk and an increase in the scope of substantive testing for the assertions affected by the control being tested. Only when the upper deviation rate found in Table 9–4 is less than or equal to the tolerable deviation rate would the sample results support the planned assessed level of control risk.

Detailed Illustration of Attributes Sampling

The following procedures for applying attribute sampling are based upon the use of the tables in Figures 9–3 and 9–4; however, only slight modifications of the approach are necessary if other tables are used.

1. Determine the objective of the test Assume that the auditors wish to test the effectiveness of the client's internal control procedure of matching receiving reports with purchase invoices as a step in authorizing payments for purchases of materials. They are, therefore, interested in assessing the clerical accuracy of the matching process and in determining whether the control procedure that requires the matching of purchase invoices and receiving reports is operating effectively.

2. Define a deviation The auditors define a deviation as any one or more of the following with respect to each invoice and the related receiving report:

a. Any invoice not supported by a receiving document.
b. Any invoice supported by a receiving document that is applicable to another invoice.
c. Any difference between the invoice and the receiving document as to quantities shipped.

For this type of test, the only testing procedure needed is inspection of the documents and matching receiving reports with invoices.

3. Define the population to be sampled The client prepares a serially numbered voucher for every purchase of materials. The receiving report and purchase invoice are attached to each voucher. Therefore, the sampling unit for the test is an individual voucher. Since the test of controls is being performed during the interim period, the population to be tested consists of 3,600 vouchers for purchases of material during the first 10 months of the year under audit. If at any point the auditor determines that the physical representation of the population (the 3,600 vouchers) has omitted vouchers that should be included in the first 10 months, the auditor should also analyze those vouchers as is appropriate.

4. Determine the method of sample selection Since the vouchers are serially numbered, the auditors decide to use a generalized audit software program to generate a list of random numbers to select a sample for testing.

5. Determining the sample size In the audits of the previous three years, the auditors observed that exceptions of the type described above produced deviation rates of 0.5 percent, 0.9 percent, and 0.7 percent. Therefore, the auditors conservatively select an ***expected deviation rate*** of 1 percent.

The auditors realize that errors in matching receiving reports with purchase orders can affect the financial statements through overpayments to vendors and misstatements of purchases and accounts payable. They also would like to rely upon this internal control procedure to limit their substantive testing of accounts payable, inventories, and the cost of goods sold. Based on these considerations, the auditors decide upon a tolerable rate of 7 percent, with a risk of assessing control risk too low of 5 percent.

Since the stipulated risk of assessing control risk too low is 5 percent, Figure 9–3 is applicable. At the intersection of the column for a tolerable deviation rate of 7 percent and the row for a 1 percent expected deviated rate, the sample size is found to be 66 items. The allowable number of deviations in the sample is one.

6. Select the sample and examine the sample items The auditors proceed to select 66 vouchers, and examine the vouchers and supporting documents for each of the types of deviations previously defined.

7. Evaluate the sample results In evaluating the sample results, the auditors must consider not only the actual number of deviations observed, but also the nature of the deviations. We will discuss three possible sets of circumstances: (1) the actual deviation rate is equal to, or less than, the allowable rate; (2) the actual deviation rate is more than the allowable rate; and (3) one or more deviations observed contain evidence of a deliberate manipulation or circumvention of internal control.

First, assume that one deviation has been identified and there is no evidence of a deliberate manipulation or circumvention of internal control. Recall that the allowable number of deviations from Figure 9–3 was one. Because the number of deviations (here, one) did not exceed the allowable number, the auditors may conclude that there is less than a 5 percent risk that the population deviation rate is greater than 7 percent. In this case, the sample results support the auditors' planned assessed level of control risk.

Next, assume that the number of deviations observed in the sample is three, and none of the observed deviations indicate deliberate manipulation or circumvention of internal control. Because this exceeds the allowable number of one deviation, the achieved upper deviation rate is greater than 7 percent. Referring to Figure 9–4 for a sample size of 65 (the highest number still less than the sample size), the auditors find that when three deviations are observed the achieved upper deviation rate is 11.5 percent. In light of these results, the auditors should increase the assessed level of control risk in this area and increase their reliance upon their substantive testing procedures (i.e., decrease detection risk). As a preliminary step to any modification of their audit program, the auditors should investigate the cause of the unexpectedly high deviation rate.

Finally, assume that one or more of the deviations discovered by the auditors indicates an irregularity such as circumvention of internal control. In such a circumstance other auditing procedures become necessary. The auditors must evaluate the effect of the deviation on the financial statements and adopt auditing procedures that are specifically designed to protect against the type of deviation observed. Indeed, the nature of the deviation may be more important than its rate of occurrence.

8. Documenting the sampling procedures Finally, each of the seven prior steps, as well as the basis for overall conclusions, should be documented in the auditors' working papers.

Other Statistical Attributes Sampling Approaches

Discovery Sampling.   Discovery sampling is actually a modified case of attributes sampling. The purpose of a discovery sample is to detect at least *one deviation,* with a predetermined risk of assessing control risk too low, if the deviation rate in the population is greater than the specified tolerable rate. One important use of discovery sampling is to locate examples of a suspected fraud.

Although discovery sampling is designed to locate relatively rare items, it cannot locate a needle in a haystack. If an extremely small number of deviations exist within a population (e.g., .1 percent or less), no sample of reasonable size can provide adequate assurance that an example of the deviation will be encountered. Still, discovery sampling can (with a very high degree of confidence) ensure detection of deviations occurring at a rate as low as .3 to 1 percent.

Discovery sampling is used primarily to search for *critical errors.* When a deviation is critical, such as evidence of fraud, any deviation rate may be intolerable. Consequently, if such deviation is discovered, the auditors may abandon their sampling procedures and undertake a thorough examination of the population. If no deviations are found in discovery sampling, the auditors may conclude (with the specified risk of assessing control risk too low) that the critical error does not occur to the extent of the tolerable rate.

To use discovery sampling, the auditors must specify their desired risk of assessing control risk too low and the tolerable rate for the test. The required sample size then may be determined by referring to an appropriate attribute sampling table, ***with the assumption that the expected deviation rate in the population is 0 percent.***

To illustrate discovery sampling, assume that auditors have reason to suspect that someone has been preparing fraudulent purchase orders, receiving reports, and purchase invoices in order to generate cash disbursements for fictitious purchase transactions. In order to determine whether this has occurred, it is necessary to locate only one set of the fraudulent documents in the client's file of paid vouchers.

Assume the auditors desire a 5 percent risk of assessing control risk too low that their sample will not bring to light a fraudulent voucher if the population contains 2 percent or more fraudulent items. Referring to Figure 9–3, the auditors find that a sample size of 149 is required for an expected population deviation rate of zero percent and a tolerable rate of 2 percent. Assuming that the auditors select and examine the 149 vouchers and no fraudulent vouchers are found, the auditors will have only a 5 percent risk that there are more than 2 percent fraudulent vouchers in the population.

Sequential (Stop-or-Go) Sampling.   Another approach used in practice is *sequential (stop-or-go) sampling.* Under a sequential sampling plan, the audit sample is taken in several stages. The auditors start by examining a small sample. Then, based on the results of this initial sample, they decide whether (1) to assess control risk at its planned level (2) to assess control risk at a higher level than planned or (3) to examine additional sample items to get more information. If the sample results do not provide enough information to make a clear-cut decision about internal control, the auditors examine additional items and repeat the decision process until the tables being used indicate that a decision as to the assessed level of control risk can be made.

The primary advantage of a sequential approach is that for very low population deviation rates, lower sample sizes may be required as compared to the fixed sample size plans. Disadvantages of sequential approaches include the fact that sample sizes may be larger for populations with moderate error rates and that the process of drawing samples at several stages may not be cost efficient.

Nonstatistical Attributes Sampling

The major differences between statistical and nonstatistical sampling in attributes sampling are the steps for determining sample size and for evaluating sample results. As is the case with statistical sampling, auditors who use nonstatistical sampling need to consider the risk of assessing control risk too low and the tolerable deviation rate when determining the required sample size. But these factors need not be quantified. When evaluating results, the auditors should compare the deviation rate of the sample to the tolerable rate. If the sample size was appropriate and the sample deviation rate is somewhat lower than the tolerable deviation rate, the auditors can generally conclude that the risk of assessing control risk too low is at an acceptable level. As the sample deviation rate gets closer to the tolerable deviation rate, it becomes less and less likely that the population's deviation rate is lower than the tolerable level. The auditors must use their professional judgment to determine the point at which the assessed level of control risk is increased.

AUDIT SAMPLING FOR SUBSTANTIVE TESTS

Substantive tests are designed to detect misstatements, both errors and fraud, that may exist in the financial statements. Accordingly, the sampling plans that are used for substantive tests are designed to estimate the dollar amount of misstatement in a particular account balance. Based on the sample results, the auditors then conclude whether there is an unacceptably high risk of material misstatement in the balance. The actual steps involved may be summarized thus:

1. Determine the objective of the test.
2. Define the population.
3. Choose an audit sampling technique.
4. Determine the sample size.
5. Choose the method of sample selection.
6. Select the sample and examine the sample items.
7. Evaluate the sample results.
8. Document the sampling procedures.

Statistical procedures that typically are used for substantive tests include classical variables and probability-proportional-to-size sampling plans. This chapter emphasizes the classical variables plans, especially the **mean-per-unit estimation** method. Appendix 1 presents an overview of the probability-proportional-to-size method.

Sampling Risk for Substantive Tests

In performing substantive tests of account balances, there are two types of sampling risk:

1. The risk of *incorrect rejection* (alpha risk) of a population. This is the possibility that sample results will indicate that an account is materially misstated when, in fact, it is not materially misstated.
2. The risk of *incorrect acceptance* (beta risk) of a population. This is the possibility that sample results will indicate that an account is *not* materially misstated when, in fact, it is materially misstated.

The nature of these risks parallel the sampling risks of tests of controls. If the auditors make the first type of error and incorrectly reject an account balance, their audit will lack *efficiency* since they will perform additional audit procedures that will eventually reveal that the account is not materially misstated. Thus, the risk of incorrect rejection relates to the efficiency, but not the effectiveness, of the audit.

The risk of incorrect acceptance of a population relates to the *effectiveness* of the audit in detecting material misstatements. This risk is of primary concern to auditors; failure to detect a material misstatement may lead to accusations of negligence and to extensive legal liability.

Variables Sampling

Although attributes sampling approaches are useful for testing internal control, they do not provide results stated in dollars. Techniques that enable auditors to estimate dollar amounts are called *variables sampling plans*. These techniques are very useful in such audit applications as estimating the dollar value of a client's inventories or accounts receivable. Widely used classical variables sampling plans include *mean-per-unit estimation, ratio estimation,* and *difference estimation.*

Mean-per-Unit Estimation

Mean-per-unit estimation enables auditors to estimate the *average* dollar value of items in a population, with specified sampling risk and allowance for sampling risk (precision) by determining the *average* dollar value of items in a sample. An estimate of the total dollar value of the population may be obtained by multiplying the average audited value in the sample (the *sample mean*) times the number of items in the population. The *projected misstatement* may then be calculated as the difference between this estimated total value of the population and the client's book value.

The assumption underlying mean-per-unit estimation is that the mean of a sample will, within a certain sampling risk and allowance for sampling risk, represent the true mean of the population. For variables sampling, even if tables are used to determine the required sample size, the auditor needs some familiarity with statistical theory and terminology. Of particular importance are the concepts of ***normal distribution*** and ***standard deviation***.

Normal Distribution.   Many populations, such as the heights of all men, may be described as normal distributions. A normal distribution is illustrated by the familiar bell-shaped curve, illustrated in Figure 9–5, in which the values of the individual items tend to congregate around the population ***mean***. Notice that the distribution of individual item values is symmetrical on both sides of the mean. There is no tendency for deviations to be to one side rather than the other.

Even when the items within the population are not normally distributed, the concept of a normal distribution is relevant to sampling theory. If auditors were to draw from any population hundreds of samples of a given size, ***the means of these samples would form a normal distribution*** around the true population mean. This characteristic allows auditors to apply mean-per-unit estimation to populations that are not normally distributed, even though only one sample is usually taken.

FIGURE 9–5   Normal Distribution

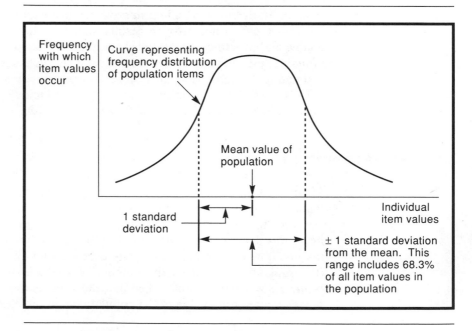

Standard Deviation. The standard deviation of a population is a measure of the *variability* or *dispersion* of individual item values about the population means.[8] The less variation among item values, the smaller the standard deviation; the greater the variation among item values, the larger the standard deviation. It is inherent in the definitions of normal distribution and standard deviation that 68.3 percent of the item values in a normal distribution fall within ±1 standard deviation of the population mean, that 95.4 percent fall within ±2 standard deviations, and that 99.7 percent fall within ±3 standard deviations. These percentage relationships hold true by definition; however, the dollar amount of the standard deviation will vary from one population to another.

Auditors may obtain a reliable estimate of the dollar amount of the standard deviation by taking a *pilot sample* of approximately 50 items.[9] (The items examined in this pilot sample become part of the larger sample used for estimating the population mean.) Generalized audit software packages also include routines designed to estimate the standard deviation of the book values of a population either from a sample or from the population itself.

Controlling Sampling Risk

The risks of incorrect acceptance and of incorrect rejection may be controlled independently of one another. For example, auditors may design a sample that limits both risks to 10 percent, or they may hold the risk of incorrect acceptance to 5 percent while allowing the risk of incorrect rejection to rise to 40 percent or more. In establishing the planned level of the risk of incorrect acceptance, auditors must consider the extent of the evidence that must be obtained from this test about the fairness of the account. This is determined by the extent to which the auditors need to restrict detection risk for the account. In stipulating the planned risk of

---

[8] The standard deviation is the square root of the following quotient: the sum of the squares of the deviation of each item value from the population mean, divided by the number of items in the population. Symbolically, the formula for calculating the standard deviation is:

$$\sqrt{\frac{\Sigma(\bar{x} - \overline{X})^2}{N}}$$

[9] An *estimate* of the standard deviation may be made from a sample by taking the square root of the following quotient: the sum of the squares of the deviation of each sample item value from the sample mean, divided by one less than the number of items in the sample. Symbolically, the formula for estimating the standard deviation is:

$$\sqrt{\frac{\Sigma(x - \bar{x})^2}{n - 1}}$$

incorrect rejection, on the other hand, they should consider the *time* and *cost* involved in performing additional audit procedures when the sample results *erroneously* indicate that a correct book balance is materially misstated. In mean-per-unit estimation, as was the case with attributes sampling, the allowance for sampling risk is used to control sampling risk. The appropriate planned allowance for sampling risk may be determined from the following formula:

$$\text{Planned allowance for sampling risk} = \frac{\text{Tolerable misstatement}}{1 + \dfrac{\text{Incorrect acceptance coefficient}}{\text{Incorrect rejection coefficient}}}$$

The tolerable misstatement is the maximum monetary misstatement that may exist in the account without causing the financial statements to be materially misstated. The **risk coefficients** are taken from a table, such as the one in Figure 9–6. Notice that the coefficients are different for the two types of risks.

FIGURE 9–6 Risk Coefficients		
Acceptable Level of Risk	*Incorrect Acceptance Coefficient*	*Incorrect Rejection Coefficient*
1.0%	2.33	2.58
4.6	1.68	2.00
5.0	1.64	1.96
10	1.28	1.64
15	1.04	1.44
20	0.84	1.28
25	0.67	1.15
30	0.52	1.04
40	0.25	0.84
50	0.00	0.67

Determination of Sample Size

The factors directly included in the sample size formula in mean-per-unit estimation are (1) population size, (2) planned risk of incorrect rejection, (3) estimated variability (standard deviation) among item values in the population, and (4) planned allowance for sampling risk. The relationship of these factors to the required sample size is expressed by the following:[10]

$$\text{Sample size} = \left(\frac{\text{Population size} \times \text{Incorrect rejection coefficient} \times \text{Estimated standard deviation}}{\text{Planned allowance for sampling risk}} \right)^2$$

Evaluating the Sample Results

Recall that the auditors determined sample size based on the planned sampling risks and on an estimate of the standard deviation of the population. When the auditors' estimate of the population's standard deviation is exactly the same as that of the subsequent sample, the planned allowance for sampling risk may be used for evaluation purposes. However, this is seldom the case. The auditors' estimate of the population standard deviation usually differs from that of the subsequent sample. When this occurs, the sample taken does not control both risks at their planned levels, because the auditors have under- or overestimated the variability of the population in computing the required sample size. Although there are various ways of adjusting the allowance for sampling risk, one that maintains the risk of incorrect acceptance at its planned level is described below:

$$\begin{array}{l} \text{Adjusted allowance} \\ \text{for sampling risk} \end{array} = \text{Tolerable misstatement} - \frac{\begin{array}{c} (\text{Population size} \times \text{Incorrect} \\ \text{acceptance coefficient} \times \\ \text{Sample standard deviation}) \end{array}}{\sqrt{\text{Sample size}}}$$

Once the auditors calculate the adjusted allowance for sampling risk, the client's book value is accepted or rejected based on whether it falls within the interval constructed by the audited sample mean ± the adjusted allowance for sampling risk. If the book value falls within the interval, the sample results support the conclusion that the account balance is materially correct. On the other hand, if the client's book value does *not* fall within the interval, the sample results indicate that there is too great a risk that the account balance is materially misstated.

---

[10] This formula is based upon an infinite population. The effect on sample size when the population is finite but of significant size is small. Symbolically, this formula may be stated:

$$n = \left(\frac{N \times U_r \times SD}{A} \right)^2$$

where n = sample size. N = population size, U_r = incorrect rejection coefficient, SD = estimated standard deviation, and A = planned allowance for sampling risk.

Detailed Illustration of Mean-per-Unit Estimation

1. Determine the Objective of the Test. Assume that the auditors wish to test the validity of recorded accounts receivable of a small public-utility client. They wish to test the book value of accounts receivable by confirming a sample of the accounts through direct correspondence with the customers.

2. Define the Population. The client's records have 100,000 accounts recorded at a total book value of $6,250,000. Figure 9–7 summarizes the accounts.

3. Choose the Audit Sampling Technique. The auditors have decided to use the mean-per-unit technique.

4. Determine the Sample Size. To calculate the required sample size the auditors must determine (1) the tolerable misstatement for accounts re-

FIGURE 9–7   Population of Accounts Receivable

ABC Company
Accounts Receivable
December 31, 19X3

Account Number	Account Name	Book Value
000,001	Aaron, Williams	$ 65.55
000,002	Adams, James	66.44
000,003	Alons, Susan	82.42
000,004	Ahohn, Jennifer	55.14
000,005	Ahrons, Kenneth	44.96
⋮	⋮	⋮
003,000	Carhon, Sandra	65.00
⋮	⋮	⋮
099,999	Zenit, Darlene	82.50
100,000	Zyen, Chem	99.20
Total book value		$6,250,000.00
Mean account value*		$62.50

* $6,250,000/100,000.

ceivable, (2) planned levels of sampling risk (the risks of incorrect acceptance and rejection), (3) an estimate of the population standard deviation, and (4) the population size.

Based on their evaluation of internal control, the auditors believe that all accounts are included in the 100,000 accounts in the clients' subsidiary ledger. In view of the materiality of the dollar amounts involved, the auditors assess the tolerable misstatement to be $364,000. Since internal control is weak, the auditors recognize that detection risk must be restricted to a low level. Therefore, the auditors decide on a 5 percent risk of incorrect acceptance. Also, based on a consideration of costs of performing the procedures, a 4.6 percent risk of incorrect rejection is planned by the auditors. From this information and by using risk coefficients obtained from Figure 9–6, the planned allowance for sampling risk may be calculated as follows:

$$\text{Planned allowance for sampling risk} = \frac{\text{Tolerable misstatement}}{1 + \dfrac{\text{Incorrect acceptance coefficient}}{\text{Incorrect rejection coefficient}}}$$

$$= \frac{\$364,000}{1 + \dfrac{1.64}{2.00}} = \$200,000$$

To estimate the standard deviation of the population, the auditors used a generalized audit software program to calculate the standard deviation of the recorded book values of the individual customers' accounts. The result was $15.

Using the sample size formula, the required sample size may now be computed:

$$\text{Sample size} = \left(\frac{\text{Population size} \times \text{Incorrect rejection coefficient} \times \text{Estimated standard deviation}}{\text{Planned allowance for sampling risk}} \right)^2$$

$$= \left(\frac{100,000 \times 2.00 \times \$15}{\$200,000} \right)^2 = \left(\frac{\$3,000,000}{\$\ 200,000} \right)^2$$

$$= 225 \text{ accounts}$$

5. Choose the Method of Sample Selection. The client's receivables are from residential customers and do not vary greatly in size. For this reason, the auditors decide to use a random number table to select an unstratified random sample.

6. Select the Sample and Examine the Sample Items. The auditors send the confirmations and perform additional procedures as appropriate.

7. Evaluate the Sample Results. Confirmation of the 225 accounts as summarized on Figure 9–8 results in a sample with a mean audited value of

FIGURE 9–8 Auditors' Sample of Accounts Receivable

ABC Company
Sample of Accounts Receivable
December 31, 19X3

Sample Item Number	Account Number	Account Name	Book Value	Audited Value	Difference
001	000,002	Adams, James	$ 66.44	$ 66.44	$ 0.00
002	000,005	Ahrons, Kenneth	44.96	43.00	1.96
003	001,100	Boynton, Willis	92.16	92.16	0.00
004	002,200	Banner, Jane	72.12	68.50	3.62
005	003,000	Carhon, Sandra	65.00	65.00	0.00
...	...	...	...	...	...
...	...	...	...	...	...
...	...	...	...	...	...
224	093,212	Yelbow Sharlene	82.50	82.50	0.00
225	100,000	Zyen, Chem	99.20	92.00	7.20
Total value (sample)			$14,175.00	$13,725.00	$450.00
Mean values (Total value/225)			63.00	61.00	2.00

382

$61 per account. Figure 9–8 also indicates that the mean *book value* of the 225 accounts in the sample was $63. Notice that this $63 mean sample book value differs somewhat from the mean book value of the entire population, $62.50 per Figure 9–7. *This difference of 50 cents per account is due to chance and is not directly used in the mean-per-unit analysis.*

As a first case, assume that the confirmation results also indicate a standard deviation of the sample's audited values of $15. Since the sample's standard deviation equals that used in planning, the adjusted allowance for sampling risk equals the planned allowance of $200,000. Therefore, the auditors' estimate of the total value of the population is $6,100,000 ($61 × 100,000 accounts) plus or minus the allowance for sampling risk of $200,000 ($5,900,000 to $6,300,000). Because the client's book value of $6,250,000 falls within this interval, the sample results indicate that the client's valuation of accounts receivable is not materially in error. However, the sample results indicate a *projected misstatement* of $150,000 ($6,250,000 − $6,100,000). This projected misstatement will be considered when the auditors are analyzing the total amount of potential misstatement in the financial statements. Also, the auditors will suggest that the client correct any accounts that their test revealed to be misstated, even though the misstatements are less than the tolerable misstatement amount.

How do the auditors evaluate the results if the sample's standard deviation differs from the estimate? The auditors may use the formula discussed above to calculate the adjusted allowance for sampling risk. For example, if the sample's standard deviation had instead been equal to $16, the adjusted allowance for sampling risk may be calculated as follows:

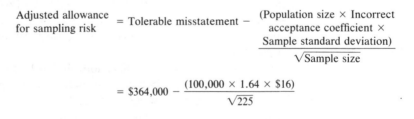

$$\begin{array}{l}\text{Adjusted allowance} \\ \text{for sampling risk}\end{array} = \text{Tolerable misstatement} - \frac{\begin{array}{c}(\text{Population size} \times \text{Incorrect} \\ \text{acceptance coefficient} \times \\ \text{Sample standard deviation})\end{array}}{\sqrt{\text{Sample size}}}$$

$$= \$364,000 - \frac{(100,000 \times 1.64 \times \$16)}{\sqrt{225}}$$

$$= \$189,067$$

Thus, the interval would be constructed as $6,100,000 ± $189,067 ($5,910,933 to $6,289,067). Because the book value ($6,250,000) falls within this interval, the sample results still indicate that the account does not contain a material misstatement.

In cases in which the client's book value falls *outside* the interval, the auditor must decide whether (1) the client's book value is actually materially misstated or (2) the sample is not representative of the population. To decide which is the case, the auditors should carefully examine the misstatements found in the sample. If few misstatements were found, this indicates that the sample may not be representative. Based on the results of this misstatement analysis, the auditors may decide (1) to increase the sample size of the test, (2) to perform other audit tests of the account, or (3) to work with the client's personnel to locate the misstatements in the account.

As in other types of sampling, the auditors should consider the qualitative aspects of any misstatements found in their sample. Questions the auditors would attempt to answer in their qualitative evaluation of the results are, What caused the misstatements? Do any of the misstatements indicate fraud? and What are the implications of the misstatements for other audit areas?

8. Document the Sampling Procedures.   Each of the prior seven steps, as well as the basis for overall conclusions, should be documented.

Ratio Estimation and Difference Estimation

Mean-per-unit estimation estimates the average item value as the basis for estimating the total value of the population. Two alternatives to this approach are ratio estimation and difference estimation. Although closely related, ratio estimation and difference estimation are two distinct sampling plans; each is appropriate under slightly different circumstances.

In ratio estimation, the auditors use a sample to estimate the *ratio* of the audited (correct) value of a population to its book value. This ratio is estimated by dividing the total audited value of a sample by the total book value of the sample items.[11] An estimate of the correct population value is obtained by multiplying this estimated ratio by the total book value of the population.

In applying difference estimation, the auditors use a sample to estimate the *average difference* between the audited value and book value of items in a population. The average difference is estimated by dividing the net difference between the audited value and book value of a sample by the

---

[11] Symbolically, this process is expressed:

$$\hat{R} = \frac{\Sigma a_j}{\Sigma b_j}$$

where $\hat{R}$ (pronounced R caret) represents the estimated ratio of audited value to book value, a_j represents the audited value of each sample item, and b_j represents the book value of each sample item.

number of items in the sample.[12] The total difference between the book value of the population and its estimated correct value is determined by multiplying the estimated average difference by the number of items in the population.

Use of Ratio and Difference Estimation. The use of ratio or difference estimation techniques requires that (1) each population item has a book value, (2) an audited value may be ascertained for each sample item, and (3) differences between audited and book values are relatively frequent. If the occurrence rate of differences is very low, a prohibitively large sample is required to disclose a representative number of misstatements. However, when these requirements are met, ratio estimation or difference estimation is often more efficient than mean-per-unit estimation.

Ratio estimation is most appropriate when the size of misstatements is nearly proportional to the book values of the items. In many cases, the size of transactions affecting an account may be nearly proportional to the account balance. Thus, mistakes in processing transactions affecting large accounts generally are larger than those affecting small accounts. In these situations, ratio estimation is more appropriate than difference estimation. When the size of misstatements is not approximately proportional to book value, difference estimation is the more appropriate technique.

Illustration of Ratio Estimation and Difference Estimation

The information presented in Figures 9–7 and 9–8 may be used to illustrate the use of ratio and difference estimation techniques. Recall that the population consists of 100,000 accounts with an aggregate book value of $6,250,000. The auditors calculate the required sample size, randomly select the accounts to be sampled, and apply auditing procedures to determine the correct account balances. In actuality, the sample size would probably differ from that obtained using the mean-per-unit method, but in this illustration we will continue to assume a sample size of 225, as summarized on Figure 9–8.

Using ratio estimation, the auditors would estimate the ratio of audited value to book value to be .96825 ($13,725/$14,175). Their estimate of the

---

[12] Symbolically, the estimated difference is computed:

$$\hat{d} = \frac{1}{n}\sum_{j=1}^{n} (a_j - b_j)$$

where $\hat{d}$ represents the estimated average difference between audited value and book value, n represents the number of items in the sample, and a_j and b_j represent the audited and book values, respectively.

total population value, therefore, would be $6,051,563 ($6,250,000 × .96825). The ratio approach thus indicates a projected misstatement of a $198,437 overstatement ($6,250,000 − $6,051,563) for accounts receivable.

If difference estimation is used, the auditors would estimate the average difference per item to be a $2 overstatement ($63 − $61). Multiplying the $2 by the 100,000 accounts in the population indicates that the projected misstatement for accounts receivable is a $200,000 overstatement. The estimated total audited value would be $6,050,000 ($6,250,000 − $200,000). Formulas are available for both ratio and difference estimation to calculate an adjusted allowance for sampling risk to control sampling risk in a manner similar to the mean-per-unit method.

Nonstatistical Variables Sampling

The major differences between statistical and nonstatistical sampling in substantive testing are in the steps for determining sample size and for evaluating sample results. When using nonstatistical sampling, the auditors may choose not to explicitly quantify the factors used to arrive at a sample size, although they should consider the relationships summarized in Figure 9–2. In evaluating the sample results, the auditors should project the misstatements found in the sample to the population and consider sampling risk, but they do not quantify the risk.

KEY TERMS

allowance for sampling risk (ASR, precision) An interval around the sample results in which the true population characteristic is expected to lie.

attributes sampling A sampling plan enabling the auditors to estimate the rate of deviation (occurrence) in a population.

confidence level The complement of the risk of assessing control risk too low (or of incorrect acceptance).

deviation rate (occurrence rate, exception rate) A defined rate of departure from prescribed control procedures. This is the characteristic measured in tests of controls.

difference estimation A sampling plan for estimating the average difference between the audited (correct) values of items in a population and their book values. Difference estimation is used in lieu of ratio estimation when the differences are not nearly proportional to book values.

discovery sampling A sampling plan for locating at least one exception, providing that the exception occurs in the population with a specified frequency.

dual-purpose test   A test designed to test an internal control procedure and to substantiate the dollar amount of an account using the same sample.

effective audit   An audit that achieves the planned degree of effectiveness in detecting any material misstatements in the client's financial statements.

efficient audit   An effective audit that is performed at the lowest possible cost.

expected deviation rate   An advance estimate of a deviation rate. This estimate is necessary for determining the required sample size in an attributes sampling plan.

mean   The average item value, computed by dividing total value by the number of items comprising total value.

mean-per-unit estimation   A sampling plan enabling the auditors to estimate the average dollar value (or other variable) of items in a population by determining the average value of items in a sample.

nonsampling risk   The aspects of audit risk not due to sampling. This risk normally relates to *human* rather than *statistical* errors.

normal distribution   A frequency distribution in which item values tend to congregate around the mean with no tendency for deviation toward one side rather than the other. A normal distribution is represented graphically by a bell-shaped curve.

physical representation of population   The population from which the auditors sample. The physical representation of the population differs from the true population when it does not include items that exist in the true population. For example, the auditors sample from a trial balance of receivables which may or may not include all actual receivables.

population   The entire field of items from which a sample might be drawn.

precision   See **allowance for sampling risk.**

random selection   Selecting items from a population in a manner in which every item has an equal chance of being included in the sample.

ratio estimation   A sampling plan for estimating the ratio of the audited (correct) values of items to their book values. Extending the book value of the population by this ratio provides an estimate of audited total population value. Ratio estimation is a highly efficient technique when misstatements are nearly proportional to item book values.

representative sample   A sample possessing essentially the same characteristics as the population from which it was drawn.

risk of assessing control risk too high   This risk is the possibility that assessed level of control risk based on the sample is greater than the true operating effectiveness of the internal control procedure.

risk of assessing control risk too low This most important risk is the possibility that the assessed level of control risk based on the sample is less than the true operating effectiveness of the internal control procedure.

risk of incorrect acceptance (beta risk) The risk that sample results will indicate that a population is *not* materially misstated when, in fact, it is materially misstated.

risk of incorrect rejection (alpha risk) The risk that sample results will indicate that a population is materially misstated when, in fact, it is not.

sampling error The difference between the actual rate or amount in the population and that of the sample. For example, if an actual (but unknown) deviation rate of 3 percent exists in the population, and the sample's deviation rate is 2 percent, the sampling error is 1 percent.

sampling risk The risk that the auditors' conclusion based on a sample might be different from the conclusion they would reach if the test were applied to the entire population. For tests of controls, sampling risks include the risks of assessing control risk too high and too low; for substantive testing, sampling risks include the risks of incorrect acceptance and rejection.

sequential sampling A sampling plan in which the sample is selected in stages, with the need for each subsequent stage being conditional on the results of the previous stage.

standard deviation A measure of the variability or dispersion of item values within a population; in a normal distribution, 68.3 percent of all item values fall within ± 1 standard deviation of the mean, 95.4 percent fall within ± 2 standard deviations, and 99.7 percent fall within ± 3 standard deviations.

stratification Dividing a population into two or more relatively homogeneous subgroups (strata). Stratification increases the efficiency of most sampling plans by reducing the variability of items in each stratum. The sample size necessary to evaluate the strata separately is often smaller than would be needed to evaluate the total population.

systematic selection The technique of selecting a sample by drawing every nth item in the population, following one or more random starting points.

tolerable misstatement An estimate of the maximum monetary misstatement that may exist in an account balance, when combined with misstatement in other accounts, without causing the financial statements to be materially misstated.

tolerable rate The maximum population rate of deviations from a prescribed control procedure that the auditor will tolerate without modifying the planned assessment of control risk.

variables sampling   Sampling plans designed to estimate a numerical measurement of a population, such as a dollar value.

GROUP I: REVIEW QUESTIONS

9–1.   Define, and differentiate between, nonstatistical (judgmental) sampling and statistical sampling.

9–2.   What statistical sampling plan appears to be most useful in accomplishing the basic objectives of tests of controls? Explain.

9–3.   In selecting items for examination, an auditor considered three alternatives: (*a*) random number table selection, (*b*) systematic selection, and (*c*) random number generator selection. Which, if any, of these methods would lead to a random sample if properly applied?

9–4.   Explain briefly the term *systematic selection* as used in auditing and indicate the precautions to be taken if a random sample is to be obtained. Is systematic selection applicable to unnumbered documents? Explain.

9–5.   Explain briefly how the auditors using statistical sampling techniques may measure the possibility that the sample drawn has characteristics not representative of the population.

9–6.   What would be the difference in an attributes sampling plan and a variables sampling plan in a test of inventory extensions?

9–7.   Distinguish between attributes sampling and variables sampling.

9–8.   Explain the meaning of *sampling without replacement* and *sampling with replacement.*

9–9.   Describe what is meant by a *sequential sampling plan.*

9–10. If a sample of 100 items indicates a deviation rate of 3 percent, should the auditors conclude that the entire population also has approximately a 3 percent deviation rate?

9–11. What relationship exists between the expected population deviation rate and sample size?

9–12. Describe the difference between sampling risk and nonsampling risk.

9–13. Explain what is meant by an allowance for sampling risk of ±1 percent with a risk of assessing control risk too low of 10 percent.

(AICPA, adapted)

9–14. The 10 following statements apply to unrestricted random sampling with replacement. Indicate whether each statement is true or false. Briefly discuss each false statement.

   a. When sampling from the population of accounts receivable, for certain objectives the auditor might sample only active accounts with balances.

   b. To be random, every item in the population must have an equal chance of being selected for inclusion in the sample.

    c. In general, all items in excess of a material misstatement need to be examined, and sampling of them is inappropriate.

    d. It is likely that five different random samples from the same population could produce five different estimates of the true population mean.

    e. A 100 percent sample would have to be taken to attain an allowance for sampling risk range of ±$0 with no sampling risk.

    f. The effect of the inclusion by chance of a very large or very small item in a random sample can be lessened by increasing the size of the sample.

    g. The standard deviation is a measure of the variability of items in a population.

    h. The larger the standard deviation of a population, the smaller the required sample size.

    i. Unrestricted random sampling with replacement results in a larger sample size than unrestricted random sampling without replacement.

    j. Unrestricted random sampling normally results in a smaller sample size than does stratified sampling.

9–15. In performing a substantive test of the book value of a population, auditors must be concerned with two aspects of sampling risk. What are these two aspects of sampling risk, and which aspect is of greater importance to auditors? Explain.

GROUP II: QUESTIONS REQUIRING ANALYSIS

9–16. Increasing attention is being given by auditors to the application of statistical techniques to audit testing.

Required:
    a. List and explain the advantages of applying statistical sampling techniques to audit testing.

    b. List and discuss the decisions involving professional judgment that must be made by the auditors in applying statistical sampling techniques to tests of controls.

    c. You have applied attributes sampling to the client's pricing of the inventory and discovered from your sampling that the sample deviation rate exceeds your maximum tolerable rate. Discuss the courses of action you can take.

                                               (AICPA, adapted)

9–17. An auditor used a nonstatistical sampling plan to audit the inventory of an auto supply company. The auditor tested the recorded cost of a sample of inventory items by reference to vendors' invoices. In performing the test, the auditor verified all the items on two pages selected at random from the client's 257-page inventory listing. The sampling plan resulted in a test of $50,000 of the total book value of $5,000,000, and the auditor found a total of $5,000 in overstatements in the sample. Since the senior indicated that a material misstatement in the inventory account was $100,000, the auditor concluded that the recorded inventory value was materially correct.

Required:

Evaluate the auditor's sampling plan and the manner in which the results were evaluated.

9–18. In performing a test of controls for sales order approvals, the auditors stipulate a maximum tolerable rate of 8 percent with a risk of assessing control risk too low of 5 percent. They anticipate a deviation rate of 2 percent.

Required:

a. What type of sampling plan should the auditors use for this test?

b. Using the appropriate table or formula from this chapter, compute the required sample size for the test.

c. Assume that the sample indicates four deviations. May the auditors conclude with a 5 percent risk of assessing control risk too low that the population deviation rate does not exceed their maximum tolerable rate of 8 percent?

9–19. One of the generally accepted auditing standards states that sufficient appropriate audit evidence should be obtained through inspection, observation, enquiries, computation, analysis, and confirmation to afford a reasonable basis for an opinion regarding the financial statements under examination. Some degree of uncertainty is implicit in the concept of "a reasonable basis for an opinion," because the concept of sampling is well established in auditing practice.

Required:

a. Explain the auditor's justification for accepting the uncertainties that are inherent in the sampling process.

b. Discuss the nature of the sampling risk and nonsampling risk. Include the effect of sampling risk on substantive tests of details and on tests of control.

(AICPA, adapted)

9–20. An auditor has reason to suspect that fraud has occurred through forgery of the treasurer's signature on company cheques. The population under consideration consists of 3,000 cheques. Can discovery sampling rule out the possibility that any forged cheques exist among the 3,000 cheques? Explain.

9–21. During an audit of Potter Company, an auditor needs to estimate the total value of the 5,000 invoices processed during June. The auditor estimates the standard deviation of the population to be $30. Determine the sample size the auditor would select to achieve an allowance for sampling risk (precision) of ±$25,000 with 4.6 percent risk of incorrect rejection.

(AICPA, adapted)

9–22. Robert Rotter, CA, is considering the use of a mean-per-unit estimation sampling plan. Explain the factors that Rotter would consider in determining:

   a. The acceptable risk of incorrect rejection.

   b. The maximum tolerable misstatement in the population.

   c. The acceptable risk of incorrect acceptance.

9–23. Cathy Williams is auditing the financial statements of Westerman Industries. In the performance of a mean-per-unit estimation of credit sales, Williams has decided to limit the risk of incorrect rejection to 25 percent and the risk of incorrect acceptance to 10 percent. Williams considers the maximum tolerable misstatement in this revenue account to be ±$500,000. Calculate the planned allowance for sampling risk.

9–24. Select the best answer for each of the following questions. Explain the reasons for your selection.

   a. Which of the following is an element of sampling risk?

   (1) Choosing an audit procedure that is inconsistent with the audit objective.

   (2) Concluding that no material misstatement exists based on taking a sample that includes no misstatements from a materially misstated population.

   (3) Failing to detect an error on a document that has been inspected by an auditor.

   (4) Failing to perform audit procedures that are required by the sampling plan.

   b. The primary purpose of using stratification as a sampling method in auditing:

   (1) To decrease the nonsampling risk of a given sample.

   (2) To determine the exact deviation rate of a given characteristic in the population being studied.

   (3) To decrease the effect of variance in the total population.

   (4) To determine the allowance for sampling risk of the sample selected.

   c. Approximately 4 percent of the items included in Gooba's finished goods inventory are believed to be defective. The auditors examining Gooba's financial statements decide to test this estimated 4 percent defective rate. They learn that a sample of 146 items from the inventory will permit a specified risk of assessing control risk too low of 5 percent with a tolerable rate of 8 percent. If the specified tolerable rate is changed to 9 percent and the risk of assessing control risk too low remains at 5 percent, the planned sample size becomes (solve without use of tables):

(1) 100
(2) 335
(3) 436
(4) 1,543

d. In assessing sampling risk, the risk of incorrect rejection and the risk of assessing control risk too high relate to:

(1) Efficiency of the audit.
(2) Effectiveness of the audit.
(3) Selection of the sample.
(4) Audit quality controls.

e. When forms are not consecutively numbered:

(1) Selection of a random sample probably is not possible.
(2) Systematic sampling may be appropriate.
(3) Stratified sampling should be used.
(4) Random number tables cannot be used.

f. If the auditors are concerned that a population may contain deviations, the determination of a sample size sufficient to include at *least* one such exception is a characteristic of:

(1) Discovery sampling.
(2) Variables sampling
(3) Random sampling
(4) Attributes sampling

(AICPA, adapted)

9–25. The professional development department of a large CA firm has prepared the following illustration to familiarize the audit staff with the relationships of sample size to population size and variability and the auditors' specifications as to the allowance for sampling risk (ASR) and the risk of incorrect acceptance.

Required:

For each of the five cases in the above illustration, indicate the relationship of the sample size to be selected from population 1 relative to the sample from population 2. Select your answer from the following numbered responses and state the reasoning behind your choice. The required sample size from population 1 is:

1. Larger than the required sample size from population 2.
2. Equal to the required sample size from population 2.

	Characteristics of Population 1 Relative to Population 2		Audit Specifications as to a Sample from Population 1 Relative to a Sample from Population 2	
	Size	Variability	Planned ASR	Planned Risk of Incorrect Acceptance
Case 1....................	Larger	Equal	Equal	Equal
Case 2....................	Equal	Larger	Wider	Equal
Case 3....................	Larger	Equal	Tighter	Equal
Case 4....................	Smaller	Smaller	Equal	Lower
Case 5....................	Smaller	Equal	Wider	Higher

    3. Smaller than the required sample size from population 2.
    4. Indeterminate relative to the required sample size from population 2.

(AICPA, adapted)

9–26.   Ratio estimation and difference estimation are two widely used variables sampling plans.

Required:
a. Under what conditions are ratio estimation or difference estimation appropriate sampling plans for estimating the total dollar value of a population?
b. What relationship determines which of these two plans will be most efficient in a particular situation?

GROUP III: PROBLEMS

9–27.   Sampling for attributes is often used to allow an auditor to reach a conclusion concerning a rate of deviation in a population. A common use in auditing is to test the rate of deviation from a prescribed internal control procedure to determine whether planned assessed level of control risk is appropriate.

Required:
a. When an auditor samples for attributes, identify the factors that should influence the auditor's judgment concerning the determination of:

(1) Acceptable level of risk of assessing control risk too low.

(2) Tolerable deviation rate.

(3) Expected population deviation rate.

b. State the effect on sample size of an increase in each of the following factors, assuming all other factors are held constant:

(1) Acceptable level of the risk of assessing control risk too low.

(2) Tolerable rate.

(3) Expected population deviation rate.

c. Evaluate the sample results of a test for attributes if authorizations are found to be missing on 7 cheque requests out of a sample of 100 tested. The population consists of 2,500 cheque requests, the tolerable rate is 8 percent, and the acceptable level of risk of assessing control risk too low is considered to be 5 percent.

d. How may the use of statistical sampling assist the auditor in evaluating the sample results described in (*c*), above?

(AICPA, adapted)

9–28. The use of statistical sampling techniques in an examination of financial statements does not eliminate judgmental decisions.

Required:

a. Identify and explain four areas in which judgment may be exercised by auditors in planning a statistical test of a control.

b. Assume that the auditors' sample shows an unacceptable deviation rate. Discuss the various actions that they may take based upon this finding.

c. A nonstratified sample of 80 accounts payable vouchers is to be selected from a population of 3,200. The vouchers are numbered consecutively from 1 to 3,200 and are listed, 40 to a page, in the voucher register. Describe four different techniques for selecting a random sample of vouchers for review.

(AICPA, adapted)

9–29. To test the pricing and mathematical accuracy of sales invoices, the auditors selected a sample of 200 sales invoices from a total of 41,600 invoices that were issued during the years under examination. The 200 invoices represented a total recorded sales of $22,880. Total sales for the year amounted to $5 million. The examination disclosed that of the 200 invoices audited, 5 were not properly priced or contained errors in extensions and footings. The 5 incorrect invoices represented $720 of the total recorded sales, and the errors found resulted in a net understatement of these invoices by $300.

Required:

Explain what conclusions that auditors may draw from the above information, assuming the sample was selected:

a. Using nonstatistical sampling.

b. As part of an attributes sampling plan using a stipulated maximum deviation rate of 5 percent, and a risk of assessing control risk too low of 5 percent.

c. As part of a difference estimation plan for estimating the total population value.

9–30. In the audit of Potomac Mills, the auditors wish to test the costs assigned to manufactured goods. During the year, the company has produced 2,000 production lots with a total recorded cost of $5.9 million. The auditors select a sample of 200 production lots with an aggregate book value of $600,000 and vouch the assigned costs to the supporting documentation. Their examination discloses misstatements in the cost of 52 of the 200 production lots; after adjustment for these misstatements, the audited value of the sample is $582,000.

Required:

a. Show how the auditors would compute an estimate of the total cost of production lots manufactured during the year using each of the following sampling plans. (Do not compute the allowance for sampling risk or risk of incorrect acceptance of the estimates.)

   (1) Mean-per-unit estimation.

   (2) Ratio estimation.

   (3) Difference estimation.

b. Explain why mean-per-unit estimation results in a higher estimate of the population value than does ratio estimation in this particular instance.

9–31. The auditors wish to use mean-per-unit sampling to evaluate the reasonableness of the book value of the accounts receivable of Smith, Inc. Smith has 10,000 receivable accounts with a total book value of $1,500,000. The auditors estimate the population's standard deviation to be equal to $25. After examining the overall audit plan, the auditors believe that the account's tolerable misstatement is $60,000, and that a risk of incorrect rejection of 5% and a risk of incorrect acceptance of 10% are appropriate.

Required:

a. Calculate the required sample size.

b. Assuming the following results:

   Average audited value   = $146
   Standard deviation of sample = $ 28

Use the mean-per-unit method to:

   (1) Calculate the point estimate of the account's audited value.

(2) Calculate the projected misstatement for the population.

(3) Calculate the adjusted allowance for sampling risk.

(4) State the auditors' conclusion in this situation.

GROUP IV: ANALYTICAL AND DISCUSSION CASE

9–32.   Sampling, whether statistical or nonstatistical (judgmental), is an integral part of the audit process. Its use raises fundamental auditing issues which have become the subject of professional literature and studies. A decision to use sampling involves a number of practical and conceptual considerations.

Required:
Describe these considerations.

(CICA, adapted)

APPENDIX 1:

PROBABILITY-PROPORTIONAL-TO-SIZE (PPS) SAMPLING

Probability-proportional-to-size (PPS) sampling[13] is a technique that applies the theory of attributes sampling to estimate the total dollar amount of misstatement in a population. It has gained popularity in practice because (1) its use may result in smaller-size samples than classical approaches, especially for populations with low error rates; (2) the method automatically results in a stratified sample in which individually significant items are identified; (3) the sample can be designed and sample selection can begin prior to the availability of the entire population; and (4) many auditors consider it easier to apply than classical variables sampling.

Whereas classical variables sampling plans define the population as a group of accounts or transactions, PPS sampling defines the population as the ***individual dollars*** comprising the population's book value. Thus, a population of 5,000 accounts receivable with a total value of $2,875,000 is viewed as a population of 2,875,000 items (dollars), rather than 5,000 items (accounts).

Determination of Sample Size

The factors affecting sample size in PPS sampling are (1) the recorded dollar amount of the population, (2) the reliability factor, (3) the tolerable misstatement, (4) the expected misstatement in the account, and (5) the

---

[13] Variations of this sampling technique are called dollar-unit sampling and monetary unit sampling.

expansion factor. Specifically, the sample size for PPS may be computed as follows:

$$\text{Sample size} = \frac{\text{Book value of population} \times \text{Reliability factor}}{\text{Tolerable misstatement} - (\text{Expected misstatement} \times \text{Expansion factor})}$$

Several of the factors in the PPS formula need very little additional explanation. The book value of the population is the recorded amount of the population being audited. The tolerable misstatement is the maximum monetary misstatement that may exist in the population without causing the financial statements to be materially misstated. The expected misstatement is the auditors' estimate of the dollar amount of misstatement in the population. The auditors estimate the expected misstatement using professional judgment based on prior experience and knowledge of the client. The other factors used to calculate sample size are based on the auditors' desired risk of incorrect acceptance and are obtained from tables, such as the ones in Figures 9–9 and 9–10. The "zero errors" row of Figure 9–9 is always used for obtaining the reliability factor for determining sample size. Thus, if a 10 percent risk of incorrect acceptance is desired, the factor is 2.31. The expansion factor comes directly from Figure 9–10. For a 10 percent risk, the factor is 1.5.

Controlling Sampling Risk

As is the case with classical variables approaches, the auditors decide on an appropriate level of risk of incorrect acceptance. This level of risk is

FIGURE 9–9   Reliability Factors for Misstatements of Overstatement

Number of Over-statement Misstatements	Risk of Incorrect Acceptance								
	1%	*5%*	*10%*	*15%*	*20%*	*25%*	*30%*	*37%*	*50%*
0*	4.61	3.00	2.31	1.90	1.61	1.39	1.21	1.00	.70
1	6.64	4.75	3.89	3.38	3.00	2.70	2.44	2.14	1.68
2	8.41	6.30	5.33	4.72	4.28	3.93	3.62	3.25	2.68
3	10.05	7.76	6.69	6.02	5.52	5.11	4.77	4.34	3.68
4	11.61	9.16	8.00	7.27	6.73	6.28	5.90	5.43	4.68
5	13.11	10.52	9.28	8.50	7.91	7.43	7.01	6.49	5.68
6	14.57	11.85	10.54	9.71	9.08	8.56	8.12	7.56	6.67
7	16.00	13.15	11.78	10.90	10.24	9.69	9.21	8.63	7.67
8	17.41	14.44	13.00	12.08	11.38	10.81	10.31	9.68	8.67
9	18.79	15.71	14.21	13.25	12.52	11.92	11.39	10.74	9.67
10	20.15	16.97	15.41	14.42	13.66	13.02	12.47	11.79	10.67

* Always used for reliability factor in sample size formula and for basic precision.

Source: AICPA, "Audit and Accounting Guide," *Audit Sampling* (New York, 1983).

FIGURE 9–10 Expansion Factors for Expected Misstatements

				Risk of Incorrect Acceptance					
	1%	*5%*	*10%*	*15%*	*20%*	*25%*	*30%*	*37%*	*50%*
Factor	1.9	1.6	1.5	1.4	1.3	1.25	1.2	1.15	1.0

Source: AICPA, "Audit and Accounting Guide," *Audit Sampling* (New York, 1983).

then used to obtain the appropriate factors to calculate sample size. The risk of incorrect rejection is indirectly controlled by the auditors' estimate of expected misstatement that is used to calculate the PPS sample size. If the auditors underestimate the expected misstatement, the sample size will not be large enough and additional testing may be necessary in order to accept the account balance as being materially correct.

Method of Sample Selection

Auditors generally use a systematic selection approach when using PPS. However, since the sampling unit is based on dollars, not individual accounts, the sampling interval is also based on dollars. The sampling interval is calculated as follows:

$$\text{Sampling interval} = \frac{\text{Book value of population}}{\text{Sample size}}$$

To illustrate this method of selection, assume that the auditors are sampling from a population of accounts receivable totaling $300,000, and the sampling interval is calculated to be $1,500. A random starting point is selected between $1 and $1,500, say, $412. Then, the sample will include the accounts receivable that contain every $1,500 from the starting point, as illustrated in Figure 9–11. The accounts included in Figure 9–11 are considered "logical units" because when applying PPS the auditors generally *cannot* audit only the dollar selected but must audit the entire account, invoice, or voucher. Consider the confirmation of accounts receivable. Sending a confirmation of a specific dollar in a selected balance is not generally feasible. The auditors usually must confirm the entire account.

Evaluation of Sample Results

After the sample has been selected and procedures applied to arrive at audited values for the individual accounts, the PPS sample may be evaluated. The PPS evaluation procedure involves calculating an **upper limit on misstatements,** which is an estimate of the maximum amount of

---

FIGURE 9–11   PPS Selection Process

Account Number	Book Value	Cumulative Total	Dollar Selected	Sample Item Book Value
0001	$1,000	$ 1,000	$ 412	$1,000
0002	42	1,042		
0003	1,700	2,742	1,912	1,700
0004	666	3,408		
0005	50	3,458	3,412	50
.	.	.	.	.
.	.	.	.	.
.	.	.	.	.
		$300,000		

---

misstatement in the account. The upper limit on misstatements has two already familiar components—the *projected misstatement* and the *allowance for sampling risk*. However, in PPS sampling, the allowance for sampling risk is made up of two other components, the *basic precision* and the *incremental allowance*. Mathematically, these relationships may be described as follows:

$$\underset{\text{on misstatements}}{\text{Upper limit}} = \underset{\text{misstatement}}{\text{Projected}} + \overbrace{\underset{\text{precision}}{\text{Basic}} + \underset{\text{allowance}}{\text{Incremental}}}^{\substack{\text{Allowance for} \\ \text{sampling risk}}}$$

As is the case with the classical approaches, the projected misstatement may be viewed as the auditors' best guess of the misstatement in the population. The *projected misstatement* in the population is determined by summing the projected misstatement for each account, or other logical unit, in the sample. Thus, when the sample includes no misstatements, the projected misstatement is zero. When misstatements do exist in the sample, the method used to project the misstatement in a particular account depends on whether or not the book value of the account found to be in error is less than the sampling interval. For accounts with book values that are less than the amount of the sampling interval, the projected misstatement is calculated by multiplying the percent of misstatement in the account, known as the *tainting,* times the sampling interval. Thus, if an account with a book value of $100 is found to have an audited value of $60, the misstatement in the account is $40 ($100 − $60) and the tainting is 40 percent ($40/$100). The tainting of 40 percent would then be multiplied by the sampling interval to get the projected misstatement for that account.

For accounts with book values equal to or greater than the sampling interval, the actual misstatement in the account is equal to the projected misstatement. The reason for the difference in the methods of calculation of the projected misstatement is that every account with a book value equal to or greater than the sampling interval will be included in the sample. These items do not represent other unselected items in the population; therefore, the actual misstatement in the account is equal to the projected misstatement. Accounts with balances less than the sampling interval represent other unselected items of similar size in the population. For these accounts the misstatement must be weighted by the sampling interval to arrive at the projected misstatement for the account.

The next step in determining the upper limit on misstatements involves calculating the two components of the allowance for sampling risk—the basic precision and the incremental allowance. The basic precision is always found by multiplying the reliability factor for zero misstatements, from Figure 9–9, by the sampling interval.

The way in which the incremental allowance is calculated varies depending on the number of accounts with book values less than the sampling interval that are found to be misstated. When no such misstatements are found in the sample, the incremental allowance is zero. When misstatements are discovered in the sample, the incremental allowance is found by (1) ranking the projected misstatements for the accounts with book values less than the sampling interval from largest projected misstatement to smallest projected misstatement, (2) mutiplying each projected misstatement by an incremental factor calculated from the reliability factors in Figure 9–9, and (3) summing the resulting amounts.

To complete the quantitative evaluation of the sample results, the auditors compute the upper limit on misstatements. When misstatements are found, the upper limit is computed by adding together the projected misstatements, the basic precision, and the incremental allowance. Of course, if no misstatements are found in the sample, the upper limit on misstatements consists only of the basic precision.

After the upper limit on misstatements is calculated, the auditors compare it to the tolerable misstatement for the account. If the upper limit on misstatements is less than or equal to tolerable misstatement, the sample results support the conclusion that the population is not misstated by more than tolerable misstatement at the specified level of sampling risk. On the other hand, if the upper limit on misstatements exceeds the amount of tolerable misstatement, the sample results do not provide the auditor with enough assurance that the misstatement in the population is less than tolerable misstatement.

Illustration of PPS Sampling

The case used to illustrate mean-per-unit sampling on pages 380 to 384 will be used to illustrate PPS sampling. The population, in that case, had a book value of $6,250,000 and the auditors decided on a tolerable misstatement for the account of $364,000 and a 5 percent risk of incorrect acceptance. Additionally, assume that based on prior audits, the auditors expected $50,000 of misstatement in the population.

Since the auditors are using a risk of incorrect acceptance of 5 percent, the reliability factor from Figure 9–9 is 3.00, and the expansion factor from Figure 9–10 is 1.6. Remember for calculating sample size that the zero error row of Figure 9–9 is always used. Using this information, the sample size and sampling interval may be calculated as follows:

$$\text{Sample size } = \frac{\text{Book value of population} \times \text{Reliability factor}}{\text{Tolerable misstatement} - (\text{Expected misstatement} \times \text{Expansion factor})}$$

$$= \frac{\$6,250,000 \times 3}{\$364,000 - (50,000 \times 1.6)} = 66$$

$$\text{Sampling interval} = \frac{\text{Book value of population}}{\text{Sample size}}$$

$$= \frac{\$6,250,000}{66} = \$95,000 \text{ (approximately)}$$

Using the PPS selection method, the auditors select the accounts for confirmation, perform confirmation procedures, and find the following three misstatements:

Book Value	Audited Value
$ 100	$ 90
2,000	1,900
102,000	102

Based on the above results, the projected misstatement, basic precision, and the incremental allowance are calculated in Figure 9–12.

The calculation of projected misstatement is straightforward, and no table values are required. Note that the tainting percentages for the first two misstatements are computed by dividing the misstatement amount by the book value of the account. Then, the tainting percentages are multiplied by the sampling interval to calculate the projected misstatement. Because the book value of the account containing the third misstatement is greater than the sampling interval, the projected misstatement for that account is equal to the amount of the misstatement.

The second element of the upper limit on misstatements, basic precision, is simply the reliability factor for zero misstatements and a risk of

---

FIGURE 9–12 PPS Illustration of Calculation of Upper Limit on Misstatements

---

Projected Misstatement

Book Value	Audited Value	Misstatement	Tainting Percentage	Sampling Interval	Projected Misstatement	
$ 100	$ 90	$ 10	10%	$95,000	$ 9,500	
2,000	1,900	100	5	95,000	4,750	
102,000	102	101,898	NA	NA	101,898	
$104,100	$2,092	$102,008				$116,148

Basic Precision

Basic precision = Reliability factor × Sampling interval

$$3.0 \quad \times \quad \$95,000 \quad = \qquad \$285,000$$

Incremental Allowance

Reliability Factor	Increment	(Increment −1)	Projected Misstatement	Incremental Allowance	
3.00	—	—	—	—	
4.75	1.75	.75	$9,500	$7,125	
6.30	1.55	.55	4,750	2,613	9,738
Upper limit on misstatements					$410,886

---

incorrect acceptance of 5 percent from Figure 9–9 multiplied by the sampling interval.

The calculation of the incremental allowance uses the projected misstatements of the accounts with book values less than the sampling interval. These projected misstatements are ranked by size from largest projected misstatement to smallest and multiplied by the incremental reliability factors, minus one. These incremental reliability factors are derived from the factors in Figure 9–9. Because a 5 percent risk of incorrect acceptance was selected and two misstatements were found in accounts with balances less than the sampling interval, the factors of 3.00, 4.75, and 6.30 are taken from Figure 9–9. An incremental factor is calculated as the difference between successive factors. For example, the incremental factor for the first error is 4.75 − 3.00, or 1.75. Then one is subtracted from each incremental factor to arrive at the factor that is multiplied by the first projected misstatement, in this case .75. This process is repeated for each additional projected misstatement.

Because the upper limit ($410,886) is in excess of the tolerable misstatement ($364,000), the auditors would not accept the population as being materially correct. Thus, adjustment of the account, expansion of the sample, or audit report modification would be appropriate.[14] In this situation, the most logical approach would be to persuade the client to adjust for the $102,008 in actual misstatements found in the sample. This would reduce the upper limit on misstatements to $308,878 ($410,886 − $102,008) and enable the auditors to accept the account as being materially correct.

Final Comments.   Although the formulas for PPS sampling at first seem difficult, once a user becomes familiar with them, they are easier to apply in practice than the classical sampling methods. Also, no estimate of the standard deviation of the population is necessary and the method does not rely upon normal distribution theory. The method also provides smaller sample sizes when few misstatements are expected in the sample.

The advantages of the PPS system do not come without cost. If there are many differences between recorded and audited amounts, the classical variables sampling methods might result in a smaller sample size. Also, when using PPS sampling, special consideration needs to be made for (1) accounts with zero balances, (2) accounts with negative balances, and (3) accounts that are understated; public accounting firms use various methods to resolve these limitations.

APPENDIX 2:

AUDIT RISK

What level of risk of incorrect acceptance is acceptable for a substantive test? Recall that in Chapter 5 the concept of audit risk was introduced. That chapter suggested that audit risk resulted from three sources—inherent risk, control risk, and detection risk. Although not meant to be a formula rigidly applied in practice, those relationships may be described as follows:

$$AR = IR \times CR \times DR$$

where

AR = Audit risk, the risk that the auditor may unknowingly fail to appropriately modify his opinion on financial statements that are materially misstated.

IR = Inherent risk, the risk of material misstatement[15] in an assertion, assuming there were no related internal controls.

---

[14] In many circumstances such as this, the client requests that the auditors expand the sample to either identify the specific errors or to determine that the account is not materially misstated.

[15] Formally, all of the component risks (inherent risk, control risk, and detection risk) relate to misstatement either material by itself or when aggregated with other misstatements.

CR = Control risk, the risk of a material misstatement occurring in an assertion and not being prevented or detected on a timely basis by internal control.

DR = Detection risk, the risk that the auditors' procedures will lead them to conclude an assertion is not materially misstated, when in fact such misstatement does exist.

Conceptually, if the auditors can quantify the planned level of audit risk and the estimated levels of inherent risk and control risk, the appropriate planned level of detection risk may be determined. This planned level of detection risk is a function of the risk of incorrect acceptance of the test being performed and of any other substantive procedures bearing on the account (e.g., analytical procedures).

Implementing this formula in practice is difficult. For example, immaterial misstatements in two more more accounts may accumulate to a material amount, and the disaggregation of a material amount to "tolerable misstatements" for individual accounts is difficult, both conceptually and practically. In addition, quantifying the various risks is difficult. Despite these difficulties, we know from the formula that in circumstances in which the auditors assess inherent risk and control risk as high, a low detection risk (the combination of the risk related to analytical procedures and tests of details) becomes appropriate. Decreases in inherent risk or control risk allow the auditors to accept a higher detection risk.

To illustrate, assume the auditors are willing to accept a 5 percent audit risk of a larger-than-tolerable misstatement in the client's accounts receivable. They believe that the inherent risk of the account is 75 percent. After considering internal control over sales and cash receipts transactions, they decide that control risk is at a level of 70 percent. The acceptable level of detection risk is:

$$DR = \frac{AR}{IR \times CR} = \frac{.05}{(.75)(.70)} = .095$$

Thus, the auditors must plan a combination of substantive tests to control detection risk at approximately a 10 percent level.

KEY TERMS

audit risk The risk that the auditors may unknowingly fail to appropriately modify their opinion on financial statements that are materially misstated.

basic precision In probability-proportional-to-size sampling, the reliability factor (for zero misstatements at the planned risk of incorrect acceptance) times the sampling interval.

control risk The risk of a material error occurring in an assertion and not being detected on a timely basis by internal control.

detection risk The risk that the auditors' procedures will lead them to conclude that an assertion is not materially misstated when in fact such misstatement does exist.

dollar-unit sampling See **probability-proportional-to-size sampling.**

incremental allowance In probability-proportional-to-size sampling, an amount determined by ranking the errors for logical units that are less than the sampling interval and considering incremental changes in reliability factors.

inherent risk The risk of material misstatement in an account, assuming there were no related internal controls.

probability-proportional-to-size sampling A variables sampling procedure that uses attributes theory to express a conclusion in monetary (dollar) amounts.

projected misstatement In probability-proportional-to-size sampling, an amount calculated for logical units less than the size of the sampling interval by multiplying the percentage of misstatement (the tainting) times the sampling interval.

tainting In probability-proportional-to-size sampling, the percentage of misstatement of an item (misstatement amount divided by book value).

upper limit on misstatements In probability-proportional-to-size sampling, the sum of projected misstatement, basic precision, and the incremental allowance. This total is used to evaluate sample results.

QUESTIONS AND PROBLEMS FROM APPENDICES

9–A–1. Barker Company has an inventory with a book value of $4,583,231, which includes 116 product lines and a total of 326,432 units. How many items comprise this population for purposes of applying a probability-proportional-to-size sampling plan? Explain.

9–A–2. Chris York is considering the use of probability-proportional-to-size sampling in examining the sales transactions and accounts receivable of Carter Wholesale Company.

Required:

a. How does the definition of the items in an accounts receivable population vary between probability-proportional-to-size sampling and mean-per-unit sampling?

b. Should a population of accounts receivable be stratified by dollar value before applying probability-proportional-to-size sampling procedures? Discuss.

9–A–3. The auditors of Dunbar Electronics want to limit the risk of material misstatement in the valuation of inventories to 2 percent. They believe that there exists only a 20 percent risk that a material misstatement could have bypassed the client's internal control and that the inherent risk in the account is 50 percent. What is the maximum detection risk the auditor may allow in their substantive tests for inventories?

9–A–4. The auditors wish to test the valuation of accounts receivable in the audit of Desert Enterprises of Bullhead City. The client has $500,000 of total recorded receivables, composed of 850 accounts. The auditors have determined the following:

Tolerable misstatement	$25,000
Risk of incorrect acceptance	.05
Expected misstatement	$ 2,000

The auditors have decided to use probability-proportional-to-size sampling.

Required:

a. For the planning of the sample, calculate:
    (1) Required sample size.
    (2) Sampling interval.

b. Assume that the auditors have tested the sample and discovered three misstatements:

Book Value	Audited Value
$ 50	47
800	760
8,500	8,100

Calculate:
    (1) Projected misstatement.
    (2) Basic precision.
    (3) Incremental allowance.
    (4) Upper limit on misstatements.

c. Explain how the auditors would consider the results calculated in (b).

9–A–5.   Edwards has decided to use probability-proportional-to-size (PPS) sampling, sometimes called dollar-unit sampling, in the audit of a client's accounts receivable balance. Few, if any, misstatements of account balance overstatement are expected. Edwards plans to use the following PPS sampling table:

Reliability Factors for Misstatements of Overstatement

Number of Overstatement Misstatements	Risk of Incorrect Acceptance				
	1%	*5%*	*10%*	*15%*	*20%*
0	4.61	3.00	2.31	1.90	1.61
1	6.64	4.75	3.89	3.38	3.00
2	8.41	6.30	5.33	4.72	4.28
3	10.05	7.76	6.69	6.02	5.52
4	11.61	9.16	8.00	7.27	6.73

Required:
a. Identify the advantages of using PPS sampling over classical variables sampling.
b. Calculate the sampling interval and the sample size Edwards should use given the following information:

Tolerable misstatement	$15,000
Risk of incorrect acceptance	5%
Estimated misstatements	0
Recorded amount of accounts receivable	$300,000

Note: Requirements *b* and *c* are ***not*** related.
c. Calculate the total projected misstatement if the following three misstatements were discovered in a PPS sample:

	Recorded Amount	*Audit Amount*	*Sampling Interval*
1st misstatement	$ 400	$ 320	$1,000
2nd misstatement	500	0	1,000
3rd misstatement	3,000	2,500	1,000

(AICPA, adapted)

INTEGRATING PROBLEM

9–A–6. *Overall background information relevant for parts a through g:*
Bill Pei, CA, is about to begin his audit of the accuracy of his
client's accounts receivable. Based on past experience, he ex-
pects that approximately 1 percent of the client's 40,000 accounts have errors. Total receivables are $5 million. Pei has
established $390,000 as the amount for tolerable misstatement, 5
percent for the risk of incorrect acceptance, and 10 percent for
the risk of incorrect rejection. The auditors estimate the standard deviation of the accounts to be $45.

Required:
a. Using mean-per-unit sampling, calculate the required sample
size.
b. Now ignore part *a*. Assume that as part of an attributes
sampling plan using a stipulated tolerable rate of 5 percent,
and a risk of assessing control risk too low of 5 percent, the
auditors wish to test the receivables valuation—that is, each
account will be considered either as correct or as a deviation.
What sample size would be required for this test?

Additional information for parts c through g: Now ignore your
(*a*) and (*b*) answers and assume that the auditors selected a
random sample of 208 accounts (square root = 14.4) representing a total book value of receivables of $40,800. They found 5
errors, representing a $300 overstatement as follows:

Misstatement	Book Value	Audited Value
1	$26,000	$25,950
2	1,000	900
3	220	200
4	180	120
5	100	30
	$27,500	$27,200

The standard deviation of the book value of the sample was $50,
while the standard deviation of the audited values of the sample
was $55. For part *g* assume a sampling interval of $24,038
($5,000,000/208).

Required:

c. Using mean-per-unit sampling, what is the projected misstatement for the population?

d. Using mean-per-unit sampling, calculate the adjusted allowance for sampling risk and use it to calculate the appropriate interval for use in deciding whether to accept or reject the population.

e. Using difference estimation, calculate the projected misstatement for the population.

f. Given the five misstatements presented above, what statistical conclusion may be made using attribute sampling (recall part *b* above)?

g. Using PPS sampling, calculate:
   (1) Projected misstatement.
   (2) Basic precision.
   (3) Incremental allowance for sampling risk.

Chapter 10

Audit Working Papers: Examination of the General Records

Chapter Objectives

After studying this chapter, you should be able to:

- Describe the functions of audit working papers.
- Explain the relationship between the working papers and legal liability of auditors.
- Discuss the factors that affect auditors' judgment as to the quality, type, and content of the working papers.
- Describe the types of working papers, and the way they are organized.
- Describe the type of general records that are examined by auditors.
- Explain the major types of laws and regulations with which auditors should be familiar.
- Describe the auditors' review and testing of the client's accounting records.

Working papers are vitally important tools of the auditing profession. To an auditor, the ability to design and use working papers efficiently is just as essential as is the surgeon's ability to use surgical instruments. In this chapter, we first discuss the basic characteristics of working papers and the roles these papers play in the audit process. We also discuss a variety of general records that auditors examine during their audits.

What Are Audit Working Papers?

Working papers are the connecting link between the client's accounting records and the auditors' report. They document all of the work performed by the auditors and provide the justification for the auditors' report.[1] The third examination standard states:

> Sufficient appropriate audit evidence should be obtained, by such means as inspection, observation, enquiries, confirmations, computation, and analysis, to afford a reasonable basis to support the content of the report.

All of this evidence must be clearly documented in the auditors' working papers.

Some working papers take the form of bank reconciliations or analyses of ledger accounts; others may consist of photocopies of minutes of directors' meetings; still others might be organization charts or flowcharts of the client's internal control. Working trial balances; audit programs; internal control questionnaires; letters of representation obtained from the client and from the client's legal counsel; notes on the level of materiality and risk used in determining the nature, extent, and timing of tests; returned confirmation forms—all of these schedules, lists, notes, and documents are part of the auditors' working papers.

Thus, the term *audit working papers* is quite comprehensive. Remember that the partner who writes and signs the auditors' report did not personally perform most of the audit procedures. The partner's opinion was developed primarily by reviewing the working papers prepared by the audit staff. Therefore, the working papers must include absolutely all of the information that is *relevant to expressing an opinion on the fairness of the client's financial statements.*

Most large public accounting firms send new staff assistants to the firm's special training sessions to learn the firm's working paper techniques. Of course, no one standard set of working papers is suitable for all engagements. As auditors move from one client to another, they encounter different business operations and different kinds of accounting records and internal controls. It follows that the auditors must tailor the type and content of their working papers to fit the circumstances of each engagement.

---

[1] CICA, *CICA Handbook* (Toronto), Section 5145.06.

Functions of Working Papers

Audit working papers assist auditors in several major ways: they (*a*) provide a means of assigning and coordinating audit work; (*b*) aid seniors, managers, and partners in supervising and reviewing the work of assistants; (*c*) provide the support for the auditors' report; (*d*) document the auditors' compliance with the generally accepted auditing standards;[2] and (*e*) aid in planning and conducting future audits of the client. In addition, working papers provide information useful in rendering additional professional services, such as preparing income tax returns, making recommendations for improving internal control, and providing management advisory services.

Assigning and Coordinating Audit Work.   Most audits are a joint effort. Several auditors, perhaps even several different offices of a public accounting firm, usually are involved in each engagement. The work of these different auditors is coordinated through the audit working papers. Work may be conveniently delegated by assigning different assistants responsibility for completing different working papers. The senior auditor might fill in the column headings on a working paper and enter one or two sample transactions, requesting that a staff assistant complete the paper. In this manner, a senior can initiate and supervise the work of several assistants simultaneously.

If an audit is to progress efficiently, information often must pass from one auditor to another. For example, assume that Macor prepared the flowcharts of a client's internal control and was then transferred to another job. Jones and Reed are now assigned responsibility for performing tests of the significant control procedures. Obviously Jones and Reed must understand how the client's control procedures operate—information previously obtained by Macor. This information is readily available in the flowchart—the audit working paper in which Macor documented his work.

Often it is not possible to complete all of the work on an account at one time. For example, cash on hand may be counted at the balance sheet date, but confirmations of bank balances may not be received until a week or so later. As each step in the verification of the client's cash balance is completed, a working paper is filed, to be expanded and updated as additional information is obtained. Thus, the audit work on a given account might be started early in the engagement by one assistant and completed later by another.

Supervising and Reviewing the Work of Assistants.   As working papers are completed by staff assistants, they are *reviewed* by the senior running

---

[2] Ibid., Section 5145.03

the job. If the senior finds any shortcomings in an assistant's work, the senior will explain the problem to the assistant and ask that the working paper be revised. Once the senior is satisfied with the working paper, it will be passed on to the manager, who will perform a similar review. If the manager has any questions or finds any problems, the working paper is again returned to the audit staff. After the manager is satisfied that the working paper documents complete and thorough audit work, the working paper is reviewed by one or more partners. This process of successive levels of review provides assurance that work of the audit staff is carefully reviewed and supervised. As each review is completed, the reviewer signs off by initialing the working paper.

Support for the Report.   The working papers must contain adequate evidence and documentation to convince the partner on the engagement that it is appropriate for the public accounting firm to issue a particular type of opinion on the client's financial statements. The partner knows that some risk always exists that investors may sustain losses and bring a lawsuit against the firm alleging an improper audit. Therefore, the partner will want to be certain that the auditors' report is supported and justified by the evidence contained in the working papers.

Compliance with Generally Accepted Auditing Standards.   As discussed in Chapter 4, auditors may find themselves liable for losses sustained by financial statement users if the auditors' examination was not performed in accordance with generally accepted auditing standards. The working papers are the principal means by which auditors can demonstrate their compliance with these standards. For example, the working papers should document adequate planning, proper execution, and proper supervision (the first examination standard); a proper understanding of internal control (second standard); and the gathering of sufficient appropriate audit evidence to afford a reasonable basis for opinion (third standard).

Planning and Conducting the Next Audit.   The working papers from the previous audit of a particular client provide a wealth of information that is useful in planning and conducting the next audit. For example, the prior year's working papers show how much time was required to perform the audit, provide insight into the client's internal control, and refresh the auditors' memory of any special problems encountered during the engagement. In addition, some working papers, such as the substantiation of land, bonds payable, or capital stock, may be updated from one year to the next with very little effort.

Finally, how do inexperienced staff assistants know which is the best way to document the results of the audit procedures they perform? Often they look at the prior year's audit working papers. The procedures performed in the prior year probably were similar to those scheduled for the current year. Furthermore, the prior year's working papers were reviewed and signed off by a senior, a manager, and at least one partner, thus providing assurance that they represent satisfactory documentation of the audit work performed. Also, exceptions noted in last year's working paper may alert the assistant to possible problems in the current year.

Some care should be taken in using the working papers of the prior year as a model. The auditor must always be alert to changes in the client's operations or internal control that may make last year's approach inappropriate for the current year. In addition, the auditor should always be looking for ways to make the current year's audit more efficient than that of the prior year. Nonetheless, the audit staff usually finds the prior year's working papers to be an invaluable guide in conducting the current year's audit.

Confidential Nature of Working Papers

To conduct a satisfactory audit, the auditors must be given unrestricted access to all information about the client's business. Much of this information is confidential, such as the profit margins on individual products, tentative plans for business combinations with other companies, and the salaries of officers and key employees. Officers of the client company would not be willing to make available to the auditors information that is carefully guarded from competitors, employees, and others unless they could rely on the auditors' maintaining a professional silence on these matters.

Much of the information gained in confidence by the auditors is recorded in their working papers; consequently, the working papers are confidential in nature. The *Rules of Professional Conduct* developed by the accounting profession stipulate that a member in public practice shall not disclose any confidential information obtained in the course of a professional engagement except with the consent of the client or by order of lawful authorities.

Although the auditor is as careful as a lawyer or physician to hold in confidence all information concerning a client, the communication between a client and a public accountant is not privileged under the common law. Thus, a public accounting firm may legally be required to produce its working papers in a court case and to disclose information regarding a client.

Under normal circumstances, auditors think of confidential information as being information that must not be divulged *outside* of the client organization. But the confidential nature of information in the auditors' working papers has another dimension—it often must not be divulged *within* the client organization. If, for example, the client does not want certain employees to know the levels of executive salaries, the auditors obviously should not defeat this policy by exposing their working papers to unauthorized client personnel. Also, the working papers may identify particular accounts, branches, or time periods to be tested by the auditors; to permit the client's employees to learn of these in advance would weaken the significance of the tests.

Since audit working papers are highly confidential, they must be safeguarded at all times. Safeguarding working papers usually means keeping them locked in a file cabinet or in an audit case during lunch and after working hours in such a manner that prevents access to the working papers by persons other than the auditors.

Ownership of Audit Working Papers

Audit working papers are the ***property of the auditors,*** not of the client.[3] At no time does the client have the right to demand access to the auditors' working papers. After the audit, the working papers are retained by the auditors for a period long enough to satisfy the legal and professional requirements.[4]

Clients may sometimes find it helpful to refer to information from the auditors' working papers from prior years. Auditors usually are willing to provide this information, but the auditors' working papers should not be regarded as a substitute for the client's own accounting records. As part of any audit engagement, the auditors should provide the client with any information that could be regarded as the client's accounting records.

Working Papers and Auditors' Liability

The auditors' working papers are the principal record of the extent of the procedures applied and evidence gathered during the audit. If the auditors, after completing an engagement, are charged with negligence, their audit working papers will be a major factor in refuting or substantiating the charge. Working papers, if not properly prepared, are as likely to injure the auditors as to protect them.

If a lawsuit is brought against the auditors, the plaintiffs will go over the auditors' working papers in great detail, looking for contradictions, omissions, or any evidence of negligence or fraud. This possibility suggests the need for public accounting firms to make their own critical review of the working papers at the end of each engagement. During this review, the auditors should bear in mind that any contradictory statements or evi-

---

[3] Ibid., Section 5145.07
[4] Ibid., Section 5145.08

dence that is not consistent with the conclusions finally reached may be used at a later date to support a charge of improper auditing.

Part of the difficulty in avoiding inconsistent and conflicting evidence in working papers is that the papers are prepared in large part by less experienced staff members. When the papers are reviewed by a supervisor or partner, the reviewer will give careful consideration to any questionable points. In studying these points, the reviewer often gives consideration to many other aspects of the audit and of the client's records with which he or she is familiar. These other factors may lead the reviewer to the conclusion that an issue raised in the working papers does not warrant any corrective action. In some instances, the reviewer may conclude that the assistant who prepared the paper has misinterpreted the situation. Years later, if a dispute arises and the working papers are being subjected to critical study by lawyers representing an injured party, these questionable points in the papers may appear in a different light. The reviewer who cleared the issue based on personal knowledge of the client's business may not be available to explain the reasoning involved. This long-range responsibility suggests that the reviewer should insert in the working papers a carefully written *memorandum* explaining the decision.

Differences of Opinion.   On occasion, inconsistencies will arise in the working papers because different members of the audit staff—say, a senior and the engagement partner—will reach different conclusions on some complex auditing or accounting issue. In such cases, the disagreeing auditors should discuss the matter to see if they can reach agreement. If they are able to do so, the working papers should be revised to reflect their common opinion. If they are not able to reach agreement, the opinion of the partner in charge of the engagement will prevail with respect to the content of the auditors' report. However, all other members of the audit team have the right to document in the working papers *their disagreement* with the ultimate decision. In the event that a staff person elects to document his or her disagreement, the partner in charge obviously should be extremely thorough in documenting the rationale underlying the firm's ultimate decision.

Types of Working Papers

Since the audit working papers document a variety of information gathered by the auditors, there are innumerable types of papers. However, there are certain general categories into which most working papers may be grouped: (1) audit administrative working papers; (2) working trial balance and lead schedules; (3) adjusting journal entries and reclassification entries; (4) supporting schedules, analyses, reconciliations, and computational working papers; and (5) corroborating documents.

Audit Administrative Working Papers. Auditing is a sophisticated activity requiring planning, supervision, control, and coordination. Certain working papers are specifically designed to aid the auditors in the planning and administration of engagements. These working papers include audit plans and programs, internal control questionnaires and flowcharts, engagement letters, and time budgets. Memoranda of the planning process and significant discussions with client management are also considered administrative working papers.

Working Trial Balance. The working trial balance is a schedule listing the balances of accounts in the general ledger for the current and previous year, and also providing columns for the auditors' adjustments and reclassifications and for the final amounts that will appear in the financial statements. A working trial balance is the backbone of the entire set of audit working papers; it is the key schedule that controls and summarizes all supporting papers. This type of working paper may appear as shown below, or in computer printout form when audit software is used.

						TB-1
	Process Company Inc.					
	Working Trial Balance					
	December 31, 1992					
Working Paper Reference	Caption	Final Dec. 31,91	Balance per Ledger Dec. 31,92	Adjustments Dr. (Cr.)	Adjusted Dec. 31,92	Reclassifications Dr. (Cr.)	Final Balance Dec. 31,92
	Assets						
	Current Assets:						
A	Cash	481413	742186		742186		742186
B	Short-Term Investments		449413		449413		449413
C	Accounts Receivable—Net	2298722	2053918	(91096)	1962822		1962822
D	Inventories	2701814	2942117	(129799)	2812318		2812318

Although most of these column headings are self-explanatory, a brief discussion of the third and fourth columns is appropriate. In the third column, the final adjusted balances from the previous year's audit are listed. Inclusion of the previous year's figures facilitates comparison with the corresponding amounts for the current year and focuses attention upon any unusual changes. Inclusion of the final figures from the prior year's audit also gives assurance that the correct starting figure is used if the auditors verify the year's transactions in a balance sheet account in order to determine the validity of the ending balance.

The fourth column provides for the account balances at the close of the year under audit; these balances usually are taken directly from the general ledger. The balances of the revenue and expense accounts should be included, even though these accounts have been closed into the Retained Earnings account prior to the auditors' arrival. Since the auditors ordinarily express an opinion on the income statement as well as the balance sheet, it is imperative that the audit working papers include full information on the revenue and expense accounts. The amount to be listed for the Retained Earnings account is the balance at the ***beginning*** of the year under audit. Dividends declared during the year are listed as a separate item, as is the computed net income for the year.

In many audits, the client furnishes the auditors with a working trial balance after all normal end-of-period journal entries have been posted. Before accepting the trial balance for their working papers, the auditors should trace the amounts to the general ledger for evidence that the trial balance is prepared accurately.

Lead Schedules.   Separate lead schedules (also called ***grouping sheets*** or ***summary schedules***) are set up to combine similar general ledger accounts, the total of which appears on the working trial balance as a single amount. For example, a lead schedule for Cash might combine the following general ledger accounts: Petty Cash, $500; General bank account, $196,240; Factory Payroll bank account, $500; and Dividend bank account, $1,000. Similar lead schedules would be set up for Accounts Receivable, Inventories, Shareholders' Equity, Net Sales, and for other balance sheet or income statement captions.

Adjusting Journal Entries and Reclassification Entries.   During the course of an audit engagement, the auditors may discover various types of misstatements in the client's financial statements and accounting records. These misstatements may be large or small in amount; they may arise from the omission of transactions or from the use of incorrect amounts; or they may result from improper classification or cutoff, or from misinterpretation of transactions. Generally, these misstatements are accidental errors; however, the auditors may discover fraud in the financial statements or accounting records.

To correct ***material*** errors or fraud discovered in the financial statements and accounting records, the auditors draft ***adjusting journal entries*** (AJEs), which they recommend for entry in the client's accounting records. In addition, the auditors develop ***reclassification journal entries*** (RJEs) for items that, although correctly recorded in the accounting records, must be reclassified for fair presentation in the client's financial statements. For example, accounts receivable with large credit balances should be ***reclassified*** as a liability in the balance sheet. Reclassification entries affect only the financial statement presentation; therefore, they are *not recorded* in the client's accounting records. Reclassification entries appear only in the auditors' working papers.

Supporting Schedules. Although all types of working papers may loosely be called schedules, auditors prefer to use this term to describe a listing of the elements or details comprising the balance in an asset or liability account at a specific date. Thus, a list of amounts owed to vendors making up the balance of the Trade Accounts Payable account is properly described as a *schedule.*

Analysis of a Ledger Account. An analysis of a ledger account is another common type of audit working paper. The purpose of an analysis is to show on one paper *all changes* in an asset, liability, equity, revenue, or expense account during the period covered by the audit. If a number of the changes are individually immaterial, they may be recorded as a single item in the analysis working paper. Account analyses are most useful in substantiating those accounts affected by relatively few transactions during the year. Examples include plant asset accounts, long-term debt accounts, capital stock accounts, and retained earnings.

To analyze a ledger account, the auditors first list the beginning balance and indicate the nature of the items comprising this balance. Next, the auditors list and investigate the nature of all debits and credits to the account during the period. These entries, when combined with the beginning balance, produce a figure representing the balance in the account as of the audit date. If any errors or omissions of importance are detected during this analysis of the account, the necessary adjusting journal entry approved by the client is entered on the working paper to produce the adjusted balance required for the financial statements.

Reconciliations. Frequently, auditors wish to prove the relationship between amounts obtained from different sources. When they do so, they prepare working papers known as reconciliations. These reconciliations provide evidence as to the accuracy of one or both of the amounts and are important to the audit of many accounts, including cash, accounts receivable, and inventories.

Computational Working Papers. Another type of supporting working paper is the computational working paper. The auditors' approach to verifying certain types of accounts and other figures is to make an independent computation and compare their results with the amounts shown by the client's records. Examples of amounts that might be verified by computation are interest expense, depreciation, payroll taxes, income taxes, pension liabilities, and earnings per share.

Corroborating Documents. Auditing is not limited to the examination of financial records, and working papers are not confined to schedules and analyses. During the course of an audit, the auditors may gather much purely expository material to substantiate their report. One common example is copies of minutes of directors' and shareholders' meetings. Other examples include copies of articles and certificates of incorporation and bylaws; copies of important contracts, bond indentures, and mortgages; memoranda pertaining to examination of records; audit confirmations; and letters of representations from the client and from the client's legal counsel.

Organization of the Working Papers

The auditors usually maintain two files of working papers for each client: (1) current files for every completed examination and (2) a permanent file of relatively unchanging data. The current file (as for the 1993 audit) pertains solely to that year's examination; the permanent file contains such things as copies of the articles of incorporation, which are of continuing audit interest.

The Current Files.   The auditors' report for a particular year is supported by the working paper contained in the current files. Many public accounting firms have found it useful to organize the current files around the arrangement of the accounts in the client's financial statements. The administrative working papers usually begin the current files, including a draft of the financial statements and the auditors' report. These working papers are followed by the working trial balance and the adjusting and reclassification entries. The remaining portion of the current files consists of working papers supporting the balances and other representations in the client's financial statements. It begins with working papers for each asset account and continues with papers for liabilities, owners' equity accounts, and revenue and expense accounts. The file containing the work on the understanding and test of internal control is often called the *interim* or *systems file*. The file covering the substantive testing is generally called the *year-end file*.

Each working paper in a file is assigned a reference number, and information is tied together through a system of cross-referencing. In this way, a reviewer may trace amounts on the working trial balance back to the supporting working papers. Figure 10–1 illustrates a system of cross-referencing and a typical arrangement of the current files after the administrative working papers.

The Permanent File.   The permanent file serves three purposes: (1) to refresh the auditors' memory on items applicable over a period of many years; (2) to provide for new staff members a quick summary of the policies and organization of the client; and (3) to preserve working papers

FIGURE 10–1 Organization of the Current Files

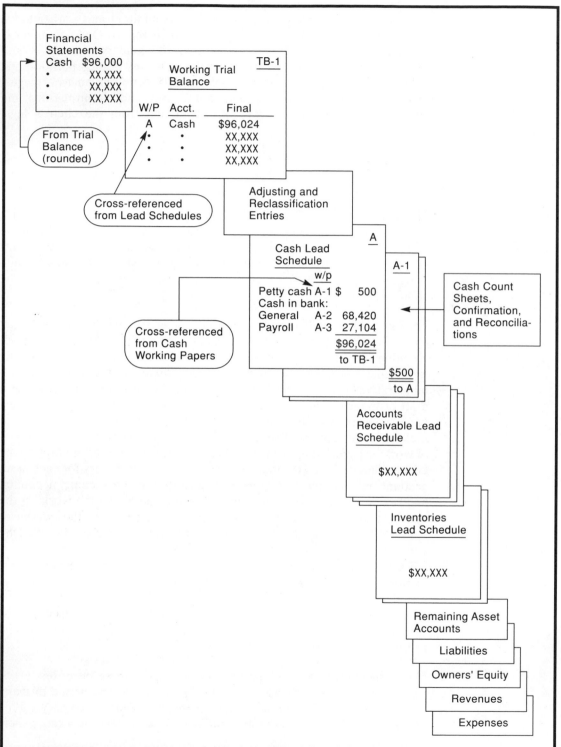

on items that show relatively few or no changes, thus eliminating the necessity for their preparation year after year.

Much of the information contained in the permanent file is gathered during the course of the first audit of a client's records. A considerable portion of the time spent on a first audit is devoted to gathering and appraising background information, such as copies of articles and certificates of incorporation and bylaws, leases, patent agreements, pension plans, labour contracts, long-term construction contracts, charts of accounts, and prior years' tax returns.[5]

Analyses of accounts that show few changes over a period of years are also included in the permanent file. These accounts may include land, buildings, accumulated depreciation, long-term investments, long-term liabilities, capital stock, and other owners' equity accounts. The initial investigation of these accounts must often include the transactions of many years. But once these historical analyses have been brought up to date, the work required in subsequent examinations will be limited to a review of the current year's transactions in these accounts. In this respect, the permanent file is a timesaving device because current changes in such accounts need only be added to the permanent papers without reappearing in the current working papers. Adequate cross-referencing in the working papers, of course, should be provided to show where in the permanent file such information is to be found.

Guidelines for Preparation of Working Papers

We can now summarize in a few short paragraphs our basic guidelines for preparing working papers that will meet current professional standards.

A separate, properly identified working paper should be prepared for each topic. Proper identification of a working paper is accomplished by a heading that includes the name of the client company, a clear description of the information presented, and the applicable date or the period covered.

Complete and specific identification of documents examined, employees interviewed, and sites visited is essential for good working paper practice. The preparer of a working paper should date and sign or initial the working paper; the signatures or initials of the senior, manager, or partner who reviewed the working paper should also appear on the paper, together with the date of the review.

All working papers should be referenced and cross-referenced to the working trial balance or relevant lead schedule. Where reference is necessary between working papers, there must be adequate cross-referencing.

---

[5] Many accounting firms have a separate file for the client's income tax matters.

The nature of verification work performed by the auditors should be indicated on each working paper. A review of paid purchase invoices, for example, might be supplemented by inspection of the related purchase orders and receiving documents to substantiate the authenticity of the invoices examined; a description of this verification procedure should be included on the working paper. As audit working papers are prepared, the auditors will use several different symbols to identify specific steps in the work performed. These symbols, or *tick marks,* provide a very concise means of indicating the auditing procedures applied to particular amounts. Whenever tick marks are employed, they must be accompanied by a legend explaining their meaning.

The working papers should include comments by the auditors indicating their conclusions on each aspect of the work. In other words, the auditors should clearly express the opinion they have formed as a result of having performed the auditing procedures summarized in the working paper. Figure 10–2 illustrates such a conclusion related to the audit of the allowance for uncollectible account, along with other aspects of a properly prepared working paper.

Computer-generated Working Papers

Traditionally, working papers have been prepared in pencil on columnar paper. Today, many working papers are prepared on portable personal computers carried by the auditors to the work site. When an adjustment is entered on computer-based working papers, it appears instantly on the appropriate lead schedules, the adjustments schedule, and the working trial balance. The necessary cross-references are automatically entered on each schedule. If the adjustment affects taxable income, the income tax expense account and the tax liability are automatically adjusted using the client's tax rate. In addition, all of the subtotals, column totals, and cross-footings in the working papers are instantly adjusted.

When working papers are maintained manually, all of these entries and changes must be made by hand with a pencil, an eraser, and a calculator. With a personal computer, an adjustment that might take a half hour or more to "push through" manual working papers can be entered in a few seconds. Thus, personal computers have taken much of the "pencil pushing" and the "number crunching" out of working paper preparation.

The Review of Audit Working Papers

Working papers are reviewed at every supervisory level of a public accounting firm. Senior auditors review the working papers of staff assistants: managers review all working papers prepared by staff assistants and

FIGURE 10-2 Preparation of a Working Paper

Maine Company, Inc.
Allowance for Uncollectible Accounts
March 31, 19X3

Balance per ledger, Mar. 31, X3		22,881.75 x
Deduct: Write-offs during fiscal 19X3		
June 12, X2 Morgan Desk Co.	6,581.44 n	
Feb. 12, X3 Baker Cabinet Co.	8,041.60 n	14,623.04
		8,258.71
Add: Provision for year ended Mar. 31, X3 based on		
aged trial balance of trade accounts		
receivable at Mar. 31, X3		6,589.81
Balance per ledger, Mar. 31, X3		14,848.52 x
A.J.E. 7- to increase allowance based on		
tests of collectibility and analytical		
review procedures on C-5-1.		5,151.48
		TB-5-2
Adjusted balance Mar. 31, X3		20,000.00

F. Footed
n. Examined Controller's authorization for write-off. — F to C
x. Agreed to general ledger.
Based on the results of the tests of collectibility
and analytical review procedures on C-6, the
adjusted balance of the allowance for
uncollectible accounts, appears to be adequate
to value the accounts receivable at net
realizable values.

B.J.P.
V.M.W.

Maine Company, Inc.
Adjusting Journal Entries
March 31, 19X3

TB-5-2
V.M.W.
4/26/X3

Working Paper Reference	Account No.	Account Title and Explanation (7)	Dr.	Cr.
C-5	524	Uncollectible Accounts Expense	5,151.48	
	126	Allowance for Uncollectible Accounts		5,151.48
		To increase the allowance for uncollectible accounts to amount considered necessary based on test work performed on C-5.		

Illustrative Case

An advertisement for computer software appearing in the *Journal of Accountancy* illustrates the time savings that can be achieved by preparing audit working papers on a personal computer. The advertisement showed time comparisons for preparing various working papers manually and by computer. The following were among the comparisons made:

	Hours	
	Manual	*Computer*
1. Prepare 30 lead schedules and a working trial balance	9	1
2. Perform initial analytical procedures	8	½
3. Prepare accounts receivable confirmation letter reports and analysis of results	20	5
4. Prepare 50 adjusting and reclassifying journal entries and post to lead schedules and working trial balance	4	½
5. Prepare comparative balance sheet, income statements, and statement of changes in financial position worksheet . . .	10	1
6. Oops! Post two *late* adjusting journal entries to lead schedules and working trial balance. Update *all* working papers as required	10	½

---

by senior auditors; the partner in charge of the engagement reviews the entire set of working papers. Many firms also require a review by a second partner.

What Do the Reviewers Look For?   All of the reviewers want to ensure that the working papers properly document the audit. However, there are differences in the nature of the reviews. The senior's review is the most technical, and it generally is performed promptly after the completion of the individual working paper. Seniors look primarily to see that the staff assistant has performed the audit procedures properly and that the assistant's findings and conclusions are clearly expressed.

The reviews by managers and partners are often performed near the *end* of the engagement, when the reviewer may examine at one time the entire set of working papers. These reviewers are primarily interested in the determining that the audit was performed in accordance with generally accepted auditing stnadards and that the working papers properly support the auditors' report that will be issued on the financial statements. There are several advantages to reviewing all of the working papers at once. The reviewer can determine that the working papers "tie together"—that is, that amounts are properly carried forward from one working paper to another. As we mentioned earlier in the chapter, these reviewers should look critically for any inconsistencies, omissions, or loose ends that might later support a plaintiff's allegations of improper auditing. In addition, the reviewer should consider whether the various immaterial discrepancies that were passed without adjustment might **cumulatively** have a material effect upon the financial statements.

The purposes of a **second partner review** are to provide assurance that all of the firm's **quality control policies** have been complied with, as well as to provide a second opinion that the audit was performed in accordance with generally accepted auditing standards. The second partner review, sometimes called a *cold review,* usually is performed by a partner with no personal or professional ties to the audit client. Multioffice firms sometimes bring in a partner from another office to perform the second partner review.

Not until all of these reviewers have signed off on the audit working papers is the public accounting firm's name signed to the auditors' report.

EXAMINATION OF THE GENERAL RECORDS

In the early stages of an audit, the external auditors must become familiar with many aspects of the client's business. For example, the auditors must obtain a knowledge of the client's organization plan, financial structure, physical facilities, products, accounting policies, and the control procedures. However, information about the internal activities of the client is not in itself sufficient. If this information is to be interpreted and evaluated in a proper perspective, the auditors must also understand the business environment in which the client operates.[6] Provincial and federal laws and regulations, pending or threatened litigation, affiliations with other companies, and contracts with suppliers and customers are only a few of the factors in the business environment that may affect the client's internal activities. The auditors can gain considerable information about both the client's business environment and internal operations by examining the client's general records. The term **general records** is used to include the following categories.

1. Nonfinancial records.
    a. Articles and certificate of corporation and bylaws.
    b. Partnership contract.
    c. Minutes of directors' and shareholders' meetings.

---

[6] CICA, *CICA Handbook* (Toronto), Section 5140.

    d. Contracts with customers and suppliers.

    e. Contracts with officers and employees, including union agreements and stock option, profit-sharing, bonus, and pension plans.

    f. Government regulations directly affecting the enterprise.

    g. Correspondence files.

2. Financial records.

    a. Income tax returns of prior years.

    b. Financial statements and annual reports of prior years.

    c. Registration statements and periodic reports filed with the securities commissions and other governmental agencies.

3. Accounting records.

    a. General ledger.

    b. General journal.

Examining these records should assist the auditors in identifying problems requiring more extensive audit attention. Also, the auditors obtain an understanding of the client's business characteristics, policies, and plans that enable them to determine whether the transactions reflected in the accounts were properly authorized and executed in accordance with the directives of management. If audit staff members are thoroughly familiar with the history and problems of the business, the duties and responsibilities of key officials, and the nature and quality of the accounting records and procedures, then they are prepared to carry out each phase of the audit with confidence and understanding. If they do not acquire this background information before beginning the work of analyzing transactions and substantiating account balances, they are almost certain to proceed in a mechanical and routine manner, unaware of the real significance of much of the evidence examined.

Articles and Certificate of Incorporation and Bylaws

In the first audit of a client's financial statements, a senior auditor will obtain copies of the articles and certificate of incorporation and the bylaws. The *articles and certificate of incorporation* are the basic documents that evidence the legal existence of a corporation. They include such information as the name of the company, date and place of incorporation, the number of authorized directors, and the authorized capital structure, including classes of capital stock, number of shares authorized, par or no-par values, liquidating preferences, voting rights, and dividend rates for preferred stock.

The *bylaws* help define the internal administrative structure of a corporation; they include the organizational structure, rules, and procedures adopted by the corporate shareholders. For example, the bylaws may stipulate the frequency of shareholders' meetings, the date and method for election of directors and selection of officers, and the powers and duties of directors and officers. Copies of the articles and certificate of incorporation and the bylaws are retained in the auditors' permanent file for convenient reference during repeat engagements.

Partnership Contract

In the audit of a business organized as a partnership, the partnership contract should be examined in much the same manner as the articles and certificate of incorporation and bylaws of corporate clients. The partnership contract represents an agreement among partners on the rules to be followed in the operation of the enterprise. The information available in a copy of the partnership contract usually includes the following:

1. The name and address of the firm.
2. The names and addresses of the individual partners.
3. The amount, date, and nature of the investment made by each partner.
4. The income-sharing ratio, partners' salaries, interest on partners' capital, and restrictions on withdrawals.
5. The duties, responsibilities, and authority of each partner.
6. The provision for insurance on the lives of partners.
7. The provisions concerning the liquidation of the firm and the distribution of assets.

In repeat examinations, the auditors must ascertain whether any modification of the partnership contract has been made and obtain copies of the modifications for the permanent file. If no change has occurred since the preceding audit, a notation to that effect should be made.

Corporate Minutes Book

The corporate minutes book is an official record of the actions taken at meetings of directors and shareholders. Typical of the actions taken at meetings of shareholders is the extension of authority to management to acquire or dispose of subsidiaries and to adopt or modify pension or profit-sharing plans for officers and employees. The shareholders also appoint a public accounting firm as external auditors. Representatives of the auditing firm attend the shareholders' meeting for the purpose of answering questions that may arise concerning internal control and the financial operations of the business.

Minutes of the directors' meetings usually contain authorizations for important transactions and contractual arrangements, such as the establishment of bank accounts, setting of officers' salaries, declaration of dividends, and formation of long-term agreements with vendors, customers, and lessors. In addition, the minutes may document discussions by the board of pending litigation, investigations by regulatory agencies, or other contingencies.

Committees of the Board.   In large corporations, the board of directors often works through committees appointed to deal with special phases of operations. Common examples include an audit committee and an investment committee. As discussed in Chapters 4 and 7, the audit committee maintains close contact with both the external auditors and the company's internal auditors and may be involved in discussions of weaknesses in internal control, accounting policies, and possible illegal or fraudulent acts by management. The investment committee periodically reviews and approves the investment activities of management. Minutes of the meetings of such committees are just as essential to the auditors' investigation as are the minutes covering the meetings of the entire board.

Procedure for Review of Minutes.   In the first audit of a client, it may be necessary to review minutes recorded in prior years. Copies of these minutes will be preserved in the permanent file; as succeeding annual audits are made, the file will be appropriately expanded.

The auditors will obtain from the secretary or other corporate officer copies of all minutes, including those of board committees, directors, and shareholders, for both regular and special meetings. These copies should be certified by a corporate officer and should be compared with the official minutes book to an extent sufficient to establish their completeness and authenticity.

In reviewing the minutes, the auditors will (1) note the date of the meeting and whether a quorum was present and (2) underscore or highlight such actions and decisions that in their judgment should influence the conduct of the audit. Nonessential material can be scanned rapidly, and highlighting can be limited to issues that warrant investigation during the course of the audit. For this phase of the audit work, there is no substitute for breadth of experience and maturity of judgment; the minutes include a wide range of information, from matters of real importance to the audit to those that may safely be passed by.

Major decisions in the minutes, such as declaration of dividends or authorization for borrowing, usually result in actions that need to be recorded in the accounting records. As the audit progresses, the auditors should trace authorized events from the minutes into the accounting records and cross-reference their copies of the minutes to the underlying account analyses. Similarly, events recorded in the accounting records that normally require authorization by directors should be traced and cross-referenced to the auditors' copies of the minutes.

Determining that All Minutes Are Made Available.   How do auditors know that copies of all minutes have been made available to them? First, they can review their permanent file to determine the identities of the boards' committees and the scheduled dates for regular meetings. Next, a typical practice at board and committee meetings is to approve the minutes of the preceding meeting. This practice enables the auditors to work backward from the most recent minutes to the oldest, noting the date of the previous minutes approved in the later meeting. Also, the auditors should obtain from management a letter representing that all minutes have been made available. The client's refusal to provide the auditors with copies of all minutes is a serious limitation of the scope of the auditors' examination.

Relationship of Corporate Minutes to Audit Objectives.   The nature of the information to be highlighted in the minutes and the usefulness of this information to the auditors can be made clear by a few examples. Figure 10–3 shows several audit objectives and indicates for each objective certain relevant events that are likely to be documented in the minutes of the board and its committees.

Contracts Held or Issued by Client

Early in the audit engagement the auditors should obtain copies of the major contracts to which the client is a party. Information obtained from an analysis of contracts may be helpful in interpreting such accounts as Advances from Suppliers, Progress Payments under Government Contracts, and Stock Options. In addition to production contracts with governmental agencies and other companies, the auditors may review contracts with suppliers for future delivery of materials, royalty agreements for use of patents, union labour contracts, leases, pension plans, stock options, and bonus contracts with officers.

The terms of existing contracts are often material factors in measuring debt-paying ability and estimating future earnings. When examinations are being made on behalf of prospective investors, creditors, or purchasers of a business, the nature of contracts with customers may outweigh all other considerations in determining a market value for the business.

The auditors may at times require the assistance of engineers, lawyers, and other specialists in the interpretation of important contracts. Most contracts include such accounting concepts as net income or working capital, but unfortunately those who draft the contracts may not in all cases understand the true meaning of the accounting terminology they employ. Skill in analyzing and interpreting the financial aspects of contracts appears to be a qualification of increasing importance to external auditors.

FIGURE 10–3 Relationship of Minutes to Audit Objectives

Audit Objectives	*Relevant Information Likely to Be Included in Minutes of the Board and Its Committees*
1. Establishing the completeness of cash balances.	1. The opening and closing of bank accounts require authorization by the board of directors.
2. Financial statement presentation and disclosure of marketable securities.	2. Pledging of securities as collateral for a loan requires approval of the investments committee of the board.
3. Establishing the completeness of liabilities.	3a. The obtaining of bank loans requires advance approval by the board.
	b. Authority for the declaration of dividends payable rests with the board.
	c. The issuance of bonds payable or other long-term debt requires approval by the board.
4. Financial statement presentation and disclosure of contingencies.	4a. Such issues as pending litigation, income tax disputes, accommodation endorsements, and other contingencies discussed by the board are documented in the minutes.
	b. Unusual purchase commitments and sales commitments may be submitted to the board for approval.
	c. The selection of legal counsel, who in turn may have information regarding pending litigation or other contingencies, is approved by the board.

Among the items auditors should usually note in reviewing contracts are the names and addresses of parties, effective date and duration of the contract, schedule for performance, provisions for price redetermination (such as cost-of-living adjustments), procedures for settlement of disputes, cancellation clauses, and provisions requiring audit of records to determine amounts owed.

Government Laws and Regulations

Although external auditors are not licensed to give legal advice or to interpret federal or provincial laws, they must be familiar with laws and regulations that affect the client's financial statements. Recall from our discussion in Chapter 2 that audits should be designed to provide reasonable assurance of detecting illegal acts having a material ***direct*** effect on financial statement amounts. While an audit does ***not*** generally provide a basis for detecting violations of laws or regulations which have an ***indirect*** effect on the financial statement, the auditor must be aware of the possibility that such violations may have occurred. When such information comes to the auditor's attention, the auditor should apply audit procedures directed towards ascertaining whether a material illegal act has occurred.

Among the laws and regulations with which auditors should be familiar are the following:

Federal and Provincial Business Corporations Acts.   Laws governing the formation and operation of corporations vary between the federal and provincial acts, and also among the provincial acts. The auditors should obtain a copy of the act of each client's place of incorporation and become familiar with provisions of the act which affect such matters as legal capital, par or no-par shares, dividend declarations, and treasury shares.

Provincial Partnership Acts.   These acts govern the operations of partnerships in areas not covered by the partnership contract.

Provincial Securities Laws.   Since securities legislation is substantially within provincial jurisdiction, the auditors should be familiar with the securities laws governing the issue and trading of their clients' securities as well as the disclosure requirements for their clients' financial statements.

Competition Act.   This act is designed to promote competition and prescribes penalties for certain unfair business and trading practices such as price fixing, predatory pricing, discriminatory allowance, and misleading advertising about price.

Labour Laws.   The federal and provincial labour codes govern collective bargaining and other labour matters.

Unemployment Insurance, Canada Pension, and Workers' Compensation Laws.   These laws are relevant to auditors because they affect payroll deductions and contributions.

Special Acts for Specific Industries.   Clients in industries such as insurance, banking, airlines, railroads, public utilities, and broadcasting are governed by special acts of both the federal and provincial governments. Auditors with clients in these industries will need to be familiar with the special laws and regulations that directly affect the operations of these companies.

Temporary Controls.   In addition to the seemingly permanent statutes listed above, various temporary regulations are occasionally imposed by government which affect the transactions subject to review by the auditors. Examples include controls over wages, prices, profits, and dividends. If violations are apparent, the auditors should inform both management and legal counsel of the client company and consider the possible existence of unrecorded liabilities in the form of fines or penalties.

Correspondence Files

The general correspondence files of the client may contain much information of importance to the external auditors, but it would be quite out of the question for them to read the great mass of general correspondence on file in search of pertinent letters. When the reading of corporate minutes, contract files, or other data indicates the existence of significant correspondence on matters of concern to the auditors, they should request the client to provide them with copies of such letters. In addition, the audit staff will usually review the client's correspondence with banks and other lending institutions, lawyers, and governmental agencies. Correspondence may generally be accepted as authentic, but if reason for doubt exists, the auditors may wish to confirm the contents of letters directly with the responsible persons.

Income Tax Returns of Prior Years

A review of federal, provincial, and foreign income tax returns of prior years will aid the auditors in planning any tax services required by the terms of the engagement. The possibility of assessment of additional income taxes exists with respect to the returns of recent years not yet cleared by tax authorities. By reviewing tax returns and assessment notices, the auditors may become aware of any matters that pose a threat of additional assessments; they may also find a basis for filing a claim for a tax refund.

Financial Statements and Annual Reports of Prior Years

Study of the financial statements and annual reports of prior years and of any available monthly or quarterly statements for the current year is a convenient way for the auditors to gain a general background knowledge of the financial history and problems of the business. If external auditors have submitted audit reports in prior years, these documents may also be useful in drawing attention to matters requiring special consideration.

Reports to the Securities Commissions and Other Governmental Agencies

Registration statements and periodic reports filed by the client with the securities commissions and other governmental agencies contain valuable information for the auditors—especially in a first audit. Included in this information will be the client's capital structure, a summary of earnings for the past five years, identity of affiliated companies, descriptions of the business and property of the client, pending legal proceedings, names of directors and executive officers of the client and their remuneration, stock option plans, and principal shareholders of the client.

Review and Testing of the Accounting Records

Early in the examination, the auditors should review the client's accounting system and assess the quality of the accounting records. A review of these records will inform the auditors as to the client's accounting procedures, the accounting records in use, and the control procedures in effect. Testing of the accounting records verifies the mechanical accuracy of the records and provides assurance that the journals and ledger are actually achieving their respective purposes of recording and classifying transaction data.

The quality of accounting records may vary widely from one engagement to the next. Many clients maintain records that are carefully designed, well maintained, and easy to comprehend. The journals and ledgers of such clients are generally up to date, in balance, and virtually free from mechanical error. When the auditors ascertain that a client's accounting records are highly reliable, the audit work necessary to substantiate account balances may justifiably be minimized. At the other extreme, the accounting records of some clients may be typified by unrecorded transactions, unsupported entries, and numerous mechanical errors. In these cases, the auditors may have to perform extensive audit work to substantiate account balances. On occasion, the accounting records may be so inadequate that the auditors must deny an opinion on the financial statements.

Extent of Testing.   If the client's accounting records and procedures are well designed and efficiently maintained, it is reasonable to devote less audit time to verifying the mechanical accuracy of the records than would be required in audits in which less satisfactory conditions prevail. The extent to which the auditors test the accounting records depends upon two factors: (1) the general appearance of the records and (2) the frequency and relative importance of any misstatements discovered during the actual testing. The first of these factors, the general appearance of the records, deserves some explanation. High-quality accounting records have basic characteristics that are readily apparent: journal entries include adequate written explanations, general journal entries are reviewed and approved by an officer before processing, and the records are up to date and properly cross-referenced. When records do not possess these characteristics, the existence of misstatements is a virtual certainty.

Testing of the accounting records may be done on a judgmental basis, or the auditors may use statistical sampling techniques. Attributes sampling, as discussed in Chapter 9, is a statistical sampling plan that may be used to estimate deviation rates with specified levels of risk of assessing control risk too low.

The General Ledger

The function of the general ledger is to accumulate and classify the transaction data posted from the journals. To ascertain that the ledger is being properly maintained, the auditors should conduct tests to determine that (1) account balances are mathematically correct, (2) entries in the ledger were posted from journal entries, and (3) journal entries were properly posted.

To test the mathematical accuracy of account balances, the auditors should verify the footings of some or all of the ledger accounts. The term **footings** is used among practicing accountants to designate column totals. To foot, as discussed in Chapter 7, means to verify the total by adding the column.

The concept of *directional testing,* discussed in Chapter 5, applies to the second and third groups of tests. For the second group, the auditors must satisfy themselves that entries in the general ledger were posted from authentic sources, that is, from entries in the journals. This procedure is important because the financial statements are drawn from the general ledger balances, and these balances conceivably could be falsified through the recording of unsupported debits or credits in the general ledger. The auditors can determine that entries in the ledger are properly supported by *tracing a sample of ledger entries back into the journals.* Ledger entries included in this sample are normally selected at random from entries made throughout the year. Of course, the auditors may test most or all of the entries in excess of some specified dollar amount. Tracing ledger entries back to journal entries may reveal transactions that are not supported and, possibly, are not valid. By extending the test and vouching the journalized transactions to the supporting documents, such as receiving reports and canceled cheques, the auditors may also obtain evidence of the validity of the journalized transactions. On the other hand, transactions that are not supported *can never* be found by tracing forward from journal entries or source documents to the ledgers.

Finally, to test the accuracy of the client's posting procedures, the auditors should *trace a sample of entries from the journals into the general and subsidiary ledgers.* In this test, the auditors are testing the *completeness* of posted transactions. If a transaction was never posted, this omission can be detected only by tracing from the source documents or the journals to the ledgers. Transactions improperly omitted from ledger accounts *cannot* be brought to light by tracing existing ledger entries back to their source. Of course, some errors, such as transposition errors in entering transactions and postings to the wrong account, may be discovered by tracing in either direction.

Computer-based Systems. It is likely that a client's accounting system will involve some form of electronic data processing. In these computer-based systems, transactions are entered into the computer either individually or in batches. The computer system then creates a journal of the transactions, and posts the transactions to the general ledger and appropriate subsidiary ledgers. Entries in the journals are linked to the ledger postings by the *audit trail* that allows journal entries to be traced to or from the ledgers. The audit trail also allows journal entries to be traced to and from the documents supporting the transactions.

Tests of the mechanical accuracy of computer-based accounting records may be performed manually by the auditors. It is generally more efficient, however, to perform the tests using *computer-assisted audit techniques,* as described in Chapter 8. Generalized audit software programs may be used to test the accuracy of accounting records.

The General Journal

The general journal is an accounting record used to record all transactions for which special journals have not been provided. In its simplest form, the general journal has only a single pair of columns for the recording of debit and credit entries, but many variations from this basic design are encountered. A third column may be added to provide for entries to subsidiary ledgers, or various multicolumn forms may be used.

Some companies maintain a system of journal vouchers. These are serially numbered documents, each containing a single, general journal entry, with full supporting details and bearing the signature of the controller or other officer authorized to approve the entry. A general journal in traditional form may be prepared from the journal vouchers, or that series of documents may be utilized in lieu of a general journal.

The auditors should conduct tests to determine that entries in the general journal are based on valid transactions and that these transactions have been properly recorded. Suggested procedures for testing the general journal follow:

1. Foot column totals of the journal.

The testing of footings in the general journal follows the pattern previously described for verification of ledger balances. The footings may be performed manually or by using computer assisted audit techniques.

2. Vouch selected entries to original documents.

To vouch a journal entry means to examine the original papers and documents supporting the entry. The term *voucher* is used to describe any type of supporting documentary evidence. For example, a journal entry recording the trade-in of a machine would be vouched by comparing it with a purchase order, supplier's invoice, sales contract, receiving report, and paid cheque—the vouchers for this entry. The auditors might not consider it necessary to examine all these documents if the evidence first examined appeared to provide adequate support for the entry. All general journal entries selected for testing should be vouched.

Entries in the general journal should include clear, informative explanations, but, unfortunately, deviations from this principle are frequently encountered. The auditors should determine whether (1) the explanation is in agreement with the supporting documentation, and (2) the entry reflects the transaction properly in the light of generally accepted accounting principles.

The supporting evidence to be examined during the review of general journal entries may include purchase orders, invoices, receiving reports, sales contracts, correspondence, the minutes book, and the partnership contract. Journal vouchers represent an internal control device; however, they should not be considered as original source documents supporting entries in the general journal. Verification of journal entries requires that the auditors refer to original invoices and other evidence previously described.

3. Scan the general journal for unusual entries.

The importance of certain types of transactions that are recorded in the general journal makes it desirable for auditors to scan this record for the entire period under audit, in addition to vouching all entries selected for testing. The following list is illustrative of the types of significant transactions for which the auditors should look in this scanning of the general journal:

a. The write-off of assets, particularly notes and accounts receivable: Collections from customers abstracted by employees and not recorded in the accounts may be permanently concealed if the accounts in question are written off as uncollectible. Any general journal entries involving loans receivable from officers require full investigation to provide assurance that such transactions are proper and have been authorized.

b. Assumption of liabilities: Transactions that create liabilities are normally recorded in special journals. Common examples of such transactions are the purchase of merchandise, materials, or equipment and the receipt of cash. General journal entries that bring liabilities into the record warrant close investigation to determine that they have received proper authorization and are adequately supported.

c. Any debits or credits to cash accounts, other than for bank charges and other bank reconciliation items: Most transactions affecting cash are recorded in special journals.

d. Creation of revenue: Transactions affecting operating revenue accounts are usually recorded in special journals. Operating revenue would be recorded in the general journal only if the underlying transaction was of an unusual nature or, for some reason, was being processed in a special manner. In either case, the auditors should verify the authenticity of the transaction and the propriety of the entry.

e. Unexplained or fragmentary transactions, the purpose and nature of which are not apparent from the journal entry: General journal entries with inadequate or unintelligible explanations suggest that the person making the entry did not understand the issues involved or was unwilling to state the facts clearly. Entries of this type, and entries that affect seemingly unrelated accounts, should be fully investigated.

f. Related party transactions: Transactions between the client and affiliated companies, directors, officers, and principal owners and their immediate families are not at arm's length and should be investigated to determine that the substance of the transactions has been fairly recorded. These transactions, as discussed in Chapter 6, should be reviewed by the auditors as to reasonableness of amounts, business purpose, and adequacy of disclosure.

Illustrative Case

In a widely publicized management fraud, the financial statements of Equity Funding Corporation of America in the United States were inflated over a period of years by more than $120 million in fictitious assets and revenue. Although falsified journal entries were prepared to record fictitious transactions, there was frequently no documentation to support the journal entries. Large amounts of revenue were also recognized in journal entries that involved debits and credits to an illogical combination of accounts. Thorough investigation of unusual revenue-creating journal entries could have alerted the company's external auditors to the fraud long before it reached mammoth proportions.

---

4. Determine that general journal entries have received the approval of an officer.

Adequate internal control includes procedures for regular review and written approval of all general journal entries by the controller or other appropriate executive. The auditors should determine that such procedures have been consistently followed. In those cases in which a client official does not regularly review and approve journal entries, the auditors may deem it desirable to review the general journal with the controller and request an approval signature on each page. In such cases, the report to the client on internal control should include a suggestion that the client undertake regular review and approval of journal entries.

Audit Working Papers for the Examination of Accounting Records

Upon completing the review and testing of the accounting records, the auditors should prepare a working paper describing the records in use, the tests of controls and other audit procedures followed, the nature and significance of the misstatements discovered, any suggestions for improving the accounting system, and the auditors' conclusion as to the overall quality of the accounting records. This working paper summarizes an important part of the auditors' consideration of internal control and may serve as a reference for determining appropriate modifications in the audit program. At the beginning of the next annual audit, a review of the working paper will enable the auditors to concentrate upon the most significant aspects of the accounting records.

KEY TERMS

adjusting journal entry   A journal entry drafted by the auditors to correct a misstatement discovered in the financial statements and accounting records.

administrative working papers   Working papers specifically designed to help the auditors in planning and administration of the engagement, such as audit programs, internal control questionnaires and flowcharts, time budgets, and engagement memoranda.

analysis   A working paper showing all changes in an asset, liability, equity, revenue, or expense account during the period covered by the audit.

articles of incorporation   That part of the application to the government to incorporate a corporation. It includes detailed information concerning the financial structure and other details of the business.

bylaws   Rules adopted by the shareholders at the inception of a corporation to serve as general guidelines in the conduct of the business.

certificate of incorporation   An official document issued by the government which shows the date on which a corporation comes into existence.

corroborating documents   Documents and memoranda included in the working papers that substantiate representations contained in the client's financial statements. These working papers include audit confirmations, lawyers' letters, copies of contracts, copies of minutes of directors' and shareholders' meetings, and letters of representations from the client's management.

journal voucher   A serially numbered document describing the details of a single journal entry and bearing the signature of the officer who approved the entry.

lead schedule   A working paper with columnar headings similar to those in a working trial balance, set up to combine similar ledger accounts, the total of which appears in the working trial balance as a single amount.

minutes book   A formal record of the issues discussed and actions taken in meetings of shareholders and of the board of directors.

permanent file   A file of working papers containing relatively unchanging data, such as copies of articles and certificate of incorporation and bylaws, copies of minutes of directors', shareholders', and committee meetings, and analyses of such ledger accounts as land and retained earnings.

reclassification entry   A working paper entry drafted by the auditors to assure fair presentation in the client's financial statements, such as an entry to transfer accounts receivable credit balances to the current liabilities section of the client's balance sheet. Since reclassification entries do not correct misstatements in the client company's accounting records, they are not posted to the client's ledger accounts.

tick mark   A symbol used in working papers by the auditor to indicate a specific step in the work performed. Whenever tick marks are used, they must be accompanied by a legend explaining their meaning.

vouch   To verify the accuracy and authenticity of entries in the accounting records by examining the original source documents supporting the entries.

working papers   Papers that document the evidence gathered by auditors to show the work they have done, the methods and procedures they have followed, and the conclusions they have developed in an examination of financial statements or other type of engagement.

working trial balance   A working paper that lists the balances of accounts in the general ledger for the current and the previous year and also provides columns for the auditors' adjustments and reclassifications and for the final amounts that will appear in the financial statements.

GROUP I: REVIEW QUESTIONS

10–1.   What are the major functions of audit working papers?

10–2.   Why are the prior year's audit working papers a useful reference to staff assistants during the current examination?

10–3.   Why are the final figures from the prior year's audit included in a working trial balance or lead schedules? Explain.

10–4.   Should the working trial balance prepared by the auditors include revenue and expense accounts if the balances of these accounts for the audit year have been closed into retained earnings prior to the auditors' arrival? Explain.

10–5.   Explain the meaning of the term *permanent file* as used in connection with audit working papers. What kinds of information are usually included in the permanent file?

10–6.   List the major types of audit working papers and give a brief explanation of each. For example, one type of audit working paper is an account analysis. This working paper shows the changes that occurred in a given account during the period under audit. By analyzing an account, the auditors determine its nature and content.

10–7.   List several guidelines to be observed in the preparation of working papers that will reflect current professional practice.

10–8.   In their review of audit working papers, what do managers and partners look for?

10–9.   Should the auditors prepare adjusting journal entries to correct all misstatements they discover in the accounting records for the year under audit? Explain.

10–10. "Audit working papers are the property of the auditors, who may destroy the papers, sell them, or give them away." Criticize this quotation.

10–11. Describe a situation in which a set of audit working papers might be used by third parties to support a charge of negligence against the auditors.

10–12. "I have finished my testing of footings of the cash journals," said the assistant auditor to the senior auditor. "Shall I state in the working papers the periods for which I verified footings, or should I just list the totals of the receipts and disbursements I have proved to be correct?" Prepare an answer to the assistant's question, stressing the reasoning involved.

10–13. What is the purpose of a "second partner review?" What should be the extent of the second partner's association with the engagement being reviewed?

10–14. During the first audit of a corporate client, the auditors will probably obtain a copy of the bylaws and review them carefully.

Required:

a. What are bylaws of a corporation?

b. What provisions of the bylaws are of interest to the auditors?

10–15. State five significant provisions for which an auditor should particularly look in examining the articles and certificate of incorporation of a company and any amendments thereto.

10–16. In connection with the annual audit of a corporation engaged in manufacturing operations, the auditors have regularly reviewed the minutes of the meetings of shareholders and of the board of directors. Name 10 important items that might be found in the minutes of the meetings held during the period under review that would be of interest and significance to the auditors.

10–17. What should be the scope of an auditors' review of the corporate minutes book during the first audit of a client? During a repeat engagement?

10–18. Should the auditors make a complete review of all correspondence in the client's files? Explain.

10–19. List three types of general journal entries that the auditors would investigate in scanning the general journal for unusual entries, and explain why the journal entries you list are unusual.

10–20. What is the nature of the working papers used by the auditors to summarize the audit work performed on the accounting records?

GROUP II: QUESTIONS REQUIRING ANALYSIS

10–21. An important part of every examination of financial statements is the preparation of audit working papers.

Required:

a. Discuss the relationship of audit working papers to each of the examination standards.

b. You are instructing an inexperienced staff assistant on her first auditing assignment. She is to examine an account. An analysis of the account has been prepared by the client for inclusion in the audit working papers. Prepare a list of the comments, commentaries, and notations that the staff assistant should make or have made on the account analysis to provide an adequate working paper as evidence of her examination. (Do not include a description of auditing procedures applicable to the account.)

(AICPA, adapted)

10–22. The preparation of working papers is an integral part of the auditors' examination of financial statements. On a recurring engagement, the auditors review the working papers from their prior examination while planning the current examination to determine the papers' usefulness for the current engagement.

Required:
a. (1) What are the purposes of functions of audit working papers?

 (2) What records of the auditors may be included in audit working papers?

b. What factors affect the auditors' judgment of the type and content of the working papers for a particular engagement?

c. To comply with generally accepted auditing standards, the auditors include certain evidence in their working papers, for example, "evidence that the engagement was adequately planned and properly executed, and work of assistants was properly supervised and reviewed." What other evidence should the auditors include in audit working papers to comply with generally accepted auditing standards?

(AICPA, adapted)

10–23. The partnership of Smith, Frank & Clark, a CA firm, has been the auditor of Greenleaf Inc. for many years. During the annual examination of the financial statements for the year ended December 31, 199X, a dispute developed over whether certain disclosures should be made in the financial statements. The dispute resulted in Smith, Frank & Clark's being dismissed and Greenleaf's engaging another CA firm. Greenleaf demanded that Smith, Frank & Clark turn over all working papers applicable to the Greenleaf audits or face a lawsuit. Smith, Frank & Clark refused. Greenleaf has instituted a suit against Smith, Frank & Clark to obtain the working papers.

Required:
a. Will Greenleaf succeed in its suit? Explain.

b. Discuss the rational underlying the rule of law applicable to the ownership of audit working papers.

(AICPA, adapted)

10–24. "Working papers should contain facts and nothing but facts," said student A. "Not at all," replied student B. "The audit working papers may also include expressions of opinion. Facts are not always available to settle all issues." "In my opinion," said student C, "a mixture of facts and opinions in the audit working papers would be most confusing if the papers were produced as a means of supporting the auditors' position when their report has been challenged." Evaluate the issues underlying these arguments.

10–25.   At 12 o'clock, when the plant whistle sounded, George Green, an assistant auditor, had his desk completely covered with various types of working papers. Green stopped work immediately, but not wanting to leave the desk with such a disorderly appearance, he took a few minutes to sort the papers into proper order, place them in a neat pile, and weight them down with a heavy ash tray. He then departed for lunch. The auditor-in-charge, who had been observing what was going on, was critical of the assistant's actions. What do you think was the basis for criticism by the auditor-in-charge?

10–26.   You have been assigned by your firm to complete the examination of the financial statements of Hamilton Manufacturing Corporation because the senior auditor and his inexperienced assistant, who began the engagement, were hospitalized as the result of an accident. The engagement is about one-half completed. Your audit report must be delivered in three weeks, as agreed when your firm accepted the engagement. You estimate that by utilizing the client's staff to the greatest possible extent consonant with independence, you can complete the engagement in five weeks. Your firm cannot assign an assistant to you.

The working papers show the status of work on the examination as follows:

a.   ***Completed***—Cash, property and equipment, depreciation, mortgage note payable, and shareholders' equity.

b.   ***Completed except as noted later***—Inventories, accounts payable, tests of controls over purchase transactions and payrolls.

c.   ***Nothing done***—Trade accounts receivable, inventory price testing, accrued expenses payable, unrecorded liability test, tests of controls over sales transactions, tests of controls over payroll deductions and observation of payroll cheque distribution, analysis of other expenses, analytical procedures, vouching of December purchase transactions, audit report, assessment of control risk, letter on internal control weaknesses, minutes, preparation of tax returns, subsequent events, and supervision and review.

Your review discloses that the assistant's working papers are incomplete and were not reviewed by the senior accountant. For example, the inventory working papers present incomplete notations, incomplete explanations, and no cross-referencing.

Required:

a.   What examination standards have been violated by the senior accountant who preceded you on this assignment? Explain why you think the standards you list have been violated.

  b. In planning your work to complete this engagement, you should scan working papers and schedule certain work as soon as possible and also identify work that may be postponed until after the audit report is rendered to the client.

   (1) List the areas on which you should plan to work first, say, in your first week of work, and explain why each item deserves early attention.

   (2) State which work you believe could be postponed until after the audit report is rendered to the client, and give reasons why the work may be postponed.

(AICPA, adapted)

10–27. Select the best answer for each of the following and give reasons for your choice:

  a. Which of the following is *not* a factor that affects the external auditors' judgment as to the quality, type, and content of working papers?

   (1) The timing and the number of personnel to be assigned to the engagement.

   (2) The nature of the financial statements, schedules, or other information upon which the auditor is reporting.

   (3) The need for supervision of the engagement.

   (4) The nature of the auditors' report.

  b. Audit working papers should be:

   (1) Kept on the client's premises to allow the client access to them for reference purposes.

   (2) The primary support for the financial statements being examined.

   (3) Considered as a part of the client's accounting records that is retained by the auditors.

   (4) Designed to meet the circumstances and the auditors' needs on each engagement.

  c. A primary purpose of the audit working papers is to:

   (1) Aid the auditors in adequately planning their work.

   (2) Provide a point of reference for future audit engagements.

   (3) Support the underlying concepts included in the preparation of the basic financial statements.

   (4) Support the auditors' opinion.

  d. An auditor should examine the minutes of board of directors' meetings:

   (1) Through the date of the financial statements.

   (2) Through the date of the audit report.

   (3) On a test basis.

   (4) Only at the beginning of the audit.

  e. A difference of opinion concerning accounting and auditing matters relative to a particular phase of the audit arises between an assistant auditor and the auditor responsible for the engagement. After appropriate consultation, the assistant auditor asks to be disassociated from the resolution of the matter. The working papers would probably:

(1) Remain silent on the matter since it is an internal matter of the auditing firm.

(2) Note that the assistant auditor is completely dissociated from responsibility for the auditor's opinion.

(3) Document the additional work required, since all disagreements of this type will require expanded substantive testing.

(4) Document the assistant auditor's position, and how the difference of opinion was resolved.

f. Which of the following statements most adequately summarizes the auditor's responsibility for reviewing the client's correspondence files?

(1) The auditor should review all correspondence for items relevant to the audit.

(2) The auditor should not review any correspondence; to do so would waste time more productively spent on gathering other evidence.

(3) The auditor should apply statistical selection techniques to draw a random sample of correspondence for review.

(4) The auditor should review correspondence with banks, other lending institutions, lawyers, and governmental agencies.

(AICPA, adapted)

10–28. In a recent court case, the presiding judge criticized the work of a senior in charge of an audit in approximately the following language: "As to minutes, the senior read only what the secretary (of the company) gave him, which consisted only of the board of directors' minutes. He did not read such minutes as there were of the executive committee of the board. He did not know that there was an executive committee; hence, he did not discover that the treasurer had notes of executive committee minutes which had not been written up."

Required:

How can the external auditors be certain the client has provided them with minutes of all meetings of the board and committees thereof? Explain.

10–29. Bonnie Cogan, CA, is a senior auditor assigned to the first examination of the financial statements of Pioneer Mfg. Company Inc. for the current year ended December 31. In scanning the client's general journal, Cogan noted the following entry dated June 30 of the current year:

Cost of Sales.................................. 186,453

Raw Materials..............................	84,916
Work in Process...........................	24,518
Finished Goods	77,019

To adjust perpetual inventories to amounts of physical inventory taken this date.

The client-prepared income statement shows net sales and net income of approximately $5,500,000 and $600,000, respectively.

Required:
Do you think Cogan should investigate the above entry? Explain fully.

10–30. Fred Murray, an audit staff assistant, was instructed to use a discovery sampling plan to search for entries in the client's ledger that were not supported by entries from the journals. Murray decided to sample from the journal entries recorded in the various journals during the year to the ledger. He wishes to obtain adequate assurance that 2 percent or less of the ledger's entries are unsupported by a journal entry, with a 5 percent risk of assessing control risk too low. A statistical table indicates that a sample size of 149 is necessary.

In conducting his test, Murray traced 149 randomly selected journal entries into the ledger and found no deviations. Based upon this test, may Murray conclude with a 5 percent risk of assessing control risk too low that at least 98 percent of the entries in the ledger are supported by journal entries? Explain fully.

GROUP III: PROBLEMS

10–31. Criticize the working paper on the following page that you are reviewing as senior auditor on the December 31, 1993 audit of Pratt Limited.

10–32. One of the practical problems confronting the auditors is that of determining whether adjusting journal entries or other corrective actions are warranted by errors, omissions, and inconsistencies. The following items were noted by the auditors during their December 31 year-end examination of a manufacturing partnership having net sales of approximately $1.6 million, net income of approximately $40,000, total assets of nearly $2 million, and total partners' capital of $300,000.

   a. Proceeds of $250 from the sale of fully depreciated office equipment were credited to Miscellaneous Revenue rather

Pratt Limited

Cash   E-2

Per bank   44,874.50 √

Deposit in transit   837.50 √

Bank charges   2.80
                    _____
                    45,714.80

Outstanding cheques
                    46.40
                    10.00
                    30.00
                    1,013.60 √
                    1,200.00 √
                    10.00
                    25.00 √
                    15.00 √
                    50.00 √
                    1,002.00 √   3,402.00
                    _____
Per ledger   42,312.80 √

√ - Verified

R. G. H.
1-15-94

than to Gain and Loss on Sale of Equipment, a ledger account that had not been used for several years.

b. The Trade Accounts Receivable control account showed a balance of $79,600. The individual accounts comprising this balance included three with credit balances of $320, $19, and $250, respectively.

c. Several debits and credits to general ledger accounts had been made directly without use of journal entries. The amounts involved did not exceed $500.

d. Credit memoranda were not serially numbered or signed, but a file of duplicates was maintained.

e. General journal entries did not include explanations for any but unusual transactions.

f. Posting references were occasionally omitted from entries in general ledger accounts.

g. An expenditure of $200 for automobile repairs was recorded as a December expense, although shown by the invoice to be a November charge.

h. Expenditures for advertising amounting to $8,000 were charged to the Advertising Expense account: other advertising expenses amounting to $3,000 had been charged to Miscellaneous Expense.

i. On September 12, the client borrowed $288,000 from First Bank by signing a 120-day note payable in the face amount of $300,000. The note matures on January 10. The client's accountant had charged the entire $12,000 interest included in the face amount of the note to the interest expense of the current year. He stated that he did not consider deferring part of the interest to the following year to be warranted by the dollar amounts involved.

Required:
You are to state clearly the position the auditors should take with respect to each of the above items during the course of an annual audit. If adjusting journal entries are necessary, include them in your solution.

10–33. Kenneth J. Bryan, secretary of Jensen Corporation, has given you the minutes of the meetings of the board of directors. Summarize, in good form for the audit working papers, those contents of the following minutes that you consider to be of significance in the conduct of an annual audit.

Meeting of February 15, 19X2

The meeting was called to order at 2:15 P.M. by H. R. Jensen, chairman of the board. The following directors were present:

John J. Savage	Ruth Andrews
Helen R. King	Dale H. Lindberg
Lee McCormick	Ralph Barker
H. R. Coleman	H. R. Jensen
George Anderson	Kenneth J. Bryan
Harold Bruce Smith	

Absent was Director J. B. Adams, who was in Quebec City on company business in connection with the opening of a sales office.

The minutes of the preceding meeting, December 15, 19X1, were read by the secretary and duly approved as read.

President John J. Savage outlined the current status of negotiations leading toward the acquisition of a new factory site in Toronto, and recommended to the board the purchase of said property at a price not to exceed $600,000.

Ms. King offered the following resolution, which was seconded by Mr. Smith, and unanimously carried:

Resolved: That Mr. Savage hereby is authorized to acquire on behalf of the company the factory site located at Exmont and Donaldson Avenues, Toronto, at a price not in excess of $600,000, to be paid for in cash from the general funds of the corporation.

Upon a motion by Mr. Savage, seconded by Ms. King and carried unanimously, the secretary was instructed to arrange for the purchase from the estate of J. B. Williams, former director, 100 shares of the company's own stock at a price not in excess of $110 per share.

Mr. Savage, after discussing the progress of the company in recent months and its curent financial condition, submitted the following resolution, which was seconded by Mr. Coleman and unanimously passed:

Resolved: That the following cash dividends are hereby declared, payable April 10, 19X2, to shareholders of record on March 31, 19X2.

(a) The regular quarterly divident of $1 per share of capital stock.
(b) A special dividend of 50 cents per share of capital stock.

There being no further business brought before the meeting, the meeting was adjourned at 4 P.M.

Kenneth J. Bryan
Secretary

Meeting of March 15, 19X2

The meeting was called to order at 2:15 P.M. by H. R. Jensen, chairman of the board. The following directors were present:

John J. Savage	Ruth Andrews
Helen R. King	Dale H. Lindberg
Lee McCormick	J. B. Adams
H. R. Coleman	H. R. Jensen
George Anderson	Kenneth J. Bryan
Harold Bruce Smith	

Absent was Director Ralph Barker.

The minutes of the preceding meeting, February 15, 19X2, were read by the secretary and duly approved as read.

Chairman H. R. Jensen stated that nominations for the coming year were in order for the positions of president, vice president in charge of sales, vice president in charge of manufacturing, treasurer, controller, and secretary.

The following nominations were made by Ms. King, and there being no further nominations the nominations were declared closed:

President	John J. Savage
Vice president—sales	Otis Widener
Vice president—manufacturing	Henry Pendleton
Treasurer	Ruth Andrews
Controller	Roger Dunn
Secretary	Kenneth J. Bryan

The above nominees were duly elected.

Mr. McCormick then offered the following resolution, which was seconded by Mr. Coleman and unanimously carried:

Resolved: That the salaries of all officers be continued for the next year at the same rates currently in effect. These rates are as follows:

John J. Savage—president	$160,000
Otis Widener—vice president—sales	80,000
Henry Pendleton—vice president—manufacturing	80,000
Ruth Andrews—treasurer	80,000
Roger Dunn—controller	80,000
Kenneth J. Bryan—secretary	60,000

Mr. Bryan offered the following resolution, which was seconded by Mrs. Andrews and unanimously carried:

Resolved: That the company establish a bank account at the United National Bank, Toronto, to be subject to cheque by either John J. Savage or Ruth Andrews.

There being no further business to come before the meeting, the meeting was adjourned at 4 P.M.

Kenneth J. Bryan
Secretary

10–34. A normal procedure in the audit of a corporate client consists of a careful reading of the minutes of meetings of the board of directors. One of the auditors' objectives in reading the minutes is to determine whether the transactions recorded in the accounting records are in agreement with actions approved by the board of directors.

Required:

a. What is the reasoning underlying this objective of reconciling transactions in the corporate accounting records with actions approved by the board of directors? Describe fully how the auditors achieve the stated objective after they have read the minutes of directors' meetings.

b. Discuss the effect each of the following situations would have on specific audit steps in the auditors' examination and on the auditors' opinion:

   (1) The minutes book does not show approval for the sale of an important manufacturing division that was consummated during the year.

   (2) Some details of a contract negotiated during the year with the labour union are different from the outline of the contract included in the minutes of the board of directors.

   (3) The minutes of a meeting of directors held after the balance sheet date have not yet been written, but the corporation's secretary shows the auditors' notes from which the minutes are to be prepared when the secretary has time.

c. What corporate actions should be approved by shareholders and recorded in the minutes of the shareholders' meetings?

(AICPA, adapted)

GROUP IV: ANALYTICAL AND DISCUSSION CASE

10–35. During the examination of Bryan Instrument Manufacturing Corporation, Dwight Bond, an assistant auditor, was assigned by the auditor-in-charge to the verification of the trade accounts receivable. The receivables totaled more than $2 million and included accounts with governmental agencies, national mail-order houses, manufacturers, wholesalers, and retailers. Bond had recently read a study of credit losses in this industry covering the past 10 years, and as a preliminary step, he computed an allowance for uncollectible accounts by applying to the total accounts receivable a percentage mentioned in the 10-year study as the average rate of uncollectible account losses for the sales of the entire industry. Application of this percentage to the Bryan Corporation's receivables indicated an uncollectible account loss of $90,000; the allowance provided by the company's management was $25,000. The working paper showing the computation of the $90,000 estimate of uncollectible account losses was placed in the file of working papers by Bond:

After making this preliminary calculation, Bond undertook a careful study of the receivables; as a first step, he obtained from the client a classification of the accounts by type of customer and by age. He made a careful analysis of individual accounts that appeared in any way doubtful, discussed all past-due accounts with the credit manager, and reviewed the company's prior history of uncollectible account losses. He then reviewed his findings with the auditor-in-charge, who, after further investigation and discussion with the client management, took the position that the allowance for uncollectible accounts must be increased from $25,000 to $40,000 or an unqualified opinion could not be given. The client management was not convinced of the need for the increase but finally agreed to make the change.

While Bond was working on the accounts receivable, another staff assistant, Carla Roberts, was engaged in verification of inventory. Roberts overheard a stock clerk remark that the finished goods inventory was full of obsolete products that could never be sold. As a result of this chance remark, Roberts made a test of a number of items in the inventory, comparing the quantities on hand with the amount of recent sales. These tests indicated that the quantities in inventory were reasonable and that the items were moving out to customers. Because of the technical nature of the instruments manufactured by the company, Roberts was not able to determine by observation whether the articles in stock were obsolete or unsalable for any other reason. She made a point of questioning officials of the company on the possibility of obsolescence in the inventory and was assured that no serious problem of obsolescence existed.

In preparing the working papers covering her investigation, Roberts included a separate memorandum quoting the remark she had overheard concerning the obsolescence of the inventory and added a suggestion of her own that this question of obsolescence be given special attention in succeeding examinations. She prepared a detailed description of certain portions of the inventory and suggested that in the succeeding examination the auditors determine whether these specific units were still on hand. During the review of the working papers, the auditor-in-charge questioned Roberts at length about the tests for obsolescence. He interviewed the employee who had made the remark about the impossibility of disposing of the finished goods inventory; the employee denied having made any such statement. The auditor-in-charge then discussed the issue with client officials and came to the conclusion that the inventory was properly valued and readily salable. In completing his review of the working papers, the auditor-in-charge added the following comment to the memorandum prepared by Roberts: "Questions of obsolescence investigated and passed, but we should give consideration to this issue in succeeding examinations."

After all the adjustments recommended by the auditors had been made, the financial statements of the company indicated a considerably weaker financial position than had existed in prior years. The president complained that the adjustments insisted on by the auditors made the company's position look so bad that it would be difficult to obtain private long-term financing for which he had been negotiating. An unqualified audit report was issued.

Two months later, Bryan Instrument Manufacturing became insolvent. The principal causes of the failure, according to the president, were unexpectedly large credit losses and inability to dispose of inventories that had become obsolete because of newly designed products being offered by competitors in recent years. The president acknowledged that the company had made sales to customers of questionable credit standing because of the need to dispose of inventories threatened by obsolescence. Creditors of the company attempted to recover their losses from the auditors, charging the public accounting firm with negligence and lack of independence in reviewing the valuation of the accounts receivable and inventory. Attention was directed to the working papers prepared by Bond and Roberts; it was charged that these papers showed the auditors had knowledge of the over-valuation of receivables and inventory but under pressure from the client had failed to disclose the facts.

Required:
a. Should the working paper showing the percentage calculation of a $90,000 allowance for uncollectible accounts have been prepared and retained? Explain.
b. Should the working paper quoting the stock clerk's remark about obsolescence have been prepared and retained? Explain.
c. Did the auditor-in-charge handle his duties satisfactorily?
d. Do you think the working papers tended to support or injure the auditors' defense against the charges of the creditors? Explain.
e. Do you consider the creditors' charges to be well founded? Give reasons for your answer.

Chapter 11

Cash and Marketable Securities

After studying this chapter, you should be able to:

- Describe the nature of cash and marketable securities.
- Explain the nature of the cash receipts and disbursements cycles.
- Explain the fundamental internal controls over cash receipts, cash disbursements, and marketable securities.
- Describe the auditors' objectives for the audit of cash and marketable securities.
- Describe the nature of appropriate audit procedures to accomplish the objectives for the audit of cash and marketable securities.

The manner in which auditors approach cash and marketable securities is discussed in this chapter. Because both types of accounts are usually extremely liquid and because companies often transfer funds between them, their consideration is combined in the chapter.

CASH

Sources and Nature of Cash

Cash normally includes general, payroll, and petty cash accounts and, less frequently, savings accounts. General accounts are chequing accounts similar in nature to those maintained by individuals. Cash sales, collections of receivables, and investment of additional capital typically increase the account; business expenditures decrease it. Under the terms of a bank loan agreement, the cash in a company's general account sometimes must be maintained at a specified minimum balance referred to as a ***compensating balance.***

Cash equivalents are often combined with cash items to create the current asset classification called *cash and cash equivalents.* ***Cash equivalents*** include temporary investments such as marketable securities, certificates of deposit, savings certificates, and other similar types of deposits. Any item that cannot be converted to cash on short notice should be classified as a receivable or prepaid expense, rather than as a cash equivalent.

Payroll and petty cash accounts are "imprest" at a low balance. When payroll is paid, a cheque from the general account is drawn to deposit funds into the payroll account. Petty cash, used for very small expenditures, is replenished as necessary.

Normal internal control policies and procedures (e.g., reconciliation of bank accounts) detect most errors that occur in these accounts. On the other hand, the liquid nature of cash increases the risk of undetected irregularities or fraud.

The Auditors' Objectives in Examination of Cash

The auditors have five ***objectives*** in the examination of cash:

1. Consider ***internal control*** over cash transactions.
2. Determine the ***existence*** of recorded cash and the client's ***ownership*** of this asset.
3. Establish the ***completeness*** of recorded cash.
4. Establish the ***clerical accuracy*** of cash schedules.
5. Determine that the ***statement presentation*** of cash, including restricted funds (such as compensating balances and bond sinking funds), is appropriate.

In connection with the audit of cash, the auditors will also verify the amounts of any interest revenue from cash deposits. As is the case with other assets, auditors are especially concerned with the likelihood of overstatements of the account; therefore, objective 2, the existence of recorded cash, is of utmost importance.

Illustrative Case

A recent research study reports the results of a study of lawsuits against accountants. A total of 129 cases were examined and none of the suits concerned misstatements involving undervalued ***assets.***

In addition to concerns about the overstatement of cash, auditors are aware that cash may have been improperly abstracted during the period, even though the year-end cash may be properly stated. To distinguish between the situations assume that the client's balance sheet shows "Cash . . . $250,000." For most clients, the primary risks are that errors, fraud, or irregularities either (1) create a situation in which $250,000 overstates actual cash, or (2) have improperly reduced the balance to $250,000.

Concerning the first risk (overstated cash), a shortage may have been concealed merely by the insertion of a fictitious cheque in the cash on hand at year-end or by the omission of an outstanding cheque from the year-end bank reconciliation. Note that the omission of an outstanding cheque may be indicative of either an error or a fraud. For example, poor internal control may result in a situation in which human error resulted in the cheque's not being recorded in disbursements. On the other hand, although recorded in cash disbursements, the cheque may be omitted from the outstanding cheque list to allow the individual who has embezzled that amount of cash to hide the fraud.

Concerning the second risk—when the year-end cash is correct, but should be higher—the auditors' problem is not misstated cash, but the fraud itself and its effect on other accounts. Consequently, the auditors have in mind such basic questions as, (1) do the client's records reflect all cash transactions that took place during the year? and (2) were all cash payments properly authorized and for a legitimate business purpose? Examples of fraud or irregularities that may be disclosed in searching for answers to these questions are:

1. Interception of cash receipts before any record is made.
2. Payment for materials not received.
3. Duplicate payments.
4. Overpayments to employees or payments to fictitious employees.
5. Payments for personal expenditures of officers or related parties.

Exceptions exist to the general rule that auditors are primarily concerned with overstatements of cash (and other assets). For example, the management of a privately held company may be motivated to understate assets (including cash) to minimize income taxes. Also, a client may maintain bank accounts not recorded on the books for purposes such as making illegal bribes. Thus, the auditors must consider whether all amounts of cash accounts are recorded (the completeness objective).

We have not included a *valuation* objective for cash. Valuation is less a concern for cash than for other assets because no allowance need be considered to arrive at a realizable value. However, when foreign subsidiaries are involved, the auditors must determine that translated currency is properly valued.

How Much Audit Time for Cash?

The factor of materiality applies to audit work on cash as well as to other sections of the examination. The counting of a small petty cash fund, which is inconsequential in relation to the company's overall financial position, accomplishes little in achieving the auditors' objective of expressing an independent opinion on the financial statements. Nevertheless, auditors do devote a larger proportion of the total audit hours to cash than might be suggested by the relatively small amount of cash shown on the balance sheet. Although the year-end balance of cash may appear relatively small, the amount flowing into and out of the cash account during the year is often greater than for any other account. Consequently, work on cash is important in virtually every audit.

Several reasons exist to explain the auditors' traditional emphasis on cash transactions. Liabilities, revenue, expenses, and most other assets flow through the cash account; that is, these items either arise from or result in cash transactions. Thus, the examination of cash transactions assists the auditors in the substantiation of many other items in the financial statements.

Another reason contributing to extensive auditing of cash is that cash is the most liquid of assets and offers the greatest temptation for theft, embezzlement, and misappropriation. Inherent risk is high for liquid assets, and auditors tend to respond to high-risk situations with more intensive investigation. However, the detection of fraud is relevant to the overall fairness of the client's financial statements only if such fraud is material in amount.

On occasion, auditors may encounter evidence of small-scale employee fraud. After determining that such fraud could *not* have a material effect upon the financial statements, the auditors should review the situation with the management and the audit committee of the board of directors before investigating the matter further. This discussion will alert the client to the situation, protect the auditors from charges of incompetence, and avoid wasting audit time on matters that are not material with respect to the financial statements and that may better be pursued by client personnel.

Internal Control over Cash Transactions

Most of the functions relating to cash handling are the responsibility of the finance department, under the direction of the treasurer. These functions include handling and depositing cash receipts; signing cheques; investing idle cash; and maintaining custody of cash, marketable securities, and other negotiable assets. In addition, the finance department must forecast cash requirements and make both short-term and long-term financing arrangements.

Ideally, the functions of the finance department and the accounting department should be integrated in a manner that provides assurance that:

1. All cash that should have been received *was* in fact received, recorded accurately, and deposited promptly.
2. Cash disbursements have been made only for authorized purposes and have been properly recorded.
3. Cash balances are maintained at adequate, not excessive, levels by forecasting expected cash receipts and payments related to normal operations. The need for obtaining loans or for investing excess cash is thus made known on a timely basis.

A detailed study of the operating routines of the individual business is necessary in developing the most efficient control procedures, but there are some general guidelines to good cash-handling practices in all types of business. These universal rules for achieving internal control over cash may be summarized as follows:

1. Do not permit any one employee to handle a transaction from beginning to end.
2. Separate cash handling from record-keeping.
3. Centralize receiving of cash as much as possible.
4. Record cash receipts immediately.
5. Encourage customers to obtain receipts and observe cash register totals.
6. Deposit each day's cash receipts intact.
7. Make all disbursements by cheque with the exception of small expenditures from petty cash.
8. Have monthly bank reconciliations prepared by employees not responsible for the issuance of cheques or custody of cash. The completed reconciliation should be reviewed promptly by an appropriate official.
9. Forecast expected cash receipts and disbursements and investigate variances from forecasted amounts.

Several good reasons exist for the rule that each day's cash receipts should be deposited intact. Daily deposits mean that less cash will be on hand to invite "borrowing"; moreover, the deposit of each day's cash receipts as a unit tends to prevent the substituting of later cash receipts to cover a shortage. Also, any delay in depositing customers' cheques increases the risk that the cheques will be uncollectible. Furthermore, undeposited receipts represent idle cash, which is not a revenue-producing asset.

Internal Control over Cash Receipts

Cash Sales. Control over cash sales is strongest when two or more employees (usually a salesclerk and a cashier) participate in each transaction with a customer. Restaurants and cafeterias often use a centrally located cashier who receives cash from the customer along with a sales ticket prepared by another employee. Theatres generally have a cashier selling prenumbered tickets, which are collected by a door attendant when the customer is admitted. If tickets or sales invoices are serially numbered and all numbers accounted for, this separation of responsibility for the transaction is an effective means of preventing fraud. In many retail establishments, the nature of the business is such that one employee must make over-the-counter sales, deliver the merchandise, receive cash, and record the transaction. In this situation, dishonesty may be discouraged by proper use of cash registers, electronic point-of-sale systems, or form-writing machines. The protective features of cash registers include (1) visual display of the amount of the sale in full view of the customer; (2) a printed receipt, which the customer is urged to take with the merchandise; and (3) accumulation of a locked-in total of the day's sales.

Electronic Point-of-Sale (POS) Systems. Many retail stores use various types of electronic cash registers, including on-line computer terminals. With some of these registers, an electronic scanner is used to read the sales price and other data from specially prepared product tags. The salesperson need only pass the tag over the scanner for the register to record the sale at the product's sale price. Thus, the risk of a salesperson recording sales at erroneous prices is substantially reduced. Besides providing strong control over cash sales, electronic registers often may be programmed to perform numerous other control functions. For example, on-line registers may verify the credit status of charge account customers, update accounts receivable and perpetual inventory records, and provide special printouts accumulating sales data by product line, salesperson, department, and type of sale.

Control Features of Form-writing Machines. Some businesses making sales over the counter find that internal control is strengthened by use of a machine containing triplicate sales invoices. As each sales invoice is written, two copies are ejected by the machine and a third copy is retained in a locked compartment. The retention of the third copy, which is not available to the salesclerk, tends to prevent a dishonest employee from changing the store's copy of the sales invoice to an amount less than that shown on the customer's copy.

Collections from Credit Customers. In many manufacturing and wholesale companies, cash receipts consist principally of cheques received

FIGURE 11–1 Flowchart of Cash Receipts Cycle

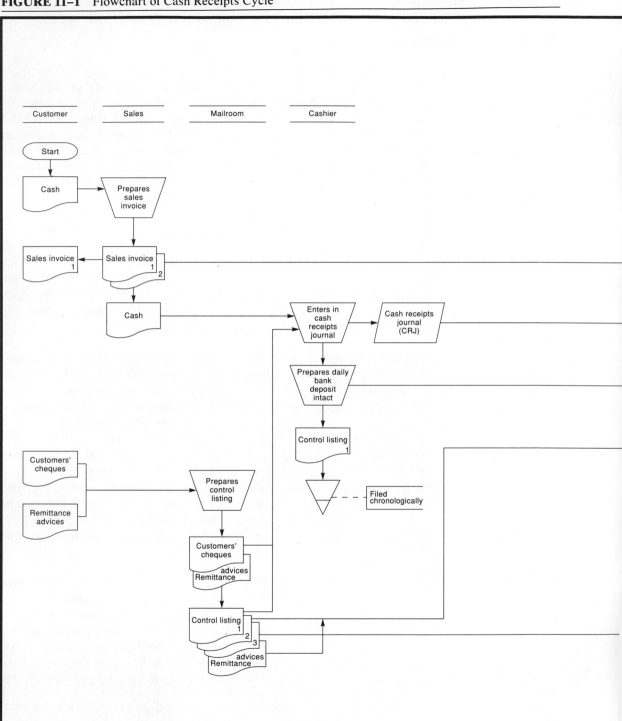

FIGURE 11–1 (*concluded*)

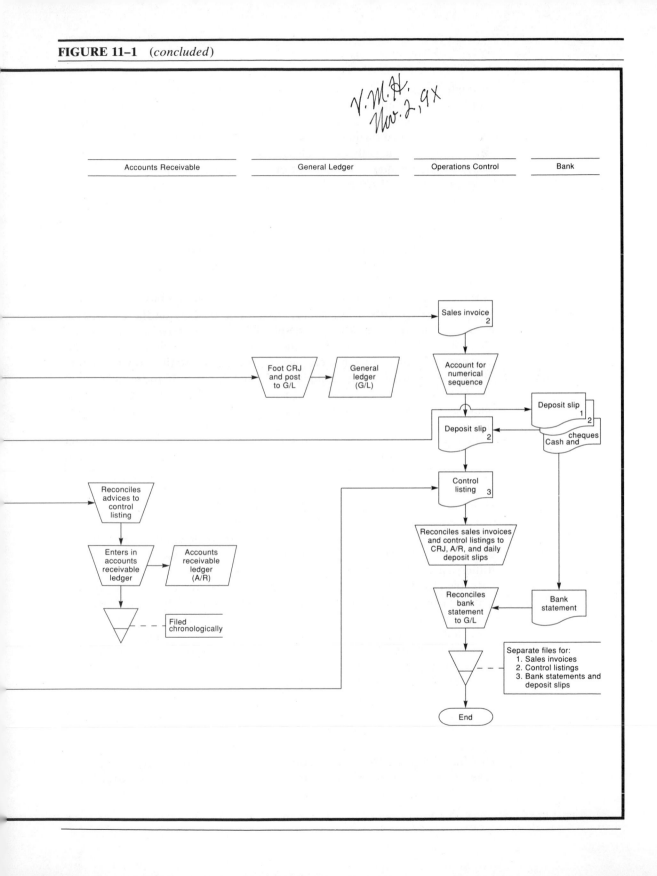

through the mail. This situation poses little threat of defalcation unless one employee is permitted to receive and deposit these cheques and also to record the credits to the customers' accounts. Typical internal control over cash received through the mail is described below.

Incoming mail usually is opened in the mail room, where an employee endorses the cheques "for deposit only" to the company's account, and prepares a *control listing* of the incoming cash receipts. This listing shows the amount received from each customer and identifies the customer by name or account number. A copy of the control listing is forwarded to the controller. Another copy of the control listing and the cash receipts are forwarded to the cashier. The remittance advices and a copy of the control listing are forwarded to the employee responsible for the customers' accounts.

Which controls tend to prevent the mail room employee from abstracting the receipts from several customers, destroying the remittance advices, and omitting these receipts from the control listing? First, incoming cash receipts consist primarily of cheques made payable to the company. Second, if customers' accounts are not credited for payments made, the customers will complain to the company. If these customers can produce paid cheques supporting their claims of payment, and these cheques do not appear on the mail room control listings, responsibility for the abstraction is quickly focused upon the mail room employee.

The cashier uses the control listing to record the cash received in the cash receipts journal. Then the cashier deposits the day's receipts intact in the bank. Control is exercised over the cashier by periodic reconciliation of the controller's copies of the mail room control listings with the cash receipts journal and the details of daily bank deposits.

The employee responsible for the customers' accounts ledger reconciles the remittance advices to his copy of the control listing and, when satisfied that all remittance advices are accounted for, posts credits to the customers' accounts. Strong internal control requires that the accounts receivable clerk have no access to the cash receipts, and that the customers' accounts be periodically reconciled with the general ledger. When the nature of operations permits, different employees should be assigned responsibility for (1) preparation of sales invoices, (2) maintenance of customers' accounts, (3) reconciliation of customers' ledgers with controlling accounts, (4) initial listing of cash receipts, (5) custody and depositing of cash receipts, and (6) collection activity and past-due accounts.

The division of responsibilities, sequence of procedures, and internal controls over cash sales and collections from customers are illustrated in the systems flowchart in Figure 11–1.

Lockbox Control over Cash Receipts.   Businesses receiving a large volume of cash through the mail often use a lockbox system to strengthen internal control and hasten the depositing of cash receipts. The lockbox is actually a post office box controlled by the company's bank. The bank picks up mail at the post office box several times a day, credits the company's account for cash received, and sends the remittance advices to the company. Internal control is strengthened by the fact that the bank has no access to the company's accounting records.

Internal Control over Cash Disbursements

All disbursements should be made by cheque, except for payment of minor items from petty cash funds. A principal advantage is the obtaining of a receipt from the payee in the form of an endorsement on the cheque. Other advantages include (1) the centralization of disbursement authority in the hands of a few designated officials—the only persons authorized to sign cheques; (2) a permanent record of disbursements; and (3) a reduction in the amount of cash kept on hand.

To secure in full the internal control benefits implicit in the use of cheques, it is essential that all cheques be prenumbered and all numbers in the series be accounted for. Unissued prenumbered cheques should be adequately safeguarded against theft or misuse. Voided cheques should be defaced to eliminate any possibility of further use and filed in the regular sequence of paid cheques. Dollar amounts should be printed on all cheques by the computer or a cheque-protecting machine. This practice prevents anyone from altering a cheque by raising its amount.

Officials authorized to sign cheques should review the documents supporting the payment and perforate (deface) these documents at the time of signing the cheque to prevent them from being submitted a second time. The official signing cheques should maintain control of the cheques until they are placed in the mail. Typically, the cheque comes to the official complete except for the signature. It is imperative that the signed cheques not be returned to the employee who prepared them for signature.

Most companies issuing a large volume of cheques use cheque-signing machines. These machines print the authorized signature, usually that of the treasurer, on each cheque by means of a facsimile signature plate. An item count of cheques signed is provided by the machine, and a key is required to retrieve the signed cheques. The facsimile signature plate should be removed from the machine and safeguarded when the machine is not in use.

Reconciliation of monthly bank statements is essential to adequate internal control over cash receipts and disbursements. Bank statements should be reconciled by an employee having no part in authorizing or accounting for cash transactions, or in handling cash. Statements from the bank should come unopened to this employee. Each month the completed bank reconciliation should be reviewed by a responsible company official and approved in writing.

Illustrative Case

One large construction company ignored basic controls over cash disbursements. Unissued cheques were stored in an unlocked supply closet, along with Styrofoam coffee cups. The company cheque-signing machine deposited signed cheques into a box that was equipped with a lock. Despite warnings from their external auditors, company officials found it "too inconvenient" to keep the box locked or to pay attention to the cheque-counter built into the machine. The company maintained very large bank balances and did not bother to reconcile bank statements promptly.

A three-week-old bank statement and a group of paid cheques were given to an employee with instructions to prepare a bank reconciliation. The employee noticed that the group of paid cheques accompanying the bank statement was not complete. No paid cheques could be found to support over $700,000 in charges on the bank statement. Further investigation revealed that more than $1 million in unauthorized and unrecorded cheques had been paid from various company bank accounts. The cheques had been issued out of sequence and had been signed by the company cheque-signing machine. The company was unable to determine who was responsible for the theft, and the money was never recovered.

Control Features of a Voucher System.   A voucher system is one method of achieving strong internal control over cash disbursements by providing assurance that all disbursements are properly authorized and reviewed before a cheque is issued. In a typical voucher system, the accounting department is responsible for assembling the appropriate documentation to support every cash disbursement. For example, before authorizing payment for merchandise purchased, the accounting department assembles copies of the purchase order, receiving report, and vendor's invoice, and determines that these documents are in agreement. After determining that the transaction is properly supported, an accounting employee prepares a voucher, which is filed in a tickler file according to the date upon which payment will be made.

A voucher, in this usage, is an authorization sheet that provides space for the initials of the employees performing various authorization functions. Authorization functions include such procedures as extending and footing the vendor's invoice; determining the agreement of the invoice, purchase order, and receiving report; and recording the transaction in the accounts. Transactions are recorded in a *voucher register* (which normally replaces a purchases journal) by an entry debiting the appropriate asset, liability, or expense accounts, and crediting Vouchers Payable.

On the payment date, the voucher and supporting documents are removed from the tickler file. A cheque is prepared *but not signed*. The voucher, supporting papers, and the cheque (complete except for signature) are forwarded to the finance department. The treasurer reviews the voucher before signing the cheque; the cheque is then mailed directly to the payee, and the voucher and all supporting documents are perforated to prevent reuse. The canceled vouchers are returned to the accounting department, where an entry is made to record the cash disbursement (a debit to Vouchers Payable and a credit to Cash). Paid vouchers usually are filed by voucher number in a paid voucher file.

Strong internal control is inherent in this system because every disbursement is authorized and reviewed before a cheque is issued. Also, neither the accounting department nor the finance department is in a position to disburse cash without a review of the transaction by the other department. The operation of a voucher system is illustrated in the flowchart in Figure 11–2.

Internal Control Aspects of Petty Cash Funds

Internal control over payments from an imprest petty cash fund is achieved at the time the fund is replenished to its fixed balance, rather than at the time of handing out small amounts of cash. When the custodian of a petty cash fund requests replenishment of the fund, the documents supporting each disbursement should be reviewed for completeness and authenticity and perforated to prevent reuse.

Audit tests of petty cash emphasize transactions rather than the year-end balance. The auditors may test one or more replenishment transactions by examining petty cash vouchers and verifying their numerical sequence.

Petty cash funds are sometimes kept in the form of separate bank accounts. The bank should be instructed in writing not to accept for deposit in such an account any cheques payable to the company. The deposits will be limited to cheques to replenish the fund and drawn payable to the bank or to the custodian of the fund. The prohibition against deposit of cheques payable to the company is designed to prevent the routing of cash receipts into petty cash, since this would violate that basic assumption of limited disbursements and review at time of replenishing the fund.

Internal Control and the Computer

Computer processing of cash transactions can contribute to strong internal control over cash. As previously discussed, control over cash sales may be strengthened by the use of on-line register terminals. Remittance advices or mail room listings of customers' payments can be processed by computer. Many companies use computers to issue cheques and, subsequently, to prepare bank reconciliations. The daily computer processing of cash receipts and cheques can provide management with a continually up-to-date cash receipts journal, cheque register, customers' accounts ledger, and cash balance. In addition to this, the computer can prepare reliable bank reconciliations even when thousands of cheques are out-

FIGURE 11–2 Flowchart of Cash Disbursements Cycle (Voucher System)

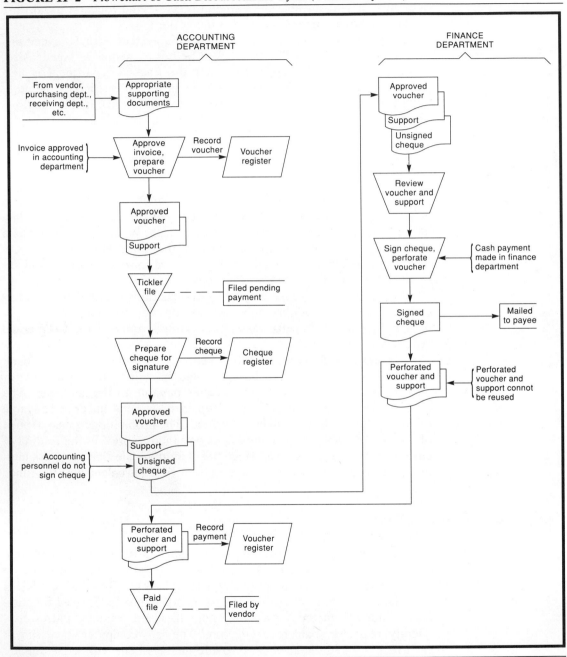

standing and can provide current information for cash planning and fore-casting.

Audit Working Papers for Cash

Auditors' working papers for cash include a flowchart or a written narra-tive of internal controls. An internal control questionnaire is also often used, especially in larger companies. A related working paper will summa-rize tests of controls for cash transactions and the assessments of control risk for the financial statement assertions about cash.

Additional cash working papers include a lead schedule, cash counts, bank confirmations, bank reconciliations, lists of outstanding cheques, lists of cheques being investigated, recommendations to the client for improving internal control, and notes concerning proper presentation of cash in the client's balance sheet.

AUDIT PROGRAM FOR CASH

The following audit program indicates the general pattern of work per-formed by the auditors in the verification of cash. Selection of the most appropriate procedures for a particular audit will be guided, of course, by the nature of the internal controls in force and by other circumstances of the engagement.

A. Consider internal control for cash.
  1. *Obtain an understanding of internal control* for cash.
  2. *Assess control risk* and *design additional tests of controls* for cash.
  3. *Perform additional tests of controls* for those controls which the auditors plan to consider in their assessment of control risk, such as:
      a. Test the accounting records and reconciliations by reper-formance.
      b. Compare the detail of a sample of cash receipts listings to the cash receipts journal, accounts receivable postings, and au-thenticated deposit slips.
      c. Compare the detail of a sample of recorded disbursements in cash payments journal to accounts payable postings, purchase orders, receiving reports, invoices, and paid cheques.
  4. *Reassess control risk* and *design substantive tests* for cash.
B. Perform substantive tests of cash transactions and balances.
  5. Obtain analyses of cash balances and reconcile to the general ledger.
  6. Send standard confirmation forms to banks to verify amounts on deposit.

7. Obtain or prepare reconciliations of bank accounts as of the balance sheet date and consider the need to reconcile bank activity for additional months.
8. Obtain a cutoff bank statement containing transactions of at least seven business days subsequent to balance sheet date.
9. Count and list cash on hand.
10. Verify the client's cutoff of cash receipts and cash disbursements.
11. Trace all bank transfers for last week of audit year and first week of following year.
12. Investigate any cheques representing large or unusual payments to related parties.
13. Evaluate proper financial statement presentation and disclosure of cash.

Figure 11–3 relates these substantive tests to the primary audit objectives.

A. Consider internal control for cash.
1. Obtain an understanding of internal control.

In the audit of a small business, the auditors may prepare a written narrative of controls in force, based upon the questioning of owners and employees and upon firsthand observation. For larger companies, a flow-chart or internal control questionnaire is usually employed to describe the internal control. An internal control questionnaire for cash receipts was illustrated in Chapter 7. Among the questions included in a questionnaire for cash disbursements are whether all disbursements (except those

---

FIGURE 11–3 Objectives of Major Substantive Tests of Cash Transactions and Balances

Substantive Tests	*Primary Audit Objectives*
Obtain analyses of cash balances and reconcile to general ledger	*Clerical accuracy*
Send standard confirmation forms to banks Obtain reconciliations of bank balances and consider reconciling bank activity Obtain bank cutoff statement Count cash on hand	*Existence and ownership*
Verify the client's cutoff of cash transactions Trace bank transfers occurring around year-end	*Existence and ownership* *Completeness*
Investigate payments to related parties Evaluate financial statement presentation and disclosure	*Statement presentation*

from petty cash) are made by prenumbered cheques and whether voided cheques are mutilated, preserved, and filed. The existence of these controls permits the auditors to determine that all disbursements have been recorded by accounting for the sequence of cheques issued or voided during the period.

Other points to be made clear by the questionnaire include (*a*) whether cheque-signing authority is restricted to selected executives not having access to accounting records or to vouchers and other documents supporting cheques submitted for signature, and (*b*) whether cheques are mailed directly to the payees after being signed. The internal control questionnaire will also cover cash disbursements for payroll and for dividends, as well as bank reconciliation procedures.

After the auditors have prepared a flowchart (or other description) of internal control, they should conduct a walk-through of the system. The term ***walk-through*** means to trace a few transactions through each step of the system to determine that transactions actually are being processed in the manner indicated by the flowchart. The walk-through allows the auditors to determine that the internal control systems and procedures as described in the working papers have actually been ***placed in operation.***

As the auditors verify their understanding of the cash receipts and disbursements cycles, they will observe whether there is appropriate segregation of duties, and enquire as to who performed various functions throughout the year. They will also inspect the various documents and reconciliations that are important to the client's internal control over cash receipts and disbursements. Cash forecasts or budgets also will be inspected, and the auditors will review the evidence of the follow-up on variances from forecasted amounts of receipts and disbursements. These tests of controls may provide the auditors with sufficient evidence to assess control risk for certain financial statement assertions at less than the maximum.

2. Assess control risk and design additional tests of controls.

After obtaining an understanding of the client's internal control for cash receipts and disbursements, the auditors perform their initial assessments of control risk. To further evaluate these assessments, the auditors must obtain additional evidence of the operating effectiveness of various internal control policies, systems, and procedures. This evidence is obtained by performing additional tests of controls. In designing these tests, the auditors must decide which ones will result in sufficient reductions in substantive tests to justify the time spent performing them.

3. Perform additional tests of controls.

Tests directed toward the effectiveness of controls help to evaluate the client's internal control and determine the extent to which the auditors are justified in reducing their assessed levels of control risk for the assertions about the cash account. Certain tests of controls are performed as the auditors obtain an understanding of the client's internal control; these were described in our discussion of that process. The following are examples of typical additional tests of controls.

a. Test the accounting records and reconciliations by reperformance.

To determine that the clients accounting procedures are operating effectively, the auditors perform tests of the mechanical accuracy of the client's journals and ledgers. In a computer-based system, journal and ledger entries are created simultaneously from the same source documents, and the auditors might choose to use generalized audit software to test the accuracy of the accounting records.

In a manual system, information on source documents is entered first in a journal; at a later date the information is summarized and posted from journals to ledgers. The auditors must manually determine that documents are accurately entered to the journals, that the journals are accurately footed, and that the data is properly posted to the ledgers.

The auditors also may decide to test the client's procedures for reconciling bank accounts. They may select a sample of the reconciliations performed during the year, noting who performed them, and *reperforming* the reconciliation process by reference to accounting records, bank statements, and canceled cheques.

b. Compare detail of cash receipts listings to cash receipts journal, accounts receivable postings, and authenticated deposit slips.

Satisfactory internal control over cash receipts demands that each day's collections be deposited intact no later than the next banking day. To provide assurance that cash receipts have been deposited intact, the auditors should compare the detail of the original cash receipts listings (mail room control listings and register tapes) to the detail of the daily deposit slips. The *detail* of cash receipts refers to a listing of the amount of each individual cheque and the total amount of currency comprising the day's receipts.

Comparison of the daily entries in the cash receipts journal with bank deposits may disclose a type of fraud known as *lapping*. Lapping means the concealment of a cash shortage by delaying the recording of cash receipts. If cash collected from customer A is withheld by the cashier, a subsequent collection from customer B may be entered as a credit to A's account. B's account will not be shown as paid until a collection from customer C is recorded as a credit to B. Unless the money abstracted by the cashier is replaced, the accounts receivable as a group remain overstated, but judicious shifting of the overstatement from one account receivable to another may avert protests from customers receiving monthly statements. The following schedule makes clear how a lapping activity may be carried on. In companies in which the cashier has access to the general accounting records, shortages created in this manner have sometimes been transferred to inventory accounts or elsewhere in the records for temporary concealment.

Date	Actually Received From	Actual Cash Receipts	Recorded as Received From	Receipts Recorded and Deposited	Receipts Withheld
Dec. 1	Abbott	$ 750			$ 750
	Crane	1,035	Crane	$1,035	
2	Barstow	750	Abbott	750	
	White	130	White	130	
3	Crawford	1,575	Barstow	750	825
	Miller	400	Miller	400	
		$4,640		$3,065	$1,575

Lapping is most easily carried on when an employee who receives collections from customers is responsible for the posting of customers' accounts. Familiarity with customers' accounts makes it relatively easy to lodge a shortage in an account that will not be currently questioned.

c. Compare the detail of a sample of recorded disbursements in cash payments journal, accounts payable postings, purchase orders, receiving reports, invoices, and paid cheques.

Satisfactory internal control over cash disbursements requires that controls exist to provide assurance that disbursements are properly authorized. Testing cash disbursements involves tracing selected items back through the cash payments journal to original source documents, including vouchers, purchase orders, receiving reports, invoices, and paid cheques. While examining these documents, the auditors have an opportunity to test many of the controls over cash disbursements. For example, they will notice whether all paid vouchers and supporting documents have been perforated or cancelled. Also, they will determine whether agreement exists among the supporting documents and note the presence of all required authorization signatures. The auditors also may review the file of paid cheques to test the client's procedures for accounting for the numerical sequence of cheques.

4. Reassess control risk and design substantive tests.

When the auditors have completed the procedures described in the preceding sections, they should reassess the extent of control risk for each financial statement assertion regarding cash. The auditors then draft the portion of the audit program devoted to the substantive tests of cash transactions and balances.

B. Substantive tests.

5. Obtain analyses of cash balances and reconcile to general ledger.

The auditors will prepare or obtain a schedule that lists all of the client's cash accounts. For cash in bank accounts, this schedule will typically list the bank, the account number, account type, and the year-end balance per books. The auditors will trace and reconcile all accounts to the general ledger as necessary.

6. Send standard confirmation forms to banks to verify amounts on deposit.

One of the objectives of the auditors' work on cash is to substantiate the existence of the amount of cash shown on the balance sheet. A direct approach to this objective is to confirm amounts on deposit, count the cash on hand, and obtain or prepare reconciliations between bank statements and the accounting records.

Confirmation of amounts on deposit by direct communication with banks is normally obtained in all audits. Account balances are confirmed with a standard form, as illustrated by Figure 11–4. This standard confirmation form, approved by the Canadian Bankers' Association and the Canadian Institute of Chartered Accountants, addresses the client's deposit, loan balances (and collateral security), contingent liabilities, and securities in safekeeping. Information identifying accounts and loans and their balances is typed on the form to assist the financial institution in completing it. Thus, the form is primarily used to *corroborate* the existence of recorded information. However, the confirmation may also lead to the *discovery* of additional accounts or loans, and it therefore provides limited evidence about the completeness of recorded amounts. Although the personnel at the banks will not conduct a detailed search of the records, they will include information about additional deposits and loans that they note while completing the confirmation.

The details of other financial arrangements are also confirmed with the banks. For example, the auditors may request the bank to corroborate compensating balance arrangements, or authorized cheque signers.

7. Obtain or prepare reconciliations of bank accounts as of the balance sheet date and consider need to reconcile bank activity for additional months.

Determination of a company's cash position at the close of the period requires a reconciliation of the balance per the bank statement at that date with the balance per the company's accounting records. Even though the auditors may not be able to begin their work for some time after the close of the year, they will prepare a bank reconciliation as of the balance sheet date or test the one prepared by the client.

If the year-end reconciliation has been made by the client before the arrival of the auditors, there is no need for duplicating the work. However, the auditors should examine the reconciliation in detail to satisfy themselves that it has been properly prepared. Inspection of a reconciliation prepared by the client will include verifying the arithmetical accuracy, tracing balances to the bank statement, the bank confirmation, and the ledger account, and investigating the reconciling items. The importance of testing the client's reconciliation is indicated by the fact that a cash short-

FIGURE 11–4

BANK CONFIRMATION

Use With No. 9
Window Envelope

CLIENT AUTHORIZED SIGNATURE

CLIENT

Longview Corporation
1000 Kingston Avenue
Windsor, Ontario
N1B 6J9

John Berksty

CHARTERED ACCOUNTANT

COOPERS, PEAT and PRICE
1368 ISLAND AVENUE
WINDSOR, ONTARIO
N8X 1L9

BANK

United National Bank
690 Ambassador Bridge Street
Windsor, Ontario
N2F 8C6

If at all possible, this Confirmation Request should arrive at the branch at least one week before Confirmation Date

Confirmation Date
December 31, 19X3
All information to be provided as at this date

BRANCH CONTACT NAME

Susan Marchand   *901 2169*

Susan Marchand

Notes To Bank

- Please complete this confirmation as at Confirmation Date noted above, include name, telephone number and sign in the space provided above. Mail original in the enclosed envelope to the chartered accountant.
- Use the ROUTING SHEET provided by your Bank to collect data from your departments, then transfer the information to this form. In the absence of a Routing Sheet, use the ROUTE TO box to ensure the Bank confirmation is circulated to the appropriate departments in your branch.
- If the space provided is inadequate, please enter totals on this form and attach a statement giving full details as called for by the headings.
- For COMPLETION INSTRUCTIONS, see the reverse of this form.

ROUTE TO
☐ ....
☐ ....
☐ ....
☐ ....
☐ ....
☐ ....

① DEPOSITS OVERDRAFTS   If none, so state

AMOUNT (Brackets if Overdraft)	If applicable ISSUE DATE	MATURITY DATE	ACCOUNT NUMBER	TYPE OF ACCOUNT AND CURRENCY	INTEREST RATE
$89,548.92			138-7190	General, Canadian funds	None
8,212.05			138-2419	Payroll, Canadian funds	None

② LOANS OTHER DIRECT LIABILITIES AND COLLATERAL SECURITY   Exclude overdrafts listed in Section ① Include bankers' acceptances. If no items, so state

AMOUNT AND CURRENCY	NATURE OF LIABILITY	DUE DATE	NATURE OF COLLATERAL LODGED BY CUSTOMER TO SUPPORT THE LIABILITIES (If none, so state)	INTEREST RATES	DATE PAID TO
$ 78,910.11	Mortgage	July 4 19x7	Building	12%	Dec. 31, 19x3
123,456.00	Credit Line	May 1, 19x4	None	13%	Dec. 31, 19x3

③ CONTINGENT LIABILITIES   If none, so state. Exclude bankers' acceptances *none*

AMOUNT AND CURRENCY	DATE OF NOTE	DUE DATE	PAYABLE BY

④ SECURITIES IN SAFE-KEEPING OTHER INFORMATION REQUESTED BY CHARTERED ACCOUNTANT   If none, so state. Exclude items already listed in Section ②

NONE

⑤ GUARANTEES COMFORT LETTERS

Were the customer's direct liabilities guaranteed or supported by comfort letters by third parties   ☐ Yes,   ☐ No

302
APPROVED 1986 · The Canadian Bankers' Association and the Canadian Institute of Chartered Accountants

age may be concealed merely by omitting a cheque from the outstanding cheque list or by purposely making an error in addition on the reconciliation.

There are many satisfactory forms of bank reconciliations. The form most frequently used by auditors begins with balance per bank and ends with unadjusted balance per the accounting records. This format permits the auditors to post adjusting entries affecting cash directly to the bank reconciliation working paper, so that the final adjusted balance can be cross-referenced to the cash grouping sheet or to the working trial balance.

The mechanics of balancing the ledger account with the bank statement by no means completes the auditors' verification of cash on deposit. The authenticity of the individual items making up the reconciliation must be established by reference to their respective sources. The balance per the bank statement, for example, is not accepted at face value but is verified by direct confirmation with the bank, as described in the preceding pages. Other verification procedures associated with the reconciliation of the bank statement will now be discussed.

The auditors should investigate any cheques outstanding for a year or more. If cheques are permitted to remain outstanding for long periods, internal control over cash disbursements is weakened. Employees who become aware that certain cheques have long been outstanding and may never be presented to the bank for payment have an opportunity to conceal a cash shortage merely by omitting the old outstanding cheque from the bank reconciliation. Such omissions will serve to increase the apparent balance of cash on deposit and may thus induce an employee to abstract a corresponding amount of cash on hand. It is good practice for the client to eliminate long-outstanding cheques of this nature by an entry debiting the Cash account and crediting an appropriate expense or liability account. This will reduce the work required in bank reconciliations, as well as lessen the opportunity for errors, fraud, and irregularities.

When internal control over the recording of cash receipts and disbursements is considered weak, the auditors may use additional reconciliation procedures such as preparing a *proof of cash*, which allows a more detailed study of the cash transactions occurring within a specified period. This is essentially a fraud detection procedure which may be used for the last month of the year or for selected months during the year.

A proof of cash for the test period of September is illustrated in Figure 11–5. Notice that this working paper is so organized that the first and last columns reconcile the cash balance per bank and the balance per accounting records at the beginning of the test period (column 1) and at the end of this period (column 4). These outside columns are equivalent to typical monthly bank reconciliations. The two middle columns reconcile the bank's record of deposits with the client's record of cash receipts (column 2) and the bank's record of paid cheques with the client's record of cash disbursements (column 3).

FIGURE 11–5 Proof of Cash

The Fairview Corporation

acct. No. 101   Proof of Cash for September 199x   A-4

December 31, 199x

	Balance Aug/31/9x	Deposits	Cheques	Balance Sept/30/9x
Per bank statement	39,736.40 Z	46,001.00 ②	40,362.90	44,874.50 Z
Deposits in transit				
at Aug/31/9x	600.00 Z	(600.00)		
at Sept/30/9x		837.50		837.50
Outstanding cheques				
at Aug/31/9x	(1,241.00) X		(1,241.00)	
at Sept/30/9x			3,402.00	(3,402.00) √
Bank service charge				
August	4.60		4.60	
September			(2.80)	2.80
Cheque of customer				
A.G. Speller charged back				
by bank Sept/12/9x				
redeposited Sept/15/9x		(900.00)	(900.00)	
Per books	38,600.00 u	45,338.50 u	41,625.70 u	42,312.80 u
			①	A-1

Z = Traced to clients' Aug/31/9x
     September bank statement.
# = Per adding machine tape at A-4-1
X = Per adding machine tape at A-4-2
√ = Per adding machine tape at A-4-3
u = Traced to general ledger
① = Vouched selected September disbursements to paid vouchers and
     other supporting documents.
② = Obtained authenticated deposit slips for September from bank
     and compared with cash receipts journal. Compared detail of
     10 deposit slips with original control listings and postings
     to customers' accounts.

Footed cash receipts journal and cheque register for September 199x.
Accounted for numerical sequence of all cheques issued
September 199x - nos. 610-792. No exceptions to tests.

V. O. N. H. Oct/16/9x

Next consider the source of the figures used in this reconciliation. The amounts "per bank statement" are taken from the September 30 bank statement. The subsequent rows of deposits, cheques, and other items are taken from the August and September bank reconciliations, and the amounts "per books" are taken from the client's cash general ledger account and from cash receipts and disbursements journals.

8. Obtain a cutoff bank statement containing transactions of at least seven business days subsequent to balance sheet date.

A *cutoff bank statement* is a statement covering a specified number of *business days* (usually 7 to 10) following the end of the client's fiscal year. The client will request the bank to prepare such a statement and deliver it directly to the auditors. This statement is used to test the accuracy of the year-end reconciliation of the company's bank accounts. It allows the auditors to examine firsthand the cheques listed as outstanding and the details of deposits in transit on the company's reconciliation.

With respect to cheques that were shown as outstanding at year-end, the auditors should determine the dates on which these cheques were paid by the bank. By noting the dates of payment of these cheques, the auditors can determine whether the time intervals between the dates of the cheque and the time of payment by the bank were unreasonably long. Unreasonable delay in the presentation of these cheques for payment constitutes a strong implication that the cheques were not mailed by the client until some time after the close of the year. The appropriate adjusting entry in such cases consists of a debit to Cash and a credit to a liability account.

In studying the cutoff bank statement, the auditors will also watch for any paid cheques issued, or clearing a bank, on or before the balance sheet date but not listed as outstanding on the client's year-end bank reconciliation. Thus, the cutoff bank statement provides assurance that the amount of cash shown on the balance sheet was not overstated by omission of one or more cheques from the list of cheques outstanding.

9. Count and list cash on hand.

Cash on hand ordinarily consists of undeposited cash receipts, petty cash funds, and change funds. The petty cash funds and change funds may be counted at any time before or after the balance sheet date; many auditors prefer to make a surprise count of these funds.

The count of cash on hand is of special importance in the audit of banks and other financial institutions. Whenever auditors make a cash count, they should insist that the ***custodian of the funds be present throughout the count.*** At the completion of the count, the auditors should obtain from the custodian a signed and dated acknowledgment that the funds were counted in the custodian's presence and were returned intact by the auditors. Such procedures avoid the possibility of an employee trying to explain a cash shortage by claiming that the funds were intact when turned over to the auditors.

A first step in the verification of cash on hand is to establish control over all negotiable assets, such as cash funds, securities and other investments, notes receivable, and warehouse receipts. Unless all negotiable assets are verified at one time, an opportunity exists for a dishonest officer or employee to conceal a shortage by transferring it from one asset category to another.

It is not uncommon to find included in cash on hand some personal cheques cashed for the convenience of officers, employees, and customers. Such cheques, of course, should not be entered in the cash receipts journal because they are merely substitutes for currency previously on hand. The auditors should determine that these cheques are valid and collectible, thus qualifying for inclusion in the balance sheet figure for cash. This may be accomplished by the auditors' taking control of the last bank deposit for the period and determining that it includes all cheques received through year-end. The auditors will retain a validated deposit slip from this deposit for comparison to any cheques subsequently charged back by the bank.

10. Verify the client's cutoff of cash receipts and cash disbursements.

The balance sheet figure for cash should include all cash received on the final day of the year and none received subsequently. In other words, an accurate cutoff of cash receipts (and of cash disbursements) at year-end is essential to a proper statement of cash on the balance sheet. If the auditors can arrange to be present at the client's office at the close of business on the last day of the fiscal year, they will be able to verify the cutoff by counting the undeposited cash receipts. It will then be impossible for the client to include in the records any cash received after this cutoff point without the auditor being aware of such actions.

Of course, auditors cannot visit every client's place of business on the last day of the fiscal year, nor is their presence at this time essential to a satisfactory verification of cash. As an alternative to a count on the balance sheet date, auditors can verify the cutoff of cash receipts by determining that deposits in transit as shown on the year-end bank reconciliation appear as credits on the bank statement on the first business day of the new year. Failure to make *immediate* deposit of the closing day's cash receipts would suggest that cash received at a later time might have been included in the deposit, thus overstating the cash balance at the balance sheet date.

To ensure an accurate cutoff of cash disbursements, the auditors should determine the serial number of the last cheque written on each bank account on the balance sheet date and should enquire whether all cheques up to this number have been placed in the mail. Some companies, in an effort to improve the current ratio, will prepare cheques payable to creditors and enter these cheques as cash disbursements on the last day of the fiscal year, although there is no intention of mailing the cheques until several days or weeks later. The auditors will be alert when examining the cutoff bank statement for an unusually large number of outstanding cheques that have not cleared the bank.

11. Trace all bank transfers for the last week of audit year and first week of following year.

The purpose of tracing bank transfers is to disclose overstatements of cash balances resulting from *kiting.* Many businesses maintain chequing accounts with a number of banks and often find it necessary to transfer funds from one bank to another. When a cheque drawn on one bank is deposited in another, several days (called the float period) usually pass before the cheque clears the bank on which it is drawn. During this period, the amount of the cheque is included in the balance on deposit at both banks. Kiting refers to manipulations that utilize such temporarily overstated bank balances to conceal a cash shortage or meet short-term cash needs.

Auditors can detect manipulations of this type by preparing a schedule of bank transfers for a few days before and after the balance sheet date. This working paper lists all bank transfers and shows the dates that the receipt and disbursement of cash were recorded in the cash journals and on the bank statements. A partial illustration of a schedule of bank transfers is shown below.

	Bank Accounts			Date of Disbursement		Date of Receipt	
Cheque No.	From	To	Amount	Books	Bank	Books	Bank
5897	General	Payroll	$30,620	Dec. 28	Jan. 3	Dec. 28	Dec. 28
6006	General	Branch 4	24,018	Jan. 2	Jan. 4	Dec. 30	Dec. 30
6029	Branch 2	General	10,000	Jan. 3	Jan. 5	Jan. 3	Dec. 31

Disclosure of Kiting. By comparing the dates in this working paper, auditors can determine whether any manipulation of the cash balance has taken place. The increase in one bank account and decrease in the other bank account should be recorded in the cash journals in the same accounting period. Notice that Cheque No. 6006 in the transfer schedule was recorded in the cash journals as a receipt on December 30 and a disbursement of January 2. As a result of recording the debit and credit parts of the transaction in different accounting periods, cash is overstated on December 31. For the cash receipts journal to remain in balance, some account must have been credited on December 30 to offset the debit to cash. If a revenue account was credited, the results of operations were overstated along with cash.

Kiting may also be used to conceal a cash shortage. Assume, for example, that a financial executive misappropriates $10,000 from a company's general account. To conceal the shortage on December 31, the executive draws a cheque transferring $10,000 from the company's branch bank account to the general account. The executive deposits the transfer cheque in the general account on December 31, but records the transfer in the accounting records as occurring early in January. As of December 31, the shortage in the general account has been replaced, no reduction has yet been recorded in the branch account, and no shortage is apparent. Of course, the shortage will reappear in a few days when the transfer cheque is paid from the branch account.

A bank transfer schedule should disclose this type of kiting because the transfer deposit appears on the general account bank statement in December, while the transaction was not recorded in the cash journals until January. Cheque No. 6029 in the transfer schedule illustrates this discrepancy.

A third type of kiting uses the float period to meet short-term cash needs. For example, assume that a business does not have sufficient cash to meet the month-end payroll. The company might draw a cheque on its general account in one bank, deposit it in a payroll account in another bank, and rely upon subsequent deposits being made to the general account before the transfer cheque is presented for payment. If the transfer is properly recorded in the accounting records, this form of kiting will not cause a misstatement of the cash balance for financial reporting purposes (e.g., Cheque No. 5897). However, banks attempt to detect this practice and may not allow the customer to draw against the deposit until the cheque has cleared the other account.

12. Investigate any cheques representing large or unusual payments to related parties.

Any large or unusual cheques payable to directors, officers, employees, affiliated companies, or cash should be carefully reviewed by the auditors to determine whether the transactions (*a*) were properly authorized and recorded and (*b*) are adequately disclosed in the financial statements.

To provide assurance that cash disbursements to related parties were authorized transactions and were properly recorded, the auditors should determine that each such transaction has been charged to the proper account, is supported by adequate vouchers or other documents, and was specifically approved in advance by an officer other than the one receiving the funds.

The need for financial statement disclosure of transactions with related parties was discussed in Chapter 6. To determine that such transactions are adequately disclosed, the auditors must obtain evidence concerning the relationship between the parties, the substance of each transaction (which may differ from its form), and the effect of each transaction upon the financial statements. Disclosure of related party transactions should include the nature of the relationships, a description of the transactions, and the dollar amounts involved.

13. Determine proper financial statement presentation and disclosure of cash.

The balance sheet figure for cash should include only those amounts that are available for use in current operations. A bank deposit that is restricted in use (e.g., cash deposited with a trustee for payments on long-term debt) should not be included in cash. Agreements to maintain *compensating balances* should be disclosed. The auditors must also make sure that the caption, "cash" or "cash and cash equivalents," on the client's balance sheet corresponds to that used in the statement of changes in financial position.

Window Dressing.   The term *window dressing* refers to actions taken shortly before the balance sheet date to improve the cash position or in other ways to create an improved financial picture of the company. For example, if the cash receipts journal is held open for a few days after the close of the year, the balance sheet figure for cash is improperly increased to include cash collections actually received after the balance sheet date. Another approach to window dressing is found when a corporate officer who has borrowed money from the corporation repays the loan just before the end of the year and then promptly obtains the loan again after the balance sheet date. This second example is not an outright misrepresentation of the cash position (as in the case of holding the cash receipts journal open), but nevertheless creates misleading financial statements that fail to portray the underlying economic position and operations of the company.

Not all forms of window dressing require action by the auditors. Many companies make strenuous efforts at year-end to achieve an improved financial picture by rushing shipments to customers, by pressing for collection of receivables, and sometimes by paying liabilities down to an unusually low level. Such efforts to improve the financial picture to be reported are not improper. Before giving approval to the balance sheet presentation of cash, the auditors must exercise their professional judgment to determine whether the client has engaged in window dressing of a nature that causes the financial statements to be misleading.

Interim Audit Work on Cash

To avoid a concentration of audit work shortly after the year-end, public accounting firms try to complete as many auditing procedures as possible on an interim basis during the year. The consideration of internal control over cash, for example, can be performed in advance of the client's year-end. The audit work on cash at year-end can then be limited to such substantive tests as a testing of the client's bank reconciliations, confirmation of year-end bank balances, investigation of the year-end cutoff, and a general review of cash transactions during the interval between the interim work on cash and the end of the period.

MARKETABLE SECURITIES

The most important group of investments, from the viewpoint of the auditors, consists of stocks and bonds because they are found more frequently and usually are of greater dollar value than other kinds of investment holdings. Commercial paper issued by corporations, mortgages and trust deeds, and the cash surrender value of life insurance policies are other types of investments often encountered.

Investment of temporarily idle cash in selected types of marketable securities is an element of good financial management. Such holdings are regarded as a secondary cash reserve, capable of quick conversion to cash at any time, yet producing a steady rate of return. Management may also choose to maintain some investments in marketable securities on a semipermanent basis. The length of time such investments are held may be determined by current security yields and by the company's income tax position, as well as by its cash requirements. Investments in securities made for the purpose of maintaining control or significant influence over affiliated companies should *not* be classified under marketable securities.

The Auditors' Objectives in Examination of Marketable Securities

The auditors have six *objectives* in the examination of marketable securities:

1. Consider *internal control* over marketable securities.
2. Determine the *existence* of recorded marketable securities and the client's *ownership* of the securities.
3. Establish the *completeness* of recorded marketable securities.
4. Determine that the *valuation* of marketable securities is in accordance with the lower-of-cost-and-market method of accounting.
5. Establish the *clerical accuracy* of schedules of marketable securities.
6. Determine that the *statement presentation* of marketable securities, including current/noncurrent classifications, are appropriate.

In conjunction with their audit of marketable securities, the auditors will also verify the related accounts of interest income and dividends, accrued interest revenue, and gains and losses on the sale of securities.

The liquid nature of marketable securities makes the potential for fraud and irregularities high. Auditors must coordinate their cash and marketable securities audit procedures to detect any possible fraud and irregularities involving unauthorized substitution (e.g., sale of securities to hide a cash shortage) between the accounts. The overall audit approach is one of assessing control over securities, inspecting certificates, confirming securities held by third parties such as banks, and determining the appropriate valuation of the securities.

Internal Control for Marketable Securities

The major elements of adequate internal control over marketable securities include the following:

1. Separation of duties between the executive *authorizing* purchases and sales of securities, the *custodian* of the securities, and the person maintaining the *record* of investments.
2. Complete detailed records of all securities owned and the related revenue from interest and dividends.
3. Registration of securities in the name of the company.
4. Periodic physical inspection of securities by an internal auditor or an official having no responsibility for the authorization, custody, or record-keeping of investments.

In many concerns, segregation of the functions of custody and record-keeping is achieved by the use of an independent safekeeping agent, such as a stockbroker, bank, or trust company. Since the independent agent has no direct contact with the employee responsible for maintaining accounting records of the investments in securities, the possibilities of concealing fraud through falsification of the accounts are greatly reduced. If securities are not placed in the custody of an independent agent, they should be kept in a bank safety-deposit box under the joint control of two or more of the company's officials. *Joint control* means that neither of the two custodians may have access to the securities except in the presence of the other. A list of securities in the box should be maintained there, and the deposit or withdrawal of securities should be recorded on this list along with the date and signatures of all persons present. The safety-deposit box rental should be in the name of the company, not in the name of an officer having custody of securities.

Complete detailed records of all securities owned, and of any securities held for others, are essential to satisfactory internal control. These records frequently consist of a subsidiary record for each security, with such identifying data as the exact name, face amount or par value (if any), certificate number, number of shares, date of acquisition, name of broker, cost, and any interest or dividends payments received. The purchase and sale of securities often is entrusted to a responsible financial executive, subject to frequent review by an investment committee of the board of directors. Actual interest and dividends are compared to budgeted amounts; any significant variances are investigated.

An internal auditor or other responsible employee should at frequent intervals inspect the securities on hand, compare the serial numbers and other identifying data of the securities examined with the accounting records, and reconcile the subsidiary record for securities with the control account. This procedure supplements the internal control inherent in the segregation of the functions of authorization, record-keeping, and custodianship.

Internal Control Questionnaire

A questionnaire used by the auditors in assessing internal controls relating to securities will include such questions as the following. Are securities and similar instruments under the joint control of responsible officials? Are all persons having access to securities properly bonded? Is an independent safekeeping agent retained? Are all purchases and sales of securities authorized by a financial executive and reviewed by an investment committee of the board of directors?

Audit Program for Securities

Listed below are procedures typically performed by auditors to achieve the objectives described earlier.

A. Consider internal control for securities.
 1. *Obtain an understanding of internal control* for securities.
 2. *Assess control risk* and *design additional tests of controls* for securities.
 3. *Perform additional tests of controls* for those controls the auditors plan to consider in their assessment of control risk, such as:
     a. Trace a number of transactions for purchases and sales of securities through the system.
     b. Review reports by internal auditors on their periodic inspection of securities.
     c. Review monthly reports on securities owned, purchased, and sold, and amounts of revenue earned and budgeted.
 4. *Reassess control risk* and *design substantive tests* for securities.

B. Perform substantive tests of securities transactions and year-end balances.
 5. Obtain or prepare analyses of the securities investment account and related revenue accounts and reconcile to the general ledger.
 6. Inspect securities on hand and compare serial numbers with those shown on previous examinations.
 7. Obtain confirmation of securities held by others.
 8. Vouch selected purchases and sales of securities during the year.
 9. Perform analytical procedures.
 10. Make independent computations of revenue from securities.

11. Verify the client's cutoff of securities transactions.
12. Determine market value of securities at date of balance sheet.
13. Evaluate the method of accounting for securities.
14. Evaluate financial statement presentation and disclosure of securities.

Figure 11–6 relates these substantive tests to the primary audit objectives.

Audit Procedures and Working Papers

The audit working papers describing internal control may include a flowchart, questionnaire, or a written narrative. Next, selected transactions for purchase or sale of securities will be traced through the system to verify that the controls are placed in operation. For example, a purchase of securities should be authorized by the appropriate officer, and documents from the stockbroker should show receipt of the order and its execution. Tracing these transactions allows the auditors to observe firsthand the segregation of duties for processing securities transactions and the documents supporting the transactions.

A written report of securities transactions can be a valuable control device. In many companies, the accounting department will submit a report monthly to the investment committee of the board of directors

FIGURE 11–6   Objectives of Major Substantive Tests of Securities

Substantive Tests	*Primary Audit Objectives*
Obtain analyses of securities and related accounts and reconcile to ledger	*Clerical accuracy*
Inspect securities on hand Obtain confirmation of securities held by others	*Existence and ownership*
Vouch selected purchases and sales of securities during the year	*Existence and ownership* *Valuation*
Perform analytical procedures Make independent computations of revenue from securities Verify the client's cutoff of securities transactions	*Existence and ownership* *Completeness*
Determine market value of securities Evaluate the method of accounting	*Valuation* *Statement presentation*
Evaluate financial statement presentation and disclosure	*Statement presentation*

showing securities owned, purchases and sales during the month, gains and losses, dividends and interest received, and variances from budgeted amounts. The auditors may inspect these reports to obtain evidence to assess control risk for marketable securities.

The client's internal auditors may perform periodic examinations of securities and issue reports describing their findings. The external auditors may consider these reports and use the evidence to reduce the extent of their substantive procedures for marketable securities. The auditors will count securities held by the client at year-end, verify that the securities are registered in the company's name, and record in the working papers a description of the securities, including the serial numbers. When the client's records indicate that a particular security has been held since the last audit, the auditors may compare the serial number on the certificate with that shown in the prior year's working papers. This may allow the auditors to detect securities that have been sold without authorization during the year and replaced before this year's examination.

The count of securities ideally is made at the balance sheet date concurrently with the count of cash and other negotiable instruments. If the securities are kept in a bank safety-deposit box, the client may instruct the bank in writing on the balance sheet date that no one is to have access to the box unless accompanied by the auditors. This arrangement makes it possible to count the securities at a more convenient time after the balance sheet date. Also, banks keep records of access to safety-deposit boxes that can be examined by the auditors to determine who has had access to the box and at what dates. A representative of the client should be present when the auditors count the securities, and that individual should acknowledge in writing that the securities were returned intact.

Most client-owned securities will be in the hands of brokers or banks for safekeeping. In such cases, the auditors send a confirmation, signed by the client, to the holders of the securities to verify the existence and ownership of the securities.

To determine that securities purchased and sold during the period are recorded properly, the auditors vouch a sample of transactions by reference to ***brokers' advices*** and cash records. In addition, they review transactions for one or two weeks after the balance sheet date. The purpose is to assure that a correct cutoff of transactions was made. Sometimes sales occur shortly before the balance sheet date but go unrecorded until the securities are delivered to the broker early in the next period.

The auditors can use analytical procedures to test the reasonableness of the amounts of recorded dividend and interest income, or they can verify the amounts by independent computation. Dividends that should have been received and recorded can be computed by referring to dividend record books published by investment advisory services. These books show dividend declarations, amounts, and payment dates for all listed stocks. Interest earned on bonds and notes also can be computed independently by the auditors and compared with recorded amounts in the client's records. This provides evidence both that the employees are not embezzling investment income and that the client actually owns the securities recorded in the accounting records.

Current market quotations for all marketable securities owned by the client can be verified by reference to financial publications, such as the *Financial Post,* or representations by securities brokers. The presentation of marketable securities in financial statements should be at the lower of the aggregate cost and market value at balance sheet date.

Long-Term Investments.   Investments that management intends to hold for the indefinite future are classified as long-term investments. Depending on the type of investment, they are valued at the lower of the aggregate cost and market value, at cost (adjusted for unamortized discount or premium), or by the equity method. When the cost method is used, the auditors determine the value by vouching the original purchase and recomputing the amount of any discount or premium amortization. To determine that there is no permanent decline in value, the auditors will obtain information about the current market value of the investment. If the investment is closely held with no active market, the auditors may have to rely upon a securities appraiser to value the security. In such cases, the auditors should consider the professional qualifications of the appraiser, and obtain an understanding of the methods and assumptions used.

Investments in common stock that give the investor company the ability to exercise significant influence over operating and financial policies of the investee require use of the equity method of accounting. Ownership of 20 percent of the voting stock of an investee is used as a general indication of ability to exert influence in the absence of evidence to the contrary. Such factors as investor representation on the investee's board of directors and material intercompany transactions also suggest an ability to exercise influence.

When auditing an investment accounted for by the equity method, the auditors must verify that the investment was recorded properly initially. They must also obtain evidence regarding subsequent amounts of income from the investment and of other adjustments to the investment account. This evidence is usually obtained from ***audited*** financial statements of the investee.

If audited financial statements of an investee are not available for the period covered by the external auditors' report on the investor, the auditors should perform a sufficient investigation of the investee's financial statements to determine the fairness of amounts recorded by the investor.

KEY TERMS

brokers' advice   A notification sent by a stockbrokerage firm to a customer reporting the terms of a purchase or sale of securities.

certificate of deposit   A receipt issued by a bank for a deposit of funds for a specified time. Usually in denominations of $100,000 or more and bearing interest at a higher rate than for most bank savings accounts.

cheque register   A journal used in a voucher system to record payment of vouchers. Since the cost distribution relating to voucher transactions is made in the voucher register, entries in the cheque register represent debits to Vouchers Payable and credits to Cash.

confirmation request—securities   A letter prepared by the client and addressed to the broker, bank, or other holder of client-owned securities, requesting the holder to respond directly to the external auditors giving full identification of the securities held.

cutoff bank statement   A bank statement covering a specified number of business days (usually 7 to 10) after the client's balance sheet date. Auditors use this statement to determine that cheques issued on or before the balance sheet date and paid during the cutoff period were listed as outstanding on the year-end bank reconciliation. Another use is to determine that reconciling items shown on the year-end bank reconciliation have cleared the bank within a reasonable time.

dividend record book   A reference book published monthly by investment advisory services reporting detailed information concerning all listed and many unlisted securities; includes dividend dates and amounts, current prices of securities, and other condensed financial data.

kiting   Manipulations causing an amount of cash to be included simultaneously in the balance of two or more bank accounts. Kiting schemes are based on the float period—the time necessary for a cheque deposited in one bank to clear the bank on which it was drawn.

lockbox   A post office box controlled by a company's bank at which cash remittances from customers are received. The bank picks up the remittances, immediately credits the cash to the company's bank account, and forwards the remittance advices to the company.

proof of cash   An audit procedure that reconciles the bank's record of cash activity with the client's accounting records for a test period. The working paper used for the proof of cash is a four-column bank reconciliation.

remittance advice   A document that accompanies cash remittances from customers identifying the customer and the amount of the remittance.

voucher   A document authorizing a cash disbursement. A voucher usually provides space for employees performing various approval functions to initial. (The term *voucher* may also be applied to the group of documents that support a cash disbursement.)

voucher register   A special journal used to record the liabilities for payment originating in a voucher system. The debit entries are the cost distribution of the transaction, and the credits are to Vouchers Payable. Every transaction recorded in a voucher register corresponds to a voucher authorizing future payment of cash.

window dressing   Action taken by the client shortly before the balance sheet date to improve the financial picture presented in the financial statements.

GROUP I: REVIEW QUESTIONS

11–1.   It is sometimes said that audit work on cash is facilitated by the existence of two independent records of the client's cash transactions, which are available for comparison by the auditors. Identify these two independent records.

11–2.   "If the auditors discover any evidence of employee fraud during their work on cash, they should extend their investigation as far as necessary to develop a complete set of facts, regardless of whether the amounts involved are or are not material." Do you agree with the quoted statement? Explain.

11–3.   Give two reasons why audit work on cash is likely to be more extensive than might appear to be justified by the relative amount of the balance sheet figure for cash.

11–4.   The auditors' work on cash may include an understanding of internal controls and performing tests of controls. Which of these two steps should be performed first? What is the purpose of tests of controls?

11–5.   Among the departments of J-R Company are a purchasing department, receiving department, accounting department, and finance department. If you were preparing a flowchart of a voucher system to be installed by the company, in which department would you show:

   a. The assembling of the purchase order, receiving report, and vendor's invoice to determine that these documents are in agreement.

   b. The preparation of a cheque.

   c. The signing of a cheque.

   d. The mailing of a cheque to the payee.

   e. The perforation of the voucher and supporting documents.

11–6.   Describe circumstances that might cause a client to understate assets such as cash and marketable securities.

11–7.   What prevents the person who opens incoming mail from being able to abstract cash collections from customers?

11–8.   Prepare a simple illustration of lapping of cash receipts, showing actual transactions and the cash receipts journal entries.

(AICPA, adapted)

11–9. During your audit of a small manufacturing firm, you find numerous cheques of large amount drawn payable to the treasurer and charged to the Miscellaneous Expense account. Does this require any action by the auditor? Explain.

11–10. What information do auditors request from a bank in the standard bank confirmation?

11–11. How can the auditors corroborate compensating balance arrangements?

11–12. What action should be taken by the auditors when the count of cash on hand discloses a shortage?

11–13. State one broad general objective of internal control for each of the following: cash receipts, cash disbursements, and cash balances.

11–14. During your reconciliation of bank accounts in an audit, you find that a number of cheques of small amount have been outstanding for more than a year. Does this situation call for any action by the auditor? Explain.

11–15. Explain the objectives of each of the following audit procedures for cash:

    a. Obtain a cutoff bank statement subsequent to the balance sheet date.

    b. Compare paid cheques returned with bank statement to list of outstanding cheques in previous reconciliation.

    c. Trace all bank transfers during the last week of the audit year and the first week of the following year.

    d. Investigate any cheques representing large or unusual payments to related parties.

11–16. Explain two procedures by which auditors may verify the client's cutoff of cash receipts.

11–17. What is the meaning of the term *window dressing* when used in connection with year-end financial statements? How might the term be related to the making of loans by a corporation to one or more of its executives?

11–18. An audit client that has never before invested in securities recently acquired more than a million dollars in cash from the sale of real estate no longer used in operations. The president intends to invest this money in marketable securities until such time as the opportunity arises for advantageous acquisition of a new plant site. He asks you to enumerate the principal factors you would recommend to create strong internal control over marketable securities.

11–19. What documents should be examined in verifying the purchases and sales of securities made during the year under audit?

11–20. How can the auditors determine that all dividends applicable to marketable securities owned by the client have been received and recorded?

11–21.   What information should be noted by the auditors during their inspection of securities on hand?

11–22.   Assume that it is not possible for you to be present on the balance sheet date to inspect the securities owned by the client. What variation in audit procedures is appropriate if the inspection is not made until two weeks after the balance sheet date?

11–23.   A well-financed audit client of your public accounting firm invests large amounts in marketable securities. As part of its internal control, the company uses a monthly report of securities transactions. The report is prepared by the controller and presented to the investment committee of the board of directors. What information should this report contain?

GROUP II: QUESTIONS REQUIRING ANALYSIS

11–24.   "When auditors are verifying a client's bank reconciliation, they are particularly concerned with the possibility that the list of outstanding cheques may include a nonexistent or fictitious cheque and also are concerned with the possibility of omission from the reconciliation of a deposit in transit." Criticize the above quotation and revise it into an accurate statement.

11–25.   During the first few months of the year, John Smith, the cashier in a small company, was engaged in lapping operations. However, he was able to restore the amount of cash "borrowed" by March 31, and he refrained from any fraudulent acts after that date. Will the year-end audit probably lead to the discovery of his lapping activities? Explain.

11–26.   An assistant auditor received the following instructions from her supervisor: "Here is a cutoff bank statement covering the first seven business days of January. Compare the paid cheques returned with the statement and dated December 31 or earlier with the list of cheques outstanding at December 31." What type of fraud or irregularity might this audit procedure bring to light? Explain.

11–27.   Henry Mills is responsible for preparing cheques, recording cash disbursements, and preparing bank reconciliations for Signet Corporation. While reconciling the October bank statement, Mills noticed that several cheques totaling $937 had been outstanding for more than one year. Concluding that these cheques would never be presented for payment, Mills prepared a cheque for $937 payable to himself, forged the treasurer's signature, and cashed the cheque. Mills made no entry in the accounts for this disbursement and attempted to conceal the theft by destroying the forged cheque and omitting the long-outstanding cheques from subsequent bank reconciliations.

Required:
a. Identify the weaknesses in Signet Corporation's internal control.

b. Explain several audit procedures that might disclose the fraudulent disbursement.

11–28. Fluid Controls, Inc., a manufacturing company, has retained you to perform an audit for the year ended December 31. Prior to the year-end, you begin to obtain an understanding of the new client's internal controls over cash.

You find that nearly all of the company's cash receipts are in the form of cheques received through the mail, but there is no prelisting of cash receipts before they are recorded in the accounts. You find that the incoming mail is opened either by the cashier or by the employee maintaining the accounts receivable subsidiary ledger, depending on which employee has time available. The controller stresses the necessity of flexibility in assignment of duties to the 20 employees comprising the office staff, in order to keep all employees busy and achieve maximum economy of operation.

Required:
a. Explain how the prelisting of cash receipts strengthens internal control.

b. List specific duties that should not be performed by an employee assigned to prelist the cash receipts in order to avoid any opportunity for that employee to conceal embezzlement of cash receipts.

(AICPA, adapted)

11–29. Although the primary objective of an external audit is not the discovery of fraud, the auditors in their work on cash take into consideration the high inherent risk associated with this asset. One evidence of this attitude is evidenced by the auditors' alertness for signs of lapping.

Required:
a. Define **lapping**.

b. Explain the audit procedures that auditors might utilize to uncover lapping.

11–30. During the examination of cash, the auditors are alert for any indications of kiting.

Required:

  a. Define **kiting**.

  b. Explain the audit procedures that should enable the auditors to uncover kiting.

11–31. Explain how each of the following items would appear in a four-column proof of cash for the month of November. Assume the format of the proof of cash begins with bank balances and ends with the unadjusted balances per the accounting records.

  a. Outstanding cheques at November 30.

  b. Deposits-in-transit at October 31.

  c. Cheque issued and paid in November, drawn payable to cash.

  d. The bank returned $1,800 in NSF cheques deposited by the client in November; the client redeposited $1,450 of these cheques in November and $350 in December, making no additional entries in the accounting records.

11–32. During your audit of Miles Company, you prepared the following bank transfer schedule:

Miles Company
Bank Transfer Schedule
December 31, 199X

Cheque Number	Bank Accounts		Amount	Date Disbursed Per		Date Deposited Per	
	From	*To*	*Amount*	*Books*	*Bank*	*Books*	*Bank*
2020	1st Natl.	Suburban	$32,000	Jan. 4	Jan. 5	Dec. 31	Jan. 3
2021	1st Natl.	Capital	21,000	Dec. 31	Jan. 4	Dec. 31	Jan. 3
3217	Royal	Suburban	6,700	Jan. 3	Jan. 5	Jan. 3	Dec. 30
0659	T-D Bank	Suburban	5,500	Dec. 30	Jan. 5	Dec. 30	Jan. 3

Required:

  a. Describe the purpose of a bank transfer schedule.

  b. Identify those transfers that should be investigated and explain the reason.

                (AICPA, adapted)

11–33. In the audit of a client with a fiscal year ending June 30, the auditors obtain a July 10 bank statement directly from the bank. Explain how this cutoff bank statement will be used:

  a. In the review of the June 30 bank reconciliation.

  b. To obtain other audit information.

                (AICPA, adapted)

11–34.   In the audit of Wheat Inc. for the year ended December 31, you discover that the client had been drawing cheques as creditors' invoices became due but had not been mailing the cheques immediately. Because of a working capital shortage, some cheques have been held for two or three weeks.

The client's controller informs you that unmailed cheques totaling $48,500 were on hand at December 31 of the current year. He states that these December-dated cheques had been entered in the cash disbursements journal and charged to the respective creditors' accounts in December because the cheques were prenumbered. However, these cheques were not actually mailed until early January. The controller wants to adjust the cash balance and accounts payable at December 31 by $48,500 because the Cash account had a credit balance. He objects to submitting to his bank the financial statements showing an overdraft of cash.

Discuss the propriety of adjusting the cash balance and accounts payable by the indicated amount of outstanding cheques.

11–35.   Select the best answer for each of the following situations and give reasons for your choice.

   a. You have been assigned to the year-end audit of a client and are planning the timing of audit procedures relating to cash. You decide that it would be preferable for the auditors to:
      (1) Count the cash in advance of the balance sheet date in order to disclose any kiting operations at year-end.
      (2) Coordinate the count of cash with the cutoff of accounts payable.
      (3) Coordinate the count of cash with the count of marketable securities and other negotiable assets.
      (4) Count the cash immediately upon the return of the bank confirmation.

   b. To gather evidence on the balance per bank in a bank reconciliation, the auditors would examine all of the following *except:*
      (1) Cutoff bank statement.
      (2) Year-end bank statement.
      (3) Bank confirmation.
      (4) General ledger.

   c. The mailing of disbursement cheques and remittance advices should be controlled by the employee who:
      (1) Signed the cheques.
      (2) Approved the vouchers for payment.
      (3) Matched the receiving reports, purchase orders, and vendors' invoices.
      (4) Verified the mathematical accuracy of the vouchers and remittance advices.

d. Which of the following is an internal control procedure that would prevent a paid voucher from being presented for payment a second time?
(1) Vouchers should be prepared by individuals who are responsible for signing cheques.
(2) Vouchers should be approved by at least two responsible officials.
(3) The date on a voucher should be within a few days of the date the voucher is presented for payment.
(4) The official signing the cheque should compare the cheque with the voucher and should perforate or otherwise deface the voucher and supporting documents.

e. In order to guard against the misappropriation of company-owned marketable securities, which of the following is the *best* course of action that can be taken by a company with a large portfolio of marketable securities?
(1) Require that one trustworthy and bonded employee be responsible for access to the safekeeping area where securities are kept.
(2) Require that employees who enter and leave the safekeeping area sign and record in a log the exact reason for their access.
(3) Require that employees involved in the safekeeping function maintain a subsidiary control ledger for securities on a current basis.
(4) Require that the safekeeping function for securities be assigned to a bank or stockbroker that will act as a custodial agent.

f. Hall Company had large amounts of funds to invest on a temporary basis. The board of directors decided to purchase marketable securities and assigned the future purchase and sale decisions to a responsible financial executive. The best person(s) to make periodic reviews of the investment activity would be:
(1) An investment committee of the board of directors.
(2) The chief operating officer.
(3) The corporate controller.
(4) The treasurer.

GROUP III: PROBLEMS

11–36. The Art Appreciation Society operates a museum for the benefit and enjoyment of the community. During hours when the museum is open to the public, two clerks who are positioned at the entrance collect a five-dollar admission fee from each nonmember patron. Members of the Art Appreciation Society are permitted to enter free of charge upon presentation of their membership cards.

At the end of each day, one of the clerks delivers the proceeds to the treasurer. The treasurer counts the cash in the presence of the clerk and places it in a safe. Each Friday afternoon the treasurer and one of the clerks deliver all cash held in the safe to the bank, and receive an authenticated deposit slip that provides the basis for the weekly entry in the cash receipts journal.

The board of directors of the Art Appreciation Society has identified a need to improve their internal control over cash admission fees. The board has determined that the cost of installing turnstiles, sales booths, or otherwise altering the physical layout of the museum will greatly exceed any benefits which may be derived. However, the board has agreed that the sale of admission tickets must be an integral part of its improvement efforts.

Smith has been asked by the board of directors of the Art Appreciation Society to review the internal control over cash admission fees and provide suggestions for improvement.

Required:
Indicate weaknesses in the existing internal control over cash admission fees, which Smith should identify, and recommend one improvement for each of the weaknesses identified.

Organize the answer as indicated in the following illustrative example:

Weakness	Recommendation
1. There is no documentation to establish the number of paying patrons.	1. Prenumbered admission tickets should be issued upon payment of the admission fee.

11–37. The following are typical questions that might appear on an internal control questionnaire for marketable securities.

1. Is custody of investment securities maintained by an employee who does not maintain the detailed records of the securities?

2. Are securities registered in the company name?

Required:
a. Describe the purpose of each of the above internal control procedures.
b. Describe the manner in which each of the above procedures might be tested.
c. Assuming that the operating effectiveness of each of the above procedures is found to be inadequate, describe how the audi-

tors might alter their substantive tests to compensate for the increased level of control risk.

11–38. John Harris, CA, has been engaged to audit the financial statements of the Spartan Drug Store, Inc. Spartan is a medium-sized retail outlet that sells a wide variety of consumer goods. All sales are for cash or cheque. Cashiers utilize cash registers to process these transactions. There are no receipts by mail and there are no credit card or charge sales.

Required:
Construct the ''processing cash collections'' segment of the internal control questionnaire on ''Cash Receipts'' to be used in the evaluation of the internal control for the Spartan Drug Store, Inc. Each question should elicit either a yes or no response. Do **not** discuss the internal controls over cash sales.

(AICPA, adapted)

11–39. The following client-prepared bank reconciliation is being examined by Kautz, CA, during an examination of the financial statements of Cynthia Company:

CYNTHIA COMPANY
Bank Reconciliation
Village Bank Account 2
December 31, 199X

Balance per bank (*a*)		$18,375.91
Deposits in transit (*b*):		
Dec. 30...	$1,471.10	
Dec. 31...	2,840.69	4,311.79
Subtotal...		22,687.70
Outstanding cheques (*c*):		
837...	6,000.00	
1941..	671.80	
1966..	320.00	
1984..	1,855.42	
1985..	3,621.22	
1987..	2,576.89	
1991..	4,420.88	(19,466.21)
Subtotal...		3,221.49
NSF cheque returned:		
Dec. 29 (*d*)		200.00
Bank charges...		5.50
Error Cheque No. 1932		148.10

Customer note collected by the bank ($2,750 plus $275 interest) (*e*)................................	(3,025.00)
Balance per books (*f*).............................	$ 550.09

Required:
Indicate one or more audit procedures that should be performed by Kautz in gathering evidence in support of each of the items, (*a*) through (*f*) above.

(AICPA, adapted)

11–40. The cashier of Mission Corporation intercepted customer A's cheque, payable to the company in the amount of $500, and deposited it in a bank account that was part of the company petty cash fund, of which he was custodian. He then drew a $500 cheque on the petty cash fund bank account payable to himself, signed it, and cashed it. At the end of the month, while processing the monthly statements to customers, he was able to change the statement to customer A to show that A had received credit for the $500 cheque that had been intercepted. Ten days later he made an entry in the cash receipts journal that purported to record receipt of a remittance of $500 from customer A, thus restoring A's account to its proper balance but overstating cash in the bank. He covered the overstatement by omitting from the list of outstanding cheques in the bank reconciliation two cheques, the aggregate amount of which was $500.

Required:
Discuss briefly what you regard as the more important deficiencies in internal control in the above situation and in addition include what you consider a proper remedy for each deficiency.

(AICPA, adapted)

11–41. You are the senior in charge of the July 31, 199X, audit of Reliable Auto Parts, Inc. Your newly hired staff assistant reports to you that she is unable to complete the four-column proof of cash for the month of April 199X, which you instructed her to do as part of the consideration of internal control for cash.

Your assistant shows you the following working paper that she has prepared:

RELIABLE AUTO PARTS, INC.
Proof of Cash for April 199X
For the Year Ended July 31, 199X

	Balance Mar. 31 9X	Deposits	Cheques	Balance Apr. 30 9X
Per bank statement	71,682.84	61,488.19	68,119.40	65,051.63
Deposits in transit:				
At Mar 31 9X	2,118.18			(2,118.18)
At Apr 30 9X		4,918.16		4,918.16
Outstanding cheques:				
At Mar 31 9X	(14,888.16)		14,888.16	
At Apr 30 9X			(22,914.70)	22,914.70
Bank service charges:				
March 199X	(22.18)		22.18	
April 199X			(19.14)	19.14
Note receivable collected by bank Apr 30 9X		18,180.00		18,180.00
NSF cheque of customer L. G. Waite, charged back by bank Mar 31, 9X, redeposited and cleared Apr 3, 9X	(418.19)	418.19		
Balances as computed	58,472.49	85,004.54	60,095.90	108,965.45
Balances per books	59,353.23	45,689.98	76,148.98	28,894.23
Unlocated difference	(880.74)	39,314.56	(16,053.08)	80,071.22

Your review of your assistant's work reveals that the dollar amounts of all of the items in her working paper are correct. You learn that the accountant for Reliable Auto Parts, Inc., makes no journal entries for bank services charges or note collections until the month following the bank's recording of the item and that Reliable's accountant makes no journal entries whatsoever for NSF cheques that are redeposited and cleared.

Required:
Prepare a corrected four-column proof of cash in good form for Reliable Auto Parts, Inc., for the month of April 199X.

11–42. During the audit of Sunset Building Supply, you are given the following year-end bank reconciliation prepared by the client:

SUNSET BUILDING SUPPLY
Bank Reconciliation
December 31

Balance per Dec. 31 bank statement	$48,734
Add: Deposits in transit	4,467
	53,201
Less: Cheques outstanding	20,758
Balance per ledger, Dec. 31	$32,443

According to the client's accounting records, cheques totaling $31,482 were issued between January 1 and January 14 of the following year. You have obtained a cutoff bank statement dated January 14 containing paid cheques amounting to $50,440. Of the cheques outstanding at December 31, $3,600 were not returned in the cutoff statement, and of those issued per the accounting records in January, $8,200 were not returned.

Required:

a. Prepare a working paper comparing (1) the total of all cheques returned by the bank or still outstanding with (2) the total per the client's records of cheques outstanding at December 31 plus cheques issued from January 1 to January 14.

b. Suggest four possible explanations for the situation disclosed in your working paper. State what action you would take in each case, including any adjusting entry you would propose.

11–43. MLG Company's auditor received confirmations and cutoff statements with related cheques and deposit slips for MLG's three general-purpose bank accounts directly from the banks. The auditor determined that internal control over cash was satisfactory and will be relied upon. The proper cutoff of external cash receipts and disbursements was established. No bank accounts were opened or closed during the year.

Required:
Prepare the audit program of substantive procedures to verify MLG's bank balances. Ignore any other cash accounts.

(AICPA, adapted)

11–44. You are in charge of the audit of the financial statements of Hawk Corporation for the year ended December 31. The corporation has had the policy of investing its surplus cash in marketable securities. Its stock and bond certificates are kept in a safety-deposit box in a local bank. Only the president or the treasurer of the corporation has access to the box.

You were unable to obtain access to the safety-deposit box on December 31 because neither the president nor the treasurer was available. Arrangements were made for your staff assistant to accompany the treasurer to the bank on January 11 to examine the securities. Your assistant has never examined securities that were being kept in a safety-deposit box and requires instructions. To inspect all the securities on hand should not require more than one hour.

Required:
a. List the instructions that you would give to your assistant regarding the examination of the stock and bond certificates kept in the safety-deposit box. Include in your instructions the details of the securities to be examined and the reasons for examining these details.
b. Upon returning from the bank, your assistant reported that the treasurer had entered the box on January 4. The treasurer stated that the purpose of the January 4 visit to the safety-deposit box had been to remove an old photograph of the corporation's original building. The photograph was reportedly loaned to the local chamber of commerce for display purposes. List the additional audit procedures that are required because of the treasurer's action.

(AICPA, adapted)

GROUP IV: ANALYTICAL AND DISCUSSION CASE

11–45. On October 21, Rand & Brink, a CA firm, was retained by Suncraft Appliance Corporation to perform an audit for the year ended December 31. A month later James Minor, president of the corporation, invited the CA firm's partners, George Rand and Alice Brink, to attend a meeting of all officers of the corporation. Mr. Minor opened the meeting with the following statement:

"All of you know that we are not in a very liquid position, and our October 31 balance sheet shows it. We need to raise some outside capital in February, and our December 31 financial statements (both balance sheet and income statement) must look reasonably good if we're going to make a favourable impression upon lenders or investors. I want every officer of this company to do everything possible during the next month to ensure that, at December 31, our financial statements look as strong as possible, especially our current position and our earnings.

"I have invited our auditors to attend this meeting so they will understand the reason for some year-end transactions that might be a little unusual. It is essential that our financial statements carry the auditors' approval, or we'll never be able to get the financing we need. Now what suggestions can you offer?"

The vice president for sales was the first to offer suggestions: "I can talk some of our large customers into placing some orders in December that they wouldn't ordinarily place until the first part of next year. If we get those extra orders shipped, it will increase this year's earnings and also increase our current assets."

The vice president in charge of production commented: "We can ship every order we have now and every order we get during December before the close of business on December 31. We'll have to pay some overtime in our shipping department, but we'll try not to have a single unshipped order on hand at year-end. Also, we could overship some orders, and the customers wouldn't make returns until January."

The controller spoke next: "If there are late December orders from customers that we can't actually ship, we can just label the merchandise as sold and bill the customers with December 31 sales invoices. Also, there are always some cheques from customers dated December 31 that don't reach us until January— some as late as January 10. We can record all those customers' cheques bearing dates of late December as part of our December 31 cash balance."

The treasurer offered the following suggestions: "I owe the company $50,000 on a call note I issued to buy some of our stock. I can borrow $50,000 from my mother-in-law about Christmas time and repay my note to the company. However, I'll have to borrow the money from the company again early in January, because my mother-in-law is buying an apartment building and will need the $50,000 back by January 15.

"Another thing we can do to improve our current ratio is to write cheques on December 31 to pay most of our current liabilities. We might even wait to mail the cheques for a few days or mail them to the wrong addresses. That will give time for the January cash receipts to cover the December 31 cheques."

The vice president of production made two final suggestions: "Some of our inventory, which we had tentatively identified as obsolete, does not represent an open and shut case of being unsalable. We could defer any write-down until next year. Another item is some machinery we have ordered for delivery in December. We could instruct the manufacturer not to ship the machines and not to bill us before January.''

After listening to these suggestions, the president, James Minor, spoke directly to Rand and Brink, the auditors. ''You can see I'm doing my best to give you full information and cooperation. If any of these suggested actions would prevent you from giving a clean bill of health to our year-end statements, I want to know about it now so we can avoid doing anything that would keep you from issuing an unqualified audit report. I know you'll be doing a lot of preliminary work here before December 31, but I'd like for you not to bill us before January. Will you please give us your reactions to what has been said in this meeting?''

Required:

a. Put yourself in the role of Rand & Brink, CAs, and evaluate **separately** each suggestion made in the meeting. What general term is applicable to most of the suggested actions?

b. Could you assure the client that an unqualified audit report would be issued if your recommendations were followed on all the matters discussed? Explain.

c. Would the discussion in this meeting cause you to withdraw from the engagement?

Chapter 12

Accounts Receivable, Notes Receivable, and Sales Transactions

Chapter Objectives

After studying this chapter, you should be able to:

- Describe the nature of receivables.
- Explain the nature of the sales (revenue) and collection transaction cycle.
- Identify and explain the fundamental internal controls over sales transactions and receivables.
- Describe the auditors' objectives for the audit of receivables and sales.
- Describe the nature of the audit procedures to accomplish the auditors' objectives for the audit of receivables and sales.

Because sales transactions and receivables from customers are so closely related, the two can best be considered jointly in a discussion of auditing objectives and procedures. In broad terms, the sales and collection cycle includes the receiving of orders from customers, the delivery and billing of merchandise to customers, and the recording and collection of accounts receivable. Receivables from customers include both accounts receivable and various types of notes receivable.

RECEIVABLES

Sources and Nature of Accounts Receivable

Accounts receivable include not only claims against customers arising from the sale of goods or services, but also a variety of miscellaneous claims such as loans to officers or employees, loans to subsidiaries, stock subscriptions receivable, claims against various other firms, claims for tax refunds, and advances to suppliers.

Trade notes and accounts receivable usually are relatively large in amount and should appear as separate items in the current assets section of the balance sheet at their net realizable value. Auditors are especially concerned with the presentation and disclosure of loans to officers, directors, and affiliated companies. These related party transactions are commonly made for the convenience of the borrower rather than to benefit the lending company. Consequently, such loans are often collected only at the convenience of the borrower. It is a basic tenet of financial statement presentation that transactions not characterized by arm's-length bargaining should be fully disclosed.

Sources and Nature of Notes Receivable

Typically, notes receivable are used for handling transactions of substantial amount; these negotiable documents are widely used by both industrial and commercial concerns. In banks and finance companies, notes receivable usually constitute the single most important asset.

An instalment note or contract is a negotiable instrument that grants possession of the goods to the purchaser but permits the seller to retain a lien on the goods until the final instalment under the note has been received. Instalment notes are widely used in the sale of industrial machinery, farm equipment, and automobiles. Other transactions that may lead to the acquisition of notes receivable include the disposal of items of plant and equipment, the sale of divisions of a company, the issuance of capital stock, and the making of loans to officers, employees, and affiliated companies.

The Auditors' Objectives in Examination of Receivables and Sales

The auditors' *objectives* in the examination of receivables and sales are:

1. To consider *internal control* over receivables and sales transactions.
2. To determine the *existence* of receivables, the client's *ownership* of these assets, and the *occurrence* of sales transactions.

3. To establish the ***completeness*** of receivables and sales transactions.
4. To establish the ***clerical accuracy*** of records and supporting schedules of receivables and sales.
5. To determine that the ***valuation*** of receivables is at appropriate net realizable values.
6. To determine that the ***statement presentation*** of receivables and sales is adequate, including the separation of receivables into appropriate categories, and adequate reporting of any receivables pledged as collateral, and related party sales and receivables.

Internal Control of Sales Transactions and Accounts Receivable

Our discussion of internal control will be developed primarily in terms of the sales activities of manufacturing companies. When internal controls over sales on account are inadequate, large credit losses are almost inevitable. For example, merchandise may be shipped to customers whose credit standing has not been approved. Shipments may be made to customers without notice being given to the billing department; consequently, no sales invoice is prepared. Sales invoices may contain errors in prices and quantities, and if sales invoices are not controlled by serial numbers, some may be lost and never recorded as accounts receivable. To avoid such difficulties, strong internal controls over credit sales are necessary. Usually internal control over credit sales is strengthened by a division of duties so that different departments or individuals are responsible for (1) preparation of the sales order, (2) credit approval, (3) issuance of merchandise from stock, (4) shipment, (5) billing, (6) invoice verification, (7) maintenance of control accounts, (8) maintenance of customers' ledgers, (9) approval of sales returns and allowances, and (10) authorization of write-offs of uncollectible accounts. When this degree of subdivision of duties is feasible, accidental errors are likely to be detected quickly through the comparison of documents and amounts emerging from independent units of the company, and the opportunity for fraud is reduced to a minimum.

Controlling Customers' Orders.   The controlling and processing of orders received from customers require carefully designed operating procedures and numerous control devices if costly errors are to be avoided. Important initial steps include the registering of the customer's purchase order, a review of items and quantities to determine whether the order can be filled within a reasonable time, and the preparation of a sales order. The sales order is a translation of the terms of the customer's order into a set of specific instructions for the guidance of various divisions, including the credit, finished goods stores, shipping, billing, and accounts receivable units. The action to be taken by the factory upon receipt of a sales order will depend upon whether the goods are standard products carried in stock or are to be produced to specifications set by the customer.

Credit Approval.   Before sales orders are processed, the credit department must determine whether goods may be shipped to the customer on open account. This department is supervised by a credit manager who reports to the treasurer or the vice president of finance. The credit department implements management's credit policies and uses them to evaluate prospective and continuing customers by studying the customer's financial statements and by reference to reports of credit agencies, such as Dun & Bradstreet.

Issuing Merchandise.   Companies that carry standard products in stock maintain a finished goods storeroom supervised by a storeskeeper. The storeskeeper issues the goods covered by a sales order to the shipping department only after the sales order has been approved by the credit department. Perpetual inventory records of finished goods should be maintained in the accounting department, not by the storeskeeper.

The Shipping Function.   When the goods are transmitted by the finished goods storeroom to the shipping department, this group must arrange for space in railroad cars, aircraft, or motor freight carriers. Shipping documents, such as bills of lading, are created at the time of loading the goods into cars or trucks. The shipping documents are numerically controlled and are entered in a shipping register before being forwarded to the billing department. When shipments are made by truck, some type of gate control is also needed to ensure that all goods leaving the plant have been recorded as shipments. This may require the surrender to the gatekeeper of special copies of shipping documents.

The Billing Function.   The term *billing* means notifying the customer of the amount due for goods or services delivered. This notification is accomplished by preparing and mailing a sales invoice. Billing should be performed by a department not under the control of sales executives. The function is generally assigned to a separate section within the accounting, data processing, or finance departments. The billing section has the responsibility of (1) accounting for the serially numbered shipping documents, (2) comparing shipping documents with sales orders and customers' purchase orders and change notices, (3) entering pertinent data from these documents on the sales invoice, (4) applying prices and discounts from price lists to the invoice, (5) making the necessary extensions and footings, and (6) accumulating the total amounts billed. In the case of government contracts, the formal contract usually specifies prices, delivery procedures, inspection and acceptance routines, method of liquidating advances, and numerous other details, so that the contract is a more important source of information for preparation of the sales invoice.

Before invoices are mailed to customers, they should be reviewed to determine the propriety and accuracy of prices, credit terms, transportation charges, extensions, and footings. Daily totals of amounts invoiced should be transmitted directly to the general ledger accounting section for entry in controlling accounts on a daily, weekly, or monthly basis. Copies of individual invoices should be transmitted to the accounts receivable section under the control of transmittal letters, with a listing by serial number of all invoices being submitted. These invoice copies may be used to post the individual accounts receivable ledger accounts.

Under this system the general ledger and the subsidiary ledger for accounts receivable are developed from separate data by employees working independently of each other, thus assuring detection of accidental errors. The subsidiary ledger should be balanced periodically with the control account by an employee from the operations control group.

Collection of Receivables.   Most receivables held by manufacturing companies are collected by receipt of customers' cheques and remittance advices through the mails. The cashier will control and deposit cheques. The remittance advices or a listing of the receipts will be forwarded to the accounts receivable section or the data processing department, which will record them in the appropriate accounts in the customers' ledger. The total reduction in accounts receivable will be posted periodically to the general ledger control account from the total of the accounts receivable column in the cash receipts journal. Internal control over collections from customers is shown in the cash receipt flowchart in Figure 11–1 of Chapter 11.

An *aged trial balance* of customers' accounts should be prepared at regular intervals for use by the credit department in carrying out its collection program.

Write-Off of Receivables.   Receivables judged by management to be uncollectible should be written off (after review by the credit department). The accounts will then either be turned over to a collection agency or retained and transferred to a separate ledger and control account. The records may be of a memorandum nature rather than part of the regular accounting system. Also, when possible—generally when the debtor is still in existence—statements requesting payment should continue to be mailed. Otherwise, any subsequent collections may be abstracted by employees without the necessity of any falsification of the records to conceal the theft.

Internal Audit of Receivables.   In some companies, the internal auditors periodically take over the mailing of monthly statements to customers or send confirmations to them and investigate any discrepancies reported;

FIGURE 12–1

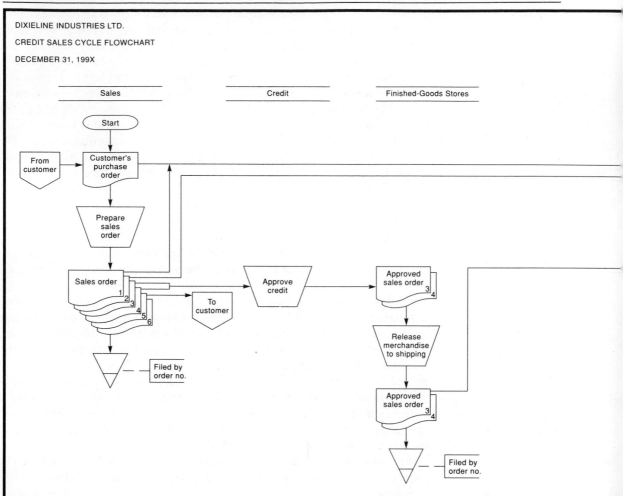

DIXIELINE INDUSTRIES LTD.

CREDIT SALES CYCLE FLOWCHART

DECEMBER 31, 199X

FIGURE 12–1 (*concluded*)

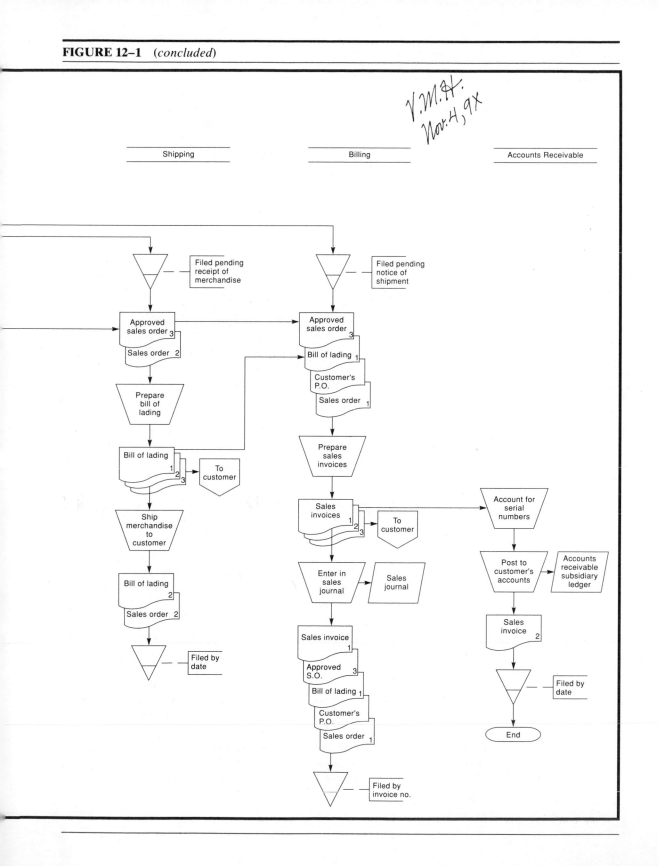

they also make extensive reviews of shipping reports, invoices, credit memoranda, and aged trial balances of receivables to determine whether authorized procedures are being carried out effectively and consistently.

The division of responsibility, sequence of procedures, and basic documentation of the handling of credit sales transactions are illustrated in the systems flowcharts in Figure 12–1.

Internal Control of Notes Receivable

As previously stated, a basic characteristic of internal control consists of the subdivision of duties. As applied to notes receivable, this principle requires that:

1. The custodian of notes receivable not have access to cash or to the general accounting records.
2. The acceptance and renewal of notes be authorized in writing by a responsible official who does not have custody of the notes.
3. The write-off of defaulted notes be approved in writing by responsible officials and effective procedures adopted for subsequent follow-up of such defaulted notes.

These rules are obviously corollaries of the general proposition that the authorization and recording functions should be entirely separate from the custodial function, especially for cash and receivables.

If the acceptance of a note from a customer requires written approval of a responsible official, the likelihood of fictitious notes being created to offset a theft of cash is materially reduced. The same review and approval should be required for renewal of a note; otherwise, an opportunity is created for the diversion of cash when a note is collected and the concealment of a shortage by unauthorized renewal of the paid note. The protection given by this procedure for executive approval of notes will be stronger if the internal auditing department periodically confirms notes directly with the makers.

The abstraction of cash receipts is sometimes concealed by failing to make any entry to record receipt of a partial payment on a note. Satisfactory control procedures for recording partial payments require that the date and amount of the payment and the new unpaid balance should be entered on the back of the instrument, with proper credit being given the debtor in the note register. Notes written off as uncollectible should be kept under accounting control because occasionally debtors may attempt to reestablish their credit in later years by paying old dishonored notes. Any credit memoranda or journal vouchers for partial payments, write-offs, or adjustment of disputed notes should be authorized by proper officials and kept under numerical control.

Adequate internal controls over notes receivable secured by mortgages and trust deeds must include follow-up procedures that assure prompt action on delinquent property taxes and insurance premiums, as well as for nonpayment of interest and principal instalments.

In many companies, internal control is strengthened by the preparation of monthly reports summarizing notes receivable transactions during the month and the details of notes owned at the end of the reporting period. These reports are often designed to focus executive attention immediately upon any delinquent notes and to require advance approval for renewals of maturing notes. In addition, a monthly report on notes receivable ordinarily will show the amounts collected during the month, the new notes accepted, notes discounted, and interest earned. The person responsible for reporting on note transactions should be someone other than the custodian of the notes.

Internal Control and the Computer

EDP systems permit instantaneous verification of customers' credit when the sales order is entered by the sales department. The computer automatically prints out a list of authorized sales for release and shipment by the finished-goods stores and shipping departments. As the goods are shipped, personnel enter the details on computer terminals, allowing the computer to update the perpetual inventory records. Then the computer compares the details of the actual shipments to authorized amounts, prepares the sales invoices, records the sales transactions, and posts to the subsidiary and general ledger accounts. At the end of the month, the computer also generates statements for mailing to customers. In these systems, the risk of clerical errors is significantly reduced. However, auditors must consider the essential internal controls over EDP operations, especially those controls over the accuracy of data entered into the system, and the improper access to the data after it is entered.

Audit Working Papers for Receivables and Sales

Besides preparing lead schedules for receivables and net sales, the auditors obtain or prepare the following working papers, among others:

1. Aged trial balance of trade accounts receivable (often a computer printout).
2. Analyses of other accounts receivable.
3. Analysis of notes receivable and related interest.
4. Analysis of allowance for uncollectible accounts and notes.
5. Comparative analyses of sales transactions by month, product, or territory, or by relating forecasted sales to actual sales.

AUDIT PROGRAM FOR RECEIVABLES AND SALES TRANSACTIONS

The following audit procedures are typical of the work done in the verification of notes, accounts receivable, and sales transactions.

A. Consider internal control for receivables and sales.

1. *Obtain an understanding of internal control* for receivables and sales.
2. *Assess control risk* and *design additional tests of controls* for receivables and sales.
3. *Perform additional tests of controls* for those controls which the auditors plan to consider in their assessment of control risk, such as:
   - *a.* Examine significant aspects of a sample of sales transactions.
   - *b.* Compare a sample of shipping documents to related sales invoices.
   - *c.* Review the use and authorization of credit memoranda.
   - *d.* Reconcile selected cash register tapes and sales invoices with sales journals.
4. *Reassess control risk* and *design substantive tests* for receivables and sales.

B. Perform substantive tests of receivables and sales transactions.

5. Obtain an aged trial balance of trade accounts receivables and analyses of other accounts receivable and reconcile to ledgers.
6. Obtain analyses of notes receivable and related interest.
7. Inspect notes on hand and confirm those not on hand with holders.
8. Confirm receivables with debtors.
9. Review the year-end cutoff of sales transactions.
10. Perform analytical procedures for accounts receivable, sales, notes receivable, and interest revenue.
11. Verify interest earned on notes and accrued interest receivable.
12. Evaluate the propriety of the client's accounting for receivables and sales.
13. Determine adequacy of allowance for uncollectible accounts.
14. Ascertain whether any receivables have been pledged.
15. Investigate any notes or accounts receivable from related parties.
16. Evaluate financial statement presentation and disclosure of receivables and sales.

Figure 12–2 relates these major substantive tests of receivables and sales to their primary audit objectives.

A. Consider internal control for receivables and sales.

1. Obtain an understanding of internal control.

The auditors' consideration of internal controls over receivables and sales may begin with the preparation of a written narrative or flowchart and the completion of an internal control questionnaire. Typical of the ques-

FIGURE 12–2   Objectives of Major Substantive Tests of Receivables and Sales Transactions

Substantive Tests	Primary Audit Objectives
Obtain aged listing of receivables and reconcile to ledgers Obtain analyses of notes receivable and related interest	*Clerical accuracy*
Inspect notes on hand and confirm those not on hand Confirm receivables with debtors	*Existence, occurrence, and ownership*
Review the year-end cutoff of sales transactions Perform analytical procedures Verify interest earned on notes receivable	*Existence, occurrence, and ownership* *Completeness*
Evaluate the propriety of client's accounting for transactions Determine adequacy of allowance for uncollectible accounts	*Valuation*
Ascertain the existence of pledged receivables Investigate receivables from related parties Evaluate financial statement presentation and disclosure	*Statement presentation*

tions comprising an internal control questionnaire for sales and receivables are the following: Are orders from customers initiated and reviewed by the sales department? Are sales invoices prenumbered and all numbers accounted for? Are all sales approved by the credit department before shipment?

After the auditors have prepared a flowchart (or other description) of the internal control policies, systems, and procedures, they will determine whether the client is actually using the policies, systems, and procedures—that is, whether they have been *placed in operation.*

As the auditors confirm their understanding of the sales and collections cycle, they will observe whether there is an appropriate segregation of duties, and enquire as to who performed various functions throughout the year. They will also perform a walk-through of the cycle; inspect various documents, such as bills of lading, sales invoices, and customer statements; and review document files to determine that the client is appropriately accounting for the sequence of prenumbered documents.

Sales forecasts or budgets will be examined and the auditors will review the evidence of follow-up on variances from forecasted amounts. These tests of controls may provide the auditors with sufficient evidence to assess control risk for certain financial statement assertions about receivables and sales at less than the maximum.

2. Assess control risk and design additional tests of controls.

After obtaining an understanding of the client's internal control for receivables and sales transactions, the auditors perform their initial assessments of control risk for the various financial statement assertions. To further evaluate these assessments, the auditors may decide to obtain additional evidence about the operating effectiveness of the client's internal control policies, systems, and procedures by designing additional tests of controls. In designing these tests, the auditors must decide which ones will result in sufficient reductions in substantive tests to justify the time spent performing them.

3. Perform additional tests of controls.

Tests directed toward the effectiveness of controls help to evaluate the client's internal control, and determine the extent to which the auditors are justified in reducing their assessed levels of control risk for the assertions about the receivables and sales accounts. Certain tests of controls are performed as the auditors obtain an understanding of the client's internal control, and were described in our discussion of that process. The following are examples of typical additional tests.

a. Examine significant aspects of a sample of sales transactions.

To determine that the internal controls portrayed in the flowchart are actually functioning in everyday operations, the auditors will examine significant aspects of a sample of sales transactions. The size of the sample and the transactions included therein may be determined by either statistical or nonstatistical sampling techniques. The auditors often use generalized computer audit programs to select the transactions to be tested.

In manufacturing companies, the audit procedure for verification of a sales transaction that has been selected for testing may begin with a comparison of the customer's purchase order, the client's sales order, and the duplicate copy of the sales invoice. The descriptions of items and the quantities, as well as the customer's name and address, are compared on these three documents and traced to the duplicate copy of the related shipping document. The credit manager's signature denoting approval of the customer's credit should appear on the sales order.

The extensions and footings on each invoice in the sample should be proved to be arithmetically correct. In addition, the date of each invoice should be compared with two other dates:

1. The date on the related shipping document.
2. The date of entry in the accounts receivable subsidiary ledger.

Consistent pricing and sales discount policies are a necessary element of good internal control over sales transactions. After discussing the policies with management, prices and discounts on the invoices selected for testing can be verified by comparison with authorized price lists, catalogues, or contracts with customers. After proving the accuracy of selected individual invoices, the auditors next trace the invoices to the sales journal and to posting in the accounts receivable subsidiary ledger.

When performing tests of sales transactions, the auditors should be alert for indications of consigned shipments treated as sales. Some companies that dispose of only a small portion of their total output by consignment fail to make any distinction between consignment shipments and regular sales.

If the subsidiary records for receivables include some accounts with large debit entries and more numerous small credit entries, this should suggest to the auditors that goods have been shipped on consignment and that payments are being received only as the consignee makes sales. Notations such as "Consignment shipment" or "On approval" are sometimes found in subsidiary ledgers or on the duplicate copies of sales invoices. Numerous large returns of merchandise are also suggestive of consignment shipments.

The auditors should also investigate the controls for sales to related parties. Effective control over intercompany or interbranch transfers of merchandise often requires the same kind of formal procedures for billing, shipping, and collection functions as for sales to outsiders; hence, these movements of merchandise are often invoiced and recorded as sales. When the operations of the several organizational units are combined or consolidated into one income statement, however, it is apparent that any transactions not representing sales to outsiders should be eliminated from consolidated sales. In the examination of a client that operates subsidiaries or branches, the auditors should investigate the procedures for recording movements of merchandise among the various units of the company.

b. **Compare a sample of shipping documents to related sales invoices.**

The preceding step in the audit program called for an examination of selected sales transactions and a comparison of the invoices with sales records and shipping documents. That procedure would not, however, disclose orders that had been shipped but not billed. To assure that all shipments are billed, the auditors may obtain a sample of shipping documents issued during the year and compare these to sales invoices. In making this test, particular emphasis should be placed upon accounting for all shipping documents by serial number. Any voided shipping documents should have been mutilated and retained in the files. The purposeful or accidental destruction of shipping documents before the creation of a sales invoice might go undetected if this type of test were not made. Correlation of serial numbers of sales orders, shipping advices, and sales invoices is highly desirable.

c. **Review the use and authorization of credit memoranda.**

All allowances to customers for returned or defective merchandise should be supported by serially numbered credit memoranda signed by an

FIGURE 12–3 Assessing Control Risk for Receivables and Sales

Internal Control Policy, System, or Procedure	Typical Tests of the Control Policy, System, or Procedure	Financial Statement Assertions				
		Existence	Completeness	Ownership	Valuation	Presentation
Segregate duties over sales and collections of receivables	Observe and make enquiries about the performance of various functions	X	X	X		
Use control listing to control cash collections	Observe, make enquiries about the process, and agree selected listings to bank and accounting records	X	X	X	X	
Obtain credit approval of sales prior to shipment	Make enquiries about credit policies; select a sample of sales transactions and examine evidence of credit approval				X	
Use prenumbered shipping and billing documents and account for the sequence	Observe and make enquiries about the use of prenumbered documents and inspect evidence of accounting for the sequence		X			

Control procedure	Audit procedure			
Match sales invoices with shipping documents	Select a sample of sales invoices and compare details to shipping documents		X	X
Review invoices after preparation for clerical accuracy and agreement to sales and shipping documents and authorized price lists	Select a sample of sales invoices, agree the details to supporting documents and test prices and clerical accuracy	X	X	
Mail monthly statements to customers and follow up on errors reported	Observe and make enquiries about the mailing of statements and review evidence of follow-up	X	X	
Use aged-trial balances and various procedures to follow up on collections	Inspect aged trial balances and enquire about follow-up procedures on collections		X	
Use sales budgets and analyze variances from actual sales	Examine budgets and evidence of follow-up on variances	X	X	

officer or responsible employee having no duties relating to handling cash or to the maintenance of customers' ledgers. Good internal control over credits for returned merchandise usually includes a requirement that the returned goods be received and examined before credit is given. The memoranda should then bear the date and serial number of the receiving report on the return shipment.

In addition to establishing that credit memoranda were properly authorized, the auditors should make tests of these documents similar to those suggested for sales invoices. Prices, extensions, and footings should be verified, and postings traced from the sales return journal or other accounting record to the customers' accounts in the subsidiary receivable ledgers.

d. **Reconcile selected cash register tapes and sales invoices with sales journals.**

In the audit of clients that make a substantial amount of sales for cash, the auditors may compare selected daily totals in the sales journal with cash register readings or tapes. The serial numbers of all sales invoices used during the selected periods should be accounted for and the individual invoices examined for accuracy of calculations and traced to the sales summary or journal.

4. Reassess control risk and design substantive tests.

When the auditors have completed the procedures described in the preceding sections, they should assess the extent of control risk for each financial statement assertion regarding receivables and sales transactions.

These assessments will determine the nature, timing, and extent of the auditors' substantive tests for receivables and sales. Figure 12–3 summarizes the relationship between these assertions, the internal control policies, systems, and procedures, and typical tests of controls. This figure illustrates which internal control policies, systems, and procedures affect the auditors' assessment of control risk for the various assertions.

B. Substantive tests.

6. Obtain an aged trial balance of trade accounts receivable and analyses of other accounts receivable and reconcile to ledgers.

An aged trial balance of trade accounts receivable at the audit date is commonly prepared by employees of the client for the auditors, often in the form of a computer printout. The client-prepared schedule illustrated in Figure 12–4 is a multipurpose format designed to display the aging of customers' accounts, the estimate of probable credit losses, and the confirmation control information. The summary of so many phases of the examination of receivables in a single working paper is practicable only for small concerns with a limited number of customers. If the client has any accounts receivable other than trade accounts, the auditors also should obtain similar analyses of those accounts.

FIGURE 12–4

The Coast Company
Acct. No. 121 — Accounts Receivable—Trade — G-1
December 31, 199X

| Confirmation No. | Customer | Balance Dec. 31, 9X | Billed In | | | Prior Months | Credit Balances | Collections Subsequent to Dec. 31, 9X | Estimated Loss Acct. No. 125 |
			December	November	October				
1	Adams & Sons	CX $8,255.60 ⁴	7,921.60 ^		334.00 ^			7,921.60	334.00
2	Baker Company, Inc.	C 205.00 ⁴		205.00 ^				205.00	
3	Cross Mfg. Co., Inc.	C 7,310.20 ⁴	1,500.20 ^	1,210.00 ^	600.00	4,100.00 ^		4,100.00	
	Douglas Supply Co.	22.00 ⁴				22.00			22.00
4	Elastic Mfg. Co., Inc.	C 1,250.00 ⁴	1,250.00 ^					1,250.00	
	J. R. Farmer	3,000.00	3,000.00 ^						
64	Young Industries	CX 1,825.00 ⁴	1,575.00 ^			250.00			912.50
	Zenith Co.	47.19 ⁴	47.19 ^					47.19	
		78,624.62	48,801.67	21,245.60	2,875.20	6,302.15	(600.00)		4,100.00
	A.J.E. 12—Correct J.R. Farmer G-2	(3,000.00)	(3,000.00)						
		75,624.62 u	45,801.67 ⁴	21,245.60 ⁴	2,875.20 u	6,302.15 u	(600.00)		4,100.00 u
		G							G

A.J.E. 12
Accounts Receivable—Officers   3,000.00
    Accounts Receivable—Trade   3,000.00
Correct classification of account
receivable from J. R. Farmer,
President.

Prepared by Client

u = Footed and cross-footed ✓ Agreed to general ledger } no differences noted
⁴ = Traced to accounts receivable subsidiary ledger }
^ = Verified aging
C = Confirmed; no exceptions.
CX = Confirmed with exceptions. See G-1-1.

See audit program (B-2) for extent of confirmation and
other auditing procedures.

Conclusion:
    The results of the confirmation and other tests described in the audit program (B-2)
provide sufficient appropriate evidence of the genuineness of trade accounts
receivable in the aggregate amount of $75,624.62.

V.M.H.
Jan. 20, 9Y

When trial balances or analyses of accounts receivable are furnished to the auditors by the client's employees, some independent verification of the listing is essential. Determination of the proper extent of testing should be made in relation to the adequacy of the internal controls over receivables. The auditors should test footings, cross-footings, and agings. In testing the aging, it is important to test some accounts classified as current, as well as those shown as past due. These selected accounts should be traced to the subsidiary ledgers. The totals of schedules prepared by client personnel should also be compared with related controlling accounts. In addition, the balances of the subsidiary ledger records should be verified by footing the debit and credit columns on a test basis. Generalized computer audit programs may be used to perform these tests when the client's accounts receivable are processed by an electronic data processing system.

6. Obtain analyses of notes receivable and related interest.

An analysis of notes receivable supporting the general ledger controlling account may be prepared for the auditors by the client's staff. The information to be included in the analysis normally will include the name of the maker, date, maturity, amount, and interest rate. In addition to verifying the accuracy of the analysis prepared by the client, the auditors should trace selected items to the accounting records and to the notes themselves.

7. Inspect notes on hand and confirm those not on hand with holders.

The inspection of notes receivable on hand should be performed concurrently with the count of cash and securities to prevent the concealment of a shortage by substitution of cash for misappropriated negotiable instruments, or vice versa. Any securities held by the client as collateral for notes receivable should be inspected and listed at the same time. Complete control over all negotiable instruments should be maintained by the auditors until the count and inspection are completed.

Notes receivable owned by the client may be held by others at the time of the examination. Confirmation in writing from the *holder* of the note is considered as an acceptable alternative to inspection; it does not, however, eliminate the need for securing confirmation from the *maker* of the note. The confirmation letter sent to a bank, collection agency, secured creditor, or other holder should contain a request for verification of the name of the maker, the balance of the note, the interest rate, and the due date.

Confirmation of notes receivable discounted or pledged as collateral with banks is obtained in connection with the verification of cash on deposit, since the standard bank confirmation form includes specific enquiry on these matters.

Printed note forms are readily available at any bank; an unscrupulous officer or employee of the client company desiring to create a fictitious note could do so by obtaining a bank note form and filling in the amount, date, maturity, and signature. The relative ease of creating a forged or fictitious note suggests that physical inspection by the auditors represents a less significant and conclusive audit procedure in verification of notes receivable than for cash or securities.

8. Confirm receivables with debtors.

The term *confirmation* was defined in Chapter 6 as a type of documentary evidence secured from outside the client organization and transmitted directly to the auditors. Direct communication with debtors is the most essential and conclusive step in the verification of accounts and notes receivable. By confirming an account receivable, the auditors prove that the customer *exists.* Written acknowledgment of the debt by the debtor serves the purposes of (*a*) establishing the existence, ownership, and gross valuation of the asset and (*b*) providing some assurance that no lapping or other manipulations affecting receivables is being carried on at the balance sheet date. However, the confirmation of a receivable provides only limited evidence about the completeness and valuation assertions, because only recorded amounts are confirmed, and debtors may acknowledge debts even though they are not able to pay them.

A better understanding of the emphasis placed on confirmation of receivables can be gained by a brief review of auditing history. Audit objectives and procedures were drastically revised in the 1940s. Before that time, the usual audit did not include procedures to assure that the receivables were genuine claims against existing companies or that inventories actually existed and had been accurately counted. For the auditors to confirm receivables (or to observe the taking of physical inventory) was considered too expensive and not particularly important. Auditors generally relied in that early era upon a written statement by management concerning the validity of receivables and the existence of inventories. This approach was drastically revised after some spectacular fraud cases in the United States involving millions of dollars in fictitious receivables and inventories showed the need for stronger audit evidence.

The following recommendation from Section 6020 of the *CICA Handbook* summarizes the current status of the confirmation procedure:

> Generally accepted auditing procedures in respect of accounts and notes receivable should include some form of direct confirmation of accounts and notes receivable by communication with debtors.
>
> In circumstances where direct confirmation would be inpracticable or is deemed to be harmful to the client's business, auditors should substitute other acceptable procedures.

All requests for confirmation of notes and accounts receivable should be mailed in envelopes bearing the public accounting firm's return address. A stamped or business reply envelope addressed to the office of the auditors should be enclosed with the request. The confirmation requests should be deposited personally by the auditors at the post office or in a government mailbox. These procedures are designed to prevent the client's employees from having any opportunity to alter or intercept a confirmation request or the customer's reply thereto. The entire process of confirming receivables will obviously contribute nothing toward the detection of overstated or fictitious accounts if the confirmation requests or replies from customers pass through the hands of the client. Requests returned as undeliverable by the post office may be of prime significance to the auditors and hence should be returned directly to their office.

An important part of confirming notes and accounts receivable is determining the validity of the debtors' addresses. The auditors should investigate thoroughly if an excessive number of *individual* debtors have addresses that are post office boxes; the boxes may have been rented under fictitious debtors' names by employees of the client company engaged in accounts receivable fraud.

Illustrative Case

In the Equity Funding Corporation of America fraud in the United States, fictitious receivables selected for confirmation by the auditors bore addresses of employees who were conspirators in the fraud. The fictitious confirmation requests were thus signed and returned to the auditors by the recipients.

To improve the response rate to confirmations, the auditors should carefully design the form to make sure that the person receiving the confirmation has easy access to the information requested. For example, customers that use a voucher system for cash disbursements may be better able to confirm unpaid transactions than the account balance. The auditors should also try to include on the form the details of the transactions, such as customers' purchase order numbers.

Positive and Negative Confirmation Requests.   There are two methods of confirming receivables by direct communication with the debtor. In each type of communication, the *client* makes the formal request for confirmation, although the auditors *control* the entire confirmation process.

The *positive method* consists of a request addressed to the debtor company asking it to confirm directly to the auditors the accuracy of the dollar amount shown on the confirmation request. The positive method calls for a reply in every case; the customer is asked to state whether the balance shown is correct or incorrect. See Figure 12–5.

FIGURE 12–5 Positive Form of Accounts Receivable Confirmation Request

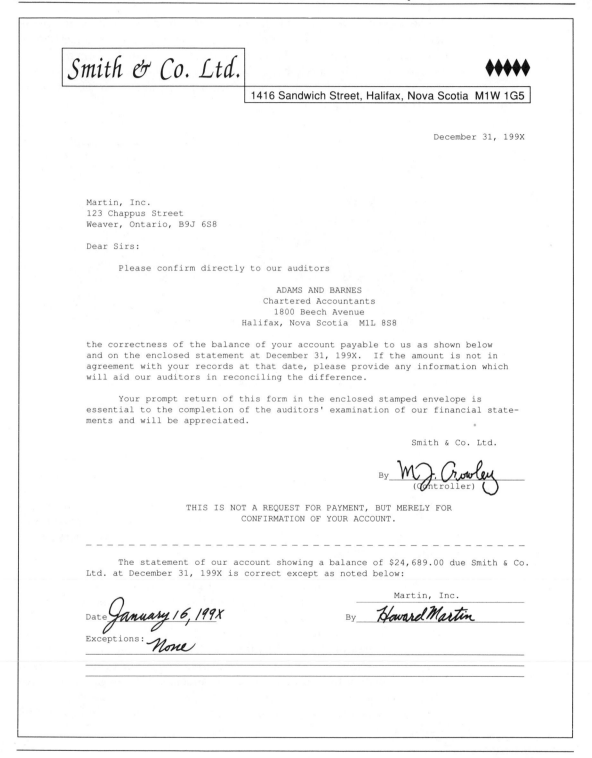

Smith & Co. Ltd.

◆◆◆◆◆

1416 Sandwich Street, Halifax, Nova Scotia M1W 1G5

December 31, 199X

Martin, Inc.
123 Chappus Street
Weaver, Ontario, B9J 6S8

Dear Sirs:

    Please confirm directly to our auditors

               ADAMS AND BARNES
           Chartered Accountants
           1800 Beech Avenue
       Halifax, Nova Scotia M1L 8S8

the correctness of the balance of your account payable to us as shown below
and on the enclosed statement at December 31, 199X. If the amount is not in
agreement with your records at that date, please provide any information which
will aid our auditors in reconciling the difference.

    Your prompt return of this form in the enclosed stamped envelope is
essential to the completion of the auditors' examination of our financial statements and will be appreciated.

                          Smith & Co. Ltd.

                      By *M. J. Crowley*
                        (Controller)

      THIS IS NOT A REQUEST FOR PAYMENT, BUT MERELY FOR
           CONFIRMATION OF YOUR ACCOUNT.

- -

    The statement of our account showing a balance of $24,689.00 due Smith & Co.
Ltd. at December 31, 199X is correct except as noted below:

                                        Martin, Inc.

Date *January 16, 199X*   By *Howard Martin*

Exceptions: *None*

The *negative method* consists of a communication addressed to the debtor company asking it to advise the auditors *only* if the balance shown is incorrect. A negative confirmation request may be in the form of a letter or it may be made merely by applying a rubber stamp to the customer's regular monthly statement, or by attaching a gummed label bearing the words shown in Figure 12–6.

FIGURE 12–6   Negative Form of Accounts Receivable Confirmation Request

---

Please examine this statement carefully. If it does not agree with your records, please report any differences to our auditors

Adams and Barnes
Chartered Accountants
1800 Beech Avenue
Halifax, Nova Scotia MIL 858

A business reply envelope requiring no postage is enclosed for your convenience.

THIS IS NOT A REQUEST FOR PAYMENT

The greater reliability of the positive form of confirmation arises from the fact that the auditors are alerted to the need for further investigation if a reply is not received. When the negative form of confirmation is used, the lack of a reply from a given customer is interpreted as satisfactory evidence when in fact the customer may simply have ignored the confirmation request. The expense of sending negative confirmation requests is considerably less than for the positive confirmation; thus, more customers can be contacted for the same cost.

Negative confirmation requests may be used for certain types of entities, but only when (*a*) the assessed level of control risk is low, (*b*) a large number of small balances is involved, and (*c*) the auditors have no reason to believe that the recipients of the requests are unlikely to give them consideration. When the auditors use negative requests, they should consider supplementing the confirmations with other substantive procedures. In many situations a combination of positive and negative forms is used, with the positive form used for large balances and the negative form for small balances.

Section 6020 of the *CICA Handbook* contains the following comments on the methods of confirming receivables:

The positive and negative forms of confirmation each have certain applications, and the choice between them will depend on circumstances. The receipt of a positive confirmation provides better evidence of the correctness of an account than does failure to receive a protest under the negative form of circularization. The negative form, however, is simpler and less time-consuming and consequently may permit coverage of a larger number of balances.

Negative confirmation suffers from the fact that it does not always receive consideration from the debtor, and consequently a failure to reply does not necessarily signify agreement. Positive confirmation will seldom produce replies to all requests, but it sometimes has the advantage of producing useful information in cases where the customer is not prepared to confirm or is unable to do so.

Positive confirmation would be preferred:

(*a*) for individual balances of relatively large amounts; or
(*b*) where there are few debtors; or
(*c*) where there is evidence or suspicion of fraud or serious errors.

For many audit engagements, a combination of positive requests for at least a sample of large accounts and negative requests for at least a sample of smaller accounts will provide a suitable coverage.

Size of Sample. In the audit of most companies, the confirmation process is limited to a sample of the accounts receivable. The sample should generally be sufficiently large to account for most of the dollar amount of the receivables, and it should always be sufficiently representative to warrant the drawing of valid inferences about the entire population of receivables.

The size of the sample will vary with the materiality of accounts receivable in comparison with total assets. If accounts receivable are a relatively large asset, the size of the sample should be relatively large. The auditors' assessment of control risk is also a factor; weaknesses in internal control call for larger samples than when internal control is strong. The results of confirmation tests in prior years serve as another guide to the auditors in setting sample size; significant exceptions in prior years' confirmations may signal the need for extensive confirmation of this year's receivables. Finally, the choice between the positive and negative forms of confirmation request influence the size of the sample. The number of confirmations is usually increased when the negative form is used.

In selecting the individual accounts to be confirmed, it is customary to include all customers with balances above a selected dollar amount and to select accounts on a random basis from the remaining receivables. Generalized computer audit programs are useful in stratifying computer-processed accounts receivable to facilitate the selection process described above.

Discrepancies in Customers' Replies.   The auditors should resolve unusual or significant differences reported by customers. The majority of such reported discrepancies arise because of normal lags in the recording of cash receipts or sales transactions, or because of misunderstanding on the part of the customer company as to the date of the balance it is asked to confirm. Some replies may state that the balance listed is incorrect because it does not reflect recent cash payments; in such instances, the auditors normally trace the reported payments to the cash records.

Alternative Audit Procedures for Nonrespondents.   The percentage of replies to be expected for positive confirmation requests will vary greatly according to the type of debtor. When using positive confirmation requests, the auditors should generally follow up with a second and sometimes a third request to produce replies. When replies are still not received, the auditors should apply alternative procedures to the accounts, unless (*a*) the amount of the nonresponses is not significant when projected as a 100 percent misstatement to the total balance of receivables, and (*b*) there are no unusual characteristics related to the nonresponses, such as all of them relating to transactions occurring very near the end of the year. Alternative procedures generally include examining subsequent cash receipts, shipping documents, customer purchase orders, and sales invoices or contracts.

Putting the Confirmation Process in Perspective.   When all expected replies to confirmation requests have been received, a summary should be prepared outlining the extent and nature of the confirmation program and the overall results obtained. Such a summary is a highly important part of the audit working papers.

The auditors face more than one type of risk in relying upon the confirmation process to form an opinion about the fairness of the accounts receivable as a whole. We have already recognized the risk that some accounts with erroneous balances may not be included in the sample confirmed, and also the risk that replies may not be received from some customers having erroneous balances. Finally, there is the risk that customers may routinely return confirmation requests without actually comparing the balance with their records. Such responses would give the auditors a false sense of security. Despite these risks, however, the confirming of accounts receivable provides valuable evidence and represents an important part of the auditors' work.

It has sometimes been said that the best proof available to the auditors as to the existence and ownership of an account receivable is its collection during the course of their examination. But this statement requires qualification, as indicated by the following situation:

Illustrative Case

During the first audit of a small manufacturing company, the auditors sent confirmation requests to all customers whose accounts showed balances in excess of $1,000. Satisfactory replies were received from all but one account, which had a balance of approximately $30,000. A second confirmation request sent to this customer produced no response, but before the auditors could investigate further, they were informed by the cashier-accountant that the account had been paid in full. The auditors asked to examine the customer's cheque and the accompanying remittance advice, but were told that the cheque had been deposited and the remittance advice destroyed. Further questioning concerning transactions with this customer evoked such vague responses that the auditors decided to discuss the account with the officers of the company. At this point the cashier-accountant confessed that the account in question was a fictitious one created to conceal a shortage and that to satisfy the auditors he had "collected" the account receivable by diverting current collections from other customers whose accounts had already been confirmed.

Reviewing and Confirming Accounts and Notes Written Off as Uncollectible.   If any accounts or notes receivable of significant amount were written off as uncollectible during the year, the auditors should determine that these write-offs were properly authorized. In the absence of proper authorization procedures, a dishonest employee could conceal permanently a theft of cash merely by a charge to accounts or notes receivable followed by a write-off of that asset.

A systematic review of the notes and accounts written off can conveniently be made by obtaining or preparing an analysis of the Allowance for Doubtful Accounts and Notes. Debits to the allowance may be traced to the authorizing documents and to the control record of accounts and notes written off; confirmation requests may be mailed to some of the debtors to determine that the account or note was genuine when it was first recorded in the accounts. Credit entries should be compared with the charges to Uncollectible Accounts and Notes Expense. Any write-off that appears unreasonable should be fully investigated. Charge-off of a note or account receivable from an officer, shareholder, or director is unreasonable on its face and warrants the most searching investigation by the auditors. The computation of percentages relating the year's write-offs to net credit sales, to uncollectible accounts expense, and to the allowance for doubtful accounts and notes may be useful in bringing to light any abnormal write-offs.

9. Review the year-end cutoff of sales transactions.

One of the more common methods of falsifying accounting records is to inflate the sales for the year by holding open the sales journal beyond the balance sheet date. Shipments made in the first part of January may be covered by sales invoices bearing a December date and included in December sales. The purpose of such misleading entries is to present a more favourable financial picture than actually exists. Since sales are frequently used as the base for computation of bonuses and commissions, an additional incentive for padding the Sales account is often present. A related abuse affecting accounts receivable is the practice of holding the cash journals open beyond the balance sheet date; auditing procedures designed to detect this practice were described in connection with the audit of cash transactions in Chapter 11.

To guard against errors in the cutoff of sales records (whether accidental or intentional), the auditors should compare the sales recorded for several days before and after the balance sheet date with the duplicate sales invoices and shipping documents. The effectiveness of this step is largely dependent upon the degree of segregation of duties between the shipping, receiving, and billing functions. If warehousing, shipping, billing, and receiving are independently controlled, it is most unlikely that records in all these departments will be manipulated to disguise shipments of one period as sales of the preceding period. On the other hand, one individual who had control over both shipping records and billing documents could manipulate both sets of records if overstatement of the year's sales were attempted.

Fictitious sales, as well as predated shipments, are occasionally recorded at year-end as a means of window-dressing the financial statements. The merchandise in question may even be shipped to customers without their prior knowledge, and subsequently returned. To guard against such manipulation, the auditors should review carefully all substantial sales returns following the balance sheet date that may apply to receivables originating in the year under audit. Consideration should be given to reflecting these returns in the current year's business by means of adjusting entries. Confirmation of accounts receivable, if made at the balance sheet date, should also serve to bring any large unauthorized shipments to the attention of the auditors.

10. Perform analytical procedures for accounts receivable, sales, notes receivable, and interest revenue.

Several ratios and relationships can be computed to indicate the overall reasonableness of the amounts shown for accounts receivable, sales, notes receivable, and interest revenue. Examples include (*a*) the gross profit rate, (*b*) accounts receivable turnover, (*c*) the ratio of accounts receivable at year-end to the year's net credit sales, (*d*) the ratio of accounts written off during the year to the ending balance of accounts receivable, (*e*) the ratio of the valuation allowance to accounts receivable, (*f*) the ratio of interest revenue to notes receivable, and (*g*) the ratio of uncollectible account expense to credit sales.

These ratios and relationships should be compared with corresponding data for the preceding years and with comparable industry averages.

11. Verify interest earned on notes and accrued interest receivable.

The most effective verification of the Interest Earned account consists of an *independent computation* by the auditors of the interest earned during the year on notes receivable. The working paper used to analyze notes receivable should show the interest rate and date of issuance of each note. The interest section of this working paper consists of four columns, which show for each note receivable owned during the year the following information:

1. Accrued interest receivable at the beginning of the year (taken from the preceding year's audit working papers).
2. Interest earned during the year (computed from the terms of the notes).
3. Interest collected during the year (traced to cash receipts records).
4. Accrued interest receivable at the end of the year (computed by the auditors).

These four columns make up a self-balancing set. The beginning balance of accrued interest receivable (first column) plus the interest earned during the year (second column) minus the interest collected (third column) should equal the accrued interest receivable at the end of the year (fourth column). The totals of the four columns should be cross-footed to ensure that they are in balance; in addition, the individual column totals should be traced to the balances in the general ledger.

If the interest earned for the year as computed by the auditors does not agree with interest earned as shown in the accounting records, the next step is an analysis of the ledger account. Any unaccounted-for credits in the Interest Earned account deserve particular attention because these credits may represent interest received on notes that have never been recorded.

For financial institutions or other clients having numerous notes receivable, the auditors may verify interest computations on only a sample of the notes. In addition, they should test the reasonableness of total interest earned for the year by applying a weighted average rate of interest to the average balance of the Notes Receivable ledger account during the year.

12. Evaluate the propriety of the client's accounting for receivables and sales.

Many instances of misstatements of financial statements have involved inappropriate recognition of sales revenue and related receivables. The auditors must carefully evaluate the propriety of the client's treatment of certain transactions. Problems that the auditors might discover include:

1. An allowance for sales returns may not be set up for goods shipped to customers who are given the right to return the goods under certain circumstances.

2. Cash receipts from franchise fees may be included in revenue and receivables when services have not been rendered to the franchisees.
3. Leases properly accounted for using the operating method of accounting may be improperly accounted for as sale-type capital leases overstating revenues and receivables.
4. Management might use the percentage-of-completion method of revenue recognition in inappropriate circumstances, or might overestimate the amount of revenue earned.

These examples make it clear that auditors must have a thorough understanding of generally accepted accounting principles and the *substance,* as well as the form, of the client's sales transactions. The auditors should carefully examine the various documents pertaining to the transactions to determine that proper accounting principles have been followed.

13. Determine adequacy of allowance for uncollectible accounts.

If the balance sheet is to reflect fairly the financial position of the business, the receivables must be stated at net realizable value, that is, at face value less an adequate allowance for doubtful notes and accounts receivable. The measurement of income requires an impartial matching of revenue and related expenses. Since one of the expenses involved is the expense caused by uncollectible notes and accounts, the auditors' review of doubtful receivables should be looked upon as the verification of both income statement and balance sheet accounts.

As the audit approaches completion, considerable time will have elapsed since the balance sheet date. Consequently, many of the accounts receivable that were past due at the balance sheet date will have been collected; the others will be further past due. Thus, the auditors have the advantage of hindsight in judging the collectibility of the receivables owned at the balance sheet date.

The auditors' best evidence of *collectibility* of accounts and notes receivable is payment in full by the debtors subsequent to the balance sheet date. The auditors should note in the working papers any such amounts received; in the illustrated trial balance of trade accounts receivable (Figure 12–4), a special column has been provided for this purpose. Since one of the auditors' objectives in the examination of notes and accounts receivable is the determination of their collectibility, it is important for the auditors to be aware of any collections on past-due accounts or matured notes during the period subsequent to the balance sheet date.

A note receivable, especially one obtained in settlement of a past-due account receivable, may involve as much credit risk as an account receivable. Provision for loss may reasonably be made for notes that have been repeatedly renewed, for instalment notes on which payments have been late and irregular, for notes received in consequence of past-due accounts receivable, for defaulted notes, and for notes of companies known to be in financial difficulties. To appraise the collectibility of notes receivable, the auditors may investigate the credit standing of the makers of any large or doubtful notes. Reports from credit-rating agencies and financial statements from the makers of notes should be available in the client's credit department.

Evaluation of any collateral supplied by the makers of notes is another step in determining the collectibility of notes receivable. The auditors should determine current market value of securities held as collateral by the client by reference to market quotations or by enquiry from brokers. Attention of the client should be called to any cases in which the market value of the collateral is less than the note; the deficiency might have to be considered uncollectible.

To conclude, as to the adequacy of management's accounting estimate for the allowance for doubtful accounts the auditors may take the following steps:

1. Compare the details to the aging of accounts receivable to prior years' aging. Examine the past-due accounts receivable listed in the aging schedule that have not been paid subsequent to the balance sheet date, noting such factors as the size and recency of payments, settlement of old balances, and whether recent sales are on a cash or a credit basis. The client's correspondence file may furnish much of this information.
2. Investigate the credit ratings for delinquent and unusually large accounts. An account with a single customer may represent a major portion of the total receivables.
3. Review confirmation exceptions for indication of amounts in dispute or other clues as to possible uncollectible accounts.
4. Summarize in a working paper those accounts considered to be doubtful of collection based on the preceding procedures. List customer names, doubtful amounts, and reasons considered doubtful.
5. Review with the credit manager the current status of significant doubtful accounts, ascertaining the collection action taken and the opinion of the credit manager as to ultimate collectibility. Indicate on the doubtful accounts working paper the credit manager's opinion as to the collectible portion of each account listed, and provide for the estimated losses on accounts considered by the auditors to be uncollectible.
6. Compute relationships, such as the number-of-days-sales in accounts receivable and the relationship of the valuation allowance to (1) accounts receivable, (2) net credit sales, and compare to comparable relationships for prior years and industry averages. Investigate any significant variations.

14. Ascertain whether any receivables have been pledged.

The auditors should enquire directly whether any notes or accounts receivable have been pledged or assigned. Evidence of the pledging of receivables may also be disclosed through the bank confirmation requests, which specifically call for a description of the collateral securing bank loans. Analysis of the interest expense accounts may reflect charges from the pledging of receivables to finance companies.

Accounts receivable that have been pledged should be plainly labeled by stamping on the copy of the sales invoice a notice such as ''Pledged to First National Bank under loan agreement of December 199X,'' and by inserting an identifying code in the accounts receivable records. Accounts labeled in this manner would be identified by the auditors in their initial review of receivables and confirmed by direct correspondence with the bank to which the accounts receivable are pledged. The auditors cannot, however, proceed on the assumption that all pledged receivables have been labeled to that effect, and they must be alert to detect any suggestions of an unrecorded pledging of accounts receivable.

15. Investigate fully any notes or accounts receivable from related parties.

Loans by a corporation to its officers, director, shareholders, or affiliates require particular attention from the auditors because these related party transactions are not the result of arm's-length bargaining by parties of opposing interests. Furthermore, such loans may be prohibited by law or by the corporation's bylaws. It is somewhat difficult to reconcile substantial loans to insiders by a nonfinancial corporation with the avowed operating objectives of such an organization. The external auditors have an obligation to shareholders, creditors, and others who rely upon audited statements to require disclosure of any self-dealing on the part of the management. It seems apparent that most loans to officers, directors, and shareholders are made for the convenience of the borrower rather than for the profit of the corporation. Because of the somewhat questionable character of such loans, they are sometimes paid off just before the balance sheet date and renewed shortly thereafter in an effort to avoid disclosure in financial statements. Under these circumstances, the renewed borrowing may be detected by the auditors through a scanning of notes and accounts receivable transactions subsequent to the balance sheet date.

16. Evaluate financial statement presentation and disclosure.

The auditors must ascertain that the financial presentation of accounts and notes receivable and the related disclosures are in accordance with generally accepted accounting principles. Related party receivables should be shown separately with disclosure of the nature of the relationships and the amounts of the transactions. Any unusual terms of notes receivable should be disclosed in the footnotes. Also, the amounts of allowances for uncollectible receivables should be shown as deductions from the related receivables.

Interim Audit Work on Receivables and Sales

Much of the audit work on receivables and sales can be performed one or two months before the balance sheet date. The interim work may consist of the consideration of internal controls and, in some cases, the confirmation of accounts receivable as well. A decision to carry out the confirmation of receivables at an interim date rather than at year-end is justified only if internal controls for receivables are reasonably strong.

If interim audit work has been done on receivables and sales, the year-end audit work may be modified considerably. For example, if the confirmation of accounts receivable was performed at October 31, the year-end audit program would include preparation of a summary analysis of postings to the Accounts Receivable controlling account for the period from November 1 through December 31. This analysis would list the postings by month, showing the journal source of each. These postings would be traced to the respective journals, such as the sales journal and cash receipts journal. The amounts of the postings would be compared with the amounts in preceding months and with the corresponding months in prior years. The purpose of this work is to bring to light any significant variations in receivables during the months between the interim audit work and the balance sheet date.

In addition to this analysis of the entries to the receivable accounts for the intervening period, the audit work at year-end would include obtaining the aging of the accounts receivable at December 31, confirmation of any large accounts in the year-end trial balance that are new or delinquent, and the usual investigation of the year-end cutoff of sales and cash receipts.

KEY TERMS

aged trial balance A listing of individual customers' accounts classified by age. Serves as a preliminary step in estimating the collectibility of accounts receivable.

confirmation A type of documentary evidence that is created outside the client organization and transmitted directly to the auditors.

consignment A transfer of goods from the owner to another person who acts as the sales agent of the owner.

interim audit work Those audit procedures that can be performed before the balance sheet date. The purpose is to facilitate earlier issuance of the audit report and to spread the auditors' work more uniformly over the year.

negative confirmation A confirmation request addressed to the debtor requesting a reply only if the balance shown on the confirmation is incorrect.

pledging of receivables To assign to a bank, factor, finance company, or other lender an exclusive claim against accounts receivable as security for a debt.

positive confirmation A confirmation request sent to the debtor asking it to confirm directly to the auditors the accuracy of the dollar amount shown on the request. Calls for a reply regardless of whether the amount is correct or incorrect.

GROUP I: REVIEW QUESTIONS

12–1. Give an example of a type of receivable originating without arm's-length bargaining. Comment on the presentation of such receivables in the balance sheet.

12–2. State briefly the objective of the billing function. What important document is created by the billing department?

12–3. Criticize the following quotation: "A credit memorandum should be issued only when an account receivable is determined to be uncollectible."

12–4. Explain the difference between a *customer's order* and a *sales order,* as these terms might be used by a manufacturing company making sales on credit.

12–5. Describe the role of the credit department in a manufacturing company.

12–6. In selecting accounts receivable for confirmation, the auditors discover that the client company's records show the addresses of several individual customers to be post office boxes. What should be the auditors' reaction to this situation?

12–7. Cite various procedures auditors employ that might lead to the detection of an inadequate allowance for doubtful accounts receivable.

(AICPA, adapted)

12–8. A public accounting firm wishes to test the client's sales cutoff at June 30, 199X. Describe the steps that the auditors should include in this test.

(AICPA, adapted)

12–9. Several accounts receivable confirmations have been returned with the notation "verifications of vendors' statements are no longer possible because of our data processing system." What alternative auditing procedures could be used to verify these accounts receivable?

(AICPA, adapted)

12–10. The confirmation of accounts receivable is an important auditing procedure. Should the formal request for confirmation be made by the client or by the auditors? Should the return envelope be addressed to the client, to the auditors in care of the client, or to the auditors office? Explain.

12–11. The controller of a new client operating a medium-size manufacturing business complains to you that he believes the company has sustained significant losses on several occasions because certain sales invoices were misplaced and never recorded as accounts receivable. What internal control procedure can you suggest to guard against such problems?

12–12. In the examination of an automobile agency, you find that instalment notes received from the purchasers of automobiles are promptly discounted with a bank. Would you consider it necessary to confirm these notes by a communication with the bank? With the makers? Explain.

12–13. Your review of notes receivable from officers, directors, shareholders, and affiliated companies discloses that several notes of small amounts were written off to the allowance for uncollectible notes during the year. Have these transactions any special significance? Explain.

12–14. In the examination of credit memoranda covering allowances to customers for goods returned, how can the auditors ascertain whether the customer actually did return merchandise in each case in which accounts receivable were reduced?

12–15. What auditing procedures, if any, are necessary for notes receivable but are not required for accounts receivable?

12–16. Among specific procedures that contribute to good internal control over accounts receivable are (*a*) the approval of uncollectible account write-offs and credit memoranda by an executive and (*b*) the sending of monthly statements to all customers. State three other procedures conducive to strong internal control.

(AICPA)

12–17. What additional auditing procedures should be undertaken in connection with the confirmation of accounts receivable where customers having substantial balances fail to reply after second request forms have been mailed directly to them?

(AICPA, adapted)

12–18. In your first examination of Hydro Manufacturing Company, a manufacturer of outboard motors, you discover that an unusually large number of sales transactions were recorded just before the end of the fiscal year. What significance would you attach to this unusual volume?

12–19. In connection with a regular annual audit, what are the purposes of a review of sales returns and allowances subsequent to the balance sheet data?

(AICPA, adapted)

12–20. An inexperienced clerk assigned to the preparation of sales invoices in a manufacturing company became confused as to the nature of certain articles being shipped, with the result that the prices used on the invoices were far less than called for in the company's price lists. What internal control procedures could be established to guard against such errors?

12–21. The accounts receivable section of the accounting department in Wind Power Inc. maintains subsidiary ledgers that are posted from copies of the sales invoices transmitted daily from the billing department. How may the accounts receivable section be sure that it receives promptly a copy of each sales invoice prepared?

12–22. A company that ships goods to its customers must establish procedures to ensure that a sales invoice is prepared for every shipment. Describe procedures to meet this requirement.

12–23. State briefly the ***audit objectives*** that are addressed by the audit procedure of "Confirm accounts receivable and notes receivable by direct communication with debtors."

GROUP II: QUESTIONS REQUIRING ANALYSIS

12–24. During the audit of Solar Technologies, Inc., the auditors sent confirmation requests to customers whose accounts had been written off as uncollectible during the year under audit. An executive of Solar protested, saying: "You people should be verifying that the receivables on the books are collectible. We know the ones we wrote off are no good."

Required:

a. What purpose, if any, is served by this audit procedure?

b. Does the Solar executive's statement suggest some misunderstanding of audit objectives? Explain.

12–25. If you were preparing a credit sales system flowchart, what document would you show as:

a. The source for posting debits to a customer's account in the accounts receivable ledger.

b. Authorization to the finished goods stores to release merchandise to the shipping department.

c. The source for preparing a sales order.

d. The source for preparing a bill of lading.

e. The source for an entry in the sales journal.

12–26. During preliminary conversations with a new staff assistant you instruct her to send out confirmation requests for both accounts receivable and notes receivable. She asks whether the confirmation requests should go to the makers of the notes or to the holders of the notes in the case of notes that have been discounted. Provide an answer to her question and give reasons for your answer.

12–27. Lakeside Company has retained you to conduct an audit so that it will be able to support its application for a bank loan with audited financial statements. The president of Lakeside states that you will have unlimited access to all records of the company and may carry out any audit procedures you consider necessary, except that you are not to communicate with customers. The president feels that contacts with customers might lead them to believe that Lakeside was in financial difficulty. Under these circumstances, will it be possible for you to issue the auditors' standard unqualified audit report? Explain.

12–28. Tom Jones, CA, is examining the financial statements of a manufacturing company with a significant amount of trade accounts receivable. Jones is satisfied that the accounts are properly summarized and classified, and are valued in accordance with generally accepted accounting principles. Jones plans to use accounts receivable confirmation requests to satisfy the third examination standard as to trade accounts receivable.

Required:
a. Identify and describe the two forms of accounts receivable confirmation requests and indicate what factors Jones should consider in determining when to use each.
b. Assume Jones has received a satisfactory response to the confirmation requests. Describe how Jones could evaluate collectibility of the trade accounts receivable.

(AICPA, adapted)

12–29. In their work on accounts receivable and elsewhere in an audit, the external auditors often make use of confirmations.
a. What is an audit confirmation?
b. What characteristics should an audit confirmation possess if a public accounting firm is to consider it as valid evidence?
c. Distinguish between a positive confirmation and a negative confirmation in the auditors' examination of accounts receivable.
d. In confirming a client's accounts receivable, what characteristics should be present in the accounts if the public accounting firm is to use negative confirmations?

(AICPA, adapted)

12–30. Elizabeth Cole, the senior auditor-in-charge of the audit of Thorne Company, a small manufacturer, was busy writing the audit report for another engagement. Accordingly, she sent Martin Joseph, a recently hired staff assistant of the public accounting firm, to begin the audit of Thorne Company, with the suggestion that Joseph start with the accounts receivable. Using the preceding year's audit working papers for Thorne Company as a guide, Joseph prepared a trial balance of Thorne's trade accounts receivable, aged them, prepared and mailed positive confirmation requests, examined underlying documents plus other support for charges and credits to the Accounts Receivable ledger account, and performed such other work as he deemed necessary to assure the existence, ownership, and collectibility of the accounts receivable. At the conclusion of Joseph's work, Cole traveled to Thorne Company to review Joseph's working papers. Cole found that Joseph had carefully followed the prior years's audit working papers.

Required:
State how the three examination standards of the generally accepted auditing standards were fulfilled, or were not fulfilled, in the audit of the accounts receivable of Thorne Company.

(AICPA, adapted)

12–31.   *a.* What are the implications to the auditors if, during their examination of accounts receivable, some of a client's customers do not respond to the auditors' request for positive confirmation of their accounts receivable?

b. What procedures should the auditors perform if there is no response to a second request for a positive confirmation?

(AICPA, adapted)

12–32.   Walter Conn is engaged to audit the financial statements of Matthews Wholesaling for the year ended December 31, 199X. Conn obtained and documented an understanding of the internal control relating to the accounts receivable and assessed control risk relating to accounts receivable at the maximum level. Conn requested and obtained from Matthews an aged accounts receivable schedule listing the total amount owed by each customer as of December 31, 199X, and sent positive confirmation requests to a sample of the customers.

Required:
What additional substantive audit procedures should Conn consider applying in auditing the accounts receivable?

(AICPA, adapted)

12–33.   An assistant auditor was instructed to "test the aging of accounts receivable as shown on the trial balance prepared by the client." In making this test, the assistant traced all past-due accounts shown on the trial balance to the ledger cards in the accounts receivable subsidiary ledger and computed the aging of these accounts. The assistant found no discrepancies and reported to the senior auditor that the aging work performed by the client was satisfactory.

Comment on the logic and adequacy of this test of the aging of accounts receivable.

12–34. Your regular audit of Palisades Inc. included the confirmation of accounts receivable. You decided to use the positive form of confirmation request. Satisfactory replies were received from all but one of the large accounts. You sent a second and third request to this customer, but received no reply. At this point an employee of the client company informed you that a cheque had been received for the full amount of the receivable. Would you regard this as a statisfactory disposition of the matter? Explain.

12–35. Select the best answer for each of the following and explain fully the reason for your selection.

a. To determine that all sales have been recorded, the auditors would select a sample of transactions *from* the:

(1) Shipping documents file.

(2) Sales journal.

(3) Accounts receivable subsidiary ledger.

(4) Remittance advices.

b. Which of the following might be detected by the auditors' review of the client's sales cutoff?

(1) Excessive goods returned for credit.

(2) Unrecorded sales discounts.

(3) Lapping of year-end accounts receivable.

(4) Inflated sales for the year.

c. To test the existence assertion for recorded receivables, the auditors would select a sample *from* the:

(1) Sales orders file.

(2) Customer purchase orders.

(3) Accounts receivable subsidiary ledger.

(4) Shipping documents (bills of lading) file.

d. Which assertion relating to sales is most directly addressed when the auditors compare a sample of shipping documents to related sales invoices?

(1) Existence or occurrence.

(2) Completeness.

(3) Ownership.

(4) Statement presentation.

e. Cooper, CA, is auditing the financial statements of a small rural municipality. The receivable balances represent residents' delinquent real estate taxes. The internal control at the municipality is weak. To determine the existence of the accounts receivable balances at the balance sheet date, Cooper would most likely:

(1) Send positive confirmation requests.

(2) Send negative confirmation requests.

(3) Examine evidence of subsequent cash receipts.

(4) Inspect the internal records such as copies of the tax invoices that were mailed to the residents.

f. Identify the control that is most likely to prevent the concealment of a cash shortage resulting from the improper write-off of a trade account receivable:

(1) Write-offs must be approved by a responsible official after review of credit department recommendations and supporting evidence.

(2) Write-offs must be approved by the accounts receivable department.

(3) Write-offs must be authorized by the shipping department.

(4) Write-offs must be supported by an aging schedule showing that only receivables overdue by several months have been written off.

GROUP III: PROBLEMS

12–36. The following are typical questions that might appear on an internal control questionnaire for accounts receivable.

1. Are sales invoices checked for proper pricing, terms, and clerical accuracy?

2. Are shipping documents prenumbered and all numbers accounted for?

3. Is customer credit approval obtained from the credit department prior to shipment of goods?

Required:

a. Describe the purpose of each of the above internal control procedures.

b. Describe the manner in which the operating effectiveness of each of the above procedures might be tested.

c. Assuming that the operating effectiveness of each of the above procedures is found to be inadequate, describe how the auditors might alter their substantive tests to compensate for the increased level of control risk.

12–37. You are conducting an annual audit of Granite Corporation, which has total assets of approximately $1 million and operates a wholesale merchandising business. The corporation is in good financial condition and maintains an adequate accounting system. Granite Corporation owns about 25 percent of the capital stock of Desert Sun, Inc., which operates a dude ranch. This investment is regarded as a permanent one and is accounted for by the equity method.

During your examination of accounts and notes receivable, you develop the information shown below concerning three short-term notes receivable due in the near future. All three of these notes receivable were discounted by Granite Corporation with its bank shortly before the balance sheet date.

a. A 13 percent, 60-day note for $50,000 received from a customer of unquestioned financial standing.

b. A 15 percent, six-month note for $60,000 received from the affiliated company, Desert Sun, Inc. The affiliated company is operating profitably, but is presently in a weak cash position because of recent additions to buildings and equipment. The president of Granite Corporation intends to make an $80,000 advance with a five-year maturity to Desert Sun, Inc. The proposed advance will enable Desert Sun, Inc., to pay the existing 15 percent, $60,000 note at maturity and to meet certain other obligations.

c. A 14 percent, $20,000 note from a former key executive of Granite Corporation whose employment had been terminated because of chronic alcoholism and excessive gambling. The maker of the note is presently unemployed and without personal resources.

Required:
Describe the proper balance sheet presentation with respect to these discounted notes receivable. Use a separate paragraph for each of the three notes, and state any assumption you consider necessary.

12–38. Milton Chambers, CA, was retained by Hall Corporation to perform an audit of its financial statements for the year ending December 31. In a preliminary meeting with company officials, Chambers learned that the corporation customarily accepted numerous notes receivable from its customers. At December 31, the client company's controller provided Chambers with a list of the individual notes receivable owned at that date. The list showed for each note the date of the note, amount, interest rate, maturity date, the name and address of the maker. After a careful consideration of the internal control relating to notes receivable, Chambers turned his attention to the list of notes receivable provided to him by the controller.

Chambers proved the footing of the list and determined that the total agreed with the general ledger control account for notes receivable and also with the amount shown in the balance sheet. Next he selected 20 of the larger amounts on the list of notes receivable for detailed investigation. This investigation consisted of confirming the amount, date, maturity, interest rate, and collateral, if any, by direct communication with the makers of the notes. By selection of the larger amounts, Chambers was able to verify 75 percent of the dollar amount of notes receivable by confirming only 20 percent of the notes. However, he also selected a random sample of another 20 percent of the smaller notes on the list for confirmation with the makers. Satisfactory replies were received to all confirmation requests.

The president of Hall Corporation informed Chambers that the company never required any collateral in support of the notes receivable; the replies to confirmation requests indicated no collateral had been pledged.

No notes were past due at the balance sheet date, and the credit manager stated that no losses were anticipated. Chambers verified the credit status of the makers of all the notes he had confirmed by reference to audited financial statements of the makers and Dun & Bradstreet credit ratings.

By independent computation of the interest accrued on the notes receivable at the balance sheet date, Chambers determined that the accrued interest receivable as shown on the balance sheet was correct.

Since Chambers found no deficiencies in any part of his examination, he issued an unqualified audit report. Some months later, Hall Corporation became insolvent and the president fled the country. Chambers was sued by creditors of the company, who charged that his audit was inadequate and failed to meet minimum professional standards. You are to comment on the audit program followed by Chambers with respect to notes receivable *only*.

12–39.   As part of his examination of the financial statements of Marlborough Corporation for the year ended March 31, 199X, Mark Wayne, CA, is reviewing the balance sheet presentation of a $1,200,000 advance to Franklin Olds, Marlborough's president. The advance, which represents 50 percent of current assets and 10 percent of total assets, was made during the year ended March 31, 199X. It has been described in the balance sheet as "miscellaneous accounts receivable" and classified as a current asset.

Olds informs the CA that he has used the proceeds of the advance to purchase 35,000 shares of Marlborough's common stock, in order to forestall a take over raid on the company. He is reluctant to have his association with the advance described in the financial statements because he does not have voting control and fears that this will "just give the raiders ammunition."

Olds offers the following four-point program as an alternative to further disclosure:

1. Have the advance approved by the board of directors. (This can be done expeditiously because a majority of the board members are officers of the company.)

2. Prepare a demand note payable to the company with interest of 12 percent (the average bank rate paid by the company).

3. Furnish an endorsement of the common stock to the company as collateral for the loan. (During the year under audit, despite the fact that earnings did not increase, the market price of Marlborough common rose from $20 to $40 per share. The common stock has maintained its $40 per share market price subsequent to year-end.)

4. Obtain a written opinion from the company lawyer supporting the legality of the company's advance and the use of the proceeds.

Required:

a. Discuss the proper balance sheet classification of the advance to Olds and other appropriate disclosures in the financial statements and footnotes. (Ignore tax effects, creditors' restrictions on stock repurchase, and the presentation of common stock dividends and interest revenue.)

b. Discuss each point of Olds's four-point program as to whether it is desirable and as to whether it is an alternative to further disclosure.

c. If Olds refuses to permit further disclosure, what action should the CA take? Discuss.

d. In his discussion with the CA, Olds warns that the raiders, if successful, probably will appoint new auditors. What consideration should the CA give to this factor? Explain.

(AICPA, adapted)

12–40. Lawrence Company maintains its accounts on the basis of a fiscal year ending October 31. Assume that you were retained by the company in August to perform an audit for the fiscal year ending October 31, 199X. You decide to perform certain auditing procedures in advance of the balance sheet date. Among these interim procedures is the confirmation of accounts receivable, which you perform at September 30.

The accounts receivable at September 30 consisted of approximately 200 accounts with balances totaling $956,750. Seventy-five of these accounts with balances totaling $650,725 were selected for confirmation. All but 20 of the confirmation requests have been returned; 30 were signed without comments, 14 had minor differences that have been cleared satisfactorily, and 11 confirmations had the following comments:

a. We are sorry, but we cannot answer your request for confirmation of our account because Moss Company uses a computerized accounts payable voucher system.

b. The balance of $1,050 was paid on September 23, 199X.

c. The above balance of $7,750 was paid on October 5, 199X.

d. The above balance has been paid.

e. We do not owe you anything at September 30, 199X, since the goods represented by our invoice dated September 30, 199X, Number 25,050, in the amount of $11,550, were received on October 5, 199X, on FOB destination terms.

f. An advance payment of $2,500 made by us in August 199X should cover the two invoices totaling $1,350 shown on the statement attached.

g. We never received these goods.

h. We are contesting the propriety of the $12,525 charge. We think the charge is excessive.

i. Amount okay. As the goods have been shipped to us on consignment, we will remit payment upon selling the goods.

j. The $10,000, representing a deposit under a lease, will be applied against the rent due to us during 199X, the last year of the lease.

k. Your credit dated September 5, 199X in the amount of $440 cancels the above balance.

Required:

What steps would you take to clear satisfactorily each of the above 11 comments?

(AICPA, adapted)

12–41. During your examination of the financial statements of Martin Mfg. Co. Ltd., a new client, for the year ended March 31, 199X, you note the following entry in the general journal dated March 31, 199X:

Notes Receivable	550,000	
Land		500,000
Gain on Sale of Land		50,000
To record sale of excess plant-site land to Ardmore Corp. for 8 percent note due five years from date. No interest payment required until maturity of note.		

Your review of the contract for sale between Martin and Ardmore, your enquiries of Martin executives, and your study of minutes of Martin's directors' meetings develop the following facts:

a. The land has been carried in your client's accounting records at its cost of $500,000.

b. Ardmore Corp. is a land developer and plans to subdivide and resell the land acquired from Martin Mfg. Co. Ltd.

c. Martin had originally negotiated with Ardmore on the basis of a 12 percent interest rate on the note. This interest rate was established by Martin after a careful analysis of Ardmore's credit standing and current money market conditions.

d. Ardmore had rejected the 12 percent interest rate because the total outlay on a 12 percent note for $550,000 would amount to $880,000 at the end of five years, and Ardmore thought a total outlay of this amount would leave it with an inadequate return on the subdivision. Ardmore held out for a total cash outlay of $770,000, and Martin Mfg. Co. Ltd. finally agreed to this position. During the discussions, it was pointed out that the present value of $1 due five years hence at an annual interest rate of 12 percent is approximately $0.567.

Required:

Ignoring income tax considerations, is the journal entry recording Martin's sale of the land to Ardmore acceptable? Explain fully and draft an adjusting entry if you consider one to be necessary.

12–42. The July 31, 199X, general ledger trial balance of Aerospace Contractors, Inc., reflects the following accounts associated with receivables. Balances of the accounts are after all adjusting journal entries proposed by the auditors and accepted by the client.

Accounts receivable—commercial	$ 595,000
Accounts receivable—Government of Canada	3,182,000
Allowance for uncollectible accounts and notes	75,000 cr.
Claims receivable—public carriers	7,000
Claims receivable—Government of Canada terminated contracts	320,000
Due from Harwood Co., investee	480,000
Notes receivable—trade	15,000

Remember that two or more ledger accounts are often combined into one amount in the financial statements in order to achieve a concise presentation. The need for brevity also often warrants the disclosure of some information parenthetically, as for example, the amount of the allowance for doubtful accounts.

Required:

a. Draft a partial balance sheet for Aerospace Contractors at July 31, 199X. In deciding upon which items deserve separate listing, consider materiality as well as the nature of the accounts.

b. Write an explanation of the reasoning employed in your balance sheet presentation of these accounts.

Chapter 13

Inventories and Cost of Goods Sold

After studying this chapter, you should be able to:

- Describe the nature of inventories and cost of goods sold.
- Explain the nature of the purchase and production (conversion) cycles.
- Identify the fundamental internal controls over inventories, purchases, and production.
- Describe the auditor's objectives for the audit of inventories.
- Describe the nature of the audit procedures to accomplish the auditors' objectives for the audit of inventories.

The interrelationship of inventories and cost of goods sold makes it logical for the two topics to be considered together. The internal controls that assure reliable accounting for inventories are found in the purchase cycle. These controls include procedures for selection of vendors, ordering merchandise or materials, inspecting goods received, recording the liability to the vendor, and authorizing and making cash disbursements. In a manufacturing business, the valuation of inventories also is affected by the production (or conversion) cycle, in which various manufacturing costs are assigned to inventories, and the cost of inventories is then transferred to the cost of goods sold.

The selection of a valuation method and the need for consistency in its application also affect both inventories and cost of goods sold. During periods of inflation, the inadequacies of historical cost affect the validity of cost of goods sold as much as they affect inventories. Thus, it is not surprising that the accounting profession in both Canada and the United States recently experimented with requiring supplemental disclosure of current replacement cost of inventories.[1]

Sources and Nature of Inventories and Cost of Goods Sold

The term *inventories* is used in this chapter to include (1) goods on hand ready for sale, either the merchandise of a trading concern or the finished goods of a manufacturer; (2) goods in the process of production; and (3) goods to be consumed directly or indirectly in production, consisting of raw (or direct) materials, purchased parts, and supplies.

Inventories have received much attention in both the accounting and auditing literature, as well as in discussions among professional accountants. The reasons for the special significance attached to inventories are readily apparent:

1. Inventories usually constitute the largest current asset of an enterprise and are very susceptible to major errors, fraud, and irregularities.
2. Numerous alternative methods for valuation of inventories are sanctioned by the accounting profession, and different methods may be used for various classes of inventories.
3. The determination of inventory value directly affects the cost of goods sold and has a major impact upon net income for the year.
4. The determination of inventory quality, condition, and value is inherently a more complex and difficult task than is the case with most elements of financial position. Many inventory items, such as precious gems, sophisticated electronic parts, and construction in progress, present significant problems of identification and valuation.

The Auditors' Objectives in Examination of Inventories and Cost of Goods Sold

The auditors' have six *objectives* in the examination of inventories and cost of goods sold:

1. To consider *internal control* over inventories and cost of goods sold.

---

[1] The CICA has proposed to rescind Section 4510 on reporting the effects of changing prices. In the United States, the requirement for mandatory disclosure of current cost information was rescinded by *FASB Statement No. 89,* ''Financial Reporting and Changing Prices.''

2. To determine the *existence* of inventories, and the client's *ownership* of these assets.
3. To establish the *completeness* of inventories.
4. To establish the *clerical accuracy* of records and supporting schedules for inventories and cost of goods sold.
5. To determine that the *valuation* of inventories and cost of goods sold is based on appropriate methods.
6. To determine that the *statement presentation* of inventories and cost of goods sold is adequate, including disclosure of classifications of inventories, accounting methods, and any inventories pledged as collateral for loans.

In conjunction with the audit of inventories and cost of goods sold, the auditors will also obtain evidence about the related purchases, sales, purchase returns, and sales returns accounts.

The responsibilities of external auditors with respect to the validity of inventories can best be understood by turning back to the time of the spectacular *McKesson & Robbins* fraud case in the United States. The hearings conducted by the SEC of the United States in 1939 disclosed that the audited financial statements of McKesson & Robbins, Inc., a drug company listed on the New York Stock Exchange, contained $19 million of fictitious assets, about one fourth of the total assets shown on the balance sheet. The fictitious assets included $10 million of nonexistent inventories. How was it possible for the external auditors to have conducted an audit and to have issued an unqualified report without discovering this gigantic fraud? The audit program followed for inventories in this case was in accordance with customary auditing practice of the 1930s. The significant point is that in that period it was customary to limit the audit work on inventories to an examination of records only; the standards of that era did not require any observation, physical count, or other actual contact with the inventories.

Up to the time of the *McKesson & Robbins* case, auditors had avoided taking responsibility for verifying the accuracy of inventory quantities and the physical existence of the goods. With questionable logic, many auditors had argued that they were experts in handling figures and analyzing accounting records but were not qualified to identify and measure the great variety of raw materials and manufactured goods found in the factories, warehouses, and store buildings of their clients.

The *McKesson & Robbins* case brought a quick end to such limited views of the auditors' responsibility. The public accounting profession was faced with the necessity of accepting responsibility for verifying the physical existence of inventories or of confessing that its audit function offered no real protection to investors or other users of financial statements. The profession met the challenge by adopting new standards requiring the auditors to establish the existence, ownership, and completeness of inventories by observing the taking of the physical inventory.

Both Section 6030 of the *CICA Handbook* and *SAS Nos. 1* and *2* of the AICPA now recommend the observation of the taking of physical inventories as one of the generally accepted auditing procedures. If such a procedure is not practicable or possible in the circumstances, the auditors should substitute other satisfactory auditing procedures, which should include observing or making some physical counts of inventories at some time other than the time of the client's inventory taking or stocktaking.[2] Where the auditors are able to obtain sufficient appropriate audit evidence through the use of other auditing procedures, they may issue an unqualified opinion without disclosing the omission of an observation of the physical inventory.

It is also important to note that *SAS No. 1* makes a distinction between companies which determine inventory quantities solely by an annual physical count and companies with well-kept perpetual inventory records. The latter companies often have strong internal control over inventories, and many of them employ statistical sampling techniques to verify the records by occasional test counts during the year rather than by a complete annual count of the entire inventory. For these clients the auditors' observation of physical inventory may be limited to such counts as they consider appropriate, and may occur during or after the end of the period being audited.

The auditors' approach to the verification of inventories and cost of goods sold should be one of awareness to the possibility of intentional misstatements, as well as to the prevalence of accidental error in the determination of inventory quantities and amounts. Purposeful misstatement of inventories has often been employed to evade income taxes, to conceal shortages arising from fraud and various irregularities, and to mislead shareholders or other inactive owners as to a company's profits and financial position.

Internal Control over Inventories and Cost of Goods Sold

The importance of adequate internal control over inventories and cost of goods sold from the viewpoint of both management and the auditors can scarcely be overemphasized. In some companies, management stresses internal controls over cash and securities but pays little attention to control over inventories. Since many types of inventories are composed of items not particularly susceptible to theft, management may consider internal controls to be unnecessary in this area. Such thinking ignores the fact that

---

[2] However, the AICPA's *SAS No. 1* stipulates that the use of alternative procedures must always include observing or making some physical counts of inventory even though this occurs after the balance sheet date.

internal control performs other functions just as important as fraud prevention.

Good internal control is a means of providing accurate cost data for inventories and cost of goods sold as well as accuracy in reporting physical quantities. Inadequate internal control may cause losses by permitting erroneous cost data to be used by management in setting prices and in making other decisions based on reported profit margins. If the accounts do not furnish a realistic picture of the cost of inventories on hand, the cost of finished goods manufactured, and the cost of goods sold, the financial statements may be grossly misleading both as to earnings and as to financial position.

Internal control procedures for inventories affect nearly all the functions involved in producing and disposing of the company's products. Purchasing, receiving, storing, issuing, processing, and shipping are the physical functions directly connected with inventories; the cost accounting system and the perpetual inventory records comprise the recording functions. Since the auditors are interested in the final products of the recording functions, it is necessary for them to understand and appraise the cost accounting system and the perpetual inventory records, as well as the various procedures and original documents underlying the preparation of financial data.

The Purchasing Function.   Adequate internal control over purchases requires, first of all, an organizational structure that delegates to a separate department of the company exclusive authority to make all purchases of materials and services. The purchasing, receiving, and recording functions should be clearly separated and lodged in separate departments. In small companies, this type of departmentalized operation may not be possible, but even in very small enterprises, it is usually feasible to make one person responsible for all purchase transactions.

Serially numbered purchase orders should be prepared for all purchases, and copies forwarded to the accounting and receiving departments. The copy sent to receiving should have the quantities blacked out to increase the probability that receiving personnel will make independent counts of the merchandise received. Even though the buyer may actually place an order by telephone, the formal purchase order should be prepared and forwarded. In many large organizations, purchase orders are issued only after compliance with extensive procedures for (1) determining the need for the item, (2) obtaining competitive bids, and (3) obtaining approval of the financial aspect of the commitment.

The Receiving Function.   All goods received by the company—without exception—should be cleared through a receiving department that is independent of purchasing, storing, and shipping departments. The receiving department is responsible for (1) the determination of quantities of goods received, (2) the detection of damaged or defective goods, (3) the preparation of a receiving report, and (4) the prompt transmittal of goods received to the stores department.

The Storing Function.   As goods are delivered to stores, they are counted, inspected, and receipted for. The stores department will then notify the accounting department of the amount received and placed in stock. In performing these functions, the stores department makes an important contribution to overall control of inventories. By signing for the goods, it fixes its own responsibility, and by notifying the accounting department of actual goods stored, it provides verification of the receiving department's work.

The Issuing Function.   The stores department, being responsible for all goods under its control, has reason to insist that for all items passing out of its hands it be given a prenumbered requisition, which serves as a signed receipt from the department accepting the goods. Requisitions are usually prepared in triplicate. One copy is retained by the department making the request, another serves as the stores department's receipt, and the third is a notice to the accounting department for cost distribution. To prevent the indiscriminate writing of requisitions for questionable purposes, some organizations establish policies requiring that requisitions be drawn only upon the authority of a bill of materials, an engineering order, or a sales order. In wholesale and retail concerns, shipping orders rather than factory requisitions serve to authorize withdrawals from stores.

The Production (Conversion) Function.   Responsibility for the goods in production must be fixed, usually on factory supervisors or superintendents. Routing sheets document the flow of the goods and related responsibility as they progress through the production process. Thus, from the time materials are delivered to the factory until they are completed and routed to a finished-goods storeroom, a designated supervisor should be in control and be prepared to answer for their location and disposition.

The internal control over goods in process may include regular inspection procedures to reveal defective work. This aids in disclosing inefficiencies in the productive system and also tends to prevent inflation of the goods in process inventory by the accumulation of cost for goods that will eventually be scrapped.

Control procedures should also assure that goods scrapped during the process of production are promptly reported to the accounting department so that the decrease in value of goods in process inventories may be recorded. Scrapped materials may have substantial salvage value, and this calls for segregation and control of scrap inventories.

The Shipping Function.   Shipments of goods should be made only after proper authorization has been received. This authorization will normally be a sales order approved by the credit department, although the shipping function also includes the returning of defective goods to suppliers. In this latter case, the authorization may take the form of a shipping authorization from a purchasing department executive.

The shipping department will prepare a prenumbered shipping document, detailing the goods shipped. One copy of the shipping document will go to the stores department, a second copy will be retained by the shipping department as evidence of shipment, and a third copy will be enclosed as a packing slip with the goods when they are shipped. The control aspect of this procedure is strengthened by the fact that an outsider, the customer, will inspect the packing slip and notify the company of any discrepancy between this list, the goods ordered, and the goods actually received.

When the goods have been shipped, the shipping department will attach to a fourth copy of each shipping document the related evidence of shipment: bills of lading, trucking bills, carriers' receipts, and freight bills. This facilitates subsequent audit by grouping together the documents showing that shipments were properly authorized and carried out. The shipping document, with the sales order and other supporting documents attached, is then sent to the billing department, where it is used as the basis for invoicing the customer.

Established shipping routines should be followed for all types of shipments, including the sale of scrap, return of defective goods, and forwarding of materials and parts to subcontractors.

The Cost Accounting System.   An adequate cost accounting system is necessary to account for the usage of raw materials and supplies, to determine the content and value of goods in process inventories, and to compute the finished goods inventory. This system comprises all the records, orders, requisitions, time tickets, and the like, needed in a proper accounting for the disposition of materials as they enter the flow of production and as they continue through the factory in the process of becoming finished goods. The cost accounting system also serves to accumulate labour costs and indirect costs that contribute to the goods in process and the finished-goods inventories. The cost accounting system thus forms an integral part of the internal control for inventories.

The figures produced by the cost accounting system should be controlled by general ledger accounts. The cost of raw materials and labour are recorded in individual goods (work) in process accounts for each job order or process. Periodically, manufacturing overhead is applied to the jobs or processes and recorded in the accounts. A single goods-in-process inventory account controls individual goods-in-process accounts.

Underlying this upper level of control between the factory records and the general ledger is a system of production orders, material requisitions, job tickets or other labour distributions, and manufacturing overhead distributions. Control is affected by various procedures that verify the accuracy of production records. Allocations of raw materials and labour costs are recomputed and reconciled to material and payroll records. Manufacturing overhead costs that are applied using predetermined rates are adjusted to actual costs at the end of the period.

Many companies have established standard cost systems that help identify the causes of ineffectiveness and waste. These systems provide for the prompt pricing of inventories and for control over operations through a study of variances between actual and standard costs. All the various types of cost accounting systems are alike in that they are designed to contribute to effective internal control by tracing the execution of managerial directives in the factory, by providing reliable inventory figures, and by safeguarding company assets.

The Perpetual Inventory System.   Perpetual inventory records constitute a most important part of internal control. These records, by showing at all times the quantity of goods on hand, provide information essential to intelligent purchasing, sales, and production-planning policies. With such a record it is possible to guide procurement by establishing points of minimum and maximum quantities for each standard item stocked.

The use of a perpetual inventory system allows companies to control the high costs of holding excessive inventory, while minimizing the risk of running out of stock. The company can control inventories through reorder points and economic order quantities, including *just-in-time* ordering systems in which inventory levels are kept to a minimum.

If perpetual inventory records are to produce the control implicit in their nature, it is desirable that the subsidiary records be maintained both in quantities and dollars for all stock, that the subsidiary records be controlled by the general ledger, that trial balances be prepared at reasonable intervals, and that both the detailed records and the general ledger control accounts be adjusted to agree with physical counts whenever taken.

Perpetual inventory records discourage inventory theft and waste, since storeskeepers and other employees are aware of the accountability over goods established by this continuous record of goods received, issued, and on hand. The records, however, must be periodically verified through the physical counting of goods.

Internal Control and the Computer

A computerized inventory system makes it much easier for the client to maintain control over inventories, purchasing, and the manufacturing process. Purchase requisitions and orders can be automatically generated by the computer when inventory levels reach predetermined reorder points. The client's purchasing system may even be linked to the system of its suppliers, allowing *electronic data interchange* to completely coordinate production and purchasing. The EDP system also maintains records of responsibility for goods as they are routed through the production process. Details of direct labour and material usage are entered, and the computer allocates these direct costs to jobs or processes, applies manufacturing overhead costs based on predetermined rates, and maintains perpetual records of the costs of goods in process, finished and sold. The computer also generates various financial reports, including *responsibility accounting reports* that indicate actual costs, standard costs, and the related variances.

Good internal control in EDP systems requires the normal segregation of functions of purchasing, receiving, storing, processing, and shipping. In addition, the client should establish appropriate EDP controls that promote the accuracy of data as it is entered into the system, and maintain its integrity after it is entered.

Audit Working Papers for Inventories and Cost of Goods Sold

A great variety of working papers may be prepared by the auditors in their verification of inventories and cost of goods sold. These papers will range in form from written comments on the manner in which the physical inventory was taken to elaborate analyses of production costs of finished goods and goods in process. Selected working papers will be illustrated in connection with the audit procedures to be described in later sections of this chapter.

AUDIT PROGRAM FOR INVENTORIES AND COST OF GOODS SOLD

The following audit procedures for the verification of inventories and cost of goods sold will be discussed in detail in the succeeding pages. The program is appropriate for a manufacturing company that takes a complete physical inventory to verify the perpetual inventories at the close of each fiscal year.

A. Consider internal control for inventories and cost of goods sold.

1. *Obtain an understanding of internal control* for inventories and cost of goods sold.
2. *Assess control risk and design additional tests of controls* for inventories and cost of goods sold.
3. *Perform additional tests of controls* for those controls which the auditors plan to consider to reduce their assessment of control risk, such as:
   a. Examine significant aspects of a sample of purchase transactions.
   b. Test the cost accounting system.

4. *Reassess control risk and design substantive tests* for inventories and cost of goods sold.

B. Perform substantive tests of inventories and cost of goods sold transactions.

5. Obtain listings of inventory and reconcile to ledgers.
6. Evaluate the client's planning of physical inventory.
7. Observe the taking of physical inventory and make test counts.
8. Review the year-end cutoff of purchases and sales transactions.
9. Obtain a copy of the completed physical inventory, test its clerical accuracy, and trace test counts.
10. Review inventory quality and condition.
11. Evaluate the bases and methods of inventory pricing.
12. Test the pricing of inventories.
13. Perform analytical procedures.
14. Determine whether any inventories have been pledged and review purchase and sales commitments.
15. Evaluate financial statement presentation of inventories and cost of goods sold, including the adequacy of disclosure.

Figure 13–1 relates the objectives of the major substantive tests of inventories and cost of goods sold to the primary audit objectives.

A. Consider internal control for inventories and cost of goods sold.

1. Obtain an understanding of internal control.

As previously indicated, the consideration of internal controls may involve the filling out of a questionnaire, the writing of descriptive memoranda, or the preparation of flowcharts depicting organizational structure and the flow of materials and documents. In obtaining an understanding of internal control over inventory, the auditors should become thoroughly conversant with the procedures for purchasing, receiving, storing, and issuing goods and for controlling production, as well as acquiring an understanding of the cost accounting system and the perpetual inventory records.

The auditors should also give consideration to the physical protection for inventories. Any deficiencies in storage facilities, in guard service, or in physical handling that may lead to losses from weather, fire, flood, or theft may appropriately be called to the attention of management.

The matters to be investigated in the auditors' consideration of internal controls over inventory and cost of sales are fairly well indicated by the following questions: Are perpetual inventory records maintained for each class of inventory? Are the perpetual inventory records verified by physical inventories at least once each year? Do the procedures for physical inventories include the use of prenumbered tags, with all tag numbers accounted for? Are differences between physical inventory counts and perpetual inventory records investigated before the perpetual records are adjusted? Is a separate purchasing department responsible for purchasing

FIGURE 13–1   Objectives of Major Substantive Tests of Inventories and Cost
of Goods Sold

Substantive Tests	*Primary Audit Objectives*
Obtain listings of inventory and reconcile to ledgers	*Clerical accuracy*
Evaluate the client's planning of physical inventory Observe the taking of the physical inventory Review the year-end cutoff of purchases and sales transactions Obtain a copy of the completed physical inventory and test its accuracy	*Existence and ownership* *Completeness*
Review inventory quality and condition Evaluate the bases and methods of inventory pricing Test the pricing of inventories	*Valuation*
Perform analytical procedures	*Existence and ownership* *Completeness* *Valuation*
Determine whether any inventories have been pledged and review commitments	*Valuation* *Statement presentation*
Evaluate financial statement presentation and disclosure	*Statement presentation*

all materials, supplies, and equipment? Are all incoming shipments, including returns by customers, processed by a separate receiving department? Are materials and supplies held in the custody of a stores department and issued only on properly approved requisitions?

After the auditors have prepared a flowchart (or other description) of internal control, they should determine that the client is using those procedures, that is, they determine whether the controls have been ***placed in operation***. This information may be obtained through enquiries of entity personnel, inspection of documents, and observation of activities. As the auditors confirm their understanding of the internal control policies systems, and procedures, they will observe whether there is an appropriate segregation of duties, and enquire who performed various functions throughout the year. They will also inspect various documents, such as purchase requisitions, purchase orders, material requisitions, time tickets, and shipping documents, and review document files to determine that the client is appropriately accounting for the sequence of prenumbered documents. Inventory and production reports will be examined, and the auditors will review the evidence of follow-up on variances from standard costs. These procedures may provide the auditors with sufficient evidence to assess control risk for certain financial statement assertions about inventories and cost of goods sold at less than the maximum.

2. Assess control risk and design additional tests of controls.

After obtaining an understanding of the client's internal control over inventories and cost of goods sold, the auditors perform their initial assessments of control risk for the various financial statement assertions. To further evaluate these assessments, the auditors must obtain additional evidence of the operating effectiveness of the client's internal control policies, systems, and procedures by designing additional tests of controls. In designing these tests, the auditors must decide which ones will result in sufficient reductions in substantive tests to justify the time spent performing them.

3. Perform additional tests of controls.

Tests directed toward the effectiveness of controls help to evaluate the client's internal control and to determine the extent to which the auditors are justified in reducing their assessed levels of control risk for the assertions about the inventory and cost of goods sold accounts. Certain tests of controls are performed as the auditors obtain an understanding of the client's internal control; they were described in our discussion of that process. The following are examples of typical additional tests.

a. **Examine significant aspects of a sample of purchase transactions.**

The proper recording of purchase transactions and of cash disbursements is essential to reliable accounting records. Therefore, the auditors test the key control procedures in the client's purchasing transaction cycle. Tests of this cycle may include the following steps:

1. Account for, on a test basis, the numerical sequence of purchase orders and receiving reports.
2. Select a sample of purchase transactions.
3. Examine the purchase requisition or other authorization and the purchase order for each purchase transaction in the sample.
4. Examine the related vendor's invoice, receiving report, and paid cheque for each purchase order in the sample. Trace transactions to the voucher register and cheque register.
5. Review vendors' invoices for approval of prices, extensions, footings, freight and credit terms, and account distribution.
6. Compare quantities and prices in the invoice, purchase order, and receiving report, and prices with suppliers' price catalogues or listings.
7. Trace postings from voucher register to general ledger and any applicable subsidiary ledgers.

b. Test the cost accounting system.

For a client in the manufacturing field, the auditors must become familiar with the cost accounting system in use as a part of their consideration of internal control. A wide variety of practices will be encountered for the costing of finished units. The cost accounting records may be controlled by general ledger accounts or operated independently of the general accounting system. In the latter case, the cost of completed units may be difficult or impossible to verify and may represent nothing more than a well-reasoned guess. Because cost accounting methods vary so widely, even among manufacturing concerns in the same industry, audit procedures for a cost accounting system must be designed to fit the specific circumstances encountered in each case.

In any cost accounting system, the three elements of manufacturing cost are raw (direct) materials costs, direct labour costs, and manufacturing overhead. Cost accounting systems may accumulate either actual costs or standard costs according to *processes* or *jobs.* The auditors' tests of the client's cost accounting system are designed to determine that costs allocated to specific jobs or processes are appropriately compiled.

To achieve this objective, the auditors test the propriety of raw materials quantities and unit costs, direct labour-hours and hourly rates, and overhead rates and allocation bases. Quantities of direct materials charged to jobs or processes are vouched to materials requisitions, and unit materials costs are traced to the raw materials perpetual inventory records or purchase invoices. The auditors examine job tickets or time summaries supporting direct labour-hours accumulations and trace direct labour hourly rates to union contracts or individual employee personnel files.

The auditors must recognize that a variety of methods is generally accepted for the application of manufacturing overhead to inventories. A predetermined rate of factory overhead, applied on the basis of machine-hours, direct labour dollars, direct labour-hours, or some similar basis, is used by many manufacturing companies. The predetermined overhead rate is usually revised periodically, but nevertheless leads each year to some underabsorbed or overabsorbed overhead. The auditors will ordinarily insist that any significant amount of under- or overabsorbed overhead be applied to a proportionate reduction in inventory and cost of sales.

A distinction between manufacturing overhead, on the one hand, and overhead costs pertaining to selling or general administration of the business, on the other, must be made under generally accepted accounting principles because selling expenses and general and administrative expenses are written off in the period incurred. The difference in the accounting treatment accorded to manufacturing overhead and to non-manufacturing overhead implies a fundamental difference between these two types of cost. Nevertheless, as a practical matter it is often impossible to say with finality that a particular expenditure, such as the salary of a vice president in charge of production, should be classified as overhead, as general and administrative expense, or perhaps be divided between the two. Despite this difficulty, a vital procedure in the audit of cost of goods sold for a manufacturing concern is determining that overhead costs are reasonably allocated in the accounts. Failure to distribute manufacturing costs to the correct accounts can cause significant distortions in the client's predetermined overhead rate and in over- or underapplied factory overhead. The auditors may find it necessary to obtain or prepare analyses of a number of the overhead subsidiary ledger accounts and to verify the propriety of the charges thereto. Then the auditors must determine the propriety of the total machine-hours, direct labour-hours, or other aggregate allocation base used by the client company to predetermine the overhead rate.

If standard costs are in use, it is desirable to compare standard costs with actual costs for representative items and to ascertain whether the standards reflect current materials and labour usage and unit costs. The composition of manufacturing overhead, the basis for its distribution by department and product, and the effect of any change in basis during the year should be reviewed. The standard costs of selected products should be verified by testing computations, extensions, and footings and by tracing charges for labour, material, and overhead to original sources.

The auditors' study of a manufacturing company's cost accounting system should give special attention to any changes in cost methods made during the year and the effect of such changes on the cost of sales. Close attention should also be given to the methods of summarizing costs of completed products and to the procedures for recording the cost of partial shipments.

4. Reassess control risk and design substantive tests.

The understanding and tests of controls of the client's internal control for inventories and cost of goods sold provide the auditors with evidence as to weaknesses and strengths of the system. Based on this information, the auditors reassess control risk for the assertions about inventories and cost of goods sold. Figure 13–2 illustrates the relationship between these assertions and the various internal control policies, systems, and procedures. It also shows how these policies, systems, and procedures are typically tested. The auditors' assessments of control risk are then used to design the substantive tests of inventories and costs of goods sold.

B. **Substantive tests.**

5. Obtain listings of inventory and reconcile to ledgers.

The auditor will obtain a schedule of listings of inventory which will be reconciled to both the general ledger and appropriate subsidiary ledgers. The nature of the listings will vary depending upon whether the client engages in manufacturing or simply sells products at wholesale or retail. The auditors' goal in performing this step is to make sure the inventory records agree with what is reported in the financial statements.

6. Evaluate the client's planning of physical inventory.

Efficient and effective inventory taking requires careful planning in advance. Cooperation between the auditors and client personnel in formulating the procedures to be followed will prevent unnecessary confusion and will aid in securing a complete and well-controlled count. A first step is the designation by the client management of an individual employee, often a representative of the controller, to assume responsibility for the physical inventory. This responsibility will begin with the drafting of procedures and will carry through to the final determination of the dollar value of all inventories.

In planning the physical inventory, the client should consider many factors, such as (1) selection of the best date or dates, (2) suspending production in certain departments of the plant, (3) segregating obsolete and defective goods, (4) establishing control over the counting process through the use of inventory tags or sheets, (5) achieving proper cutoff of sales and purchase transactions, and (6) arranging for services of engineers or other specialists to determine the quantity or quality of certain goods or materials.

Once the plan has been developed, it must be documented and communicated in the form of written instructions to the personnel taking the physical inventory. These instructions normally will be drafted by the client and reviewed by the auditors, who will judge their adequacy. In evaluating the adequacy of the instructions, the auditors should consider the nature and materiality of the inventories, as well as the existing internal control. Normally, the auditors will insist that the inventory be taken at or near the balance sheet date. However, if the client has effective internal control, including perpetual records, the auditors may be satisfied to observe inventory counts performed during the year. If the client plans to use a statistical sampling technique to estimate the quantities of inventories, the auditors will evaluate the statistical validity of the sampling method and the adequacy of the level of risk of assessing control risk too low and allowance for sampling risk (precision).[3] If the instructions for taking inventory are adequate, then the auditors' responsibility during the count is largely a matter of seeing that the instructions are followed conscientiously.

Some companies prepare two sets of instructions for the physical inventory: one set for the supervisors who will direct the count and a second set for the employees who will perform the detailed work of counting and listing merchandise. A set of instructions prepared by the controller of a large clothing store for use by supervisors is shown in Figure 13–3.

---

[3] Some sources use the term *confidence level* to represent the complement of the risk of assessing control risk too low. Thus, a 95 percent confidence level is identical to a 5 percent risk of assessing control risk too low (100 percent − 5 percent).

FIGURE 13–2 Assessing Control Risk for Inventories, Production and Purchases

Internal Control Policy, System, and Procedure	• Typical Tests of the Control Policy, System, or Procedure	Financial Statement Assertions				
		Existence	Completeness	Ownership	Valuation	Presentation
Segregate duties over purchases, production, and custody of inventories	Observe and make enquiries about the performance of various functions	X	X	X		
Use prenumbered requisitions, purchase orders, and receiving reports and account for the sequence of documents	Observe and make enquiries about the use of prenumbered documents and inspect evidence of accounting for the sequence		X			
Establish procedures for authorizing purchase transactions, reconciling purchase invoices to purchase orders and receiving reports, and verifying the clerical accuracy of purchase invoices	Observe and make enquiries about purchase procedures, and test a sample of purchase transactions by comparing the details to authorized purchase orders and receiving reports, and recomputing the invoice amounts	X		X	X	
Establish general ledger control of inventories of raw materials, goods in process, and finished goods and periodically reconcile to production records	Inspect accounting and production records and enquire about and inspect selected reconciliations	X		X	X	X

Internal control	Related audit procedure					
Establish a cost accounting system that accumulates appropriate inventory costs on a job order or process cost basis	Test the raw material costs by reference to requisitions and purchase invoices, direct labour costs by reference to payroll records and union contracts, and recompute overhead application rates					X
Analyze variances from standard costs	Inspect inventory reports and examine evidence of follow-up on variances	X	X	X	X	
Use perpetual records to control inventories	Enquire about the perpetual inventory procedures, and test the records by reference to purchase invoices and production records		X	X	X	
Use appropriate procedures for taking the physical inventory	Review the inventory instructions and observe the inventory taking procedures		X	X	X	
Establish appropriate physical controls over inventories	Observe and enquire about the physical control policies, systems, and procedures			X	X	

FIGURE 13–3

GLEN HAVEN DEPARTMENT STORES, INC.

Instructions for Physical Inventory,
August 5, 199X

TO ALL SUPERVISORS:

A complete physical inventory of all departments in each store will
be taken Sunday, August 5, 199x, beginning at 8:30 a.m. and continuing
until completed. Employees are to report at 8:15 a.m. to receive their
final briefing on their instructions, which are appended hereto.

Within one week prior to August 5, supervisors should make sure
that merchandise in departments is well organized. All merchandise with
the same stock number should be located together. Merchandise that is
damaged should be segregated for separate listing on inventory sheets.

Each count team should be formed and started by a supervisor, and
should be periodically observed by that supervisor to assure that instructions are being complied with in the counting and listing processes.

A block of sequential prenumbered inventory sheets will be issued
to each supervisor at 8:00 a.m. August 5, for later issuance to count
teams. Each supervisor is to account for all sheets--used, unused, or
voided. In addition, each supervisor will be furnished at that time with
a listing of count teams under his supervision.

When a count team reports completion of a department, that team's
supervisor should accompany a representative of the external auditors,
McDonald & Company, in performing test counts. A space is provided on
each inventory sheet for the supervisor's signature as reviewer. When
the auditors have "cleared" a department, the supervisor responsible
should take possession of the count sheets. All completed count sheets
are to be placed in numerical sequence and turned over to me when the
entire inventory has been completed.

Before supervisors and employees leave the stores Saturday evening,
August 4, they are to make certain that "housekeeping" is in order in
each department, and that all merchandise bears a price ticket.

If you have any questions about these instructions or any other aspect of the physical inventory, please see me.

J. R. Adams

J. R. Adams
Controller
July 24, 199x

Advance planning by the senior auditor-in-charge is also necessary to assure efficient use of audit staff members during the inventory taking. The auditor-in-charge should determine the dates of the counts, the extent of the test counts, the number of auditors needed at each location, and the estimated time required. The senior should then assign auditors to specific locations and provide them with a written statement of their duties. The senior may also wish to arrange for the cooperation of the client's internal auditing staff during the count, and possibly for the assistance of the company's engineers or independent specialists.

When written instructions are prepared by the auditing firm for use of its staff in a particular engagement, these instructions are not made available to the client. Their purpose is to make sure that all auditors understand their assignments and can therefore work efficiently during the physical inventory. An example of inventory instructions prepared by a public accounting firm for the use of its own staff members is presented in Figure 13–4. These instructions relate to the same audit engagement described in the client's instructions to supervisors illustrated in Figure 13–3. The audit staff members should have copies of the client's inventory instructions in their possession during the inventory observation.

7. Observe the taking of physical inventory and make test counts.

It is not the auditors' function to *take* the inventory or to control or supervise the taking; this is the responsibility of management. The auditors *observe* the inventory taking in order to obtain sufficient appropriate evidence as to the existence and completeness of audit objectives. In brief, observation of inventory taking gives the auditors a basis for an opinion as to the credibility of representations by management of inventory quantities.

To observe the inventory taking, however, implies a much more active role than that of a mere spectator. Observation by the auditors also includes determining that all usable inventory owned by the client is included in the count and that the client's employees comply with the written inventory instructions. As part of the process of observing the physical inventory, the auditors will be alert to detect any obsolete or damaged merchandise included in inventory. Such merchandise should be segregated by the client and written down to net realizable value. In short, during the inventory observation, the auditors are alert for, and follow up on, any unusual problems not anticipated in the client's written inventory instructions or improperly dealt with by the client's inventory teams.

The auditors will also *make a record of the serial number of the final receiving and shipping documents issued before the taking of inventory* so that the accuracy of the cutoff can be determined at a later date. Shipments or receipts of goods taking place during the counting process should be closely observed and any necessary reconciliations made. Observation of the physical inventory by the auditors also stresses determining that the client is controlling properly the inventory tags or sheets. These should be prenumbered so that all tags can be accounted for.

FIGURE 13–4

McDONALD and COMPANY

CHARTERED ACCOUNTANTS

Glen Haven Department Stores, Inc.
Inventory Observation--Instructions for Audit Staff
August 5, 199X

We will observe physical inventory taking at the following stores of Glen Haven Department Stores, Inc., on August 5, 199X:

Store	Store Manager	Our Staff
Wilshire	J. M. Baker	John Rodgers, Faye Arnold
Crenshaw	Roberta Bryan	Weldon Simpkins
Valley	Hugh Remington	Roger Dawson

Report to assigned stores promptly at 8:00 a.m. Attached are copies of the company's detailed instructions to employees who are to take the physical inventories and to supervisors who are to be in charge. These instructions appear to be complete and adequate; we should satisfy ourselves by observation that the instructions are being followed.

All merchandise counted will be listed on prenumbered inventory sheets. We should make test counts of approximately 5 percent of the stock items to ascertain the accuracy of the physical counts. A majority of the counts should be performed on the high-value stock, as described on the enclosed listing. Test counts are to be recorded in working papers, with the following information included:

> Department number
> Inventory sheet number
> Stock number
> Description of item, including season letter and year
> Quantity
> Selling price per price tag

We should ascertain that adequate control is maintained over the prenumbered inventory sheets issued. Also, we should prepare a listing of the last numbers used for transfers, markdowns, and markups in the various departments and stores. Inventory sheets are not to be removed form the departments until we have "cleared" them; we should not delay this operation.

Each staff member's working papers should include an opinion on the adequacy of the inventory taking. The papers should also include a summary of time incurred in the observation.

No cash or other cutoff procedures are to be performed as an adjunct to the inventory observation.

During their inventory observation, the auditors will make test counts of selected inventory items. The extent of the test counts will vary widely, depending upon the inherent risk and materiality of the client's inventory and the extent of the client's internal controls. A representative number of test counts should be recorded in the audit working papers for subsequent comparison with the completed inventory listing.

Serially numbered inventory count tags are usually attached to each lot of goods during the taking of a physical inventory. The design of the tag and the procedures for using it are intended to guard against two common pitfalls: (*a*) accidental omission of goods from the count and (*b*) double counting of goods.

Many companies use two-employee teams to count the inventories. Each team is charged with a sequence of the serially numbered tags and is required to turn in to the physical inventory supervisor any tags voided or not used.

The actual counting, the filling in of inventory tags, and the pulling of these tags are done by the client's employees. While the inventory tags are still attached to the goods, the auditors may make such test counts as they deem appropriate in the circumstances. The auditors will list in their working papers the tag numbers for the test counts that were made. The client employees will ordinarily not collect (pull) the inventory tags until the auditors indicate that they are satisfied with the accuracy of the count.

In comparing their test counts to the inventory tags, the auditors are alert for errors not only in quantities but also in part numbers, descriptions, units of measure, and all other aspects of the inventory item. For test counts of goods in process inventory, the auditors must ascertain that the percentage or stage of completion indicated on the inventory tag is appropriate.

If the test counts made by the auditors indicate discrepancies, the goods are recounted at once by the client's employees and the error corrected. If an excessive number of errors is found, the inventory for the entire department or even for the entire company should be recounted.

The information listed on the inventory tags often is transferred by the client to serially numbered inventory sheets. These sheets are used in pricing the inventory and in summarizing the dollar amounts involved. After the inventory tags have been collected, the client employee supervising the inventory will determine that all tags are accounted for by serial number. The auditors should ascertain that numerical control is maintained over both inventory tags and inventory sheets.

Clients using electronic data processing equipment may facilitate inventory counting and summarizing through machine-readable inventory tags. Prior to the physical inventory, the tags may be encoded with tag numbers, part numbers, descriptions, and unit prices. After the physical inventory, the information from the tags is entered into the computer, which extends quantity times unit price for each inventory item and prints out a complete inventory summary.

The test counts and tag numbers listed by the auditors in their working papers will be traced later to the client's inventory summary sheets. A discrepancy will be regarded not as an error in counting but as a mistake in copying data from the tags, a purposeful alteration of a tag, or creation of a fictitious tag.

Illustrative Case

The auditors of Cenco Incorporated in the United States did not adequately review the control of physical inventory tags, even though their CPA firm's procedures required such a review. According to the SEC (*Accounting and Auditing Enforcement Release No. 1,* par. 4552), Cenco personnel altered quantities on the final inventory computer listings and created bogus inventory tags; the result was a $39 million overstatement of inventory with a reported value of $119 million. The auditors ignored several indications of the inventory overstatement, including numerous differences between the client's inventory computer listings and the auditors' test counts, lack of vendor invoices to support the purchase of quantities of certain inventory items reported to be on hand, and unusual adjustments of perpetual records to physical counts.

During the observation of physical inventories, the auditors should make enquiries to ascertain whether any of the materials or goods on hand are the property of others, such as goods held on consignment or customer-owned materials sent in for machine work or other processing.

Audit procedures applicable to goods held by the client on consignment may include a comparison of the physical inventory with the client's records of consigned goods on hand, review of contracts and correspondence with consignors, and direct written communication with the consignors to confirm the quantity and value of goods held at the balance sheet date and to disclose any client liability for unremitted sales proceeds or from inability to collect consignment accounts receivable.

Working papers will be prepared by each auditor participating in the observation of the inventory. These papers should indicate the extent of test counts, describe any deficiencies noted, and express a conclusion as to whether the physical inventory appeared to have been properly taken in accordance with the client's instructions. The auditor-in-charge should prepare a concise summary memorandum indicating the overall extent of observation and the percentage of inventory value covered by quantity tests. The memorandum may also include comments on the consideration given to the factors of quality and condition of stock, the treatment of consigned goods on hand, and the control of shipments and receipts during the counting process. Figure 13–5 illustrates this type of memorandum.

Inventories in Public Warehouses and on Consignment. The examination of warehouse receipts is not sufficient verification of goods stored in public warehouses. Section 6030 of the *CICA Handbook* suggests the examination of "independent documentary evidence." The AICPA in the

FIGURE 13–5

THE WILSHIRE CORPORATION
Comments on Observation of Physical Inventory   D9

December 31, 199X

1. Advance Planning of Physical Inventory.

   A physical inventory was taken by the client on December 31, 199X. Two
weeks in advance of this date we reviewed the written inventory instructions
prepared by L. D. Frome, Controller. These instructions appeared entirely
adequate and reflected the experience gained during the counts of previous
years. The plan called for a complete closing down of the factory on
December 31, since the preceding year's count had been handicapped by movements of productive material during the counting process. Training meetings
were conducted by Frome for all employees assigned to participate in the
inventory; at these meetings the written instructions were explained and
discussed.

2. Observation of Physical Inventory.

   We were present throughout the taking of the physical inventory on
December 31, 199X. Prior to the count, all materials had been neatly arranged, labeled, and separated by type. Two-employee inventory teams were
used: one employee counting and calling quantities and descriptions; the
other employee filling in data on the serially numbered inventory tags. As
the goods were counted, the counting team tore off the "first count" portion
of the inventory tag. A second count was made later by another team working
independently of the first; this second team recorded the quantity of its
count on the "second count" portion of the tag.
   We made test counts of the numerous items, covering approximately 30
percent of the total inventory value. These counts were recorded on our
working papers and used as noted below. Our observation throughout the plant
indicated that both the first and second counts required by the inventory
instructions were being performed in a systematic and conscientious manner.
The careful and alert attitude of employees indicated that the training
meetings preceding the count had been quite effective in creating an understanding of the importance of an accurate count. Before the "second count"
portions of the tags were removed, we visited all departments in company with
Frome and satisfied ourselves that all goods had been tagged and counted.
   No goods were shipped on December 31. We ascertained that receiving
reports were prepared on all goods taken into the receiving department on
this day. We recorded the serial numbers of the last receiving report and
the last shipping report for the year 199X. (See D-9-1.) We compared the
quantities per the count with perpetual inventory records and found no
significant discrepancies.

3. Quality and Condition of Materials

   Certain obsolete parts had been removed from stock prior to the count and
reduced to a scrap carrying value. On the basis of our personal observation
and questions addressed to supervisors, we have no reason to believe that any
obsolete or defective materials remained in inventory. During the course of
inventory observation, we tested the reasonableness of quantities of 10
items, representing 40 percent of the value of the inventory, by comparing
the quantity on hand with the quantity used in recent months; in no case did
we find that the quantity in inventory exceeded three months' normal usage.

V.M.H.
Jan. 3, 9Y

United States has recommended direct confirmation in writing from outside custodians of inventories, and supplementary procedures when the amounts involved represent a significant proportion of the current assets or of the total assets of a concern. These supplementary procedures include review of the client's procedures for investigating prospective warehouses and evaluating the performance of warehouses having custody of the client's goods. The auditors should also consider obtaining auditors' reports on the warehouses' internal controls relevant to custody of stored goods. If the amounts are quite material, or if any reason for doubt exists, the auditors may decide to visit the warehouses and observe a physical inventory of the client's merchandise stored at the warehouses.

The verification of goods in the hands of consignees may conveniently be begun by obtaining from the client a list of all consignees and copies of the consignment contracts. Contract provisions concerning the payment of freight and other handling charges, the extension of credit, computation of commissions, and frequency of reports and remittances require close attention. After review of the contracts and the client's records of consignment shipments and collections, the auditors should communicate directly with the consignees and obtain full written information on consigned inventory, receivables, unremitted proceeds, and accrued expenses and commissions as of the balance sheet date.

Often, the client may own raw materials that are processed by a subcontractor before being used in the client's production process. The auditors should request the subcontractor to confirm quantities and descriptions of client-owned materials in the subcontractor's possession.

Inventory Verification When Auditors Are Engaged after the End of the Year.   A company desiring an independent audit should engage the auditors well before the end of the year, so they can participate in advance planning of the physical inventory and be prepared to observe the actual counting process. Occasionally, however, auditors are not engaged until after the end of the year and therefore find it impossible to observe the taking of inventory at the close of the year. For example, the illness or death of a company's sole practitioner public accountant near the year-end might lead to the engagement of new auditors shortly after the balance sheet date.

Under these circumstances, the auditors may conclude that sufficient appropriate evidence cannot be obtained concerning inventories to permit them to express an opinion on the overall fairness of the financial statements. On the other hand, if circumstances are favourable, the auditors may be able to obtain satisfaction concerning the inventories by alternative auditing procedures. These favourable circumstances might include the existence of strong internal control, perpetual inventory records, availability of instructions and other records showing that the client had carried out a well-planned physical inventory at or near the year-end, and the making of test counts by the newly appointed auditors. If the auditors are to express an unqualified opinion, their investigation of inventories should include some physical contact with items of inventory and should be thorough enough to compensate for the fact that they were not present when the physical inventory was taken. Whether such alternative auditing procedures will be feasible and will enable the auditors to satisfy themselves depends upon the circumstances of the particular engagement.

8. Review the year-end cutoff of purchases and sales transactions.

An accurate cutoff of purchases is one of the most important factors in verifying the existence and completeness of the year-end inventory. Assume that a shipment of goods costing $10,000 is received from a supplier on December 31, but the purchase invoice does not arrive until January 2 and is entered as a January transaction. If the goods are included in the December 31 physical inventory but there is no December entry to record the purchase and the liability, the result will be an overstatement of both net income for the year and retained earnings and an understatement of accounts payable, each error being in the full amount of $10,000 (ignoring income taxes).

An opposite situation may arise if a purchase invoice is received and recorded on December 31, but the merchandise covered by the invoice is not received until several days later and is not included in the physical inventory taken at the year-end. The effect on the financial statements of recording a purchase without including the goods in the inventory will be to understate net income, retained earnings, and inventory.

How can the auditors determine that the liability to suppliers has been recorded for all goods included in inventory? Their approach is to *examine on a test basis the purchase invoices and receiving reports for several days before and after the inventory date.* Each purchase invoice in the files should have a receiving report attached; if an invoice recorded in late December is accompanied by a receiving report dated December 31 or earlier, the goods must have been on hand and included in the year-end physical inventory. However, if the receiving report carried a January date, the goods were not included in the physical count made on December 31.

A supplementary approach to the matching of purchase invoices and receiving reports is to examine the records of the receiving department. For each shipment received near the year-end, the auditors should determine that the related purchase invoice was recorded in the same period.

The effect on the financial statements of failing to include a year-end in-transit purchase as part of physical inventory is often not a serious one, *provided* the related liability is not recorded until the following period. In other words, a primary point in effecting an accurate *cutoff of purchases is that both sides of a purchase transaction must be reflected in the same accounting period.* If a given shipment is included in the year-end physical inventory of the purchaser, the entry debiting Inventories and crediting

Accounts Payable must be made. If the shipment is not included in the purchaser's year-end physical inventory, the purchase invoice must not be recorded until the following period.

Adjustments to achieve an accurate cutoff of purchases should, of course, be made by the client's staff; the function of the auditors should be to review the cutoff and determine that the necessary adjustments have been made.

Chapter 12 includes a discussion of the audit procedures for determining the accuracy of the sales cutoff. The sales cutoff is mentioned again at this point to emphasize its importance in determining the fairness of the client's inventory and cost of goods sold as well as accounts receivable and sales.

9. Obtain a copy of the completed physical inventory, test its clerical accuracy, and trace test counts.

The testing of extensions and footings on the final inventory listing may disclose misstatements of physical inventories. Often this test consists of "sight-footing" to the nearest hundred dollars or thousand dollars of the inventory listings. Generalized audit software may also be used to test extensions and footings.

In testing extensions, the auditors should be alert for two sources of substantial errors—misplaced decimal points and incorrect extension of *count* units by *price* units. For example, an inventory listing that extends 1,000 units times $1C (per hundred) as $1,000 will be overstated by $990. An inventory extension of 1,000 sheets of steel times $1 per pound will be substantially understated if each sheet of steel weighs more than one pound.

The auditors also should trace to the completed physical inventory their test counts made during the observation of physical inventory. During this tracing, the auditors should be alert for any indications that inventory tags have been altered or that fictitious inventory tags have been created. The auditors also compare inventory tag number sequences in the physical inventory listing to tag numbers noted in their audit working papers for the inventory observation. This procedure is designed to determine that the client has not omitted inventory items from the listing, or included additional items that were not present during the physical inventory.

Another test of the clerical accuracy of the completed physical inventory is the reconciliation of the physical counts to inventory records. Both the quantities and the values of the items should be compared to the company's perpetual records. The totals of various sections of inventory should also be compared with the corresponding control accounts. All substantial discrepancies should be investigated fully. The number, type, and cause of the discrepancies revealed by such comparisons are highly significant in assessing control risk for inventories.

10. Review inventory quality and condition.

The auditors should also be alert during the course of their inventory observation for any inventory of questionable quality or condition. Excessive dust or rust on raw materials inventory items may be indicative of obsolescence or infrequent use.

The auditors should also review perpetual inventory records for indications of slow-moving inventory items. Then, during the course of observing inventory taking, the auditors should examine these slow-moving items and determine that the client has identified the items as obsolete if appropriate.

To discharge their responsibility for inventory quality and condition, the auditors may also have to rely upon the advice of a specialist. For example, the auditors of a retail jeweler might request the client to hire an independent expert in jewelry to assist the auditors in identifying the precious stones and metals included in the client's inventory. Similarly, the auditors of a chemical producer might rely upon the expert opinion of an independent chemist as to the identity of components of the client's inventories. Guidelines for using the work of a specialist are in Chapter 6.

11. Evaluate the bases and methods of inventory pricing.

The auditors are responsible for determining that the bases and methods of pricing inventory are in accordance with generally accepted accounting principles. The investigation of inventory pricing often will emphasize the following three questions:

1. What method of pricing does the client use?
2. Is the method of pricing the same as that used in prior years?
3. Has the method officially selected by the client been applied consistently and accurately in practice?

For the first question—a method of pricing—a long list of alternatives is possible, including such methods as cost; cost and market, whichever is lower; the retail method; and quoted market price (as for metals and staple commodities traded on organized exchanges). The cost method, of course, includes many diverse systems, such as last-in, first-out (LIFO); first-in, first-out (FIFO); specific identification; weighted average; and standard cost.

The second question raised in this section concerns a change in method of pricing inventory from one year to the next. For example, let us say that the client has changed from the FIFO method to the LIFO method. The nature and justification of the change in method of valuing inventory and its effect on income should be disclosed in accordance with the recommendations of the *CICA Handbook,* Section 1506, "Accounting Changes." In addition, the new method should be applied retroactively to prior periods.

The third question posed deals with consistent, accurate application in practice of the method of valuation officially adopted by the client. To answer this question, the auditors must test the pricing of a representative number of inventory items.

12. Test the pricing of inventories.

The testing of prices applied to inventories of raw materials, purchased parts, and supplies by a manufacturing company is similar to the testing of prices of merchandise in a trading business. In both cases, cost of inventory items, whether LIFO, FIFO, weighted average, or specific identification, is readily verified by reference to purchase invoices. An illustration of a working paper prepared by an auditor in making price tests of an inventory of raw materials and purchased parts is presented in Figure 13–6.

Audit procedures for verification of the inventory values assigned to goods in process and finished goods are not so simple and conclusive as in the case of raw materials or merchandise for which purchase invoices are readily available. To determine whether the inventory valuation method used by the client has been properly applied, the auditors must make tests of the pricing of selected items of finished goods and goods in process. The items to be tested should be selected from the client's inventory summary sheets after the quantities established by the physical inventory have been priced and extended. Items of large total value will be selected for testing so that the tests will encompass a significant portion of the dollar amount of inventories.

Lower-of-Cost-and-Market Test.   As a general rule, inventories should not be carried at an amount in excess of replacement cost or net realizable value. The lower-of-cost-and-market rule is a common means of measuring any loss of utility in the inventories. If the inventory includes any discontinued lines or obsolete or damaged goods, the client should reduce these items to net realizable value, which is often scrap value.

Illustrative Case

During the first audit of an automobile agency, the auditors were observing the taking of the physical inventory of repair parts. They noticed a large number of new fenders of a design and shape not used on the current model cars. Closer inspection revealed that the fenders (with a total inventory valuation of several thousand dollars) were for a model of automobile made seven years ago. The records showed that only one of this type of fender had been sold during the past two years. The automobile dealer explained that these fenders had been included in the parts inventory when he purchased the agency two years ago and that he had no idea why such a large stock had originally been acquired. He agreed that few, if any, of this model of fender would ever be sold. It had not occurred to him to write down the carrying value of these obsolete parts, but he readily agreed with the auditors' suggestion that the fenders, being virtually unsalable, should be reduced to scrap value.

---

13. Perform analytical procedures.

Material errors in counting, pricing, and calculating the physical inventory, as well as fictitious or obsolete inventory, may be disclosed by analytical procedures designed to establish the general reasonableness of the inventory figures.

A comparative summary of inventories classified by major types, such as raw materials, goods in process, finished goods, and supplies, should be

FIGURE 13–6

The Wilshire Corporation

Tests of Pricing—Raw Materials and Purchased Parts (FSSO)   P-5

December 31, 1994

Part No.	Description	Per Inventory Quantity	Per Inventory Price	Vendor	Per Vendor Date	Per Vendor No.	Invoice Quantity	Invoice Price
82 182	Aluminum 48 x 144 x .025	910 shts	10.10	Hardy & Co.	Dec. 18,94	5418	1,000	10.10 u
82 195	Aluminum 45 x 72 x .032	804 shts	9.01	Watson Mfg. Co.	Nov. 28,94	2845	500	9.01 u
					Dec. 22,94	3207	500	9.01 u
K 1125	Stainless steel .025 x 23	80,625 lbs.	80	Ajax Steel Co.	Dec. 3, 94	K182	100,000	80 u
K 1382	Stainless steel .031 x 17	652 lbs.	82	Ajax Steel Co.	Dec. 3, 94	K192	75000	82 u
XL 3925	10 H.P. Electronic Motor	50 ea.	400.00	Cronyn Mfg. Co.	Nov. 18, 94	253	100	400.00 u
XJ 3821	¾ H.P. Electronic Motor	645 ea.	30.50	Jones & Co.	Dec. 29, 94	E9824	650	30.50 u

Inventory value of raw materials and purchased parts selected for price testing — $301,825.56.

% of total raw materials and purchased parts selected for price testing — $\frac{\$301,825.56}{503,615.10} = 60\%$

See audit program B-4 for method of selecting raw materials and purchased parts for price testing

u — agreed to prices on the vendor's invoice

Conclusion:
   Based on our tests, it appears that the pricing of raw materials and purchased parts is materially correct.

Prepared by: C.M.B.
         Jan. 4, 94

Reviewed by W.B.
         Jan. 7, 94

obtained or prepared. Explanations should be obtained for all major increases or decreases from the prior year's amounts.

In certain lines of business, particularly retail and wholesale companies, gross profit margins may be quite uniform from year to year. Any major difference between the ending inventory estimated by the gross profit percentage method and the count of inventory at year-end should be investigated fully. The discrepancy may reflect theft of merchandise, or unrecorded or fictitious purchases or sales. On the other hand, it may be the result of changes in the basis of inventory valuation or of sharp changes in sales prices.

Another useful test is the computation of rates of inventory turnover, based on the relationship between the cost of goods sold for the year and the average inventory as shown on the monthly financial statements. These turnover rates should be compared with the rates prevailing in prior years. A decreasing rate of turnover suggests the possibility of obsolescence or of unnecessarily large inventories. Deliberate stockpiling in anticipation of higher prices or shortages of certain strategic materials will, of course, be reflected by a declining inventory turnover rate. Rates of turnover are most significant when computed for individual products or by departments; if compared on a companywide basis, substantial declines in turnover in certain sections of the client company's operations may be obscured by compensating increases in the turnover rates for other units of the organization.

The auditors should also make certain that aggregate or unit inventories do not exceed the capacity of the client's production or storage facilities. For example, in the audit of a manufacturer of chemicals, the auditors should ascertain the total storage capacity of the client's containers, and determine that the aggregate quantity of chemicals reported in inventories does not exceed that capacity.

The auditors' analytical procedures for purchase transactions will often include a comparison of the volume of transactions from period to period. In this study, the purchase transactions may be classified by vendor and also by type of product; comparisons made in this manner sometimes disclose unusual variations of quantities purchased or unusual concentration of purchases with particular vendors, indicating a possible conflict of interest.

In addition to performing analytical procedures, the auditors should review all general ledger accounts relating to cost of sales to make certain that they contain no apparent irregularities. Adjustments of substantial amount should be investigated to determine the propriety of their inclusion in the cost of goods sold. If this review of general ledger accounts were not made, the door would be left open for all types of gross errors to remain undetected—such obvious errors, for example, as closing miscellaneous revenue and expense into cost of goods sold.

The auditors of a manufacturer client should obtain from the client or prepare an analysis of cost of sales by month, broken down into raw materials, direct labour, and manufacturing overhead elements. The analysis should also include a description of all unusual and nonrecurring charges or credits to cost of goods sold. These cost analyses may be compared to various production statistics, such as direct labour-hours and machine-hours.

14. Determine whether any inventories have been pledged and review purchase and sales commitments.

The verification of inventories includes a determination by the auditors as to whether any goods have been pledged or subjected to a lien of any kind. Pledging of inventories to secure bank loans should be brought to light when bank balances and indebtedness are confirmed.

A record of outstanding purchase commitments is usually readily available, since this information is essential to management in maintaining day-to-day control of the company's inventory position and cash flow.

In some lines of business, it is customary to enter into firm contracts for the purchase of merchandise or materials well in advance of the scheduled delivery dates. Comparison by the auditors of the prices quoted in such commitments with the vendors' prices prevailing at the balance sheet date may indicate substantial losses if firm purchase commitments are not protected by firm sales contracts. Such losses should be reflected in the financial statements.

The quantities of purchase commitments should be reviewed in the light of current and prospective demand, as indicated by past operations, the backlog of sales orders, and current conditions within the industry. If quantities on order appear excessive by these standards, the auditors should seek full information on this phase of operations. Purchase commitments may need to be disclosed in the financial statements.

Sales commitments are indicated by the client's **backlog** of unfilled sales orders. Losses inherent in firm sales commitments are generally recognized in the lower-of-cost-and-market valuation of inventories, with **market** being defined as the net realizable value of the goods in process or finished goods inventories applicable to the sales commitments. In addition, the backlog may include sales orders for which no production has been started as of the balance sheet date. The auditors must review the client's cost estimates for these sales orders. If estimated total costs to produce the goods ordered exceed fixed sales prices, the indicated loss and a related liability should be recorded in the client's financial statements for the current period.

15. Evaluate financial statement presentation of inventories and cost of goods sold, including the adequacy of disclosure.

One of the most important factors in proper presentation of inventories in the financial statements is disclosure of the inventory pricing method (or methods) in use. To say that inventories are stated at **cost** is not sufficient because cost may be determined under several alternative assumptions, each of which leads to a substantially different valuation.

From the standpoint of analyzing the current earnings of the company, it is extremely important to know whether the reported profits have been inflated by price changes, as has often been the case under FIFO, or that the effect of price rises has been limited through the LIFO method of valuation. The users of the financial statements also need to know whether the carrying value of inventory approximates current cost (as with FIFO) or whether inventories are stated at cost of an earlier period (as with the LIFO method).

Other important points in presenting inventories in the financial statements include the following:

1. Changes in methods of valuing inventory should be disclosed, and the dollar effect and justification for the change reported, in accordance with the *CICA Handbook* Section 1506, "Accounting Changes."
2. A separate listing is desirable for the various classifications of inventory, such as finished goods, goods in process, and raw materials.
3. If any portion of the inventory has been pledged to secure liabilities, full disclosure of the arrangement should be made.

Problems Associated with Inventory of First-Year Audit Clients

The need for the auditors to be present to observe the taking of the ending inventory has been strongly emphasized in auditing literature. However, the figure for beginning inventory is equally significant in determining the cost of goods sold and the net income for the year. In the initial examination of a client, the auditors may not have been present to observe the taking of inventory at the beginning of the year. What procedures can they follow to obtain evidence that the beginning inventories are fairly stated?

The first factor to consider is whether the client was audited by another firm of public accountants for the preceding year. If a review of the predecessor firm's working papers indicates compliance with generally accepted auditing standards, the new auditors can accept the beginning inventories with a minimum of investigation. That minimum might include the following steps: (*a*) study of the inventory valuation methods used; (*b*) review of the inventory records; (*c*) review of the inventory sheets used in taking the preceding year's physical inventory; and (*d*) comparison of the beginning and ending inventories, broken down by product classification.

If there had been no satisfactory audit for the preceding year, the investigation of the beginning inventories would include not only the procedures mentioned above but also the following steps: (*a*) discussion with the person in the client's organization who supervised the physical inventory at the preceding balance sheet date, (*b*) study of the written instructions used in planning the inventory, (*c*) tracing of numerous items from the inventory tags or count sheets to the final summary sheets, (*d*) tests of the perpetual inventory records for the preceding period by reference to supporting documents for receipts and withdrawals, and (*e*) tests of the overall reasonableness of the beginning inventories in relation to sales, gross profit, and rate of inventory turnover. An investigation along these lines will sometimes give the auditors definite assurance that the beginning inventory was carefully compiled and reasonable in amount; in other cases, these procedures may raise serious doubts as to the validity of the beginning inventory figure. In these latter cases, the auditors will not be able to issue an unqualified opinion *as to statements of income.* They may be able, however, to give an unqualified opinion on the *balance sheet,* since this financial statement does not reflect the beginning inventories.

KEY TERMS

bill of lading   A document issued by a common carrier acknowledging the receipt of goods and setting forth the provisions of the transportation agreement.

confirmation   A type of documentary evidence that is created outside the client organization and transmitted directly to the auditors.

consignment   A transfer of goods from the owner to another person who acts as the sales agent of the owner.

observation   The auditors' evidence-gathering technique that provides physical evidence.

periodic inventory system   A method of accounting in which inventories are determined solely by means of a physical inventory at the end of the accounting period.

perpetual inventory system   A method of accounting for inventories in which controlling accounts and subsidiary ledgers are maintained to record receipts and issuances of goods, both in quantities and in dollar amounts. The accuracy of perpetual inventory records is tested periodically by physical inventories.

purchase commitment   A contractual obligation to purchase goods at fixed prices, entered into well in advance of scheduled delivery dates.

routing sheet   A schedule that accompanies a specific job through the production process and specifies the processes required for the job.

sales commitment   A contractual obligation to sell goods at fixed prices, entered into well in advance of scheduled delivery dates.

specialist   A person or firm possessing special skill or knowledge in a field other than accounting or auditing, such as an actuary.

GROUP I:REVIEW QUESTIONS

13–1. Many auditors consider the substantiation of the figure for inventory to be a more difficult and challenging task than the verification of most other items on the balance sheet. List several specific factors that support this view.

13–2. Explain the significance of the purchase order to adequate internal control over purchase transactions.

13–3. What segregation of duties would you recommend to attain maximum internal control over purchasing activities in a manufacturing concern?

13–4. Do you believe that the normal review of purchase transactions by the auditors should include examination of receiving reports? Explain.

13–5. The client's cost accounting system is often the focal point in the auditors' examination of the financial statements of a manufacturing company. For what purposes do the auditors consider the cost accounting system?

(AICPA, adapted)

13–6. What part, if any, do the external auditors play in the planning for a client's physical inventory?

13–7. What are general objectives or purposes of the auditors' observation of the taking of the physical inventory? (Do not discuss the procedures or techniques involved in making the observation.)

(AICPA)

13–8. For what purposes do the auditors make and record test counts of inventory quantities during their observation of the taking of the physical inventory? Discuss.

(AICPA)

13–9. Once the auditors have completed their test counts of the physical inventory, will they have any reason to make later reference to the inventory tags used by the client's employees in the counting process? Explain.

13–10. When perpetual inventory records are maintained, is it necessary for a physical inventory to be taken at the balance sheet date? Explain.

13–11. What charges and credits may be disclosed in the auditors' analysis of the Cost of Goods Sold account of a manufacturing concern?

13–12. A client company wishes to conduct its physical inventory on a sampling basis. Many items will not be counted. Under what general conditions will this method of taking inventory be acceptable to the auditors?

13–13. ''A well-prepared balance sheet usually includes a statement that the inventories are valued at cost.'' Evaluate this quotation.

13–14. Darnell Equipment Company uses the FIFO method of valuation for part of its inventories and weighted-average cost for another portion. Would you be willing to issue an unqualified opinion under these circumstances? Explain.

13–15. "If the auditors can determine that all goods in the physical inventory have been accurately counted and properly priced, they will have discharged fully their responsibility with respect to inventory." Evaluate this statement.

13–16. How do the external auditors use the client's backlog of unfilled sales orders in the examination of inventories?

13–17. The controller of a new client company informs you that most of the inventories are stored in bonded public warehouses. He presents warehouse receipts to account for the inventories. Will careful examination of these warehouse receipts constitute adequate verification of these inventories? Explain.

13–18. Hana Ranch Company, which has never been audited, is asked on October 1 by its bank to arrange for a year-end audit. The company retains you to make this audit and asks what measures, if any, it should take to ensure a satisfactory December 31 year-end physical inventory. Perpetual inventories are not maintained. How would you answer this enquiry?

13–19. Enumerate specific steps to be taken by the auditors to ascertain that a client's inventories have not been pledged or subjected to a lien of any kind.

GROUP II: QUESTIONS REQUIRING ANALYSIS

13–20. You are engaged in the audit of Reed Limited, a new client, at the end of its first fiscal year, June 30, 19X1. During your work on inventories, you discover that all of the merchandise remaining in stock on June 30, 19X1, had been acquired July 1, 19X0, from Andrew Reed, the sole shareholder and president of Reed Limited, for an original selling price of $10,000 cash and a note payable due July 1, 19X3, with interest at 15 percent, in the amount of $90,000. The merchandise had been used by the president when he operated a similar business as a sole proprietor.

How can you verify the pricing of the June 30, 19X1, inventory of Reed? Explain.

13–21. The observation of a client's physical inventory is a mandatory auditing procedure when practicable and possible for the auditors to carry out and when inventories are material.

Required:

a. Why is the observation of physical inventory a mandatory auditing procedure? Explain.

b. Under what circumstances is observation of physical inventory impracticable or impossible?

c. Why is the auditors' review of the client's control of inventory tags important during the observation of physical inventory? Explain.

13–22. You have been asked to examine the financial statements of Wilson Corporation, a roadbuilding contractor that has never before been audited by public accountants. During your interim work, you learn that Wilson excludes a significant inventory item from its annual balance sheet. This inventory item, which Wilson management claims is approximately the same amount each year, is gravel that has been processed for use in road building and is placed at different road construction sites wherever it might be used. Wilson's controller states that any unused gravel at the completion of a construction contract is never moved to another job site; in fact, the gravel often disappears because of thefts during winter months when road construction is suspended.

Would you be able to issue an unqualified opinion on the financial statements of Wilson Corporation? Explain.

13–23. Grandview Manufacturing Company employs standard costs in its cost accounting system. List the audit procedures that you would apply to ascertain that Grandview's standard costs and related variance amounts are acceptable and have not distorted the financial statements. (Confine your audit procedures to those applicable to raw materials.)

(AICPA, adapted)

13–24. At the beginning of your annual audit of Crestview Manufacturing Company's financial statements for the year ended December 31, 199X, the company president confides in you that Henry Ward, an employee, is living on a scale in excess of that which his salary would support.

The employee has been a buyer in the purchasing department for six years and has been in charge of purchasing all general materials and supplies. He is authorized to sign purchase orders for amounts up to $500. Purchase orders in excess of $500 require the countersignature of the general purchasing agent.

The president understands that the usual examination of financial statements is not designed, and cannot be relied upon, to disclose fraud or conflicts of interest, although their discovery may result. The president authorizes you, however, to expand your regular audit procedures and to apply additional audit procedures to determine whether there is any evidence that the buyer has been misappropriating company funds or has been engaged in activities that were conflicts of interest.

Required:

List the audit procedures you would apply to the company records and documents in an attempt to discover evidence within the purchasing department of fraud being committed by the buyer. Give the purpose of each audit procedure.

(AICPA, adapted)

13–25. A number of companies employ outside service companies that specialize in counting, pricing, extending, and footing inventories. These service companies usually furnish a certificate attesting to the value of the physical inventory.

Assuming that the service company took the client company's inventory on the balance sheet date:

a. How much reliance, if any, can the auditors place on the inventory certificate of outside specialists? Discuss.

b. What effect, if any, would the inventory certificate of outside specialists have upon the type of report the auditors would render? Discuss.

c. What reference, if any, would the auditors make to the certificate of outside specialists in their audit report?

(AICPA)

13–26. Santa Rosa Corporation is a closely held furniture manufacturing company employing approximately 1,000 employees. On December 15, the corporation retained the firm of Warren and Wood, Chartered Accountants, to perform a December 31 year-end audit. The president of the corporation explained that perpetual inventory records were maintained and that every attention was given to maintaining strong internal control. A complete count of inventories had been made at November 30 by the company's own employees; in addition, extensive test counts had been made in most departments at various intervals during the year. Although the company was not large, it employed an internal auditor and an assistant who had devoted their full time to analysis of internal control and appraisal of operations in the various organizational units of the company.

The chartered accountant who had audited Santa Rosa Corporation for several years had died during the current year, and the company had decided to forgo an annual audit. The physical inventory had therefore been taken at November 30 without being observed by an independent public accountant. Shortly thereafter, a major shareholder in the company had demanded that new auditors be retained. The president explained to Warren and Wood that the company was too far behind on its delivery schedules to take time out for another physical inventory, but that all the papers used in the recent count were available for their review. The auditors reviewed these papers, made a thorough analysis of the internal controls over inventory, and made test counts at December 31 of large items representing 10 percent of the total value of inventory. The items tested were traced to the perpetual inventory records, and no significant discrepancies were found. Inventories at December 31 amounted to $4 million out of total assets of $9 million.

Required:
Assume that the auditors find no shortcomings in any aspect of the examination apart from the area of inventories. You are to prepare:
  a. An argument setting forth the factors that indicate the auditors should issue an unqualified audit opinion.

  b. An opposing argument setting forth the factors that indicate the auditors should not issue an unqualified opinion.

13–27. One of the problems faced by the auditors in their verification of inventory is the possibility that slow-moving and obsolete items may be included in the goods on hand at the balance sheet date. In the event that such items are identified in the physical inventory, their carrying value should be written down to an estimated scrap value or other recoverable amount.

Prepare a list of the auditing procedures that the auditors should employ to determine whether slow-moving or obsolete items are included in the physical inventory.

13–28. During your observation of the November 30 physical inventory of Jay Company, you note the following unusual items:
  a. Electric motors in finished goods storeroom not tagged. Upon enquiry, you are informed that the motors are on consignment to Jay Company.

  b. A cutting machine (one of Jay's principal products) in the receiving department, with a large REWORK tag attached.

  c. A small, isolated storeroom with five types of dusty raw materials stored therein. Inventory tags are attached to all of the materials, and your test counts agree with the tags.

Required:
What additional procedures, if any, would you carry out for each of the above? Explain.

13–29. Ace Corporation does not conduct a complete annual physical count of purchased parts and supplies in its principal warehouse, but uses statistical sampling instead to estimate the year-end inventory. Ace maintains a perpetual inventory record of parts and supplies and believes that statistical sampling is highly effective in determining inventory values and is sufficiently reliable to make a physical count of each item of inventory unnecessary.

Required:

a. Identify the audit procedures that should be used by the external auditor that change or are in addition to normal required audit procedures when a client utilizes statistical sampling to determine inventory value and does not conduct a 100 percent annual physical count of inventory items.

b. List at least 10 normal audit procedures that should be performed *to verify physical quantities* whenever a client conducts a periodic physical count of all or part of its inventory.

(AICPA, adapted)

13–30. Nolan Manufacturing Limited retains you on April 1 to perform an audit for the fiscal year ending June 30. During the month of May, you made extensive studies of internal control over inventories.

All goods purchased pass through a receiving department under the direction of the chief purchasing agent. The duties of the receiving department are to unpack, count, and inspect the goods. The quantity received is compared with the quantity shown on the receiving department's copy of the purchase order. If there is no discrepancy, the purchase order is stamped ''OK— Receiving Dept.'' and forwarded to the accounts payable section of the accounting department. Any discrepancies in the quantity or variations from specifications are called to the attention of the purchasing agent by returning the purchase order to him with an explanation of the circumstances. No records are maintained in the receiving department, and no reports originate there.

As soon as goods have been inspected and counted in the receiving department, they are sent to the factory production area and stored alongside the machines in which they are to be processed. Finished goods are moved from the assembly line to a storeroom in the custody of a stock clerk, who maintains a perpetual inventory record in terms of physical units, but not in dollars.

What weaknesses, if any, do you see in the internal control over inventories?

13–31. Select the best answer for each of the following and explain fully the reason for your selection.

a. Instead of taking a physical inventory count on the balance sheet date the client may take physical counts prior to the year-end if internal control policies, systems, and procedures are adequate and:

(1) Computerized records of perpetual inventory are maintained.

(2) Inventory is slow-moving.

(3) EDP error reports are generated for missing prenumbered inventory tickets.

(4) Obsolete inventory items are segregated and excluded.

b. The auditor's analytical procedures will be facilitated if the client:
   (1) Uses a standard cost system that produces variance reports.
   (2) Segregates obsolete inventory before the physical inventory count.
   (3) Corrects material weaknesses in internal control before the beginning of the audit.
   (4) Reduces inventory balances to the lower of cost and market.

c. When perpetual inventory records are maintained in quantities and in dollars, and internal control over inventory is weak, the auditor would probably:
   (1) Want the client to schedule the physical inventory count at the end of the year.
   (2) Insist that the client perform physical counts of inventory items several times during the year.
   (3) Increase the extent of tests for unrecorded liabilities at the end of the year.
   (4) Have to deny an opinion on the income statement for that year.

d. Which of the following is the best audit procedure for the discovery of damaged merchandise in a client's ending inventory?
   (1) Compare the physical quantities of slow-moving items with corresponding quantities of the prior year.
   (2) Observe merchandise and raw materials during the client's physical inventory taking.
   (3) Review the management's inventory representations letter for accuracy.
   (4) Test overall fairness of inventory values by comparing the company's turnover ratio with the industry average.

e. McPherson Corp. does not make an annual physical count of year-end inventories, but instead makes weekly test counts on the basis of a statistical plan. During the year, Sara Mullins, CA, observes such counts as she deems necessary and is able to satisfy herself as to the reliability of the client's procedures. In reporting on the results of her examination, Mullins:
   (1) Can issue an unqualified opinion without disclosing that she did not observe year-end inventories.
   (2) Must comment in the scope paragraph as to her inability to observe year-end inventories, but can nevertheless issue an unqualified opinion.
   (3) Is required, if the inventories were very material, to deny an opinion on the financial statements taken as a whole.

(4) Must, if the inventories were material, qualify her opinion.

f. The primary objective of an auditor's observation of a client's physical inventory count is:

(1) To discover whether a client has counted a particular inventory item or group of items.

(2) To obtain direct knowledge that the inventory exists and has been properly counted.

(3) To provide an appraisal of the quality of the merchandise on hand on the day of the physical count.

(4) To allow the auditor to supervise the conduct of the count so as to obtain assurance that inventory quantities are reasonably accurate.

(AICPA, adapted)

GROUP III: PROBLEMS

13–32. You have been engaged by the management of Alden, Inc., to review its internal controls over the purchase, receipt, storage, and issue of raw materials. You have prepared the following comments, which describe Alden's procedures.

a. Raw materials, which consists mainly of high-cost electronic components, are kept in a locked storeroom. Storeroom personnel include a supervisor and four clerks. All are well trained, competent, and adequately bonded. Raw materials are removed from the storeroom only upon written or oral authorization of one of the production first-line supervisors.

b. There are no perpetual inventory records; hence, the storeroom clerks do not keep records of goods received or issued. To compensate for the lack of perpetual records, a physical-inventory count is taken monthly by the storeroom clerks, who are well supervised. Appropriate procedures are followed in making the inventory count.

c. After the physical count, the storeroom supervisor matches quantities counted against a predetermined reorder level. If the count for a given part is below the reorder level, the supervisor enters the part number on a materials requisition list and sends this list to the accounts payable clerk. The accounts payable clerk prepares a purchase order for a predetermined reorder quantity for each part and mails the purchase order to the vendor from whom the part was purchased.

d. When ordered materials arrive at Alden, they are received by the storeroom clerks. The clerks count the merchandise and agree the counts to the carrier's bill of lading. All bills of lading are initialed, dated, and filed in the storeroom to serve as receiving reports.

Required:

Describe the weaknesses in internal control and recommend improvements of Alden's procedures for the purchase, receipt, storage, and issuance of raw materials. Organize your answer sheet as follows:

Weaknesses	Recommended Improvements

(AICPA, adapted)

13–33. The following are typical questions that might appear on an internal control questionnaire for inventory:
1. Are written procedures prepared by the client for the taking of the physical inventory?
2. Do the client's inventory taking procedures include a requirement to identify damaged inventory items?
3. Does the client maintain perpetual inventory records?

Required:
a. Describe the purpose of each of the above internal control procedures.
b. Describe the manner in which each of the above procedures might be tested.
c. Assuming that the operating effectiveness of each of the above procedures is found to be inadequate, describe how the auditors might alter their substantive tests to compensate for the increased level of control risk.

13–34. David Anderson, CA, is engaged in the examination of the financial statements of Redondo Manufacturing Corporation for the year ended June 30, 1992. Redondo's inventories at year-end include finished merchandise on consignment with consignees and finished merchandise stored in public warehouses. The merchandise in public warehouses is pledged as collateral for outstanding debt.

Required:
Normal inventory and notes payable auditing procedures have been satisfactorily completed. Describe the specific additional auditing procedures that Anderson should undertake with respect to:

a. Consignments out.

b. Finished merchandise in public warehouses pledged as collateral for outstanding debt.

(AICPA, adapted)

13–35. You are an audit manager of the rapidly growing public accounting firm of Raye and Coye. You have been placed in charge of three new audit clients, which have the following inventory features:

a. Canyon Cattle Co., which maintains 15,000 head of cattle on a 1,000 square kilometre ranch, mostly unfenced, near the south rim of a western province.

b. Rhoads Mfg. Co. Ltd., which has raw materials inventories consisting principally of pig iron loaded on gondola freight cars on a siding at the company's plant.

c. Strawser Company, which is in production around the clock on three shifts, and which cannot shut down production during the physical inventory.

Required:

What problems do you anticipate in the observation of physical inventories of the three new clients, and how would you deal with the problems?

13–36. Royal Meat Processing Limited buys and processes livestock for sale to supermarkets. In connection with the examination of the company's financial statements, you have prepared the following notes based on your review of inventory procedures:

a. Each livestock buyer submits a daily report of his or her purchases to the plant superintendent. This report shows the dates of purchase and expected delivery, the vendor and the number, and weights and type of livestock purchased. As shipments are received, any available plant employee counts the number of each type received and places a check mark beside this quantity on the buyer's report. When all shipments listed on the report have been received, the report is returned to the buyer.

b. Vendors' invoices, after a clerical review, are sent to the appropriate buyer for approval and returned to the accounting department. A disbursement voucher and a cheque for the approved amount are prepared in the accounting department. Cheques are forwarded to the treasurer for signature. The treasurer's office sends signed cheques directly to the buyer for delivery to the vendor.

c. Livestock carcasses are processed by lots. Each lot is assigned a number. At the end of each day, a tally sheet reporting the lots processed, the number and type of animals in each lot, and the carcass weight is sent to the accounting department, where a perpetual inventory record of processed carcasses and their weights is maintained.

d. Processed carcasses are stored in a refrigerated cooler located in a small building adjacent to the employee parking lot. The cooler is locked when the plant is not open, and a company guard is on duty when the employees report for work and leave at the end of their shifts. Supermarket truck drivers wishing to pick up their orders have been instructed to contact someone in the plant if no one is in the cooler.

e. Substantial quantities of by-products are produced and stored, either in the cooler or elsewhere in the plant. By-products are initially accounted for as they are sold. At this time the sales manager prepares a two-part form: one copy serves as authorization to transfer the goods to the customer, and the other becomes the basis for billing the customer.

Required:

For (*a*) to (*e*) above, state the weaknesses, if any, in the present inventory procedures and your suggestions, if any, for improvement.

(AICPA, adapted)

13–37. Payne Press Limited is engaged in the manufacture of large-size presses under specific contracts and in accordance with customers' specifications. Customers are required to advance 25 percent of the contract price. The company records sales on a shipment basis and accumulates costs by job orders. The normal profit margin over the past few years has been approximately 5 percent of sales, after provision for selling and administrative expenses of about 10 percent of sales. Inventories are valued at the lower of cost and market.

Among the jobs you are reviewing in the course of your annual examination of the company's December 31 financial statements is Job No. 2357, calling for delivery of a three-colour press at a firm contract price of $50,000. Costs accumulated for the job at the year-end aggregated $30,250. The company's engineers estimated that the job was approximately 55 percent complete at December 31. Your audit procedures have been as follows:

1. Examined all contracts, noting pertinent provisions.
2. Observed physical inventory of jobs in process and reconciled details to job order accounts.
3. Tested controls over input of labour, material, and overhead charges into the various jobs to determine that such charges were authentic and had been posted correctly.

4. Confirmed customers' advances at year-end.

5. Reconciled goods in process job ledger with control account.

Required:
With respect to Job No. 2357:

a. State what additional audit procedures, if any, you would follow and explain the purpose of the procedures.

b. Indicate the manner and the amount at which you would include Job No. 2357 in the balance sheet.

(AICPA, adapted)

13–38.   Late in December, your public accounting firm accepted an audit engagement at Nash Jewelers, Inc., a corporation that deals largely in diamonds. The corporation has retail jewelry stores in several eastern cities and a diamond wholesale store in Toronto. The wholesale store also sets the diamonds in rings and other quality jewelry.

The retail stores place orders for diamond jewelry with the wholesale store in Toronto. A buyer employed by the wholesale store purchases diamonds in the Toronto diamond market; the wholesale store then fills orders from the retail stores and from independent customers and maintains a substantial inventory of diamonds. The corporation values its inventory by the specific identification cost method.

Required:
Assume that at the inventory date you are satisfied that Nash Jewelers, Inc. has no items left by customers for repair or sale on consignment and that no inventory owned by the corporation is in the possession of outsiders.

a. Discuss the problems the auditors should anticipate in planning for the observation of the physical inventory on this engagement because of the:
(1) Different locations of inventories.
(2) Nature of the inventory.

b. Assume that a shipment of diamond rings was in transit by corporation messenger from the wholesale store to a retail store on the inventory date. What additional audit steps would you take to satisfy yourself as to the gems that were in transit from the wholesale store on the inventory date?

(AICPA, adapted)

13–39.   Smith is the partner in charge of the audit of Blue Distributing Corporation, a wholesaler that owns one warehouse containing 80 percent of its inventory. Smith is reviewing the working papers that were prepared to support the firm's opinion on Blue's financial statements, and Smith wants to be certain essential audit records are well-documented.

Required:

What substantive tests should Smith expect to find in the working papers to document management's assertion about completeness as it relates to the inventory quantities at the end of the year?

(AICPA, adapted)

GROUP IV: ANALYTICAL AND DISCUSSION CASE

13–40. Western Trading Company is a sole proprietorship engaged in the grain brokerage business. At December 31, 199X, the entire grain inventory of the company was stored in outside bonded warehouses. The company's procedure of pricing inventories in these warehouses includes comparing the actual cost of each commodity in inventory with the market price as reported for transactions on the commodity exchanges at December 31. A write-down is made on commodities in which cost is in excess of market. During the course of the 199Y examination, the auditors verified the company's computations. In addition to this, they compared the book value of the inventory with market prices at February 15, 199Y, the date of the audit report. The auditors noted that the market price of several of the commodities had declined sharply subsequent to year-end, until their market price was significantly below the commodities' book values.

The inventory was repriced by the auditors on the basis of the new market price, and the book value of the inventory was found to be in excess of market value on February 15 by approximately $21,000. The auditors proposed that the inventories be written down to this new market value. The management protested this suggestion, stating that in their opinion the market decline was only temporary and that prices would recover in the near future. They refused to allow the write-down to be made. Accordingly, the auditors qualified their audit opinion for a departure from generally accepted accounting principles.

Required:

a. Were the auditors justified in issuing a qualified opinion in this situation? Discuss fully, including alternative courses of action.

b. State your opinion as to the course of action that was appropriate in this situation.

Chapter 14

Property, Plant, and Equipment: Depreciation and Depletion

Chapter Objectives

After studying this chapter, you should be able to:
- Describe the nature of property, plant, and equipment, and of depreciation and depletion.[1]
- Explain the fundamental internal controls over property, plant, and equipment.
- Describe the auditors' objectives for the audit of property, plant, and equipment.
- Describe the nature of the procedures to accomplish the auditors' objectives for the audit of property, plant, and equipment, and depreciation.

The term *property, plant, and equipment* includes all tangible assets with a service life of more than one year that are used in the operation of the business and are not acquired for the purpose of resale. Three major subgroups of such assets are generally recognized:

1. *Land,* such as property used in the operation of the business, has the significant characteristic of not being subject to depreciation.
2. *Buildings, machinery, equipment, and land improvements,* such as fences and parking lots, have limited service lives and are subject to depreciation.

---

[1] *CICA Handbook* section 3060 uses "amortization" rather than "depreciation" and "depletion", even though these latter terms are still commonly used.

3. *Natural resources* (wasting assets), such as oil wells, coal mines, and tracts of timber, are subject to depletion as the natural resources are extracted or removed.

Acquisitions and disposals of property, plant, and equipment are usually large in dollar amount, but concentrated in only a few transactions. Individual items of plant and equipment may remain unchanged in the accounts for many years.

The Auditors' Objectives in Examination of Property, Plant, and Equipment

The auditors' *objectives* in the examination of property, plant, and equipment are as follows:

1. To consider *internal control* over property, plant, and equipment.
2. To determine the *existence* of recorded property, plant, and equipment, and the client's *ownership* of these assets.
3. To establish the *completeness* of recorded property, plant, and equipment.
4. To establish the *clerical accuracy* of schedules of property, plant, and equipment.
5. To determine that the *valuation or allocation* of the cost of property, plant, and equipment is in accordance with generally accepted accounting principles.
6. To determine that the *statement presentation* of property, plant, and equipment, including disclosure of depreciation methods, is appropriate.

In conjunction with the audit of property, plant, and equipment, the auditors also obtain evidence about the related accounts of depreciation expense, accumulated depreciation, and repairs and maintenance expense.

Contrast with Audit of Current Assets

In many companies, the investment in plant and equipment amounts to 50 percent or more of the total assets. However, the audit work required to verify these properties is usually a much smaller proportion of the total audit time spent on the engagement. The verification of plant and equipment is facilitated by several factors not applicable to audit work on current assets.

First, a typical unit of property or equipment has a high dollar value, and relatively few transactions may lie behind a large balance sheet amount. Second, there is usually little change in the property accounts from year to year. The Land account often remains unchanged for a long span of years.

The durable nature of buildings and equipment also tends to hold accounting activity to a minimum for these accounts. By way of contrast, such current assets as accounts receivable and inventory may have a complete turnover several times a year.

A third point of contrast between the audit of plant assets and the audit of current assets is the significance of the year-end cutoff of transactions. For current assets, the year-end cutoff is a critical issue; for plant assets, it is generally not. For example, in our discussion of inventories in Chapter 13, we emphasized the importance of an accurate year-end cutoff of the transactions for purchases and sales of merchandise. An error in the cutoff of a $50,000 purchase or sales transaction may cause a $50,000 error in the year's pretax net income. The possibility of such errors is substantial because a large volume of merchandise transactions is normal at year-end. For plant assets, on the other hand, a year-end cutoff error in recording an acquisition or retirement ordinarily will not affect net income for the year. Moreover, for many companies, there may be no transactions in plant assets occurring at the year-end. Of course, a cutoff error relating to acquisition or retirement of plant assets could cause slight inaccuracies in depreciation or in the timing of gains or losses on disposals. The problem of year-end cutoff for plant assets, however, must be considered a minor one in contrast to the audit of current assets.

Internal Controls over Plant and Equipment

The principal purposes of internal controls relating to plant and equipment are *to ensure the reliability of the accounting data and to obtain maximum efficiency from the dollars invested in plant assets.*

The amounts invested in plant and equipment represent a large portion of the total assets of many industrial concerns. The expenses of maintenance, rearrangement, and depreciation of these assets are a major factor in the income statement. The sheer size of the amounts involved makes strong internal controls essential to the production of reliable financial statements. Errors in measurement of income will be material if assets are scrapped without their cost being removed from the accounts or if the distinction between capital and revenue expenditures is not maintained consistently. The losses that inevitably arise from uncontrolled methods of acquiring, maintaining, and retiring plant and equipment are often greater than the losses from fraud in cash handling.

The Plant and Equipment Budget

In large enterprises, the auditors may expect to find an annual plant budget used to forecast and to control acquisitions and retirements of plant and equipment. Many small companies also forecast expenditures for plant assets. Successful utilization of a plant budget presupposes the existence of reliable and detailed accounting records for plant and equipment. A detailed knowledge of the kinds, quantities, and condition of existing equipment is an essential basis for intelligent forecasting of the need for replacements and additions to the plant.

If the auditors find that acquisitions of plant and equipment, whether by purchase or construction, are made in accordance with prior budgetary authorizations and that any necessary expenditures not provided for in the budget are made only upon approval of a top-level executive, they will be able to minimize the testing of the year's acquisitions. Reference to the reports of the internal auditors is often a convenient method for the external auditors to become familiar with the scope and dependability of the budgetary controls over plant and equipment.

Other Major Control Devices

Other important internal controls applicable to plant and equipment are as follows:

1. A subsidiary ledger consisting of a separate record for each unit of property. An adequate plant and equipment ledger facilitates the auditors' work in analyzing additions and retirements, in verifying the depreciation provision and maintenance expenses, and in comparing authorizations with actual expenditures.
2. A system of authorizations requiring advance executive approval of all plant and equipment acquisitions, whether by purchase, lease, or construction. Serially numbered capital work orders are a convenient means of recording authorizations.
3. A reporting procedure assuring prompt disclosure and analysis of variances between authorized expenditures and actual costs.
4. An authoritative written statement of company policy distinguishing between capital and revenue expenditures. A dollar minimum ordinarily will be established for capitalization; any expenditures of lesser amount automatically are classified as charges against current revenue.
5. A policy requiring all purchases of plant and equipment to be handled through the purchasing department and subjected to standard routines for receiving, inspection, and payment.
6. Periodic physical inventories, designed to verify the existence, location, and condition of all property listed in the accounts and to disclose the existence of any unrecorded units.
7. A system of retirement procedures, including serially numbered retirement work orders, stating reasons for retirement and bearing appropriate approvals.

Audit Working Papers

The key audit working paper for property, plant, and equipment is a summary analysis such as that illustrated in Figure 14–1. This working paper follows the approach we have previously described of *emphasizing changes during the year under audit.* The working paper shows the beginning balances for the various types of plant assets; these amounts are the ending balances shown in the prior year's working papers. Next, the working paper shows the additions and retirements during the year. These are the transactions upon which the auditors' attention will be focused. A final column shows the ending balances that must equal the beginning balances plus the additions and minus the retirements. A similar set of four columns is used to summarize the changes in the accounts for accumulated depreciation.

Among the other audit working papers for property, plant, and equipment are analyses of the year's additions and retirements, analyses of repairs and maintenance expense accounts, and tests of depreciation. The analyses of plant additions and retirements and the tests of depreciation are cross-indexed to the summary analysis, as illustrated in Figure 14–1. In the audit of larger companies, it is common practice for the client to prepare for the auditors both a listing of the year's additions and a schedule of the year's disposals.

Initial Audits and Repeat Engagements

The auditing procedures listed in subsequent pages are applicable to repeat engagements and therefore concern only transactions of the current year. In the auditors' first examination of a new client that has changed auditors, the beginning balances of property, plant, and equipment may be substantiated by reference to the predecessor firm's working papers. If, in previous years, audits were made by other reputable firms of public accountants, it is not customary in a first audit to go beyond a general review of the past history of the property, plant, and equipment as recorded in the accounts.

In a first audit of a company for which audits by external public accountants have not been made previously, the ideal approach is a complete historical analysis of the property accounts. By thorough review of all major charges and credits to the property accounts since their inception, the auditors can establish the validity of the beginning balances of property, plant, and equipment and accumulated depreciation.

If the client has been in business for many years, the review of transactions in earlier years must be performed on a test basis in order to stay within reasonable time limits. However, the importance of an anlysis of transactions of prior years deserves emphasis. Only by this approach can

FIGURE 14-1

The Mandeville Corporation

Summary of Property, Plant and Equipment, and Accumulated Depreciation

December 31, 19X2

K-1

Account No.	Description	Assets				Method	Rate	Accumulated Depreciation			
		Balance Dec. 31, X1	Additions	Retirements	Balance Dec. 31, X2			Balance Dec. 31, X1	Depreciation	Retirements	Balance Dec. 31, X2
151	Land	500,000.00	151,000.00		651,000.00						
152,3	Land improvements	125,000.00	10,000.00		145,000.00	st.l.	5%	13,500.00	7,000.00		20,500.00 4
154,5	Buildings	4,300,000.00	475,000.00		4,775,000.00	st.l	3%	282,000.00	142,740.00		424,740.00 4
156,7	Equipment	900,000.00	110,000.00	60,000.00	350,000.00 4	d.l.	10%	235,000.00	70,400.00	50,500.00	255,000.00 4
		5,925,000.00	746,000.00	60,000.00	6,641,000.00			540,500.00	220,240.00	50,400.00	710,340.00
			K-1-1		K			K-1-2		K-1-1	K

4 – Footed property, plant and equipment subsidiary ledger cards. No exceptions.

Conclusions:

As result of our audit procedures for property, plant and equipment and related depreciation, it is our opinion that the Dec. 31, 19X2 balances above are fairly stated. V.M.H.

V.T.H.
Jan. 7, X3

the auditors be in a sound position to express an opinion as to the propriety of the current period's depreciation. If repair and maintenance expenses have been capitalized, or asset additions have been recorded as operating expenses, or retirements of property have gone unrecorded, the depreciation expense will be misstated regardless of the care taken in the selection of depreciation rates. The auditors should make clear to the client that the initial examination of property, plant, and equipment requires procedures that need not be duplicated in subsequent engagements.

AUDIT PROGRAM FOR PROPERTY, PLANT, AND EQUIPMENT

The following procedures are typical of the work required in many engagements for the verification of property, plant, and equipment. The procedures for accumulated depreciation are covered in a separate program on pages 611–13.

A. Consider internal control for property, plant, and equipment.
1. *Obtain an understanding of internal control* for property, plant, and equipment.
2. *Assess control risk and design additional tests of controls for property, plant, and equipment.*
3. *Perform additional tests of controls* for those controls which the auditors plan to consider to reduce their assessment of control risk.
4. *Reassess control risk* for each of the major financial statement assertions about property, plant, and equipment based on the results of tests of controls, *and design substantive tests.*

B. Perform substantive tests of property, plant, and equipment, and of related revenue and expenses.
5. Obtain a summary analysis of changes in property, plant, and equipment owned and reconcile to ledgers.
6. Vouch additions to property, plant, and equipment during the year.
7. Make physical inspection of major acquisitions of plant and equipment.
8. Analyze repair and maintenance expense accounts.
9. Investigate the status of property, plant, and equipment not in current use.
10. Test the client's provision for depreciation.
11. Investigate retirements of property, plant, and equipment during the year.
12. Examine evidence of legal ownership of property, plant, and equipment.
13. Review rental revenue from land, buildings, and equipment owned by the client but leased to others.

14. Examine lease agreements on property, plant, and equipment leased to and from others.
15. Perform analytical procedures for property, plant, and equipment.
16. Evaluate financial statement presentation and disclosure for plant assets and for related revenue and expenses.

These substantive audit procedures are summarized in Figure 14–2 along with the primary audit objectives.

A. Consider internal control for property, plant, and equipment.

1. Obtain an understanding of internal control.

In obtaining an understanding of the internal control for property, plant, and equipment, the auditors may utilize a written narrative, flowcharts, or

FIGURE 14–2 Objectives of Major Substantive Tests of Property, Plant, and Equipment, and of Depreciation

Substantive Tests	*Primary Audit Objectives*
Obtain a summary analysis of changes in property, plant, and equipment owned and reconcile to ledgers	*Clerical accuracy*
Vouch additions during year Make physical inspection of major acquisitions	*Existence and ownership* *Valuation or allocation*
Analyze repair and maintenance expense accounts Investigate the status of property, plant, and equipment not in current use Test the client's provision for depreciation	*Valuation or allocation*
Investigate retirements of property, plant, and equipment during the year Examine evidence of legal ownership Review rental revenue	*Existence and ownership*
Examine lease agreements Perform analytical procedures	*Existence and ownership* *Completeness* *Valuation or allocation*
Evaluate financial statement presentation and disclosure	*Statement presentation*

an internal control questionnaire. The following are typical of the questions included in a questionnaire: Are plant ledgers regularly reconciled with general ledger controlling accounts? Are periodic physical inventories of plant assets compared with the plant ledgers? Are variances between plant budgets and actual expenditures for plant assets subject to review and approval of executives? Does the sale, transfer, or dismantling of equipment require written executive approval on a serially numbered retirement work order? Is there a written policy for distinguishing between capital expenditures and revenue expenditures?

After preparing a description of internal control, the auditors will determine whether the policies, systems, and procedures as described to them have been ***placed in operation.*** To confirm their understanding of these policies, systems, and procedures, they will observe whether there is an appropriate segregation of duties over the acquisition of plant assets, and enquire who performed various functions throughout the period. They will also inspect the subsidiary ledger of property, plant, and equipment, the serially numbered work orders, and the plant and equipment budget, and examine evidence of the follow-up on variances from the budget. These procedures may provide the auditors with sufficient evidence to assess control risk for certain financial statement assertions about property, plant, and equipment at less than the maximum.

2. Assess control risk and design additional tests of controls.

After obtaining an understanding of the client's internal control for property, plant, and equipment, the auditors develop their initial assessments of control risk for the various financial statement assertions. To further evaluate these assessments of control risk, the auditors must obtain additional evidence of the operating effectiveness of the client's internal control policies, systems, and procedures by designing additional test of controls. In designing these tests, the auditors must decide which ones will result in sufficient reductions in substantive tests to justify the time spent performing them.

3. Perform additional tests of controls.

Tests directed toward the effectiveness of controls are used to evaluate the client's internal control and to determine the extent to which the auditors are justified in reducing their assessed levels of control risk for the assertions about property, plant, and equipment accounts. Certain tests of controls are performed as the auditors obtain an understanding of the client's internal control, and these were described in our discussion of that process. However, the auditors may decide to perform additional tests of controls to further reduce their assessments of control risk. For example, the auditors may select a sample of purchases of property, plant, and equipment to test the controls related to authorization, receipt, and proper recording of the transactions. A sample of recorded retirements also may be tested for proper authorization and supporting retirement work orders. These tests often will be combined with the substantive tests of additions and retirements.

4. Reassess control risk and design substantive tests.

The final step in the auditors' consideration of internal control involves a reassessment of control risk based on the results of the tests of controls. The auditors then select the substantive tests necessary to provide sufficient appropriate evidence as to the audit objectives for the client's property, plant, and equipment. The extent of the substantive tests is determined in relation to the auditors' final assessment of control risk.

B. Substantive tests.

5. Obtain a summary analysis of changes in property, plant, and equipment owned and reconcile to ledgers.

The auditors may verify the beginning balances of property, plant, and equipment by reference to the prior year's audit working papers. In addition to beginning balances, the summary analysis will show the additions and retirements of property, plant, and equipment during the year under audit. As the audit progresses, the auditors will examine a sample of these additions and retirements. The detailed working papers showing this verification will support and be cross-indexed to the summary analysis worksheet.

Before making a detailed analysis of changes in property, plant, and equipment accounts during the year, the auditors will want to be sure that the amounts in the subsidiary ledgers agree in total with the balances in the controlling accounts. Reconciliation of the subsidiary ledgers with the controlling accounts can be performed very quickly with the use of generalized audit software.

6. Vouch additions to property, plant, and equipment during the year.

The vouching of additions to the property, plant, and equipment accounts during the period under audit is one of the most important substantive tests. The extent of the vouching is dependent upon the auditors' assessment of control risk for existence and valuation of property, plant, and equipment. The vouching process utilizes a working paper analysis of the general ledger controlling accounts and includes the tracing of entries through the journals to original documents, such as contracts, deeds, construction work orders, invoices, cheques, and authorization by officers and directors.

The specific steps to be taken in investigating the year's additions usually will include the following:

1. Review changes during the year in construction in progress and examine supporting work orders, both incomplete and closed.
2. Trace transfers from the Construction in Progress account to the property accounts, observing propriety of classification. Determine that all completed items have been transferred.
3. On a test basis, vouch purchases of property, plant, and equipment to invoices, deeds, contracts, or other supporting documents. Test extensions, footings, and treatment of discounts. Make certain revenue expenditures were not improperly capitalized.

4. Investigate all instances in which the actual cost of acquisitions substantially exceeded authorized amounts. Determine whether such excess expenditures were analyzed and approved by appropriate officials.
5. Investigate fully any debits to property, plant, and equipment accounts not arising from acquisition of physical assets.
6. Determine that the total cost of any property, plant, and equipment purchased on the instalment plan is reflected in the asset accounts and that the unpaid instalments are set up as liabilities. Ascertain that all plant and equipment leases that in effect are instalment purchases are accounted for as assets acquired. Interest charges should not be capitalized as a cost of the asset acquired.

The accounting for plant assets acquired in a trade-in or other exchange is specified by *CICA Handbook,* Section 3830, "Non-monetary Transactions." No gain or loss is recognized when a plant asset is exchanged for a similar plant asset. The asset acquired in the exchange is valued at the carrying amount of the asset given up plus any additional cash paid or amount financed.

Assets constructed by a company for its own use should be recorded at the cost of direct material, direct labour, and applicable overhead cost. However, auditors usually apply the additional test of comparing the total cost of self-constructed equipment with bids or estimated purchase prices for similar equipment from outside suppliers, and they carefully examine the capitalization of costs in excess of the amount for which the asset could have been purchased and installed.

Related Party Transactions. Assets acquired from affiliated corporations, from promoters or shareholders, or by any other type of related party transaction not involving arm's-length bargaining between buyer and seller, have sometimes been recorded at inflated amounts. The auditors should enquire into the methods by which the sales price was determined, the cost of the property to the vendor, length of ownership by vendor, and any other available evidence that might indicate an arbitrarily determined valuation. Related party transactions must be disclosed in the notes to the financial statements.

7. Make a physical inspection of major acquisitions of plant and equipment.

The auditors usually make a physical inspection of major units of plant and equipment acquired during the year under audit. This step is helpful in maintaining a good working knowledge of the client's operations and in interpreting the accounting entries for both additions and retirements.

The audit procedure of physical inspection may flow in either direction between the plant assets and the records of plant assets. By tracing items in the plant ledger to the physical assets, the auditors prove that the assets shown in the accounting records *actually exist* and are in current use. The alternative testing procedure is to inspect selected assets in the plant and trace these assets to the detailed records. This test provides evidence that existing assets are recorded.

The physical inspection of plant assets may be limited to major units acquired during the year or may be extended to include tests of older equipment as well. In a few situations (especially when control risk is very high), the auditors may conclude that the taking of a complete physical inventory is needed. Bear in mind, however, that a complete physical inventory of plant and equipment is a rare event. If such an inventory is required, the auditors' role is to *observe* the physical inventory.

Let us consider an example of a situation in which the auditors might conclude that a complete physical inventory of plant and equipment was needed. Assume that a client is engaged in commercial construction work and that the client owns and operates a great many units of costly mobile equipment. Such equipment may often be scrapped or sold upon the authorization of a field supervisor. Under these circumstances, the auditors might regard a complete physical inventory of plant and equipment as essential. Similarly, in the audit of clients owning a large number of automobiles and trucks, the auditors may insist upon observing a physical count, as well as examining legal title.

Some large companies, as part of their internal control, perform occasional physical inventories of plant and equipment at certain locations or in selected departments. The *observation* of these limited counts is often carried out by the client's internal auditing staff rather than by the external auditors.

8. Analyze repair and maintenance expense accounts.

The auditors' principal objective in analyzing repair and maintenance expense accounts is to discover items that should have been capitalized. Many companies have a written policy setting the minimum expenditure to be capitalized. For example, company policy may prescribe that no expenditure for less than $300 shall be capitalized regardless of the service life of the item purchased. In such cases, the auditors will analyze the repair and maintenance accounts with a view toward determining the consistency of application of this policy as well as compliance with generally accepted accounting principles. To determine that the accounts contain only bona fide repair and maintenance charges, the auditors will trace the larger expenditures to written authorizations for the transaction. The accuracy of the client's accounting for the expenditure may be verified by reference to vendors' invoices, to material requisitions, and to labour time records.

One useful means of identifying any capital expenditures that are buried in the repair and maintenance accounts is to obtain or prepare an analysis of the monthly amounts of expense with corresponding amounts listed for the preceding year. Any significant variations from month to month or between corresponding months of the two years should be fully investigated. If maintenance expense is classified by the departments serviced, the variations are especially noticeable.

9. Investigate the status of property, plant, and equipment not in current use.

Land, buildings, and equipment not in current use should be investigated thoroughly to determine the prospects for their future use in operations. Plant assets that are temporarily idle need not be reclassified, and depreciation may be continued at normal rates. On the other hand, idle equipment that has been dismantled, or that for any reason appears unsuitable for future operating use, should be written down to an estimated realizable value and excluded from the plant and equipment classification. In the case of standby equipment and other property not needed at present or prospective levels of operation, the auditors should consider whether the carrying value is recoverable through future use in operations.

Illustrative Case

During the 1970s, many large public utility companies began the construction of nuclear power plants which were believed to be the best source of electricity for the future. By the mid-1980s, however, a number of these projects had turned into financial nightmares. In many cases, the cost to date of a half-completed nuclear plant was several times the original estimate of total cost. Construction had ground virtually to a halt, and the prospects for getting these nuclear plants into operation were dim. Efforts of the antinuclear lobby and legal battles combined with engineering problems to raise doubts whether nuclear plants representing investments in the billions would ever become operational.

These developments created a most difficult situation for the public accounting firms having "nuclear utilities" as clients. Should the costly nuclear facilities be written off even though such action would wipe out the shareholders' equity? Should the uncompleted facilities be carried at cost in the companies' financial statements despite the distinct possibility they would never be completed? Most auditing firms felt that they must modify their audit reports to indicate that the future solvency of the client company rested on a favourable solution to the problem of the uncompleted nuclear plant.

---

10. Test the client's provision for depreciation.

See the separate *depreciation* program following this audit program.

11. Investigate retirements of property, plant, and equipment during the year.

The principal purpose of this procedure is to determine whether any property, plant, or equipment has been replaced, sold, dismantled, or abandoned without such action being reflected in the accounting records. Nearly every thorough physical inventory of property, plant, and equipment reveals missing units—units disposed of without a corresponding reduction of the accounts.

If a machine is sold for cash or traded in on a new machine, the transaction generally will involve the use of documents, such as a cash receipts form or a purchase order; the processing of these documents may bring the retirement to the attention of accounting personnel. However, plant assets may be scrapped rather than being sold or traded in on new equipment; consequently, there may be no paper work to evidence the disappearance of a machine. How is the accounting department expected to know when the asset has been retired?

One method of guarding against unrecorded retirements is enforcement of a companywide policy that no plant asset shall be retired from use without prior approval on a special type of serially numbered work order. A copy of the retirement work order is routed to the accounting department, thus providing some assurance that retirements will be reflected in the accounting records.

What specific steps should the auditors take to discover any unrecorded retirements? The following measures often are effective:

1. If major additions of plant and equipment have been made during the year, ascertain whether old equipment was traded in or replaced by the new units.
2. Analyze the Miscellaneous Revenue account to locate any cash proceeds from sale of plant assets.
3. If any of the company's products have been discontinued during the year, investigate the disposition of plant facilities formerly used in manufacturing such products.
4. Enquire of executives and supervisors whether any plant assets have been retired during the year.
5. Examine retirement work orders or other source documents for authorization by the appropriate official or committee.
6. Investigate any reduction of insurance coverage to determine whether this was caused by retirement of plant assets.

12. Examine evidence of legal ownership of property, plant, and equipment.

To determine that plant assets are the property of the client, the auditors look for such evidence as a deed, invoices, property tax bills, receipts for payments to mortgagee, and fire insurance policies. Additionally, the fact that rental payments are not being made is supporting evidence of ownership.

It is sometimes suggested that the auditors may verify ownership of real property and the absence of liens by examination of public records. This step is seldom taken. Inspection of the documentary evidence listed above usually provides adequate proof of ownership. If some doubt exists as to whether the client has clear title to property, the auditors should obtain the opinion of the client's legal counsel or request that a title search be performed.

Possession of a deed is not proof of present ownership because when real property is sold, a new deed is prepared and the old one is retained by the seller. Better evidence of continuing ownership is found in property tax bills made out in the name of the client and in fire insurance policies, rent receipts from lessees, and regular payments of principal and interest to a mortgagee or trustee.

The disclosure of liens on property is considered during the examination of liabilities, but in the audit work on plant and equipment the auditors should be alert for evidence indicating the existence of liens. Purchase contracts examined in verifying the cost of property may reveal unpaid balances. Insurance policies may contain loss payable endorsements in favour of a secured party.

The ownership of automobiles and trucks can readily be ascertained by the auditors by reference to certificates of title and registration documents. The ease of transfer of title to automotive equipment, plus the fact that it is often used as collateral for loans, makes it important that the auditors examine the title to such property.

13. Review rental revenue from land, buildings, and equipment owned by the client but leased to others.

In testing rental revenue from land and buildings, it is often desirable for the auditors to obtain or to sketch a map of the property and to make a physical inspection of each unit. This may disclose that premises reported as vacant are in fact occupied by lessees and are producing revenue not reflected in the accounting records. If the client's property includes an office or apartment building, the auditors should obtain a floor plan of the building as well as copies of all lease contracts. In this way, they can account for all available rental space as revenue producing or vacant and can verify reported vacancies by physical inspection at the balance sheet date. If interim audit work is being performed, vacancies should also be verified by inspection and discussion with management during the year.

Examination of leases will indicate whether tenants are responsible for the cost of electricity, water, gas, and telephone service. These provisions should be reconciled with utility expense accounts. Rental revenue accounts should be analyzed and the amount compared with lease agreements and cash records.

14. Examine lease agreements on property, plant, and equipment leased to and from others.

The preceding step addressed rental revenue from leases. Also related to leases, the auditors must be aware that generally accepted accounting principles require differing accounting treatments, depending upon whether they qualify as an operating or a capital lease. The auditors should carefully examine lease agreements to determine whether the accounting for the assets involved is proper. For example, the auditors must determine whether assets leased by the client should be capitalized.

15. Perform analytical procedures for property, plant, and equipment.

The specific trends and ratios used in judging the overall reasonableness of recorded amounts for plant and equipment will vary with the nature of the client's operations. Among the ratios and trends often used by auditors for this purpose are the following:

1. Total cost of plant assets divided by annual output in dollars or other units.
2. Total cost of plant assets divided by cost of goods sold.
3. Comparison of repairs and maintenance expense on a monthly basis and from year to year.
4. Comparison of acquisitions for the current year with prior years and with budget.
5. Comparison of retirements for the current year with prior years and with budget.

Acquisitions and retirements may vary widely from year to year; however, it is essential that the auditors be aware of these variations and judge their reasonableness in the light of trends in the client's past and present operations. Analytical procedures relating to depreciation are discussed later in this chapter as part of the audit program for depreciation.

16. Evaluate financial statement presentation and disclosure for plant assets and for related revenue and expenses.

The balance sheet or accompanying notes should disclose balances of major classes of depreciable assets. Accumulated depreciation may be shown by major class or in total, and the method or methods of computing depreciation should be stated. The total amount of depreciation should be disclosed in the income statement or supporting notes.

In addition, adequate financial statement presentation and disclosure will ordinarily reflect the following principles:

1. The basis of valuation should be explicitly stated. At present, cost is the generally accepted basis of valuation for property, plant, and equipment; property not in use should be valued at estimated realizable value.
2. Property pledged to secure loans should be clearly identified.
3. Property not in current use should be segregated in the balance sheet.

DEPRECIATION

The Auditors' Perspective toward Depreciation

The auditors' approach to verification of depreciation expense is influenced by two factors not applicable to most other expenses. First, we must recognize that depreciation expense is an **estimate.** Determining the annual depreciation expense involves two decisions by the client company: first, an estimate of the useful economic lives of various groups of assets; second, a choice among several depreciation methods, each of which would lead to a different answer. The wide range of possible amounts for annual depreciation expense because of these decisions by the client suggests that the auditors should maintain a perspective of looking for assurance of overall reasonableness. Specifically, overall tests of the year's depreciation expense are of special importance.

Among the methods of computing depreciation expense most frequently encountered are the straight-line method and the declining-balance methods. Less common, although quite acceptable, are methods based on units of output or hours of service. The most widely adopted types of accelerated depreciation methods are fixed percentage of declining balance, and sum-of-the-years' digits. The essential characteristic of these and other, similar methods is that depreciation is greatest in the first year and becomes smaller in succeeding years.

The Auditors' Objectives in Auditing Depreciation

As we discussed earlier, depreciation relates most directly to the ***valuation or allocation*** audit objective. To meet this objective, the auditors in examining depreciation methods and amounts determine (*a*) that the methods in use are acceptable, (*b*) that the methods are being followed consistently, and (*c*) that the calculations required by the chosen methods are accurate. A more detailed picture of the auditors' objectives is conveyed by the audit program in the following section.

Audit Program—Depreciation Expense and Accumulated Depreciation

The following outline of substantive tests to be performed by the auditors in reviewing depreciation is stated in sufficient detail to be largely self-explanatory. Consequently, no point-by-point discussion will be presented. Techniques for testing the overall reasonableness of the client's provision of depreciation for the year are, however, discussed immediately following the audit program.

1. Review the depreciation policies set forth in company manuals or other management directives. Determine whether the methods in use are designed to allocate costs of plant and equipment assets equitably over their service lives.

   a. Enquire whether any extra working shifts or other conditions of accelerated production are present that might warrant adjustment of normal depreciation rates.

   b. Discuss with executives the possible need for recognition of obsolescence resulting from inventions or economic developments. For example, assume that a new, improved model of computer has recently become available and that it would fit the company's needs most effectively. Should the remaining estimated useful life of an older computer presently owned by the company be reevaluated in the light of this technological advance?

2. Obtain or prepare a summary analysis (see Figure 14–1) of accumulated depreciation for the major property classifications as shown by the general ledger control accounts, listing beginning balances, provisions for depreciation during the year, retirements, and ending balances.

   a. Compare beginning balances with the audited amounts in last year's working papers.

   b. Determine that the totals of accumulated depreciation recorded in the plant and equipment subsidiary records agree with the applicable general ledger controlling accounts.

3. Test the provisions for depreciation.

   a. Compare rates used in the current year with those employed in prior years, and investigate any variances.

   b. Test computations of depreciation provisions for a representative number of units and trace to individual records in the property ledger. Be alert for excessive depreciation on fully depreciated assets. Generalized audit software can be used to prove the depreciation calculations in the client's subsidiary ledger for plant and equipment. The computation of depreciation expense for groups of assets can be verified quickly if the client maintains a computer-based subsidiary ledger.

   c. Compare credits to accumulated depreciation accounts for the year's depreciation provisions with debit entries in related depreciation expense accounts.

4. Test deductions from accumulated depreciation for assets retired.

   a. Trace deductions to the working paper analyzing retirements of assets during the year.

   b. Test the accuracy of accumulated depreciation to date of retirement.

5. Perform analytical procedures for depreciation.

   a. Compute the ratio of depreciation expense to total cost of plant and compare with prior years.

   b. Compare the percentage relationships between accumulated depreciation and related property accounts with that prevailing in prior years. Discuss significant variations from the normal depreciation program with appropriate members of management.

Testing the Client's Provision for Depreciation for Overall Reasonableness

We have emphasized the importance of determining the overall reasonableness of the amount of depreciation expense, which is usually a very material amount on the income statement. An *overall* test of the annual provision for depreciation requires the auditors to perform the following steps:

1. List the balances in the various asset accounts at the beginning of the year.
2. Deduct any fully depreciated assets, since these items should no longer be subject to depreciation.
3. Add one half of the asset additions for the year.
4. Deduct one half of the asset retirements for the year (exclusive of any fully depreciated assets).

These four steps produce average amounts subject to depreciation at the regular rates in each of the major asset categories. By applying the appropriate rates to these amounts, the auditors determine on an overall average basis the amount of the provision for depreciation. The computed amount is then compared with the client's figures. Precise agreement is not to be expected, but any material difference between the depreciation expense computed in this manner and the amount set up by the client should be investigated fully.

Examination of Natural Resources

In the audit of companies operating properties subject to depletion (mines, oil and gas deposits, timberlands, and other natural resources), the auditors follow a pattern similar to that used in evaluating the provision for depreciation expense and accumulated depreciation. They determine whether depletion has been recorded consistently and in accordance with generally accepted accounting principles, and they test the mathematical accuracy of the client's computations.

The depletion of timberlands is usually based on physical quantities established by cruising. (The term *cruising* means the inspection of a tract of forestland for the purpose of estimating the total lumber yield.) The determination of physical quantities to use as a basis for depletion is more difficult in many mining ventures and for oil and gas deposits. The auditors often rely upon the opinions of such specialists as mining engineers and geologists about the reasonableness of the depletion rates being used for such resources. Under these circumstances, the auditors must comply with the provisions of Section 5360 of the *CICA Handbook,* "Using the Work of a Specialist" (discussed in Chapter 6).

If the number of tonnes of ore in a mining property could be accurately determined in advance, an exact depletion cost per tonne could be computed by dividing the cost of the mine by the number of tonnes available for extraction. In reality, the contents of the mine can only be estimated, and the estimates may require significant revision as mining operations progress.

The auditors investigate the ownership and the cost of mining properties by examining deeds, leases, tax bills, vouchers, paid cheques, and other records in the same manner that they verify the plant and equipment of a manufacturing or trading concern. The costs of exploration and development work in a mine customarily are capitalized until such time as commercial production begins. After that date, additional development work generally is treated as expense. The costs of drilling oil wells are capitalized if the wells are productive. Under this "successful-efforts" policy, the costs of drilling wells which prove not to be productive are immediately written off. However, some smaller companies follow an alternative of "full-cost" policy, under which all drilling costs are capitalized and amortized over future years.

Examination of Intangible Assets

The balance sheet caption *Intangible Assets* includes a variety of assets. All intangible assets are characterized by a lack of physical substance. Furthermore, they do not qualify as current assets, and they are nonmonetary—that is, they do not represent fixed claims to cash.

Among the more prominent intangible assets are goodwill, patents, trademarks, franchises, and leaseholds. Notice that investment in securities is *not* included in our list of intangibles. Since intangible assets are lacking in physical substance, their value lies in the rights or economic advantages afforded in their ownership. Because of their intangible nature, these assets may be more difficult to identify than units of plant and equipment. When a client treats an expenditure as creating an intangible asset, the auditors must look for objective evidence that a genuine asset has come into existence.

The auditors' substantiation of intangible assets may begin with an analysis of the ledger accounts for these assets. Debits to the accounts should be traced to evidence of payment having been made, and to documentary evidence of the rights or benefits acquired. Credits to the accounts should be reconciled with the client's program of amortization or traced to appropriate authorization for the write-off of the asset.

One intangible asset that may be large in amount yet of questionable future economic benefit is *goodwill*. Goodwill arises in accounting for business combinations in which the price paid to acquire another company exceeds the fair value of the identifiable net assets acquired. When business combinations result in the recording of goodwill, the auditors should review the allocation of the lump-sum acquisition cost among tangible assets, identifiable intangible assets, and goodwill. Any allocation of total acquisition cost to goodwill should be considered for reasonableness and also traced to the authorization and subsequent approval in the minutes of the directors' meetings.

As part of an analysis of intangible asset accounts, the auditors should review the reasonableness of the client's amortization program. Amortization is ordinarily computed by the straight-line method over the years estimated to be benefited, but not in excess of 40 years.

Examination of Plant and Equipment in Advance of the Balance Sheet Date

Most of the audit work on plant and equipment can be done in advance of the balance sheet date. For the initial audit of a new client, the time-consuming task of reviewing the records of prior years and establishing the beginning balances in the plant accounts for the current period should be completed before the year-end.

In repeat engagements, as well as in first examinations, the consideration of internal control can be carried out at any convenient time during the year. Many auditing firms lighten their year-end work loads by performing interim work during October and November, including the analysis of the plant and equipment ledger accounts for the first 9 or 10 months of the year. After the balance sheet date, the work necessary on property accounts is then limited to the final two or three months' transactions.

KEY TERMS

capital expenditure An expenditure for property, plant, and equipment that is properly charged to an asset account.

cruising The inspection of a tract of forestland for the purpose of estimating the total lumber yield.

revenue expenditure An expenditure for property, plant, and equipment that is properly charged to an expense account.

work order A serially numbered accounting document authorizing the acquisition of plant assets. A separate series of retirement work orders may be used to authorize the retirement or disposal of plant assets, and a third variety consists of documents authorizing repair or maintenance of plant assets.

GROUP I: REVIEW QUESTIONS

14–1. Identify at least three elements of strong internal control for property, plant, and equipment.

14–2. What documentary evidence is usually available to the auditors in the client's office to substantiate the legal ownership of property, plant, and equipment?

14–3. Moultrie Company discovered recently that a number of its property and equipment assets had been retired from use several years ago without any entries being made in the accounting records. The company asks you to suggest procedures that will prevent unrecorded retirement of assets.

14–4. Does a failure to record the retirement of machinery affect net income? Explain.

14–5. The auditors' verification of plant and equipment is facilitated by several factors not applicable to audit work on current assets. What are these factors?

14–6. Do the auditors question the service lives adopted by the client for plant assets, or do they accept the service lives without investigation? Explain.

14–7. Should the external auditors observe a physical inventory of property and equipment in every audit engagement? Discuss.

14–8. Hamlin Metals Company has sales representatives covering several provinces and provides automobiles for them and for its executives. Describe any substantive tests you would consider appropriate for the company's fleet of more than 100 automobiles, other than the verification procedures generally applicable to all property and equipment.

14–9. Explain the use of a system of authorizations for additions to plant and equipment.

14–10. What is a principal objective of the auditors in analyzing a Maintenance and Repairs expense account?

14–11. In response to threats from a terrorist organization, Technology International installed protective measures consisting of chain-link fences, concrete road barriers, electronic gates, and underground parking at its manufacturing facilities. The costs of these installations were debited to the Land account. Indicate your reasons for approval or disapproval of this accounting treatment.

14–12. Gibson Manufacturing Company acquired new factory machinery this year and ceased using the old machinery. The old equipment was retained, however, and is capable of being used if the demand for the company's products warrants additional production. How should the old machinery be handled in the accounting records and on the financial statements?

14–13. What are the auditors' objectives in the audit of plant assets?

14–14. Explain how the existence of lease agreements may result in understated plant and equipment.

14–15. The auditor's verification of current assets such as cash, securities, and inventories emphasizes observation, inspection, and confirmation to determine the physical existence of these assets. Should the auditors take a similar approach to establish the existence of the recorded plant asset? Explain fully.

14–16. K–J Corporation has current assets of $5 million and approximately the same amount of plant and equipment. Should the two groups of assets require about the same amount of audit time? Give reasons.

14–17. You are making your first examination of Clarke Manufacturing Company. Plant and equipment represent a very substantial portion of the total assets. What verification, if any, will you make of the balances of the ledger accounts for Plant and Equipment as of the beginning of the period under audit?

14–18. Cite various substantive tests the auditors could employ that might detect unrecorded retirements of property, plant, and equipment.

(AICPA, adapted)

14–19. Suggest several comparisons to be made as part of the auditors' analytical procedures for:

a. Plant and equipment.

b. Depreciation.

14–20. Should the auditors examine public records to determine the legal title of property apparently owned by the client?

14–21. Mellon Inc. wants to use the same depreciation methods for financial statement purposes that the corporation uses for tax purposes. Is this appropriate? Explain.

GROUP II: QUESTIONS REQUIRING ANALYSIS

14–22. Give the purposes of each of the following procedures that may be included in internal control and explain how each procedure contributes to strong internal control:

a. Forecasting (budgeting) of expenditures for property, plant, and equipment.

b. Maintaining a plant ledger for property, plant, and equipment.

(AICPA, adapted)

14–23. Kadex Corporation, a small manufacturing company, did not use the services of external auditors during the first two years of its existence. Near the end of the third year, Kadex retained Jones & Scranton, CAs, to perform an audit for the year ended December 31. Officials of the company requested that the CA firm perform only the audit work necessary to provide an audit report on the financial statements for the current year.

During the first two years of its operation, Kadex had erroneously treated some material acquisitions of plant and equipment as revenue expenditures. No such errors occurred in the third year.

a. Under these circumstances, would Jones & Scranton, CAs, be likely to learn of the transactions erroneously treated as revenue expenditures in Years 1 and 2? Explain.

b. Would the income statement and balance sheet prepared at the end of Year 3 be affected by the above accounting errors made in Years 1 and 2? If so, identify the specific items. Explain fully.

14–24. List and state the purpose of all audit procedures that might reasonably be applied by the auditors to determine that all property and equipment retirements have been recorded in the accounting records.

(AICPA)

14–25. Your new client, Ross Products, Inc., completed its first fiscal year March 31, Year 10. During the course of your examination you discover the following entry in the general journal, dated April 1, Year 9.

Building	2,400,000	
Mortgage Note Payable		1,400,000
Common Stock		1,000,000

To record (1) acquisition of building constructed by J. A. Ross Construction Co. (a sole proprietorship); (2) assumption of Ross Construction Co. mortgage loan for construction of the building; and (3) issuance of entire authorized common stock (10,000 shares, $100 par value) to J. A. Ross.

Required:
Under these circumstances, what steps should the auditors take to verify the $2,400,000 recorded cost of the building? Explain fully.

14–26. An executive of a manufacturing company informs you that no formal procedures have been followed to control the retirement of machinery and equipment. A physical inventory of plant assets has just been completed. It revealed that 25 percent of the assets carried in the ledger were not on hand and had presumably been scrapped. The accounting records have been adjusted to agree with the physical inventory. You are asked to outline internal control practices to govern future retirements.

14–27. Allen Fraser was president of three corporations: Missouri Metals Corporation, Kansas Metals Corporation, and Iowa Metals Corporation. Each of the three corporations owned land and buildings acquired for approximately $500,000. An appraiser retained by Fraser in 19X1 estimated the current value of the land and buildings in each corporation at approximately $3,000,000. The appraisals were recorded in the accounts. A new corporation, Midwest Corporation, was then formed, and Fraser became its president. The new corporation purchased the assets of the three predecessor corporations, making payment in capital stock. The balance sheet of Midwest Corporation shows land and buildings "valued at cost" in the amount of $9,000,000, the carrying values to the vendor companies at the time of transfer to Midwest Corporation. Do you consider this treatment acceptable? Explain.

14–28. Shortly after you were retained to examine the financial statements of Case Corporation, you learned from a preliminary discussion with management that the corporation had recently acquired a competing business, the Mall Company. In your study of the terms of the acquisition, you find that the total purchase price was paid in cash and that the transaction was authorized by the board of directors and fully described in the minutes of the directors' meetings. The only aspect of the acquisition of the Mall Company that raises any doubts in your mind is the allocation of the total purchase price among the several kinds of assets acquired. The allocation, which had been specifically approved by the board of directors of Case Corporation, placed very high values on the tangible assets acquired and allowed nothing for goodwill.

You are inclined to believe that the allocation of the lump-sum price to the several types of assets was somewhat unreasonable because the total price for the business was as much or more than the current replacement cost of the tangible assets acquired. However, as an auditor, you do not claim to be an expert in property values. Would you question the propriety of the directors' allocation of the lump-sum purchase price? Explain fully.

14–29. Select the best answer for each of the questions below and explain fully the reason for your selection.

    a. With respect to an internal control measure that will assure accountability for fixed asset retirements, management should implement internal control that includes:

        (1) Continuous analysis of miscellaneous revenue to locate any cash proceeds from sale of plant assets.

        (2) Periodic enquiry of plant executives by internal auditors as to whether any plant assets have been retired.

        (3) Utilization of serially numbered retirement work orders.

        (4) Periodic observation of plant assets by the internal auditors.

b. The auditors may conclude that depreciation charges are insufficient by noting:
  (1) Insured values greatly in excess of book values.
  (2) Large amounts of fully depreciated assets.
  (3) Continuous trade-ins of relatively new assets.
  (4) Excessive recurring losses on assets retired.

c. Which of the following is an internal control weakness related to factory equipment?
  (1) Cheques issued in payment of purchases of equipment are not signed by the controller.
  (2) All purchases of factory equipment are required to be made by the department in need of the equipment.
  (3) Factory equipment replacements are generally made when estimated useful lives, as indicated in depreciation schedules, have expired.
  (4) Proceeds from sales of fully depreciated equipment are credited to other income.

d. Which of the following accounts should be reviewed by the auditors to gain reasonable assurance that additions to property, plant, and equipment are *not* understated?
  (1) Depreciation.
  (2) Accounts payable.
  (3) Cash.
  (4) Repairs.

e. When there are numerous property and equipment transactions during the year, an auditor planning to assess control risk at the miminum level usually plans to obtain an understanding of internal control and to perform:
  (1) Tests of controls and extensive tests of property and equipment balances at the end of the year.
  (2) Extensive tests of current year property and equipment transactions.
  (3) Tests of controls and limited tests of current year property and equipment transactions.
  (4) Analytical procedures for property and equipment balances at the end of the year.

f. To strengthen internal control over the custody of heavy mobile equipment, the client would most likely institute a policy requiring a periodic:
  (1) Increase in insurance coverage.
  (2) Inspection of equipment and reconciliation with accounting records.
  (3) Verification of liens, pledges, and collateralizations.
  (4) Accounting for work orders.

(AICPA, adapted)

GROUP III: PROBLEMS

14–30. The following are typical questions that might appear on an internal control questionnaire relating to plant and equipment.
1. Has a dollar minimum been established for expenditures to be capitalized?
2. Are subsidiary ledgers for plant and equipment regularly reconciled with general ledger controlling accounts?

Required:
   a. State the purpose of each of the above internal control procedures.
   b. Describe the manner in which each of the above procedures might be tested.
   c. Assuming that the operating effectiveness of each of the above procedures is found to be inadequate, describe how the auditors might alter their substantive tests to compensate for the increased level of control risk.

14–31. Chem-Lite Inc. maintains its accounts on the basis of a fiscal year ending March 31. At March 31, 19X1, the Equipment account in the general ledger appeared as shown below. The company uses straight-line depreciation, 10-year life, and 10 percent salvage value for all its equipment. It is the company's policy to take a full year's depreciation on all additions to equipment occurring during the fiscal year, and you may treat this policy as a satisfactory one for the purpose of this problem. The company has recorded depreciation for the fiscal year ended March 31, 19X1.

Equipment

Apr. 1, 19X0 Bal. forward	100,000
Dec. 1, 19X0	10,500
Jan. 2, 19X1	1,015
Feb. 1, 19X1	1,015
Mar. 1, 19X1	1,015

Upon further investigation, you find the following contract dated December 1, 19X0, covering the acquisition of equipment:

List price	$30,000
5% sales tax	1,500
Total	31,500
Down payment	10,500
Balance	21,000
8% interest, 24 months	3,360
Contract amount	$24,360

Required:

Prepare in good form, including full explanations, the adjusting entry (entries) you would propose as auditor of Chem-Lite Inc. with respect to the equipment and related depreciation accounts at March 31, 19X1 (assume that all amounts given are material).

(AICPA, adapted)

14–32. Nova Land Development Corporation is a closely held corporation engaged in purchasing large tracts of land, subdividing the tracts, and installing paved streets and utilities. The corporation does not construct buildings for the buyers of the land and does not have any affiliated construction companies. Undeveloped land usually is leased for farming until the corporation is ready to begin developing it.

The corporation finances its land acquisitions by mortgages; the mortgagees require audited financial statements. This is your first audit of the company, and you have now begun the examination of the financial statements for the year ended December 31.

Required:

The corporation has three tracts of land in various stages of development. List the audit procedures to be employed in the verification of the physical existence and title to the corporation's three landholdings.

(AICPA, adapted)

14–33. J. Barnes, CA, has been retained to audit a manufacturing company with a balance sheet that includes the caption Property, Plant, and Equipment. Barnes has been asked by the company's management if audit adjustments or reclassifications are required for the following material items that have been included in or excluded from Property, Plant, and Equipment.

a. A tract of land was acquired during the year. The land is the future site of the client's new headquarters, which will be constructed in the following year. Commissions were paid to the real estate agent used to acquire the land, and expenditures were made to relocate the previous owner's equipment. These commissions and expenditures were expensed and are excluded from Property, Plant, and Equipment.

b. Clearing costs were incurred to make the land ready for construction. These costs were included in Property, Plant, and Equipment.

c. During the land-clearing process, timber and gravel were recovered and sold. The proceeds from the sale were recorded as other income and are excluded from Property, Plant, and Equipment.

d. A group of machines was purchased under a royalty agreement, which provides royalty payments based on units of production from the machines. The cost of the machines, freight costs, unloading charges, and royalty payments were capitalized and are included in Property, Plant, and Equipment.

Required:

a. Describe the general characteristics of assets, such as land, buildings, improvements, machinery, equipment, and fixtures, that should normally be classified as Property, Plant, and Equipment, and identify audit objectives (i.e., how an auditor can obtain audit satisfaction) in connection with the examination of Property, Plant, and Equipment. ***Do not discuss specific audit procedures.***

b. Indicate whether each the above items (*a*) through (*d*) requires one or more audit adjustments or reclassifications, and explain why such adjustments or reclassifications are required or not required. Organize your answer as follows:

Item Reference	Is Audit Adjustment or Reclassification Required? Yes or No	Reasons Audit Adjustment or Reclassification Is Required or Not Required

(AICPA, adapted)

14–34. You are engaged in the examination of the financial statements of Holman Corporation for the year ended December 31, 1992. The accompanying analyses of the Property, Plant, and Equipment, and related accumulated depreciation accounts have been prepared by the chief accountant of the client. You have traced the beginning balances to your prior year's audit working papers.

HOLMAN CORPORATION
Analysis of Property, Plant, and Equipment, and
Related Accumulated Depreciation Accounts
Year Ended December 31, 1992

Description	Final Dec. 31, 91	Assets		Per Ledger Dec. 31, 92
		Additions	Retirements	
Land...	$422,500	$ 5,000		$427,500
Buildings.....................................	120,000	17,500		137,500
Machinery and equipment	385,000	40,400	$26,000	399,400
	$927,500	$62,900	$26,000	$964,400

Description	Final Dec. 31, 91	Accumulated Depreciation		Per Ledger Dec. 31, 92
		Additions*	Retirements	
Buildings.....................................	$ 60,000	$ 5,150		$ 65,150
Machinery and equipment	173,250	39,220		212,470
	$233,250	$44,370		$277,620

* Depreciation expense for the year.

All plant assets are depreciated on the straight-line basis (no residual value taken into consideration) based on the following estimated service lives: building, 25 years; all other items, 10 years. The company's policy is to take one half-year's depreciation on all asset additions and disposals during the year.

Your examination revealed the following information:

a. On April 1, the company entered into a 10-year lease contract for a die-casting machine, with annual rentals of $5,000 payable in advance every April 1. The lease is cancelable by either party (60 days' written notice is required), and there is no option to renew the lease or buy the equipment at the end of the lease. The estimated service life of the machine is 10 years with no residual value. The company recorded the die-casting machine in the Machinery and Equipment account at $40,400, the present value at the date of the lease, and $2,020 applicable to the machine has been included in depreciation expense for the year.

b. The company completed the construction of a wing on the plant building on June 30. The service life of the building was not extended by this addition. The lowest construction bid received was $17,500, the amount recorded in the Buildings account. Company personnel constructed the addition at a cost of $16,000 (materials, $7,500; labour, $5,500; overhead, $3,000).

c. On August 18, $5,000 was paid for paving and fencing a portion of land owned by the company and used as a parking lot for employees. The expenditure was charged to the land account.

d. The amount shown in the machinery and equipment asset retirement column represents cash received on September 5 upon disposal of a machine purchased in July 1988 for $48,000. The chief accountant recorded depreciation expense of $3,500 on this machine in 1992.

e. Harbour City donated land and building appraised at $100,000 and $400,000, respectively, to Holman Corporation for a plant. On September 1, the company began operating the plant. Since no costs were involved, the chief accountant made no entry for the above transaction.

Required:

Prepare the adjusting journal entries that you would propose at December 31, 1992, to adjust the accounts for the above transactions. Disregard income tax implications. The accounts have not been closed. Computations should be rounded off to the nearest dollar. Use a separate adjusting journal entry for each of the above five paragraphs.

(AICPA, adapted)

14–35. You are the senior accountant in the audit of Granger Grain Corporation, whose business primarily involves the purchase, storage, and sale of grain products. The corporation owns several elevators located along navigable water routes and transports its grain by barge and rail. Your staff assistant submitted the following working paper analysis for your review:

GRANGER GRAIN CORPORATION
Advances Paid on Barges under Construction—a/c 210
December 31, 1993

Advances made:

Jan. 15, 93—Cheque No. 3463—Jones Barge Construction Co.	$100,000*
Apr. 13, 93—Cheque No. 4129—Jones Barge Construction Co.	25,000*
June 19, 93—Cheque No. 5396—Jones Barge Construction Co.	63,000*
Total payments	188,000
Deduct cash received Sept. 1, 93 from City Life Insurance Co.	188,000†
Balance per general ledger—Dec. 31, 93	$ –0–

* Examined approved cheque request and paid cheque and traced to cash disbursements journal.
† Traced to cash receipts journal and to duplicate deposit ticket.

Required:

a. In what respects is this brief analysis incomplete for audit purposes? (Do not include any discussion of specific auditing procedures.)

b. What two different types of contractual arrangements may be inferred from your assistant's analysis?

c. What additional auditing procedures would you suggest that your staff assistant perform before you accept the working paper as being complete?

(AICPA, adapted)

14–36. CA has been the auditor of W Ltd. for many years. The company is a large manufacturer with 11 factories located across Canada; the factories maintain their own accounting records. Three years ago the company appointed an internal auditor, R, who works out of the corporate head office and is independent of any factory. CA's practice has been to examine R's audit programs, discuss them with him, and review the results of his work.

R visits each factory at least once annually; until now, he has never concerned himself with plant assets. This year, however, he intends to carry out the following procedures at all factories:

a. Obtain listings of plant asset additions and disposals from the beginning of the fiscal year to the date of his visit.

b. Trace all additions to the head office "Authorization for Capital Expenditure" forms, and to "Supplementary Authorizations" if the expenditures exceed original estimates.

c. Ensure that additions for each factory are within the limits of authorized capital budgets.

d. See that the additions are charged to the proper general ledger accounts.

e. Check repair and maintenance control records to ensure that assets are maintained in good condition.

f. Ascertain that assets are adequately insured.

g. Enquire as to possible obsolescence of any machinery that the machine-hour records show to be idle for extended periods.

Required:
State the alterations or additions to R's proposed audit program covering plant assets that CA might suggest to increase the program's effectiveness.

(CICA, adapted)

Chapter 15

Accounts Payable and Other Liabilities

After studying this chapter, you should be able to:

- Describe the nature of accounts payable and other liabilities.
- Explain the fundamental internal controls over purchase transactions and payables.
- Describe the auditors' objectives for the audit of accounts payable.
- Describe the nature of appropriate procedures to accomplish the auditors' objectives for the audit of accounts payable.
- Describe the nature of appropriate procedures for auditing other liabilities.

Now that the chapters dealing with the audit of assets have been completed, we are ready to consider the examination of liability accounts. In this chapter we discuss accounts payable and other current liabilities. Chapter 16 includes material on long-term debt (as well as equity capital and contingencies).

ACCOUNTS PAYABLE

Sources and Nature of Accounts Payable

The term *accounts payable* (often referred to as *vouchers payable* for a voucher system) is used to describe short-term obligations arising from the purchase of goods and services in the ordinary course of business. Typical transactions creating accounts payable include the acquisition on credit of merchandise, raw materials, plant assets, and office supplies. Other sources of accounts payable include the receipt of services, such as legal and accounting services, advertising, repairs, and utilities. Interest-bearing obligations should not be included in accounts payable but shown separately as bonds, notes, mortgages, or instalment contracts.

Accounts payable arising from the purchase of goods or services and most *other liabilities* are usually evidenced by invoices and statements received from the suppliers. However, *accrued liabilities* (sometimes called *accrued expenses*) generally accumulate over time, and management must make accounting estimates of the year-end liability. Such estimates are often necessary for salaries, pensions, interest, rent, taxes, and similar items.

The Auditors' Objectives in Examination of Accounts Payable

The auditors' *objectives* in the examination of accounts payable are as follows:

1. To consider *internal control* over accounts payable.
2. To determine the *existence* of recorded accounts payable and that the client has *obligations* to pay these liabilities.
3. To establish the *completeness* of recorded accounts payable.
4. To determine that the *valuation* of accounts payable is in accordance with generally accepted accounting principles.
5. To establish the *clerical accuracy* of schedules of accounts payable.
6. To determine that the *statement presentation* of accounts payable is appropriate.

Virtually all lawsuits against public accounting firms allege that the auditors failed to detect an overstatement of earnings. Management, especially of publicly held firms, is often under some pressure to report increased earnings. In previous chapters, we discussed the auditors' concern about exaggeration of earnings that results from the overstatement of assets. In the audit of liabilities, the auditors are primarily concerned with the possibility of understatement, or omission, of liabilities. An *understatement of liabilities* will exaggerate financial strength of a company and conceal fraud just as effectively as *overstatement of assets*. Furthermore, the understatement of liabilities is usually accompanied by the understatement of expenses and an overstatement of net income. For example, delaying the recording of bills for December operating expenses until January overstates income while understating accounts payable. Therefore, audit procedures for liabilities should have as a primary objective determining the *completeness* of recorded payables.

Audit procedures for detection of such understated liabilities differ from those used to detect overstated assets. Overstating an asset account usually requires an improper entry in the accounting records, as by the recording of a fictitious transaction. Such improper entries can be detected by the auditors through examination of the individual entries making up the balance of an asset account. Once a fictitious entry is detected, the individual responsible for the fraud has little alternative but to admit his acts. By way of contrast, understating a liability account is generally possible merely by *failing to make an entry* for a transaction creating a liability. The omission of an entry is less susceptible of detection than is a fictitious entry. If the omission is detected, it is much easier to pass it off as an accidental error. Auditors have long recognized that the most difficult type of irregularity to detect is fraud based on the *nonrecording* of transactions.

When accounts payable entries have been recorded, the existence of a definite financial commitment makes accomplishment of the valuation audit objective less difficult than for assets (other than cash). The situation with accrued liabilities is different. As we suggested earlier, in many circumstances exact measurement of these accounts will be difficult; the auditors must examine management's accounting estimates.

Internal Control over Accounts Payable

In thinking about internal control for accounts payable, it is important to recognize that the accounts payable of one company are the accounts receivable of other companies. It follows that there is little danger of errors being overlooked permanently since the client's creditors will generally maintain complete records of their receivables and will inform the client if payment is not received. This feature also aids auditors in the discovery of irregularities, since the perpetrator must be able to obtain and respond to the demands for payment. Some companies, therefore, may choose to minimize their record-keeping of liabilities and to rely on creditors to call attention to any delay in making payment. This viewpoint is not an endorsement of inaccurate or incomplete records of accounts payable, but merely a recognition that the self-interest of creditors constitutes an effective control in accounting for payables that is not present in the case of accounts receivable.

Discussions of internal control applicable to accounts payable may logically be extended to the entire purchase or acquisition cycle. In an effective purchasing system, a stores, or inventory control, department will prepare and approve the issuance of a purchase requisition that will be sent to the purchasing department. A copy of the purchase requisition will be filed numerically and matched with the subsequently prepared purchase order and finally with a copy of the receiving report.

The purchasing department, upon receiving the purchase requisition, will (1) determine that the item should be ordered and (2) select the appropriate vendor, quality, and price. Then a serially numbered purchase order is issued to order the goods. Copies of the purchase order should be sent to stores, receiving, and the accounts payable department. The copy sent to receiving is generally "blind" in that quantity information is not included so as to encourage receiving department counting of quantities. But the fact that a vendor's packing slip (with quantities specified) is almost always included when goods are received decreases the effectiveness of this control.

The receiving department should be independent of the purchasing department. When goods are received, they should be counted and inspected. Receiving reports should be prepared for all goods received. These documents should be serially numbered and prepared in a sufficient number of copies to permit prompt notification of the receipt of goods to the stores department, the purchasing department, and the accounts payable department.

Within the accounts (vouchers) payable department, all forms should be stamped with the date received. Vouchers and other documents originating within the department can be controlled through the use of serial numbers. Each step in the verification of an invoice should be evidenced by entering a date and signature on the voucher. Comparison of the quantities listed on the invoice with those shown on the receiving report and purchase order will prevent the payment of charges for goods in excess of those ordered and received. Comparison of the prices, discounts, and terms of shipment as shown on the purchase order and on the vendor's invoice provides a safeguard against the payment of excessive prices.

The separation of the function of invoice verification and approval from the function of cash disbursement is another step that tends to prevent errors and irregularities. Before invoices are approved for payment, written evidence must be presented to show that all aspects of the transaction have been verified. The official who signs cheques should stamp or perforate the voucher and supporting documents so that they cannot be presented to support payment a second time.

Another control procedure that the auditors may expect to find in a well-managed accounts payable department is the monthly balancing of the detailed records of accounts payable (or vouchers) to the general ledger control account. These reconciliations should be preserved as evidence of the performance of this procedure and as an aid in locating any subsequent errors.

Monthly statements from vendors should be reconciled promptly with the accounts payable ledger or list of open vouchers, and any discrepancies fully investigated. In some industries, it is common practice to make advances to vendors, which are recovered by making percentage deductions from invoices. When such advances are in use, the auditors should ascertain that procedures are followed to assure that deductions from the invoices are made in accordance with the agreement.

The operation of a purchase or acquisition transaction cycle is illustrated in Figure 15–1.

Internal Control and the Computer

Computer processing of purchase transactions can strengthen internal control. Purchase requisitions and purchase orders may be generated by a computer which maintains on-line perpetual inventory records. When goods are received, information may be keyed into the computer system with subsequent automated preparation of a receiving report and updating of inventory records. The computer can match the information from purchase orders, receiving reports, and vendors' invoices and approve appropriate payments of accounts payable. As indicated in Chapter 11, computer processing of both cash receipts and disbursements can provide management with a continually up-to-date cash record. However, the EDP controls discussed in Chapter 8 must be implemented to ensure the accuracy of computer input, processing, and output.

Audit Working Papers for Accounts Payable

The principal working papers are a lead schedule for accounts payable, trial balances of the various types of accounts payable at the balance sheet date, and confirmation requests for accounts payable. The trial balances are often in the form of computer printouts. In addition, the auditors may prepare a listing of **unrecorded** accounts payable discovered during the course of the audit, as illustrated in Figure 15–4.

AUDIT PROGRAM

The following procedures are typical of the work required in many engagements for the verification of accounts payable.

A. Consider internal control for accounts payable.
1. *Obtain an understanding of internal control* for accounts payable.
2. *Assess control risk and design additional tests of controls* for accounts payable.
3. *Perform additional tests of controls* for those controls which the auditors plan to consider to reduce their assessed level of control risk.
4. *Reassess control risk and design substantive tests* for accounts payable.

FIGURE 15–1 Flowchart of a Purchase Transaction Cycle

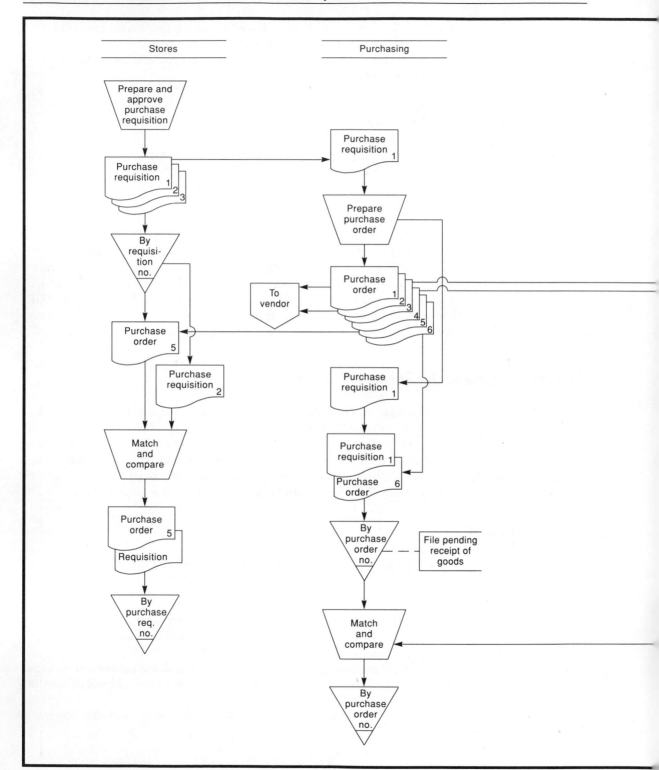

FIGURE 15–1 (*Concluded*)

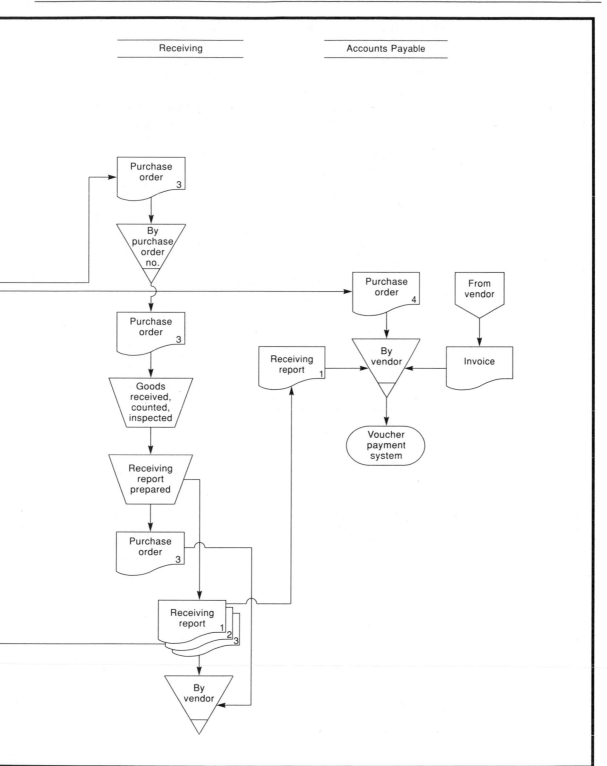

B. Substantive tests of accounts payable transactions and balances.

5. Obtain a trial balance of accounts payable as of the balance sheet date and reconcile with the general ledger.
6. Vouch balances payable to selected creditors by inspection of supporting documents.
7. Reconcile liabilities with monthly statements from creditors.
8. Confirm accounts payable by direct correspondence with vendors.
9. Perform analytical procedures for accounts payable and related accounts.
10. Search for unrecorded accounts payable.
11. Perform procedures to identify accounts payable to related parties.
12. Evaluate proper balance sheet presentation and disclosure of accounts payable.

Figure 15–2 relates the objectives of the major substantive tests of accounts payables to the primary audit objectives.

A. Consider internal control for accounts payable.

1. Obtain an understanding of internal control.

One approach used by auditors in becoming familiar with a client's internal control for accounts payable is to prepare a flowchart or to use flowcharts prepared by the client. In some engagements, the auditors may choose to prepare a narrative description covering such matters as the

FIGURE 15–2 Objectives of Major Substantive Tests of Accounts Payable

Substantive Tests	*Primary Audit Objectives*
Obtain trial balance of payables and reconcile with the ledgers	*Clerical accuracy*
Vouch balances payable to selected creditors to supporting documents	*Existence and obligations* *Valuations*
Reconcile liabilities with creditors' monthly statements	*Completeness* *Existence and obligations*
Confirm accounts payable	*Valuation*
Perform analytical procedures	
Search for unrecorded accounts payable	*Completeness*
Perform procedures to identify accounts payable to related parties	*Statement presentation*
Evaluate balance sheet presentation and disclosure	

independence of the accounts payable department and the receiving department from the purchasing department. The auditors might also use a questionnaire to obtain a description of accounts payable controls. Typical of the questions are the following: Is an accounts payable trial balance prepared monthly and reconciled to the general ledger control account? Are monthly statements from vendors reconciled with accounts payable ledgers or unpaid vouchers? Are advance payments to vendors recorded as receivables and controlled in a manner that assures that they will be recovered by offset against vendors' invoices? Are debit memos issued to vendors for discrepancies in invoice prices, quantities, or computations? Are debit balances in vendors' accounts brought to the attention of the credit and purchasing departments?

After the auditors have prepared a flowchart (or other description) of internal control, they determine whether the client is actually using the internal controls described to them; that is, they determine whether the controls have been *placed in operation.* The auditors will typically perform a walk-through of several purchase transactions and observe the implementation of the various internal control policies, systems, and procedures.

As the auditors verify their understanding of internal control, they will observe and enquire about the segregation of duties for purchases and cash disbursements. They will also inspect the various documents and reconciliations that are important to the client's internal control over accounts payable. For example, the reconciliations of monthly statements from vendors to the payables ledger will be inspected. Budgets for cash disbursements will be inspected, and the auditors will review the evidence of the follow-up on variances from budgeted amounts of disbursements. These tests of controls may provide the auditors with sufficient evidence to assess control risk for certain financial statement assertions about accounts payable at less than the maximum.

2. Assess control risk and design additional tests of controls.

After obtaining an understanding of the client's internal control for accounts payable, the auditors perform their initial assessments of control risk. To further evaluate these assessments, the auditors must obtain additional evidence of the operating effectiveness of various internal control policies, systems, and procedures. This evidence is obtained by performing additional tests of controls. In designing these tests, the auditors must decide which ones will result in sufficient reductions in substantive tests to justify the time spent performing them.

3. Perform additional tests of controls.

Tests directed toward the effectiveness of controls help to evaluate the client's internal control and to determine the extent to which the auditors are justified in reducing their assessed levels of control risk for the assertions about the accounts payable. A number of tests of controls relating to accounts payable have already been discussed in Chapters 11 and 13 on cash and inventories. In this chapter we briefly recap several significant tests.

a. Verify a sample of postings to the accounts payable control account.

The validity of the amount in the general ledger control account for accounts payable is established by tracing postings to the voucher register and cash payments journal. This work is performed before the balance sheet date as part of a general test of postings to all records. At the same time, the auditors should scrutinize all entries to the control account for the entire period under audit and should investigate any unusual entries.

b. Vouch to supporting documents a sample of entries in the voucher register or in selected accounts of the accounts payable subsidiary ledger.

Testing the voucher register or the accounts payable ledgers by tracing specific entries back through the cash payments journal, purchases journal, and other journals to original documents (such as purchase orders, receiving reports, invoices, and paid cheques) is necessary to determine the operating effectiveness of certain internal control policies, systems, and procedures. If the functions of purchasing, receiving, invoice verification, and cash disbursement are delegated to separate departments and if internal controls appear adequate, the tracing of individual entries from the register or ledgers to the original records may provide the auditors with sufficient evidence to assess control risk for the assertions related to accounts payable at a low level.

The auditors may also make tests by following the audit trail in the opposite direction. By tracing a representative sample of entries from the source documents to the register or accounts payable ledger, the auditors can verify that accounts payable are accurately recorded on a timely basis.

4. Reassess control risk and design substantive tests.

Completion of the above audit procedures enables the auditors to perform a final assessment of control risk for each of the major financial statement assertions about accounts payable. The internal control assessment provides the basis for selecting the necessary substantive tests for verification of accounts payable at the balance sheet date.

An assessment of low control risk over accounts payable often means that the auditors have found that serially numbered receiving reports are prepared promptly by the client for all goods received, that serially numbered vouchers are promptly prepared and recorded in the voucher register, and that payments are made promptly on the due dates and immediately recorded in the cheque register or cash payments journal and accounts payable subsidiary ledger. Finally, at the end of each month, an employee who does not participate in processing accounts payable compares the individual accounts in the accounts payable subsidiary ledger with vendors' statements, and also compares the total of the subsidiary record with the general ledger control account. Such favourable internal control would enable the auditors to minimize substantive testing of accounts payable.

On the other hand, an assessment of high control risk over accounts payable often means that the auditors have found that the subsidiary record of accounts payable is not in agreement with the general ledger control account, that even receiving reports and vouchers are serially numbered but are not accounted for and are used haphazardly, that purchase transactions often are not recorded until payment is made, and that many accounts payable are long past due. In this situation, the auditors must undertake extensive work if they are to determine that the balance sheet amount for accounts payable includes all liabilities in existence at the balance sheet date.

B. Substantive tests.

5. Obtain a trial balance of accounts payable as of the balance sheet date and reconcile with the general ledger.

One purpose of this procedure is to prove that the liability figure appearing in the balance sheet is in agreement with the individual items comprising the detail records. A second purpose is to provide a starting point for substantive testing. The auditors will use the list of vouchers or accounts payable to select a representative group of items for careful examination.

The client company usually furnishes the auditors with a year-end trial balance. The auditors should verify the footing and the accuracy of individual amounts in the trial balance. If the schedule of individual items does not agree in total with the control account, the cause of the discrepancy must be investigated. In most situations, the auditors will arrange for the client's staff to locate such errors and make the necessary adjustments. Agreement of the control account and the list of individual account balances is not absolute proof of the total indebtedness; invoices received near the close of the period may not be reflected in either the control account or the subsidiary records, and other similar errors may exist without causing the accounts to be out of balance.

6. Vouch balances payable to selected creditors by inspection of supporting documents.

The vouching of selected creditors' balances to supporting vouchers, invoices, purchase orders, and receiving reports is a substantive test of the existence and valuation of accounts payable.

For companies that use a voucher system, the verification of the individual vouchers is made most conveniently at the balance sheet date, when the vouchers will be together in the unpaid voucher file. The content of the unpaid voucher file changes daily; as vouchers are paid, they are removed from the file and filed alphabetically by vendor. Consequently, it is important that the client maintain a list of year-end unpaid vouchers. This listing should show the names of vendors, voucher numbers, dates, and amounts.

7. Reconcile liabilities with monthly statements from creditors.

In some companies, it is a regular practice each month to reconcile vendors' statements with the detailed records of payables. If the auditors find that this reconciliation is regularly performed by the client's staff, they may limit their examination of vendors' statements to determining that the reconciliation work has been satisfactory.

If the client's staff has not reconciled vendors' statements and accounts payable, the auditors may do so. When control risk for accounts payable is high, the auditors may control incoming mail to assure that all vendors' statements received by the client are made available to the auditors. Among the discrepancies often revealed by reconciliation of vendors' statements are charges by the vendor for shipments not yet received or recorded by the client. Although conceptually all goods on which title has passed should be included in inventory (thus, items shipped FOB shipping point as of year-end and not yet received should be included), normal accounting procedures do not provide for recording invoices as liabilities until the merchandise has been received. In-transit shipments on which title has passed should be listed and a decision reached as to whether they are sufficiently material to warrant year-end adjustment.

The cutoff of accounts payable is closely connected with the cutoff of purchase invoices in determining the year-end inventory. When observing the taking of a physical inventory on December 31, the auditors will make a record of the serial number of the last receiving report issued. This number should be identified with the corresponding vendor's invoice on the list of accounts payable at December 31. Any invoices corresponding to earlier receiving reports represent liabilities at December 31; any invoices associated with later receiving reports should not be part of the year-end amount for accounts payable. In other words, the year-end cutoff must assure that a liability is recorded for any goods received on the last day of the year *and included in the physical inventory*. Otherwise, net income would be overstated by the full amount of the omitted invoice.

If a shipment of merchandise arrives on December 31 after the physical inventory has been completed, income will not be affected if the goods are omitted from inventory and the related vendor's invoice is omitted from purchases and accounts payable. Although the omission is a cutoff error, it is far less *material* than if the goods had been included in inventory but the liability had not been recorded.

In more general terms, we can say that in judging the materiality of unrecorded liabilities, the auditors should consider the related unrecorded debits. If recording the transaction would mean adding an asset as well as a liability, the effect on the financial statements would be less significant than recording an invoice of like amount for which the debit belonged in an expense account. The auditors must be sure, however, that invoices have been recorded as liabilities for all goods received and included in the year-end physical inventory.

8. Confirm accounts payable by direct correspondence with vendors.

Confirmation of accounts payable is not a mandatory procedure as is the confirmation of accounts receivables. One reason is that for accounts payable the auditors will find in the client's possession externally created evidence such as vendors' invoices and statements that substantiate the accounts payable. No such external evidence is on hand to support accounts receivable. Another reason confirmation of payables is not mandatory is that the greatest risk in the verification of liabilities is the possibility of unrecorded amounts. To confirm the ***recorded accounts payable*** does little to determine whether any ***unrecorded accounts payable*** exist. It is difficult to adequately address the completeness assertion with confirmations. To mitigate this problem, accounts payable confirmation requests often are designed differently from that for accounts receivable. Notice that the account payable confirmation request in Figure 15–3 asks the vendor to fill in the amount of the liability; it is a ***blank confirmation*** designed to detect unrecorded amounts as well as to provide evidence as to the amount of recorded payable. Also, accounts payable confirmation requests should be mailed to vendors from whom substantial purchases have been made during the year, regardless of the size of their accounts at the balance sheet date (even to suppliers whose accounts show ***zero balances***). These substantial suppliers may be identified by reference to cash disbursement records or computer printouts of purchase volume by individual supplier; enquiry of purchasing department personnel, as well as examination of the accounts payable subsidiary ledger. Other accounts that often are confirmed by the auditors include those for which monthly statements are not available, accounts reflecting unusual transactions, accounts with parent or subsidiary corporations, and accounts secured by pledged assets.

9. Perform analytical procedures for accounts payable and related accounts.

To gain assurance as to the overall reasonableness of accounts payable, the auditor may compute ratios such as accounts payable divided by purchases, and accounts payable divided by total current liabilities. These ratios are compared with ratios for prior years to disclose trends that warrant investigation. The amounts owing to individual creditors should be compared with balances in prior years. By studying yearly variations in purchases and other accounts closely related to accounts payable, the auditors may become aware of errors in accounts payable. Finally, the portion of accounts payable which is past due at the year-end should be compared with corresponding data for previous years.

The auditors may test purchase discounts by computing the ratio of cash discounts earned to total purchases during the period and comparing this ratio from period to period. Any significant decrease in the ratio might indicate a change in terms of purchases, failure to take discounts, or fraudulent manipulation.

10. Search for unrecorded accounts payable.

Throughout the audit the auditors must be alert for any unrecorded payables. For example, the preceding three steps of this program, reconciliation, confirmation, and analytical procedures, may disclose un-

FIGURE 15–3

PACKAGING SYSTEMS, INC.
9200 Thunder Street
Bridgetown, Ontario M8F 6K7

January 2, 19X2

Grayline Container, Inc.
8600 Randolph Street
Windsor, Ontario N9E 2S8

Dear Sirs:

　　Our auditors, Nelson and Gray, CAs, are making an examination of our
financial statements. For this reason, please inform them in the space
provided below the amount, if any, owed to you by this company at December 31,
19X1.

　　Please attach an itemized statement supporting any balance owed, showing
all unpaid items. Your reply should be sent directly to Nelson & Gray, CAs,
6500 Lane Avenue, Bridgetown, Ontario, M8F 5R9. A stamped addressed envelope
is enclosed for your reply. Thank you.

　　　　　　　　　　　　　　　　　　Sincerely,

　　　　　　　　　　　　　　　　　Robert W. Jones

　　　　　　　　　　　　　　　　　Robert W. James
　　　　　　　　　　　　　　　　　Controller

- -

Nelson & Gray, CAs

　　Our records show that the amount of $___26,800___was owed to us by
Packaging Systems, Inc., at December 31, 19X1, as shown by the itemized statement attached.

Date:___Jan.6,X2___　　　　　　　　　Signature　*Sharon Steele*

　　　　　　　　　　　　　　　　　　Title　　*Controller*

recorded liabilities. In addition to normal trade payables that may be unrecorded, other examples include unrecorded liabilities related to customers' deposits recorded as credits to accounts receivable, obligations for securities purchased but not settled at the balance sheet date, unbilled contractor or architect fees for a building under construction at the audit date, and unpaid lawyer or insurance broker fees.

In addition to the prior audit steps, when searching for unrecorded accounts payable the auditors will audit transactions that were recorded following year-end. A comparison of cash payments occurring after the balance sheet date with the accounts payable trial balance is generally the most effective means of disclosing unrecorded accounts payable. All liabilities must eventually be paid, and will, therefore, be reflected in the accounts at least by the time they are paid. Regular monthly expenses, such as rent and utilities, are often posted to the ledger accounts directly from the cash disbursements journal without any account payable or other liability having been set up.

The auditors should also consider sources of potential unrecorded payables such as the following:

1. Unmatched invoices and receiving reports. These documents are called *work in process* in a voucher system. The auditors should review such unprocessed documents at the balance sheet date to ascertain that the client has recorded an account payable where appropriate.
2. Vouchers payable entered in the voucher register subsequent to the balance sheet date. Inspection of these records may uncover items that should have been recorded as of the balance sheet date.
3. Invoices received by the client after the balance sheet date. Not all vendors send invoices promptly when goods are shipped or services are rendered. Accordingly, the auditors' review of invoices received by the client in the *subsequent period* may disclose unrecorded accounts payable as of the balance sheet date.

A form of audit working paper used to summarize unrecorded accounts payable discovered by the auditors is illustrated in Figure 15–4.

When unrecorded liabilities are discovered by the auditors, the next question is whether the omissions are sufficiently material to warrant proposing an adjusting entry. Will the adjustment cause a sufficient change in the financial statements to give a different impression of the company's current position or of its earning power? As previously indicated in the discussion of the reconciliation of vendors' statements with accounts payable, auditors seldom propose adjustments for the purpose of adding shipments in transit to the year-end inventory unless the shipments are unusually large.

As a further illustration of the factors to be considered in deciding upon the *materiality* of an unrecorded transaction, let us use as an example the December 31 annual audit of a small manufacturing company in good

FIGURE 15–4

The Palerno Company

Unrecorded Accounts Payable   M-1-1

December 31, 19X3

Invoice Date	No.	Vendor and Description	Account Charged	Amount
Dec. 31, X3	2858	Hayes Mfg. Co. – invoice and shipment in transit	Inventories	10,650.00
— —		Fox & Williams – unpaid legal fees – see M-4	Legal Expenses	1,000.00
Dec. 28, X3	428	Hart & Co. – machinery repairs (paid Jan. 1, X4)	Repairs Exp.	12,600.00
Dec. 31, X3	—	Allen Enterprises – Dec. 19 account sales for consigned goods	Sales	25,680.00
— —		Grant Co. – shipment received Dec. 31, X3 per receiver no. 2907; invoice not yet received.	Inventories	15,820.00
— —		Arthur & Baker – earned but unpaid architects' fee for building under construction – see K-5	Construction in Progress	23,370.00
				89,120.00
				M-1

A.J.E. 8	131	Inventories	26,470.00	
	156	Construction in Progress	23,370.00	
	401	Sales	25,680.00	
	518	Legal Expenses	1,000.00	
	527	Repairs Expense	12,600.00	
	203	Accounts Payable		89,120.00

To record unrecorded accounts payable at Dec. 31, X3

    Above payables were developed principally in the audit of accounts payable. See audit program B-4 for procedures employed. In my opinion the $89,120 adjustment includes all material unrecorded accounts payable.

V. M. H.

Jan. 28, X4

financial condition with total assets of $1 million and preadjustment net income of $100,000. The auditors' procedures bring to light the following unrecorded liabilities:

1. An invoice of $1,400, dated December 30 and bearing terms of FOB shipping point. The goods were shipped on December 30 but were not received until January 4. The invoice was also received and recorded on January 4.

   In considering the materiality of this omission, the first point is that net income is not affected. The adjusting entry, if made, would add equal amounts to current assets (inventories) and to current liabilities; hence, it would not change the amount of working capital. The omission does affect the current ratio very slightly. The auditor would probably consider this transaction as not sufficiently material to warrant adjustment.

2. Another invoice for $4,000, dated December 30 and bearing terms of FOB shipping point. The goods arrived on December 31 and were included in the physical inventory taken that day. The invoice was not received until January 8 and was entered as a January transaction.

   This error should be corrected because the inclusion of the goods in the physical inventory without recognition of the liability has caused an error of $4,000 in pretax income for the year. Since the current liabilities are understated, both the amount of working capital and the current ratio are exaggerated. The owners' equity is also overstated. These facts point to the materiality of the omission and constitute strong arguments for an adjusting entry.

3. An invoice for $1,500, dated December 31, for a new office safe. The safe was installed on December 31, but the invoice was not recorded until paid on January 15.

   Since the transaction involved only asset and liability accounts, the omission of an entry did not affect net income. However, working capital and the current ratio are affected by the error since the debit affects a noncurrent asset and the credit affects a current liability. Most auditors would probably not propose an adjusting entry for this item.

4. An invoice for $3,000, dated December 31, for advertising services rendered during October, November, and December. The invoice was not recorded until paid on January 15.

   The argument for treating this item as sufficiently material to warrant adjustment is based on the fact that net income is affected, as well as the amount of working capital and the current ratio. The adjusting entry should probably be recommended in these circumstances.

The preceding examples suggest that a decision as to the materiality of an unrecorded transaction hinges to an important extent on whether the transaction affects net income. Assuming that an omitted transaction does affect net income and there is doubt as to whether the dollar amount is large enough to warrant adjustment, the auditors should bear in mind that almost half of the effect of the error on net income may be eliminated by corporate income taxes. In other words, an adjusting entry to record an omitted expense item of $10,000 may reduce after-tax income by only $5,000. If the adjusting entry is not made, the only ultimate effect is a shift of $5,000 between the net income of two successive years. As a general rule, the auditors should avoid proposing adjusting entries for errors in the year-end cutoff of transactions unless the effect on the statements is significant. However, it should be borne in mind that a number of insignificant individual misstatements may be material in their *cumulative* effect on the financial statements. Therefore, the auditors will accumulate the effects of these misstatements.

11. Perform procedures to identify accounts payable to related parties.

Payables to a corporation's officers, directors, shareholders, or affiliates require particular attention by the auditors since they are not the result of arm's-length bargaining by parties of opposing interests. Here the auditors should consider the possibility that these payables relate to purchases of inventory or other asset items for which there may be valuation questions.

The auditors must search for such payables. All material payables to related parties must be disclosed in the financial statements.

12. Evaluate proper balance sheet presentation and disclosure of accounts payable.

Proper balance sheet presentation of accounts payable requires that any material amounts payable to related parties (directors, principal shareholders, officers, and employees) be listed separately from amounts payable to trade creditors.

Debit balances of substantial amount sometimes occur in accounts payable because of such events as duplicate payments made in error, return of merchandise to vendors after payment had been made, and advances to suppliers. If these debit balances are material, a reclassification entry should be made in the audit working papers so that the debit balances will appear as assets in the balance sheet rather than being offset against other accounts payable with credit balances.

If the client company acts as a consignee of merchandise, it is possible that sales of consigned goods shortly before the year-end may not have been set up as a liability to the consignor. An accurate determination of any amounts owing to consignors at the balance sheet date is one step in proper balance sheet presentation of liabilities.

Accounts payable secured by pledged assets should be disclosed in the balance sheet or a note thereto, and cross-referenced to the pledged assets.

OTHER LIABILITIES

Notes payable are discussed in the next chapter. In addition to the accounts payable previously considered, other items classified as current liabilities include:

1. Amounts withheld from employees' pay.
2. Sales taxes payable.
3. Unclaimed wages.
4. Customers' deposits.
5. Accrued liabilities.

Amounts Withheld from Employees' Pay

Payroll deductions are many; among the more important are unemployment insurance taxes and individual income taxes. Although the governments do not specify the exact form of records to be maintained, they do require that records of amounts earned and withheld be adequate to permit a determination of compliance with tax laws.

Income taxes withheld from employees' pay and not remitted as of the balance sheet date constitute a liability to be verified by the auditors. Accrued employer payroll taxes may be audited at the same time. This verification usually consists of tracing the amounts withheld to the payroll summary sheets, testing computations of taxes withheld and accrued, determining that taxes have been deposited or paid in accordance with the governmental laws and regulations, and reviewing tax returns.

Payroll deductions also are often made for union dues, charitable contributions, retirement plans, insurance, savings bonds, and other purposes. Besides verifying the liability for any such amounts withheld from employees and not remitted as of the balance sheet date, the auditors should review the adequacy of the withholding procedures and determine that payroll deductions have been properly authorized and accurately computed.

Sales Taxes Payable

Business concerns are required to collect sales taxes, such as the goods and services tax, imposed by governments on retail sales. These taxes do not represent an expense to the business; the retailer merely acts as a collecting agent. Until the amounts collected from customers are remitted to the taxing authority, they constitute current liabilities of the business. The auditors' verification of this liability includes a review of the client's periodic tax returns. The reasonableness of the liability also is tested by a computation applying the tax rate to total taxable sales. In addition, the auditors should examine a number of sales invoices to ascertain that customers are being charged the correct amount of tax. Debits to the liability account for remittances to the taxing authority should be traced to copies of the tax returns and should be vouched to the paid cheques.

Unclaimed Wages

Unclaimed wages are, by their very nature, subject to misappropriation. The auditors, therefore, are particularly concerned with the adequacy of internal control over this item. A list of unpaid wages should be prepared after each payroll distribution. The payroll cheques should not be left for more than a few days in the payroll department. Prompt deposit in a special bank account provides much improved control. The auditors will analyze the Unclaimed Wages account for the purpose of determining that (1) the credits represent all unclaimed wages after each payroll distribution and (2) the debits represent only authorized payments to employees, remittances to the government under unclaimed property laws, or transfers back to general cash funds through approved procedures.

Customers' Deposits

Many companies require that customers make deposits on returnable containers. Public utilities and common carriers also may require deposits to guarantee payment of bills or to cover equipment on loan to the customer. A review of the procedures followed in accepting and returning deposits should be made by the auditors with a view to disclosing any shortcomings in internal control. In some instances, deposits shown by the records as refunded to customers may in fact have been abstracted by employees.

The verification should include obtaining a list of the individual deposits and a comparison of the total with the general ledger controlling account. If deposits are interest-bearing, the amount of accrued interest should also be tested for reasonableness. As a general rule, the auditors do not attempt to confirm deposits by direct communication with customers, but this procedure is desirable if the amounts involved are substantial or the internal control is considered to be deficient.

Accrued Liabilities

Most accrued liabilities represent obligations payable sometime during the succeeding period for services or privileges received before the balance sheet date. Examples include interest payable, accrued property taxes, accrued payrolls and payroll taxes, income taxes payable, and amounts accrued under service guarantees.

Because accrued items are based on client estimates of amounts which will subsequently become payable, subjective (as well as objective) factors may make it difficult to establish control over them. As a result, these estimates may be particularly susceptible to misstatement, especially in circumstances in which management is under pressure to show increased earnings.

The basic auditing steps for accrued liabilities are:

1. Examine any contracts or other documents on hand that provide the basis for the accrual.
2. Appraise the accuracy of the detailed accounting records maintained for this category of liability.
3. Identify and evaluate the reasonableness of the assumptions made that underlie the computation of the liability.
4. Test the computations made by the client in setting up the accrual.
5. Determine that accrued liabilities have been treated consistently at the beginning and end of the period.
6. Consider the need for accrual of other accrued liabilities not presently considered (i.e., test completeness).

The following sections describe the nature of the audit of various accrued liabilities.

Accrued Property Taxes.   Property tax payments are usually few in number and substantial in amount. It is, therefore, feasible for the audit working papers to include an analysis showing all of the year's property tax transactions. Tax payments should be verified by inspection of the property tax bills issued by local government units and by reference to the related paid cheques. If the tax accruals at the balance sheet date differ significantly from those of prior years, an explanation of the variation should be obtained. The auditors should verify that property tax bills have been received on all taxable property or that an estimated tax has been accrued.

Accrued Payrolls.   The examination of payrolls from the standpoint of appraising the adequacy of internal controls and substantiating the expenditures for the period under audit is considered in Chapter 17. The present consideration of payrolls is limited to the procedures required for the testing of accrued payrolls at the balance sheet date.

Accrued gross salaries and wages appear on the balance sheets of virtually all concerns. The accuracy of the amount accrued is significant in the determination of total liabilities and also in the proper matching of costs and revenue. The verification procedure consists principally of comparing the amounts accrued to the actual payroll of the subsequent period and reviewing the method of allocation at the balance sheet date. Payments made at the first payroll dates of the subsequent period are reviewed to determine that no significant *unrecorded* payroll liability existed as of the balance sheet date.

Pension Plan Accruals.   Auditing procedures for the accrued liability for pension costs may begin with a review of the copy of the pension plan in the auditors' permanent file. The auditors must determine that the client's accrued pension liability is presented in accordance with *CICA Handbook* Section 3460, "Pension costs and obligations." In auditing these pension obligations the auditors will obtain representations from an actuary and confirm the activity in the plan with the trustee. In evaluating the evidence from the actuary, the auditors should comply with the requirements of *CICA Handbook* Section 5360, "Using the Work of a Specialist" (discussed in Chapter 6).

Accrued Vacation Pay.   Closely related to accrued salaries and wages is the liability that may exist for accrued vacation pay. This type of liability arises from two situations: (1) an employee entitled by contract to a vacation during the past year may have been prevented from taking it by an emergency work schedule, and (2) an employee may be entitled to a future vacation of which part of the cost must be accrued to achieve a proper matching of costs and revenue.

The auditors' verification of accrued vacation pay may begin with a review of the permanent file copy of the employment contract or agreement stipulating vacation terms. The computation of the accrual should then be verified for both arithmetical accuracy and agreement with the terms of the company's vacation policy.

Product Warranty Liabilities.   The products of many companies are sold with a guarantee of free service or replacement during a rather extended warranty period. The costs of rendering such services should be recognized as expense in the year the product is sold rather than in a later year in which the replacement is made or repair service performed. If this policy is followed, the company will make an annual charge to expense and credit to a liability account based on the amount of the year's sales and the estimated future service or replacement. As repairs and replacements take place, the costs will be charged to the liability account.

The auditors should review the client's annual provision for estimated future expenditures and compute the percentage relationship between the amount in the liability account and the amount of the year's sales. If this relationship varies sharply from year to year, the client should be asked for an explanation. The auditors should also review the charges month by month to the liability account and be alert for the improper recording of other expenses in this account. Sudden variations in the monthly charges to the liability account require investigation. In general, the auditors should determine that the balance in the liability account for product warranty moves in reasonable relationship with the trend of sales. The auditors also should be alert for changes in the client's products or repair costs that might affect the amount of the warranty liability.

Accrued Commissions and Bonuses.   Accrued commissions to sales representatives and bonuses payable to managerial personnel also require verification. The essential step in this case is reference to the authority for the commission or bonus. The basic contracts should be examined and traced to minutes of directors' meetings. If the bonus or commission is based on the total volume of sales or some other objective measure, the auditors should verify the computation of the accrual by applying the prescribed rate to the amount used as a base.

Income Taxes Payable.   Federal, provincial, and foreign income taxes on corporations represent a material factor in determining both net income and financial position. The auditors cannot express an opinion on either the balance sheet or income statement of a corporation without first obtaining evidence that the provision for income taxes has been properly computed. In the audit of small- and medium-size companies, it is customary for the audit engagement to include the preparation of the client's tax returns. If the income tax returns have been prepared by the client's staff or other persons, the auditors must nevertheless verify the reasonableness of the tax liability if they are to express an opinion on the fairness of the financial statements. In performing such a review of a tax return prepared by the client's staff or by others, the auditors may sometimes discover an opportunity for a tax saving that has been overlooked; obviously such a discovery tends to enhance the client's appreciation of the services rendered by the auditors.

For businesses organized as sole proprietorships or partnerships, no provision for income taxes appears on the income statement because taxes on the profits of these enterprises are payable by the individual owner or owners.

The tax expected to be paid by a corporation often differs from the actual tax paid due to temporary differences between taxable income and pretax accounting income. These differences result in the need to establish deferred tax liabilities or assets. The auditors determine the amount of deferred tax liabilities using schedules referred to as *tax accrual* working papers, which usually are reviewed by one of the public accounting firm's tax specialists.

The auditors should analyze the Income Taxes Payable account and vouch all amounts to income tax returns, paid cheques, or other supporting documents. The final balance in the Income Taxes Payable account will ordinarily equal the computed federal, provincial, and foreign taxes on the current year's income tax returns, less any payments thereon.

Besides reviewing the computation of the income tax liability for the current year, the auditors should determine the date to which income tax returns for prior years have been examined by Revenue Canada and the particulars of any disputes or additional assessments. Review of the assessment notices is also an essential step. In the first audit of a new client, the auditors should review any prior years' income tax returns not yet examined by Revenue Canada to make sure that there has been no substantial underpayment of taxes that would warrant presentation as a liability.

Accrued Professsional Fees.   Fees of professional firms include charges for the services of lawyers, public accountants, consulting engineers, and other specialists who often render services of a continuing nature but present bills only at infrequent intervals. By enquiry of officers and by review of corporate minutes, the auditors may learn of professional services received for which no liability has yet been reflected in the accounts. Review of the expense account for legal fees is always essential because it may reveal damage suits, tax disputes, or other litigation warranting disclosure in the financial statements.

Balance Sheet Presentation

Accrued expenses—interest, taxes, rent, and wages—are included in the current liability section of the balance sheet and sometimes combined into one figure. Income taxes payable, however, may be sufficiently material to be listed as a separate item. Deferred income taxes resulting from tax allocations should be classified as current liabilities if they relate to current assets. Otherwise, deferred income taxes are classified as long term.

Deferred credits to revenue for such items as rent or interest collected in advance that will be taken into earnings in the succeeding period are customarily included in current liabilities. Deposits on contracts and similar advances from customers also are accorded the status of current liabilities because the receipt of an advance increases the current assets total and because the goods to be used in liquidating the advance are generally included in current assets.

Time of Examination

The nature and amount of trade accounts payable may change greatly within a few weeks' time; consequently, the auditors' verification of these rapidly changing liabilities is most effective when performed immediately after the balance sheet date. As stressed at the beginning of this chapter, failure to record a liability will cause an overstatement of financial position. Audit work on accounts payable performed before the balance sheet date is of little value if the client fails to record important liabilities coming into existence during the remaining weeks of the year under audit.

For this reason, many auditors believe that most of the audit work on accounts payable should be performed *after the balance sheet date.* Certainly, the auditors' search for unrecorded liabilities must be made after the balance sheet date because this search is concentrated on the transactions occurring during the first few weeks of the new year.

Some current liability accounts other than accounts payable are more suitable for preliminary audit work. The documents relating to accrued property taxes, for example, may be available in advance of the balance sheet date. Amounts withheld from employees' pay can be reviewed before the end of the year. The propriety of amounts withheld and of amounts remitted to the tax authorities during the year can be verified before the pressure of year-end work begins. The working papers relating to such liability accounts then may be completed very quickly after the end of the accounting period.

KEY TERMS

accrued liabilities (accrued expenses)   Short-term obligations for services of a continuing nature that accumulate on a time basis. Examples include interest, taxes, rent, salaries, and pensions. Generally not evidenced by invoices or statements.

confirmation   Direct communication with vendors or suppliers to determine the amount of an account payable. Represents high-quality evidence because it is a document created outside the client organization and transmitted directly to the auditors.

consignment   A transfer of goods from the owner to another person who acts as the sales agent of the owner.

subsequent period   The time extending from the balance sheet date to the date of the auditors' report.

trade accounts payable   Current liabilities arising from the purchase of goods and services from trade creditors, generally evidenced by invoices or statements received from the creditors.

vendor's statement   A monthly statement prepared by a vendor (supplier) showing the beginning balance, charges during the month for goods or services, amounts collected, and ending balance. This externally created document should correspond (except for timing differences) with an account in the client's accounts payable subsidiary ledger.

voucher   A document authorizing a cash disbursement. A voucher usually provides space for employees performing various approval functions to initial. The term *voucher* may also be applied to the group of supporting documents used as a basis for recording liabilities or for making cash disbursements.

voucher register   A special journal used in a voucher system to record liabilities requiring cash payment in the near future. Every liability recorded in a voucher register corresponds to a voucher authorizing future payment.

GROUP I: REVIEW QUESTIONS

15–1.   If a corporation overstates its earnings, are its liabilities more likely to be overstated or understated? Explain.

15–2.   Lawsuits against public accounting firms are most likely to allege that the auditors were negligent in not detecting which of the following? (*a*) overstatement of liabilities and earnings, (*b*) understatement of assets and earnings, (*c*) overstatement of owners' equity. Explain the reasoning underlying your choice.

15–3.   Assume that a highly placed employee has stolen company assets and is now planning to conceal the fraud by failing to make an accounting entry for a large transaction. Would the omission probably be for a transaction creating an asset or a liability? Explain.

15–4.   Suggest two reasons why the adjustments proposed by external auditors more often than not call for reducing recorded earnings.

15–5.   Explain how the auditors coordinate the year-end cutoff of accounts payable with their observation of the year-end physical inventory.

15–6.   Identify three audit procedures (other than "Search for unrecorded accounts payable") that are concerned directly or indirectly with disclosing unrecorded accounts payable.

15–7.   What is the purpose of the auditors' review of cash payments subsequent to the balance sheet date?

15–8.   The auditors usually find in the client's possession documentary evidence, such as invoices, supporting both accounts receivable and accounts payable. Is there any difference in the quality of such evidence for accounts receivable and for accounts payable? Explain.

15–9.   Describe briefly an internal control procedure that would prevent a paid disbursement voucher from being presented for payment a second time.

15–10.   Is the confirmation of accounts payable by direct communication with vendors as useful and important an audit procedure as is the confirmation of accounts receivable? Explain fully.

(AICPA)

15–11.   During the verification of the individual invoices comprising the total of accounts payable at the balance sheet date, the auditors discovered some receiving reports indicating that the merchandise covered by several of these invoices was not received until after the balance sheet date. What action should the auditors take?

15–12. What do you consider to be the most important single procedure in the auditors' search for unrecorded accounts payable? Explain.

15–13. Whitehall Company records its liabilities in accounts payable subsidiary ledgers. The auditors have decided to select some of the accounts for confirmation by direct communication with vendors. The largest volume of purchases during the year had been made from Ranchero Company, but at the balance sheet date this account had a zero balance. Under these circumstances should the auditors send a confirmation request to Ranchero Company, or would they accomplish more by limiting their confirmation program to accounts with large year-end balances?

15–14. Compare the auditors' approach to the verification of liabilities with their approach to the verification of assets.

15–15. Most auditors are interested in performing as many phases of an examination as possible in advance of the balance sheet date. The verification of accounts payable, however, generally is regarded as something to be done after the balance sheet date. What specific factors can you suggest that make the verification of accounts payable less suitable than many other accounts for interim work?

15–16. The operating procedures of a well-managed accounts payable department will provide for the verification of several specific points before a vendor's invoice is recorded as an approved liability. What are the points requiring verification?

15–17. List the major responsibilities of an accounts payable department.

15–18. In achieving adequate internal control over operations of the accounts payable department, a company should establish procedures that will ensure that extensions and footings are proved on all invoices and that the propriety of prices is reviewed. What is the most effective means of assuring consistent performance of these duties?

15–19. Which do you consider the more significant step in establishing strong internal control over accounts payable transactions: the approval of an invoice for payment, or the issuance of a cheque in payment of an invoice? Explain.

15–20. Outline a method by which the auditors may test the propriety of cash discounts taken on accounts payable.

15–21. For which documents relating to the accounts payable operation would you recommend the use of serial numbers as an internal control procedure?

15–22. What internal control procedure would you recommend to call attention to failure to pay invoices within the discount period?

15–23. As part of the investigation of accounts payable, auditors sometimes vouch entries in selected creditors' accounts back through the journals to original documents, such as purchase orders, receiving reports, invoices, and paid cheques. What is the principal purpose of this procedure?

15–24. Vendors' statements and accounts payable confirmations are both forms of documentary evidence created outside the client organization and useful in audit work on accounts payable. Which of these two represents higher quality evidence? Why?

15–25. What documentary evidence created outside the client's organization is particularly important to the auditors in verifying accrued property taxes?

15–26. What differences should auditors expect to find in supporting evidence for accrued liabilities as contrasted with accounts payable?

GROUP II: QUESTIONS REQUIRING ANALYSIS

15–27. Early in your first audit of Star Corporation, you notice that sales and year-end inventory are almost unchanged from the prior year. However, cost of goods sold is less than in the preceding year, and accounts payable also are down substantially. Gross profit has increased, but this increase has not carried through to net income because of increased executive salaries. Management informs you that sales prices and purchase prices have not changed significantly during the past year, and there have been no changes in the product line. Star Corporation relies on the periodic inventory system. Your initial impression of internal control is that several weaknesses may exist.

You are to suggest a possible explanation for the trends described, especially the decrease in accounts payable while sales and inventory were constant and gross profit increased. Explain fully the relationships involved.

15–28. Compare the confirmation of accounts receivable with the confirmation of accounts payable under the following headings:

   a. Generally accepted auditing procedures. (Justify the differences revealed by your comparison.)

   b. Selection of accounts to be confirmed.

(AICPA, adapted)

15–29. In connection with their examination of the financial statements of Davis Limited, the auditors reviewed the Income Taxes Payable account.

Required:

    a. Discuss reasons why the auditors should review the income tax returns for prior years and the assessment notices from Revenue Canada.

    b. What information will these reviews provide? (Do not discuss specific tax return items.)

(AICPA, adapted)

15–30. The *subsequent period* in an audit is the time extending from the balance sheet date to the date of the auditors' report.

Required:

Discuss the importance of the subsequent period in the audit of trade accounts payable.

15–31. During the course of any audit, the auditors are always alert for unrecorded accounts payable or other unrecorded liabilities.

Required:

For each of the following audit areas (1) describe an unrecorded liability that might be discovered and (2) state what auditing procedure(s) might bring it to light.

    a. Construction in progress (property, plant, and equipment).

    b. Prepaid insurance.

    c. License authorizing the client to produce a product patented by another company.

    d. Minutes of directors' meetings.

15–32. Describe the audit steps that generally would be followed in establishing the propriety of the recorded liability for federal income taxes of a corporation you are auditing for the first time. Consideration should be given the status of (*a*) the liability for prior years and (*b*) the liability arising from the current year's taxable income.

(AICPA)

15–33. In the course of your initial examination of the financial statements of Sylvan Company, you ascertain that of the substantial amount of accounts payable outstanding at the close of the period, approximately 75 percent is owed to six creditors. You have decided to confirm the balances owing to these six creditors by communicating with the creditors, but the president of the company is against such confirmation on the grounds that correspondence in regard to the balances—all of which contain some overdue items—might give rise to demands on the part of the creditors for immediate payment of the overdue items and thereby embarrass Sylvan Company.

    In the circumstances, what alternative procedure would you

adopt in an effort to satisfy yourself that the accounting records show the correct amounts payable to these creditors?

(AICPA, adapted)

15–34. Select the best answer for each of the following and explain the reason for your selection.

a. Which of the following procedures is **least** likely to be completed before the balance sheet date?
(1) Confirmation of receivables.
(2) Search for unrecorded liabilities.
(3) Observation of inventory.
(4) Review of internal control over cash disbursements.

b. An examination of the balance in the accounts payable account is ordinarily *not* designed:
(1) To detect accounts payable that are substantially past due.
(2) To verify that accounts payable were properly authorized.
(3) To ascertain the reasonableness of recorded liabilities.
(4) To determine that all existing liabilities at the balance sheet date have been recorded.

c. Which of the following is the **best** audit procedure for determining the existence of unrecorded liabilities?
(1) Examine confirmation requests returned by creditors whose accounts appear on a subsidiary trial balance of accounts payable.
(2) Examine unusual relationships between monthly accounts payable balances and recorded purchases.
(3) Examine a sample of invoices a few days prior to and subsequent to year-end to ascertain whether they have been properly recorded.
(4) Examine a sample of cash disbursements in the period subsequent to year-end.

d. Auditor confirmation of accounts payable balances at the balance sheet date may be **unnecessary** because:
(1) This is a duplication of cutoff tests.
(2) Accounts payable balances at the balance sheet date may *not* be paid before the audit is completed.
(3) Correspondence with the audit client's lawyer will reveal all legal action by vendors for nonpayment.
(4) There is likely to be other reliable external evidence available to support the balances.

e. A client erroneously recorded a large purchase twice. Which of the following internal control measures would be most likely to detect this error in a timely and efficient manner?
(1) Footing the purchases journal.
(2) Reconciling vendors' monthly statements with subsidiary payable ledger accounts.

(3) Tracing totals from the purchases journal to the ledger accounts.

(4) Sending written quarterly confirmation to all vendors.

f. For effective internal control, the accounts payable department should compare the information on each vendor's invoice with the:

(1) Receiving report and the purchase order.

(2) Receiving report and the voucher.

(3) Vendor's packing slip and the purchase order.

(4) Vendor's packing slip and the voucher.

GROUP III: PROBLEMS

15–35. The following are typical questions that might appear on an internal control questionnaire for accounts payable.

a. Are monthly statements from vendors reconciled with the accounts payable listing?

b. Are vendors' invoices matched with receiving reports before they are approved for payment?

Required:

a. Describe the purpose of each of the above internal control procedures.

b. Describe the manner in which each of the above procedures might be tested.

c. Assuming that the operating effectiveness of each of the above procedures is found to be inadequate, describe how the auditors might alter their substantive tests to compensate for the increased level of control risk.

15–36. Taylor, CA, is engaged in the audit of Rex Wholesaling for the year ended December 31. Taylor obtained an understanding of internal control relating to the purchasing, receiving, trade accounts payable, and cash disbursement cycles, and has decided not to proceed with tests of controls. Based upon analytical procedures, Taylor believes that the trade accounts payable on the balance sheet as of December 31 may be understated.

Taylor requested and obtained a client-prepared trade accounts payable schedule listing the total amount owed to each vendor.

Required:

What additional substantive audit procedures should Taylor apply in examining the trade accounts payable?

15–37. As part of your first examination of the financial statements of Marina del Rey, Inc., you have decided to confirm some of the accounts payable. You are now in the process of selecting the individual companies to whom you will send accounts payable confirmation requests. Among the accounts payable you are considering the following:

Company	Amount Payable at Year-End	Total Purchases from Vendor during Year
Dayco, Inc.	$ —	$1,980,000
Gearbox, Inc.	22,650	46,100
Landon Co.	65,000	75,000
Western Supply	190,000	2,123,000

Required:

a. Which two of the above four accounts payable would you select as the most important to confirm? Explain your choice in terms of the audit objectives in sending accounts payable confirmation requests.

b. Assume that you are selecting accounts receivable to be confirmed. Assume also that the four companies listed above are customers of your client rather than suppliers and that the dollar amounts are accounts receivable balances and total sales for the year. Which two companies would you select as the most important to confirm? Explain your choice.

15–38. James Rowe, CA, is the external auditor of Raleigh Corporation. Rowe is considering the audit work to be performed in the accounts payable area for the current year's engagement.

The prior year's working papers show that confirmation requests were mailed to 100 of Raleigh's 1,000 suppliers. The selected suppliers were based on Rowe's sample that was designed to select accounts with large dollar balances. A substantial number of hours was spent by Raleigh employees and by Rowe resolving relatively minor differences between the confirmation replies and Raleigh's accounting records. Alternative audit procedures were used for those suppliers that did not respond to the confirmation requests.

Required:

a. Identify the accounts payable audit objectives that Rowe must consider in determining the audit procedures to be followed.

b. Identify situations in which Rowe should use accounts payable confirmations and discuss whether Rowe is required to use them.

c. Discuss why the use of large dollar balances as the basis for selecting accounts payable for confirmation might not be the most efficient approach, and indicate what more efficient procedures could be followed when selecting accounts payable for confirmation.

(AICPA, adapted)

15–39. During the current year, your audit client, Video Corporation, was licensed to manufacture a patented type of television screen. The licensing agreement called for royalty payments of 50 cents for each screen manufactured by Video Corporation. What procedures would you follow in connection with your regular annual audit at December 31 to obtain evidence that the liability for royalties is correctly stated?

(AICPA, adapted)

15–40. Nancy Howe, your staff assistant on the April 30, 19X2, audit of Wilcox Limited was transferred to another audit engagement before she could complete the audit of unrecorded accounts payable. Her working paper, which you have reviewed and are satisfied is complete, appears on page 660.

Required:
Prepare a proposed adjusting journal entry for the unrecorded accounts payable of Wilcox Limited at April 30, 19X2. The amounts are material. (Do not deal with income taxes.)

15–41. You were in the final stages of your examination of the financial statements of Scott Corporation for the year ended December 31, 19X0, when you were consulted by the corporation's president, who believes there is no point to your examining the 19X1 voucher register and testing data in support of 19X0 entries. He stated that (1) bills pertaining to 19X0 that were received too late to be included in the December voucher register were recorded as of the year-end by the corporation by journal entry, (2) the internal auditors made tests after the year-end, and (3) he would furnish you with a letter representing that there were no unrecorded liabilities.

Required:
a. Should the external auditors' test for unrecorded liabilities be affected by the fact that the client made a journal entry to record 19X0 bills that were received late? Explain.
b. Should the external auditors' test for unrecorded liabilities be affected by the fact that a letter is obtained in which a responsible management official represents that to the best of his knowledge all liabilities have been recorded? Explain.

c. Should the external auditors' test for unrecorded liabilities be eliminated or reduced because of the internal audit tests? Explain.

d. Assume that the client company, which handled some govern-

---

Wilcox Limited

Unrecorded Accounts Payable   M–1–1

April 30, 19x2

Invoice Date	Vendor and Description	Amount
	Hill & Harper – unpaid legal fees at Apr. 30, x2 (see lawyer's letter at M–4)	1000 ✓
Apr. 1, x2	Drew Insurance Agency – unpaid premium on fire insurance for period Apr. 1, x2 – Mar. 31, x3 (see insurance broker letter at g–1–1)	1800 ✓
Apr. 30, x2	Mays & Sage, Stock Brokers – advice for 100 shares of Madison Ltd. Common stock (settlement date May 7, x2)	2125 ✓
	Lane Company – shipment received Apr. 30, x2 per receiver no. 3361 and included in Apr. 30, x2 physical inventory; invoice not yet received (amount is per purchase order)	5863 ✓
		10 788 –

✓ – Examined document described.

In my opinion, the $10,788 adjustment includes all material unrecorded accounts payable.

N. A. H.
May 29, x2

ment contracts, had no internal auditors but that auditors for a government agency spent three weeks auditing the records and were just completing their work at this time. How would the external auditors' unrecorded liability test be affected by the work of the auditors for a government agency?

e. What sources in addition to the 19X1 voucher register should the external auditors consider to locate possible unrecorded liabilities?

(AICPA, adapted)

GROUP IV: ANALYTICAL AND DISCUSSION CASE

15-42. CA has been the auditor of X Ltd., a medium-sized clothing retailer with six stores, for several years. Each store has its own inventory, and the inventories at the stores comprise all of X Ltd.'s inventory. Invoices for inventory purchases are paid by a central office and are approved for payment only after they are matched with receiving reports sent in from the stores.

Every year, CA has verified X Ltd.'s accounts receivable by direct communication with debtors. However, accounts payable (which consists of about 200 accounts) has been verified by checking creditors' monthly statements to the records rather than by direct communication with creditors.

This year, on reviewing his audit program, CA decided that he should use direct communication in verifying accounts payable. He conveyed this decision to X, the manager and principal shareholder of X Ltd., when they were making arrangements for the annual visit of CA's staff. X had never been happy about CA's direct communication with debtors but over the years had gradually accepted the need for it. When he learned that CA now planned to communicate directly with creditors, he was furious. "Why," he said, "would you want to communicate with creditors when you have statements from them for almost all of the accounts and certainly all of the larger ones? You've asked us to keep the statements that come in, and we've gone out of our way to do so, but now you're saying that they're not good enough. I've gone along with you writing to our debtors because they don't send out statements, but our creditors do. What you're proposing would only serve to remind our creditors that we owe them money, and there are some I don't want to remind because then we'll have to pay them faster. Anyway, I understand your main purpose in verifying accounts payable is to detect unrecorded liabilities, not that there would be any, and surely communicating with existing creditors is not going to help you do that. I can see why you have to verify accounts receivable this way, but accounts payable are completely different. Besides, it'll cost me more money because it will take you more time to do the audit."

Required:
The points CA would make in replying to X. Explain.

(CICA, adapted)

Debt and Equity Capital; Contingencies

After studying this chapter, you should be able to:

- Describe the nature of debt and equity capital.
- Explain the fundamental internal control for the financing cycle.
- Describe the auditors' objectives for the audit of debt and equity capital.
- Describe the nature of accounting and auditing responsibilities for contingencies.

Business corporations obtain substantial amounts of their financial resources by incurring interest-bearing debt and by issuing capital stock. The acquisition and repayment of debt and capital is referred to as the *financing cycle.* This cycle includes the sequence of procedures for authorizing, executing, and recording transactions that involve bank loans, mortgages, bonds payable, and capital stock as well as the payment of interest and dividends. In this chapter we present material on the auditors' approach to both debt and equity capital accounts. In addition, we present information on contingencies. These contingencies involve situations in which there is possible impairment of assets, or possible existence of a liability.

INTEREST-BEARING DEBT

Sources and Nature of Interest-bearing Debt

Nearly every business borrows. A business with an excellent credit reputation may find it possible to borrow from a bank on a simple unsecured note. A business of lesser financial standing may find that obtaining bank credit requires the pledging of specific assets as collateral or that it must agree to certain restrictive covenants, such as the suspension of dividends.

Long-term debt usually is substantial in amount and often extends for periods of 15 years or more. Debentures, secured bonds, and notes payable (sometimes secured by mortgages or trust deeds) are the principal types of long-term debt. Debentures are backed only by the general credit of the issuing corporation and not by liens on specific assets. Since in most respects debentures have the characteristics of other corporate bonds, we shall use the term *bonds* to include both debentures and secured bonds payable.

The formal document creating bonded indebtedness is called the *indenture* or *trust indenture.* When creditors supply capital on a long-term basis, they often insist upon placing certain restrictions on the borrowing company. For example, the indenture often provides that a company may not declare dividends unless the amount of working capital is maintained above a specified amount. The acquisition of plant and equipment or the increasing of managerial salaries may be permitted only if the current ratio is maintained at a specified level and if net income reaches a designated amount. Another device for protecting the long-term creditor is the requirement of a sinking fund or redemption fund to be held by a trustee. If these restrictions are violated, the indenture may provide that the entire debt is due on demand.

The Auditors' Objectives in Examination of Interest-bearing Debt

The auditors' *objectives* in the examination of interest-bearing debt are:

1. To consider *internal control* over interest-bearing debt.
2. To determine the *existence* of recorded interest-bearing debt, and that the client has an *obligation* to pay these liabilities.
3. To establish the *completeness* of recorded interest-bearing debt.
4. To determine that the *valuation* of interest-bearing debt is in accordance with generally accepted accounting principles.
5. To establish the *clerical accuracy* of schedules of interest-bearing debt.
6. To determine that the *statement presentation* of interest-bearing debt is appropriate, including disclosure of the major provisions of loan agreements.

In conjunction with the audit of interest-bearing debt, the auditors will also obtain evidence about interest expense, interest payable, and bond discount and premium.

Many of the principles related to accounts payable also apply to the audit of interest-bearing debt. As is the case for accounts payable, the understatement of debt is considered to be a major potential audit problem. Related to disclosure of interest-bearing debt, the auditors must determine that the company has met all requirements and restrictions imposed upon it by debt contracts.

Internal Control over Interest-bearing Debt

Authorization by the Board of Directors.   Effective internal control over interest-bearing debt begins with the authorization to incur the debt. The bylaws of a corporation usually require that borrowing be approved by the board of directors. The treasurer of the corporation will prepare a report on any proposed financing, explaining the need for funds, the estimated effect of borrowing upon future earnings, the estimated financial position of the company in comparison with others in the industry both before and after the borrowing, and alternative methods of raising the amount desired. Authorization by the board of directors will include review and approval of such matters as the choice of a bank or trustee, the type of security, registration with the securities commission, agreements with investment bankers, compliance with requirements of the corporate legislation, and listing of bonds on a securities exchange. After the issuance of long-term debt, the board of directors should receive a report stating the net amount received and its disposition, for example, as acquisition of plant assets, addition to working capital, or other purposes.

Use of an Independent Trustee.   Bond issues are always for large amounts—usually many millions of dollars. Therefore, only relatively large companies issue bonds; small companies obtain long-term capital through mortgage loans or other sources. Any company large enough to issue bonds and able to find a ready market for the securities will almost always utilize the services of a large financial institution as an independent trustee.

The trustee is charged with the protection of the creditors' interests and must monitor the issuing company's compliance with the provisions of the indenture. The trustee also maintains detailed records of the names and addresses of the registered owners of the bonds, cancels old bond certificates and issues new ones when bonds change ownership, follows procedures to prevent overissuance of bond certificates, distributes interest payments, and distributes principal payments when the bonds mature. Use of an independent trustee largely solves the problem of internal control over bonds payable. Internal control is strengthened by the fact that the trustee does not have access to the issuing company's assets or accounting records and that the trustee is a large financial institution with legal responsibility for its actions.

Interest Payments on Bonds and Notes Payable. The auditors' appraisal of internal controls relating to bonds and notes payable must extend to the handling of interest payments. In the case of a note payable, there may be only one recipient of interest, and the disbursement may be controlled in the same manner as other cash payments.

Many corporations assign the entire task of paying interest to the trustee for either *bearer bonds* or *registered bonds.* Highly effective control is then achieved, since the company will issue a single cheque for the full amount of the semiannual interest payment on the entire bond issue. In the case of bearer bonds (coupon bonds), the trustee upon receipt of this cheque will make payment for coupons presented, cancel the coupons, and file them numerically. A second count of the coupons is made at a later date; the coupons then are destroyed and a cremation certificate delivered to the issuing company. The trustee does not attempt to maintain a list of the holders of coupon bonds, since these securities are transferable by the mere act of delivery. If certain coupons are not presented for payment, the trustee will hold the funds corresponding to such coupons for the length of time prescribed by statute. In the case of registered bonds, the trustee will maintain a current list of holders and will remit interest cheques to them in the same manner as dividend cheques are distributed to shareholders.

Audit Working Papers

A copy of the loan agreement or the indenture relating to a bond issue should be placed in the auditors' permanent file. A listing of the restrictions placed on the company is extracted from these documents to facilitate the auditors' tests of compliance with the debt provisions. Analyses of ledger accounts for notes and bonds payable, and the related accounts for interest and discount or premium, should be obtained for the current working papers file or the permanent file. A lead schedule is seldom required for short-term notes payable or for long-term debt.

AUDIT PROGRAM FOR INTEREST-BEARING DEBT

This audit program does not provide for the usual distinction between substantive testing and internal control testing. This is because individual transactions will generally be examined for all large debt agreements. The auditors will usually prepare a written narrative or a flowchart, as well as an internal control questionnaire. Questions included on a typical questionnaire are the following: Are amounts of new interest-bearing debt authorized by appropriate management? Is an independent trustee used for all bond issues? Does a company official monitor compliance with debt provisions?

Because transactions are few in number, but large in dollar amount, the auditors are generally able to substantiate the individual transactions. Therefore, testing of controls occurs through what amounts to dual-purpose transaction testing.

Audit procedures appropriate for interest-bearing debt include the following:

1. Obtain or prepare analyses of interest-bearing debt accounts and related interest, premium, and discount accounts.
2. Examine copies of notes payable and supporting documents.
3. Confirm interest-bearing debt with payees or appropriate third parties.
4. Vouch borrowing and repayment transactions to supporting documents.
5. Perform analytical procedures to test the overall reasonableness of interest-bearing debt and interest expense.
6. Test the computations of interest expense, interest payable, and amortization of discount and premium.
7. Evaluate whether debt provisions have been met.
8. Trace authority for issuance of interest-bearing debt to the corporate minutes.
9. Review notes payable paid or renewed after the balance sheet date.
10. Perform procedures to identify notes payable to related parties.
11. Send confirmation letters to financial institutions to obtain information about financing arrangements.
12. Evaluate financial statement presentation and disclosure of interest-bearing debt and related transactions

Figure 16–1 relates these substantive tests to their primary audit objectives.

1. Obtain or prepare analyses of interest-bearing debt accounts and related interest, premium, and discount accounts.

A notes payable analysis shows the beginning balance, if any, of each individual note, additional notes issued and payments on notes during the year, and the ending balance of each note. In addition, the beginning balances of interest payable or prepaid interest, interest expense, interest paid, and ending balances of interest payable or prepaid interest may be presented in the analysis working paper.

An analysis of the Notes Payable account will serve a number of purposes: (*a*) the payment or other disposition of notes listed as outstanding in the previous year's audit can be verified, (*b*) the propriety of individual

FIGURE 16-1   Objectives of Major Substantive Tests of Interest-bearing Debt Transactions and Balances

Substantive Tests	*Primary Audit Objectives*
Obtain analyses of interest-bearing debt and related accounts	*Clerical accuracy*
Examine copies of notes payable and supporting documents Confirm interest-bearing debt	*Completeness* *Existence and obligations*
Vouch borrowing and repayment transactions	*Existence and obligations*
Perform analytical procedures Test computation of interest expense, interest payable, and amortization of discount and premium	*Completeness* *Existence and obligations* *Valuation*
Evaluate whether debt provisions have been met Trace authority for issuance of debt to corporate minutes Review notes payable paid or renewed after the balance sheet date Perform procedures to identify notes payable to related parties Send confirmation letters about financing arrangements Evaluate financial statement presentation and disclosure	*Statement presentation*

debits and credits can be established, and (*c*) the validity of the year-end balance of the account is proved through the step-by-step examination of all changes in the account during the year.

In the first audit of a client, the auditors will analyze the ledger accounts for Bonds Payable, Bond Issue Costs, and Bond Discount (or Bond Premium) for the years since the bonds were issued. The working paper is placed in the auditors' permanent file; in later audits, any further entries in these accounts may be added to the analysis.

2. Examine copies of notes payable and supporting documents.

The auditors should examine the client's copies of notes payable and supporting documents such as mortgages and trust deeds. The original documents will be in the possession of the payees, but the auditors should make certain that the client has retained copies of the debt instruments and that their details correspond to the analyses described in the first procedure of this audit program.

3. Confirm interest-bearing debt with payees or appropriate third parties.

Notes payable to financial institutions are confirmed as part of the confirmation of deposit balances. The standard bank confirmation form illustrated in Chapter 11 includes a request that the financial institution confirm all borrowings by the depositor.

Confirmation requests for notes payable to payees other than financial institutions should be drafted on the client's letterhead stationery, signed by the controller or other appropriate executive, and mailed by the auditors. Payees should be requested to confirm dates of origin, due dates, unpaid balances of notes, interest rates, dates to which interest has been paid, and collateral for the notes.

The auditors may also substantiate the existence and amount of a mortgage liability outstanding by direct confirmation with the mortgagee. The information received should be compared with the client's records and the audit working papers. When no change in the liability account has occurred in the period under audit, the only major procedure necessary will be this confirmation with the creditor. At the same time that the mortgagee is asked to confirm the debt, it may be asked for an indication of the company's compliance with the mortgage or trust deed agreement.

Bond transactions usually can be confirmed directly with the trustee. The trustee's reply should include an exact description of the bonds, including maturity dates and interest rates; bonds retired, purchased for the treasury, or converted into stock during the year; bonds outstanding at the balance sheet date; and sinking fund transactions and balances.

4. Vouch borrowing and repayment transactions to supporting documents.

The auditors must obtain evidence that transactions in interest-bearing debt accounts were valid. To accomplish this objective, the auditors trace the cash received from the issuance of notes, bonds, or mortgages to the validated copy of the bank deposit slip and to the bank statement. Any remittance advices supporting these cash receipts are also examined. The auditors can find further support for the net proceeds of a bond issue by referring to the underwriting contract and to the prospectus filed with the securities commissions.

Debits to a Notes Payable or a Mortgages Payable account generally represent payments in full or in instalments. The auditors should examine paid cheques for these payments; in so doing, they also will account for payments of accrued interest. The propriety of instalment payments should be verified by reference to the repayment schedule set forth in the note or mortgage copy in the client's possession.

A comparison of canceled notes payable with the debit entries in the Notes Payable account provides further assurance that notes indicated as paid during the year have, in fact, been retired. The auditors' inspection of these notes should include a comparison of the maturity date of the note with the date of cash disbursement. Failure to pay notes promptly at maturity is suggestive of financial weakness.

There is seldom any justification for a paid note to be missing from the files; a receipt for payment from the payee of the note is not a satisfactory substitute. If, for any reason, a paid note is not available for inspection, the auditors should review the request for a cheque or other vouchers supporting the disbursement and should discuss the transaction with an appropriate official.

In examining the canceled notes, the auditors should also trace the disposition of any collateral used to secure these notes. A convenient opportunity for diversion of pledged securities or other assets to an unauthorized use may be created at the time these assets are regained from a secured creditor.

5. Perform analytical procedures to test the overall reasonableness of interest-bearing debt and interest expense.

One of the most effective ways to determine the overall reasonableness of interest-bearing debt is to examine the relationship between recorded interest expense and the average principal amount of debt outstanding during the year. If the client is paying interest on debt that is not recorded, this relationship will not be in line with the interest rate at which the client company should be able to borrow. Therefore, the auditors can use these procedures as a test of the *completeness* of recorded interest-bearing debt.

The auditors also compare the year-end amount of interest-bearing debt with the amount in the prior year's balance sheet. A similar comparison is made of interest expense for the current year and the preceding year.

6. Test the computations of interest expense, interest payable, and amortization of discount or premium.

The auditors may test the accuracy of the client's computations of interest expense and interest payable. In addition, they may examine paid cheques supporting interest payments and review the confirmations received from payees to verify the dates on which interest on each note or mortgage has been paid. A close study of interest payments is another means of bringing to light any unrecorded interest-bearing liabilities.

The total bond interest expense for the period usually reflects, not only the interest actually paid and accrued, but also amortization of bond premium or discount. The auditors may also test the amounts amortized by independent computations.

7. Evaluate whether debt provisions have been met.

In the first audit of a client or upon the issuance of a new bond issue, the auditors will obtain a copy of the bond indenture for the permanent file. The indenture should be carefully studied, with particular attention to such points as the amount of bonds authorized, interest rates and dates, maturity dates, descriptions of property pledged as collateral, provisions for retirement or conversion, duties and responsibilities of the trustee, and any restrictions imposed on the borrowing company.

The indenture provisions frequently require maintenance of a sinking fund, maintenance of stipulated minimum levels of working capital, and insurance of pledged property. The indenture also may restrict dividends to a specified proportion of earnings, limit management compensation, and prohibit additional long-term borrowing, except under stipulated conditions.

The auditors will perform tests to evaluate whether the company is in compliance with these provisions. For example, the auditors will examine evidence of insurance coverage, vouch payments to the sinking fund, and compare the amounts of management compensation and dividends paid to amounts allowed by the agreements. If the company has not complied fully with the requirements, the auditors should inform both the client and the client's legal counsel of the violation. In some cases of violation, the entire bond issue may become due and payable on demand, and hence a current liability. When the client is in violation of an indenture provision and the penalty is to make the debt become payable upon demand, the client usually will be able to obtain a waiver of compliance with the provision. In other words, creditors often choose not to enforce contract terms fully. To enable the liability to be presented as long-term, the waiver must waive compliance for a period of one year from the balance sheet date. Even if a waiver of compliance is obtained, the matter should be disclosed in the notes to the client's financial statements.

Illustrative Case

In the audit of a large construction company, the auditors found the client's working capital to be far below the minimum level stipulated in the indenture of long-term secured bonds payable. In addition to this, the client had allowed the required insurance coverage of pledged assets to lapse. These violations of the indenture were sufficient to cause the bond issue to become payable on demand.

Although the client agreed to reclassify the bond issue as a current liability and disclose the problem in the financial statements, the auditors were unable to satisfy themselves that the client could meet the obligation if the bondholders demanded payment. Also, if the bondholders foreclosed on the pledged assets, the ability of the client to continue as a going concern would be questionable. Thus, even after the liability was reclassified as current, the client had to add a note to the financial statements referring to the uncertainty regarding the company's ability to meet its obligations and remain a going concern.

Auditors do not judge the legality of a bond issue; this is a problem for the client's lawyers. The auditors should be familiar, however, with the principal provisions of the securities and corporate legislation applicable to the client's debt issues. They should ascertain that the client has obtained a lawyer's opinion on the legality of the bond issuance. In doubtful cases, they should consult the client's legal counsel.

8. Trace authority for issuance of interest-bearing debt to the corporate minutes.

The authority to issue interest-bearing debt generally lies with the board of directors. To determine that the bonds outstanding were properly authorized, the auditors should read the passages in the minutes of directors' (and shareholders') meetings concerning the issuance of debt. The minutes usually will cite the applicable sections of the corporate bylaws permitting the issuance of debt instruments and may also contain reference to the opinion of the company's counsel concerning the legality of the issue.

9. Review notes payable paid or renewed after the balance sheet date.

If any of the notes payable outstanding at the balance sheet date are paid before completion of the audit engagement, such cash payments will provide the auditors with additional evidence on the liability. Renewal of notes maturing shortly after the balance sheet date may alter the auditors' thinking as to the proper classification of these liabilities.

In the discussion of notes receivable in Chapter 12, emphasis was placed on the necessity of close scrutiny of loans to officers, directors, and affiliates because of the absence of arm's-length bargaining in these related party transactions. Similar emphasis should be placed on the examination of notes payable to insiders or affiliates, although the opportunities for self-dealing are more limited than with receivables. The auditors should scan the notes payable records for the period between the balance sheet date and the completion of examination so that they may be aware of any unusual transactions, such as the reestablishment of an insider note that had been paid just prior to the balance sheet date.

10. Perform procedures to identify notes payable to related parties.

As has been the case in other portions of the audit, the auditors must perform procedures to determine that any related party debt is properly disclosed. Note here that the lower number of transactions makes discovery of such transactions less difficult than in accounts with a large number of transactions, such as accounts payable.

11. Send confirmation letters to financial institutions to obtain information about financing arrangements.

Financing arrangements and transactions can be very complex, and the details of these arrangements and transactions must be adequately disclosed in the notes to the financial statements. If the auditors determine that additional evidence is needed to verify these details, they will send a *separate* confirmation letter to the financial institution. For example, confirmation letters may be used to obtain information about lines of credit, compensating balance arrangements, letters of credit, or futures contracts. These letters are signed by the client and specifically addressed to the client's loan officer, or another official at financial institution that is knowledgeable about the information. This expedites a response to the confirmation and enhances the quality of the evidence received. Figure 16–2 is an example of a letter to confirm information about lines of credit.

FIGURE 16–2   Illustrative Letter for Confirmation of Lines of Credit

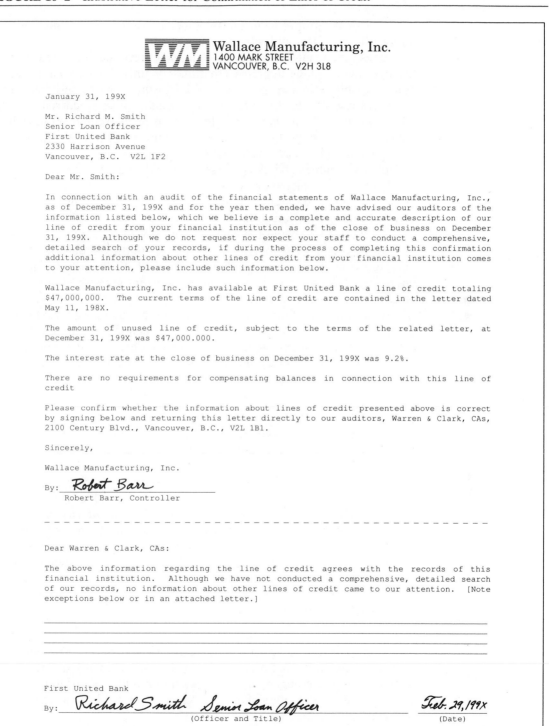

Wallace Manufacturing, Inc.
1400 MARK STREET
VANCOUVER, B.C. V2H 3L8

January 31, 199X

Mr. Richard M. Smith
Senior Loan Officer
First United Bank
2330 Harrison Avenue
Vancouver, B.C. V2L 1F2

Dear Mr. Smith:

In connection with an audit of the financial statements of Wallace Manufacturing, Inc., as of December 31, 199X and for the year then ended, we have advised our auditors of the information listed below, which we believe is a complete and accurate description of our line of credit from your financial institution as of the close of business on December 31, 199X. Although we do not request nor expect your staff to conduct a comprehensive, detailed search of your records, if during the process of completing this confirmation additional information about other lines of credit from your financial institution comes to your attention, please include such information below.

Wallace Manufacturing, Inc. has available at First United Bank a line of credit totaling $47,000,000. The current terms of the line of credit are contained in the letter dated May 11, 198X.

The amount of unused line of credit, subject to the terms of the related letter, at December 31, 199X was $47,000.000.

The interest rate at the close of business on December 31, 199X was 9.2%.

There are no requirements for compensating balances in connection with this line of credit

Please confirm whether the information about lines of credit presented above is correct by signing below and returning this letter directly to our auditors, Warren & Clark, CAs, 2100 Century Blvd., Vancouver, B.C., V2L 1B1.

Sincerely,

Wallace Manufacturing, Inc.

By: *Robert Barr*
    Robert Barr, Controller

– –

Dear Warren & Clark, CAs:

The above information regarding the line of credit agrees with the records of this financial institution. Although we have not conducted a comprehensive, detailed search of our records, no information about other lines of credit came to our attention. [Note exceptions below or in an attached letter.]

_____
_____
_____
_____

First United Bank
By: *Richard Smith* *Senior Loan Officer*   *Feb. 29, 199X*
                    (Officer and Title)   (Date)

12. Evaluate proper financial statement presentation and disclosure of interest-bearing debt and related transactions.

Because of the interest of creditors in the current liability section of the balance sheet and the inferences that may be drawn from various uses of notes payable, adequate informative disclosure is extremely important. Classification of notes by types of payees, as well as by current or long-term maturity, is desirable. Separate listing is needed for notes payable to banks, notes payable to trade creditors, and notes payable to officers, directors, shareholders, and affiliates.

Secured liabilities and pledged assets should be cross-referenced to one another with an explanation in the notes to the financial statements. In the event of financial difficulties and dissolution, creditors expect to share in the assets in proportion to their respective claims; and if choice assets, such as current receivables, have been pledged to one creditor, the risk to unsecured creditors is increased. Current liabilities should include not only those notes maturing within a period of 12 months (or a longer operating cycle) but also any instalments currently payable on long-term obligations such as mortgages.

The essential point in balance sheet presentation of long-term liabilities is that they be adequately described. Each category of long-term debt should be stated under a separate title, which describes the type of debt, amounts authorized and issued, interest rate, maturity date, and any conversion or subordination features.

Long-Term Debt Payable in the Current Period.   Long-term liabilities include all debts that will not be liquidated with the use of current assets. In other words, any bonds or notes falling due in the coming operating cycle that are to be paid from special funds or refinanced will be classified as long-term obligations regardless of maturity date. Before approving a long-term classification for maturing obligations, auditors must satisfy themselves that the client has both the *intent* and the *ability* to refinance the obligation on a long-term basis. Intent and ability to refinance are demonstrated by the client through either (1) refinancing the obligation on a long-term basis before the issuance of the financial statements, or (2) entering into a financing agreement by that date, which clearly permits such refinancing. Any debt maturing currently and payable from current assets will be a current liability.

Restrictions Imposed by Long-Term Debt Agreements.   The major restrictions imposed on the company by long-term loan agreements are significant to the company's investors and creditors. Consequently, the nature of the restrictions should be clearly set forth in a note to the financial statements.

Unamortized Bond Premium or Discount.   Unamortized premium should be added to the face amount of the bonds or debentures in the liability section of the balance sheet. Similarly, unamortized discount should be deducted from the face amount of the debt.

Time of Examination—Interest-bearing Debt

Analysis of the ledger accounts for interest-bearing debt and interest expense takes very little time in most audits because of the small number of entries. Consequently, most auditors prefer to wait until the end of the year before analyzing these accounts.

Audit procedures intended to bring to light any unrecorded liabilities cannot very well be performed in advance of the balance sheet date. Such steps as the confirmation of outstanding interest-bearing debt, tests of interest expense, and the investigation of notes paid or renewed shortly after the balance sheet date must necessarily await the close of the period being audited. We must conclude, therefore, that the opportunities for performing audit work in advance of the balance sheet date are much more limited in the case of interest-bearing debt than for most of the asset groups previously discussed.

EQUITY CAPITAL

Sources and Nature of Owners' Equity

Most of this section is concerned with the audit of shareholders' equity accounts of corporate clients; the audit of owners' equity in partnerships and sole proprietorships is discussed briefly near the end of the chapter.

Owners' equity for corporate clients consists of capital stock accounts (preferred and common) and retained earnings. Balances in the capital stock accounts change when the corporation issues or repurchases stock.[1] The account balances are not affected by transfer of ownership of shares from one shareholder to another. Retained earnings are normally increased by earnings and decreased by dividend payments. Additionally, a few journal entries (e.g., prior period adjustments) may directly affect retained earnings. Transactions in the owners' equity accounts are generally few in number, but material in amount. Often no change will occur during the year in the capital stock accounts, and perhaps only one or two entries will be made to the retained earnings account.

---

[1] The terms *stock* and *share* are used interchangeably.

The Auditors' Objectives in Examination of Owners' Equity

The auditors' *objectives* in the examination of owners' equity are:

1. To consider *internal control* over owners' equity.
2. To determine the *existence* of recorded owners' equity.
3. To establish the *completeness* of recorded owners' equity.
4. To determine that the *valuation* of owners' equity is in accordance with generally accepted accounting principles.
5. To establish the *clerical accuracy* of schedules of owners' equity.
6. To determine that the *statement presentation* of owners' equity is appropriate.

In conjunction with the audit of owners' equity accounts, the auditors will also obtain evidence about the related accounts of dividends payable and contributed capital accounts. Evidence is also gathered regarding the proper cutoff of cash receipts and disbursements relating to the equity accounts.

Because the transactions are few in number but material in amount, each requires careful attention. Additionally, to properly audit the owners' equity accounts, the auditors often need some familiarity with corporate and securities laws.

For a continuing client, the auditors will often find that audit time required will be small in relation to the dollar amounts in these accounts and much less than is required for assets, liabilities, revenue, or expense. Thus, while the capital stock account often has a larger balance than the cash account, the audit work required for capital stock is usually far less.

Internal Control for Owners' Equity

The principal elements of strong internal control over capital stock and dividends are threefold: (1) the proper authorization of transactions by the board of directors and corporate officers, (2) the segregation of duties in handling these transactions (especially the use of independent agents for stock registration and transfer and for dividend payments), and (3) the maintenance of adequate records.

Control of Capital Stock Transactions by the Board of Directors

All changes in capital stock accounts should receive formal approval by the board of directors. The substantive tests for verifying an entry in a Capital Stock account, therefore, should include tracing the entry to an authorization in the minutes of directors' meetings.

Let us consider for a moment some of the specific steps relating to capital stock transactions that require authorization by directors. The board of directors must determine the number of shares to be issued and the price per share; if an instalment plan of payments is to be used, the terms must be prescribed by the board. If plant and equipment, services, or any consideration other than cash are to be accepted in payment for shares, the board of directors must set the valuation on the noncash assets received. Transfers from retained earnings to the Capital Stock and Contributed Capital accounts, as in the case of stock dividends, are initiated by action of the board. Stock splits and changes in par value of shares also require formal authorization by the board.

Authority for all dividend actions rests with the directors. The declaration of a dividend must specify not only the amount per share, but also the date of record and the date of payment.

If a corporation handles its own capital stock transactions rather than utilizing the services of an independent registrar and stock transfer agent, the board of directors should pass a resolution designating those officers who are authorized (1) to sign stock certificates, (2) to maintain records of shareholders, (3) to have custody of unissued certificates, and (4) to sign dividend cheques. The signatures of two officers are generally required on stock certificates.

Independent Registrar and Stock Transfer Agent

In appraising the internal control over capital stock, the first question that the auditors consider is whether the corporation employs the services of an independent stock registrar and a stock transfer agent or handles its own capital stock transactions. Internal control is far stronger when the services of an independent stock registrar and a stock transfer agent are utilized because the banks or trust companies acting in these capacities will have the experience, the specialized facilities, and the trained personnel to perform the work in an expert manner. Moreover, by placing the responsibility for handling capital stock certificates in separate and independent organizations, the corporation achieves to the fullest extent the internal control concept of separation of duties.

The primary responsibility of the stock registrar is to avoid any overissuance of stock. The danger of overissuance is illustrated by the old story of a promoter who sold a 25 percent interest in a new corporation to each of 10 investors. To prevent such irregularities, the registrar must verify that stock certificates are issued in accordance with the articles of incorporation and the formal authorizations by the board of directors. The registrar obtains copies of the documents authorizing the total shares to be issued and maintains records of total shares issued and canceled. Each new certificate must be presented to the registrar for examination and registration before it is issued to a shareholder. The dangers of fraud and accidental error relating to improper issuance of stock certificates are greatly reduced when an independent registrar is employed.

Corporations with actively traded securities also employ independent *stock transfer agents.* Although the stock transfer agent maintains a record of the total shares outstanding, its primary responsibility is maintaining detailed shareholder records (name and address of each shareholder) and carrying out transfers of stock ownership.

The Stock Certificate Book

If the corporation does not utilize the services of an independent registrar and stock transfer agent, these functions usually are assigned by the board of directors to the secretary of the company. The stock certificates should be serially numbered by the printer, and from the time of delivery to the company until issuance, they should be in the exclusive custody of the designated officer.

The certificates often are prepared in bound books, with attached stubs similar to those in a chequebook. Each stub shows the certificate number and contains blank spaces for entering the number of shares represented by the certificate, the name of the shareholder, and the serial number of any previously issued certificate surrendered in exchange for the new one. Certificates should be issued in numerical sequence and not signed or countersigned until the time of issuance. When outstanding shares are transferred from one holder to another, the old certificate is surrendered to the company. The designated officer cancels the old certificate by perforating and attaching it to the corresponding stub in the certificate book.

The Shareholders Ledger

The stock certificate book is not in itself an adequate record of the capital stock outstanding. The certificates appear in the book in serial number order, and a single shareholder may own several certificates listed at various places in the certificate book.

A shareholders ledger provides a separate record for each shareholder, thus making it possible to determine at a glance the total number of shares owned by any one person. This record may be used in compiling the list of dividend cheques or for any other communication with shareholders.

Internal Control over Dividends

The nature of internal control over the payment of dividends, as in the case of stock issuance, depends primarily upon whether the company performs the function of dividend payment itself or utilizes the services of an independent dividend-paying agent. If an independent dividend-paying agent is used, the corporation will provide the agent with a certified copy of the dividend declaration and with a cheque for the full amount of the dividend. The bank or trust company serving as stock transfer agent is usually appointed to distribute the dividend, since it maintains the detailed records of shareholders. The agent issues dividend cheques to the individual shareholders and sends the corporation a list of the payments made. The use of an independent fiscal agent is to be recommended from the standpoint of internal control, for it materially reduces the possibility of fraud or error arising in connection with the distribution of dividends.

Audit Working Papers for Owners' Equity

In addition to the lead schedule for owners' equity accounts, an analysis of each equity account is prepared by the auditors for the permanent file. A detailed analysis is essential for all aspects of a stock option plan: options authorized, issued, and outstanding. For a closely held corporation not served by a transfer agent, the auditors will often prepare for the permanent file a list of shareholders and the number of shares owned by each.

AUDIT PROGRAM—CAPITAL STOCK

The following procedures are typical of the work required in many engagements for the audit of capital stock:

1. Obtain an understanding of internal control over capital stock transactions.
2. Review articles or certificate of incorporation, bylaws, and minutes for provisions relating to capital stock.
3. Obtain or prepare analyses of the capital stock accounts.
4. Account for all proceeds from stock issues.
5. Confirm shares outstanding with the independent registrar and stock transfer agent.
6. For a corporation acting as its own stock registrar and transfer agent, reconcile the shareholder records with the general ledger.
7. Determine compliance with stock option plans and with other restrictions and preferences pertaining to capital stock.

Capital stock transactions are usually few in number; consequently, the auditors usually substantiate all transactions rather than obtain evidence to reduce their assessment of control risk. In addition to the preceding steps, the auditors must determine the appropriate financial statement presentation of capital stock. This topic will be discussed later in this chapter, along with the financial statement presentation of other elements of owners' equity.

1. Obtain an understanding of internal control over capital stock transactions.

Even though the examination of capital stock consists primarily of substantive tests, the auditors must acquire an understanding of the client's procedures for authorizing, executing, and recording capital stock transactions. This may be achieved by preparing a written narrative or flowchart of the system, or by filling in an internal control questionnaire. If the questionnaire approach is employed, typical questions to be answered might include the following: Does the company utilize the services of an independent registrar and stock transfer agent? Are shareholder ledgers and transfer journals maintained? Are entries in owners' equity accounts reviewed periodically by an appropriate officer? These questions should be regarded as identifying the areas to be investigated, rather than as items requiring simple yes or no answers.

2. Review articles or certificate of incorporation, bylaws, and minutes for provisions relating to capital stock.

In a first audit, copies of the articles or certificate of incorporation, bylaws, and minutes of the meetings of directors and shareholders obtained for the permanent file should be read carefully. The information required by the auditors for each issue of capital stock includes the number of shares authorized and issued, the par value, if any, dividend rates, call and conversion provisions, stock splits, and stock options. By gathering evidence on these points, the auditors will have some assurance that capital stock transactions and dividend payments have been in accordance with legal requirements and specific authorizations by shareholders and directors. Also, they will be able to judge whether the balance sheet contains all necessary information to describe adequately the various stock issues and other elements of corporate capital.

3. Obtain or prepare analyses of the capital stock accounts.

In an initial audit engagement, capital stock accounts should be analyzed from the beginning of the corporation to provide the auditors with a complete historical picture of corporate capital. Analysis of capital stock includes an appraisal of the nature of all changes and the vouching of these changes to the supporting documents and records. All changes in capital stock should bear the authorization of the board of directors.

The analyses of capital stock accounts may be prepared in a manner that permits additions during later audit engagements. After the initial audit, if the analyses are kept in the auditors' permanent file, all that will be necessary is to record the current period's increases and decreases and to vouch these transactions. The auditors then will have working papers showing all changes in capital stock from the inception of the corporation.

The auditors also should analyze any treasury stock account and prepare a list showing the number of shares of treasury stock on hand. All certificates on hand then may be inspected. If the certificates are not on hand, they should be confirmed directly with the custodian.

In their review of treasury stock transactions, the auditors should refer to permanent file copies of the minutes of directors' meetings to determine that (*a*) the acquisition or reissuance of treasury stock was authorized by directors, (*b*) the price paid or received was in accordance with prices specified by the board, and (*c*) the acquisition and disposition of treasury stock are in compliance with corporate legislation.

4. Account for all proceeds from stock issues.

Closely related to the analyses of Capital Stock accounts is the audit procedure of accounting for the receipt and proper disposition of all funds derived from the issuance of capital stock. The proceeds should be traced to the cash records and bank statements. Registration statements filed with the securities commissions and contracts with underwriters may also be available as evidence of the amounts received from stock issues.

When assets other than cash are received as consideration for the issuance of capital stock, the entire transaction requires careful study. Generally the value of assets and services received in exchange for capital shares is established by action of the board of directors. The auditors must determine that these accounting estimates made by the client result in a reasonable valuation.

5. Confirm shares outstanding with the independent registrar and stock transfer agent.

The number of shares issued and outstanding on the balance sheet date may be confirmed by direct communication with the independent registrar and stock transfer agent. The confirmation request should be written by the client on the client's letterhead, but it should be mailed by the auditors. Confirmation replies should be sent directly to the auditors, not to the client. All information contained in these replies should be traced to the corporate records. It is essential that the general ledger controlling accounts agree with the amount of stock issued as reported by the independent registrar and stock transfer agent. Because of the strong internal controls usually maintained over stock certificates, it is not customary to communicate with individual shareholders in establishing the number of shares outstanding.

6. For a corporation acting as its own stock registrar and transfer agent, reconcile the shareholder records with the general ledger.

When a corporation acts as its own transfer agent and registrar, the auditors must adopt alternative procedures to obtain evidence that is not available by direct confirmation with outside parties. These procedures include (*a*) accounting for stock certificate numbers, (*b*) examining canceled certificates, and (*c*) reconciling the shareholder ledger and stock certificate book with the general ledger.

The audit working papers should include a record of the last certificate number issued during the year. Reference to the working papers for the preceding audit, combined with the verification of certificate numbers issued during the current period, will enable the auditors to account for all certificates by serial number.

A working paper prepared during the auditors' examination of the stock certificate book of a small, closely held corporation is designed to be utilized during several audits; it may be retained in the permanent file or forwarded to successive current files. Additionally, it is desirable for the auditors to inspect the unissued certificates to determine that all certificates purported to be unissued are actually on hand and blank.

Adequate internal control for corporations not utilizing the services of an independent registrar and stock transfer agent requires that all canceled stock certificates be perforated or marked in a manner precluding the possibility of further use. Canceled certificates should be attached to the corresponding stubs in the stock certificate book and permanently preserved. If reacquired certificates are not canceled properly, the danger exists that they may be reissued fraudulently by officers or employees. Auditors, therefore, will examine all canceled stock certificates on hand, noting in particular that they have been voided.

The general ledger account for capital stock shows the total par value or the total consideration received of all shares outstanding, plus any treasury shares. The subsidiary record for capital stock includes an account for each shareholder. The stock certificate book contains all canceled certificates and also open stubs for outstanding certificates. These three records (general ledger control account, shareholder ledger, and stock certificate book) must be reconciled by the auditors to establish the amount of outstanding stock and to rule out the possibility of an overissuance of shares. If this verification were not made, it would be possible for a dishonest official to issue unlimited amounts of stock and to withhold the proceeds from such sales.

A trial balance of the subsidiary shareholder records may be obtained from the client or prepared by the auditors and compared with the general ledger control account. In conjunction with this procedure, the total shares outstanding, as shown by the stock certificate book stubs, should also be reconciled with the control account and with the subsidiary trial balance. These procedures assure the auditors of the accuracy of the ledger account balances for capital stock.

7. Determine compliance with stock option plans and with other restrictions and preferences pertaining to capital stock.

Many corporations grant stock options to officers and key employees as an incentive type of compensation plan. When stock options are granted, a portion of the authorized but unissued stock must be held in reserve by the corporation so that it will be in a position to fulfill the option agreements. Similarly, corporations with convertible debentures or convertible preferred stocks outstanding must hold in reserve a sufficient number of common shares to meet the demands of preferred shareholders and debenture holders who may elect to convert their securities into common stock.

The auditors must become thoroughly familiar with the terms of any stock options and stock purchase plans and with the conversion features of debenture bonds and preferred stock, so that they can determine whether the financial statements make adequate disclosure of these agreements. The auditors must also verify the shares issued during the year through conversion or exercise of stock options and must ascertain that the number of shares held in reserve at the balance sheet date does not exceed the corporation's authorized but unissued stock.

RETAINED EARNINGS AND DIVIDENDS

Audit work on retained earnings and dividends includes two major steps: (1) the analysis of retained earnings and any appropriations of retained earnings, and (2) the review of dividend procedures for both cash and stock dividends.

The analysis of retained earnings and any appropriations of retained earnings should cover the entire history of these accounts. Such an analysis is prepared for the permanent file and is added to in each annual audit. Credits to the Retained Earnings account ordinarily represent amounts of net income transferred from the Income Summary account. Debits to the Retained Earnings account may include entries for net losses, cash, and stock dividends, and for the creation or enlargement of appropriated reserves. Appropriations of retained earnings require specific authorization by the board of directors. The only verification necessary for these entries is to ascertain that the dates and amounts correspond to the actions of the board.

In the verification of cash dividends, the auditors usually will perform the following steps:

1. Determine the dates and amounts of dividends authorized.
2. Verify the amounts paid.
3. Determine the amount of any preferred dividends in arrears.
4. Review the treatment of unclaimed dividend cheques.

When reviewing minutes of the directors' meetings, the auditors should note the date and amount of each dividend declaration. This serves to establish the authority for dividend disbursements. The dividend payment may then be verified by multiplying the total number of shares as shown by the general ledger control account by the dividend per share.

The auditors' review of dividend declarations may reveal the existence of cash dividends declared but not paid. These declared but unpaid dividends must be shown as liabilities in the balance sheet. The auditors also may review the procedures for handling unclaimed dividends and ascertain that these items are recognized as liabilities. The amount of any accumulated dividends in arrears on preferred stock should be computed. In the verification of stock dividends, there is an additional responsibility of determining that the proper amounts have been transferred from retained earnings to capital stock and contributed capital accounts.

Time of Examination—Shareholders' Equity

The ledger accounts for capital stock, contributed capital, and retained earnings ordinarily receive very few entries during the year. Consequently, most auditors agree that nothing can be gained by making a preliminary analysis of these accounts for a fraction of the year. It usually is more efficient to make the analysis in one step after the close of the period. Other audit procedures, such as the examination of the stock certificate book or the confirmation of outstanding shares with the independent registrar and stock transfer agent, also are performed at the year-end. In the first audit of a new client, some preliminary work can be done advantageously in obtaining and reviewing copies of the articles or certificate of incorporation and bylaws and in analyzing the capital accounts. For repeat engagements, however, there is usually little opportunity to perform audit work on owners' equity accounts before the end of the period.

Financial Statement Presentation of Shareholders' Equity

The presentation of capital stock in the balance sheet should include a complete description of each issue. Information to be disclosed includes the title of each issue; par or no par value; dividend rate, if any; dividend preference; conversion and call provisions; number of shares authorized, issued, and in treasury; dividends in arrears, if any; and shares reserved for stock options or for conversions.

Treasury stock should be shown in the shareholders' equity section, at cost, as a deduction from the combined total of contributed capital and retained earnings. In many jurisdictions, an amount of retained earnings equivalent to the cost of the treasury shares must be restricted. This restriction is disclosed by a note to the financial statements.

Changes in retained earnings during the year may be shown in a separate statement or combined with the income statement. In such form of presentation, the amount of retained earnings at the beginning of the year is added to the net income figure, dividends paid are subtracted from the subtotal, and the final figure represents the new balance of retained earnings.

One of the most significant points to consider in determining the presentation of retained earnings in the balance sheet is the existence of any restriction on the use of this retained income. Agreements with banks, bondholders, and other creditors very commonly impose limitations on the payment of dividends. These restrictions must be fully disclosed in the notes to the financial statements.

AUDIT OF SOLE PROPRIETORSHIPS AND PARTNERSHIPS

Perhaps the most common reason for a small business to arrange for an external audit is the need for audited financial statements in order to obtain a bank loan. Often, a banker, when approached by the owner of a small business applying for a loan, will request audited financial statements as an aid to reaching a decision on the loan application.

Procedures for Audit of Partners' Accounts. A most significant document underlying the partnership form of organization is the partnership contract. The auditors are particularly interested in determining that the distribution of net income has been carried out in accordance with the profit-sharing provisions of the partnership contract. Maintenance of partners' capital accounts at prescribed levels and restriction of drawings by partners to specified amounts are other points often covered in the contract; compliance with these clauses should be verified by the auditors in determining the propriety of the year's entries in the capital accounts. Partners' loan accounts also require reference to the partnership contract to determine the treatment intended by the partners.

Occasionally auditors may find that a partnership is operating without any written agreement of partnership. This situation raises a question of whether profits have been divided in accordance with the understanding existing between the partners. The auditors may appropriately suggest that the firm develop a written partnership contract; for their own protection, the auditors may wish to obtain from each partner a written statement confirming the balance in his or her capital account and approval of the method used in dividing the year's earnings.

In general, the same principles described for the audit of corporate capital are applicable to the examination of the capital accounts and drawing accounts of a sole proprietorship or partnership. Analyses are made of all proprietorship accounts from the beginning of the business, the initial capital investment and any additions are traced to the cash and asset records, and the net income or loss for the period and any withdrawals are verified. In the case of a sole proprietorship, a common source of difficulty is the practice of intermingling business and personal transactions, making it necessary for the auditors to segregate personal net worth from business capital. Adjustments may also be required to transfer from expense accounts to the owner's drawing account any personal expenditures paid with company funds.

DISCLOSURE OF CONTINGENCIES

A *loss contingency* may be defined as a *possible* loss, stemming from past events, that will be resolved as to existence and amount by some future event. Central to the concept of a contingent loss is the idea of uncertainty—uncertainty concerning both the amount of loss and whether, in fact, any loss has been incurred. This uncertainty is resolved when some future event occurs or fails to occur.

Most loss contingencies may also appropriately be called *contingent liabilities. Loss contingencies,* however, is a broader term, encompassing the possible impairment of assets as well as the possible existence of liabilities. The audit problem with respect to loss contingencies is twofold. First, the auditors must determine the existence of the loss contingencies. Because of the uncertainty factor, most loss contingencies do not appear in the accounting records, and a systematic search is required if the auditors are to have reasonable assurance that no important loss contingencies have been overlooked. Second, the auditors must appraise the probability that a loss has been incurred. This is made difficult both by the uncertainty factor and by the tendency of the client management to maintain at least an outward appearance of optimism.

Section 3290 of the *CICA Handbook* sets forth the criteria for accounting for loss contingencies. Such losses should be reflected in the accounting records when both of the following conditions are met: (1) information available prior to the issuance of the financial statements indicates that it is *likely* that a loss had been sustained at the balance sheet date, *and* (2) the amount of the loss can be *reasonably estimated.* Recognition of the loss may involve either recognition of a liability or reduction of an asset. When a loss contingency has been accrued in the accounts, it is usually desirable to explain the nature of the contingency in a note to the financial statements and to disclose any exposure to loss in excess of the amount accrued.

Loss contingencies that do not meet both of the above criteria should still be disclosed when there is at least a *reasonable possibility* that a loss has been incurred. This disclosure should describe the nature of the contingency and, if possible, provide an estimate of the possible loss. If the amount of possible loss cannot be reasonably estimated, the disclosure should include either a range of loss or a statement that an estimate cannot be made. Accordingly, Section 3290 recommends:

The existence of a contingent loss at the date of the financial statements should be disclosed in notes to the financial statements when:

(1) the occurrence of the confirming future event is likely but the amount of the loss cannot be reasonably estimated; or
(2) the occurrence of the confirming future event is likely and an accrual has been made but there exists an exposure to loss in excess of the amount accrued; or
(3) the occurrence of the confirming future event is not determinable.

The procedures undertaken by auditors to ascertain the existence of loss contingencies and to assess the probability of loss vary with the nature of the contingent item. To illustrate these types of procedures, we will discuss several of the more frequent types of contingencies warranting financial statement disclosure.

1. Litigation.

Perhaps the most common loss contingency appearing in financial statements is that stemming from pending or threatened litigation. An *enquiry letter* to the client's legal counsel is the auditors' primary means of obtaining evidence to confirm pending or threatened litigation.

Section 6560 states that "an enquiry letter, prepared by the client, should be sent by the auditor to each law firm identified as handling claims which are outstanding or possible claims." This enquiry letter should include, among other items, (*a*) a list of outstanding *claims* and *possible claims,* together with a description of their nature and current status; (*b*) an evaluation by the client of the likelihood of loss and the estimated amount thereof for each claim and possible claim; and (*c*) a request for an evaluation by the law firms regarding these claims. The law firms are then required to send a *response letter* to the client, with a separate signed copy sent directly to the auditors, indicating whether the claims or possible claims have been properly described and reasonably evaluated by the client and whether the client has included all outstanding claims. The law firms are not required to indicate any possible claims not listed in the enquiry letter. However, if there is such an omission of possible claims, the law firms will discuss with the client to ensure that the client is advised of its responsibility to inform the auditors and make any appropriate adjustment to or disclosure in the financial statements.

The auditors should review the response letter for any restriction that may constitute a limitation on the scope of their examination. If there is a restriction and it cannot be satisfactorily resolved, the auditors should either qualify their opinion or deny an opinion in their report, depending on the materiality of the restriction.

2. Income tax disputes.

The necessity of estimating the income tax liability applicable to the year under audit was discussed in Chapter 15. In addition to the taxes relating to the current year's income, uncertainty often exists concerning the amount ultimately payable for prior years. A lag of two or three years often exists between the filing of income tax returns and the final settlement after review by Revenue Canada. Disputes between the taxpayer and Revenue Canada may create contingent liabilities not settled for several more years. The auditors should determine whether Revenue Canada has examined any returns of the client since the preceding audit, and if so, whether any additional taxes have been assessed.

3. Accommodation endorsements and other guarantees of indebtedness.

The endorsement of notes of other concerns or individuals is very seldom recorded in the accounts, but may be reflected in the minutes of directors' meetings. The practice is more common among small concerns—particularly when one person has a propietary interest in several companies. Officers, partners, and sole proprietors of small organizations should be questioned as to the existence of any contingent liability from this source. Enquiry should also be made as to whether any collateral has been received to protect the company. The auditors should confirm written or oral guarantees or other contingent liabilities with appropriate financial institutions, using the standard bank confirmation illustrated in Chapter 11.

4. Accounts receivable sold or assigned with recourse.

When accounts receivable are sold or assigned *with recourse,* a guarantee of collectibility is given. Authorization of such a transaction should be revealed during the auditors' reading of the minutes, and a clue also may be found during the examination of transactions and correspondence with financial institutions. Confirmation by direct communication with the purchaser or assignee is necessary for any receivables sold or assigned.

Commitments

Closely related to contingent liabilities are obligations termed *commitments.* The auditors may discover during their examination many of the following commitments: inventory purchase commitments, commitments to sell merchandise at specified prices, contracts for the construction of plant and equipment, pension or profit-sharing plans, long-term operating leases of plant and equipment, employee stock option plans, and employment contracts with key officers. A common characteristic of these commitments is the contractual obligation to enter into transactions *in the future.*

To illustrate the relationship of a commitment to a loss contingency, assume that a manufacturer agrees to sell at a fixed price a substantial part of its output over the next three years. At the time of forming the agreement, the manufacturer, of course, believes the arrangement to be advantageous. However, it is possible that rising price levels could transform the fixed-price sales agreement into an unprofitable one, requiring sales to be made at prices below manufacturing cost. Such circumstances could warrant recognition of a loss in the financial statements.

All classes of material commitments may be described in a single note to the financial statements, or they may be included in a "Contingencies and Commitments" note to the financial statements.

General Risk Contingencies

In addition to loss contingencies and commitments, all businesses face the risk of loss from numerous factors called *general risk contingencies.* A general risk contingency represents a loss that *might occur in the future,* as opposed to a loss contingency that *might have occurred in the past.* Examples of general risk contingencies are the threat of a strike or a consumer boycott, the risk of price increases in essential raw materials, and the risk of a natural catastrophe.

General risk contingencies *should not be disclosed* in financial statements. Such disclosure would be confusing to investors, since the events that might produce a loss actually have not occurred, and since these risks are part of the general business environment. The lack of insurance coverage is a general risk contingency. However, it may be desirable to disclose in the financial statements the lack of adequate insurance against *material* risk that is *normally* insured.[2]

Audit Procedures for Loss Contingencies

Although audit procedures vary with the individual type of loss contingency, the following steps are taken in most audits as a means of discovering these conditions:

1. Review the minutes of directors' meetings to the date of the audit report. Important contracts, lawsuits, and dealings with subsidiaries are typical of matters discussed in board meetings that may involve loss contingencies.
2. Request the client to prepare an enquiry letter to its lawyers asking for their evaluation of the completeness of the claims listed and of the reasonableness of the client's description and evaluation of the claims and possible claims. This letter is sent by the auditors, and the lawyers' response to it is sent directly to the auditors.
3. Review the client's income tax files, income tax assessment notices, and correspondence with Revenue Canada for contingent liabilities.
4. Review correspondence with financial institutions for evidence of accommodation endorsements, guarantees of indebtedness, or sales or assignments of accounts receivable.
5. Obtain a representations letter from the client indicating that all liabilities known to officers are recorded or disclosed.

Liability Representations

Since contingent liabilities often are not entered in the accounting records, the officers of the company may be the only persons aware of the contingencies. It is therefore important that the auditors should ask the officers to disclose all liabilities and contingencies of which they have knowl-

---

[2] CICA, *CICA Handbook* (Toronto), Section 3290.16; emphasis added.

edge. To emphasize the importance of the request and to guard against any possible misunderstanding, the officers should be asked to sign a written liability representation, stating that all liabilities known to them are reflected in the accounts or otherwise disclosed in the financial statements.

Financial Presentation of Loss Contingencies

Current practice utilizes supporting footnotes as a means of disclosure of loss contingencies that are not accrued in the financial statements. Presentation of information concerning loss contingencies should be limited to specific factual situations, such as accommodation endorsements, guarantees, and pending lawsuits. To fill the financial statements with vague generalities about the uncertainties of the future is more akin to fortune-telling than to financial reporting.

KEY TERMS

claim   A matter involving the client which is or may become litigious, with respect to which (*a*) a law firm has been engaged to represent or advise the client and (*b*) a demand or an indication of a demand has been communicated to or by the client, carrying with it the possibility of future loss or gain.

commitment   A contractual obligation to carry out a transaction at specified terms in the future. Material commitments should be disclosed in the financial statements.

contingent liability   A possible liability, stemming from past events, that will be resolved as to existence and amount by some future event.

contributed capital (or premium on capital stock)   Capital contributed by shareholders in excess of the par value of the shares issued.

debenture bond   An unsecured bond, dependent on the general credit of the issuer.

enquiry letter   A letter prepared by the client and sent by the auditors to the client's legal counsel requesting an evaluation of the client's listing, description, and assessment of claims and possible claims.

general risk contingency   An element of the business environment that involves some risk of a future loss. Examples include the risk of accident, strike, price fluctuations, or natural catastrophe. General risk contingencies usually should not be disclosed in financial statements.

indenture   The formal agreement between bondholders and the issuer as to the terms of the debt.

liability representation   A written representation provided by key officers of the client that all liabilities and loss contingencies known to them are disclosed in the financial statements.

loss contingency   A possible loss, stemming from past events, that will be resolved as to existence and amount by some future event. Loss contingencies should be disclosed in notes to the financial statements if there is a reasonable possibility that a loss has been incurred. When loss contingencies are considered likely and can be reasonably estimated, they should be accrued in the accounts.

possible claim   A matter involving the client which is or may become litigious, with respect to which a law firm has been engaged to represent or advise the client but a demand or indication of demand has not been communicated to or by the client.

shareholders ledger   A record showing the number of shares owned by each shareholder. This is the basic record used for preparing dividend payments and other communications with shareholders.

sinking fund   Cash or other assets set aside for the retirement of a debt.

stock certificate book   A book of serially numbered certificates with attached stubs. Each stub shows the corresponding certificate number and provides space for entering the number of shares represented by the certificate, name of the shareholder, and serial number of the certificate surrendered in exchange for the new one. Surrendered certificates are canceled and replaced in the certificate book.

stock option plan   A formal plan granting the right to buy a specified number of shares at a stipulated price during a specified time. Stock option plans are frequently used as a form of executive compensation. The terms of such plans should be disclosed in financial statements.

stock registrar   An institution charged with responsibility for avoiding overissuance of a corporation's stock. Every new certificate must be presented to the registrar for examination and registration before it is issued to a shareholder.

stock transfer agent   An institution responsible for maintaining detailed records of shareholders and handling transfers of stock ownership.

treasury stock   Shares of its own stock acquired by a corporation for the purpose of being reissued or canceled at a later date.

GROUP I: REVIEW QUESTIONS

16–1.   Mansfield Corporation has outstanding an issue of 15-year bonds payable. There is no sinking fund for these bonds. Under what circumstances, if any, should this bond issue be classified as a current liability?

16–2. What does the trust indenture used by a corporation in creating long-term bonded indebtedness have to do with the payment of dividends on common stock?

16–3. In addition to verifying the recorded liabilities of a company, the auditors must also give consideration to the possibility that other unrecorded liabilities exist. What specific steps may be taken by the auditors to determine that all of their client's interest-bearing liabilities are recorded?

16–4. Two assistant auditors were assigned by the auditor-in-charge to the examination of long-term liabilities. Some time later, they reported to the auditor-in-charge that they had determined that all long-term liabilities were properly recorded and that all recorded long-term liabilities were genuine obligations. Does this determination constitute a sufficient examination of long-term liabilities? Explain.

16–5. Palmer Company has issued a number of notes payable during the year, and several of these notes are outstanding at the balance sheet date. What sources of information should the auditors use in preparing a working paper analysis of the notes payable?

16–6. If the federal income tax returns for prior years have not as yet been reviewed by federal tax authorities, would you consider it necessary for the client to disclose this situation in notes to the financial statements? Explain.

16–7. What is the principal reason for testing the reasonableness of the interest expense account in conjunction with the examination of notes payable?

16–8. Is the confirmation of notes payable usually correlated with any other specific phase of the audit? Explain.

16–9. Audit programs for examination of accounts receivable and notes receivable often include investigation of selected transactions occurring after the balance sheet date as well as transactions occurring during the year under audit. Are the auditors concerned with note payable transactions subsequent to the balance sheet date? Explain.

16–10. Most corporations with bonds payable outstanding utilize the services of a trustee. What relation, if any, does this practice have to the maintenance of adequate internal control?

16–11. "Auditors are not qualified to pass on the legality of a bond issue; this is a question for the company's lawyers. It is therefore unnecessary for the auditors to inspect the bond indenture." Criticize the quotation.

16–12. What is the meaning of the term *commitment?* Give examples. Do commitments appear in financial statements? Explain.

16–13. Long-term creditors often insist upon placing certain restrictions upon the borrowing company for the term of the loan. Give three examples of such restrictions, and indicate how each restriction protects the long-term creditor.

16–14. What information should be requested by the auditors from the trustee responsible for an issue of debentures payable?

16–15. What are *general risk contingencies?* Do such items require disclosure in the financial statements?

16–16. Compare the auditors' examination of owners' equity with their work on assets and current liabilities. Among other factors to be considered are the relative amounts of time involved and the character of the transactions to be reviewed.

16–17. What do you consider to be the most important internal control device a corporation can adopt with respect to capital stock transactions?

16–18. You have been retained to perform an audit of Valley Products, a small corporation which has not been audited during the previous 10 years of its existence. How will your work on the Capital Stock account in this initial audit differ from that required in a repeat engagement?

16–19. Comment on the desirability of audit work on the owners' equity accounts before the balance sheet date.

16–20. Name three situations that might place a restriction on retained earnings limiting or preventing dividend payments. Explain how the auditors might become aware of each such restricting factor.

16–21. Delta Limited has issued stock options to four of its officers permitting them to purchase 5,000 shares each of common stock at a price of $25 per share at any time during the next five years. The president asks you what effect, if any, the granting of the options will have upon the balance sheet presentation of the shareholders' equity accounts.

16–22. Describe the significant features of a stock certificate book, its purpose, and the method of using it.

16–23. In the audit of a small corporation not using the services of an independent stock registrar and stock transfer agent, what use is made of the stock certificate book by the auditors?

16–24. What is the primary responsibility of an independent registrar with respect to capital stock?

16–25. What is the usual procedure followed by the CA in obtaining evidence regarding pending and threatened litigation against the client?

16–26. What are *loss contingencies?* How are such items presented in the financial statements? Explain.

16–27. What errors are commonly encountered by the auditors in their examination of the capital and drawing accounts of a sole proprietor?

16–28. Corporations sometimes issue their own capital stock in exchange for services and various assets other than cash. As an auditor, what evidence would you look for to determine the propriety of the values used in recording such transactions?

16–29. In your second annual examination of a corporate client, you find a new account in the general ledger, treasury stock, with a balance of $306,000. Describe the procedures you would follow to verify this item.

16–30. In examining the financial statements of Foster Limited, you observe a debit entry for $200,000 labeled as Dividends in the Retained Earnings account. Explain in detail how you would verify this entry.

16–31. Your new client, Black Angus Valley Ranch, is a small corporation with less than 100 shareholders, and does not utilize the services of an independent stock registrar or transfer agent. For your first audit, you want to obtain or prepare a year-end list of shareholders showing the number of shares owned by each. From what source or record should this information be obtained? Explain.

GROUP II: QUESTIONS REQUIRING ANALYSIS

16–32. Stan Jones, CA, the continuing auditor of Sussex, Inc., is beginning the audit of the common stock and treasury stock accounts. Jones has decided to design substantive tests without reliance on internal control.

Sussex has no par value common stock and acts as its own registrar and transfer agent. During the past year Sussex both issued and reacquired shares of its own common stock, some of which the company still owned at year-end. Additional common stock transactions occurred among the shareholders during the year.

Common stock transactions can be traced to individual shareholders' accounts in a subsidiary ledger and to a stock certificate book. The company has not paid any cash or stock dividends. There are no other classes of stock, stock rights, warrants, or option plans.

Required:

What substantive audit procedures should Jones apply in examining the common stock and treasury stock accounts?

(AICPA, adapted)

16–33. The only long-term liability of Range Corporation is a note payable for $1 million secured by a mortgage on the company's plant and equipment. You have audited the company annually for three preceding years, during which time the principal amount of the note has remained unchanged. The maturity date is 10 years from the current balance sheet date. You are informed by the president of the company that all interest payments have been made promptly in accordance with the terms of the note. Under these circumstances, what audit work, if any, is necessary with respect to this long-term liability during your present year-end audit?

16–34. Current CICA recommendations require that under certain circumstances loss contingencies *be accrued* in the financial statements. Under other circumstances, loss contingencies require *disclosure only in notes* to the financial statements. Identify the circumstances for each of these two categories.

16–35. During your annual audit of Walker Distributing Co., your assistant, Jane Williams, reports to you that although a number of entries were made during the year in a general ledger account, Notes Payable to Officers, she decided that it was not necessary to audit the account because it had a zero balance at year-end.

Required:

Do you agree with your assistant's decision? Discuss.

(AICPA)

16–36. In an audit of a corporation that has a bond issue outstanding, the trust indenture is reviewed and confirmation as to the issue is obtained from the trustee. List eight matters of importance to the auditors that might be found either in the indenture or in the confirmation obtained from the trustee. Explain briefly the reason for the auditors' interest in each of the items.

(AICPA)

16–37. You are retained by Columbia Corporation to make an examination of its financial statements for the fiscal year ended June 30, and you begin work on July 15. Your survey of internal control indicates a fairly satisfactory condition, although there are not enough employees to permit extensive subdivision of duties. The company is one of the smaller units in the industry, but has realized net income of about $500,000 in each of the last three years.

Near the end of your audit you overhear a telephone call received by the president of the company while you are discussing the audit with him. The telephone conversation indicates that on May 15 of the current year the Columbia Corporation made an accommodation endorsement of a 60-day, $430,000 note issued by a major customer, Brill Corporation, to its bank. The purpose of the telephone call from Brill was to inform your client that the note had been paid at the maturity date. You had not been aware of the existence of the note before overhearing the telephone call.

Required:

a. Do you think the auditors would be justified from an ethical standpoint in acting on information acquired in this manner?

b. Should the balance sheet as of June 30 disclose the contingent liability? Give reasons for your answer.

c. Prepare a list of auditing procedures that might have brought the contingency to light. Explain fully the likelihood of detection of the accommodation endorsement by each procedure listed.

16–38. You are the audit manager in the examination of the financial statements of Midwest Grain Storage, Inc., a new client. The company's records show that as of the balance sheet date, approximately 15 million bushels of various grains are in storage for the Commodity Credit Corporation.

In your review of the audit senior's working papers, you ascertain the following facts:

a. All grain is stored under an agreement which holds Midwest responsible for the quantity and quality of the grain.

b. Losses due to shrinkage, spoilage, and so forth are inherent in the storage of grain. Midwest's losses, however, have been negligible due to the excellence of its storage facilities.

c. Midwest carries a warehouseman's bond covering approximately 20 percent of the value of the stored grain.

In the loss contingencies section of the working papers, the senior auditor has made the following notation: "I propose recommending to Midwest's controller that the contingent liability for grain spoilage and shrinkage be disclosed in a note to the financial statements."

Required:

Do you concur with the senior's proposal? Explain.

16–39. Linda Reeves, CA, receives a telephone call from her client, Lane Limited. The company's controller states that the board of directors of Lane has entered into two contractual arrangements with Ted Forbes, the company's former president, who has recently retired. Under one agreement, Lane will pay the ex-president $7,000 per month for five years if he does not compete with the company during that time in a rival business. Under the other agreement, the company will pay the ex-president $5,000 per month for five years for such advisory services as the company may request from the ex-president.

Lane's controller asks Reeves whether the balance sheet as of the date the two agreements were signed should show $144,000 in current liabilities and $576,000 in long-term liabilities, or whether the two agreements should be disclosed in a contingencies note to the financial statements.

Required:
How should Linda Reeves reply to the controller's questions? Explain.

16–40. You are engaged in the examination of the financial statements of Armada Corporation for the year ended August 31, 199X. The balance sheet, reflecting all of your audit adjustments accepted by the client to date, shows total current assets, $9,000,000; total current liabilities, $7,500,000; and shareholders' equity, $1,500,000. Included in current liabilities are two unsecured notes payable—one payable to United National Bank in the amount of $900,000 due October 31, 199X; the other payable to First Bank in the amount of $800,000 due September 30, 199X. On September 30, the last scheduled date for your audit work, you learn that Armada Corporation is unable to pay the $832,000 maturity value of the First Bank note, that Armada executives are negotiating with First Bank for an extension of the due date of the note, and that nothing definite has been decided as to the extension.

Required:
a. Should this situation be disclosed in footnotes to Armada Corporation's August 31 financial statements?

b. After the question of financial statement disclosure has been resolved to the auditor's satisfaction, might this situation have any effect upon the audit report?

16–41. During an audit engagement, Robert Wong, CA, has satisfactorily completed an examination of accounts payable and other liabilities and now plans to determine whether there are any loss contingencies arising from litigation, claims, or assessments.

Required:
What are the audit procedures Wong should follow with respect to the existence of loss contingencies arising from litigation, claims, or assessments? Do not discuss reporting requirements.

16–42. Valley Corporation has a stock option plan designed to provide extra incentive to its officers and key employees. A footnote to the financial statements includes a description of the plan and lists the number of options for shares that have been authorized, the number granted, the number exercised, and the number expired. The option price and the market price per share on the grant dates and the exercise dates are also shown.

Required:

a. In view of the fact that the information concerning the stock option plan appears in a note to, rather than in the body of, the financial statements, what responsibility, if any, do the external auditors have for this information?

b. List the audit procedures, if any, that you believe should be applied to the stock option plan information.

16–43. Select the best answer choice for each of the following, and justify your selection in a brief statement.

a. With respect to which of the following is the audit procedure of confirmation *least* appropriate?

(1) The trustee of an issue of bonds payable.

(2) Holders of common stock.

(3) Holders of notes receivable.

(4) Holders of notes payable.

b. The performance of audit procedures prior to the balance sheet date is an efficient auditing approach for some items but not for others. For which of the following is audit work prior to the balance sheet date most feasible?

(1) Capital stock.

(2) Unrecorded liabilities.

(3) Trade accounts payable.

(4) Plant and equipment.

c. In the audit of a manufacturing company of medium size, which of the following areas would you expect to require the least amount of audit time?

(1) Owners' equity.

(2) Revenue.

(3) Assets.

(4) Liabilities.

d. How can the auditors best verify a client's bond sinking fund transactions and year-end balance?

(1) Recomputation of interest expense, interest payable, and amortization of bond discount or premium.

(2) Confirmation with individual holders of retired bonds.

(3) Confirmation with bond trustee.

(4) Examination and count of the bonds retired during the year.

e. The auditors' program for the examination of long-term debt should include steps that require:

(1) Verification of the existence of the bondholders.

(2) Examination of copies of debt agreements.

(3) Inspection of the accounts payable subsidiary ledger.

(4) Investigation of credits to the bond interest income account.

f. Where should all corporate capital stock transactions ultimately be traced?
(1) Minutes of the board of directors.
(2) Cash receipts journal.
(3) Cash disbursements journal.
(4) Numbered stock certificates.

(AICPA, adapted)

GROUP III: PROBLEMS

16–44. In your first audit of Hydrafoil Limited, a manufacturer of specially designed boats capable of transporting passengers over water at very high speeds, you find that sales are made to commercial transportation companies. The sales price per unit is $400,000, and with each unit sold, the client gives the purchasing company a certificate reading as follows:

> Hydrafoil Limited promises to pay _____ the sum of $24,000 when the boat designated as Serial No. _____ is permanently retired from service and evidence of such retirement is submitted.

The president of Hydrafoil explains to you that the purpose of issuing the certificates is to ensure contact with customers when they are in the market for new equipment. You also learn that the company makes no journal entry to record a certificate when it is issued. Instead, the company charges an expense account and credits a liability account $200 per month for each outstanding certificate, based on the company's experience that its hydrafoil boats will be rendered obsolete by new, more efficient models in approximately 10 years from the date of sale.

Required:
Do you concur with Hydrafoil's accounting for the certificates? You may assume that the 10-year service life of the product (and therefore of the certificates) is an accurate determination. Explain your position clearly.

16–45. You have been retained to audit the financial statements of Midwest Products Inc. for the year ended December 31. During the current year, Midwest had obtained a long-term loan from its bank in accordance with a financing agreement which provided the following:

1. The loan was to be secured by the company's inventory and accounts receivable.

2. The company was to maintain a debt-to-equity ratio not to exceed two to one.

3. The company was not to pay dividends without permission from the bank.

4. Monthly instalment payments were to commence July 1 of the next year.

In addition, during the current year, Midwest Products Inc. borrowed, on a short-term basis, from its president, including substantial amounts just prior to the year-end.

Required:

a. For the purpose of your audit of the financial statements of Midwest Products Inc., what procedures would you employ in examining the above described items? Do not discuss internal control.

b. What financial statement disclosures are appropriate with respect to the loans from the president?

(AICPA, adapted)

16–46. The following covenants are extracted from the indenture of a bond issue of Case Limited. The indenture provides that failure to comply with its terms in any respect automatically advances the due date of the loan to the date of noncompliance (the regular due date is 20 years hence). Give any audit procedures or reporting requirements you think should be taken or recognized in connection with each of the following:

a. "The debtor company shall endeavour to maintain a working capital ratio of two to one at all times; and in any fiscal year following a failure to maintain said ratio, the company shall restrict compensation of officers to a total of $2,000,000. Officers for this purpose shall include chairman of the board of directors, president, all vice presidents, secretary, controller, and treasurer."

b. "The debtor company shall keep all property that is security for this debt insured against loss by fire to the extent of 100 percent of its actual value. Policies of insurance comprising this protection shall be filed with the trustee."

c. "The debtor company shall pay all taxes legally assessed against property that is security for this debt within the time provided by law for payment without penalty, and shall deposit receipted tax bills or equally acceptable evidence of payment of same with the trustee."

d. "A sinking fund shall be deposited with the trustee by semiannual payments of $900,000, from which the trustee shall, in its discretion, purchase bonds of this issue.''

(AICPA, adapted)

16–47. You are engaged in the first audit of Microdent, Inc. The corporation has both a stock transfer agent and an independent registrar for its capital stock. The transfer agent maintains the record of shareholders, and the registrar determines that there is no over-issue of stock. Signatures of both are required to validate stock certificates.

It has been proposed that confirmations be obtained from both the transfer agent and the registrar as to the stock outstanding at the balance sheet date. If such confirmations agree with the accounting records, no additional work is to be performed as to capital stock.

If you agree that obtaining the confirmations as suggested would be sufficient in this case, give the justification for your position. If you do not agree, state specifically all additional steps you would take and explain your reasons for taking them.

(AICPA, adapted)

16–48. You are engaged in the audit of Phoenix Corp., a new client, at the close of its first fiscal year, April 30, 19X1. The accounts had been closed before the time you began your year-end work.

You review the following shareholders' equity accounts in the general ledger:

Capital Stock

May 1, X0 CR1	500,000
Apr. 28, X1 J12–5	50,000

Premium on Capital Stock

May 1, X0 CR1	250,000
Feb. 2, X1 CR10	2,500

Retained Earnings

Apr. 28, X1 J12–5	50,000	Apr. 30, X1 J12–14	800,000

Treasury Stock

Sept. 14, X0 CP5	80,000	Feb. 2, X1 CR10	40,000

Income Summary

Apr. 30, X1 J12–13	5,200,000	Apr. 30, X1 J12–12	6,000,000
Apr. 30, X1 J12–14	800,000		

Other information in your working papers includes the following:
1. Phoenix's articles of incorporation filed April 17, 19X0, authorized 100,000 shares of no-par-value capital stock.
2. Directors' minutes include the following resolutions:
   Apr. 18, X0 Established $50 per share stated value for capital stock.
   Apr. 30, X0 Authorized issue of 10,000 shares to an underwriting syndicate for $75 per share.
   Sept. 13, X0 Authorized acquisition of 1,000 shares from a dissident holder at $80 per share.
   Feb. 1, X1 Authorized reissue of 500 treasury shares at $85 per share.
   Apr. 28, X1 Declared 10 percent stock dividend, payable May 18, 19X1, to shareholders of record May 4, 19X1.
3. The following costs of the May 1, 19X0, and February 2, 19X1, stock issuances were charged to the named expense accounts: Printing Expense, $2,500; Legal Fees, $17,350; Accounting Fees, $12,000; and Other Fees, $150.
4. Market values for Phoenix Corp. capital stock on various dates were:

Sept. 13, X0	$78.50
Sept. 14, X0	79.00
Feb. 2, X1	85.00
Apr. 28, X1	90.00

5. Phoenix Corp.'s combined federal and provincial income tax rates total 55 percent.

Required:

a. Adjusting journal entries at April 30, 19X1.

b. Shareholders' equity section of Phoenix Corp.'s April 30, 19X1, balance sheet.

16–49. Robert Hopkins was the senior office employee in Griffin Equipment Company and enjoyed the complete confidence of the owner, William Barton, who devoted most of his attention to sales, engineering, and production problems. All financial and accounting matters were entrusted to Hopkins, whose title was office manager. Hopkins had two assistants, but their only experience in accounting and financial work had been gained under Hopkins's supervision. Barton had informed Hopkins that it was his responsibility to keep him (Barton) informed on financial position and operating results of the company but not to bother him with details.

The company was short of working capital and would occasionally issue notes payable in settlement of past-due open accounts to suppliers. The situations warranting issuance of notes were decided upon by Hopkins, and the notes were drawn by him for signature by Barton. Hopkins was aware of the weakness in internal control and finally devised a scheme for defrauding the company through understating the amount of notes payable outstanding. He prepared a note in the amount of $24,000 payable to a supplier to whom several invoices were past due. After securing Barton's signature on the note and mailing it to the creditor, Hopkins entered the note in the Notes Payable account of the general ledger as $4,000, with an offsetting debit of $4,000 to Accounts Payable, and the accounts payable subsidiary ledger of the supplier.

Several months later when the note matured, a cheque for $24,000 plus interest was issued and properly recorded, including a debit of $24,000 to the Notes Payable account. Hopkins then altered the original credit in the account by changing the figure from $4,000 to $24,000. He also changed the original debit to Accounts Payable from $4,000 to $24,000. This alteration caused the Notes Payable account to have a balance in agreement with the total of other notes outstanding. To complete the fraud, Hopkins called the supplier to whom the cheque had been sent and explained that the cheque should have been for only $4,000 plus interest.

Hopkins explained to the supplier that the note of $24,000 originally had been issued in settlement of a number of past-due invoices, but that while the note was outstanding, cheques had been sent in payment of all the invoices. "In other words," said Hopkins over the telephone, "we made the mistake of giving you a note for those invoices and then going ahead and sending you cheques for them as soon as our cash position had improved. Then we paid the note at maturity. So please excuse our mistakes and return the overpayment.'' After reviewing the record of invoices and cheques received, the supplier agreed he had been overpaid by $20,000 plus interest and promptly sent a refund, which Hopkins abstracted without making any entry in the accounts.

Required:

a. Assuming that an audit by independent auditors was made while the note was outstanding, do you think that the $20,000 understatement of the Notes Payable account would have been detected? Explain fully the reasoning underlying your answer.

b. If the fraud was not discovered while the note was outstanding, do you think that an audit subsequent to the payment of the note would have disclosed the fraud? Explain.

c. What internal control procedures would you recommend for Griffin Equipment Company to avoid fraud of this type?

Chapter 17

Further Verification of Revenue and Expenses: Completing the Audit

After studying this chapter, you should be able to:

- Describe the audit objectives for revenue and expense accounts.
- Describe appropriate audit procedures for the audit of revenue and expense accounts.
- Explain the fundamental internal controls over payroll and be able to identify weaknesses.
- Describe the steps involved in completing the audit.

Throughout the previous chapters on balance sheet accounts we have discussed related procedures for income statement accounts. In this chapter we provide further information on the audit of revenues and expenses as well as present information on procedures involved with completing the audit.

Nature of Revenue and Expenses

Today, with greater emphasis being placed upon corporate earnings as an indicator of the health and well-being of corporations as well as of the overall economy, the income statement is of fundamental importance to management, shareholders, creditors, employees, and government. The relative level of corporate earnings is often a key factor in the determination of such issues as wage negotiations, income tax rates, subsidies, and government fiscal policies. In fact, accountants generally agree that the measurement of income is the most important single function of accounting.

Throughout Chapters 11 through 16, we have emphasized the relationships of revenues and expenses to the various balance sheet accounts. Put briefly, the principles used in making accounting decisions for balance sheet accounts often have a direct effect upon the measurement of income.

The Auditors' Approach in Examination of Revenues and Expenses

The doctrine of conservatism is a powerful force influencing decisions on revenues and expenses. The concept remains important in large part due to the subjectivity involved with many accounting estimates (as for expected future credit losses on receivables, lives of assets, and the warranty of products sold). Conservatism in the valuation of assets means that when two (or more) reasonable alternative values are indicated, the accountant will choose the lower amount. For valuation of liabilities, the higher amount is chosen. Therefore, when applied to the income statement, the conservatism concept results in a low, or conservative, income figure.

Most auditors have a considerable respect for the doctrine of conservatism. In part, this attitude springs from the concept of legal liability to third parties. Financial statements that *understate* financial position and operating results almost never lead to legal action against the auditors involved. Nevertheless, auditors must recognize that overemphasis on conservatism in financial reporting is a narrow and shortsighted approach to meeting the needs of our society. To be of greatest value, financial statements should present fairly, rather than understate, financial position and operating results.

A fair, informative income statement is surely as important as, if not more important than, the balance sheet. Nevertheless, audits continue to be organized in terms of balance sheet topics. The reasons for organizing audit work in this manner were discussed in Chapter 10.

As the significance of the income statement increased, auditors began to verify income statement accounts concurrently with related balance sheet accounts. Depreciation expense, for example, is most conveniently verified along with the plant and equipment accounts. Once the existence and cost of depreciable assets are established, the verification of depreciation expense is merely an additional step. On the other hand, to verify depreciation expense without first establishing the nature and amount of assets owned and subject to depreciation would obviously be a cart-before-the-horse approach. The same line of reasoning tells us that the auditors' work on inventories, especially in determining that inventory transactions were accurately cut off at the end of the period, is a major step toward the verification of the income statement figures for sales and cost of goods sold. Much of the material in the preceding six chapters of this book has related to income statement accounts, although the sequence of topics has followed a balance sheet arrangement.

When the balance sheets at the beginning and end of an accounting period have been fully verified, the net income for the year is fairly well established, although considerable additional work remains to be done before the auditors can express a professional opinion that the income statement presents fairly the results of operations.

Let us emphasize the fact that the auditors' examination of revenue and expense transactions should be much more than an incidental by-product of the examination of assets and liabilities. They use a combination of cross-referencing, analytical procedures, and analysis of specific transactions to bring to light errors, omissions, and inconsistencies not disclosed in the examination of balance sheet accounts.

Specifically, the auditors' *objectives* in the examination of revenues and expenses are:

1. To consider *internal control* over revenues and expenses.
2. To determine the *occurrence* of recorded revenue and expense transactions.
3. To establish the *completeness* of recorded revenue and expense transactions.
4. To determine that the *valuation* of revenue and expense transactions is in accordance with generally accepted accounting principles.
5. To establish the *clerical accuracy* of schedules of revenues and expenses.
6. To determine that the *statement presentation* of revenue and expense accounts is appropriate.

REVENUE

The auditors' review of sales activities was considered in connection with accounts receivable in Chapter 12. In this section, we discuss (1) the relationship of revenue to balance sheet accounts and (2) the miscellaneous revenue account.

Relationship of Revenue to Balance Sheet Accounts

As pointed out previously, most revenue accounts are verified by the auditors in conjunction with the audit of a related asset or liability. The following list summarizes the revenue verified in this manner:

Balance Sheet Item	*Revenue*
Accounts receivable	Sales
Notes receivable	Interest
Securities and other investments	Interest, dividends, gains on sales, share of investee's income
Property, plant, and equipment	Rent, gains on sale
Intangible assets	Royalties

Miscellaneous Revenue

One category of revenue not included in the above listing, but of interest to the auditors, is miscellaneous revenue. Miscellaneous revenue, by its very nature, is a mixture of minor items, some nonrecurring and others likely to be received at irregular intervals. If the client's personnel receive a cash payment and are not sure of the source, it is likely that it will be recorded as miscellaneous revenue. Because of the nature of items often recorded in the Miscellaneous Revenue account, the auditors will obtain an analysis of the account. Among the items the auditors might find improperly included as miscellaneous revenue are the following:

1. Collections on previously written-off accounts or notes receivable. These collections should be credited to the allowance for doubtful accounts and notes receivable.
2. Write-offs of old outstanding cheques or unclaimed wages. If unclaimed properties revert to the government after statutory periods, these write-offs should be credited to a liability account rather than to miscellaneous revenue.
3. Proceeds from sales of scrap. Scrap sale proceeds should generally be applied to reduce cost of goods sold, under by-product cost accounting principles.
4. Rebates or refunds of insurance premiums. These refunds should be offset against the related expense or unexpired insurance.
5. Proceeds from sales of plant assets. These proceeds should be accounted for in the determination of the gain or loss on the assets sold.

The auditors should propose adjusting journal entries to classify correctly any material items of the types described above that have been included in miscellaneous revenue by the client. Before concluding the work on revenue, the auditors should perform analytical procedures and investigate unusual fluctuations. Material amounts of unrecorded revenue may be discovered by these procedures, as well as significant misclassifications affecting revenue accounts.

EXPENSES

The auditors' work relating to purchases and cost of goods sold was covered, along with inventories, in Chapter 13. We are now concerned with audit procedures for other types of expenses.

Relationship of Expenses to Balance Sheet Accounts

Let us consider for a moment the number of expense accounts for which we have already outlined verification procedures in the chapters dealing with balance sheet topics:

Balance Sheet Item	*Expenses (and Costs)*
Accounts and notes receivable	Uncollectible accounts and notes expense
Inventories	Purchases and cost of goods sold
Property, plant, and equipment	Depreciation, repairs and maintenance, and depletion
Prepaid expenses and deferred charges	Various related expenses, such as rent, property taxes, advertising, postage, and others
Intangible assets	Amortization
Accrued liabilities	Commissions, fees, bonuses, product warranty expenses, and others
Interest-bearing debt	Interest

In the following sections, we shall complete our review of expenses by considering additional audit procedures for payrolls, and for selling general, and administrative expenses other than those listed above. The audit of payroll is presented as a unit without regard to the division of salaries and wages between manufacturing operations and other operations. Manufacturing salaries and wages are, of course, charged to inventories, either directly or by means of the allocation of manufacturing overhead.

Audit Program for Selling, General, and Administrative Expenses

For other expenses not verified in the audit of balance sheet accounts, the following substantive tests are appropriate:

1. Perform analytical procedures related to the accounts.
   a. Develop an expectation of the account balance.

    b. Determine the amount of difference from the expectation that can be accepted without investigation.

    c. Compare the company's account balance with the expected account balance.

    d. Investigate significant deviations from the expected account balance.

2. Obtain or prepare analyses of selected expense accounts.
3. Obtain or prepare analyses of critical expenses in income tax returns.

1. Perform analytical procedures related to the accounts.

***a*. Develop an expectation of the account balance.**

Auditors develop an expectation of the account balance by considering factors such as budgeted levels, the prior year audited balances, industry averages, relationships among financial data, and relevant nonfinancial data.

An effective budgeting program will reduce control risk since budgets provide management with information as to expected amounts. The existence of these expected expense amounts increases the likelihood that errors will be detected by management, since any significant discrepancy between budgeted and actual amounts receives timely attention.

The existence of a good budgeting program also helps the auditors in their audit of expense accounts. When the control over budgeting has been found to be effective, the budgeted amounts often provide the auditors with very good expected amounts for their analytical procedures.

The issue of classification is most important as between manufacturing overhead costs, on the one hand, and selling, general, and administrative expenses on the other. Manufacturing overhead costs may properly be carried forward as part of inventory cost, whereas the expenses of selling, general, and administrative functions usually are deducted from revenue in the period incurred. Consequently, an error in classification may cause an error in the net income of the period. The auditors' review of the propriety of classification of expenses can be linked conveniently with the comparison of monthly amounts of the various expenses. Comparison of yearly totals is accomplished by inclusion of amounts for the preceding year on the auditors' lead schedules or working trial balance, but this procedure may be supplemented by comparison of expenses on a month-by-month basis.

Comparison of expense (as well as revenue) accounts with industry and nonfinancial data is another means of bringing to light circumstances that require investigation. Unexpected deviations from industry averages should be investigated. Also, unusual relationships between financial and nonfinancial information, such as between production records stated in litres or kilograms and the dollar amounts of sales, should be investigated.

***b*. Determine the amount of difference from the expectation that can be accepted without investigation.**

The auditors use their estimates of materiality to arrive at which differences are to be investigated and which might be expected to occur by chance. However, the extent of the assurance desired from the analytical procedure must also be considered.

c. Compare the company's account balance with the expected account balance.

The expense accounts may be compared to the auditors' expected values developed in (*a*) above. For example, the current year's selling expenses as a percentage of sales may be compared with the percentage for the preceding year, with industry averages, or with budgeted percentages. Significant differences may then be identified. Figure 17–1 illustrates a working paper that compares major income statement categories for the year under audit with the prior year amounts and industry averages.

d. Investigate significant deviations from the expected account balance.

The starting point for investigating significant variations in expenses is enquiry of management. The auditors substantiate management's explanations for significant variations by various means, including analyses of accounts. Analyses of expense accounts involves tracing entries in the accounts back to the voucher register or to the cash disbursements journal. From these accounting records, reference may be made to invoices, receiving reports, purchase orders, or other supporting evidence.

2. Obtain or prepare analyses of selected expense accounts.

As a result of the above procedure, the auditors will have chosen certain expense accounts for further verification. The client should be requested to furnish analyses of the accounts selected, together with related vouchers and other supporting documents, for the auditors' review.

Which expense accounts are most likely to contain misstatements or to indicate other audit problems and are most important for the auditors to analyze? The accounts often analyzed are (1) advertising, (2) research and development, (3) legal expenses and other professional fees, (4) maintenance and repairs, and (5) rents and royalties.

The analyses of legal and other professional fees may disclose legal and audit fees properly chargeable to costs of issuing stock or debt instruments, or to costs of business combinations. Also, the analysis of professional fees expense furnishes the names of lawyers to whom letters should be sent requesting information as to pending litigation and other loss contingencies. Figure 17–2 illustrates an analysis of the professional fees expense account.

3. Obtain or prepare analyses of critical expenses in income tax returns.

Income tax returns generally require schedules for charitable donations, royalties, management fees, and registered pension plan contributions. Accordingly, the auditors should obtain or prepare analyses of any of these expenses that were not analyzed when performing other audit steps. The auditors should bear in mind that details of these expenses will probably be closely scrutinized when Revenue Canada examines the client's tax returns.

FIGURE 17–1

Cheviot Corporation
Comparative Income Statement   R-1-4
Year Ended December 31, 19X3

| | 19X2 | | 19X3 | | Industry Statistics |
	$	%	$	%	%
Sales	548784 – √	100	610740 – √▽	100	100
Cost of Goods Sold	374658 – √	68	403070 – √∅	66	65
Gross Profit	174126 –	32	207670 – ∅	34	35
Selling Expenses	55784 – √	10	85654 – √△	14	15
General and Administrative Expenses	79654 – √	15	87557 – √∅	14	12
Income before Taxes	39008 –	7	34459 – ∅	6	8
Taxes	12873 – √	2	6869 – √✗	1	3
Net Income	26135 –	5	27590 – ∅	5	5

∧ Footed.
√ Agreed to the general ledger.
✗ Agreed to the prior year working papers.

∅ Amount appears reasonable in relation to
    prior year results and industry statistics.
▽ See audit procedures performed on sales, R-1-2.
△ Large increase in selling expenses is due to
    the addition of a salesman to the sales staff.
    Based on a review of the payroll records the
    increase in the account appears reasonable.

✗ Decrease in tax rate is due to the realization of
    several thousand dollars in tax credits. See tax
    accrual working paper, O-3.

Conclusion:
The comparative analysis revealed no unusual
fluctuations that could not be adequately explained.

V.M.H.   Concur: C.M.
Jan. 15, X4   C.M.   Jan. 19, X4

FIGURE 17–2   Analysis of Professional Fees

Cheviot Corporation

Acct. No. 547   Professional Fees Expense   R-3-7

Year Ended December 31, 199X

Date	Reference	Payee	Description	Amount	
Various	Various	Hale & Hale	Monthly retainer for legal services – 12 × $500 v	6,000 –	
Mar 5, 9x	CD 411	Jay & Wall, CAs	Fee for the audit	7,500 –	y
May 2, 9x	CD 602	Hale & Hale	Fee for legal services relating to acquisition of real property adjoining Vancouver plant	3,000 –	y
Sept 13, 9x	CD 1018	Hale & Hale	Fee for legal services relating to modification of instalment sales contract forms.	400 –	y
Dec 31, 9x			Balance per ledger	16,900 –	
Dec 31, 9x	A.J.E. 41		To capitalize May 2, 9x disbursement as part of cost of land X-1	(3,000 –)	
Dec 31, 9x			Adjusted balance	13,900	∧
				R-3	

A.J.E. 41

Land   3,000 –
   Professional Fees   3,000 –
To capitalize legal
fees re obtaining land.

Prepared by client

∧ – Footed and agreed to general ledger balance.
y – Examined billing and copy of client's cheque in payment thereof.

Conclusion:
   Professional fees expense is fairly presented
in the adjusted amount of $13,900.

V.M.H.   J. Agra
Jan 7, 9x   C.M. 9x   C.M.
                  Jan 12, 9x   Jan 12, 9x

THE AUDIT OF PAYROLL

The payroll in many companies is by far the largest operating cost and, therefore, deserves the close attention of the auditors. In the past, payroll frauds were common and often substantial. Today, however, such frauds may be more difficult to conceal for several reasons: (1) extensive subdivision of duties relating to payroll; (2) use of computers, with proper controls, for preparation of payrolls; and (3) necessity of filing frequent reports to the government, listing employees' earnings and tax withholdings.

Internal Control

The establishment of strong internal control over payrolls is particularly important for several reasons. Although payroll frauds are less frequent today, the possibility of large-scale payroll fraud still exists. Such frauds may involve listing fictitious persons on the payroll, overpaying employees, and continuing employees on the payroll after their separation from the company. A second reason for emphasizing internal control over payrolls is that a great mass of detailed information concerning hours worked and rates of pay must be processed quickly and accurately if workers are to be paid promptly and without error. Good employee relations demand that paycheques be ready on time and be free from error. As pointed out in previous chapters, internal control is a means of securing accuracy and dependability in accounting data, as well as a means of preventing fraud.

Still another reason for emphasizing the importance of internal control over payrolls is the existence of various payroll tax laws and income tax laws which require that certain payroll records be maintained and that payroll data be reported to the employee and to governmental agencies.

Methods of Achieving Internal Control

Budgetary Control of Labour Costs.   To control payroll costs means to avoid waste and to obtain the maximum production from the dollars expended for services of employees. As a means of establishing control over payroll costs, many companies delegate to department heads and other supervisors responsibility for the control of costs in their respective units of the business. The supervisor may be requested at the beginning of each year to submit for the budget an estimate of departmental labour costs for the coming period. As the year progresses and actual labour costs are compiled, the controller submits monthly reports to top management comparing the budgeted labour costs and the actual labour costs for each department. The effectiveness of this control device will depend largely upon the extent to which top management utilizes these reports and takes action upon variances from the budget.

Reports to Governmental Agencies.   Another important internal control over payroll lies in the necessity of preparing reports to government agencies showing the earnings and tax deductions for all employees. This type of control is not concerned with holding labour costs to a minimum, but is an effective means of preventing and detecting payroll fraud. In a few cases, falsified reports to government agencies have been prepared as part of a payroll fraud, but this involves such extensive scheming and falsification of records as to make fraud of this type less likely.

Subdivision of Duties.   Most important of all internal controls over payroll is the division of payroll work among several departments of the company. Payroll activities include the functions of employment, timekeeping, payroll preparation and record-keeping, and the distribution of pay to employees. For strong internal control, each of these functions should be handled by a separate department of the company. Combination of these functions in a single department or under the authority of one person opens the door to payroll fraud. These several phases of payroll activities will now be considered individually.

The Employment Function

The first significant step in building strong internal control over payrolls is taken by the personnel department when a new employee is hired. At this point, the authorized rate of pay should be entered on a pay-rate record. The employee also should sign a payroll deduction authorization specifying any amounts to be withheld and a personal tax credit return form (TDI). These records should be kept in the personnel department, but a notice of the hiring of the new employee, the rate of pay, and the payroll deductions should be sent to the payroll department. Notice of employment and of the authorized pay rate also is sent to the head of the department in which the employee is to work.

Under no circumstances is the payroll department justified in adding a name to the payroll without having received the formal authorization notice from the personnel department. When an employee's rate of pay is changed, the new rate will be entered on the pay-rate record that is maintained in the personnel department. An authorization for the new rate must be sent to the payroll department before the change can be made effective on the payroll. Upon the termination of an employee, notice of termination is sent from the personnel department to the payroll department. The work of the payroll department and the propriety of names and pay rates used in preparing the payroll, therefore, rest upon formal documents originating outside the payroll department.

Adequate internal control demands that the addition and removal of names from the company payroll, as well as rate changes and reclassification of employees, be evidenced by written approval of an executive in the personnel department and by the head of the operating department concerned. To permit the payroll department to initiate changes in pay rates, or to add names to the payroll without formal authorization from the personnel department, is to invite payroll fraud.

Timekeeping

The function of timekeeping consists of determining the number of hours (or units of production) for which each employee is to be paid. The use of electronic time-recording equipment is of considerable aid in establishing adequate internal control over the timekeeping function. Reports prepared by timekeepers who travel through the plant and contact an employee only once or twice during the day may be less dependable than time reports prepared by supervisors, whose duties keep them in continuous contact with a small group of employees.

Internal control can be improved by the practice of regular comparison of the time reports prepared by timekeepers or supervisors with time clock records showing arrival and departure times of employees. If pay is based on piecework, a comparison may be made between the reports of units produced and the quantities that are added to the perpetual inventory records.

Salaried employees receiving a fixed monthly or weekly salary may not be required to use time clocks. Some companies require salaried employees to fill out a weekly or semimonthly report indicating the time devoted to various activities. If a salaried employee is absent, the department head usually has authority to decide whether a pay reduction should be made.

Payroll Records and Payroll Preparation

The payroll department has the responsibility of computing the amounts to be paid to employees and of preparing all payroll records. It is imperative that the payroll department should *not* perform the related functions of timekeeping, employment, or distribution of pay to employees. The output of the payroll department may be thought of as (1) the payroll cheques (or pay envelopes, if wages are paid in cash); (2) individual employee statements of earnings and deductions; (3) a payroll journal; (4) an employees' ledger, summarizing earnings and deductions for each employee; (5) a payroll distribution schedule, showing the allocation of payroll costs to direct labour, overhead, and various departmental expense accounts; and (6) regular reports to the government showing employees' earnings and taxes withheld. If the client utilizes an electronic data processing installation, many of these functions may be delegated to the data processing department.

The payroll department computes the payroll using the work hours reported by the timekeeping department, and the authorized pay rates and payroll deductions reported by the personnel department. In addition to preparing the payroll journal, the payroll department prepares the payroll cheques or the pay envelopes, if wages are paid in cash. Cheques are then forwarded to the treasurer for signature.

The auditors may find payroll records and procedures varying in complexity from a manual "write it once" system to the most sophisticated computerized techniques. In addition, pay is sometimes deposited directly into employee bank accounts. Regardless of the system used, however, the auditors should expect the client's system to include such basic records as timecards, payroll journals, labour distributions, and employee earnings records.

Distributing Paycheques or Cash to Employees

The distribution of paycheques or pay envelopes to employees should be the task of the paymaster, an individual who performs no other payroll activity, and *not to the employees' supervisors.* If employees are paid in cash, the paymaster will use a copy of the payroll journal and the information on the payroll envelopes (both prepared by the payroll department) to fill the payroll envelopes with cash.

The paymaster will require proof of identity when distributing cheques or cash to employees, and require them to sign a receipt for any cash received. A cheque or pay envelope for an absent employee should be retained and neither returned to the payroll department nor turned over to another employee for delivery.

Most companies that pay employees by cheque use a special payroll bank account. A voucher for the entire amount of the weekly payroll may be prepared in the general accounting department based on the payroll summary prepared in the payroll department. This voucher is sent to the treasurer, who issues a cheque on the general bank account for the amount of the payroll. The cheque is deposited in the special payroll bank account, and cheques to individual employees are drawn on this bank account. It also is the practice of some companies to have printed on the cheque a statement that this type of cheque is not valid if issued for an amount in excess of a specified dollar amount.

If wages are paid in cash, any unclaimed wages should be deposited in the bank and credited to a special liability account. Subsequent disbursement of these funds to employees then will be controlled by the necessity of drawing a cheque and preparing supporting documents. The dangers inherent in permitting unclaimed pay envelopes to be retained by the paymaster, returned to the payroll clerk, or intermingled with petty cash are apparent.

Description of Internal Control for Payroll

Typical of the questions to be answered by the auditors for the completion of an internal control questionnaire, a systems flowchart, or other record of payroll internal controls are the following: Are employees paid by cheque? Is a payroll bank account maintained on an imprest basis? Are the activities of timekeeping, payroll compilation, payroll cheque signing, and paycheque distribution performed by separate departments or employees? Are all operations involved in the preparation of payrolls subjected to independent verification before the paycheques are distributed? Are employee time reports approved by supervisors? Is the payroll bank account reconciled monthly by an employee having no other payroll duties?

Audit Program for Payrolls

The following audit procedures are representative of the work generally completed to establish the propriety of payments for salaries, wages, bonuses, and commissions:

1. Obtain an understanding of the internal control for payrolls.
2. Perform tests of controls over payroll transactions for selected pay periods, including the following specific procedures:
    a. Trace names and wage or salary rates to records maintained by the personnel department.
    b. Trace time shown on payroll to timecards and time reports approved by supervisors.
    c. If payroll is based on piecework rates rather than hourly rates, reconcile earnings with production records.
    d. Determine basis of deductions from payroll and compare with records of deductions authorized by employees.
    e. Test extensions and footings of payroll.
    f. Compare total of payroll with total of payroll cheques issued.
    g. Compare total of payroll with total of labour cost summary prepared by cost accounting department.
    h. If wages are paid in cash, compare receipts obtained from employees with payroll records.
    i. If wages are paid by cheque, compare paid cheques with payroll and compare endorsements to signatures on personal tax credit returns.

3. Observe the use of time clocks by employees reporting for work, and investigate timecards not used.
4. Plan a surprise observation of one of the pay distributions, including control of payroll records and an accounting for all employees listed.
5. Perform analytical procedures to test the reasonableness of payroll expense (e.g., develop an expectation about the amount of payroll expense by multiplying the amount of one pay period by the number of pay periods in the year).
6. Obtain or prepare a summary of compensation of officers for the year and trace to contracts, minutes of directors' meetings, or other authorization.
7. Investigate any extraordinary fluctuations in salaries, wages, and commissions.
8. Test computations of compensation earned under profit-sharing plans.
9. Test commission earnings by examination of contracts and detailed supporting records.
10. Test pension payments by reference to authorized pension plans and to supporting records.

The fourth procedure in the above list, calling for the auditors to plan a surprise observation of a regular distribution of pay to employees, deserves special consideration. The auditors' objective in observing the distribution of cheques or cash to employees on a regular payday is to determine that every name on the company payroll is that of a bona fide employee presently on the job. This audit procedure is desirable if the various phases of payroll work are not sufficiently segregated by departments to afford good internal control. The history of payroll frauds shows that permitting one person to have custody of employment records, timecards, paycheques, and employees' earnings records has often led to the entering of fictitious names on the payroll, and to other irregularities, such as use of excessive pay rates and continuance of pay after the termination of an employee.

The auditors first will determine that they have possession of all the cheques or envelopes comprising the payroll. They will then accompany representatives of the client around the plant as all the cheques or envelopes are distributed to employees. The whole procedure will be meaningless unless the auditors establish the identity of each employee receiving payment.

INCOME STATEMENT PRESENTATION

How Much Detail in the Income Statement?

One of the more interesting problems of statement presentation of revenue and expenses is the question of how much detailed operating information may be disclosed without causing the income statement to become unreasonably long and complex. As a minimum, the income statement should show the sales revenue, income from investments, government assistance credited directly to income, and amortization expenses (such as depreciation, depletion), interest expense, cost of goods sold, selling expenses, general and administrative expenses, income taxes, discontinued operations, extraordinary items, net income, and earnings per share. However, the auditors should ensure that the income statement is presented in accordance with the disclosure requirements of Section 1520 of the *CICA Handbook* and the relevant corporation laws.

Reporting Earnings per Share

After the net income figure, per share figures should be reported for income before discontinued operations and extraordinary items, and for net income. The computations should be based on the weighted-average number of common shares outstanding during the year. In addition to these basic earnings per share, companies with a complex capital structure may be required to report *fully diluted* earnings per share. The auditors should ensure, as a minimum, that the earnings per share presentation is in accordance with Section 3500 of the *CICA Handbook*.

Reporting by Diversified Companies

The business combination movement in recent years has created many large conglomerate corporations by bringing together companies in quite unrelated industries. Although the word *conglomerate* is usually applied to a large family of corporations created by business combinations, other companies have achieved the same degree of diversification among unrelated industries through internal development and expansion. The term *diversified company* is therefore more appropriate for our use in considering the special financial reporting problems created by the emergence of this new type of business entity.

For the diversified company carrying on operations in several unrelated industries, we may well question whether the traditional form of income statement constitutes a fair presentation. Would the income statement be more useful to financial analysts and others if it showed separately the revenue and operating results of the various industry segments comprising the diversified company? In the past an investor or financial analyst easily could associate a given corporation with a specific industry. Since this is hardly possible for many large, diversified companies, a worthwhile analysis of the income statement may require disclosure of profitability of the several industry segments.

Accordingly, Section 1700 of the *CICA Handbook* recommends that an enterprise whose securities are traded in a public market or which is required to file financial statements annually with a securities commission should disclose segmented information. Such segmented information includes the disclosure of the enterprises's total operations by industry and by geographic area, as well as the amount of export sales. The auditors should ensure that the segmented information is fairly presented in accordance with the standards specified in this section of the *Handbook*. As presented in Chapter 4, Regulation 47 of the Canada Business Corporations Act provides certain guidelines for segmented reporting. It should be noted, however, that the *CICA Handbook* standards override these regulation guidelines.

Similarly, the Financial Accounting Standards Board in the United States requires companies with shares owned by the public to include certain business segment information in their annual financial statements. This disclosure includes information concerning the company's operations in different industries, its foreign operations, and its sales to major customers. Since the information is required for fair presentation of the financial statements in conformity with generally accepted accounting principles, it must be audited to provide a basis for an unqualified opinion of the financial statements. Accordingly, the AICPA's *SAS 21* (AU 435), "Segment Information," states that the auditors should perform the following procedures related to the business segment information:

1. Evaluate the reasonableness of management's methods of compiling the information.
2. Consider whether the information is presented in sufficient detail; apply analytical procedures to test its reasonableness.
3. Evaluate the reasonableness of methods used in allocating operating expenses among segments.

Examination of the Statement of Changes in Financial Position

The statement of changes in financial position is prepared from other financial statements and from analyses of increases and decreases in selected account balances. The amounts included in this statement are audited in conjunction with the audit of balance sheet and income statement accounts. Thus, limited substantive testing is necessary. The auditors merely trace the amounts included in the statement of changes in financial position to other financial statement balances and amounts included in audit working papers.

Since cash flows must be classified in the statement of changes in financial position as to whether they are from operating, investing, or financing activities, the presentation and disclosure audit objective is especially important. The auditors must determine that the concept of cash or cash and cash equivalents analyzed in the statement agrees with an amount shown on the balance sheet.

COMPLETING THE AUDIT

The remainder of this chapter will review the audit procedures and other considerations involved in completing the audit engagement. These procedures and judgments are completed on, or near, the date of the audit report, and they are important in determining the nature and content of the auditors' opinion.

Audit Procedures

The auditors' opinion on the client's financial statements is based on all evidence gathered by the auditors up to the date of the audit report, and any information that *comes to their attention* after that date. To be effective, certain audit procedures described in previous chapters cannot be completed before the end of the audit. Among the procedures that must be performed at, or near, the date of the audit report are the following.

Obtain the Lawyer's Letter.　The letter of enquiry from the client's legal counsel must be obtained near the end of the audit and should bear the same date as the audit report. As discussed in Chapter 16, the purpose of the lawyer's enquiry letter is to obtain information regarding pending or threatened litigation against the client. The lawyer's assessment of the probable outcome of significant litigation is important to the auditors' evaluation of the financial statement presentation of contingent liabilities.

Obtain the Representations Letter.　Chapter 6 included a general description of the letter of representations that the auditors must obtain from management. The primary purpose of the representations letter is to have the client's principal officers acknowledge that they are primarily responsible for the fairness of the financial statements. Since the financial statements must reflect all material subsequent events, the representations letter should bear the same date as the audit report.

Perform Other Procedures to Identify Subsequent Events.　Other audit procedures that are designed to identify significant subsequent events also must be completed near the end of the engagement. These audit procedures (described in Chapter 6) include review of the minutes of meetings of the shareholders and of the board of directors, enquiry of client officers, and review of interim accounting records and financial statements.

Perform Overall Review Using Analytical Procedures.　The discussion of analytical procedures in Chapter 6 pointed out that they must be performed in planning as well as for overall review purposes at the completion of the audit. Analytical procedures performed as a part of the overall review assist the auditors in assessing the validity of the conclusions reached, including the opinion to be issued. This overall review may identify areas that need to be examined further as well as provide a consideration of the adequacy of data gathered in response to usual or unexpected relationships identified during the audit.

Complete the Search for Unrecorded Liabilities. As discussed in Chapter 16, the search for unrecorded liabilities includes procedures performed through the date of the audit report.

Review the Working Papers. The work of the audit staff should be reviewed to ensure that it was adequately performed and that the results are consistent with the conclusions to be presented in the audit report. This review of the work of the audit staff is primarily accomplished through a review of the audit working papers. The seniors on audit engagements typically perform their review of the audit working papers as the papers are completed. While audit partners and managers will generally communicate with seniors and other staff members throughout the audit, their review of the working papers generally is performed at or near the end of the audit. The audit partner and manager will devote special attention to those accounts that have a higher risk of material misstatement, such as the significant accounting estimates of inventory obsolescence and warranty obligations. If a second partner review is required by the public accounting firm's quality control policies, this review is usually performed just prior to issuance of the audit report.

Review the Financial Statement Disclosures. The recent proliferation of accounting standards makes it difficult for the auditors to evaluate the adequacy of financial statement disclosures. It is not effective to rely on the auditors' memories to evaluate the adequacy of disclosures, and it is not efficient for them to research the required disclosures each time they review a set of financial statements. Thus, many public accounting firms have developed *disclosure checklists* that list all specific disclosures required by the *CICA Handbook* and the securities and corporation legislation. The auditors complete the checklist as a part of their review of the completed financial statements.

Evaluating Audit Findings

Throughout the course of the audit, the auditors will propose adjusting entries for all *material misstatements* (errors, fraud, and irregularities) that are discovered in the client's financial records. Any *material* misstatement that the auditors find must be corrected; otherwise, the auditors cannot issue an unqualified opinion on the financial statements. In evaluating whether an individual misstatement is material, the auditors consider both quantitative and qualitative factors. For example, a $10,000 related party transaction might be considered material for a particular audit, whereas a misstatement of trade accounts receivable of the same amount would not be considered material. Immaterial misstatements that are discovered by the auditors are accumulated on a working paper with a title such as "Adjusting Entries Passed."

To issue an unqualified opinion, the auditors must conclude that there is a low level of risk of material misstatement of the financial statements. In evaluating this risk the auditors develop an estimate of the *total likely misstatement* of the financial statements, which is made up of the following three components.

1. *Known misstatements* include those that the client has not corrected because they are individually immaterial. These individually immaterial misstatements could be material on a combined basis.
2. *Projected misstatements* are those that are calculated when the auditors employ audit sampling, as described in Chapter 9. For example, if the book value of accounts receivables is $6,250,000 and the auditors, using audit sampling, estimate the audited value to be $6,100,000, the projected misstatement would be the difference of $150,000. However, it should be noted that this projected misstatement includes the amount of known misstatement used to calculate it.
3. *Other estimated misstatements* are those estimated by techniques other than audit sampling, like analytical procedures. One significant source of these estimated misstatements is differences related to accounting estimates, such as inventory obsolescence, uncollectible receivables, and product warranty obligations. For these items, the estimated misstatement is the difference between the client's estimate and the closest amount that the auditors consider to be reasonable. An example would be a situation in which the management estimates the company's product warranty liability to be $100,000 and the auditors develop an estimate of between $120,000 and $140,000 for the account. The estimated misstatement is $20,000 ($120,000 − $100,000).

Obviously, if the auditors estimate that the total likely misstatement is material to the financial statements, they would conclude that the risk of material misstatement is too high to issue an unqualified opinion on the financial statements. Even if the total likely misstatement in the financial statements is estimated to be somewhat less than a material amount, the auditors, recognizing that the actual misstatement might be greater than their estimate, might still conclude that the risk of material misstatement of the financial statements is too high. If so, the auditors will ask management to adjust the financial statements for the known misstatements, or they will perform additional audit procedures to further reduce detection risk. The auditors should never issue an unqualified opinion on financial statements in which the risk of material misstatement is considered to be excessive.

The auditors will conclude that the risk of material misstatement is sufficiently low to issue an unqualified opinion only when *total likely misstatement is significantly less than a material amount.* The relationship between total likely misstatement and materiality is often documented in a working paper similar to Figure 17–3. As illustrated, the auditors must consider the effects of the likely misstatements on the various components of the financial statements, such as current assets and net income. As we have emphasized throughout the textbook, whether an amount is material depends on its specific effects on the financial statements.

Responsibility for Information in the Annual Report

Audit reports on the financial statements of large enterprises usually are included in an annual report to the shareholders. Such an annual report includes a multitude of *other information* in addition to audited financial statements and the audit report. The auditors should (1) determine whether the audited financial statements and the audit report are *accurately reproduced* in the annual report, and (2) read the other information in the annual report and consider whether any of this information is *inconsistent* with the audited financial statements.[1] In most cases, any error in the reproduction of the audited financial statements and the audit report as well as any inconsistency in the other information will be satisfactorily resolved between the auditors and management of the enterprise.

However, when an inconsistency is a result of an error in the audited financial statements and management refuses to correct the error, the auditors should express a reservation in their report. On the other hand, when an inconsistency requires a revision in the other information in the annual report and management refuses to make such a revision, the auditors should formally notify the board of directors of the situation and consider any further action.

When the auditors discover a material misstatement of fact in the other information in the annual report, they should discuss this matter with management, including the board of directors and its audit committee. If management refuses to take any corrective action, the auditors should formally notify the board of directors and consider any further actions.[2]

---

[1] CICA, *CICA Handbook* (Toronto), Sections 7500.19 and .13.

[2] Ibid., Section 7500.20.

FIGURE 17-3

Earthmade Products, Inc.

Accumulated Likely Misstatement

December 31, 199X

W/P REF.		Financial Statement Effects					
		Current Assets	Total Assets	Current Liabilities	Total Liabilities	Stockholders' Equity	Net Income
	Uncorrected Known Misstatements:						
D-8	Error in prepaid expenses	(6,500)	(6,500)			(6,500)	(6,500)
F-6	Error in prior years depreciation		10,200			10,200	
M-4	Unrecorded liabilities			11,215	11,215	(11,215)	(11,215)
	Projected Misstatements:						
C-5	Accounts receivable confirmation	(30,000)	(30,000)			(30,000)	(30,000)
	Other estimated Misstatements:						
C-10	Allowance for uncollectible accounts	(5,000)	(5,000)			(5,000)	(5,000)
	Total Likely Misstatements	(41,500)	(31,500)	(11,215)	(11,215)	(42,714)	(52,715)
	Amount of a material misstatement	100,000	150,000	100,000	150,000	250,000	100,000

Conclusion:
Total likely misstatement is low enough in relation to the amounts considered to be material misstatements.

KEY TERMS

analytical procedures Evaluations of financial information made by a study of plausible relationships between financial and nonfinancial information.

basic earnings per share A presentation of earnings per share based on outstanding common shares and those securities that are in substance equivalent to common shares.

conservatism An accounting doctrine for asset valuation in which the lower of two alternative acceptable asset valuations is chosen.

disclosure checklist A list of specific disclosures required by the *CICA Handbook* and securities and corporation legislation that are used to evaluate the adequacy of the disclosures in a set of financial statements.

fully diluted earnings per share A pro forma presentation that reflects the dilution of earnings per share that would have occurred if all contingent issuances of common stock that individually would reduce earnings per share had taken place at the beginning of the period.

likely misstatements in the financial statements Misstatements in the financial statements that are estimated by the auditors based on the results of audit procedures. For example, the projected misstatement from an audit sample is an estimate of the likely misstatement in the audit population.

segment A component of an entity whose activities represent a separate major line of business or class of customer.

GROUP I: REVIEW QUESTIONS

17–1. Identify three revenue accounts that are verified during the audit of balance sheet accounts; also, identify the related balance sheet accounts.

17–2. Identify three expense accounts that are verified during the audit of balance sheet accounts; also, identify the related balance sheet accounts.

17–3. How are analytical procedures used in the verification of revenue?

17–4. Identify three items often misclassified as miscellaneous revenue.

17–5. For which expense accounts should the auditors obtain or prepare analyses to be used in preparation of the client's income tax returns?

17–6. When you are first retained to examine the financial statements of Wabash Company, you enquire whether a budget is used to control costs and expenses. The controller, James Lowe, replies that he personally prepares such a budget each year, but that he regards it as a highly confidential document. He states that you may refer to it if necessary, but he wants you to make sure that no employee of the firm sees any of the budget data. Comment on this use of a budget.

17–7.   What division of duties among independent departments is desirable to achieve maximum internal control over payrolls?

17–8.   What specific procedures are suggested by the phrase "test of controls over payroll transactions"?

17–9.   What safeguards should be employed when the inaccessibility of banking facilities makes it desirable to pay employees in cash?

17–10. You are asked by a client to outline the procedures you would recommend for disposing of unclaimed wages. What procedures do you recommend?

17–11. Why does the auditors' examination of the statement of changes in financial position usually not involve substantiation of the statement amounts?

17–12. What auditing procedure can you suggest for determining the reasonableness of selling, general, and administrative expenses?

17–13. Describe how the auditors use analytical procedures in the examination of selling, general, and administrative expenses.

17–14. What standards did the CICA recommend for disclosures of operating details on the income statements of diversified companies?

17–15. How should the auditors advise the client to present discontinued operations in the income statement?

17–16. List the audit procedures that must be completed near the end of audit (the date of the audit report).

17–17. Describe a disclosure checklist. What is its purpose?

17–18. During an initial audit, you observe that the client is not complying with government regulations concerning wages and hours. Would you (*a*) report the violation to regulatory authorities, (*b*) discuss the matter with the client, (*c*) ignore the matter completely, (*d*) withdraw from the engagement, or (*e*) follow some other course of action? Explain.

17–19. Describe the manner in which the auditors evaluate their audit findings.

17–20. What is the auditors' obligation with respect to information in client-prepared annual reports to shareholders, other than the audit report and the audited financial statements?

GROUP II: QUESTIONS REQUIRING ANALYSIS

17–21. In a properly planned examination of financial statements, the auditors coordinate their reviews of specific balance sheet and income statement accounts.

Required:
Why should the auditors coordinate their examinations of balance sheet accounts and income statement accounts? Discuss and illustrate by examples.

(AICPA, adapted)

17–22. Your new audit client, Coin-O-Mat Company, leases coin-operated laundry equipment to military bases. Usage of the equipment requires the insertion of coins into metered receptacles, which record expired time of equipment operation. How can you determine whether all revenue earned by Coin-O-Mat Company has been recorded in the accounting records?

17–23. In your first examination of the financial statements of Willman Company, you discover that the company has included in the miscellaneous revenue account a $10,000 commission from Bradley Realtors, Inc. Your investigation discloses that Bradley negotiated Willman's purchase for $500,000 of a tract of land from Payne Company, and that Payne had paid Bradley's commission of $50,000 on the sale.

Required:
Would you take exception to Willman Company's accounting for the commission received from Bradley Realtors, Inc.? Explain.

17–24. During your regular audit of Payton Company, you discover that the company signed a 10-year lease on a building at the beginning of the company's fiscal year. The lease, which is an operating lease, requires monthly rental payments of $1,000 per month for the last nine years of the lease only. Nancy James, controller of Payton Company, explains that the lessor waived the first year's rent because the building had remained vacant for a long period. James states that, in her view, Payton Company had incurred no rent expense for the fiscal year your audit covers. Do you agree? Explain.

17–25. Bowden Company owed property taxes of $5,972. Through error, Morton Bryant, who served the company as office manager, cashier, and accountant, paid the tax bill twice. Realizing his error after having mailed the second cheque, he wrote to the county officials requesting a refund.

When the refund was received some weeks later, Bryant substituted the cheque from the city for cash receipts and abstracted $5,972 in currency.

Would this error and theft probably be discovered in an audit by independent public accountants? Indicate what auditing procedure, if any, would disclose the facts.

17–26. Barton Limited is a highly diversified public company with segments that manufacture and sell antibiotics, dairy products, hospital supplies, toiletries, and chemicals. In what form should the income statement of Barton Limited be prepared?

17–27. Select the best answer for each of the following, and explain fully the reason for your selection.

a. As a result of analytical procedures, the auditors determine that the gross profit percentage has declined from 30 percent in the preceding year to 20 percent in the current year. The auditors should
   (1) Express an opinion that is qualified due to the inability of the client company to continue as a going concern.
   (2) Evaluate management's performance in causing this decline.
   (3) Require footnote disclosure.
   (4) Consider the possibility of a misstatement in the financial statements.

b. Which of the following is the *best* way for the auditors to determine that every name on a company's payroll is that of a bona fide employee presently on the job?
   (1) Examine personnel records for accuracy and completeness.
   (2) Examine employees' names listed on payroll tax returns for agreement with payroll accounting records.
   (3) Make a surprise observation of the company's regular distribution of paycheques.
   (4) Visit the working areas and confirm with employees their badge or identification numbers.

c. Which of the following *best* describes the auditors' approach to obtaining satisfaction concerning depreciation expense in the income statement?
   (1) Verify the mathematical accuracy of the amounts charged to income as a result of depreciation expense.
   (2) Determine the method for computing depreciation expense and ascertain that it is in accordance with generally accepted accounting principles.
   (3) Reconcile the amount of depreciation expense to those amounts credited to accumulated depreciation accounts.
   (4) Establish the basis for depreciable assets and verify the depreciation expense.

d. Proper internal control over payroll paid in cash would mandate which of the following?
   (1) The payroll clerk should fill the envelopes with cash and a computation of the net wages.
   (2) Unclaimed pay envelopes should be retained by the paymaster.
   (3) Each employee should be asked to sign a receipt.
   (4) A separate bank account for payroll should be maintained.

  e. The auditor's performance of analytical procedures will be facilitated if the client:

   (1) Uses a standard cost system that produces variance reports.

   (2) Segregates obsolete inventory before the physical inventory count.

   (3) Corrects material weaknesses in internal control before the beginning of the audit.

   (4) Reduces inventory balances to the lower of cost and market.

  f. An auditor accepted an engagement to audit the December 31, 19X8 financial statements of EFG Corporation and began the audit work on September 30, 19X8. EFG gave the auditor the 19X8 financial statements on January 17, 19X9. The auditor completed the audit work on February 10, 19X9, and delivered the report on February 16, 19X9. The client's representations letter normally would be dated:

   (1) December 31, 19X8.

   (2) January 17, 19X9.

   (3) February 10, 19X9.

   (4) February 16, 19X9.

                 (AICPA, adapted)

GROUP III: PROBLEMS

17–28. The following are typical questions that might appear on an internal control questionnaire for payroll procedures:

  1. Is there adequate separation of duties between employees who maintain personnel records and employees who approve payroll disbursements?

  2. Is there adequate separation of duties between personnel who maintain timekeeping or attendance records for employees and personnel who distribute payroll cheques?

Required:

 a. Describe the purpose of each of the above internal control procedures.

 b. Describe the manner in which each of the above procedures might be tested.

 c. Assuming that the operating effectiveness of each of the above procedures is found to be inadequate, describe how the auditors might alter their substantive tests to compensate for the increased level of control risk.

17–29. In connection with an examination of the financial statements of Olympia Company, the auditors are reviewing procedures for accumulating direct labour-hours. They learn that all production is by job order and that all employees are paid hourly wages, with time and a half for overtime hours.

Olympia's direct labour-hour input process for payroll and job-cost determination is summarized in the flowchart shown below. Steps A and C are performed in timekeeping, Step B in the factory operating departments, Step D in payroll audit and control, Step E in data preparation (keypunch), and Step F in computer operations.

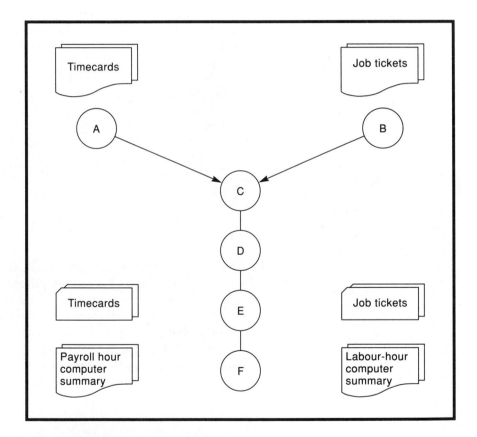

Required:

For each input processing Step A through F:

a. List the possible errors or discrepancies that may occur.

b. Cite the corresponding control procedure that should be in effect for each error or discrepancy.

Note: Your discussion of Olympia's procedures should be limited to the input for direct labour-hours, as shown in Steps A through F in the flowchart. Do not discuss personnel procedures for hiring, promotion, termination, and pay-rate authorization. In Step F, do not discuss equipment, computer program, and general computer operational controls.

Organize your answer for each input-processing step as follows:

Step	Possible Errors or Discrepancies	Control Procedures
A		

(AICPA, adapted)

17–30. Rita King, your staff assistant on the April 30, 19X2, audit of Maxwell Company, was transferred to another assignment before she could prepare a proposed adjusting journal entry for Maxwell's Miscellaneous Revenue account, which she had analyzed per the working paper on page 734. You have reviewed the working paper and are satisfied with King's procedures. You are convinced that all the Miscellaneous Revenue items should be transferred to other accounts.

Required:

Draft a proposed adjusting journal entry at April 30, 19X2, for Maxwell Company's Miscellaneous Revenue account.

17–31. Rowe Manufacturing Company has about 50 production employees and uses the following payroll procedures.

The factory supervisor interviews applicants and on the basis of the interview either hires or rejects the applicants. After being employed, the applicant prepares a personal tax credit return (TDI) and gives it to the supervisor. The supervisor writes the hourly rate of pay for the new employee in the corner of the TDI and then gives it to a payroll clerk as notice that the applicant has been employed. The supervisor verbally advises the payroll department of pay rate adjustments.

A supply of blank timecards is kept in a box near the entrance to the factory. Each employee takes a timecard on Monday morning, signs it, and notes in pencil on the timecard the daily arrival and departure times. At the end of the week, the employees drop the timecards in a box near the door to the factory.

The completed timecards are taken from the box on Monday morning by a payroll clerk. Two payroll clerks divide the cards alphabetically between them, one taking the A to L section of the

Maxwell Company

Acctg. No. 430   Miscellaneous Revenue   O-2

Year Ended April 30, 19X2

C.H. May 19, X2

Date	Description	Reference	Amount	
May 8, X1 through April 7, X2	Proceeds of sale of scrap from manufacturing process (total of 12 monthly sales).	Various CR	5843	✓
July 18, X1	Write-off of old outstanding cheques nos. 118-$500; 214-$400; 407-$200	G.J. 7-4	1100	✓
Sept. 22, X1	Recovery of previously written-off account receivable from Wilson Company.	C.R. 9-1	4381	✓
Feb. 6, X2	Cash proceeds from sale of machine. Cost of $10,000 and accumulated depreciation of $8,000 as of Feb. 6, X2 not removed from accounts.	C.R. 2-1	3500	✓
April 28, X2	Refund of premium overcharge on fire insurance policy no. 1856, for period April 1, X2 - Mar. 31, X3	C.R. 4-1	600	✓
April 30, X2	Balance per ledger		15424	

✓ - Traced to cash receipts journal or general journal; vouched to appropriate supporting documents.

R. A. K.
May 15, X2

payroll, and the other taking the M to Z section. Each clerk is fully responsible for one section of the payroll. The payroll clerks compute the gross pay, deductions, and net pay; post the details to the employees' earnings records; and prepare and number the payroll cheques. Employees are automatically removed from the payroll when they fail to turn in a timecard.

The payroll cheques are manually signed by the chief accountant and given to the supervisor, who distributes the cheques to the employees in the factory and arranges for the delivery of the cheques to the employees who are absent. The payroll bank account is reconciled by the chief accountant, who also prepares the various payroll tax reports.

Required:
List your suggestions for improving Rowe Manufacturing Company's internal control for factory hiring practices *and* payroll procedures.

(AICPA, adapted)

17–32. Your client owns and operates a shopping centre with 30 store tenants. All leases with the store tenants provide for a fixed rent plus a percentage of sales, net of sales taxes, in excess of a fixed dollar amount computed on an annual basis. Each lease also provides that the lessor may engage CAs to audit all records of the tenant for assurance that sales are being properly reported to the lessor.

You have been requested by your client to audit the records of Traders Restaurant to determine that the sales totaling $390,000 for the year ended December 31, 19X2 have been properly reported to the lessor. The restaurant and the shopping centre entered into a five-year lease on January 1, 19X1. Traders Restaurant offers only table service; no liquor is served. During meal times there are four or five waitresses in attendance, who prepare handwritten prenumbered restaurant cheques for the customers. Payment is made at a cash register, operated by the proprietor, as the customer leaves. All sales are for cash. The proprietor also is the accountant. Complete files are kept of restaurant cheques and cash register tapes. A daily journal and general ledger are also maintained.

Required:
List the auditing procedures that you would employ to verify the total annual sales of Traders Restaurant.

(AICPA, adapted)

17–33. City Loan Limited has 100 branch loan offices. Each office has a manager and four or five employees who are hired by the manager. Branch managers prepare the weekly payroll, including their own salaries, and pay employees from cash on hand. The employees sign the payroll sheet signifying receipt of their salary. Hours worked by hourly personnel are inserted in the payroll sheet from time reports prepared by the employees and approved by the manager.

The weekly payroll sheets are sent to the home office, along with other accounting statements and reports. The home office compiles employee earnings records and prepares all payroll tax returns from the weekly payroll sheets.

Salaries are established by home office job-evaluation schedules. Salary adjustments, promotions, and transfers of full-time employees are approved by a home office salary committee based upon the recommendations of branch managers and area supervisors. Branch managers advise the salary committee of new full-time employees and terminations. Part-time and temporary employees are hired without referral to the salary committee.

Required:

a. How might funds for payroll be diverted in the above system?

b. Prepare a payroll internal audit program to be used in the home office to audit the branch office payrolls of City Loan Limited.

(AICPA, adapted)

Chapter 18

Auditors' Reports

Chapter Objectives

After studying this chapter, you should be able to:

- Describe the auditors' standard report.
- Discuss how materiality affects the consideration of the type of audit report to be issued.
- Identify the circumstances that may result in a qualified opinion, an adverse opinion, and a denial of opinion.

Expressing an independent and expert opinion on the fairness of financial statements is the most important and valuable service rendered by the public accounting profession. The third reporting standard states:

> The [auditors'] report should contain either an expression of opinion on the financial statements or an assertion that an opinion cannot be expressed. In the latter case, the reasons therefor should be stated.

In Chapter 2, we saw that the auditors' standard report meets this standard (*a*) by stating that the audit was performed in accordance with generally accepted auditing standards and (*b*) by expressing an opinion that the client's financial statements are presented fairly in accordance with generally accepted accounting principles. However, if the client's financial statements are affected by a departure from generally accepted accounting principles or a scope limitation in the audit, auditors ***cannot*** issue the standard report. Instead, they must carefully modify their report to make these problems known to users of the audited financial statements.

In this chapter, we shall discuss the different types of reports that auditors may issue in order to indicate clearly the character of their examination and the degree of responsibility they are taking for the client's financial statements.

Financial Statements

The reporting phase of an auditing engagement begins when the auditors have substantially completed their examination.[1] Before writing their report, the auditors must review the client-prepared financial statements for form and content, or draft the financial statements on behalf of the client.

The financial statements on which the auditors customarily report are the balance sheet, the income statement, the statement of retained earnings, and the statement of changes in financial position. Financial statements generally are presented in comparative form for the current year and the preceding year and are accompanied by explanatory notes. The financial statements for a parent corporation usually are consolidated with those of the subsidiaries.

Financial Statement Disclosures

The purpose of notes to financial statements is to achieve adequate disclosure when information in the financial statements proper is insufficient to attain this objective. Although the notes, like the financial statements themselves, are representations of the client, the auditors generally assist in drafting the notes. The writing of notes to financial statements is a challenging task because complex issues must be summarized in a clear and concise manner. Adequate disclosure in the notes to the financial statements is necessary for the auditors to issue an unqualified opinion on the financial statements.

The types of information provided in notes to financial statements may be classified into the following broad categories:

1. Financial Data.   These data are included as notes either to simplify the structure of the financial statements or to clarify certain items in the financial statements—for example, details of certain assets and liabilities such as long-term investments and long-term debts, segmented information, and lawsuits or possible judgments against the company.

---

[1] The term *substantially completed* or *substantial completion* has a technical meaning and is defined in Section 5405.03 of the *CICA Handbook*. It will be discussed in detail in the section on dating the report.

2. Accounting Information. This area deals essentially with accounting matters such as explanations of the accounting principles used and changes therein, and with the existence of commitments—for example, disclosure of accounting policies such as the bases for consolidation and inventory valuation, and disclosure on commitment regarding assets pledged or liabilities secured, and restrictions on declaration of dividends.

3. Other Matters. This category includes information and explanations which do not directly affect the financial statements but which may be essential for a proper understanding of the future prospects of the company—for example, events subsequent to the balance sheet date or differences between Canadian and U.S. accounting principles.

Much of the information included in notes to financial statements is required by the *CICA Handbook* recommendations and the various corporations and securities acts. The following listing represents a few of the most common requirements:

1. Significant accounting policies, such as principles of consolidation and the basis for valuation of assets.
2. Changes in accounting principle and practice.
3. Significant events between the date of the financial statements and the date of the auditors' report.
4. Segmented information.
5. Related party transactions.

In drafting financial reporting disclosures, the auditors should keep in mind that disclosures are meant to supplement the information in the financial statements and not to *correct* improper financial statement presentation. Thus, a note or supplementary schedule, no matter how skillfully drafted, does not compensate for the erroneous presentation of an item in the financial statements.

The Auditors' Standard Report

For convenient reference, the auditors' standard (unqualified) report, which was introduced and discussed in Chapter 2, is presented again:

Auditors' Report

To the Shareholders of XYZ Limited

We have audited the balance sheet of XYZ Limited as at December 31, 19— and the statements of income, retained earnings, and changes in financial position for the year then ended. These financial statements are the responsibility of the company's management. Our responsibility is to express an opinion on these financial statements based on our audit.

We conducted our audit in accordance with generally accepted auditing standards. Those standards require that we plan and perform an audit to obtain reasonable assurance whether the financial statements are free of material misstatement. An audit includes examining, on a test basis, evidence supporting the amounts and disclosures in the financial statements. An audit also includes assessing the accounting principles used and significant estimates made by management, as well as evaluating the overall financial statement presentation.

In our opinion, these financial statements present fairly, in all material respects, the financial position of the company as at December 31, 19— and the results of its operations and the changes in its financial position for the year then ended in accordance with generally accepted accounting principles.

Windsor, Ontario
February 26, 19XX

Blue, Gray + Company
Chartered Accountants

Before continuing, let us mention a few details about this report. Recall that it was adopted in 1990 by the Auditing Standards Board. Unlike the previous standard report, it has three, rather than two, paragraphs. The first paragraph is referred to as the ***introductory paragraph.*** It clearly indicates that (1) the financial statements identified in the report have been audited, (2) the financial statements are the responsibility of management, and (3) the auditors' responsibility is to express an opinion on them. The second paragraph, which describes the nature of an audit, is called the ***scope paragraph.*** Finally, the ***opinion paragraph*** presents the auditors' opinion on whether the financial statements are in accordance with generally accepted accounting principles.

Notice that the report is signed with the name of the CA *firm,* not the name of an individual partner in the firm. This signature stresses that it is the *firm,* not an individual, that takes responsibility for the auditors' report. If the CA performing the audit is an individual practitioner, the report will be signed with the CA's personal signature. In addition, a sole practitioner should use the word *I* instead of *we* in the auditors' report.

Also notice the date of the report. This is the date by which the auditors have substantially completed their examination. Recall from Chapter 6 that this date is quite significant in determining the auditors' responsibility for events occurring subsequent to the balance sheet date.

An unqualified auditors' report may be issued only when both of the following conditions have been met:

1. The financial statements are presented in accordance with ***generally accepted accounting principles;*** that is, there is no material departure from generally accepted accounting principles.
2. The audit was performed in accordance with generally accepted audi-

ting standards; that is, there were no material or significant *scope limitations* preventing the auditors from gathering the evidence necessary to support their opinion.

EXPRESSION OF AN OPINION

The auditors' options when expressing an opinion on financial statements may be summarized as follows:

1. *An unqualified opinion—standard report.* This report represents a "clean opinion" and may be issued when the two conditions listed above have been met.
2. *A qualified opinion.* A qualified opinion is basically a positive opinion. It asserts that the financial statements, viewed as a whole, are not misleading. Qualified reports are issued when the financial statements depart materially from generally accepted accounting principles, or when a material limitation is placed on the scope of the auditors' procedures. The problems, while material, *do not overshadow the overall fairness of the statements.*
3. *An adverse opinion.* This is a *negative opinion,* asserting that the financial statements *are not* a fair presentation. Auditors will issue an adverse opinion when the deficiencies in the financial statements are *so significant* or *so pervasive* that the financial statements taken as a whole are misleading.
4. *A denial of opinion.* A denial of opinion means that due to very significant scope restriction or limitation, the auditors *were unable to form an opinion* on the fairness of the financial statements. A denial is neither a positive nor a negative opinion—it simply means that the auditors do not have an adequate basis for expressing an opinion.

All significant reasons for the issuance of a qualified, adverse, or denial of opinion should be set forth in a reservation paragraph between the scope and opinion paragraphs.

Materiality

The *CICA Handbook* provides the following general guidance for determining materiality:

> A misstatement or the aggregate of all misstatements in financial statements is considered to be material if, in the light of surrounding circumstances, it is probable that the decision of a person who is relying on the financial statements, and who has a reasonable knowledge of business and economic activities (the user), would be changed or influenced by such misstatement or the aggregate of all misstatements.[2]

[2] CICA, *CICA Handbook* (Toronto), Section 5130.05. Also see Section 1000.17.

Auditors must qualify their report whenever there are *material* deficiencies in the client's financial statements. However, when these deficiencies are *immaterial,* an unqualified report may be issued. Accordingly, auditors must exercise professional judgment to evaluate the materiality of any such departures. As discussed in Chapter 17, the auditors, in evaluating audit findings, consider the effects of misstatements on the various components of the financial statements. At this stage of the audit, the auditors should consider both the *quantitative* and *qualitative* effects of the deficiencies. For example, a related party transaction of a relatively small amount would be considered to be material.

Auditors are required to issue an adverse opinion when the deficiencies in financial statements are *"so significant"* that a qualified opinion would be inappropriate. A qualified opinion is considered *insufficient* when the deficiencies in financial statements are so material that they *overshadow the fairness of the financial statements viewed as a whole.* For example, misstatements that make an insolvent business appear to be solvent would be considered sufficiently material as to overshadow the fairness of the statements viewed as a whole.

The distinction between problems that are material but do not overshadow the fairness of the statements and those problems that do overshadow the fairness of the statements is again a matter of professional judgment. In our following discussions, it will not be practical to present sufficient detail for readers to make these judgments. Therefore, we will use the term *material* to describe problems sufficient to require qualification of the auditors' report, but which do not overshadow the fairness of the statements. Problems overshadowing the fairness of the statements will be described as *very material, very significant,* or as causing the statements to be *misleading.*

Fair Presentation, GAAP, and Professional Judgment

As pointed out in Chapter 2, auditors' professional judgment on the fair presentation of financial statements must be made within the framework of GAAP. Such a judgment includes the consideration on the appropriateness of the selection and application of generally accepted accounting principles and their overall effect on the financial statements.[3] Thus, the GAAP used must be *appropriate* in the circumstances, individually and collectively.

Since recommendations in the *CICA Handbook* are considered "generally accepted," a departure from such recommendations represents a departure from GAAP. A departure is permitted only when compliance with a recommendation in a specific situation would make financial

---

[3] Ibid., Section 5400.15.

statements *misleading*.[4] In such a case, the auditors would be able to express an unqualified opinion (i.e., an opinion without reservation), provided the reasons for not following *Handbook* recommendations are adequately disclosed.[5]

However, neither the auditors' personal disagreement with a *Handbook* recommendation nor the auditors' alternative choice of an equally appropriate accounting principle (i.e., an alternative principle that also results in an appropriate presentation) constitutes a valid reason for departure from a *Handbook* recommendation.[6] Thus, in either case, the auditors cannot express an unqualified opinion.

The Unqualified Report

Auditors express an unqualified opinion on the client's financial statements when there has been no material departure from GAAP and there have been no material unresolved restrictions on the scope of their audit.

The unqualified opinion is, of course, the most desirable report from the client's point of view. The client usually will make any necessary adjustments to the statements to enable the auditors to issue this type of opinion.

Under certain circumstances, however, auditors may consider it appropriate to *add additional wording* to the standard report even though they are issuing an unqualified opinion. This additional wording is *not regarded as a reservation* because it does *not lessen* the auditors' responsibility for the financial statements. Rather, the additional wording merely *draws attention* to certain statutory requirements or a specific matter.

Statutory Requirements.   Governing statutes under which the audit is performed may require certain additional information to be provided by the auditors in their standard report. The auditors should modify the wording of their standard report in order to meet such statutory requirements. When statutory information is lengthy, Section 5701 of the *CICA Handbook* suggests that such information "should be set out in a separate paragraph after the opinion paragraph, with a reference, if appropriate, to the particular governing statute which makes it necessary to provide the additional information."

For example, since the current standard report no longer contains a reference to the consistency application of GAAP but such a reference is required by some legislation, auditors may add a statement to the opinion

---

[4] Ibid., Section 5400.22.
[5] Ibid., Section 5400.19.
[6] Ibid., Sections 5400.16 and 5400.23.

paragraph, explaining the situation. The auditing guideline on "Legislative requirements to report on the consistency application of generally accepted accounting principles" suggests the following sentence to be added to the opinion paragraph: "As required by [specify legislation or regulation], I report that, in my opinion, these principles have been applied on a basis consistent with that of the preceding year."

Emphasis of a Matter.   Another modification of the standard audit report is the auditors' emphasis on a matter regarding the client's financial statements. For example, the auditors may add a separate paragraph after the opinion paragraph to their unqualified audit report, calling attention to a significant subsequent event described in a note to the financial statements. If the conventional wording is used in the opinion paragraph, such an audit report is unqualified. However, this type of modification should be used only in very unusual cases. Also, if comparative financial statements were audited by another auditor or there was a reservation on the comparative financial statements which affect the fair presentation of the current financial statements, the situation should be disclosed in a separate paragraph after the opinion paragraph.

Reservation

The term *reservation* is used to signify the auditors' inability to express an unqualified opinion. The reservation paragraph (between the scope and opinion paragraphs) is focused on the reasons for a qualified opinion, an adverse opinion, or a denial of opinion. In addition, the scope or opinion paragraph or both (in the case of scope limitation) should contain appropriate wording to warn users of financial statements that the auditors are limiting their responsibility for the fairness of the statements. Examples of the reservation paragraphs and the appropriate wording for the scope and opinion paragraphs will be discussed in detail in the following sections of this chapter.

Qualified Opinions

A qualified opinion restricts the auditors' responsibility for fair presentation in some area of the financial statements. The opinion states that *except for* the effects of some material departure from GAAP, or some material limitation in the scope of the auditors' examination, *the financial statements are presented fairly*.

The auditors' reports for all qualified opinions should have a *separate reservation paragraph* disclosing the reasons for the qualification. The opinion paragraph of a qualified report includes the appropriate qualifying language such as "except for," "except that," or "except as" (phrases such as "with the foregoing explanation" or "subject to" are not acceptable) and a reference to the reservation paragraph.

What constitutes a departure from generally accepted accounting principles? The following are some of the specific circumstances:

1. an inappropriate accounting treatment, such as accounting for a capital lease as an operating lease or a failure to record a liability,
2. an inappropriate valuation such as the lack of or inadequate provision for inventory obsolescence, and
3. a failure to disclose essential information or to present information in an appropriate manner, such as inadequate explanation of a contingency or a failure to classify an individual or enterprise as a related party and disclose the information related thereto.[7]

[7] Ibid., Section 5510.06.

On the other hand, the specific circumstances that constitute a scope limitation are as follows:

1. the timing of the auditors' appointment and the audit work, such as the appointment of auditors during the year and thus the auditors are unable to observe the physical inventory at the beginning of the year;
2. the unavailability of accounting and other records caused by factors beyond the control of the client or the auditor, such as a destruction of accounting records in a fire; and
3. the inability to perform the necessary audit procedures created by the client, such as a refusal to allow confirmation of accounts receivable, or a failure of the client to maintain adequate accounting records.[8]

[8] Ibid., Section 5510.09.

The nature of the circumstances (whether the circumstances are a departure from generally accepted accounting principles or a scope limitation) and the materiality of the matter involved govern the types of reservations that are expressed in the audit report. A departure from generally accepted accounting principles will require either a qualified or an adverse opinion, depending on the materiality of the matter involved (i.e., if material, qualify; if very material, adverse). On the other hand, the materiality of a scope limitation will dictate either a qualified opinion or a denial of opinion (i.e., if material, qualify; if very material, deny).

Qualifications as to Accounting Principles. The auditors sometimes must qualify their opinion because they do not agree with the accounting principles used in preparing the statements or because they believe disclosures in the statements are inadequate. Usually, when the auditors' objections are carefully explained, the client will agree to change the statements in an acceptable manner. If the client does not agree to make the suggested changes, the auditors will be forced to qualify their opinion (or if the exception is so material or so pervasive, to issue an adverse opinion). An example of an audit report, showing only the reservation and opinion paragraphs, qualified as to the accounting principles follows (the standard introductory and scope paragraphs are unchanged):

Note 1 to the financial statements describes the depreciation policy with respect to the company's manufacturing plants and equipment. The note also indicates that the company is not depreciating its head office building, which it acquired five years ago, on the grounds that it is not a producing asset and is maintaining its value as a potential rental or resale property. In this respect the financial statements are not in accordance with generally accepted accounting principles. The estimated useful life of similar buildings is usually considered to be between 30 and 40 years. If depreciation had been provided on the basis of an estimated useful life of, say, 35 years, depreciation for the current year would have been increased by $200,000 (1992, $220,000), net income after taxes would have been decreased by $100,000 (1992, $110,000), accumulated depreciation would have been increased by $200,000 (1992, $220,000) and the closing balance of retained earnings would have been reduced by $610,000 (1992, $510,000).

In our opinion, *except for the effects of the failure to record depreciation as described in the preceding paragraph,* these financial statements present fairly, in all material respects, the financial position of the company as at December 31, 1993 and the results of its operations and the changes in its financial position for the year then ended in accordance with generally accepted accounting principles.[9] (Emphasis added.)

---

[9] Adapted from *CICA handbook,* Section 5510.A.

If the auditors consider disclosures in, or notes to, the client's financial statements to be inadequate, they generally will issue a qualified audit report. For example, if the client fails to adequately disclose matters affecting its ability to continue as a going concern, the auditors should word their report as follows after the standard introductory and scope paragraphs:

The accompanying financial statements, in our opinion, do not draw attention explicitly to doubts concerning the company's ability to realize its assets and discharge its liabilities in the normal course of business. These doubts arise because it is uncertain whether the company will be able to refinance long-term debt in the amount of $10,000,000 due on March 26, 1993, in view of the existence of recurring operating losses in the past five years and the deficiency in working capital of $2,000,000 at December 31, 1992. If refinancing cannot be arranged, it is not known whether the company can sell its hotel property for an amount sufficient to realize its carrying value of $9,000,000 and to generate adequate funds to repay this debt.

In our opinion, *except for the omission of the disclosure described in the preceding paragraph,* these financial statements present fairly, in all material respects, the financial position of the company as at December 31, 1992 and the results of its operations and the changes in its financial position for the year then ended in accordance with generally accepted accounting principles.[10] (Emphasis added.)

---

[10] *CICA Handbook,* Section 5510.F, adapted.

Some corporate legislation grants a company the right to apply to a specified authority, such as a court, for permission to omit certain essential information (e.g., sales) from its financial statements on the ground that the disclosure would be detrimental to the company's interest. Also, a specified authority may, in some cases, direct a company not to disclose certain essential information in the financial statements. In those cases where a company is permitted or required by a specified authority to omit essential information from its financial statements, the auditors must express a reservation, usually a qualified opinion, on the statements because such an omission represents a departure from generally accepted accounting principles. In addition, the auditors must identify the authority and must not quantify the effects of the omission on the financial statements.[11]

Consistency of Accounting Principles.   If a client company makes a change in accounting principle, the nature of, justification for, and effect of the change should be reported in a note to the financial statements for the period in which the change was made. Any such change having a material effect on the financial statements should be adequately disclosed. Until November 1980, a change in accounting principle was one of the circumstances for a reservation. Since then, a reservation for consistency has *not* been required when the change in accounting principle is applied retroactively to prior periods, or prospectively if retroactivity is impracticable in the circumstances.[12] Thus, when a change in accounting principle is applied retroactively or prospectively as permitted by Section 1506 of the *CICA Handbook,* and is adequately disclosed in the financial statements, the auditors can issue an unqualified opinion.[13] However, a failure to apply a change retroactively when practicable, or a lack of adequate disclosure

---

[11] Ibid., Section 5510.37.
[12] Ibid., Section 1506.10.
[13] Ibid., Section 5400.19.

of the change, represents a departure from generally accepted accounting principles. Under such circumstance a reservation in the auditors' report is required.[14]

Limitations on Scope of Examination. We have pointed out that limitations on the scope of an audit may result from the inability of the auditors to perform necessary auditing procedures, for example, because of restrictions created by the client or because of inability to verify the beginning inventories of a new client. If the scope limitations are not so material as to require a denial of opinion, the auditors would issue a qualified opinion such as the following (the introductory paragraph is unchanged):

Except as explained in the following paragraph, we conducted our audit in accordance with generally accepted auditing standards. Those standards require that we plan and perform an audit to obtain reasonable assurance whether the financial statements are free of material misstatement. An audit includes examining, on a test basis, evidence supporting the amounts and disclosures in the financial statements. An audit also includes assessing the accounting principles used and significant estimates made by management as well as evaluating the overall financial statement presentation.

Because we were appointed auditors of the company during the current year, we were not able to observe the counting of physical inventories at the beginning of the year or satisfy ourselves concerning those inventory quantities by alternative means. Since opening inventories enter into the determination of the results of operations and changes in financial position, we were unable to determine whether adjustments to cost of sales, income taxes, net income for the year, opening retained earnings and cash provided from operations might be necessary.

In our opinion, *except for the effect of adjustments, if any, which we might have determined to be necessary had we been able to examine opening inventory quantities, as described in the preceding paragraph,* the statements of income, retained earnings, and changes in financial position present fairly, in all material respects, the results of operations, and the changes in financial position of the company for the year ended December 31, 1993 in accordance with generally accepted accounting principles. Further, in our opinion, the balance sheet presents fairly, in all material respects, the financial position of the company as at December 31, 1993 in accordance with generally accepted accounting principles.[15] (Emphasis added.)

---

[15] Ibid., Section 5510.J, adapted.

Reliance on Other Auditors. On occasion, it may be necessary for the primary auditors of a company to rely on another accounting firm (the secondary auditors) to perform a portion of the audit work. The most

---

[14] Ibid., Section 5400.20.

common situation in which the primary auditors rely on the work of the secondary auditors is in the audit of consolidated entities. If certain subsidiaries are audited by other accounting firms, the auditors of the parent company may rely on the work of these secondary auditors. In order to justify such a reliance on the secondary auditors, the primary auditors must perform the procedures outlined in Section 6930 of the *CICA Handbook:*

1. consider the professional qualifications, competence, and integrity of the secondary auditor;
2. communicate with the secondary auditor regarding such matters as the requirements of the primary auditor and any significant audit problems encountered by the secondary auditor;
3. read the report of the secondary auditor and the related financial statements;
4. obtain a written communication from the secondary auditor acknowledging the primary auditor's intention to rely on the secondary auditor's report and setting out the representations required by the primary auditor; and
5. review the work of the secondary auditor.

When the primary auditors are satisfied with the results of these procedures, they can reasonably rely on the report and work of the secondary auditors. Under such circumstances, the primary auditors should be in a position to express an unqualified opinion and should *not* refer to the secondary auditors in the audit report. However, when the primary auditors have not been able to satisfy themselves with the results of their procedures with respect to the report and work of the secondary auditors, the primary auditors should express a reservation in their audit report. In this case, the primary auditors may refer in the audit report to their inability to rely on the secondary auditors.

Major Uncertainty Affecting a Client's Business. A major uncertainty affecting a client's business can range from a contingency as defined in Section 3290 of the *CICA Handbook* to a serious doubt of a client's ability to continue as a going concern. Until November 1980, the auditors were required to express a reservation of opinion when there was a major uncertainty affecting the financial statements. Since then, Section 5510 of the *CICA Handbook* has recommended that so long as the accounting treatment, disclosure, and presentation of the uncertainties are in accordance with generally accepted accounting principles, the auditors should not express a reservation of opinion or refer to the uncertainties in their report. Thus, the "subject to" qualified opinion and the denial of opinion based on uncertainty of major contingencies and going concern problems are no longer permitted.

Why was this change needed? Among the most important reasons are the following: (1) it is the client's responsibility to provide sufficient disclosure to inform the users of financial statements about major uncertainties, (2) it is the auditors' responsibility to review and evaluate the adequacy of such disclosure, (3) highlighting only contingencies or going concern problems in the auditors' report may overshadow other important matters in the financial statements, and (4) the use of a "subject to" qualification to alert financial statements users of a contingency does not necessarily provide additional legal protection for the auditors.

When the auditors encounter a major contingency during the course of an audit, they should obtain sufficient appropriate audit evidence to ensure that the accounting treatment, disclosure, and presentation of the contingency are in accordance with generally accepted accounting principles (the discussion on contingencies is presented in Chapter 17). The auditors should express a reservation of opinion only when they have been precluded from obtaining the appropriate available audit evidence or when the contingency is not accounted for, disclosed, or presented in accordance with generally accepted accounting principles.

During their examination, the auditors may become aware of conditions that seriously threaten the client's continued existence. Conditions that cast doubt on a company's ability to continue as a going concern include recurring operating losses, serious deficiencies in working capital, negative cash flows from operations, defaults on loan agreements, inability to obtain sufficient financing for continued operations, adverse financial ratios, and loss of primary assets. When such conditions come to the auditor's attention, they should consider whether the conditions are mitigated by other factors. For example, management may have other available sources of financing, creditors may be willing to restructure the client's debts, or unprofitable segments of the business may be offered for sale. After considering evidence contrary to the assumption of a going concern, and also after considering any mitigating factors and management's plans, the auditors may conclude that a substantial doubt remains about the client's ability to continue in operation. In such a case, the auditors must ensure that the situation of the client is accounted for, disclosed, and presented in accordance with generally accepted accounting principles, particularly the principle that the disclosure of information be adequate to explicitly draw the attention of the financial statement users to the possibility that the client may be unable to continue as a going concern. When the client has complied with the requirements of generally accepted accounting principles, no reservation of opinion is necessary. If, for example, there is a lack of adequate disclosure of the situation, the auditors must express a reservation of opinion because there is a departure from generally accepted accounting principles. An illustration of such a reservation was presented earlier in this section.

Two or More Qualifications

An auditors' report may be qualified for two or more reasons. For example, the report may be qualified because of both a scope limitation and a separate problem involving accounting principles. The wording of such a report would include the appropriate qualifying wording and the reservation paragraphs from both types of qualifications.

When there are several reasons for qualifying an opinion, the auditors should consider the cumulative effects of these problems. If the effect of the problems is to overshadow the fairness of the statements viewed as a whole, or to prevent the auditors from forming an overall opinion, a qualified opinion would be inappropriate. In such cases, the auditors should issue either an adverse opinion or a denial of opinion, depending upon the circumstances.

Adverse Opinions

An adverse opinion is the opposite of an unqualified opinion; it is an opinion that the financial statements **do not** present fairly the financial position, results of operations, and changes in financial position of the client, in accordance with generally accepted accounting principles. When the auditors express an adverse opinion, they must have accumulated sufficient appropriate evidence to support their unfavourable opinion.

The auditors should express an adverse opinion if the statements are so lacking in fairness that a qualified opinion would not be warning enough. These statements are unfair and misleading or virtually useless, even when read in conjunction with the auditors' report, because the impact of the departure from generally accepted accounting principles is so pervasive or so significant that the auditors are unable to describe clearly its effect or that it overshadows a clear description of the effect on the statements. Whenever the auditors issue an adverse opinion, they should disclose in a separate paragraph of their report the reasons for the adverse opinion and the principle effects of the adverse opinion on the client company's financial position and operating results.

Thus, an audit report that included an adverse opinion might include the standard introductory and scope paragraphs, a paragraph describing the reasons for the adverse opinion and the principle effects of the subject matter of the adverse opinion, and an opinion paragraph, such as the one following:

> In our opinion, *because of the effects of the matters discussed in the preceding paragraph,* these financial statements *do not present fairly* the financial position of the company as at December 31, 1993, and the results of its operations and changes in its financial position for the year then ended, in accordance with generally accepted accounting principles. (Emphasis added.)

Adverse opinions are rare because most clients follow the recommendations of the auditors with respect to fair presentation in financial statements. One possible source of adverse opinions is the actions of regulatory agencies that prescribe accounting practices not in accordance with generally accepted accounting principles.[16]

Denial of Opinions

A denial of opinion is no opinion.[17] In an audit engagement, a denial is required when *very significant* restrictions on the scope of the audit preclude compliance with generally accepted auditing standards.

In some engagements, the client will impose restrictions limiting the auditors' compliance with generally accepted auditing standards. Examples are the prohibition of inventory observation and receivables confirmation. Since inventories and receivables are usually important factors in determining both financial position and operating results, the auditors (if prohibited by the client from observing the physical inventory or confirming receivables) must make a reservation in the scope paragraph of their report. Generally, failure to observe the physical inventory or to confirm receivables will represent such a material shortcoming in the scope of the examination that the auditors will not be able to express an opinion on the fairness of the financial statements taken as a whole.

Another example of a client-imposed restriction on the scope of the audit is the client's denial of permission for the auditors to examine the financial statements of a very or extremely significant subsidiary company or branch, or to apply required auditing procedures to the financial statements of a very or extremely significant investee company.

However, it may not be legally permissible for auditors to accept any statutory audit engagement containing limitations which infringe on their statutory duties. If significant limitations are imposed by the client during the audit, the auditors should seriously consider resigning from the audit engagement. In any event, auditors encountering client-imposed limitations on the scope of their audit examination should seek legal advice on their course of action.

When the client imposes restrictions that limit very significantly the scope of the audit, the CA firm *must deny an opinion* on the client's financial statements. In a separate paragraph of the audit report, the auditors should describe all substantive reasons for the denial of opinion, and should disclose any reservations they have regarding the fairness of the financial statements. In a denial of opinion, the auditors should not describe the auditing procedures actually performed; to do so might dilute the impact of the denial.

---

[16] Ibid., Section 5400.24.

[17] In the United States, the term *disclaimer* is used instead of the term *denial*.

In addition, a very significant scope limitation may be caused by the timing of the auditors' appointment and their audit work or by factors beyond the control of the client or the auditors, rather than by restrictions imposed by the client. For example, the auditors may be appointed after the client's physical inventory has been taken and may be unable to satisfy themselves by other procedures as to the fairness of the inventory, or the accounting records may be destroyed in a fire or other accidents. When these situations are very significant, the auditors must deny an opinion on the financial statements.

The following is an example of a denial of opinion due to the timing of appointment and serious deficiencies in the accounting records and internal control (with the standard introductory paragraph omitted):

> ***Except as explained in the following paragraph,*** we conducted our audit in accordance with generally accepted auditing standards. Those standards require that we plan and perform an audit to obtain reasonable assurance whether the financial statements are free of material misstatement. An audit includes examining, on a test basis, evidence supporting the amounts and disclosures in the financial statements. An audit also includes assessing the accounting principles used and significant estimates made by management, as well as evaluating the overall financial statement presentation.
>
> We were not appointed auditor until after [year-end date] and thus did not observe the taking of physical inventories at either the beginning of the year or the end of the year and were not able to satisfy ourselves concerning inventory quantities by alternative means. Also, our examination indicated serious deficiencies in the accounting records and in internal control. As a consequence, we were unable to satisfy ourselves that all revenues and expenditures of the company had been recorded, nor were we able to satisfy ourselves that the recorded transactions were proper. As a result, we were unable to determine whether adjustments were required in respect of recorded or unrecorded assets, recorded or unrecorded liabilities, and the components making up the statements of income, retained earnings, and changes in financial position.
>
> ***In view of the possible material effects on the financial statements of the matters described in the preceding paragraph, we are unable to express an opinion*** whether these financial statements are presented fairly in accordance with generally accepted accounting principles.[18] (Emphasis added.)
>
> ——————
> [18] *CICA Handbook*, Section 5510.M, adapted.

Summary of Auditors' Reports

Figure 18–1 summarizes the types of auditors' reports that should be issued under different conditions. Figure 18–2 summarizes the format and the appropriate wording for each of the different reports.

FIGURE 18–1   Summary of Appropriate Auditors' Reports

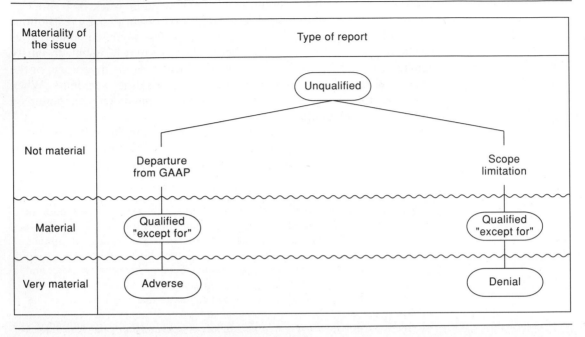

Different Opinions on Different Statements

It is acceptable for the auditors to express an unqualified opinion on one of the financial statements while expressing a qualified, adverse, or denial of opinion on the others. Such a situation may arise, for example, when the auditors are retained *after* the client has completed its *beginning* physical inventory. In this case, the auditors may satisfy themselves as to the amounts in the year-end balance sheet, but not as to the statements of income, retained earnings, and changes in financial position. Therefore, the auditors may be able to perform a useful service by using an unqualified opinion on the balance sheet and a reservation of opinion on the other statements.

Comparative Financial Statements in Audit Reports

The CICA has long supported the presentation of comparative financial statements for a series of accounting periods in annual or interim reports to shareholders. Comparative statements show changes and trends in the financial position and operating results of a company over an extended period, and thus are more useful to investors and creditors than are financial statements for a single period.

When comparative financial statements are presented by the client company, the auditors' report covers only the current period unless an extension to cover the statements of a prior period is specifically stated in their report. However, when the comparative financial statements were reported on by the other auditors, this fact should be disclosed in the notes to the financial statements or in a separate paragraph of the auditors' report following the opinion paragraph. Similar disclosure should be made when comparative financial statements are unaudited and are not clearly identified as such.

If reservations were expressed in the auditors' report for the prior period that may impair comparability with the current period, the auditors should refer to such reservations in their report for the current period.

In the United States, however, the auditors should report on the comparative financial statements if the CPA firm has examined them. The scope paragraph would describe the periods for which the statements were examined, and the opinion paragraph of an unqualified audit report would be worded as follows:

> In our opinion, the financial statements referred to above present fairly, in all material respects, the financial position of X Company as of December 31, 19x7, and December 31 19x8, and the results of its operations and its cash flows for the years then ended in conformity with generally accepted accounting principles.

Dating and Double Dating the Auditors' Report

The date of the auditors' report signifies to the users of financial statements the date as of which the auditors form their opinion on the financial statements. Thus, the auditors are responsible for all significant information affecting the financial statements up to this date. However, the date the report is actually signed and released to the client is usually later than the date of the report.

In the *CICA Handbook,* Section 5405.06 recommended that the date of *"substantial completion of examination"* (emphasis added) should be used as the date for the auditors' report. The term *substantial completion of examination* means that the auditors have "identified and sought all the audit evidence" required to support their opinion and have "obtained and examined substantially all such evidence" but are "awaiting receipt of specific corroborating evidence or documentation before signing and releasing" their report.[19] However, if this evidence or documentation is in

---

[19] Ibid., Section 5405.03.

FIGURE 18–2

Type of Report	Introductory Paragraph	Scope Paragraph	Reservation Paragraph	Opinion Paragraph	Opinion Paragraph or after Opinion Paragraph
		Modifications Required in the Auditors' Report			
Unqualified opinions:					
Statutory requirements	None	None	No reservation paragraph	None	Describe matter
Emphasis of a matter	None	None	No reservation paragraph	None	Describe matter
Qualified opinions:					
Departure from GAAP	None	None	Describe departure and effects	". . . except for [the departure] these financial statements present fairly. . . ."	None

Scope restriction	None	"Except as explained in the following paragraph . . ."	Describe scope restriction	". . . except for the effects of adjustments . . . these financial statements present fairly . . ."	None
Adverse Opinion: Departure from GAAP (very material)	None	None	Describe reasons for adverse opinion	". . . the financial statements do not present fairly . . ."	None
Denial of Opinion: Scope limitation (very material)	None	"Except as explained in the following paragraph . . ."	Describe scope restriction and reservations	". . . we do not express an opinion on the financial statements" or "we are unable to express an opinion . . ."	None

conflict with what was anticipated, the auditors should consider the nature and extent of the conflicting information. If the conflict is significant but isolated and the financial statements are adjusted, the date of substantial completion of the examination is still used. On the other hand, if the conflict is so significant or pervasive as to undermine previously obtained audit evidence, the auditors need to consider whether to update their work and opinion. An updating will extend the auditors' responsibility for their opinion on the financial statements to the later date.[20]

If an event subsequent to the date of substantial completion of examination, but prior to the release of the auditors' report, requires disclosure in a note to the financial statements, the auditors have two options for dating their report. They may use *double dating,* such as "February 16, 19—, except for Note 7, which is as of February 28, 19—," or they may date their report as of the later date. In the first option, the auditors are responsible only for examining evidence related to the specific subsequent event. In the second option, the auditors' responsibility extends to the later date for both the specific subsequent event and the financial statements as a whole.[21]

Auditors' Responsibility for Information in the Annual Report

Audit reports on the financial statements of large enterprises usually are included in an annual report to shareholders. Such an annual report includes a multitude of *other information* in addition to audited financial statements and the audit report. Thus, the question arises as to what extent the auditors are responsible for the information in the annual report. In response, the CICA's Auditing Standards Board set forth certain recommendations in Section 7500 of the *Handbook,* "The Auditor's Involvement with Annual Reports." These recommendations require the auditors (1) to determine whether the audited financial statements and the audit report are *accurately reproduced* in the annual report, and (2) to read the other information in the annual report and consider whether any of this information is *inconsistent* with the audited financial statements. The objective of these recommendations is to "identify matters that could undermine the credibility" of the auditors' reports and the audited financial statements rather than to "provide assurance as to the accuracy or reliability of management's assertions in the other information."[22] In most cases, any errors in the reproduction of the audited financial statements and the

---

[20] Ibid., Section 5405.08.
[21] Ibid., Section 5405.11.
[22] Ibid., Section 7500.05.

audit report, as well as any inconsistency in the other information, will be satisfactorily resolved between the auditors and management of the enterprise before the annual report is released.

If an error in the reproduction of the audited financial statements or the audit report is not corrected before the annual report is released or if an error is discovered after the annual report has been released, the auditors should ensure that reasonable efforts have been made by management to notify users that the error has occurred. If the auditors conclude that such efforts have not been made, they should formally notify the board of directors and consider further appropriate action.

When an inconsistency resulting from an error in the audited financial statements occurs, the auditors' action would depend on whether the audit report has been released and whether the error is corrected. If the report has not been released and the error is not corrected, the auditors should express a reservation in their report. On the other hand, if the report has been released, the auditors should issue a revised report if the error is corrected or seek legal advice as to what action they should take to discharge their responsibility if the error is not corrected. Generally, corporation laws in Canada require the auditors to notify each member of the board of directors of an error or misstatement in the audited financial statements discovered subsequent to their release.

When an inconsistency requires a revision in the other information in the annual report and management refuses to make such a revision, the auditors should formally notify the board of directors of the situation and consider further appropriate action.

When the auditors discover a material misstatement of fact in the other information in the annual report, they should discuss this matter with management, including the board of directors and its audit committee. If management refuses to take any corrective action, the auditors should formally notify the board of directors and consider further appropriate action.

Similarly, the AICPA in the United States set forth guidelines for the auditors with respect to the other information in the annual report in its *SAS 8*. It requires the auditor to read the other information and consider whether it, or its manner of presentation, is materially inconsistent with information appearing in the audited financial statements or notes. If the other information is inconsistent, and the auditors conclude that neither the audited financial statements nor the audit report requires revision, they should request the client to revise the other information. If the client refuses to do so, the auditors should consider such alternatives as (1) revising the audit report to describe the inconsistency, (2) withholding use of their audit report by the client, or (3) withdrawing from the engagement. The auditors should also be alert for, and discuss with the client, any other types of material misstatements included in the other information.

Reports to the SEC in the United States

Many publicly owned corporations in the United States and those Canadian companies listed on the stock exchanges in the United States are subject to the financial reporting requirements of the federal laws administered by the SEC. Thus, it is important for Canadian auditors to be familiar with these reporting requirements. Two principal laws, the Securities Act of 1933 and the Securities Exchange Act of 1934, provide for a multitude of reports requiring audited financial statements. The most important of these reports, or *forms,* are the following:

1. **Forms S-1 through S-18.** These forms are the "registration statements" for clients planning to issue securities to the public. They are accompanied by an audited balance sheet and three years' statements of income and cash flows.
2. **Form 8-K.** This is a "current report" filed for any month in which significant events occur for a company subject to the Securities Acts. If the significant event is a business combination, audited financial statements of the acquired company often are required in the current report.
3. **Form 10-Q.** This form is filed quarterly with the SEC by publicly owned companies. It contains unaudited financial information. The companies' auditors may perform reviews of this data, but their work is substantially less in scope than an audit.
4. **Form 10-K.** This report is filed annually with the SEC by publicly owned companies. The report includes audited financial statements and other detailed financial information.

The preceding points represent only a brief summary of the complex reporting requirements of the SEC. The auditors dealing with these reports should be well versed in the requirements of each form, as well as in the provisions of the SEC's *Regulation S-X,* which governs the form and content of financial statements and supporting schedules required to be filed with the various forms.

KEY TERMS

adverse opinion An opinion that the financial statements *do not* present fairly financial position, results of operations, and changes in financial position, in accordance with generally accepted accounting principles.

dating the report Selecting the date for the auditors' report to signify the date as of which the auditors form their opinion on the financial statements and are responsible for all significant information affecting the statements. Such a date is usually earlier than the date the report is actually signed and released. The date of substantial completion of examination is usually the date of the report.

denial of opinion   A form of report in which the auditors state that they do not express an opinion on the financial statements.

double dating   Dating of audit reports with two dates: the date of substantial completion of examination and the date of a significant subsequent event described in a note to the financial statements. The latter date is later than the former.

fair presentation   Fair presentation, or "present fairly," is judged within the framework of GAAP; in other words, it means the financial statements are in accordance with the GAAP appropriate for the circumstances.

introductory paragraph   The paragraph of the auditors' report in which the auditors indicate that they have audited the financial statements, that the financial statements are the responsibility of management, and that they are responsible for their opinion on the financial statements.

material   Being of substantial importance. Significant enough to affect evaluations or decisions by users of financial statements. Information that should be disclosed in order that financial statements constitute a fair presentation. Involves both quantitative and qualitative criteria.

opinion paragraph   The paragraph of an auditors' report that communicates the degree of responsibility that the auditors are taking for the financial statements.

other information   All the information stated in the annual report other than the audit report and the audited financial statements. The auditors are responsible to read this information for any inconsistency with the audited financial statements and any misstatement of fact.

primary auditors   Auditors who use the work and reports of other auditors who have examined the financial statements of one or more subsidiaries, branches, or other segments of the primary auditors' client.

qualified opinion   A modification of the auditors' standard report, employing an *except for* clause to limit the auditors' opinion on the financial statements. A qualified opinion indicates that except for some limitation on the scope of the examination or some departure from generally accepted accounting principles, the financial statements are fairly presented.

reservation   A term used to signify the auditors' inability to express an unqualified opinion; it covers a qualified opinion, an adverse opinion, or a denial of opinion.

reservation paragraph   An explanatory paragraph inserted in an auditors' report between the scope and opinion paragraphs. Used by the auditors to explain the reasons for giving something other than an unqualified opinion.

scope limitation   Something that prevents the auditors from being able to apply all of the audit procedures that they consider necessary under the circumstances. Scope limitations may be client imposed or may stem from other factors.

scope paragraph   The paragraph of an auditors' report in which the auditors describe the character of their examination.

standard report   The "standard wording" of an unqualified auditors' report, not including such modifications as emphasis of a matter or disclosure of statutory requirements.

substantial completion of examination   A term used for selecting an appropriate date for the audit report. It means that the auditor have identified and sought all the audit evidence required for their opinion and have examined substantially all such evidence except for some specific corroborating evidence.

unqualified opinion   An opinion that the financial statements present fairly financial position, results of operations, and changes in financial position, in accordance with generally accepted accounting principles.

GROUP I: REVIEW QUESTIONS

18–1.   What basic conditions must be met before auditors can issue an unqualified auditors' report?

18–2.   Identify the four basic types of opinions that an auditor may issue and explain when each is appropriate.

18–3.   Howard Green is a partner with Cary, Loeb & Co. On February 20, Green substantially completed the audit of Baker Manufacturing for the year ended last December 31. It is now March 1, and Green is about to sign the auditors' report. How should Green sign and date the report?

18–4.   What is meant by the term *reservation?*

18–5.   Explain two situations in which the wording of an *unqualified* opinion might depart from the auditors' standard report.

18–6.   The auditors do not believe that certain lease obligations have been reflected in conformity with generally accepted accounting principles in the client's financial statements. What type of opinion should the auditors issue if they decide that the departure is immaterial? Material? Very material?

18–7.   Can the client change a set of financial statements to receive an unqualified opinion instead of an opinion qualified as to disclosure? Can the client change the financial statements to avoid a report modified because of a scope limitation? Explain.

18–8. Why are adverse opinions rare?

18–9. What type of report should auditors issue when the client has imposed very significant scope limitations?

18–10. The auditors know that the client's accounting for deferred income taxes is not in accordance with generally accepted accounting principles, but because of a very significant scope limitation, they have not been able to form an opinion on the financial statements taken as a whole. What type of report should they issue?

18–11. Only one type of qualified opinion modifies the wording in both the scope paragraph and the opinion paragraph. What is the reason for this type of qualification?

18–12. What is the function of notes to financial statements?

18–13. Cite three specific circumstances that constitute:

a. A departure from generally accepted accounting principles.

b. A scope limitation.

18–14. What procedures should the primary auditors perform in order to determine whether they can reasonably rely on the report and work of the secondary auditors.

18–15. Under what situation should the primary auditors refer to the secondary auditors in the audit report? In such a situation, what type of opinion should the primary auditors express in the audit report?

18–16. Under what circumstances would the auditors express a reservation in their report for a client with a major uncertainty affecting its business.

18–17. What are the main reasons for the deletion of the **subject to** qualification due to uncertainty?

18–18. Which date should the auditors use for their report and what is the significance of such a date?

18–19. Explain the meaning of the term **substantial completion of examination**.

18–20. What is the auditors' obligation with respect to information in client-prepared annual reports to shareholders other than the audit report and the audited financial statements?

18–21. Wade Corporation has been your audit client for several years. At the beginning of the current year, the company changed its method of inventory valuation from average cost to LIFO. The change, which had been under consideration for some time, was in your opinion a logical and proper step for the company to take. What effect, if any, will this situation have on your audit report for the current year?

GROUP II: QUESTIONS REQUIRING ANALYSIS

18–22. The following statement is representative of attitudes and opinions sometimes encountered by public accountants in their professional practices: "It is important to read the notes to financial statements, even though they often are presented in technical language and are incomprehensible. The auditors may reduce their exposure to third-party liability by stating something in the notes that contradicts completely what they have presented in the balance sheet or income statement."

Required:
Evaluate the above statement and indicate:
a. Areas of agreement with the statement, if any.
b. Areas of misconception, incompleteness, or fallacious reasoning included in the statement, if any.

(AICPA, adapted)

18–23. Rowe & Myers are the primary auditors of Dunbar Electronics. During the audit, Rowe & Myers engaged Jones & Abbot, an American public accounting firm, to audit Dunbar's wholly owned U.S. subsidiary.

Required:
a. Must Rowe & Myers make reference to the other auditors in their audit report? Explain.
b. Assume that Jones & Abbot issued a qualified report on the U.S. subsidiary. Must Rowe & Myers include the same qualification in their report on Dunbar Electronics?

18–24. What type of audit report (unqualified opinion, qualified opinion, adverse opinion, denial of opinion) should the auditors **generally** issue in each of the following situations? Explain.
a. Client-imposed restrictions limit very significantly the scope of the auditors' procedures.
b. The auditors decide that it is necessary to make reference to their report of another public accounting firm (the secondary auditors).
c. The auditors believe that the financial statements have been stated in conformity with generally accepted accounting principles in all respects other than the treatment and disclosure of a material uncertainty.

18–25. While performing your audit of Williams Paper Limited, you discover evidence that indicates that Williams may not have the ability to continue as a going concern.

Required:

    a. Discuss the types of information that may indicate a going-concern problem.

    b. Explain the auditors' reporting obligation in such situations.

18–26. Select the best answer for each of the following and explain fully the reason for your selection:

    a. A material departure from generally accepted accounting principles will result in auditor consideration of:

        (1) Whether to issue an adverse opinion rather than a denial of opinion.

        (2) Whether to issue a denial of opinion rather than an *except for* opinion.

        (3) Whether to issue an adverse opinion rather than qualified opinion.

        (4) Nothing, because none of these opinions is applicable to this type of exception.

    b. The auditors' report should be dated as of the date the:

        (1) Report is delivered to the client.

        (2) Examination is substantially completed.

        (3) Fiscal period under audit ends.

        (4) Review of the working papers is completed.

    c. In the report of the primary auditor, reference to the fact that a portion of the audit was made by another auditor is:

        (1) Not to be construed as a reservation, but rather as a division of responsibility between the two public accounting firms.

        (2) Not in accordance with generally accepted auditing standards.

        (3) An indication of a reservation by the primary auditor.

        (4) An example of a dual opinion requiring the signatures of both auditors.

    d. Assume that the opinion paragraph of an auditor's report begins as follows: "With the foregoing explanation, these financial statements present fairly. . . ." This is:

        (1) An unqualified opinion.

        (2) A denial of opinion.

        (3) An *except for* opinion.

        (4) An *except for* qualified opinion with improper wordings.

    e. The auditor who wishes to indicate that the entity has significant transactions with related parties should disclose this fact in:

        (1) An explanatory paragraph to the auditors' report.

        (2) An explanatory note to the financial statements.

(3) The body of the financial statements.

(4) The ''summary of significant accounting policies'' section of the financial statements.

f. When restrictions that significantly limit the scope of the audit are imposed by the client, the auditor should generally issue which of the following opinions?

(1) Qualified.

(2) Denial.

(3) Adverse.

(4) Unqualified.

(AICPA, adapted)

GROUP III: PROBLEMS

18–27. Sturdy Corporation owns and operates a large office building in a desirable section of the city's financial centre. For many years, the management of Sturdy Corporation has modified the presentation of their financial statements by:

a. Reflecting a write-up to appraisal values in the building accounts.

b. Accounting for depreciation expense on the basis of such valuations.

Wyley, CA, was asked to examine the financial statements of Sturdy Corporation for the year ended December 31, 19X3. After completing the examination, Wyley concluded that, consistent with prior years, an adverse opinion would have to be expressed because of the materiality of the deviation from the historical cost principle.

Required:

a. Describe in detail the appropriate content of the explanatory paragraph of the auditor's report on the financial statements of Sturdy Corporation for the year ended December 31, 19X3. ***Do not discuss deferred taxes.***

b. Write a draft of the opinion paragraph of the auditor's report on the financial statements of Sturdy Corporation for the year ended December 31, 19X3.

18–28. What type of auditors' report would be issued in each of the following cases? Justify your choice.

a. Draves Corporation owns substantial properties, which have appreciated significantly in value since the date of purchase. The properties were appraised and are reported in the balance sheet at the appraised values with full disclosure. The CA firm believes that the values reported in the balance sheet are reasonable.

b. London Limited has material investments in stocks of subsidiary companies. Stocks of the subsidiary companies are not actively traded in the market, and the CA firm's engagement does not extend to any subsidiary company. The CA firm is able to determine that all investments are carried at original cost, and the auditors have no reason to suspect that the amounts are not stated fairly.

c. Slade Ltd. has material investments in stocks of subsidiary companies. Stocks of the subsidiary companies are actively traded in the market, but the CA firm's engagement does not extend to any subsidiary company. Management insists that all investments shall be carried at original costs, and the CA firm is satisfied that the original costs are accurate. The CA firm believes that the client will never ultimately realize a substantial portion of the investments, and the client has fully disclosed the facts in notes to the financial statements.

(AICPA, adapted)

18–29. Roscoe and Jones, CAs, have completed the examination of the financial statements of Excelsior Corporation as at, and for, the year ended December 31, 1994. Roscoe also examined and reported on the Excelsior financial statements for the prior year. Roscoe drafted the following report for 1994.

We have audited the balance sheet of Excelsior Corporation Inc. as of December 31, 1994 and the statements of income and retained earnings for the year then ended. These financial statements are the responsibility of the company's management. Our responsibility is to express an opinion on these financial statements based on our audit.

We conducted our audit in accordance with generally accepted auditing standards. Those standards require that we plan and perform the audit to obtain reasonable assurance whether the financial statements are free of material misstatement. An audit includes examining, on a test basis, evidence supporting the amounts and disclosures in the financial statements. An audit also includes assessing the accounting principles used and significant estimates made by management, as well as evaluating the overall financial statement presentation.

In our opinion, these financial statements present fairly, in all material respects, the financial position of Excelsior Corporation as of December 31, 1994 and the results of its operations for the year then ended in accordance with generally accepted accounting principles, applied on a basis consistent with that of the preceding year.

March 15, 1995   Roscoe & Jones, CAs

Other information:

a. Excelsior does not wish to present a statement of changes in financial position for 1994.

b. During 1994, Excelsior changed its method of accounting for long-term construction contracts and properly reflected the effect of the change in the current year's financial statements and restated the prior year's statements. Roscoe and Jones are satisfied with Excelsior's justification for making the change. The change is properly discussed in note 12.

c. Roscoe and Jones were unable to perform normal accounts receivable confirmation procedures, but alternate procedures were used to satisfy them as to the validity of the receivables.

d. Excelsior Corporation is the defendant in litigation, the outcome of which is highly uncertain. If the case is settled in favour of the plaintiff, Excelsior will be required to pay a substantial amount of cash that might require the sale of certain fixed assets. The litigation and the possible effects have been properly disclosed in note 11.

e. Excelsior issued debentures on January 31, 1993, in the amount of $10 million. The funds obtained from the issuance were used to finance the expansion of plant facilities. The debenture agreement restricts the payment of future cash dividends to earnings after December 31, 1993. Excelsior declined to disclose this essential data in the notes to the financial statements.

Required:
Consider all the facts given and rewrite the auditors' report in acceptable and complete format, incorporating any necessary departures from the standard report.

Do not discuss the draft of the report, but identify and explain any items included in "*Other information*" that need not be part of the auditors' report.

(AICPA, adapted)

18–30. Brown & Brown, CAs, was engaged by the shareholders of Cook Industries Inc. to audit Cook's calendar year 19X8 financial statements. The following report was drafted by an audit assistant at the completion of the engagement. It was submitted to Brown, the partner with client responsibility for review on March 7, 19X9, the date of the substantial completion of the examination. Brown has reviewed matters thoroughly and properly concluded that an adverse opinion was appropriate.

Brown also became aware of a March 14, 19X9, subsequent event which the client has properly disclosed in the notes to the financial statements. Brown wants responsibility for subsequent events to be limited to the specific event referred to in the applicable note to the client's financial statements.

The financial statements of Cook Industries Inc. for the calendar year 19X7 were examined by predecessor auditors who expressed an adverse opinion and have not reissued their report. The financial statements for 19X7 and 19X8 are presented in comparative form.

To the President of Cook Industries, Inc.:

We have audited the balance sheet of Cook Industries Inc. as of December 31, 19X8 and the statements of income, retained earnings, and changes in financial position for the year then ended. These financial statements are the responsibility of the company's management. Our responsibility is to express an opinion on these financial statements based on our audit. As discussed in Note K to the financial statements, the company has properly disclosed a subsequent event dated March 14, 19X9.

We conducted our audit in accordance with generally accepted auditing standards. Those standards require that we plan and perform the audit to obtain reasonable assurance whether the financial statements are free of material misstatement. An audit includes examining, on a test basis, evidence supporting the amounts and disclosures in the financial statements. An audit also includes assessing the accounting principles used and significant estimates made by management, as well as evaluating the overall financial statement presentation.

In our opinion, except for the matters discussed in the first and the final paragraphs of this report, these financial statements present fairly, in all material respects, the financial position of Cook Industries Inc. as of December 31, 19X8 and the results of its operations and the changes in its financial position for the year then ended in accordance with generally accepted accounting principles applied on a basis consistent with that of the preceding year.

As discussed in Note G to the financial statements, the company carries its property and equipment at appraisal values, and provides depreciation on the basis of such values. Further, the company does not provide for income taxes with respect to differences between financial income and taxable income arising because of the use, for income tax purposes, of the instalment method of reporting gross profit from certain types of sales. We believe that these appraisal values are reasonable.

March 7, 19X9   Brown & Brown, CAs

Required:
Identify the deficiencies in the draft of the proposed report. Do *not* redraft the report or discuss corrections.

(AICPA, adapted)

18–31.   Explain the reporting and disclosure implications that you should consider in each of the following unrelated situations.

  a. You are the auditor of X Ltd., a company which at December 31, 1993, had working capital of $200,000, total assets of $2,500,000, and total liabilities of $2,200,000. During the three years ended December 31, 1993, the company has sustained accumulated operating losses totaling $700,000. Management has been informed that current debenture holders will not renew a debenture of $500,000 maturing September 30, 1994, and presently included in long-term liabilities. Although preliminary discussions have already been held with various commercial lenders, it presently appears uncertain as to whether or not X Ltd. will be able to refinance its debt. As X Ltd. has had liquidity problems from time to time, it may be unable to obtain adequate financing both to refinance its debenture and to provide additional working capital.

  b. Your client, ABC Ltd., owns 15 percent of the share of Y Company Ltd. The 1993 pretax net income of ABC Ltd. is $1 million, and its shareholders' equity is $3 million.

  The investment in Y Company Ltd. is carried on the balance sheet of ABC Ltd. (as of December 31, 1993) at $250,000, which represents original cost. Y Company Ltd. has incurred significant losses in the past few years. A current appraisal by a qualified business evaluator indicates that the current market value of 100 percent of the issued and outstanding shares of Y Company Ltd. is $1 million. You are also aware that an investor who held 20 percent of the shares of Y Company Ltd. recently sold those shares for $180,000.

  Your client, ABC Ltd., insists that the shares be shown at their original cost of $250,000 but is willing to expand note disclosure.

(CICA, adapted)

18–32.   Your client, Quaid Limited, requests your assistance in rewriting the note presented below, to make it clearer and more concise.

Note 6. The indenture relating to the long-term debt contains certain provisions regarding the maintenance of working capital, the payment of dividends, and the purchase of the company's capital stock. The most restrictive of these provisions requires that (*a*) working capital will be maintained at not less than $4,500,000; (*b*) the company cannot pay cash dividends or purchase its capital stock if, after it has done so, working capital is less than $5,000,000; and (*c*) cash dividends paid since January 1, 1992, plus the excess of capital stock purchased over the proceeds of stock sold during the same period, cannot exceed 70 percent of net earnings (since January 1, 1992) plus

$250,000. At December 31, 1995, $2,441,291 of retained earnings were available for the payment of dividends under this last provision, as follows:

Net earnings since January 1, 1992	$5,478,127
70 percent of above	$3,834,688
Additional amount available under indenture	250,000
	4,084,688
Cash dividends paid since January 1, 1992.	1,643,397
Retained earnings available.	$2,441,291

Required:

Rewrite the note in accordance with your client's instructions.

18–33. On September 30, 1994, White & Co., CAs, was engaged to audit the consolidated financial statements of National Motors Inc. for the year ended December 31, 1994. The consolidated financial statements of National had not been audited the prior year. National's inadequate inventory records precluded White from forming an opinion as to the proper or consistent application of generally accepted accounting principles to inventory balances on January 1, 1994. Therefore, White decided not to express an opinion on the results of operations for the year ended December 31, 1994. National decided not to present comparative financial statements.

Rapid Parts Limited, a consolidated subsidiary of National, was audited for the year ended December 31, 1994, by Green & Co., CAs. Green completed its work on February 28, 1995, and submitted an unqualified opinion on Rapid's financial statements on March 7, 1995. Rapid's statements reflect total assets and revenues of $7,000,000 and $8,000,000, respectively, of the consolidated totals of National. White decided to assume responsibility for the work of Green. Green's report on Rapid does not accompany National's consolidated statements.

White completed its audit work on March 28, 1995, and submitted its auditors' report to National on April 4, 1995.

Required:

Prepare the auditors' report on the consolidated financial statements of National Motors Inc.

Chapter 19

Special Auditing, Accounting, and Other Services

After studying this chapter, you should be able to:
- Distinguish between auditing and accounting services.
- Identify the types of special reports.
- Distinguish between review and compilation services.
- Identify the reports under the accounting and auditing guidelines.
- Discuss the issuance of comfort letters.
- Describe the nature of public accountants' reports on financial forecasts and internal control.

In the preceding chapters, we have emphasized the auditors' principal attest function—the audit of a company's financial statements to determine the fairness of presentation in accordance with generally accepted accounting principles. There are, however, other special auditing services. For example, an audit may be performed on financial information other than financial statements. Also, an audit may be performed on the compliance with contractual agreements.

Furthermore, audits are not the only services rendered by the professional staff of a public accounting firm. These individuals also perform a variety of accounting services, such as a review or compilation of financial statements, and the issuance of reports on financial forecasts or on the client's internal control.

It is important to distinguish special auditing services from accounting services. In performing special auditing services, public accountants are required to comply with the applicable generally accepted auditing standards. In performing accounting services, however, public accountants are not required to comply with these auditing standards, although they are required to comply with other standards recommended by the CICA. Also, the scope of an audit on financial statements and a special auditing service is much wider than that of an accounting engagement, and thus the level of assurance provided is much higher. Furthermore, public accountants refer to themselves as auditors when they are performing an audit on financial statements or a special auditing service. When public accountants are rendering accounting services, they refer to themselves as accountants.

In this chapter, we shall discuss the special auditing, review, and compilation services, and other special services rendered by public accountants.[1]

SPECIAL AUDITING SERVICES

There are a number of auditing services besides the audit of annual financial statements for businesses. The most common ones are the audit of financial information, compliance with contractual agreement, cash basis financial statements, and personal financial statements. These services are discussed in the following sections.

Special Reports

Auditors use the term *special reports* to describe reports issued on any of the following:[2]

1. Financial information other than financial statements, such as specific financial statement items (e.g., gross sales for a specific location of the company), grant application data, or the costs of a capital project.
2. Compliance with contractual agreements such as bond indentures.
3. Results of applying specified auditing procedures to financial information other than financial statements.

Sections 5805 and 5815 of the *CICA Handbook* provide guidance for the first two items, respectively. In these two situations the form of commu-

---

[1] Other services, such as management consulting and tax services, are not discussed in this chapter.

[2] CICA, *CICA Handbook,* Section 5800.

nication is called the ***auditors' report,*** and the auditors must comply with the general and examination standards of the generally accepted auditing standards. Section 5810 governs the third item. In this situation the communication is in the form of a letter or an accountants' report, and compliance with the general and the first examination standards of the generally accepted auditing standards is required. These three types of special reports are discussed in the following paragraphs.

Auditors may be engaged to express an opinion on financial information such as specified elements, accounts, or items of a financial statement. For example, auditors are often requested by lessees to provide reports solely on their revenues. Such reports are required by the provisions of their lease agreements and are used to compute lease payments that are contingent on the lessee's revenue. In such cases the auditors modify the standard report to indicate the information examined, the basis of accounting used, and whether the information is presented fairly on that basis. It should be noted that materiality for such engagements is determined in relation to the information presented; it is generally less than would be used in the audit of the financial statements. The following is a suggested report provided in Section 5805.

Auditors' Report on Schedule of Gross Sales

To Landlord Limited:

At the request of Client Limited, we have audited the schedule of gross sales (as defined in paragraph 2 of the lease agreement dated May 3, 19—, with Landlord Limited) at the Main Street store, (city, province) for the year ended December 31, 19—. This financial information is the responsibility of the management of Client Limited. Our responsibility is to express an opinion on this financial information based on our audit.

We conducted our audit in accordance with generally accepted auditing standards. Those standards require that we plan and perform an audit to obtain reasonable assurance whether the financial information is free of material misstatement. An audit includes examining, on a test basis, evidence supporting the amounts and disclosures in the financial information. An audit also includes assessing the accounting principles used and significant estimates made by management, as well as evaluating the overall presentation of the financial information.

In our opinion, this schedule presents fairly, in all material respects, the gross sales of Client Limited at its Main Street store (city, province) for the year ended December 31, 19—, in accordance with the provisions of paragraph 2 of the lease agreement referred to above.

[signed]

City
Date   Chartered Accountant

Debt agreements often require companies to provide compliance reports prepared by their independent auditors. A common example of such reports is those prepared for bond trustees as evidence of the company's compliance with restrictions contained in the bond indenture. Maintenance of certain financial ratios and restrictions on the payment of dividends are provisions that are commonly contained in such documents. If the auditors have audited the applicable financial statements of the company, they usually can issue a report that provides an opinion on the client's compliance with the requirements contained in the bond indenture. In certain cases the auditors may have to perform additional procedures in order to give such an assurance. The following is an example of a report in which an opinion on compliance is expressed, as suggested in Section 5815.

Auditors' Report on Compliance with Agreement

To a Trust Company Limited:

We have audited Client Limited's compliance as at December 31, 19X1 with the criteria established by (describe nature of provisions to be complied with) described in Sections _____ to _____ inclusive of (name of agreement) dated _____, 19— with (name of party to agreement) and the interpretation of such agreement as set out in note 1 attached. Compliance with the criteria established by the provisions of the agreement is the responsibility of the management of Client Limited. Our responsibility is to express an opinion on this compliance based on our audit.

We conducted our audit in accordance with generally accepted auditing standards. Those standards require that we plan and perform an audit to obtain reasonable assurance whether Client Limited complied with the criteria established by the provisions of the agreement referred to above. Such an audit includes examining, on a test basis, evidence supporting compliance, evaluating the overall compliance with the agreement, and where applicable, assessing the accounting principles used and significant estimates made by management.

In our opinion, Client Limited is in compliance, in all material respects, with the criteria established by (the provisions to be complied with) described in Sections _____ to _____ of this agreement.

[signed]

City

Date   Chartered Accountant

The auditors' engagement to report on *the application of specified auditing procedures* to financial information is different from the engagements discussed above because the specified auditing procedures are not intended to enable the public accountants to form an audit opinion or to provide negative assurance on the financial information. Therefore, it is very important that the *report is restricted* to informed individuals who have a clear understanding of the procedures performed. A discussion between the public accountants and the individuals or their representatives concerning the extent of the procedures will generally accomplish this objective. The public accountants' report on the results of applying specified auditing procedures should (1) specifically identify the financial information to which the auditing procedures were applied, (2) specify the procedures performed, (3) state only the factual results of those procedures and not express any form of negative assurance, (4) state that an audit has not been performed on the financial information and disclaim an opinion thereon, (5) indicate any restrictions on distribution of the report, and, (6) disclose the addressee, the name of the public accountant (or firm), the date of the report, and the place of issue.

Other Special Reports

In addition to these three special reports described in the preceding paragraphs, auditors are sometimes requested to perform an audit on financial statements prepared on a basis of accounting other than generally accepted accounting principles and on personal financial statements.

Report on Cash-Basis Statements.   Perhaps the most common type of financial statements prepared on a basis other than GAAP is cash-basis statements. Auditors must describe in their report the basis of accounting being used and the fact that the statements are *not* presented in accordance with GAAP. Moreover, the auditors should be cautious about the titles given to the financial statements. Titles such as "balance sheet" and "income statement" are generally associated with financial statements presented in accordance with GAAP. Consequently, auditors should insist on more descriptive titles for statements that are prepared on a cash basis. For example, a cash-basis "balance sheet" is more appropriately titled "statement of assets and liabilities arising from cash transactions."

An unqualified special report on cash-basis statements is shown below. The distinctive wording has been emphasized.

We have audited the accompanying *statement of assets and liabilities arising from cash transactions* of XYZ Company as of December 31, 19—, and the statement of revenue collected and expenses paid for the year then ended. These financial statements are the responsibility of the company's management. Our responsibility is to express an opinion on these financial statements based on our audit.

We conducted our audit in accordance with generally accepted auditing standards. Those standards require that we plan and perform the audit to obtain reasonable assurance whether the financial statements are free of material misstatement. An audit includes examining, on a test basis, evidence supporting the amounts and disclosures in the financial statements. An audit also includes assessing the accounting principles used and significant estimates made by management, as well as evaluating the overall financial statement presentation.

As described in Note 1, these financial statements were prepared on the ***basis of cash receipts and disbursements*** and ***are not intended to be a presentation in accordance with generally accepted accounting principles.***

In our opinion, these financial statements present fairly, in all material respects, the ***assets and liabilities arising from cash transactions*** of XYZ Company as of December 31, 19—, and the ***revenue collected and expenses paid*** during the year then ended, ***on the basis of accounting described in Note 1.***

The essence of the audit report is the expression of an opinion as to whether the statements fairly present what they purport to present. The wording of the footnote mentioned in the report will vary from case to case in order to give an accurate indication of the content of the statements, because the cash basis or modified cash basis usually includes accounting records of various assets other than cash.

Reports on Personal Financial Statements.   In recent years, a number of politicians have had their personal financial statements audited and made them public. Audited personal financial statements also may be required with loan applications, or when an individual seeks to purchase a business using his or her personal credit.

Personal financial statements are unique in several respects. For example, the generally accepted accounting principles used in these statements are quite different from those applicable to business entities. In personal financial statements, assets are shown at their ***estimated current values.*** Thus, auditors must apply audit procedures that will substantiate these estimates, rather than substantiating historical costs. On occasion, the auditors may need to rely upon appraisers, following the guidelines set forth in *CICA Handbook,* Section 5360, "Using the Work of a Specialist."

The "balance sheet" for an individual is termed a ***statement of financial condition.*** This statement shows the individual's ***net worth*** in lieu of "owner's equity," and includes a liability for income taxes on the differences between the estimated current values of assets and their income tax bases. The "income statement" for an individual is called the ***statement of changes in net worth.*** In addition to showing revenue and expenses, this statement includes the changes in the estimated current values of assets and in the estimated amounts of liabilities during the period.

The accounting principles for personal financial statements are described in *Statement of Position 82–1,* issued by the Auditing Standards

Division of the AICPA in the United States.[3] In addition, the AICPA has issued a *Personal Financial Statements Guide* to provide auditors with guidelines in auditing personal financial statements.[4] While the CICA has no official pronouncement in this area, it has published a report by a study group.[5] The report issued on personal financial statements are standard in form and similar to the audit report on financial statements.

Completeness—A Special Problem in Personal Financial Statements.

One of the assertions that a client makes regarding its financial statements is that the statements are complete—that is, that they reflect all of the client's assets, liabilities, and transactions for the period. Determining the completeness of financial statements may be especially difficult in the audit of personal financial statements for several reasons. First, there is generally poor internal control—all aspects of each transaction usually are under the control of the individual. Second, some individuals may seek to omit assets and income from their personal financial statements. The motivation to conceal earnings or assets may stem from income tax or estate tax considerations, anticipation of a divorce, or illegal sources of income.

Illustrative Case

The fact that hidden assets are difficult to substantiate can be demonstrated by the court-ordered investigation in the spectacular bankruptcy of a company specializing in trading foreign currencies. When the company was forced into bankruptcy, it was suspected that over $100 million in investors' money was on deposit in various foreign banks. The bankruptcy court engaged a public accounting firm to track down the money. After several months of investigation, the public accounting firm had been able to locate only one or two million dollars and was uncertain whether any additional deposits actually existed.

The omission of assets and income from financial statements is far more difficult for auditors to detect than is the overstatement of assets and income. Thus, auditors should assess the risk that an individual may be concealing assets in deciding whether to accept a personal financial statement audit engagement. If auditors conclude during an engagement that the individual is concealing assets, it is doubtful that they can ever

---

[3] AICPA, *Statement of Position 82–1,* "Accounting and Financial Reporting for Personal Financial Statements" (New York, 1982).

[4] AICPA, *Personal Financial Statements Guide* (New York, 1983).

[5] CICA, "Report of the Study Group on the Preparation of Personal Financial Statements and Compilation, Review and Audit Engagements Involving Such Statements" (Toronto, 1986).

develop confidence that their audit procedures have located all of the concealed assets. Therefore, they should withdraw from the engagement.

ACCOUNTING SERVICES

Public accounting firms generally provide both auditing and accounting services. Accounting services such as review and compilation of financial statements represent a significant portion of the total practice of many public accounting firms, particularly the smaller ones. The review and compilation services are usually provided for smaller businesses that do not need or are not required by law to have an audit.

Audits are clearly cost justified for publicly owned corporations. The two major factors accounting for this are (1) the separation of ownership from management in such corporations and (2) economies of scale in auditing—as the size of the company increases, the cost of auditing does not increase on a pro rata basis.

For smaller companies, however, the cost of an audit may exceed the benefits derived. Consider, for example, a small company applying for a $20,000 bank loan. If the bank were to require the company to supply annual audit financial statements as a condition of the loan, the company's annual audit fees might be as much as its annual interest expense for the loan. Such added significant cost is clearly unjustifiable. Thus, audits should not be performed unless the benefits are expected to exceed the cost. Also, the needs of these smaller companies may differ significantly from those of publicly owned companies. Whereas publicly owned companies have large accounting departments that prepare financial statements internally, a small company might not even employ a full-time accountant. Therefore, these smaller companies may turn to a public accounting firm for the preparation of its financial statements and may occasionally need a *review* to add credibility to their financial statements. The preparation (or compilation) or review of financial statements is a lot less costly than an audit.

The following discussion will be focused on the review and compilation services, based on the *CICA Handbook,* Sections 8100 (general review standards), 8200 (reviews of financial statements), 8500 (reviews of financial information), 8600 (reviews of compliance with agreements and regulations), and 9200 (compilation engagements).

Review Services

A *review* is described in the *CICA Handbook,* Section 8100, as consisting "primarily of enquiry, analytical procedures, and discussion" related to the information provided by the enterprise. The purpose of a review is to add a measure of credibility by assessing the *plausibility* of the information in the circumstances within the framework of appropriate criteria. For example, when financial statements or other financial information are involved, the criteria would be an appropriate disclosed basis of accounting, which, except in special instances, would be generally accepted accounting principles. When compliance with agreements is involved, the criteria would be the relevant provisions of the agreements. When statistical information of a nonfinancial nature is involved, the criteria would be the terms of the engagement.

Since the objective of a review is to add a degree of credibility, public accountants should ensure, before accepting an engagement, that (1) the subject matter of the review is within their professional expertise and (2) there are appropriate criteria for the evaluation of the subject matter. In accepting a review engagement, public accountants should secure an understanding and agreement with the client, preferably in writing in the form of an engagement letter, as to the nature and terms of the engagement. This letter would normally include the following matters:

1. The public accountants will conduct the review in accordance with generally accepted standards for review engagements and will *not* express an audit opinion.
2. The public accountants will indicate the anticipated form and content, and any restrictions on the use, of their report.
3. The client's management is responsible to provide accurate and complete information required by the public accountants.
4. The client cannot rely upon a review to prevent or detect fraud and error.

When public accountants are engaged to perform a review, they should comply with the following professional standards set forth in Section 8100 of the *CICA Handbook:*

General Standard

The review should be performed and the review engagement report prepared by a person or persons having adequate technical training and proficiency in conducting reviews, with due care and with an objective state of mind.

Review Standards

(i) The work should be adequately planned and properly executed. If assistants are employed, they should be properly supervised.
(ii) The public accountant should possess or acquire sufficient knowledge of the business carried on by the enterprise so that intelligent enquiry and assessment of information obtained can be made.
(iii) The public accountant should perform a review with the limited objective of assessing whether the information being reported on is plausible

in the circumstances within the framework of appropriate criteria. Such a review should consist of:

(*a*) enquiry, analytical procedures, and discussion; and

(*b*) additional or more extensive procedures when the public accountant's knowledge of the business carried on by the enterprise and the results of the enquiry, and analytical procedures and discussion cause him or her to doubt the plausibility of such information.

Reporting Standards

(i) The review engagement report should indicate the scope of the review. The nature of the review engagement should be made evident and be clearly distinguished from an audit.

(ii) The report should indicate, based on the review:

(*a*) whether anything has come to the public accountant's attention that causes him or her to believe that the information being reported on is not, in all material respects, in accordance with appropriate criteria; or

(*b*) that no assurance can be provided.

The report should provide an explanation of the nature of any reservations contained therein and, if readily determinable, their effect.

While these standards are generally self-explanatory, certain areas such as "adequate technical training and proficiency in conducting reviews," "sufficient knowledge of the business," "plausible," and "assurance," need further clarification. The phrase "adequate technical training and proficiency in conducting reviews" means that the reviewers have obtained formal education and experience in accounting and auditing, particularly their training and experience in conducting reviews. "Sufficient knowledge of the business" includes a general understanding of the enterprise operations such as the type of industry, the nature of the business, the manner of organization, the nature of assets and liabilities, the sources of revenue and the types of expenses, and the accounting matters peculiar to the enterprise and its industry. "Plausible" means "appearing to be worthy of belief." Finally, "assurance" means negative assurance, which indicates that as a result of a review, nothing has come to the reviewers' attention to lead them to conclude that the information is not, in all material respects, in accordance with an appropriate disclosed basis of accounting. It should be noted that the assurance is stated in a negative rather than positive fashion, as in the case of an audit opinion. Thus, the nature and level of assurance provided by a review is quite different from an audit.

Section 8100 of the *CICA Handbook* also provides general guidance regarding the three key elements—enquiry, analytical procedures, and discussion—as follows:

1. enquiries concerning financial, operating, contractual, and other information, and considering responses that, in addition to oral responses, may take the form of listings, schedules, or other documents,
2. applying analytical procedures such as comparing the current and prior period information and considering the reasonableness of financial and other interrelationships.
3. discussions with appropriate officials of the enterprise concerning information received and the information being reported on.

The same section of the *CICA Handbook* recommends that the ***review engagement report*** should include the following matters so as to clearly convey to the users of the nature of the public accountants' involvement:

1. specifically identify the subject matter reported on,
2. state that the review was made in accordance with generally accepted standards for review engagements,
3. state that the review consisted primarily of enquiry, analytical procedures, and discussion related to information supplied by the enterprise, and
4. state that the review does not constitute an audit and disclaim an audit opinion,
5. except when reservations are required, state that nothing has come to the public accountants' attention as a result of their review that causes them to believe that the information is not, in all material respects, in accordance with an appropriate disclosed basis of accounting, which except in special circumstances should be generally accepted accounting principles, or in the case of nonfinancial information other appropriate criteria.

The report is normally addressed to the party who has engaged the public accountants. However, when the addressee is someone other than the client, it may be appropriate to indicate the name of the client. In addition, each page of the information covered by the report should be conspicuously marked as "unaudited."

Under some circumstances, public accountants may not be in a position to express an unqualified negative assurance. These circumstances include (1) departure from the appropriate criteria such as generally accepted accounting principles, (2) inappropriate or unreasonable interpretation of provisions of an agreement referred to in the report, and (3) unavailability of or inability to obtain satisfactory information. Accordingly, the public accountants should express a reservation in their report in the form of a qualification, an adverse statement, or a denial of an assurance, depending on the nature and materiality of the circumstances. The public accountant should insert a reservation paragraph preceding the negative assurance paragraph. The negative assurance paragraph should contain a reference to the reservation paragraph, and in the case of a scope limitation, both the scope and negative assurance paragraphs should contain a reference to the reservation paragraph. The reservation paragraph should provide the reasons for and the effects of, if readily determinable, the reservation.

In a review engagement, public accountants may add a final paragraph to their report to indicate the specific purposes of or any restriction on the use of their report. The following example is suggested in the proposed Section 8100:

> This report is intended to be used solely for [indicate specific use] and is not to be referred to nor distributed to any person not a member of management of Client Limited or [name of person to whom the report is addressed].

Review engagement is classified into three types: (1) interim and annual financial statements, (2) financial information other than financial statements, and (3) compliance with agreements and regulations. The additional requirements for each of them are discussed in the following paragraphs.

Interim and Annual Financial Statements.   In this type of review engagement, public accountants should follow the additional requirements stipulated in Section 8200 of the *CICA Handbook*. Specifically, this section states that the public accountants would normally perform the following procedures:

> (*a*) making enquiries concerning the business activities of the enterprise and the industry of which it is a part,
> (*b*) making enquiries concerning the accounting system as it relates to the preparation of the financial statements, to obtain an understanding of the manner in which transactions are recorded, classified, and summarized,
> (*c*) performing analytical procedures which could include:
>   (i) comparing the financial statements with those of the immediately preceding period and with any budgets for the current period, and
>   (ii) considering interrelationships of key elements of financial statements that would be expected to conform to a predictable pattern based on the experience of the enterprise,
>   and obtaining explanations for relationships and individual items that appear to be unusual,

(*d*) considering the results of previous engagements, including accounting adjustments required, and the effect that any reservation in the reports thereon might have on the financial statements,

(*e*) enquiring concerning matters discussed at meetings, if any, of shareholders and directors and committees thereof that may affect the financial statements,

(*f*) making enquiries of and having discussions with management concerning matters such as:

  (i) the accounting principles being followed and whether they are consistently applied,

  (ii) the existence of major commitments, contractual obligations, and contingencies,

  (iii) the occurrence of events subsequent to the date of the financial statements that could have a material effect on such statements, and

  (iv) the occurrence of transactions with related parties.

(*g*) advising other public accountants, if any, who have reviewed or audited the financial statements of significant components of the reporting enterprise of the intention to rely on their reports, reading such reports, and communicating with them concerning any matters arising therefrom,

(*h*) discussing the financial statements and proposed review engagement report with the client, and

(*i*) obtaining a letter of representation from the client as to the accuracy and completeness of the financial statements.

After satisfactory performance of the above procedures, the public accountants are usually in a position to express an unqualified negative assurance. The following is an example of a report containing such an assurance, as suggested by Section 8200.

Review Engagement Report

To (person engaging the public accountants):

We have reviewed the balance sheet of Client Limited as at . . . , 19 . . . and the statements of income, retained earnings, and changes in financial position for the year then ended. Our review was made in accordance with generally accepted standards for review engagements and accordingly consisted primarily of enquiry, analytical procedures, and discussion related to information supplied to us by the company.

A review does not constitute an audit, and consequently we do not express an audit opinion on these financial statements.

Based on our review, nothing has come to our attention that causes us to believe that these financial statements are not, in all material respects, in accordance with generally accepted accounting principles.

        (signed)

City

Date   Chartered Accountants

Financial Information Other than Financial Statements.   This engagement includes specific financial statement items such as sales of a location, grant application data, and amounts calculated for insurance or trust deed purposes. The review procedures for this engagement are similar to those set out for the interim and annual financial statements above. In addition, public accountants should refer to Section 5805 of the *CICA Handbook* for guidance for such matters as materiality considerations and disclosures of the basis of accounting and significant interpretations of the provisions of an agreement or regulation covered by the engagement. The review engagement report should include, if applicable, a description of the significant interpretations of the provisions of an agreement or regulation or a reference to such disclosure in the financial information. The following is an example of the wording for a report suggested by Section 8500:

Review Engagement Report

To ABC Company:

At the request of Client Limited, we have reviewed the (name of financial information) of Client Limited as at March 31, 19— (calculated in accordance with the provisions of Section X of the . . . agreement with ABC Company dated May 5, 19— and the interpretations set out in Note 1). Our review was made in accordance with generally accepted standards for review engagements and accordingly consisted primarily of enquiry, analytical procedures and discussion related to information supplied to us by the company.

    A review does not constitute an audit, and consequently we do not express an audit opinion on this (name of financial information).

    Based on our review, nothing has come to our attention that causes us to believe that this [name of financial information] is not, in all material respects, in accordance with (the basis of accounting).

(signed)

City
Date   Chartered Accountants

Compliance with Agreements and Regulations.   Examples for this type of engagement include loan agreements and bond indentures which usually impose certain conditions and restrictions on such matters as dividend payments, amount of working capital, and use of proceeds of sales of property. Section 8600 states that public accountants should follow the applicable review procedures set forth in Section 8200 for interim and annual financial statements, as described earlier. In addition, the public accountants need (1) to read the applicable provisions of the agreement or regulation, (2) to make enquiries regarding the information maintained by the enterprise to monitor its compliance, and (3) to consider consistency in the application of interpretation of the provisions of the agreement or regulation. In their report, the public accountants should identify the provisions and describe any significant interpretations of the provision, as well as significant changes in the interpretations from those of the preceding report. The following is an example of the wording for a report suggested by Section 8600:

Review Engagement Report

To (person engaging the public accountants):

We have reviewed Client Limited's compliance as at December 31, 19—, with (covenants or conditions to be complied with) described in Sections . . . to . . . inclusive of the agreement dated November 3, 19—, with (party to agreement) (and the following interpretation of certain provisions of such agreement—describe interpretations). Our review was made in accordance with generally accepted standards for review engagements and accordingly consisted primarily of enquiry, analytical procedures and discussion related to information supplied to us by the company.

A review does not constitute an audit, and consequently we do not express an audit opinion on this matter.

Based on our review, nothing has come to our attention that causes us to believe that the company is not in compliance with (covenants or conditions to be complied with) described in sections . . . to . . . inclusive of the agreement (and related interpretations) referred to above.

(signed)

City
Date   Chartered Accountants

Compilation Services

A *compilation* involves the *preparation* of financial statements from the information provided by the client. The purpose of a compilation is to organize the client's information into a format of financial statements. A compilation is *not* intended to provide *any* assurance that the information in the financial statements is accurate or complete. Consequently, the public accountants should be involved with a compilation engagement only when (1) there is no reason to believe that the financial statements to be compiled are false or misleading, and (2) they believe the client understands that these financial statements may not be appropriate for general purpose use, and uninformed readers could be misled unless they are aware of the possible limitations of the statements and of the very limited involvement of the public accountants.

In accepting a compilation engagement, public accountants should secure an understanding and agreement with the client, preferably in writing in the form of an engagement letter, as to the nature and extent of services to be provided. This letter would normally include such matters as (1) the public accountants will conduct the engagement in accordance with the standards applicable to compilation engagements, (2) the client is responsible to provide accurate and complete information required to compile the financial statements which are the client's representation, (3) the compilation engagement cannot be relied on to prevent or detect fraud and error, (4) the financial statements may not be appropriate for general-purpose use, (5) no assurance will be expressed on the financial statements, (6) uninformed readers could be misled if they are not aware of the limitations of the statements and the very limited involvement by the public accountants, and (7) the anticipated form and content of the ***notice to readers*** that will accompany the financial statements.

The professional standards for a compilation engagement, as set forth in Section 9200 of the *CICA Handbook,* are as follows:

1. the services should be performed and the communication should be prepared by a person or persons having adequate technical training and proficiency in accounting, and with due care,
2. the work should be adequately planned and properly executed and, if assistants are employed, they should be properly supervised.

Public accountants performing a compilation must not accept patently unreasonable information. If they become aware that the client's information is obviously incorrect, incomplete, or otherwise unsatisfactory, the public accountants should insist upon additional or revised information. If the client refuses to provide revised information, the public accountants should withdraw from the engagement.

Section 9200 of the *CICA Handbook* also recommends that the "Notice to Reader" should include the following matters so as to clearly convey to the readers the nature of the public accountants' involvement:

1. state that the statement was compiled by the public accountants from information provided by management,
2. state that the public accountants have not audited, reviewed, or otherwise attempted to verify the accuracy or completeness of such information,
3. caution readers that the statement may not be appropriate for their purposes, and
4. not express any form of opinion or negative assurance.

The "Notice to Reader" should be either on each page of the financial statements or on a separate page, provided the notice identifies the financial statements. In addition, each page of the financial statements should be conspicuously marked "unaudited—see Notice to Reader."

The suggested wording for the "Notice to Reader" to be placed on a page separate from the financial statements, based on Section 9200, is as follows:

Notice to Reader

We have compiled the balance sheet of Client Limited as at December 31, 19—, and the statements of income, retained earnings, and changes in financial position for the (period) then ended from information provided by management (the proprietor). We have not audited, reviewed, or otherwise attempted to verify the accuracy or completeness of such information. Readers are cautioned that these statements may not be appropriate for their purposes.

(printed or signed)

City
Date   Chartered Accountants

Since a compilation is not intended to provide any assurance on the financial statements, public accountants may perform the services even when they are not independent of the client. However, the accountants should indicate their lack of independence in the "Notice to Reader" and the reasons thereof. The following, presented as a last sentence added to the notice to reader, is an example for disclosing the lack of independence together with reasons:

I am not independent of X Limited because my spouse owns 25 percent of the shares of the company.

Reporting and Other Matters Governed by the Auditing and Related Services Guidelines

The auditing and related services guidelines represent the opinions of the Auditing Standards Steering Committee of the CICA and do not have the authority of the recommendations issued by the Auditing Standards Board. Furthermore, these guidelines may be withdrawn due to changes in legislation or may be superseded by *CICA Handbook* recommendations.

However, these guidelines should be useful to auditors. At present, the guidelines include the following: (1) related party transactions and economic dependence, (2) auditor involvement with supplementary information about the effects of changing prices, (3) audit of pension costs and obligations, (4) performance of a review of financial statements, (5) services on matters relating to solvency, (6) compilation engagements—financial statement disclosures, (7) examination of a financial forecast or projection included in a prospectus or other offering document, (8) communications with audit committees (or equivalent), (9) applying materiality and audit risk concepts in conducting an audit, (10) auditor's report on comparative financial statements, (11) Canada-United States reporting conflicts, and (12) legislative requirements to report on the consistent application of generally accepted accounting principles.

Comfort Letters to Securities Commissions and Underwriters

In Canada, the independent auditors who examine the financial statements included in a prospectus are often required by regulatory authorities such as the securities commissions to submit *comfort letters* and *letters of consent.*

The purpose of a *comfort letter* is to inform the regulatory authority of the status of the auditors' examination and to bring to the regulatory authority's attention any reservations the auditors may have on the financial statements before they render an opinion on these statements. A comfort letter, filed with a preliminary prospectus, is addressed to the regulatory authority and usually covers the following:

1. Identify the company involved and the security to be issued.
2. Specify the financial statements included in the preliminary prospectus.
3. State the status of the examination and the reason for not expressing an opinion on the financial statements.
4. Provide a negative assurance on the financial statements.
5. State that the letter is for the sole use of the regulatory authority.

Sometimes unaudited interim financial statements, in addition to the audited statements, are included in a prospectus filed with regulatory authorities. In such a case the authorities may require a comfort letter in respect of the unaudited statements from the independent auditors. This comfort letter should be addressed to the regulatory authority and should include the following:

1. State the relationship between the independent auditors and the company, and describe the security to be issued.
2. Identify both the audited financial statements and the unaudited interim financial statements.
3. Specify that no audit was performed and that no opinion is expressed on the interim financial statements.

4. Provide a negative assurance on the unaudited interim financial statements, based on procedures performed on those statements by the auditors.
5. State that the letter is solely for the use of the regulatory authority.

A letter signed by the independent auditors consenting to the use of their audit report on financial statements included in a prospectus is called a *letter of consent*. Such a letter is required by most jurisdictions in Canada. In issuing a letter of consent, the independent auditors should comply with the requirements recommended by Section 7100 of the *CICA Handbook*.

Underwriters involved in a securities issue often request the independent auditors who examined the financial statements included in the prospectus to issue a letter to the underwriters. This letter, commonly called a *comfort letter,* usually covers, among others, the following:

1. A statement as to the auditors' independence.
2. An opinion as to whether the audited financial statements included in the prospectus comply in all material respects with the applicable requirements of the appropriate provincial securities act and the related rules and regulations.
3. Specify that no audit was performed and that no opinion is expressed on the interim financial statements.
4. Provide a negative assurance on the unaudited interim financial statements, based on procedures performed on those statements by the auditors.
5. State that the letter is solely for the use of the underwriter.

When auditors are involved in issuing comfort letters and letters of consent, they should be familiar with the provisions in Sections 4000 and 7100 of the *CICA Handbook*.

Reporting on Future-oriented Financial Statements

Securities analysts, loan officers, and other users are giving increasing attention to future-oriented financial statements. Although such statements may be prepared in various forms, the most common are financial forecasts and financial projections. A financial forecast presents information about the entity's *expected* results such as financial position, results of operations, and changes in financial position. On the other hand, a financial projection presents expected results, given one or more hypothetical assumptions. For example, a projection might present expected results assuming the company expanded its plant. Both financial forecasts and projections must include certain minimum future-oriented financial statement items, background information, and a list of the major assumptions and accounting policies.

Users of financial forecasts and projections often request assurance that this future-oriented information is properly presented and based upon reasonable assumptions. To provide such an assurance, public accountants may be engaged to examine future-oriented financial statements. In examining these statements, the public accountants gather evidence relating to the client's procedures for preparation of the statements, evaluate the underlying assumptions, obtain a written representation letter from the client, and evaluate whether the statements are presented in accordance with the presentation and disclosure standards established by the CICA and whether the underlying assumptions provide a reasonable basis for the statements. In no circumstance is an accountant's report to vouch for the achievability of the forecast or projection.

Following is an example of an unqualified forecast examination report.[6]

Auditors' Report on Financial Forecast

To the Directors of X Limited:

The accompanying financial forecast of X Limited, consisting of a balance sheet as at [date] and the statements of income, retained earnings and changes in financial position for the [period(s)] then ending, has been prepared by management using assumptions with an effective date of [effective date]. We have examined the support provided by management for the assumptions, and the preparation and presentation of this forecast. Our examination was made in accordance with the applicable Auditing Guideline issued by The Canadian Institute of Chartered Accountants. We have no responsibility to update this report for events and circumstances occurring after the date of our report.

In our opinion:

- as at the date of this report, the assumptions developed by management are suitably supported and consistent with the plans of the company, and provide a reasonable basis for the forecast;
- this forecast reflects such assumptions; and
- the financial forecast complies with the presentation and disclosure standards for forecasts established by The Canadian Institute of Chartered Accountants.

Since this forecast is based on assumptions regarding future events, actual results will vary from the information presented and the variations may be material. Accordingly, we express no opinion as to whether this forecast will be achieved.

[signed]

City
Date   Chartered Accountants

---

[6] CICA, *CICA Handbook,* Auditing and Related Service Guidelines, "Examination of a Financial Forecast or Projection Included in a Prospectus or Other Public Offering Document."

A projection report is similar, but it has to state that (1) the projection has been prepared based on assumptions including a hypothesis; (2) the public accountants' procedures for the hypothesis were limited to evaluating its consistency with the purpose of the projection; and (3) whether, in the public accountants' opinion, the hypothesis is consistent with the purpose of the projection.

Reports on Internal Control

We have pointed out in earlier chapters that the auditors, following their consideration of internal control, usually issue an internal control letter to the client describing weaknesses in the existing internal control and making recommendations for improvement. An internal control letter should not be confused with a report to regulatory agencies or other outside groups on a company's internal control. The internal control letter is an informal report intended only for management. Since it is an informal communication, no standard format has been developed. The letter is written for internal use by persons who have a detailed knowledge of the company's operations and are interested in making improvements in internal control. Such a letter need not carry the extensive warnings and precautions needed in a report to outsiders.

In recent years, groups outside the client company have become interested in obtaining internal control reports prepared by public accounting firms. Regulatory agencies may want such reports because of the reports' relevance to regulatory purposes or to the agencies' examination functions. However, if a report on internal control similar to the internal control letter were sent to regulatory agencies or other outside groups, they might misinterpret it and reach unwarranted conclusions. In summary, a report on internal control to be sent to regulatory agencies or other outsiders should employ the most careful and cautious wording. The report should make clear that it relates to accounting controls only, that the extent of internal control is limited by cost factors, that fraud or errors may occur despite the existence of controls, and that controls functioning at the time of the review may no longer be in force. In the United States, *SAS 30* (AU 642), "Reporting on Internal Accounting Control," provides guidelines for the form and content of such a report.

Opinions on Internal Control.   The objectives of internal control are to provide management with reasonable assurance that assets are safeguarded and financial records are reliable for the preparation of financial statements. The public accountants' opinion on internal control expresses an assurance as to whether the client's existing controls are sufficient to meet these objectives. If their study and evaluation disclose material weaknesses in internal control, those weaknesses should be described in the report.

When reviewing internal control for the purpose of expressing an opinion, the public accountants should (1) plan the scope of the engagement, (2) review the internal control design, (3) test the operating effectiveness of the prescribed procedures, and (4) evaluate the test results. These steps are similar to those used in the auditors' consideration of internal control for audit purposes, but tests of controls for audit purposes are not comprehensive. Consequently, the auditors' consideration of internal control for audit purposes generally is not adequate to express an opinion on the internal control taken as a whole.

Reporting on Condensed Financial Statements

Occasionally, a client prepared document will include *condensed financial statements* developed from audited basic financial statements. These statements typically include considerably less detail than the complete financial statements. The public accountants who have issued an audit report on the basic financial statements may be asked to report on the condensed statements. In such a case, the auditors should issue a report indicating that they have audited the basic financial statements, the date and type of opinion expressed, and whether the condensed information is fairly stated in all material respects in relation to the basic financial statements. While there is no office pronouncement in Canada in this area, the AICPA's *SAS 42* (AU 552), ''Reporting on Condensed Financial Statements and Selected Financial Data,'' provides guidance for these types of reports.

Illustrative Case

Recently, a number of corporations in the United States began experimenting with issuing summary annual reports which were distributed to shareholders. These reports generally include condensed financial statements and refer shareholders desiring more detailed information to the annual report filed with the SEC (Form 10-K). The auditors of the companies involved issue a report on the condensed information which refers to the report included with the Form 10-K.

KEY TERMS

comfort letter   A letter issued by the independent auditors to the securities commissions and to the underwriters.

compilation   The preparation of financial statements from the information provided by the client.

financial forecast Estimates of a company's most probable financial position, results of operations, and changes in financial position for one or more future periods.

financial projection Future-oriented financial statements that present expected results, given one or more hypothetical assumptions.

letter of consent A letter signed by independent auditors consenting to the use of their report on the financial statements in the prospectus filed with the regulatory authority. This letter is required by most jurisdictions in Canada.

negative assurance An assertion by a public accountant that, after performing a review, nothing has come to his or her attention that causes him or her to believe that the information or statement is not in all material respects, in accordance with an appropriate disclosed basis of accounting or, in the case of nonfinancial information, other appropriate criteria.

plausible Appearing to be worthy of belief. The term generally applies to review engagements.

report on internal control A formal report by public accountants on the adequacy of a company's internal control. Depending upon the extent of the public accountants' investigation, the report may be worded as an opinion on the adequacy of internal control, or as a disclaimer of opinion accompanied by disclosure of material weaknesses coming to their attention.

review Consisting primarily of enquiry, analytical procedures, and discussion to determine the plausibility of the information provided by an enterprise.

review services The services encompassing the review of interim and annual financial statements, financial information other than financial statements, and compliance with agreements and regulations.

special reports A report issued on any of the following: (1) financial information other than financial statements, such as specific financial statement items, grant application data, or the costs of a capital project; (2) compliance with contractual agreement such as bond indentures; and (3) results of applying specified auditing procedures to financial information other than financial statements.

GROUP I: REVIEW QUESTIONS

19–1. Can auditors express an unqualified opinion on financial statements that are not presented in accordance with generally accepted accounting principles? Explain.

19–2. In communications with clients, should public accountants refer to themselves as auditors or as accountants? Explain.

19–3.   Does the issuance of a special report based on specified auditing procedures indicate an audit engagement? Why?

19–4.   Evaluate this statement: ''All companies should be audited annually.''

19–5.   Describe the three types of engagements under the *CICA Handbook*, Section 5800, ''Special Reports.''

19–6.   Name the professional standards for the three types of special reports in Section 5800 of the *CICA Handbook*.

19–7.   How are the assets in personal financial statements valued, and what constitutes a special problem in personal financial statements?

19–8.   What is a review, and what is its purpose?

19–9.   Describe the professional standards for review engagements.

19–10. Identify the matters that should be stated in a review engagement report.

19–11. What is meant by the term **plausible**?

19–12. What matters should normally be included in a review engagement letter?

19–13. What is a compilation, and what is its purpose?

19–14. What matters should normally be included in a compilation engagement letter?

19–15. Describe the professional standards for a compilation engagement.

19–16. Identify the matters that should be included in a ''Notice to Reader.''

19–17. How does a review of financial statements differ from an audit?

19–18. What are the types of procedures performed during the review of the financial statements?

19–19. Are engagement letters needed for review and compilation services? Explain.

19–20. What is the purpose of a comfort letter to an regulatory authority? Discuss.

19–21. What is the objective of an examination of a financial forecast?

19–22. Can a public accounting firm vouch for the achievability of a financial forecast? Explain.

19–23. Can public accountants issue an opinion of internal control as the result of their consideration of internal control performed during an audit? Explain.

19–24. List the steps involved in expressing an opinion on internal control.

GROUP II: QUESTIONS REQUIRING ANALYSIS

19–25. Many public accounting firms are engaged to report on financial information other than financial statements under *CICA Handbook*, Section 5800.

Required:

a. Discuss the two types of special reports that may be provided for financial information other than financial statements.

b. Why should reports on the application of specified auditing procedures to information be restricted as to its distribution?

19–26.   You have been asked by Ambassador Hardware Co., a small family-owned company, to submit a proposal for the audit of the company. After performing an investigation of the company, including its management and accounting system, you advise the president of Ambassador that the audit fee will be approximately $10,000. Ambassador's president was somewhat surprised at the fee, and after discussion with members of the board of directors, he concluded that the company could not afford an audit at this time.

Required:

a. Discuss management's alternatives to having their financial statements audited in accordance with generally accepted auditing standards.

b. What should Ambassador's management consider when selecting the type of service that you should provide? Explain.

19–27.   Andrew Wilson, CA, has reviewed the financial statements of Texas Mirror Co., a small company. He had not performed an audit of the financial statements in accordance with generally accepted auditing standards. Wilson is confused about the standards applicable to this type of engagement.

Required:

a. Explain where Wilson should look for guidance concerning this engagement.

b. Explain Wilson's responsibilities with respect to a review of financial statements.

c. How would Wilson's responsibilities be different if this were a compilation rather than a review? Explain.

19–28.   You have been engaged by the management of Pippin, Inc., to review the company's financial statements for the year ended December 31, 1993.

Required:

a. Discuss the procedures required for the performance of a review of financial statements.

b. Explain the content of the report on a review of financial statements.

c. Discuss your responsibilities if you find that the financial statements contain a material departure from generally accepted accounting principles.

19–29. You are a public accountant retained by the manager of a cooperative retirement village to do write-up work. You are expected to compile unaudited financial statements accompanied by a standard compilation communication. In performing the work you discover that there are no invoices to support $25,000 of the manager's claimed disbursements. The manager informs you that all the disbursements are proper.

Required:
Explain the steps that you should take in this situation.

(AICPA, adapted)

19–30. In connection with a public offering of first-mortgage bonds by Guizzetti Corporation, the bond underwriter has asked Guizzetti's independent auditors to furnish them with a comfort letter giving as much assurance as possible on Guizzetti's unaudited financial statements for the three months ended March 31. The independent auditors had expressed an unqualified opinion on Guizzetti's financial statements for the year ended December 31, the preceding year; they also performed a review of Guizzetti's financial statements for the three months ended March 31. Nothing has come to their attention that would indicate that the March 31 statements are not properly presented.

Required:
a. Explain what can be stated about the unaudited interim financial statements in the letter.
b. Discuss **other** matters that are typically included in such a comfort letter.

19–31. The management of Williams Co. Ltd. is considering issuing corporate debentures. To enhance the marketability of the bond issue, management has decided to include a financial forecast in the prospectus. Williams management has requested that your accounting firm examine the financial forecast to add credibility to the prospective information.

Required:
a. Explain what is involved in the examination of a financial forecast.
b. Discuss the content of the report on an examination of a financial forecast. (Do not write a report.)

19–32. Select the best answer for each of the following and explain fully the reason for your selection.

a. Special reports are appropriate for:
   (1) Reviews of interim statements.
   (2) Compliance with contractual agreements.
   (3) Forecasts.
   (4) Feasibility studies.

b. Which of the following procedures is *not* performed in a review engagement?
   (1) Enquiries of management.
   (2) Enquiries regarding events subsequent to the balance sheet date.
   (3) Any procedures designed to identify relationships among data that appear to be unusual.
   (4) A consideration of internal control.

c. In which of the following reports or notice should a public accountant *not* express negative assurance?
   (1) A standard compilation notice on financial statements.
   (2) A standard review report on interim financial statements of a public entity.
   (3) A standard review report on annual financial statements.
   (4) A comfort letter on financial statements to the regulatory authority.

GROUP III: PROBLEMS

19–33. Loman, CA, who has examined the financial statements of the Broadwell Corporation for the year ended December 31, 1993, was asked to perform a review of the financial statements of Broadwell Corporation for the period ending March 31, 1994. The engagement letter stated that a review does not provide a basis for the expression of an audit opinion.

Required:
a. Explain why Loman's review will *not* provide a basis for the expression of an opinion.
b. What are the review procedures which Loman should perform, and what is the purpose of each procedure? Structure your responses as follows:

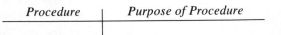

Procedure	*Purpose of Procedure*

(AICPA, adapted)

19–34. Jiffy Clerical Services is a company that furnishes temporary office help to its customers. The company maintains its accounting records on a basis of cash receipts and cash disbursements. You have audited the company for the year ended December 31, 199X, and have concluded that the company's financial statements represent a fair presentation on the basis of accounting described above.

Required:
a. Draft an unqualified auditors' report you would issue covering the financial statements (a statement of assets and liabilities and the related statement of revenue collected and expenses paid) for the year ended December 31, 199X.
b. Briefly discuss and justify your modifications of the conventional standard auditors' report on accrual-basis statements.

19–35. Norman Lewis, an inexperienced member of your staff, has compiled the financial statements of Williams Grocery. He has submitted the following "Notice to Reader" for your review:

The accompanying financial statements have been compiled by us. A compilation is an accounting service, but we also applied certain analytical procedures to the financial data.

As explained in Note 3, the company changed accounting principles in accounting for its inventories. We have not audited or reviewed the accompanying financial statements, but nothing came to our attention to indicate that they are in error.

Required:
Describe the deficiencies in the notice, give reasons why they are deficiencies, and briefly discuss how the report should be corrected. Do not discuss the addressee, signature, and date. Organize your answer sheet as follows:

Deficiency	Reason	Correction

19–36. The following report on the basic financial statements was drafted by a staff assistant at the completion of the review engagement of Delano Limited, a continuing client for the year ended September 30, 1991.

> To the Board of Directors of Delano Limited:
>
> We have reviewed the balance sheet of Delano Limited at September 30, 1991, and the statements of income and retained earnings for the year then ended, in accordance with generally accepted auditing standards. Our review included such tests of the accounting records as we considered necessary in the circumstances.
>
> A review consists principally of enquiries of company personnel. It is substantially less in scope than an audit, but more in scope than a compilation. Accordingly, we express only limited assurance on these financial statements.
>
> Based on our review, we are not aware of any material modifications that should be made to these financial statements in order for them to be in accordance with generally accepted accounting principles applied on a consistent basis.
>
> Halifax, N.S.   Anston & Co. CAs
> November 2, 1991

Required:
Identify the deficiencies in the draft of the proposed report on the financial statements. Group the deficiencies by paragraph.

19–37. The financial statements of Tiber Company have never been audited by independent auditors. Recently Tiber's management asked Anthony Burns, CA, to provide an opinion on Tiber's internal control; this management advisory services engagement will not include an examination of Tiber's financial statements. Following completion of his consideration of internal control, Burns plans to prepare a report on internal control.

Required:
a. Describe the inherent limitations that should be recognized in considering the potential effectiveness of internal control.
b. Explain and contrast the consideration of internal control that Burns might make as part of an examination of financial statements with his consideration of internal control to express an opinion on the internal control, covering each of the following:
  (1) Objective.
  (2) Scope.
  (3) Nature and content of reports.
Organize your answer for (b) as follows:

Examination of Financial Statements	Opinion on Internal Control
1. Objective	1. Objective
2. Scope	2. Scope
3. Report	3. Report

(AICPA, adapted)

19–38. Brown, CA, received a telephone call from Calhoun, the sole owner and manager of a small corporation. Calhoun asked Brown to review the financial statements for the corporation and emphasized that the statements were needed in two weeks for external financing purposes. Calhoun was vague when Brown enquired about the intended use of the statements. Brown was convinced that Calhoun thought Brown's work would constitute an audit. To avoid confusion, Brown decided not to explain to Calhoun that the engagement would only be to review the financial statements. Brown, with the understanding that a substantial fee would be paid if the work was completed in two weeks, accepted the engagement and started the work at once.

During the course of the work, Brown discovered an accrued expense account labeled Professional Fees and learned that the balance in the account represented an accrual for the cost of Brown's services. Brown suggested to Calhoun's bookkeeper that the account name be changed to Fees for Limited Audit Engagement. Brown also reviewed several invoices to determine whether accounts were being properly classified. Some of the invoices were missing. Brown listed the missing invoice numbers in the working papers with a note indicating that there should be a follow-up on the next engagement. Brown also discovered that the available records included the fixed asset values (a material amount relative to the financial statements) at estimated current replacement costs. Based on the records available, a balance sheet, income statement, and statements of retained earnings and changes in financial position were prepared. In addition, Brown drafted the notes to the financial statements, but decided that any mention of the replacement costs would only mislead the readers. Brown suggested to Calhoun that readers of financial statements would be better informed if they received a separate letter from Calhoun explaining the meaning and effect of the estimated replacement costs of the fixed assets. Brown mailed the financial statements and the notes to Calhoun with the following notation included on each page:

The accompanying financial statements are submitted to you without complete audit verification.

Required:
Identify the inappropriate actions of Brown, and indicate what Brown should have done to avoid each inappropriate action. (Do not discuss the sufficiency of the procedures.) Organize your answer sheet as follows:

Inappropriate Action	*What Brown Should Have Done to Avoid Inappropriate Action*

(AICPA, adapted)

19–39. The limitations on the public accountants' professional responsibilities when they are associated with unaudited financial statements are often misunderstood. These misunderstandings can be substantially reduced if the public accountants follow professional pronouncements in the course of their work, and take other appropriate measures.

Required:
The following list describes several situations public accountants may encounter, or contentions they may have to deal with in their association with and preparation of **unaudited** financial statements. Briefly discuss the extent of the public accountants' responsibilities and, if appropriate, the actions they should take to minimize any misunderstandings. Number your answers to correspond with the numbering in the following list.

1. The public accountants were engaged by telephone to perform write-up work, including the compilation of financial statements. The client believes that the public accountants have been engaged to audit the financial statements and examine the records accordingly.

2. A group of investors who own a farm that is managed by an independent agent engage public accountants to compile quarterly unaudited financial statements for them. The public accountants prepare the financial statements from information given to them by the independent agent. Subsequently, the investors find the statements were inaccurate because their

independent agent was embezzling funds. They refuse to pay the public accountants' fees and blame them for allowing the situation to go undetected, contending that they should not have relied on representations from the independent agent.

3. In comparing the trial balance with the general ledger, the public accountants find an account labeled Audit Fees in which the client has accumulated the public accountants' quarterly billings for accounting services, including the review of quarterly unaudited financial statements.

4. To determine appropriate account classification, the public accountants looked at a number of the client's invoices. They noted in their working papers that some invoices were missing, but did nothing further because it was felt that the invoices did not affect the unaudited financial statements they were compiling. When the client subsequently discovered that invoices were missing, he contended that the public accountants should not have ignored the missing invoices when compiling financial statements and had a responsibility at least to inform him that they were missing.

5. The public accountants were engaged to review the financial statements of a client. While reviewing the draft of financial statements with their client, the CAs learned that the land and building were recorded at appraisal value.

(AICPA, adapted)

GROUP IV: ANALYTICAL AND DISCUSSION CASE

19–40. You are a young CA just starting your own practice in Toronto, after five years' experience with a national firm. You have several connections in the entertainment industry and hope to develop a practice rendering income tax, auditing, and accounting services to celebrities and other wealthy clients.

One of your first engagements is arranged by John Forbes, a long-established business manager for a number of celebrities and a personal friend of yours. You are engaged to audit the personal statement of financial condition (balance sheet) of Dallas McBain, one of Forbes' clients. McBain is a popular rock star, with a net worth of approximately $10 million. However, the star also has a reputation as an extreme recluse who is never seen in public except at performances.

Forbes handles all of McBain's business affairs, and all of your communications with McBain are through Forbes. You have never met McBain personally and have no means of contacting the star directly. All of McBain's business records are maintained at Forbes's office. Forbes also issues cheques for many of McBain's personal expenses, using a cheque-signing machine and a facsimile plate of McBain's signature.

During the audit, you notice that during the year numerous cheques, totaling approximately $240,000, have been issued payable to Cash. In addition, the proceeds of a $125,000 sale of marketable securities were never deposited in any of McBain's bank accounts. In the accounting records, all of these amounts have been charged to the account entitled "Personal Living Expenses." There is no further documentation of these disbursements.

When you bring these items to Forbes's attention, he explains that celebrities such as McBain often spend a lot of cash supporting various "hangers-on," whom they don't want identified by name. He also states, "Off the record, some of these people also have some very expensive habits." He points out, however, that you are auditing only the statement of assets and liabilities, not McBain's revenue or expenses. Furthermore, the amount of these transactions is not material in relation to McBain's net worth.

Required:

a. Discuss whether or not the undocumented disbursements and the missing securities' proceeds should be of concern to you in a balance sheet–only audit.

b. Identify the various courses of action that you might at least consider under these circumstances. Explain briefly the arguments supporting each course of action.

c. Explain what you might do and justify your decision.

d. Assume that you are a long-established CA, independently wealthy, and that the McBain account represents less than 5 percent of the annual revenue of your practice. Would this change in circumstances affect your conclusion in (c)? Discuss.

Chapter 20

Internal, Operational, and Compliance Auditing

After studying this chapter, you should be able to:

- Distinguish between internal, operational, and compliance auditing.
- Describe the functions performed by internal auditors.
- Identify the standards for the professional practice of internal auditing.
- Explain the nature and the purpose of an operational audit.
- Describe the nature and purpose of compliance auditing and the related reports.

To this point in the text, we have focused primarily on audits of financial statements by independent public accountants. This chapter describes several other types of auditing: internal, operational, and compliance auditing.

INTERNAL AUDITING

Virtually every large corporation today maintains an internal auditing staff. This staff function has developed extremely rapidly; prior to 1940, internal auditing departments were found in relatively few entities. In 1941, the Institute of Internal Auditors (IIA) was founded with only 25 members. Now the Institute is a worldwide organization with over 30,000 members and local chapters in principal cities throughout much of the world. The growth of IIA has paralleled the recognition of internal auditing as an essential control function in all types of organizations.

What Is the Purpose of Internal Auditing?

The IIA defines internal auditing as follows:

> [It is] an independent appraisal activity established within an organization as a service to the organization. It is a managerial control, which functions by measuring and evaluating the effectiveness of other controls.

The job of the internal auditors is to assist members of an organization in the effective discharge of their responsibilities by furnishing them with analyses, appraisals, recommendations, and counsel. In performing these functions, internal auditors can be thought of as a part of the organization's internal control. They represent a high-level control that functions by measuring and evaluating the effectiveness of other internal control policies and procedures. One aspect of an organization's control environment is management's control methods for monitoring, investigating, and following up on performance, including internal auditing.

Internal auditors are not merely concerned with the organization's financial controls. Their work encompasses the entire internal control of the organization. They evaluate and test the effectiveness of internal control policies and procedures designed to help the organization meet all of its objectives.

Evolution of Internal Auditing

Internal auditing has evolved to meet the needs of business, governmental, and nonprofit organizations. Originally, a demand for internal auditing arose when managers of large corporations recognized that annual audits of financial statements by external auditors were insufficient. A need existed for timely internal auditing involvement beyond that of the external auditors to ensure accurate, timely financial records and to prevent fraud. These original internal auditors focused their efforts on financial and accounting matters.

Subsequently, the role of internal auditors expanded as a result of demands by the major stock exchanges and securities commission for increased management responsibility for the reliability of published financial statements. These demands resulted in increased internal auditor responsibilities, including more detailed analysis of internal control, as well as testing of interim and other accounting information not then considered in annual audits performed by external auditors. Moreover, the role of internal auditors expanded to encompass overall operational policies and procedures. For example, certain companies recognized the need for reliable operating reports which were used extensively by management to make decisions. The reports often were expressed, not in dollars, but in terms of operating factors, such as quantities of inventories in short supply, adherence to schedules, and quality of the product.

As organizations became larger and more complex, they encountered additional operational problems that lent themselves to solution by internal auditing. The internal auditors' role of determining whether operating units in the organization are following authorized accounting and financial policies was readily extended to determine whether they are following all of the organization's operating policies, and whether the established policies provide sound and effective control over all operations. The extension of internal auditing into these operational activities required internal auditors with specialized knowledge in other disciplines, such as economics, law, finance, statistics, electronic data processing, engineering, and taxation.

Several recent events that occurred in the United States also have been important to the evolution of the internal auditing profession. The first was the enactment of the Foreign Corrupt Practices Act of 1977. The accounting provisions of that act require public companies to establish and maintain effective internal accounting control. To assure compliance with these provisions, many companies in the United States established or augmented their internal auditing departments.

Another event that affected the internal auditing profession was the issuance of the *Report of the National Commission on Fraudulent Financial Reporting.* This report contains the commission's findings and recommendations about preventing fraudulent financial reporting by public companies. Among its recommendations was a suggestion that public companies in the United States establish an internal auditing function staffed with appropriately qualified personnel and fully supported by top management. The commission also recommended that the companies help ensure the internal auditing function's objectivity by positioning it suitably within the organization, maintaining a director of internal auditing with appropriate stature, and establishing effective reporting relationships between the director of internal auditing and the audit committee of the board of directors.

The current scope of internal auditing is summarized in the IIA's *Statement of Responsibilities of Internal Auditors,* which states that "the scope of internal auditing encompasses the examination and evaluation of the adequacy and effectiveness of the organization's system of internal control and the quality of performance in carrying out assigned responsibilities.'' Specifically, the scope includes:

1. Reviewing the reliability and integrity of financial and operating information and the means used to identify, measure, classify, and report such information.
2. Reviewing the systems established to ensure compliance with those policies, plans, procedures, laws, and regulations which could have a significant impact on operations and reports, and determining whether the organization is in compliance.
3. Reviewing the means of safeguarding assets and, as appropriate, verifying the existence of such assets.
4. Appraising the economy and efficiency with which resources are employed.
5. Reviewing operations or programs to ascertain whether results are consistent with established objectives and goals and whether the operations or programs are being carried out as planned.

Professional Standards of Internal Auditing

A relatively new development in the internal auditing profession is the issuance of the IIA's *Standards for the Professional Practice of Internal Auditing*. These standards set forth the criteria by which the operations of an internal auditing department should be evaluated and measured. They cover the various aspects of auditing within an organization, and are divided into five general sections:

1. Independence.
2. Professional proficiency.
3. Scope of work.
4. Performance of audit work.
5. Management of the internal auditing department.

These general standards and the specific standards that support them are summarized in Figure 20–1.

To provide interpretations of the *Standards for the Professional Practice of Internal Auditing,* the IIA also has issued a series of *Statements on Internal Auditing Standards*. To date, statements have been issued covering a variety of topics such as control concepts and responsibilities, preventing and investigating fraud, quality assurance, audit working papers, and relationships with external (independent) auditors.

Independence.   The first category of *Standards for the Professional Practice of Internal Auditing* deals with independence. Since internal auditors are employees of the organization, they cannot have the perceived independence of external auditors. However, independence is still

100 **Independence.** Internal auditors should be independent of the activities they audit.

  110 *Organizational Status.* The organizational status of the internal auditing department should be sufficient to permit the accomplishment of its audit responsibilities.

  120 *Objectivity.* Internal auditors should be objective in performing audits.

200 **Professional Proficiency.** Internal audits should be performed with proficiency and due professional care.

  The Internal Auditing Department

  210 *Staffing.* The internal auditing department should provide assurance that the technical proficiency and educational background of internal auditors are appropriate for the audits to be performed.

  220 *Knowledge, Skills, and Disciplines.* The internal auditing department should possess or should obtain the knowledge, skills, and disciplines needed to carry out its audit responsibilities.

  230 *Supervision.* The internal auditing department should provide assurance that internal audits are properly supervised.

  The Internal Auditor

  240 *Compliance with Standards of Conduct.* Internal auditors should comply with professional standards of conduct.

  250 *Knowledge, Skills, and Disciplines.* Internal auditors should possess the knowledge, skills, and disciplines essential to the performance of internal audits.

  260 *Human Relations and Communications.* Internal auditors should be skilled in dealing with people and in communicating effectively.

  270 *Continuing Education.* Internal auditors should maintain their technical competence through continuing education.

  280 *Due Professional Care.* Internal auditors should exercise due professional care in performing internal audits.

300 **Scope of Work.** The scope of the internal audit should encompass the examination and evaluation of the adequacy and effectiveness of the organization's system of internal control and the quality of performance in carrying out assigned responsibilities.

  310 *Reliability and Integrity of Information.* Internal auditors should review the reliability and integrity of financial and operating information and the means used to identify, measure, classify, and report such information.

  320 *Compliance with Policies, Plans, Procedures, Laws, and Regulations.* Internal auditors should review the systems established to ensure compliance with those policies, plans, procedures, laws, and regulations which could have a significant impact on operations and reports and should determine whether the organization is in compliance.

  330 *Safeguarding of Assets.* Internal auditors should review the means of safeguarding assets and, as appropriate, verify the existence of such assets.

  340 *Economical and Efficient Use of Resources.* Internal auditors should appraise the economy and efficiency with which resources are employed.

  350 *Accomplishment of Established Objectives and Goals for Operations or Programs.* Internal auditors should review operations or programs to ascertain whether results are consistent with established objectives and goals and whether the operations or programs are being carried out as planned.

400 **Performance of Audit Work.** Audit work should include planning the audit, examining and evaluating information, communicating results, and following up.

  410 *Planning the Audit.* Internal auditors should plan each audit.

FIGURE 20–1   *(concluded)*

420 *Examining and Evaluating Information.* Internal auditors should collect, analyze, interpret, and document information to support audit results.

430 *Communicating Results.* Internal auditors should report the results of their audit work.

440 *Following Up.* Internal auditors should follow up to ascertain that appropriate action is taken on reported audit findings.

500 **Management of the Internal Auditing Department.** The director of internal auditing should properly manage the internal auditing department.

510 *Purpose, Authority, and Responsibility.* The director of internal auditing should have a statement of purpose, authority, and responsibility for the internal auditing department.

520 *Planning.* The director of internal auditing should establish plans to carry out responsibilities of the internal auditing department.

530 *Policies and Procedures.* The director of internal auditing should provide written policies and procedures to guide the audit staff.

540 *Personnel Management and Development.* The director of internal auditing should establish a program for selecting and developing the human resources of the internal auditing department.

550 *External Auditors.* The director of internal auditing should coordinate internal and external audit efforts.

560 *Quality Assurance.* The director of internal auditing should establish and maintain a quality assurance program to evaluate the operations of the internal auditing department.

Source: *Standards for the Professional Practice of Internal Auditing* (Altamonte Springs, Fla.: Institute of Internal Auditors, 1980), pp. 3–4.

very important to internal auditors. The IIA's standards point out that independence is enhanced when the director of internal audit reports to a level of management of sufficient stature to ensure broad audit coverage and adequate consideration and implementation of the auditors' recommendations. Ideally, the director should report directly to the audit committee of the board of directors. Independence is also enhanced when potential conflicts of interest are considered in assigning staff to audit assignments. For example, it would be a conflict of interest for an internal auditor to audit an area in which that individual was recently employed. It is difficult, if not impossible, to remain objective in evaluating one's own operating decisions.

Professional Proficiency.   An internal auditing department should establish policies and procedures that provide assurance that staff members are competent to fulfill their assignments with professional proficiency. Ideally, the internal auditing department collectively should possess the skills, disciplines, and knowledge necessary to fulfill all the audit requirements of the organization. These skills, disciplines, and knowledge may be acquired through effective employment practices and continuing education programs.

Professional proficiency is also enhanced by establishing appropriate staffing and supervisory policies and procedures. An internal auditing department should establish policies for assigning staff members to audit areas so that the auditors will be competent to successfully complete those assignments. Once assigned to a task, the work of staff members should be adequately supervised and reviewed.

Scope of Work.   As described earlier, the scope of the internal auditors' work should extend beyond accounting and financial controls to include compliance with all types of internal control policies and procedures and operational auditing. The IIA's standards in this general section provide more detailed guidance about the appropriate scope of internal auditors' work.

Performance of Audit Work.   The IIA's standards in this category recognize that if audit work is to be effective, it must be adequately planned. Guidance is also provided for the internal auditors in collecting and evaluating evidence, communicating the results of the audit, and following up to ascertain that appropriate action is taken on reported audit findings.

Management of the Internal Auditing Department.   This group of standards provides guidance for the director of internal auditing in managing the internal auditing function. The director of internal auditing is responsible for properly managing the department to help assure that (1) the audit work is performed in accordance with professional standards and fulfills the general purposes and responsibilities developed by management of the organization, and (2) the resources of the internal auditing department are efficiently and effectively employed.

Certification of Internal Auditors

Since 1974, the IIA has administered the *Certified Internal Auditor (CIA)* program. To become certified, a candidate must have a baccalaureate degree from an accredited university and must successfully complete a two-day examination that is offered semiannually in principal cities throughout the world. The examination consists of four parts: principles of internal auditing, internal auditing techniques, principles of management, and disciplines related to internal auditing. Another requirement of certification is at least two years of work experience in internal auditing or its equivalent, although an advanced academic degree may be substituted for one year of work experience in meeting this requirement. Once internal auditors become certified, they must meet requirements for continuing professional education. More information on internal auditing and the CIA examination is available from the Institute of Internal Auditors, 249 Maitland Avenue, Altamonte Springs, Florida, U.S.A., 32701.

OPERATIONAL AUDITING

The term *operational audit* refers to a comprehensive examination of an operating unit or a complete organization to evaluate its performance, as measured by management's objectives. Whereas a *financial audit* focuses on measurement of financial position, results of operations, and changes in financial position of an entity, an operational audit focuses on the *efficiency, effectiveness,* and *economy* of operations. The operational auditor appraises management's operating controls over such varied activities as purchasing, data processing, receiving, shipping, office services, advertising, and engineering.

Objectives of Operational Audits

Operational audits often are performed by internal auditors for their organizations. The major users of operational audit reports are managers at various levels, including the board of directors. Top management needs assurances that every component of an organization is working to attain the organization's goals. For example, management needs the following:

1. Assessments of the unit's performance in relation to management's objectives or other appropriate criteria.
2. Assurance that its plans (as set forth in statements of objectives, programs, budgets, and directives) are comprehensive, consistent, and understood at the operating levels.
3. Objective information on how well its plans and policies are being carried out in all areas of operations and regarding opportunities for improvement in effectiveness, efficiency, and economy.
4. Information on weaknesses in operating controls, particularly as to possible sources of waste.
5. Reassurance that all operating reports can be relied on as a basis for action.

Governmental auditors, such as those employed by the Office of the Auditor General of Canada, perform operational audits of governmental programs that are administered by both governmental and nongovernmental organizations. Operational auditing is especially applicable to governmental programs where the effectiveness of the programs cannot be evaluated in terms of profits; they must be evaluated in measures such as, for example, the number of families relocated, the number of individuals rehabilitated, or the extent of the improvement in environmental conditions. In addition to internal and governmental auditors, public accounting firms perform operational audits for clients through their management advisory services departments.

General Approach to Operational Audits

In many respects the auditor's work in performing an operational audit is similar to that of a financial statement audit, but there are some significant differences. The steps of an operational audit might be set forth as (1) definition of purpose, (2) familiarization, (3) preliminary survey, (4) program development, (5) field work, (6) reporting the findings, and (7) follow-up. The operational audit process is illustrated by Figure 20–2.

Definition of Purpose.   The broad statement of purpose of an operational audit is usually to appraise the performance of a particular organization, function, or group of activities. However, this broad statement must be elaborated to specify precisely the purpose and scope of the audit and the nature of the report. The auditors must determine specifically which poli-

FIGURE 20–2   The Operational Audit

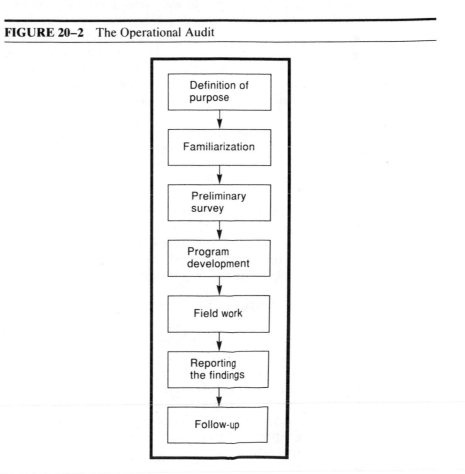

cies and procedures are to be appraised and how they relate to the specific objectives of the organization.

Familiarization.   Before starting the operational audit, the auditors must obtain a comprehensive knowledge of the objectives, organizational structure, and operating characteristics of the unit being audited. This familiarization process might begin with a study of organizational charts, statements of the functions and responsibilities assigned, management policies and directives, and operating policies and procedures. At this stage, the auditors may read some of the published material available on the subject to acquaint themselves as fully as possible with the functions performed. This background information equips the auditor to visit the organization's facilities and interview supervisory personnel to determine their specific objectives, the standards used to measure accomplishment, and the principal problems encountered in achieving the objectives. During these visits, the auditors will also observe the operations and inspect the available records and reports.

In summary, the auditors attempt to familiarize themselves as thoroughly as possible with the function being performed, particularly from the standpoint of administrative responsibility and control. The auditors' understanding of the organization is documented with questionnaires, flowcharts, and written narratives.

Preliminary Survey.   The auditors' preliminary conclusions about the critical aspects of the operations and potential problem areas are summarized in the auditors' preliminary survey. This survey serves as a guide for the development of the audit program.

Program Development.   The operational audit program is tailor-made to the particular engagement. It contains all the tests and analyses the auditors believe are necessary to evaluate the organization's operations. Based on the nature and difficulty of the audit work, appropriate personnel will be assigned to the engagement, and the work will be scheduled.

Field Work.   The field work phase involves executing the operational audit program. The auditors select the items to be reviewed to determine the adequacy of the procedures and how well they are followed. Just as in financial statement audits, the auditors will frequently select representative samples of the transactions from the records and review them to determine whether proper procedures have been followed and to discover the nature and extent of the problems encountered. In other cases they may resort to enquiry or direct observation to satisfy themselves that the employees understand their instructions and are carrying out their work as intended.

governmental organizations, the auditors often must perform tests of compliance with laws and regulations to determine that violations do not have a *direct* and *material* effect on line-item financial statement amounts. The auditors also may be engaged to provide additional reports based on these compliance procedures, or to extend their procedures to test compliance with other laws and regulations.

Generally, the objectives of compliance auditing procedures are (1) to determine whether there have been violations of laws and regulations that may have a material effect on the organization's financial statements, and (2) to provide a basis for additional reports on compliance.

Compliance auditing may be classified in two categories:

1. Compliance audit as part of a financial statement audit.
2. Compliance audit on specific programs.

Compliance Audit as Part of a Financial Statement Audit

As discussed in Chapter 2, auditors should design their audits to provide reasonable assurance of detecting material misstatements resulting from violations of laws and regulations that have a ***direct and material effect*** on line-item amounts in the financial statements. Governmental organizations are subject to a variety of laws and regulations that affect their financial statements—many more than affect typical business enterprises. An important aspect of generally accepted accounting principles for governmental organizations is the recognition of various legal and contractual requirements. These requirements are reflected in their bases of accounting, fund structure, and other accounting principles. Therefore, in performing an audit of a governmental organization's financial statements, the auditors are more likely to encounter laws and regulations that have a direct and material effect on the amounts in the organization's financial statements.

Governmental organizations receive funds from various sources, including taxes, special assessments, and bond issues. Laws and regulations often dictate the way the funds may be spent. While certain funds may be used for general purposes, others are restricted for specific purposes, such as for schools, libraries, or highways. The funds may even be restricted further. For example, a housing program may restrict the disbursement of funds to individuals meeting certain eligibility requirements.

A governmental organization also may receive financial assistance from other governmental organizations in the form of grants, shared revenues, or loans. This financial assistance often is provided only if certain requirements are met. For example, a federal agency may provide financial assistance, but only to the extent that the funds are matched with local funds. These restrictions apply not only to governmental organizations but they may also be important considerations in the audit of the financial statements of nonprofit organizations and business enterprises that receive government financial assistance.

The auditors perform a number of procedures to identify the laws and regulations that have a direct effect on an organization's financial statements, including (1) discussing laws and regulations with management, program and grant administrators, and government auditors; (2) reviewing relevant grant and loan agreements; and (3) reviewing minutes of the legislative body of the governmental organization. The auditors also obtain written representations from management about the completeness of the laws and regulations identified and acknowledging their responsibility for compliance with them.

Once the auditors have an understanding of the important laws and regulations, they assess the risks that financial statement amounts might be materially misstated by violations. In making these assessments, the auditors consider the internal control policies and procedures designed to prevent violations, such as policies regarding acceptable operating practices, codes of conduct, and assignment of responsibility for complying with regulatory requirements. These assessments are then used to design the nature, timing, and extent of the auditors' substantive tests of compliance.

Upon the completion of the audit, the auditors issue two ***additional*** reports: one on compliance with laws and regulations, and the other on the organization's internal control. To provide these additional reports, the auditors are ***not*** required to perform audit procedures beyond those required by generally accepted auditing standards.

Reporting of Compliance with Laws and Regulations.   This compliance report is based on the auditors' tests of compliance with laws and regulations that have a direct and material effect on the amounts in the financial statements—tests that are required by generally accepted auditing standards for the audit of financial statements. The report expresses positive assurance of compliance with laws and regulations that were tested. On items not tested, the report expresses negative assurance that nothing came to the auditors' attention that caused them to believe that the organization had not complied, in all material respects, with certain provisions of laws, regulations, contracts, and grants. A report on compliance with laws and regulations when the auditors' procedures discloses no material violations is illustrated in Figure 20–4.

The auditors may discover violations of provisions of laws, regulations, contracts, or grants that result in what they estimate to be a material misstatement of the organization's financial statements. Such violations are known as ***material instances of noncompliance.*** In these circumstances, the auditors must consider the effect of their opinion on the financial statements. The resulting misstatement, if left uncorrected,

FIGURE 20–4

To the Members of Council, Inhabitants,
and Ratepayers of the Corporation of the
City of Rosebud, Ontario

We have audited the financial statements of the Corporation of the City of Rosebud, Ontario, as at and for the year ended June 30, 19x2, and have issued our report thereon dated August 15, 19x2.

We conducted our audit in accordance with generally accepted auditing standards. Those standards require that we plan and perform the audit to obtain reasonable assurance whether the financial statements are free of material misstatement.

Compliance with laws, regulations, contracts, and grants applicable to the Corporation of the City of Rosebud, Ontario, is the responsibility of the City's management. As part of obtaining reasonable assurance whether the financial statements are free of material misstatement, we performed tests of the City's compliance with certain provisions of laws, regulations, contracts, and grants. However, our objective was not to provide an opinion on overall compliance with such provisions.

The results of our tests indicate that, with respect to items tested, the Corporation of the City of Rosebud, Ontario, complied, in all material respects, with the provisions referred to in the preceding paragraph. With respect to items not tested, nothing came to our attention that caused us to believe that the Corporation of the City of Rosebud, Ontario, had not complied, in all material respects, with those provisions.

This report is intended for the information of the audit committee, management, and [specify legislative or regulatory body]. This restriction is not intended to limit the distribution of this report, which is a matter of public record.

Rosebud, Ontario   Mark, McKay & McEwan
August 15, 19x2   Chartered Accountants

would normally require the auditors to issue a qualified or adverse opinion. Of course, management will usually decide to correct the financial statements, allowing the auditors to issue an unqualified opinion. Even though the financial statements are corrected, the auditors must still modify their report on compliance with laws and regulations, and include a description of the material instances of noncompliance.

The auditors should also report a description of any indications found of illegal acts that could result in criminal prosecution. Although these violations of laws and regulations may be included in the auditors report on compliance with laws and regulations, the auditors may instead discharge this responsibility by promptly reporting the illegal act in a separate written report to the organization's audit committee or governing legislative body. When the illegal act involves funds received from another government organization and management does not take appropriate action, the auditors may be required to report the matter to the officials of the other organization.

Reporting on Internal Control.   In an audit in accordance with generally accepted auditing standards, the auditors usually communicate, in the form of an internal control letter, internal control deficiencies encountered during an audit. When performing a compliance audit as part of a financial statement audit, this report becomes the third report, and it should be prepared in writing.

The report on internal control differs in other ways from the internal control letter. This report includes an identification and discussion of the implications of internal control deficiencies (weaknesses). It also includes an identification of the categories of the organization's internal control. For a government agency, for example, the internal controls over the disbursements cycle might be subdivided into categories such as grants, loans, payroll, and property and equipment. Other items in the report include (1) an indication that management is responsible for establishing and maintaining the internal control, and (2) a description of the scope of the auditors' work in obtaining an understanding of the internal control and in assessing control risk. An example report on internal control required is presented in Figure 20–5.

Compliance Audit on Specific Programs

Auditors may be engaged to perform a compliance audit on specific programs and to report on (1) compliance with laws and regulations that may have a material effect on the programs, and (2) the internal control policies and procedures relevant to the programs.

Designing Compliance Procedures for the Programs.   The auditors approach a compliance audit on specific programs in much the same way they approach a compliance audit as part of a financial statements audit. However, the former is concerned with compliance with laws and regulations that could have a *material* effect on the specific *programs,* while the latter is concerned with compliance with laws and regulations that could have a *direct* and *material* effect on the organization's *financial statements.* Because it must be considered on a program-by-program basis, materiality for planning the compliance procedures will typically be much less than what is appropriate as part of a financial statement audit. Also, an amount that is material to one program may not be material to another program of a different size or nature. This lower level of planning materiality results in an increase in the extent of the compliance auditing procedures.

In designing the compliance procedures, the auditors first assess the risk of material noncompliance with laws and regulations applicable to each program by considering various factors, such as the amount of the program expenditures and any changes made in the program. The auditors then

FIGURE 20–5

To the Member of Council, Inhabitants,
and Ratepayers of the Corporation of the
City of Rosebud, Ontario

We have audited the financial statements of the Corporation of the City of Rosebud, Ontario as at and for the year ended June 30, 19x2, and have issued our report thereon dated August 15, 19x2.

We conducted our audit in accordance with generally accepted auditing standards. Those standards require that we plan and perform the audit to obtain reasonable assurance whether financial statements are free of material misstatement.

In planning and performing our audit of the financial statements of the Corporation of the City of Rosebud, Ontario, for the year ended June 30, 19x2, we considered its internal control in order to determine our auditing procedures for the purpose of expressing our opinion on the financial statements and not to provide assurance on the internal control.

The management of the Corporation of the City of Rosebud, Ontario, is responsible for establishing and maintaining internal control. In fulfilling this responsibility, estimates and judgments by management are required to assess the expected benefits and related costs of internal control policies and procedures. The objectives of internal control are to provide management with reasonable, but not absolute, assurance that assets are safeguarded against loss from unauthorized use or disposition, and that transactions are executed in accordance with management's authorization and recorded properly to permit the preparation of financial statements in accordance with generally accepted accounting principles. Because of inherent limitations in any internal control, errors, irregularities, or fraud may nevertheless occur and not be detected. Also, projection of any evaluation of the internal control to future periods is subject to the risk that procedures may become inadequate because of changes in conditions or that the effectiveness of the design and operation of policies and procedures may deteriorate.

For the purpose of this report, we have classified the significant internal control policies and procedures in the following categories: revenue/receipts, purchases/disbursements, and payroll.

For all of the internal control categories listed above, we obtained an understanding of the design of relevant policies and procedures and whether they have been placed in operation, and we assessed control risk.

We noted certain significant deficiencies in the design or operation of the internal control that, in our judgment, could adversely affect the entity's ability to record, process, summarize, and report financial data consistent with the assertions of management in the financial statements.

1. Although temporary loans between funds are now being reconciled, they are not reconciled on a timely basis. We suggest that the accounting manager reconcile the funds' loans monthly.
2. The computer-prepared revenue, expenditure, and vouchers payable reports are not always reconciled to the general ledger accounts on a timely basis. We recommend that the chief accountant reconcile these reports monthly.

A significant deficiency is a condition in which the design or operation of the specific internal control elements does not reduce to a relatively low level the risk that errors, irregularities, or fraud in amounts that would be material in relation to the financial statements being audited may occur and not be detected within a timely period by employees in the normal course of performing their assigned functions.

We also noted other matters involving the internal control and its operation that we have reported to the management of the Corporation of the City of Rosebud, Ontario, in a separate letter dated August 15, 19x2.

This report is intended for the information of the audit committee, management, and [specify legislative or regulatory body]. This restriction is not intended to limit the distribution of this report, which is a matter of public record.

Rosebud, Ontario   Mark, McKay & McEwan
August 15, 19x2   Chartered Accountants

assess the *control risk* related to the organization's administration of the programs. The auditors should also perform a review of the internal control used in managing such programs. As part of this review, the auditors should test whether the internal control is *functioning* as designed. Based on the auditors' assessments of the risks of material noncompliance and the related levels of control risk, the auditors design sufficient substantive procedures to test each program for compliance with applicable laws and regulations.

Evaluating the Results of Compliance Procedures of the Programs.   In evaluating whether an entity's noncompliance is material to a program, the auditors should consider the frequency of noncompliance, and whether it results in a material amount of questioned costs. A *questioned cost* is an expenditure that is not allowed by the requirements of the program, not adequately supported with documentation, or unnecessary or unreasonable. An example of a questioned cost is an expenditure of financial assistance to an individual who does not need the eligibility requirements of the program. In evaluating the effect of the questioned cost on their reports, the auditors not only consider the actual amount; they must also develop an estimate of the total amount of the questioned costs. Thus, when the auditors use audit sampling to select expenditures for testing, they consider the *projected amount* of questioned costs from the sample. Regardless of whether this estimated total questioned cost is material enough to affect the auditors' opinion on compliance, the auditors should report any instances of noncompliance found and the resulting amounts of questioned costs.

Reporting on Internal Controls Relevant to the Programs.   The auditors report whether the organization's internal control provides reasonable assurance that it is managing the programs in accordance with applicable laws and regulations. Accordingly, the auditors must (1) obtain an understanding of the internal control used to administer the programs, and (2) perform tests of controls to determine whether the systems are operating effectively. This report on internal control does not include an opinion on the internal control. It is similar to the internal control report illustrated on page 821. In fact, the two reports may be combined by adding to that report an indication of the additional tests performed on the internal controls relevant to the programs and the related findings.

KEY TERMS

certified internal auditor   An individual who has passed an examination administered by the IIA and has met the experience requirements necessary to be certified.

compliance auditing   Performing procedures to test compliance with laws and regulations.

Institute of Internal Auditors (IIA)   The international professional organization of internal auditors.

internal auditing   An independent appraisal activity established within an organization as a service to the organization. It is a control that functions by examining and evaluating the adequacy and effectiveness of other controls.

noncompliance   The failure to act in accordance with laws or regulations.

operational auditing   The process of reviewing a department or other unit of a business, governmental, or nonprofit organization to measure the effectiveness, efficiency, and economy of operations.

questioned costs   Those costs paid with government assistance that appear to be in violation of a law or regulation, inadequately documented, or unreasonable in amount.

GROUP I: REVIEW QUESTIONS

20–1.   Define internal auditing.

20–2.   Describe specifically the scope of internal auditing.

20–3.   Identify the knowledge and skills that are necessary to the performance of modern internal auditing.

20–4.   "The principal distinction between public accounting and internal auditing is that the latter activity is carried on by an organization's own salaried employees rather than by independent professional auditors." Criticize this quotation.

20–5.   Describe the requirements for becoming a certified internal auditor.

20–6.   Evaluate this statement: "Internal auditors cannot be independent of the activities that they audit."

20–7.   Describe how the organizational status of the internal audit department affects its independence.

20–8.   Identify the five general categories of the IIA's *Standards for the Professional Practice of Internal Auditing*.

20–9.   Briefly describe the factors that are important to the management of an internal auditing department.

20–10.   Nearly every large corporation now maintains an internal auditing department, but 50 years ago relatively few companies carried on a formal program of internal auditing. What have been the principal factors responsible for this rapid expansion?

20–11.   Should the internal auditors generally disclose their findings to operating personnel of the department involved before transmitting the report to top management? Explain.

20–12. Compare the objectives of internal auditors with those of external auditors.

20–13. Differentiate between financial statement audits and operational audits.

20–14. Describe the purpose of an operational audit.

20–15. Explain the auditors' responsibility for testing compliance with laws and regulations in an audit of financial statements in accordance with generally accepted auditing standards.

20–16. Identify two categories of compliance audit.

20–17. "In a compliance audit as part of a financial statement audit, the auditors must perform additional tests beyond those which are required by generally accepted auditing standards. They also issue two additional reports." Evaluate this statement.

20–18. Explain why compliance with laws and regulations is so important in the audit of governmental organizations.

20–19. Describe what is meant by a *questioned cost*.

20–20. Describe the two additional audit reports issued by the auditors in a compliance audit as part of a financial statement audit.

GROUP II: QUESTIONS REQUIRING ANALYSIS

20–21. Throughout this book, emphasis has been placed on the concept of independence as the most significant single element underlying the development of the public accounting profession. The term *independent auditor* is sometimes used to distinguish the public accountant (external auditor) from an internal auditor. Nevertheless, the Institute of Internal Auditors points to the factor of independence as essential to an effective program of internal auditing. Distinguish between the meaning of *independence* as used in describing the function of the public accountant and the meaning of *independence* as used by the Institute of Internal Auditors to describe the work of the internal auditor.

20–22. In order to function effectively, the internal auditor must often educate auditees and other parties about the nature and purpose of internal auditing.

Required:
a. Define internal auditing.

b. Briefly describe three possible benefits of an internal auditing department's program to educate auditees and other parties about the nature and purpose of internal auditing.

(CIA, adapted)

20–23. Steve Ankenbrandt, president of Beeb Corp., has been discussing the company's internal operations with the presidents of several other multidivision companies. Ankenbrandt discovered that most of them have an internal audit staff. The activities of the staffs at other companies include financial audits, operational audits, and sometimes compliance audits.

Required:
Describe the meaning of the following terms as they relate to the internal auditing function:
a. Financial auditing.
b. Operational auditing.
c. Compliance auditing.

(CIA, adapted)

20–24. You are conducting the first audit of the marketing activities of your organization. Your preliminary survey has disclosed indications of deficient conditions of a serious nature. You expect your audit work to document the need for substantial corrective action. You feel certain that your audit report will contain descriptions of a number of serious defects.

Your preliminary meeting with the director of the marketing division and the principal subordinates gave you reason to believe that they will be defensive, that your audit report will receive a chilly reception, that your stated facts are likely to be challenged, and that any deficient conditions reported will be denied or minimized.

Required:
a. Identify those aspects of the *Standards for the Professional Practice of Internal Auditing* that apply to the problems described above.
b. Describe four techniques that you might use to improve the chances that your report will be well received and that appropriate corrective action will be taken.

(CIA, adapted)

20–25. Carol Warren, CA has performed an audit of the City of Ryan in accordance with generally accepted auditing standards.

Required:
a. Must Carol be concerned with the City of Ryan's compliance with laws and regulations? Explain.
b. How does Carol decide on the nature and extent of the tests of compliance that should be performed in the audit?

20–26. Wixon & Co., CAs, are performing an audit of the City of Brummet for the year ended June 30, 1993. During the course of the audit, Gerald Yarnell, a senior auditor, discovers violations of laws and regulations that constitute material instances of non-compliance.

Required:

a. Explain how these violations may affect the auditors' reports.

b. How would your answer to (*a*) change if management elected to correct the financial statements for the violations?

20–27. Select the best answers for each of the following questions. Explain the reasons for your selection.

a. Internal auditing can best be described as:
   (1) An accounting function.
   (2) A compliance function.
   (3) An activity primarily to detect fraud.
   (4) A control function.

   (CIA, adapted)

b. The independence of the internal auditing department will most likely be assured if it reports to the:
   (1) Audit committee of the board of directors.
   (2) President.
   (3) Controller.
   (4) Treasurer.

   (CIA, adapted)

c. When performing an operational audit, the purpose of a preliminary survey is:
   (1) To determine the objective of the activity to be audited.
   (2) To determine the scope of the audit.
   (3) To identify areas that should be included in the audit program.
   (4) All of the above.

   (CIA, adapted)

d. Operational auditing is primarily oriented toward:
   (1) Future improvements to accomplish the goals of management.
   (2) Ensuring the accuracy of the data in management's financial reports.
   (3) The determination of the fairness of the entity's financial statements.
   (4) Compliance with laws and regulations.

e. A compliance audit as part of a financial statement audit requires the auditors:
   (1) To perform additional compliance auditing procedures.
   (2) To perform additional tests of the internal control.
   (3) To issue additional reports on compliance with laws and regulations and on internal control.
   (4) To fulfill all of the above requirements.

GROUP III: PROBLEMS

20–28.   You are the director of internal auditing of a large hospital. You receive monthly financial reports prepared by the accounting department, and your review of them has shown that total accounts receivable from patients have steadily and rapidly increased over the past eight months.

Other information in the reports shows the following conditions:

1. The number of available hopsital beds has not changed.

2. The bed occupancy rate has not changed.

3. Hospital billing rates have not changed significantly.

4. The hospitalization insurance contracts have not changed since the last modification 12 months ago.

Your internal audit department performed a financial and operational audit of the accounts receivable accounting function 10 months ago. The working paper file for that assignment contains financial information, a record of the preliminary survey, documentation of the study, evaluation of internal controls, documentation of the procedures used to produce evidence about the validity and collectibility of the accounts, and a copy of your report that commented favourably on the controls and collectibility of the receivables.

However, the current increase in receivables has alerted you to the need for another audit. You remember news stories last year about the manager of the city water system who got into big trouble because his accounting department double-billed all the residential customers for three months. You plan to perform a preliminary survey of the problem to ascertain whether a problem indeed exists.

Required:

a. Write a memo to your senior auditor listing at least eight questions that should be used to guide and direct the preliminary survey. (*Hint:* The questions used in the last preliminary survey were these: Who does the accounts receivable accounting? What data processing procedures and policies are in effect? and How is the accounts receivable accounting done? This time, you will add a fourth question: What financial or economic events have occurred in the past 10 months?)

b. Describe the phases of the audit that would be performed after the preliminary survey is completed.

(CIA, adapted)

20–29.   The auditors issue a communication on internal control deficiencies in both an audit in accordance with generally accepted auditing standards and a compliance audit as part of a financial statement audit. One is in the form of an internal control letter, the other is in the form of a report.

Required:

a. Describe the differences between these two forms of communication.

b. Describe the major aspects of the *report* on internal control in a compliance audit as part of a financial statement audit.

20–30. In performing a compliance audit as part of a financial statement audit, the auditors are required to issue two additional reports, one on compliance with laws and regulations and one on internal control.

Required:

a. Describe the nature of the procedures that the auditors must perform beyond those required by generally accepted auditing standards to provide a basis for these reports.

b. Describe the specific contents of the auditors' compliance report.

c. Describe the specific contents of the auditors' report on internal control.

20–31. You have been engaged by the Corporation of the City of Rancho Costa to perform an audit. Randall Young, a new assistant, has drafted the following report on compliance with laws and regulations.

To the Members of Council, Inhabitants,
and Ratepayers of the Corporation of the City of
Rancho Costa:

We have audited the financial statements of the Corporation of the City of Rancho Costa, as at and for the year ended June 30, 19X1, and have issued our report thereon dated August 21, 19X1.

We conducted our audit in accordance with generally accepted auditing standards. Those standards require that we plan and perform the audit to obtain reasonable assurance that the city has not violated significant laws and regulations.

The results of our tests indicate that the Corporation of the City of Rancho Costa complied with all significant laws and regulations.

Required:

List and explain the deficiencies and omissions in the report and explain how it might be corrected. Organize your answer as follows:

Deficiency or Omission	*Correction*

Index